THE WOMAN
WHO DEFIED
KINGS

THE WOMAN
WHO DEFIED
KINGS

The life and times of Doña Gracia Nasi—
a Jewish leader during the Renaissance

Andrée Aelion Brooks

PARAGON HOUSE
St. Paul, Minnesota

First edition, 2002
First paperback printing, 2003

Published in the United States by
Paragon House
1925 Oakcrest Avenue, Suite 7
St. Paul, MN 55113

Library of Congress Cataloging-in-Publication Data

Brooks, Andrée Aelion.
    The woman who defied kings : the life and times of Doña Gracia Nasi—a Jewish leader during the Renaissance / Andrée Aelion Brooks.
        p. cm.
    Includes bibliographical references.
    ISBN 1-55778-805-7 cloth
    ISBN 1-55778-829-4 paper
    1. Nasi, Gracia, ca.1510-1569. 2. Jews—Mediterranean Region—Biography. 3. Marranos—Mediterranean Region—Biography. 4. Sephardim—Mediterranean Region—Biography. 5. Jewish women—Mediterranean Region—Biography. 6. Jews in public life—Mediterranean Region—Biography. 7. Women bankers—Mediterranean Region—Biography. I. Title.

DS 135.M43 N372 2002
909'.04924'0092—dc21
[B]
                                                                2001051161

10 9 8 7 6 5 4 3 2

For current information about all releases from Paragon House,
visit the web site at http://www.ParagonHouse.com

Before there was the House of Rothschild there was the House of Mendes and at its head was...a woman

This book is dedicated to my children and grandchildren: a legacy

Artist's Representation of Doña Gracia from
The Last Days of Shylock; *illustration by Arthur Sykes*

ACKNOWLEDGEMENTS

A book that delves into the remote corners of history and uncovers information contained in fading documents and obscure works written in thirteen different languages—Dutch, Old French, Latin, Italian, Spanish, Croatian, Old English, Ladino, Portuguese, German, Hebrew, Aramaic and Turkish written in Arabic script—requires a worldwide "army" of translators and handwriting specialists. It would have been beyond the capacity of any one individual to have all these skills.

In this respect I was truly blessed. I would particularly like to thank Emily Zaiden for her labors in the archives of Venice and Ferrara and for translating many of the Italian documents. Claudia Chierichini, Cristiana Sogno and Daniel Solomon, graduate students at Yale, were equally helpful in translating the Latin and other Italian texts and providing insights into some of the legalistic conventions of the era. Claudia also labored tirelessly on behalf of this project in archives of the Vatican, Ferrara and Modena. Edward Tilson, another graduate student at Yale, did wonders with countless documents in Old French. Tilson's understanding of the period was especially helped in placing the material in context. Maureen McKenna, yet another Yale student, helped with modern Portuguese translations and Tatjana Cisijia assisted with the Croatian. Dr. Aviva Ben-Ur, a Sephardic specialist and professor of Jewish history, was willing to take on some difficult *responsa* (Jewish legal) documents. Not only did these works keep slipping from Hebrew into Aramaic and back again, and occasionally even into Judeo-Spanish, but they were also written in archaic Rashi script. Special thanks to Hanania Cohen and Dr. Hagitte Gal-Ed for their work with other Hebrew documents, most of which were equally difficult to comprehend. As the writers of those days were not accustomed to using punctuation, it made the task of these translators all the more challenging. Thanks also to Dr. Ino Benmayor for his thoughtful and beautifully worded translations of some key chapters in modern Hebrew journals.

The novelist, Richard Zimler of Porto, and Elena Piatok, a cultural emissary in Lisbon, became indispensable in Portugal and also supportive friends. Without the thoughtful intervention of the historian Edgar Samuel in London, I might have never stumbled upon the papers of Lucien Wolf, the noted Jewish historian whose archival research on the Mendes family and the refugees entering Antwerp during the 1530's and 1540's lay untouched and unpublished for nearly a century.

I am also grateful to the experts in Mediterranean Jewish history who took time to read early chapters and give me their comments: Professor Libby Garshowitz at the University of Toronto, Professor David Gitlitz at the University of Rhode Island and Professor Ivan Marcus at Yale University. My thanks also to Professor Abraham David, Professor Yom Tov Assis and Professor Howard Adelman, all of Hebrew University in Jerusalem, Professor Herman Prins Salomon at the State University of New York at Albany, Professor Stanislao Pugliese of Hofstra University and Professor Benjamin Ravid of Brandeis University, all of whom assisted me in a variety of important ways. Historians Beki Bahar of Istanbul and Nikos Stavroulakis of Crete shared their specialized knowledge of Ottoman court life in the 16th century. Gad Nassi and Aliza Yehezkiel took equal care of my needs in Israel. Rabbi Leah Novick in Carmel, Calif., became a wise source for my understanding of Kabbalistic lore. The Bet Hatefutsoth Museum of the Diaspora in Tel Aviv was generous in sharing material it had amassed when compiling a visual exhibit centered around the House of Mendes some years ago.

A special note of gratitude must also go to the staff at the various Yale libraries who gave unstintingly of their time to help locate material that had not been touched in decades, as well as obtain books so obscure that often only one or two copies were still extant. Without unlimited access to their stacks I probably could not have reached a fraction of the information lurking in arcane works.

I would also like to acknowledge the friendship and support of Judith Liebmann who kept me going whenever I thought of giving up (and helped with German translations), and Ellen Graham, a marvelous editor formerly with the Wall Street Journal, who fell in love with the story and gave her professional appraisal and recommendations after a draft of the manuscript was completed.

Finally, and perhaps most of all, I would like to thank Carolyn French, my agent at the Fifi Oscard Agency in New York, for having faith in me and this extraordinary story.

A NOTE ON THE SPELLING OF FAMILY NAMES: We have continued to use the spellings and names in common usage among scholars who have written about the family. However, we would like to note differences where we found actual signatures (in the archives of Modena and Ferrara) that were clearly legible. Diogo Mendes signed his name as "Diego Mendez." La Chica signed as "Gracia Benvenista." Don Joseph Nasi signed as "Josef Nasy." His brother similarly signed as "Samuel Nasy." We do not have a signature for Doña Gracia, but we did find her first name sometimes spelled "Grazia."

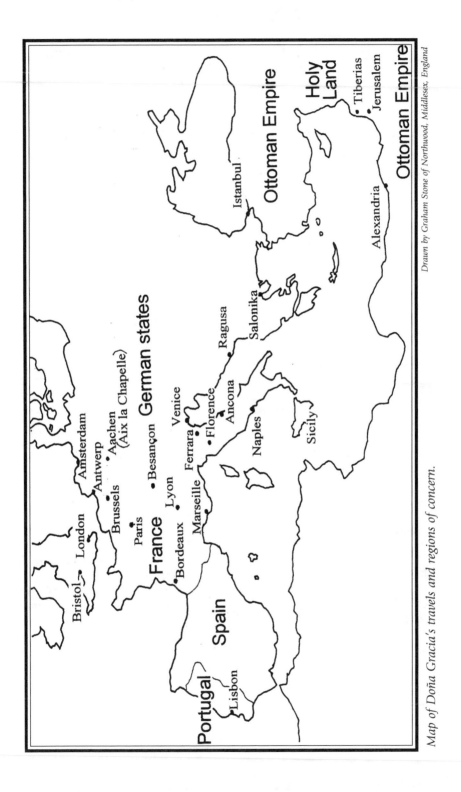

Map of Doña Gracia's travels and regions of concern.

Drawn by Graham Stone of Northwood, Middlesex, England

FAMILY TREE: MENDES (BENVENISTE)–DE LUNA FAMILIES

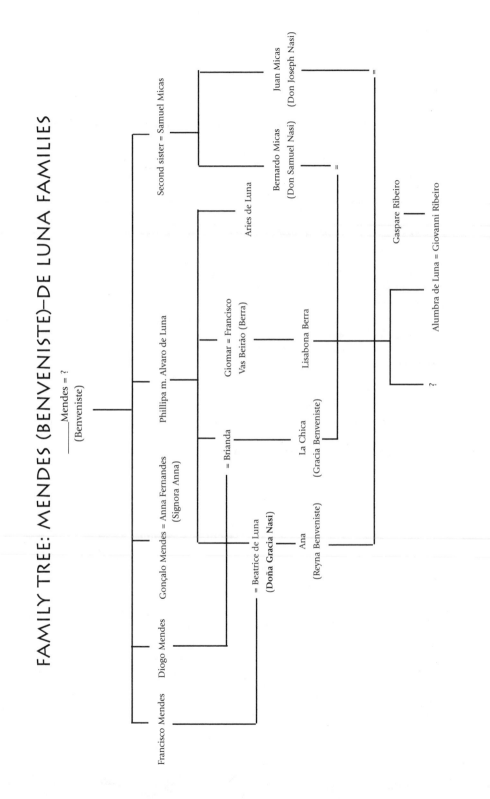

Mendes = ?
(Benveniste)

Francisco Mendes

Diogo Mendes

Gonçalo Mendes = Anna Fernandes
(Signora Anna)

Phillipa m. Alvaro de Luna

Second sister = Samuel Micas

= Beatrice de Luna
(Doña Gracia Nasi)

= Brianda

Ana
(Reyna Benveniste)

La Chica
(Gracia Benveniste)

Giomar = Francisco
Vas Beirão (Berra)

Aries de Luna

Bernardo Micas
(Don Samuel Nasi)

Juan Micas
(Don Joseph Nasi)

Lisabona Berra

=

Gaspare Ribeiro

?

Alumbra de Luna = Giovanni Ribeiro

Giovanni Ribeiro

=

CHRONOLOGY OF DOÑA GRACIA'S LIFE

1478: Pope authorizes the establishment of an Inquisition in Spain
1483 (?): Francisco Mendes (Benveniste) born in Spain
1485: Diogo Mendes (Benveniste) born in Spain
1492: expulsion of the Jews from Spain
1497: forced conversions of all Jews in Portugal
1506: massacre of *conversos* in Lisbon
1510 (?) : birth of Beatrice de Luna (Doña Gracia Nasi) in Lisbon
1512: Diogo Mendes sent to Antwerp to develop northern European business
1522: birth of Bernardo Micas (Don Samuel Nasi)
1524: birth of Juan Micas (Don Joseph Nasi)
1526: last mention in records of Alvaro de Luna, Doña Gracia's father
1528 (?): marriage of Doña Gracia to Francisco Mendes (Benveniste)
1531: creation of Antwerp bourse
1531-6: authorization of an Inquisition in Portugal amid numerous delays
1531-1555 (?): escape network for *conversos* developed, supported and expanded
1534 (?): birth of Ana Mendes (Reyna Benveniste), daughter of Francisco and Doña
   Gracia
1535: death of Francisco Mendes
1537: departure of Doña Gracia and family member from Lisbon and arrival in
   Antwerp
1539: Diogo Mendes marries Brianda, Doña Gracia's sister, in Antwerp
1540: birth of La Chica (Gracia Benveniste) Doña Gracia's niece, in Antwerp
1543: death of Diogo Mendes
1544: Queen Marie and Emperor Charles try to wed Ana to disreputable nobleman
1545: Doña Gracia and family members flee Antwerp and arrive in Venice
1548: Doña Gracia leaves hurriedly for Ferrara
1549-1552: Doña Gracia becomes a patron of printing and literature
1552: Doña Gracia returns to Venice and departs for Ottoman Empire
1553: Doña Gracia arrives in Constantinople
1553: abduction of La Chica in Venice
1554: Ana (Reyna) weds Don Joseph Nasi in Constantinople
1555: roundup of *conversos* in Ancona and Inquisition trials of family agents in Venice
1556: burning of *conversos* in Ancona and death of Brianda in Ferrara
1557: La Chica marries Don Samuel Nasi in Ferrara
1560: Doña Gracia acquires lease on Tiberias and fosters Jewish resettlement
1566: death of Sultan Suleiman and accession of Sultan Selim II
1566: Don Joseph becomes Duke of Naxos
1569: death of Doña Gracia and Don Samuel
1579: death of Don Joseph
1599 (?): death of Ana (Reyna)

CONTENTS

PROLOGUE

One wintry day early in 1535, merchant banker Francisco Mendes lay dying in his whitewashed, tile-roofed home near the royal palace in Lisbon. It was a pivotal moment for his elegant wife Beatrice, later known as Doña Gracia Nasi, and for their infant daughter, Ana. Not only were they losing a husband and father. The death of Francisco would have larger implications that Doña Gracia, still in her twenties, must have feared almost more than widowhood.

In time, Francisco's death would catapult his spirited, strong-willed young widow to the helm of one of the foremost banking houses of Renaissance Europe. But her inherited wealth would prove as much a burden as a boon. At her dying husband's side, Doña Gracia would have known even then that ruthless courtiers were plotting to seize his estate. Francisco had been a powerful confidante of Portugal's King João III. He had been regularly supplying the crown with indispensable loans. These connections had always shielded her and Ana while he was alive. No longer.

Moreover, if she chose to retain control of her life and fortune and fulfill her political goals, she was well aware that the emotional and social comforts of remarriage, or even a publicly-recognized lover, would be off limits to her for the remainder of her days. It was a classic 16th century woman's dilemma and an agonizing prospect indeed.

Doña Gracia's apprehensions were well-founded, as we shall see. Yet with her shrewd intelligence, taste for intrigue and exquisite timing, she was to become more than a match for any of the royal adversaries she would confront during her turbulent life. While steering Francisco's sprawling business interests, she would defy her enemies by spending most of her fortune on a humanitarian enterprise that would engross her more than the profitable royal loans, spice monopolies, syndications and currency arbitrage favored by her husband.

The Inquisition, which would spread throughout the Catholic world, was just beginning its terror, torture and burning. She would become the self-appointed protector and political liaison for its chief targets: the *conversos*. These were the Spanish and Portuguese Jews who, like her own family, had been forcibly converted to Catholicism in the decades prior to her birth in 1510. These converts were being subjected to ethnic cleansing by Inquisition officials who were making wholesale arrests on the spurious charge that they had relapsed into Jewish practice, whether true or not.

Because the *conversos* on the Iberian Peninsula constituted a significant segment of world Jewry at this time (the settlements of Central and Eastern Europe were still relatively small or nonexistent) her mission was critical. To her, and those in her circles, it looked as though the permanent loss of these tortured souls to Catholicism or death might seriously undermine the future of the Jewish people. Still, to enable these *conversos* to undertake and survive the arduous journey to lands beyond the reach of the Inquisition was to embark upon a mission of Moses-like proportions. That she succeeded in saving thousands of them underscores her vital role at a crossroads of Jewish history.

Ultimately the *conversos*, and most of the openly-professing Jews of the Eastern Mediterranean, would view Doña Gracia as their unquestioned leader. She would be revered as much for her wisdom and compassion as her capacity to stand up to tyranny; not to mention her willingness to give up her fortune to ensure the survival of this "remnant" of Israel, as her people were called in those days.

Here was a woman who made sure that she was constantly looking out for their welfare as they became a continual stream of frightened refugees, wandering stateless through the mountain passes, walled towns, hostile duchies and muddy roads of Europe. Here was a woman who would become so furious upon learning that Inquisition officials had burned twenty-three of her people in the Italian port of Ancona that she would organize a shipping boycott that would bring the city to its knees. And when they arrived in the safety of the Ottoman Empire, it was she who supported the building of synagogues and *yeshivas* that enabled them to reconnect with their ancestral faith. Moreover, in her final years, it was she who would make one of the earliest organized attempts to re-settle some of the refugees on sacred soil, four hundred years before the founding of modern state of Israel.

In her personal life, she would have the courage to stand face to face with Queen Marie, Regent of the Low Countries and sister of Charles V, the powerful Holy Roman Emperor, and say she would rather see her only daughter "drown" than marry the disreputable Catholic nobleman the monarchs had commanded the girl to wed. As a patron she reflected the best of Renaissance culture by supporting the creative works of her own people. In business, her name was repeated so prominently, and in so many documents, as to imply she was not simply the titular head of any enterprise. She ran it. And whenever she found herself in a tight corner, she regularly pursued a number of options simultaneously, rather than rely upon any single course of action. There are lessons here for us all.

Her people fell in love with her daring and regal spirit at a time when the pride of a people—any people—was bound up in the personality and accomplishments of its monarch. She gave the Jews and *conversos* a sense that they had a leader of substance and style, just like the Christians and Muslims. Her death would be lamented by the great rabbis of her day as equal to the destruction of the Temple in Jerusalem. Sa'adiah Longo, a leading poet-scholar in the Jewish world of those times, even admitted that his views of the capacity of women for wisdom and leadership had changed on account of her amazing deeds and strength of character. "All heed(ed) her discipline," he recalled in *Shivrei Lukhot*, a collection of elegies published in Salonika in 1594, some two decades after she died. "Trembling seized them (in her presence)…she grew a name like the name of the holy greats." If the qualities of a true leader, as has been said, combine an inborn love of power, an ability to penetrate to the origin of all things, organizational skills, a capacity to inspire others, a knack for exploiting the weaknesses in one's adversaries, then she had them all.

Nevertheless, Doña Gracia would swiftly vanish into the cluttered attic of history. Maybe it was because she was a woman. Perhaps she was too confrontational in an era when appeasement was considered the best option for Jewish survival. She would be remembered only by a few academics who themselves would make only limited reference to her while discussing more important themes. For all practical purposes she would be lost to the great masses of the Jewish people. This would be so even though other women leaders of her day—among them Catherine de Medici of France and Elizabeth of England— would overwhelm the stage on which they strode.

The oversight continued until late in the 20th century when women began entering the corridors of political and economic power in substantial numbers. It was then that they slowly started to rediscover Doña Gracia. The sum of her days—with their equal proportion of achievement and power, loneliness and personal agonies—resonated with their own. They relished each and every anecdote that demonstrated her refusal to give in to intimidation, whether on account of her gender or her Jewish blood. Though they possessed mere shards of information, they would use this slim foundation to build her into a folk hero and a spiritual cult figure while yearning to know more.

Consider: in the late 1980s Rabbi Leah Novick of Carmel, California, began introducing business, professional and artistic women to the life of Doña Gracia as part of her regular workshops and meditation sessions on women leaders in Jewish history. Rabbi Leah's sessions on Doña Gracia, bathed in soft candlelight and cradled by the gentle music of Judeo-Spanish melodies, became haunting evenings. The women—and even the men—said they came to the rabbi's tiny upstairs office to derive strength from the energies of a "great lady" whom they considered the embodiment of healing, wisdom and love.

I myself stumbled upon Doña Gracia quite by accident while preparing a curriculum in Sephardic history and culture for Jewish congregational schools under a grant from the Maurice Amado Foundation. There was an instant bond. As a journalist who had covered the women's movement in the later 70s and early 80s, I sensed a woman who pre-dated our efforts by centuries. In the early 90s, when I established The Women's Campaign School at Yale University, Doña Gracia struck me as just the sort of woman I would have been delighted to have had at my side. As a Spanish and Portuguese Jewess with the same heritage as Doña Gracia, I realized that she had possibly saved some of my own ancestors.

Others were becoming similarly intrigued. To the spiritually inclined (and the chroniclers of her day) she was the embodiment of an angel of God brought to earth to fight Satan. To Catholics of Jewish ancestry in the southwestern United States who were just beginning to probe their Jewish roots, she was an inspirational icon. Here was one of their own who faced many of the same conflicting emotions that they were facing today. To lovers of Jewish history she was a revelation, lifting their images of bygone Jewish womanhood off the birthing stool and into the sophisticated salons of Europe just as Michelangelo and Titian were creating their masterpieces.

Late in 1998, there was an art exhibition at the Platt Gallery in Los Angeles. The central piece was an 8ft by 6ft painting of Doña Gracia recently completed by Barbara Mendes, a local artist who had become an Orthodox Jew late in life. Some years ago Barbara became convinced that she was directly descended from Doña Gracia, viewing it as a source of pride and inspiration. No matter that there were no documents to prove it was true. Just a family legend insisting it was so. Her relatives even gave Barbara a symbolic heirloom—a replica of a bronze portrait medal of Doña Gracia's niece, struck in Ferrara in 1558.

Barbara's grandfather was eager for her to hold on to it as a sort of sacred trust. That Barbara's family were indeed descendants of Doña Gracia was also the conviction of her great-grandfather, Henry Pereira Mendes, a nineteenth century rabbi at Congregation Shearith Israel in New York—the first Jewish congregation on North American soil and one that was initially made up of the descendants of *conversos*. However, since Mendes was a common Hispanic family name taken by many forced converts in 16th century Portugal, and Doña Gracia had no direct descendants, the familial connection may never be proven. But that did not trouble Barbara. She felt a strong spiritual tie. The portrait she painted, on display at the gallery for two months, drew larger-than-normal crowds. Interest was so intense, Mendes recalled, that she found it necessary to develop a lecture to explain why she felt so passionately about creating an artistic impression of this woman.

The time had therefore come to go beyond the fantasizing and make-believe to give Doña Gracia the serious research and study she deserved. To date, there had only been one small non-fiction book dedicated to her life. It was written by Cecil Roth, a British historian, just after World War II. Although limited in scope, it remained the only easily available source of facts.

But how to embark upon such a complex project? Initial research at Yale University's outstanding libraries soon sent me scurrying to archives across three continents. It was a journey that was as absorbing as anything I have ever encountered. Everything about Doña Gracia lay buried in scholarly journals and among documents with another purpose and classification. The search became addictive. A shred of information from a Vatican source placed side by side with a document from the National Archives in Brussels would suddenly explain a seemingly senseless action; such as Doña Gracia's eagerness, while in Antwerp, to win the right to visit a pan-European order of cloistered nuns four times each year. Had the holy order become the escape network's mail drop? Were their convents, scattered across Europe and linked by their own couriers, being used as a web of safe houses?

A commercial document written by her nephew, Don Samuel, discovered in the Ferrara archives, brought new insights into her trading practices. An elegantly-worded letter, dated 1537, from a certain John Hussee to a woman named Lady Lisle, mentioning Doña Gracia's visit to England and found among the papers of Henry VIII, initiated a hunt to discover who these British aristocrats were and their role in British history and that of the Mendes family at this time. Mention of Doña Gracia in the collected letters of the Papal Nuncios in Portugal led to the discovery of a flamboyant character named Duarte da Paz. He had been sent by family members to Rome to lobby against the coming of an Inquisition to Portugal. It was an act that in itself brought into question the popular misconception that Jews of those days were passive recipients of their fate.

There was also magic in fingering fading documents that she had watched being prepared, as happened during a visit to an ornate *palazzo* in Ferrara that currently houses the city's archives. Or sitting in the vaulted grandeur of the Yale Medical History Library and turning the tissue-thin pages of an original copy of a 16th century medical book written by her physician—a copy that she herself might have owned. Or visiting an eminent historian in the outer reaches of Istanbul and delving into the mysteries of Ottoman court life as seen through Turkish eyes.

However, after I had encountered documents in thirteen languages located in seven different countries—requiring a team of scholars to help transcribe and translate them all—and the key characters lurking under a plethora of different spellings and pseudonyms, I realized there was a far more practical reason why her story had never been fully researched. But I persevered, fascinated by an astounding tale of courage and dogged persistence in the face of horrendous odds.

Let her life story—intertwined as it is with her family, her people, her fortune and the hazardous times in which she lived— begin.

BLESSED IS THE LORD OUR GOD, RULER OF
THE UNIVERSE, CREATOR OF ALL THE SPICES.

*—From the Havdalah service recited at the close
of the Jewish Sabbath*

PART I

PORTUGAL: 1510–1537

Bridge at Castelo de Vide, Portugal, used by thousands of Jews fleeing Spain at the time of the expulsion

CHAPTER 1

A Time to be Born

B y the start of the 16th century, the port of Lisbon had
become one of the most frenzied in all of Europe. From
early morning to sundown, hungry seagulls soared and
dipped around the thicket of bare rigging atop the wooden decks
of three-masted caravels and larger carracks at anchor in the harbor. The gulls' screeching was often so loud it almost overpow-
ered the clatter of barrels rolling onto the cobblestone wharf.
Together they produced a deafening cacophony that added to
the sense of urgency surrounding the business at hand.

Down on the docks, outside the *Casa da Mina*, a special customs building and warehouse designed to oversee these valuable imports in the name of the crown, merchants haggled in a
mix of Portuguese, German, Spanish and Italian. They were setting prices for their share of the shipments of pepper, ginger,
tamarind, aloe-wood, indigo, gold, silks, cottons, porcelain,
coconuts and other wondrous merchandise arriving in those
barrels and giant spice jars from Portugal's newly-developed trading centers in Africa and India. There was much to be settled.[1]

For it had only been a handful of years since Vasco da Gama, the celebrated Portuguese explorer, had dared to challenge the unknown, sailing through mast-bending gales around the Cape of Good Hope to the east coast of Africa and on to India. The voyage had catapulted Portugal from a small and relatively backward fishing nation on the westerly tip of Europe into a formidable seagoing commercial empire. Da Gama's 10,000-mile southeasterly journey in 1498 would never compete in history and legend with the more romantic exploits of his contemporary, Christopher Columbus, who had gambled instead upon a westerly route to the riches of the spice islands of the East. Yet da Gama would achieve far more for the immediate prosperity of Portugal than Columbus would do by discovering the Americas for Spain.[2]

The Portuguese ocean-going feat had been exquisitely-timed. The modest material demands of medieval life were giving way to modern-day capitalism and a frenzy of worldwide demand for luxury commodities from faraway lands. A profusion of consumer goods arriving directly by sea from exotic places around the globe had created an entirely new social elite—that of merchant prince.[3] Vast private fortunes were piling up in Lisbon and elsewhere, seemingly overnight. It was a prelude to what would take place at the end of the 19th century and again at the end of the 20th century when rapid technological innovation would enable formerly unpretentious folk to acquire great wealth in a hurry and indulge in an orgy of conspicuous consumption.

It was also the height of the Renaissance. New ideas were being devoured as avidly as products. Machiavelli was analyzing the true basis of power politics at the same moment as Botticelli, Titian, Raphael, Michelangelo, Holbein and Leonardo da Vinci were creating dazzling works of art. Erasmus, Calvin and Luther were examining new avenues of thought and belief systems, while Copernicus was revolutionizing the theory of the cosmos, and Rabelais and Thomas More were exploring the human condition. It was as though a veritable star burst of creative energy had descended from the heavens.

Other currents of change and upheaval, equally profound in their ultimate effect upon the emerging century, were coursing through the interior towns and villages of Portugal. Garcia de Resende, aging chamber attendant to João II, King of Portugal from 1481 to 1495, noted them in a memoir of his king. Resende had given his opus a most fitting title, as he saw it: *Chronicle of the Valorous and Distinguished Deeds of King João of Glorious Memory.*

"Chapter CLXIII," he wrote in a careful hand. "On the Entry of the Jews of Castile into Portugal...the same year (1492) that King Ferdinand and Queen Isabella of Castile, as Catholic princes, expelled all the Jews from their (Spanish) kingdoms...the Jews, helpless and yet with their stubbornness in not wanting to become Christians, resorted to our king (João II) and asked him as a favor that he harbor them...in his kingdoms...for which they would provide him with a large sum of money..."[4]

That, in a nutshell, had been the real reason behind King João II's seemingly humanitarian gesture of allowing thousands of desperate Spanish Jews to enter Portugal a handful of years earlier: easy cash. Even Resende had been open about it. King João II was no fool. In crisis the king had seen opportunity. Eager to continue his conquests along the west coast of Africa and being hard-up as usual, despite the growing prosperity around him, King João II viewed the actions of his neighboring monarchs as a rare chance to raise funds for a world-class army and fighting fleet. It was in keeping with his avowed wish to conquer even more territory from the infidel Moors. And, as Resende put it, "provide to God much service...without inflicting hardship on his people," who naturally hated being taxed.[5]

Needing the backing of his advisors and courtiers to carry

out his plan, King João II then convened a council in Sintra, a hill town northeast of Lisbon. Before anyone could utter a word he told them he had made up his mind. So, "submitting to his wishes only to please him," they gave their approval, reported Rui de Pina, a diplomat and historian who wrote his own recollections of these events.[6]

In truth, admitted de Pina, the king's counselors didn't like the idea one bit. It was contrary, they told each other, to the king's role as Defender of the (Christian) Faith. He should not harbor people, who—as non-believers—even the monarchs of Spain had thought unworthy of remaining any longer in their most Christian of lands. The counselors believed that King João II had not been realistic when he suggested that in the eight month period he would allow these Jews to remain in Portugal, they might be tempted to convert to the "true" faith (an ongoing pursuit among the monarchs of Christian Europe who believed that converting Jews was a sacred duty). The experience in other European countries had proved otherwise. The Jews had stubbornly clung to their faith and, for the most part, accepted expulsion over conversion. Not all of them, admittedly. But enough to make it seem as though King João II was hiding behind a weak excuse.[7]

Besides, the specter of a ragtag horde of dispossessed Jews swarming over the border was justifiably creating a sense of alarm among the villagers who would be squarely in refugees' path. If the incoming Jews were starving, might they rob and kill? What about pestilence? There were reasons to loathe these Jews even before a single one had crossed over. True, there had been Jews in Portugal for centuries. Some had arrived as early as biblical times when Jewish traders regularly sailed all the way west to the Spanish port of Cadiz on the Atlantic coast, adjacent to the Portuguese border. Once known as Tartessus, Cadiz was believed to have been the biblical city of Tarshish.[8] But there had never been more than 10,000 to 20,000 Jews in a country of one million Portuguese Christians, although the numbers had been swelling in recent years as tolerance for Jews throughout Spain had been dwindling.[9] Still, except for the occasional outburst against them, they had lived peaceably in their own neighborhoods, governing themselves in matters of daily life.[10] This was different. Though the king would make money, it would not be "without...great injury, losses and danger which the whole kingdom (would receive) from their coming," concluded de Pina.[11]

The problem was that the king was not talking about a handful of Jews. Over 50,000—nearly half the entire population of Jews being expelled from Spain and nearly triple the number already in Portugal—were expected.[12] Despite the fact that they would have to cross the almost impenetrable mountain ranges of Estremadura to reach Portugal, it made sense for them to make the relatively brief overland journey to a country with a similar Iberian culture and language. The alternative was a dangerous sea voyage arranged in haste on a jam-packed and probably leaky ship to distant lands they could not even envision.

There had been no opportunity for these Spanish Jews to trek north into France or the Low Countries. Almost all Western Europe had closed its doors to the Jews by the end of the 1400's, save a handful of minor Italian and German states. The reasons were manifold. For one, the Jews' economic role in the early Middle Ages as merchants and moneylenders in countries that had not yet developed a merchant class, or where Christians had not been permitted to lend money at a profit, was becoming less and less critical. The local population was increasingly assuming these roles and had become eager to expunge the competition. It had always been expedient to expel the Jews whenever a Jewish community gained some affluence. Since expulsion was normally accompanied by a confiscation of assets, it was easier and quicker to raise revenues this way than to resort to unpopular taxation. Unlike other minorities, the Jews could not easily fight back. They had lost their national power base in the year 70 of the Christian Era (CE), after their Roman overlords had sacked Jerusalem as a reprisal for repeated uprisings, scattering them throughout the Roman Empire.

By the late Middle Ages, the authorities in most European countries, especially the clergy, were insisting that because the Jews refused to acknowledge Jesus as their savior, they must surely be evil people. The common folk were genuinely convinced that it was indeed the Jews who poisoned their wells, used the blood of good Christians for ritual purposes and were responsible for any and every epidemic that came their way. In addition, the presence of Jews in their midst undermined the absolute power of the Catholic Church. So the order of the day was to convert or get out. Once converted, they could become fully assimilated into the population. And, after a generation or two of intermarriage, disappear entirely.[13]

The situation in Spain had been different. That is why this most recent order of expulsion had been so surprising and, from a Jewish point of view, monstrous in the extreme. For one, Jews had been neither latecomers nor a powerless minority in Spain. They had lived on the Iberian Peninsula since antiquity (some say they had first arrived as traders in the days of King Solomon).[14] They had been property owners, farmers, artisans and merchants as early as Roman times. Spain had also been the one country in Europe dominated for centuries by the Muslims who had swept north across the Straits of Gibraltar during the first millennium. And the Muslims were far more tolerant of the Jews.

As a result, in subsequent centuries, Jews had risen to key positions at the Muslim courts of Spain. They had become diplomats, treasurers, interpreters, land owners, tax collectors, courtiers, scribes, royal physicians, scientists, poets and philosophers.

Rather than live as a small and relatively unimportant minority, they had been among the most distinguished citizens of the Spanish kingdoms.

Even when the Christian kings began to snatch the Peninsula back from the Muslims around the 11th century, the talents and know-how of these educated and wealthy Jews had been equally critical to the Christian kings advancing their own conquests. It was a culture of castles and knights, ballads and troubadours, chivalry and heroics on the battlefield. Never suspecting their collaboration was only considered a temporary expedient, the Jews had become eager participants. But gradually, as the Christian kings grew more and more powerful, they started chipping away at Jewish privileges in line with the dictates of the pope in Rome and the other Christian monarchs of Europe.[15]

The beginning of the end came in 1391. A period of famine and plague provoked a wave of massacres that left hundreds of Jews dead on blood-stained cobblestones outside their tightly-packed homes. An equally large number, desperate to save their lives and those of their loved-ones, chose conversion. It had not been too difficult, at least for some. Unlike their brethren in Northern Europe, many of these Iberian Jews had never been particularly religious. A tolerant society lasting for hundreds of years had created an assimilated Jew for whom conversion was less problematic. Moreover, the Iberian Peninsula had a history of intermittent waves of coerced conversion since the time of the Visigoths. It was hardly a new concept.

By the early 1400's, a new critical mass was therefore emerging on the Iberian Peninsula; the descendants of those converted during the 1391 massacres and the immediate years thereafter. Known interchangeably as *conversos* or New Christians, there had been thousands of them. On the street they were dubbed *marranos*, a pejorative for pigs. Among the Jews they would henceforth be known as *anusim*, a Hebrew term born of compassion but later tinged with contempt and mistrust. Freed from the restrictions increasingly governing the life and livelihood of those who had remained steadfast in their ancestral faith, the *conversos* soared with discomforting speed through the ranks of the burghers, officials and even the clergy of the various cities and provinces.[16] All of which produced resentment among both openly-professing Jews living under increasingly difficult circumstances and the surrounding Old Christian population. Rumors soon began circulating that many of these *conversos* had never become true Christians. Rather, they were opportunists, taking full advantage of Christian goodwill and privileges while keeping their Jewish identity intact in the privacy of their homes. The *conversos* would either deny it or insist it was hardly surprising, given the brutal circumstances of their conversions.

Aiding and abetting this duplicitous religious behavior, alleged the authorities, were those Jews who had managed to survive and stick to their faith. Thus, in 1481, at the urging of the clerics and with the permission of the pope, a Holy Inquisition Against Depraved Heresy was established to root out backsliding among the *conversos*, and save the rot from infecting the rest of Christian Spain. It was not a new idea. Since the 13th century, the pope had regularly used this sort of tribunal to enforce discipline and rid the church of heretics, although never on such a large scale. True, an Inquisition only had jurisdiction over Christians. But the *conversos* were now Christian, which made it all so convenient. Yet, despite the arrests, the confiscation of property, the dank prison cells, the brutal tortures and the public spectacle of *conversos* roasting alive at the stake—the infamous *autos-da-fé*—that took place in major city squares to the squeals of pleasure from the multitude, the duplicitous behavior continued.

Thus, after the last Muslim kingdom on the Iberian Peninsula fell to Christendom in January, 1492—a triumph that cried out for a religious gesture of gratitude and a quick infusion of confiscated assets into a treasury depleted by war—King Ferdinand and Queen Isabella, the current monarchs, won enough popular support to get rid of the infidel Jews and their pernicious influence forever. On March 31 of that year, in a majestic room in the Alhambra Palace, the monarchs signed the Edict of Expulsion. All Jews were to leave Spain by the end of July, unless willing to convert, after which they could stay on indefinitely. The idea was that without openly-professing Jews all around them, the duplicitous behavior of the *conversos* would quickly die out. Even more important, everyone left would now be Christian. They could legally come under the jurisdiction of the Holy Office, the sanitized term for the Inquisition authorities. Any sign of a relapse could be exposed and stamped out immediately.[17]

At least 40,000, or one-third of the openly practicing Jews, grabbed this final chance to stay in their beloved land of dappled sunshine, haunting music, gentle pastures and citrus groves. Despite recent setbacks, they had prospered, each under his own vine and fig tree. For centuries life had been good.[18] By contrast, it was a terrifying prospect to leave one's ancestral home and abandon a solid livelihood to set off for an unknown land.

And what if the present monarchs suddenly died and the next one had a more liberal Jewish policy? Better to lie low and temporarily convert, many concluded. In some places entire Jewish villages took this approach. It was an idea that had worked before. Why not again?

Not all agreed. The most committed Jews were prepared to abandon almost everything they owned to literally keep the faith. Property values in their neighborhoods plunged. Andrés Bernáldez, a contemporary historian, tells how a Jewish house was bartered for a single mule and a Jewish vineyard for a small piece of cloth.[19] A legend sprung up, told from generation to generation, recounting how some of the Jews pocketed the keys to the wrought iron gates of their homes. They hoped these keys could prove ownership of the property,[20] once cooler heads prevailed and the Edict was rescinded, as many felt would happen.[21] But it was not to be. Jews would be officially barred from Spain until the monarchy itself was abolished, albeit temporarily, early in the 20th century.

Based upon the attitude among the European monarchs in the 1400's, the actions of the King of Portugal had thus been unusual. Nevertheless, despite the concerns of his regional lords, and the panic it provoked, the king's wishes prevailed.

The terms worked out between the anxious leaders of the Spanish Jews and King João II's emissaries seemed reasonable enough. For the privilege of crossing the common land border with Spain at predetermined checkpoints, the incoming Jews from Spain would each pay an entry tax for which they would be given a certificate. Anyone found wandering about Portugal without a certificate would immediately become a prisoner of the king and sold into slavery, whereupon an arm or leg would be scorched with a branding iron. The king had probably counted on dozens of refugees trying to sneak in without paying the fee, although the wealthy Jews of Spain offered to give generously for the purpose.[22]

Labor was in short supply and slavery was the easiest and cheapest way to amass the manpower needed for any number of capital projects. According to Bernáldez "more than a thousand souls" became captive because "they had not paid the cruzados required for entry."[23]

Later, historians would suggest that King João II had known all along there would be a triple benefit from admitting the Jews: money from those who paid his entry tax; manpower from those who could not pay; and know-how from those with special talents or great wealth to help build his nascent commercial empire.[24]

The entry tax was to be administered on a sliding scale. In

the general category were the common folk. They would each pay eight cruzados[25] for the privilege of remaining for eight months, after which they also would be sold into slavery if they had not departed. The king would provide safe shipping, at his own expense, to take them to more hospitable lands on or before the expiration date. The breathing spell was crucial. Ferdinand and Isabella had allotted barely three months from the moment when their Edict of Expulsion could be "proclaimed in the plazas and customary places," to the final deadline. It had given everyone scant time to arrange passage to anywhere. Any Jew found in Spain after that date—August 2, 1492—was to be immediately put to death with their belongings confiscated "for our treasury."[26] The Spanish monarchs were not going to let a stray ducat or two end up in someone else's money pouch if they could avoid it.

The second category was a luxury one. An entry tax of one hundred cruzados per household would be payable by some six hundred of Spain's wealthiest Jewish families. They would thereby gain the privilege of residing indefinitely, at the pleasure of the king, where they wished, including key cities like Lisbon. Artisans, cartographers, inventors and craftsmen were placed in the same category as the wealthy.[27] Though the Edict prohibited the Jews from taking gold and silver jewelry or coin with them, the rich found ways to export their wealth through bills of exchange or letters of credit made possible through their international trading contacts. The common folk by-passed the prohibition by swallowing gold and silver coins or sewing them into the lining of their garments.[28]

Still, even Bernáldez felt a measure of pity as the refugees trudged for endless miles along dusty Spanish roads scorched by a white hot midsummer sun. Whether headed for the sea ports of Spain or the mountain passes into Portugal, "They took to the difficulty of the road," he wrote later in *Historia de los*

Reyes Católicos Don Fernando y Doña Isabel, "the small and the large, the old and the young, on foot and riding on donkeys...and on carts... with great difficulties and misfortune, some falling, others rising up, others dying, others being born, others becoming sick... there was not a Christian who did not feel their pain... the rabbis (asked) the women and young men sing and play timbrels and frame drums (as they went) in order to make them happy."[29]

The "harsh pestilence" that Rui de Pina had predicted—probably plague—ravaged the countryside as they filtered into Portugal and clustered in makeshift camps. Lacking shelter, decent food and on a forced march, it was bound to happen. "An infinite number of them died and were buried on the roads, mountains and deserted places in the kingdoms," wrote de Pina.[30] Once again, the local people noted that it was the Jews who had been responsible for an epidemic. Only this time it was true. The king never did provide any promised protection. Consequently, many were robbed and even killed by farmers or roving bands of highwaymen who had no reason to want to help these newcomers.[31]

King João II also procrastinated about providing ships. He had good reason. Ultimately, in the allotted time, the hundreds of Jews who could not find ships or pay for passage from Portugal would add to the number of slaves he would squeeze out of the deal. Meanwhile, the children of those bound into slavery were shipped to the Portuguese West African jungle island of San Tomé. Away from their parents, it was alleged, they could be better raised as good Christians. In fact, it was a way to populate a newly-acquired desolate island that the Portuguese themselves had been reluctant to settle. But, according to Samuel Usque, a Jewish chronicler of the era, most of the children "wasted away from hunger and abandonment" or "were swallowed up by the huge lizards."[32]

So maybe those Jews who had chosen conversion as the only way to remain in their Spanish villages had not been wrong after all. For there was one more outrage awaiting the ones who had given up everything to adhere to their faith—one that would shape the attitudes of their children, soon to be born in exile inside Portugal.

Laid low by dropsy, King João II died three years later, in October, 1495. Manuel, his 28-year-old cousin, inherited the throne. Fair, thin, diligent, sparing in his food and drink and single, Manuel sorely needed a wife. He quickly settled upon Isabel, eldest daughter of Ferdinand and Isabella. But Isabel insisted that she would marry him only if he banished the Jews from Portugal as her parents had done from Spain.[33] Many of the Portuguese officials scoffed, saying that it had nothing to do with religious zeal. They reasoned that Spain had grown jealous of the riches that the banished Jewish merchants were bringing to this formerly insignificant neighbor nation.

It was true. Manuel had no intention of parting with such a valuable community. He could ill afford to eliminate the very people whose commercial skills were playing an important a role in Portuguese expansion and exploration.[34] He and his loyal counselors therefore devised a secret plan. On December 5, 1496, they promulgated the desired Edict of Expulsion. It required all Jews to leave by October, 1497, thereby fulfilling the wishes of the bride. A few Jews left immediately. It was none too soon. By spring, it was announced that the rest of the departing Jews could only embark from the port of Lisbon. Like his predecessor, King Manuel promised to provide the ships.[35]

Hearing the news, about 20,000 of them congregated in the center of the city, arriving from all parts of the country. As no ships were yet ready, King Manuel arranged for them to be ushered into a large city plaza known as Rossio—a rectangular arena that normally hosted circuses, religious pageants and later the

Portuguese *autos-da-fé*. With soldiers guarding all exit routes, he made them a final offer: freedom and refuge from expulsion if they would convert on the spot. But they resisted. After all, these were the diehards who had given up the comfort and security of their homes in Spain to adhere to their ancestral way of life. What did he expect?

He had already tried to break down their morale by having their children snatched from their arms and forcibly baptized. Now he left them in the open without food or water for three days, roasting their bodies under a burning sun. Friars and other clergymen visited them periodically, trying to persuade them that their lives, and the return of their children, were more important than their faith. Some could resist no longer. Others stood fast, after which the king pleaded with them yet again to be baptized. Then realizing, "if he starved them any longer they would perish (which would defeat his purpose) he dragged some by their legs and others by their hair and beards...bringing them to the churches where the waters of baptism were thrown over them," wrote Samuel Usque, the Jewish chronicler.[36] Soon King Manuel could go back to his bride and honestly say there was not a Jew left in the land. He even had an Edict of Expulsion to prove it.

Though this is the traditional view of what happened, modern historians have since argued that 20,000 people could not fit into the Rossio plaza. Nor could they have been simultaneously dragged to the baptismal font. It was much more likely that the original numbers were much smaller. The baptisms became a negotiated resolution as soon as the Jews realized Manuel was not about to back down. Under the deal, they would all agree to accept baptism peacefully, provided their children would be immediately returned. And, for at least twenty years, there would be no official enquiry into their private religious practices. It was a way for Manuel to get what he needed in a hurry without bloodshed. For the Jews it was a way to win a breathing spell...and who knew what might happen at the end of twenty years?[37]

The expulsion of Jews from Portugal, a touchstone of Jewish history, was thus a fraud; a travesty that many believed was worse than eviction for those who suffered through it. It never occurred the way it was billed. Instead, the king created thousands of bitter, outraged and defiant *converso* families. In subsequent years, many would quietly find ways to move to other lands, even though restrictions against emigration would persist for generations. But the idea that most Jews left Portugal as openly practicing Jews was a fiction, despite the fact that some of their descendants would eventually return to the faith elsewhere. Even today, many Jews who trace their ancestry to Portugal bristle at the notion that their forebears once lived as Catholics.[38]

As these newly-minted Christians resumed their lives as bankers, tax collectors, artisans, cartographers, merchants, tailors, dyers, cobblers, weavers, goldsmiths, lapidaries, booksellers, scribes, dressmakers, midwives, physicians and the like, it also became an act of defiance to surreptitiously hang onto their faith, especially as Portugal did not yet have an Inquisition to snoop into their private practices. "As a result of this violence," wrote Usque, "(which was) contrary to divine and human laws, the bodies of the Jews were made Christian but no stain ever touched their souls."[39] Indeed, Portuguese *conversos* would become the most committed crypto Jews living in any Christian land where Judaism had been outlawed.[40] They would privately perpetuate certain Jewish rites for generations; eventually without even knowing why.

In their devious and self-serving ways, King João II and King Manuel had been right about scooping up the talent and wealth of the most prominent Jews on the Iberian Peninsula and forcing them to stay. The talents, financial expertise, international business savvy and wealth of these compulsory converts helped to quickly propel the tiny nation of Portugal to the forefront of European commerce. Many of the formerly outraged *conversos* even reveled in their newfound wealth and freedoms.[41]

The subsequent years therefore became a time of attempted truce. The laws of May 1497, restricting anyone from delving into the personal religious practices of the *conversos* for twenty years, were honored, although contempt still festered silently among the Old Christian masses. The *conversos* had been expressly granted equal trading and property rights. They were now free to live anywhere in Lisbon, a cosmopolitan and rapidly-growing city teeming with some 50,000 souls of diverse racial and national origins; a populace that had already spread beyond the city's old medieval walls.

Still, many *conversos* remained in or close to the Juderia Grande, one of three original Jewish quarters. They preferred being among their own. Moreover, it occupied one of the most convenient areas in that city, adjacent to the commercial district and the royal square. It was also not far from the harbor where King Manuel had recently moved his own residence. Preferring the center of commerce to the isolation of a medieval hilltop castle, the king had left his old Moorish stronghold for the hub of his emerging empire.[42]

The aristocratic elite also favored the river front, building elegant mansions with private docks and spacious courtyards down by the water. To satisfy this whim, the old city walls running along the Tagus River were demolished or incorporated into the new manor houses. These residences, along with the bustling activity around the quay, encouraged the development of markets, shops, taverns, eating houses and hostels alongside the river. [43]

It was no doubt in this newly-fashionable district near the harbor, in one of its many whitewashed row houses with its vernacular terra-cotta tile roof, that another event of consequence was about to occur.

The year was now 1510 or thereabouts.[44] A girl was born into a family that numbered among the wealthy six hundred Jewish families from Spain that had been permitted an indefinite stay.[45] Within days, in keeping with their outwardly Christian life as *conversos*, this baby was baptized, most probably in the private chapel of the family's home, as was the custom of Lisbon's wealthier citizens. The name she was given was Beatrice de Luna.[46] The urgency of such a ceremony would have been a concern at a time of high infant mortality, and in an era when safeguarding the immortal soul was considered as important as rescuing the corporal body. Besides, an epidemic of unknown origin—possibly typhoid, influenza or dysentery—was raging throughout Lisbon at the time.[47] The odor of death was everywhere. Whether the family recited Hebrew prayers over the infant will never be known. If they did, it would have been done in private and perhaps even silently.

As the daughter of rich and influential parents, the arrival of Beatrice de Luna (later known as Doña Gracia Nasi) would have been celebrated with a sumptuous feast for family members, friends and important business associates. In lavish reception rooms with walls half-covered with Portuguese decorative tiles and richly furnished with tapestries from Flanders, damasks and velvets from Italy, rugs from India and silks and porcelain from the Far East, a long buffet table would have been filled with elaborately-prepared savory and sweet dishes, many of them incorporating an almost ridiculous amount of sugar and cinnamon—expensive status symbols of the New Discoveries, as they were called.[48]

———••❧••———

The child was the daughter of Alvaro and Phillipa de Luna.[49] Portuguese historians believe they had originally come from Aragon, a formerly independent kingdom in northeastern Spain. Doña Gracia's father, Alvaro de Luna, traded in silver, among other commodities. We assume he did so because a man named Alvaro de Luna is listed in key commercial registers as having deposited substantial amounts of silver for his own account at the *Casa da Moeda* between 1517 and 1526 , the national bank that also acted as a mint. In 1526 alone, he deposited 90 lbs of silver, placing him among a rarified few with large sums at their disposal.[50] It would have been exceptional, if not impossible, to find two men with this kind of wealth in the same city at the same time.

Moreover, silver deposits were directly connected with the Indies trade. And coming from Aragon, it would have made sense for him to become involved in overseas trading.[51] The possibility that he is our man is heightened by his identification in certain lists as Spanish (*"nacionalidade espanhol"*), a classification that may well have meant country of birth, or trade affiliation, rather than current place of residence. In another, he is clearly identified as someone who is currently operating in Lisbon.[52] If so, he was no doubt also sought after in court circles for his vital international contacts and know-how—highly prized at a time when trade links to the rest of Europe and the remainder of the known world were of great concern to the crown.

The taking of the name Beatrice de Luna at an official christening of our infant begins the curious story of the multiple names by which all *conversos* were known at this time. Each *converso* typically carried two sets of names: the Christian names under which they were baptized and another full set of first and last names corresponding to a Jewish identity, if they still had one. Beatrice de Luna certainly did, as later evidence would prove.

The taking of multiple names dated back to pre-expulsion Spain when Jews were being coerced en masse into Christianity. From the outset, it was customary for any Jew undergoing baptism to assume a set of Christian names. The church considered it mandatory, a symbolic gesture to affirm that the person's soul was being "reborn" as a Christian soul, separate from its past. The first new name might correspond to the Christian saint on whose day the individual was being baptized. Often the *conversos* took—or were forcibly given—the Hispanic family name of their sponsor (converts typically had a sponsor who assumed a role similar to that of godparent, standing by them at the baptismal font). Or they might simply agree to a name common among local Christian families. This could have meant incorporating both the names of the mother and the father, and even the town where they lived, such as Juan Gomez Martinez d'Avila. The rules concerning family names were only beginning to be standardized.[53]

Later, that Christian family name would become the recognized name by which the descendants of these *conversos* would also be known, much as any family name passes down through the generations. Even so, certain names became more closely associated with *converso* families, such as Alvarez, Gomez, Peirera, Oliveira, Enriquez (Henriques), Fonseca, Lopez, Fernandes, Nunes, Mendes. It helps explain why so many Sephardic Jews have Hispanic-sounding family names.

The name of Beatrice would therefore have been her official or *converso* first name. Fashionable and upscale, it was widely used in royal circles.[54] The Christian last name of de Luna would have come down from her parents in the traditional way. The reasons for her adopting the Jewish family name of Nasi when she reached the Ottoman Empire would emerge later in life.

Bearing the family name of de Luna begins to explain a tradition of community leadership that seems to have permeated the entire family. The name had been prominent in Aragon for generations among *conversos*, Old Christians and even a handful of Jewish families;[55] originating, no doubt, in a mountain town called Luna in the northeast—the expression de Luna literally meaning someone "from Luna." Morever, Luna had been known since the Middle Ages for its Jewish residents.[56] One of the most renowned individuals carrying that name had been yet another Alvaro de Luna, chief minister to King Juan II of Castile who reigned from 1419 to 1454—less than a hundred years before our story begins. Dominating even the king, and reputed to have had a private army of three thousand lances, this particular Alvaro de Luna had put his awesome power and reputation squarely behind the needs of both Jews and *conversos* when such an act ran counter to the trends of his time. Was this an indication of his Jewish origins? We know that he was the illegitimate son of an Aragonese nobleman.[57] So he could well have had a mother who was Jewish. Under Alvaro's stewardship, *conversos* rose to positions of leadership in almost every aspect of national life,[58] an advancement that tragically proved incendiary in the end.

Upon being forcibly converted in 1497, it would therefore have been quite likely that a distinguished Jew from Aragon would have wanted to preempt the name of someone he admired, rather than accept any Christian name, even if the name had never been in the family before. Perhaps one of the children of the original Alvaro de Luna had fled to Portugal, standing as godfather to our Alvaro at the time of the mass baptisms.[59] Or it could have simply denoted the family's village of origin.

Young Beatrice's mother, Phillipa,[60] acquired an equally distinguished first name upon baptism. Her name had originally been brought to Portugal a hundred years earlier when Phillipa of Lancaster, daughter of John of Gaunt, married King João I. It had remained fashionable thereafter. Phillipa was also the name of the spirited woman, heir to the southern French duchy of Toulouse, who had married the king of Aragon in the 11ᵗʰ century. This Phillipa had been deeply involved in the creation of the Order of Fontevrault whose abbey became a refuge for battered wives and penitent prostitutes, as well as enhancing the prestige of women in general and promoting their rights. She also happened to be the grandmother of Eleanor of Aquitaine, the most politically active and astute woman of her day,[61] reminding us that women were not passive bystanders during these centuries.

Beatrice was known at home as Gracia,[62] the Iberian equivalent of the Hebrew name of Hannah. Later, upon openly returning to Judaism at mid life, she would be publicly known as Gracia (Grace). The Spanish language honorific of Doña would automatically have been placed before the first name of anyone of noble or distinguished lineage.

As we begin to look at the influences that may have shaped her personality, actions and character during her formative years, we discover dozens of women from prominent families emerging to take center stage in business and politics during this era. She was hardly alone.

Women, especially widows, were already prevalent in the business world. They enjoyed equal inheritance rights under law in most European countries and would often find themselves thrust into commerce following the early death of their husbands.[63]

Those who also had a chance to govern often excelled. Doña Gracia had only to look over the mountains at Queen Isabella of Spain to see what a woman with a strong sense of mission could accomplish. Isabella's stubborn will and resulting achievements—waging the final battle against the Moorish presence in

Spain, championing Columbus's voyage to the New World, to name just a few—must have surely been the stuff of her history lessons.

Also discussed in educated circles would have been the fiery independence of the notorious Lucrezia Borgia (1480-1519) and Caterina Sforza (1463-1509), both of whom coveted leadership, albeit of smaller Italian city-states. Equally well known would have been Isabella d'Este (1474-1539), one of the most accomplished diplomats and patrons of the arts during the Renaissance. Later, in 1558, after a bronze portrait medal had been struck in Ferrara bearing the likeness of Doña Gracia's teenage niece, a French historian would remark that it was hard to distinguish this likeness from that of Isabella or Lucrezia. They wore the same ornaments in their hair, the same costumes and even had similar profiles on their portrait medals.[64]

Closer to her own age would have been Mary Tudor, the highly educated daughter of King Henry VIII of England, who reigned briefly as Mary I, Queen of England, at mid century. Mary's life, from 1516 to 1558, parallels that of Doña Gracia almost to the year. They may have even met as young women during Doña Gracia's brief stay in England. Certainly Doña Gracia was known to Thomas Cromwell, one of Henry's counselors who also played a role in Mary Tudor's life.[65]

Considering all her later dealings with the French crown, Doña Gracia would have been well aware of Catherine de Medici, daughter of the noted Italian family who became Queen of France. Catherine was directly involved in diplomacy and government as regent during the minority of her son. Catherine's life, from 1519 to 1589, also runs chronologically parallel to that of Doña Gracia.

There was also Marie of the House of Habsburg who became Queen of Hungary and later Regent of the Netherlands. Marie's life span—from 1505 to 1558—made her another contemporary of Doña Gracia. Marie knew precisely what it meant to be a woman leader. She would eventually match wits directly with Doña Gracia.[66]

And what about the great Jewish biblical saviors like Judith and Esther? She would have surely read about them. In addition, veneration of the saintly Mary was unusually strong at this moment, especially in Portugal.[67] Thus, the idea of a woman as a miracle worker and protectress[68] may well have seeped into Doña Gracia's impressionable mind during the countless hours when she would have been attending Mass. Later on, and significantly, the Jewish people in the Ottoman Empire would embrace this most traditional of Christian terminologies for Doña Gracia herself, dubbing her simply *La Señora*.[69] In spirit, although not literally, she became *our* lady, or *our* mother.

Jewish women were becoming equally accomplished and influential in her own day. Shortly before Doña Gracia was born, a Talmud Torah *for girls* had opened in Rome; its women graduates emerged as poets, writers and patrons of the arts. A woman known as Pomona da Modena, living in Ferrara at the beginning of the century, was said to be as well versed in Talmud "as any man." Another member of Pomona's family, Fioretta, was constantly engaged in Hebrew and rabbinic learning. Others worked as scribes.[70]

Then there was Bienvenida Abravanel, a niece of the famous Don Isaac Abravanel, the man who led the Jews out of Spain at the time of the Expulsion and later settled in Naples. Bienvenida was so smart and well educated that she became the tutor, and later advisor, to Leonora, daughter of the viceroy of Naples. When the Jews were expelled from Naples in 1530, it was Bienvenida who maneuvered through her court connections to have the order rescinded. After the death of Bienvenida's banker husband, Samuel, Bienvenida continued to run his banking business and use her wealth to ransom Jewish refugees captured by pirates.

Doña Gracia and Bienvenida were to live in the same Italian city of Ferrara in the prime of both their lives.[71]

The 16th century view of Jewish women's capabilities did not end there. By the time Doña Gracia was born, Jewish business women were routinely working alongside their husbands. In Constantinople they handled commercial transactions for Muslim women who were prohibited from doing so. Jewish women also won the right to be purveyors to the women of the Sultan's harem. Esther Kyra, the most renowned and influential of them all, worked the corridors of the *saray*, or women's palace, during Doña Gracia's lifetime.[72]

A role model for Doña Gracia's personal commitment to the Jewish community could have come from a Spanish ancestor named Tolosana—possibly a great grandmother, although it is doubtful whether an irrefutable family connection could ever be proven. Still, there are haunting similarities between the two.

During the early 1400's, Tolosana, a devout Jew from the town of Saragossa in Aragon, watched in horror as five of her seven children converted to Christianity in the tidal wave of conversions following the 1391 massacres. She even tried to stop one daughter from converting by temporarily keeping her under house arrest. It was no doubt this trauma that motivated her to provide in her will for long-term financial support of a local synagogue, Talmud Torah and other Jewish institutions that helped to keep what was left of Judaism alive in Aragon.

Further, the bequest came with exactly the sort of limitations that Doña Gracia would have established. Tolosana, widow of Don Benvenist de la Cavalleria, the richest Jew in Aragon,[73] stipulated in her will, read in 1443, that if the synagogue were ever turned into a church—then a common occurrence—the money should be transferred to another Jewish community. Among her children's first names: Beatrice, Brianda and Reyna, the same names that crop up in Doña Gracia's family. Even though they were common first names at the time, it's almost too much to believe that all three would appear yet again within a single family in less than a century without some filial tradition being responsible for the parallels.[74]

Tolosana's *converso* descendants would play a prominent role in helping the Jews during the Expulsion period. The accomplishments of a woman like Tolosana could have thus become the inspirational sub-text of family legends.[75]

CHAPTER 2

Growing Up

D oña Gracia always behaved towards her siblings as if she were her parent's first born child—at least the oldest surviving child—a birth order that would have further conditioned her to leadership. The record indicates that she had a younger sister named Brianda, a brother named Aries, and a second sister named Giomar who died early in married life.[1] There were probably others who did not participate in her later activities, and thus were not included in written documents, some of whom may not have even survived childhood, as would have been typical of the times.

Brianda was the only sibling to share much of Doña Gracia's adult life. This had more to do with the fact that their husbands were brothers than any kinship of spirit. Their public squabbles when they moved on to Italy would explode in an anger so intense it would reverberate four hundred years later from faded documents still preserved in the Venetian and Ferrara archives. Doña Gracia was determined and calculating. She also had a strong sense of mission, as we shall see. Doña Brianda was weaker-willed and less disciplined. She was more attracted by the glamor of Renaissance life.

It is doubtful whether Doña Gracia was a natural beauty. This was an era of chivalry when odes to beautiful women were penned at the wink of a suggestive eye, or the teasing shrug of a bare shoulder. Though her contemporaries would wax lyrical about her other qualities, and even her beauty of character, there is nary a mention of physical attributes, save among later historians who appear to be attributing sex appeal where none existed.[2] Unfortunately, we have no portraits to tell us either way. Still, she clearly took great pride in a stylish appearance. Being well-dressed at this time was a key sign of social status. It was also a way to show contempt for the sumptuary laws that for centuries had humiliated the Jews by restricting them from wearing fashionable attire. She would refuse to submit to those rules even when she openly reclaimed her Judaism.[3]

Though a multitude of documents tell a great deal about Doña Gracia's adult life, there are no first-hand accounts of her childhood. But much can be deduced. In the early decades of the 16th century her upbringing undoubtedly followed the expected rituals and traditions typical of an upper-class girl from a family with connections at court. For a start, she would have been immediately handed over to a wet nurse who would have been from a *converso* family that had retained similar Jewish leanings. These families were exceedingly cautious concerning the loyalties of the servants they hired, tending to choose from among their own. Providing employment to *conversos* in need was also a way to fulfill the family's commitment towards their less fortunate brethren. This becomes clear from testimony given later in Antwerp by a 75-year-old *conversa* refugee who had served as a wet nurse. Doña Gracia would continue the tradition for her own household.[4]

The manner in which she would later handle her business affairs confirms that Doña Gracia must have been exceptionally bright and a quick learner. She would have been offered a solid education even though she was a girl. Jewish women from leading families, as we have noted, tended to be well educated at this time. The coming of the Renaissance enhanced that ideal. Setting funds aside for education even became a clause in a legal contract connected with the upbringing of her niece.[5]

Her studies would have been conducted privately at home with a tutor—who probably taught her siblings at the same time. Once again, the choice of tutor would have been made from within the family's own circles. This can again be deduced from the way she would later choose the noted *converso* writer of the era, Alonso Nuñez de Reinoso, as a tutor for her own daughter and niece—a man whose writings confirm that he retained a strong Jewish identity and shared her outlook.[6]

As well as her native Portuguese, Doña Gracia would have probably understood or even spoken Spanish because her parents, uncles and aunts had all grown up in Spain.[7] Significantly, both her future husband and brother-in-law wrote their wills in Spanish even though they were no longer living in Spain.[8] She would have been taught to read and write in several additional languages, including Latin and French. She may well have learned some basic math as well as history and politics, even if some of these subjects were picked up informally. Otherwise she could never have coped with the complexities of her later business dealings and certainly would not have been handed control of a large international banking house. Litigation before the rabbinic courts over control of her family's fortune many years later implies an ability to read and personally understand the complex terms of her husband's will even as a young woman.[9] A notarial document from Ferrara, dated 1562, mentions that a certain contract had been "signed by the very hand of Doña Gracia."[10]

The study of poetry and the classics would have been expected of a refined girl of her class at the height of the Renaissance—a background that would later enable her to host a cultural and literary salon in Ferrara.[11] Music lessons would have included playing the *oud* or *vihuela*, both 16th century guitar-like instruments of Moorish origin highly popular on the Iberian Peninsula at this time. She would have learned to dance the fashionable *galliard* in order that she might participate in social events. The domestic arts—embroidery, weaving and sewing—would not have been overlooked either, as well as the management of a household. A solid education in Catholic devotions would have been a must. Though her parents probably found this troubling, especially whenever the priests thundered on about the wickedness of the Jews and the family was forced to confront the grotesque images of their brethren that had been an integral part of religious art and sculpture since the Middle Ages, such familiarity would be of great value to Doña Gracia. She would later be able to operate seamlessly in Christian society.

Manners and a meticulous understanding of the social protocols expected of her would have been of the utmost importance. The value placed upon such protocols would be underscored some twenty years later in a letter written by King João III. The aim of the missive was to invite Doña Gracia—by then a mother—to bring her infant daughter to be raised in the royal household. The idea that the child would thereby "learn all the fine customs" was considered sufficiently compelling for the newly-widowed young mother to agree.[12]

Luxurious clothing, an obsession among the upper-classes in Lisbon at this time, was similarly dictated by convention, even for a child: soft Indian cotton next to the skin, topped with an elaborate floor-length dress of brocade or velvet, sporting a tight bodice and bell sleeves. Over the bodice was typically strung multiple strands of pearls. The head and hair were encased at all times in a cap or a nun-like hood. Heavy perfumes camouflaged the lack of regular bathing, while the odor of the dirty clothes was smothered by keeping sandalwood bars in drawers and closets—a new custom derived from the exotic products arriving in Lisbon from faraway lands. She would have had to wear the obligatory crucifix around her neck.[13] How that meshed with her parents' continued commitment to Judaism would serve an early lesson in the art of balancing a double life—of which she would prove a true master.

Outside the shuttered windows of her home, purposely kept small to filter out the glare of the strong sunlight, Doña Gracia would have grown up in an overstuffed city alive with the sights, sounds and smells of lives squashed together inside and outside tiny dwellings. These houses, attached to one another on both sides to conserve space inside the city walls, provided shelter for untold numbers of relatives. Whenever one house was not roomy enough for all its residents, as well as the family enterprise, two or three adjacent houses might be leased—as her future brother-in-law would do on the Rua de Lava Cabeças, a bustling street in the old Juderia Grande.[14] Large or small, these homes were further squeezed into a tight mosaic of narrow streets and alleys that snaked like ski trails down the steep hillside on which Lisbon was perched—all the way from the Moorish castle at the very top to the harbor below. The angle of some of the alleyways was so sharp that they evolved into giant granite staircases cut into the hillside.

Her time spent at study, or play with cousins and siblings, inside the rooms or courtyard of her own home, were doubtless punctuated by the sights and sounds of the harsh street life outside. Shrill cries of *"agua vai"* ("there goes water") warned passers-by to get out the way before slops and overflowing chamber pots were dumped from a high window, splashing into the fetid alleys. The stench was overpowering, fed by the crush of bodies inside tiny dwellings, the ubiquitous fish mongers and butcher stalls, plus the dozens of open-air garbage dumps just over the city wall.[15]

The city was noisy, too. Pounding hoofs would regularly merge with the rattling of carriages and sedan chairs, the chatter of the public washerwomen walking by with woven baskets perched precariously on their heads, the songs of water-carriers similarly balancing ceramic jugs on their heads, the barnyard sounds of pigs, chickens and stray dogs devouring slops, the occasional outburst of angry voices as sailors settled personal squabbles with knives, the constant hammering from the busy shipyards, and the hawking cries of street vendors as they sold sweet rice and other culinary delights from collapsible wooden tray tables.

At least once a month and on significant saints' days, there would have been any number of religious processions offering the horrifying sight of bleeding flagellants along with majestic and solemn priests in flowing cassocks swinging incense and carrying colorful icons and jeweled crucifixes. These processions typically wove through city streets and open squares adorned with gushing fountains, ending up at the Rossio plaza where an outdoor Mass or pageant would follow.[16]

That would have been when Doña Gracia went about town accompanied by parents or relatives. Attendance at church on saints' days was mandatory. Families like her own typically traveled by personal carriage or sedan chair, rather than on foot through the dirty and dangerous streets. If she were lucky, she might have even caught a glimpse of the king taking a procession of tigers, parrots, elephants, and scantily-clad black slaves— all exotic sights newly-arrived from Africa and the Orient—through the streets of his capital city to the gasps and adulation of his people.[17]

The rhythm of daily life inside the home would have been overlaid by the family's clandestine perpetuation of Jewish rituals, a secret that may not have been fully revealed to her until she was ten years old.[18] The likelihood that the de Lunas remained committed to Judaism is confirmed by her parents' actions: they gave her in marriage to Francisco Mendes, the man who served as the covert "rabbi" of the *converso* community. This, of course, was before the Inquisition brought a halt to such practices.[19] By contrast, if they were no longer interested in perpetuating their Jewish heritage, the de Lunas would have promised their daughter to a fine Old Christian family. Disenchanted *conversos* of substantial means were rapidly shedding their tainted Jewish blood this way, hopefully for good.

Her parents clearly agonized over their discarded Judaism because years later, Doña Gracia would devise a complex maneuver to have their remains disinterred from a Catholic cemetery in Portugal and brought to her in Italy for reburial on sacred ground in Jerusalem. She would do the same for her late husband.[20]

Perpetuation of Jewish customs tended to center upon domestic rituals: the changing of clothes and washing weekly each Friday, just before the Sabbath; refraining from work or cooking on the Sabbath itself. Dietary laws were observed by avoiding shellfish and pork (at least in the privacy of their homes). Many continued to eat their favorite "Jewish" foods like chickpeas and eggplant. The substitution of the popular Portuguese sausage of pork, breading and spices, with an identical-looking one made of partridge, quail or chicken, even led to a new variety of local sausage called *alheiras*. But, over time, even these customs faded, especially after the Inquisition arrived in Portugal in 1536 and classified such domestic practices as proof of backsliding.[21]

Leading a double life, religiously speaking, was not easy. It lead to terrible feelings of guilt and confused identity. Throughout the century, Portuguese *conversos* would cry out in anguish over their hybrid existence whenever they set down their feelings in literature.[22] What made matters worse was that religion was not separated from the core of a person's existence and identity. It was a fundamental way of interpreting the world before the advent of scientific explanations. Besides, many brooded over the fact that following the "wrong" faith could condemn their souls to hell.[23]

As a child of first-generation *conversos* living in Portugal before the coming of the Inquisition, Doña Gracia had the chance for a rudimentary Jewish education. The family may even have had Hebrew books in the house. A curious exemption to the laws of 1497, offered by King Manuel as part of his negotiated settlement, had permitted newly-converted physicians and surgeons to keep Hebrew books.[24] Many of the best medical treatises of the times were written in Hebrew or Arabic, a legacy dating from the days when advanced Muslim culture was revered on the Iberian Peninsula and Jewish doctors even more so. And Doña Gracia had at least one uncle who was a physician.[25]

Two outside events would have helped to shape her sense of mission. The first was the Lisbon Massacre of 1506. About five years before Doña Gracia was born, Lisbon had been subjected to one of its periodic outbreaks of plague.[26] These epidemics would typically follow a series of bad harvests and malnutrition that weakened the people. This time there were so many victims that the king ordered two new cemeteries dug outside the city walls. Hysteria and fear gripped every citizen in the city. The more prosperous among them, including the royal court, fled elsewhere until the epidemic ran its course. Added to the agony were drought and hunger. The situation became so dire that daily street processions were mounted to plead with the Almighty for water and mercy. It did no good. After five bone-dry weeks the people were so terrified they were ready to do anything to save what was left of their lives. By early in 1506, everything was in place for a fearful explosion of pent-up emotions.

First, a rumor spread that their hunger was primarily due to the *conversos* who now numbered among the city's most active grain speculators. It was said that they exported grain to foreign countries at huge profits to themselves, while leaving the local population without bread.[27] Then a group of *conversos* was arrested in April for secretly celebrating the Passover Seder. Two days later yet another *converso* was accused of showing contempt for Christianity by mocking a miracle as it was actually occurring: the Virgin Mary appearing in a "divine light" that had suddenly illuminated a crucifix on an altar of a convent chapel. All was ready for the kind of unrestrained mayhem that had regularly plagued Jewish communities throughout the Middle Ages. The tinder had been lit.[28]

That these were now *conversos*, and no longer openly-practicing Jews, was of no consequence in the eyes of the masses. They were seeking a way out of their current miseries. And they were certain that people of Jewish blood were once again responsible for their troubles. Any number of baptisms or public expressions of Christian piety was not about to change that view. It was not only the grain speculation. A lifting of the old legal barriers had allowed too many *conversos* to become too prosperous too fast. Nobody else, they argued, was getting a chance to benefit from the wealth pouring into the country from the New Discoveries.

The young *converso* who allegedly mocked the miracle was dragged to the door of the church and pelted with stones until dead. His body was dismembered on the spot. When his brother arrived to find out what was going on, the mob turned on him, too. A fire was lit and both bodies were burned, the foul odor of burning flesh signaling everyone else to build similar pyres. Even the foreign sailors joined in, contributing money for the wood.[29]

The crowd was now thirsting for *converso* blood, crying out that if the king would not punish these people—and thus appease their God—the people would have to do the job themselves. The royal court, miles away in the safety of Evora, appeared paralyzed. Moreover, it was accused of having favored the *conversos* for too long. Certainly it was out of touch. The local authorities were overwhelmed. Thousands of men, women and even children were soon running amok. Their hunt was made easy because it had only been nine years since the mass conversions had taken place, and fourteen years since many of these *conversos* had arrived from Spain. Everyone knew them by sight. Or, if not, the residents of each parish knew exactly which houses they occupied. The mob was soon throwing *conversos* out of upper story windows, slicing their limbs from their bodies, tossing them alive on the roasting pyres. By the time order was restored four days later around 2,000 *conversos* lay dismembered or burned. There was not a *converso* family left in Lisbon that did not mourn someone close to them. Even the de Luna family, which had probably fled weeks earlier with the court to Evora, no doubt lost relatives or friends.[30]

No amount of wealth, connections or repeated reciting of Catholic devotions, would make them feel safe again. No amount of baptismal water tossed over them would wash away centuries of hatred. The idea of being vulnerable because of Jewish blood, and not because of Jewish practice, became a new and unsettling concept. This was ethnic cleansing. Their homes became places of perpetual fear. There was hardly a single one among them who did not create a hidden cellar, a concealed door or tunnel leading from their houses in case of surprise attack.[31] It was a rude awakening, particularly among members of the younger generation who did not have the same attachment to the faith of their fathers as their parents. Tolerance, the historians have since decided, would have done far more to eradicate Judaism than persecution.

It did not end there. When Doña Gracia was five years old, placards designed once again to turn the people against the *conversos* began appearing all over Lisbon.[32] Since the bulk of the population was not yet literate, they doubtless proclaimed their messages using grotesque cartoons. She would have had no trouble understanding their meaning even as a small child. One can only think how painful it must have been for her mother to explain. It was an ominous warning. As an adult, Doña Gracia always behaved as though she knew, deep down, that the *conversos* would never been acceptable to the Christian world.

Why most of the *conversos* did not leave Lisbon immediately can only be explained by the on-again, off-again policies of the crown concerning their right to leave, and the terms under which they would be permitted to depart. There were also personal hurdles: livelihood considerations, the difficulty liquidating and transferring assets, the problem of leaving behind family members who could not travel, an atavistic sense that the Iberian Peninsula was still their rightful home and the continued difficulty of safely reaching any place where Jews would truly be welcome. It could further be explained by the age-old delusion that tomorrow will surely be a better day. Finally, it's tough to run away from an economic boom. So many of them were personally prospering.

Yet, if a dread of indiscriminate annihilation became a constant companion in the childhood of Doña Gracia, so too did its counterpart, the messianic concept that divine deliverance would surely follow a series of calamities like the ones so recently suffered by all Portuguese *conversos*.

Divine deliverance, in the Jewish messianic sense, means the coming of a purely human, albeit charismatic man (a Messiah), probably a descendent of King David, who defeats the enemies of Israel, restores the Jewish people to their rightful place in the Holy Land and introduces a period of spiritual and physical bliss for all humankind. No longer subject to cruel whims of alien rulers, the Jews would once again enjoy self-determination under just and upright leaders. This man would serve as a prophet, warrior, judge, king and teacher, just like King David. Not only would his coming be preceded by an agonizing period of trouble and turbulence, he would also be tested in battle. Reports were beginning to arrive from Jerusalem suggesting his coming would also be associated with the reappearance of the Ten Lost Tribes of Israel.[33]

In those days, both Christian and Jew believed that every occurrence, however magnificent or mundane, had a symbolic meaning and purpose. Accordingly, the twin events—a massacre and a portent of divine deliverance—must have combined to make a powerful statement in the mind of a young girl who would one day have the power and money to nudge these implications forward in a practical way.

The man who gave the portent of divine deliverance a sense of imminence arrived by ship at Tavira, a port in southern Portugal, in 1525.[34] His timing could not have been better. The morale of the *converso* community had collapsed once again. Three years earlier a new king—King João III—had come to the throne. Considered by all to be an intolerant man of limited intelligence, he loathed anyone with Jewish blood. And he was heavily influenced by unyielding clerics.[35] A contemporary portrait shows him with a steely gaze, a flat forehead and protruding ears. He is wearing a seven-pointed crown. Over his shoulders is draped an ermine cape, on top of which lies the heavy gold chain of office.[36]

Nobody was therefore much surprised when he soon began badgering the pope for the right to establish a Spanish-style Inquisition in Portugal. He was convinced that his *conversos* would never totally relinquish their Jewish practices unless forced to do so under threat of death and torture. The outlook was grim.[37]

The man arriving at Tavira went by the name of David Reubeni. Elaborate tales are told of this charismatic adventurer who quickly captivated the hearts and minds of *conversos* and rulers alike. Reubeni, a tiny runt of a man with a skeletal frame from fasting and prayer, told everyone that he hailed from an obscure location in Africa, an area that today comprises Ethiopia. Indeed, he could well have been an Ethiopian Jew. In fact, much of what he said about himself, his goals and his biblical beliefs make even more sense today in the context of what we have now learned about Ethiopian Jews and their culture.[38] Diogo Mendes, Doña Gracia's future brother-in-law, would refer to Reubeni in no uncertain terms as "short and black" (*"petit, noir"*)when being asked, seven years later, what he knew about the man during an interrogation in Antwerp.[39] If Reubeni had been African, rather than having Caucasian features like most Ethiopians, the term *negre* would have been used.

Reubeni maintained that he belonged to a warrior sect of Jews. Also, that he was the son of a king called Solomon and the brother of another king called Joseph, both of whom ruled the lost tribes of Reuben, Gad and Manasseh in the faraway land that was his home. He even produced a "pedigree" tracing his ancestry back to King David. His most fluent language was Arabic, although he also seemed familiar with Hebrew. His mission was to obtain firearms and cannon with which to fight the dreaded Muslims. He wanted to drive them out of the holy city of Jerusalem, returning it to all Judeo-Christian peoples. But he desperately needed the armaments because his people were not advanced technologically. Their only weapons were "the sword, lance and bow." Whenever he addressed a group of Portuguese *conversos* he would tell them that he intended to go on to conquer the entire Holy Land. Afterwards, he promised, he would send his captains "to gather the dispersed of Israel" from all over Europe and North Africa and deliver them back to their rightful homeland.[40]

Reubeni had first surfaced in Italy, two years earlier, arriving by ship in Venice and then riding into Rome on a white horse. He was so convincing that he even persuaded Pope Clement VII of the value of an alliance between his state and the Christian world. He told the pope he was seeking help for a new crusade against the Muslims, whose recent conquests in Turkey and the Balkans had begun to terrify the leaders of Western Europe. He clearly knew how to capitalize on the political concerns of the day. The pope decided to send him from Rome to Lisbon with a personal letter of introduction to the king of Portugal. The Portuguese king was considered most appropriate, on account of Portugal's seagoing expertise and its ongoing campaigns against the Muslims along the West African coast.

Reubeni was thus beginning to fulfill all the requirements of a messianic contender: he had a charismatic personality, he was a member of a lost tribe, he was purportedly born of the House of David and he had been charged with a military mission.

He had one more ace up his damask sleeve. He knew that Portugal had long been obsessed with forming an alliance with Prester John, the legendary chief of the African kingdom of Ethiopia and the only Christian king in a region dominated by Muslims. The Portuguese and Ethiopians had even exchanged diplomats. The Portuguese hoped to neutralize the encroaching military muscle of the Muslims by attacking from the East as well as the West. So when David Reubeni—who was clearly from the same region and also bore the same first name as the current Ethiopian emperor—showed up, it was viewed by the royal court as a major breakthrough.[41]

In truth, it was probably a coincidence and a confusion of facts. The Portuguese had been eagerly awaiting the return from Ethiopia of one of their diplomatic missions. They mistakenly thought Reubeni had been sent by their own emissaries. The potential benefit to Portugal was considered so great that even Reubeni's Jewish identity was temporarily ignored.

He was soon being received at court with all the honors of an important ambassador. The *converso* community flocked to meet him, taking his presence as a signal that their moment had finally come. Even if it didn't work out as planned, it was nevertheless a "sign" that messianic redemption was at hand. Faux Messiahs had appeared throughout the ages without the messianic idea itself losing credibility. Besides, Reubeni had been quick to dismiss any notions that he was a Messiah—maybe a precursor of a Messiah, he hinted, but not the fellow himself. Such hoopla and its glorious potential could not have failed to impress the teenage Doña Gracia who lived in daily fear of her neighbors. Whether they actually met face to face is not known. But it's highly possible; Reubeni is known to have visited the homes of the leading *converso* families of the day.[42]

Reubeni kept a private journal during this period.[43] In it he reported that the Portuguese *converso* community had invited him to stay at their houses, even covering all his expenses during the year he remained in Portugal. His strategy with King João III, he revealed, was to offer to support Portuguese spice trading ventures in the East against attacks from Muslim traders. In exchange, he wanted Portugal to support his efforts to free Jerusalem.

However, at least one high official at court insisted Reubini should not be trusted. His true mission, the official maintained, was to restore the *conversos* to their ancestral faith. At first nobody listened. But then a crisis occurred. A *converso* courtier became so obsessed by Reubeni and his message that he had himself circumcised. Reubeni claimed that he had hoped this would not happen as he was well aware it would put "all the *conversos*...in great danger." It certainly changed the mood of the court. Negotiations for "eight ships armed with 4,000 large and small firearms" immediately fell apart. Reubeni was lucky to escape with his life. He left the *conversos* "fearful and weeping" but promised that the struggle was not yet over. "This time," he told them, "I only come to give you good tidings that salvation will soon come."[44]

He was tragically wrong. The backdrop to Doña Gracia's later teenage years would be one of even greater fear. Accusations of sacrilege, like setting fire to a crucifix or stamping upon the cross, multiplied irrespective of reality. When the government failed to stop the hate-mongering, the accusations became even bolder. King João III had recently wed Catherine, a granddaughter of Ferdinand and Isabella of Spain. From personal experience she insisted that an Inquisition was therefore indispensable.[45]

The threat of the imminent establishment of an Inquisition in Portugal must have become an obsession within Doña Gracia's family circle. Both her future husband and his brother—who were related to her even before her marriage—were among those who would devote untold hours to help finance a well-organized lobbying effort at the Vatican to prevent its coming.[46] Without the needed bull from the pope there could be no Inquisition. Even when that overture failed (although the lobbyists did manage to win a delay) the leading *conversos* kept hammering away to mitigate the tribunal's excesses.[47]

It was quickly becoming a family tradition to fight back with every tool in its arsenal, the seeds of which may have been planted decades earlier. We know of at least one plot in Aragon in 1485, spearheaded by Aragonese *conversos*, to prevent the coming of the Inquisition to that region. They had chosen murder as their weapon of choice, hunting down and killing some of the incoming Inquisition officials in the hope of deterring others. They also raised bribe money and petitioned the Spanish crown—all of which led to nothing.[48] What is not known is whether any of Doña Gracia's family had been part of this earlier effort. In the relatively tight circles of the courtier Jews of 15th century Aragon, it's entirely possible.

But for a young girl quickly blossoming into womanhood this was no time to dwell on outside concerns. She could well have been mourning the death of her parents, both of whom disappear from the record very early on. Besides, the year was now 1528. She had reached her eighteenth birthday.[49] And she was about to be formally betrothed and wed to the most sophisticated, wealthy and prominent merchant in Lisbon.

CHAPTER 3

Marriage

At first blush, it was a glittering match. Doña Gracia's husband-to-be, Francisco Mendes, would have made any bride's heart flutter, and the mother of the bride sing for joy. He was not simply rich—one of a number of *arrivistes* about Lisbon at a time when the very piers were paved with profits. Rather, he was the quintessence of old money, a brilliant member of an illustrious Jewish courtier family from Aragon. Before the mass conversions of 1497, they had been known by their Jewish family name of Benveniste.[1] The family had been so prominent in state affairs on the Iberian Peninsula for so many generations that Francisco was singled out for unusual treatment. His Jewish family name continued to be cited in official documents for years after the conversions, alongside his far more mundane baptized name. Even Vatican documents refer to him as Francisco Mendes Benveniste.[2]

Though the family name of Benveniste has since become commonplace among the Sephardim, its use at the dawn of the 16th century was far more limited. Anyone bearing this name was likely to be related to Francisco in one way or another. The name first shows up around 1080 in documents in the Provence region of France and the adjacent kingdoms of northeastern Spain.

Among Francisco's illustrious ancestors was Sheshet ben Isaac Benveniste, a 12th century physician and diplomat at the courts of King Alfonso II and King Pedro II of Aragon; Isaac Ben Joseph Benveniste, yet another royal physician who, during the 13th century, used his court connections to persuade the king not to force the Jews of Aragon to wear the hated Jewish "badge," required at the time by the Pope Honorius III. Then there was Benveniste ibn Benveniste and Benveniste de la Porta, both of whom became important translators of medical works from Arabic into Catalan in the 14th century. Don Vidal Ben Veniste was one of the Jewish scholars present at the famous Tortosa disputation of 1413, arguing the relative merits of Christian versus Jewish attitudes concerning the Messiah. The Jews had been summoned there by Pope Benedict XIII, also known as Pedro de Luna (the first tantalizing connection between the two family names).

The most powerful of all was Abraham Benveniste, chief justice and treasurer during the reign of King Juan II of Castile during the 15th century. Once again, here was a Benveniste who used his position to strengthen the rights of the Jews, this time in Castile. This particular Benveniste served under Alvaro de Luna, the *de facto* dictator of Castile at that time, and a man who bore the same first and last name as Doña Gracia's father. The close alliance of the two men offer us an intriguing historical connections between de Lunas and Benvenistes even before Francisco and Doña Gracia were born. An additional connection was implied in the marriage of Tolosana to a man named Don Benvenist de la Cavalleria.

It was the powerful Abraham Benveniste, a man of fabulous

riches and the highest connections, who was probably Francisco's direct ancestor, perhaps a grandfather. Finally, and within the lifetime of Francisco himself, was Vidal Benveniste de la Caballería who negotiated the entry tax between King João II of Portugal and the incoming refugees from Spain.[3]

Here, therefore, was a bridegroom who had been bred through the generations to the role of intermediary between the Jews and their secular lords. Little wonder he was even able to charm a king as anti-Semitic as Portugal's King João III.[4] And no doubt his young bride as well.

Francisco Mendes was born around 1482 in the Aragonese town of Soria or Saragossa.[5] Ten years later, his parents were among those 600 wealthy Jewish families fervent enough in their beliefs to give up their ancestral homes, and a sizeable chunk of their assets, to emigrate rather than convert. When Francisco (his Jewish first name is unknown)[6] made the journey to Portugal he would have been about ten—old enough to have remembered the ordeal. We are certain he left Spain that fateful year because a letter of King João III, dated August 28, 1532, makes it clear that Francisco had entered the country forty years earlier.[7]

Francisco would have therefore been around fifteen when forcibly converted in Portugal and baptized under the name of Francisco Mendes. It must have been a traumatic experience for an adolescent so well versed in his religious studies that a rabbinic court ruling would later refer to him as a *rabbi anus*, the term used for a rabbi converted by force who also leads *conversos* in prayer.[8] He appears to have been the eldest boy in a large brood that included at least two other brothers: Diogo, born 1485 (the only brother with a birth date that is certain)[9] and Gonçalo,[10] who was probably younger than Diogo. Considering their likely ages, all three would have been born before the family left Spain. Thus, they would have had a full-scale Jewish education, which doubtless included familiarity with Hebrew, Jewish attitudes towards daily life and the important rituals and prayers.

Patching together fragments of information gleaned from later testimony before various Antwerp tribunals and documents found in the Ferrara archives, Francisco also had two sisters. One was the mother of Don Joseph Nasi, the man who became Doña Gracia's protégé and business partner and eventually her son-in-law. The other sister was Doña Gracia's mother. This is disturbing. It meant that Doña Gracia was marrying her uncle.[11] Certainly, the penchant among the courtier Jews on the Iberian Peninsula to intermarry to a degree that is shocking by today's standards was well-known at the time.[12] They managed to perpetuate the tradition even though it was contrary to canon law (church officials were apparently content to look the other way whenever their palms were sufficiently greased). Doña Gracia's own daughter, Ana,[13] and her niece, Gracia la Chica, would follow the same tradition. They would marry a pair of brothers who were also their first cousins.[14]

At the age of eighteen, Doña Gracia was therefore not only marrying her uncle, but also being wed to a man more than twice her age. But even this was a time-honored practice that dated back to the early Middle Ages, so she probably thought nothing of it.[15] Besides, marrying one's uncle was an even more ancient and time-honored custom in Judaism. The Mishnah (Jewish civil and religious law codified around the second century CE) and the Talmud (expansion and commentaries on this law) both fostered the idea, arguing that the affection a man had for his sister would extend to protect her daughter.[16]

Still, from a modern perspective, the perfect spouse was not so perfect after all.

Yet judged within the context of the marriage traditions observed among wealthy and aristocratic families of the 16th century, the match made perfect sense. These marriages had everything to do with financial alliances, the preservation of wealth and heritage inside a particular family, security and familiarity for the young bride and broader political ambitions.[17] They had nothing whatsoever to do with compatibility or sexual attraction. Rather, a marriageable daughter from such a family would have been viewed as a commodity, a key bargaining chip who might be profitably traded for important business or diplomatic links, or even an infusion of cash. It would have also been in keeping with the strong secular belief in the importance of marrying a social equal. The downside was the flawed genetic consequence of all this inbreeding, as the royal families of Europe were to find out. It could have also been a factor that contributed to the demise of the House of Mendes so soon after Doña Gracia's death.

Doña Gracia would have been expected to bring a dowry to the marriage table that in some way complemented the economic status of her husband-to-be—a further reason to believe that the man named Alvaro de Luna who shows up in the commercial registers during Doña Gracia's childhood was her father. Since Alvaro de Luna disappears from those registers two years before the marriage, and Doña Gracia was described as an "orphan" at the time of her wedding,[18] (an expression used for the loss of father but not necessarily a mother) her widowed mother might have had an even greater incentive to conclude the match. It would have meant that a man as competent as Francisco Mendes would be managing her daughter's sizeable inheritance.

There might have even been a prior contract written with that goal in mind. A custom had existed among the Jews on the Iberian Peninsula, at least since the 11th century, whereby a betrothal document was drawn up quite early between a bride's father and his future son-in-law, outlining the financial obligations on both sides. It would even include the penalties that might befall either party if the deal fell through.[19] Sometimes the match was even agreed upon informally at birth, suggesting Doña Gracia might well have been promised to Francisco from childhood.[20] The fact that her younger sister, Brianda, would marry Francisco's younger brother, Diogo, underscores the likelihood of an early marriage agreement, especially since Diogo never had the chance to become acquainted with Brianda beforehand. He moved to Antwerp so early on she must still have been a baby.[21]

Even more to the point, considering conditions in Portugal at this time, both parties could keep their Jewish identity alive, free from the fear of "outsiders" finding out, and pass along the depth of their feelings to their children.[22]

At the time of the marriage, Francisco Mendes had become so rich that King João III could comfortably describe him as a man who had "accumulated enormous wealth here,"[23] and a gentleman who numbered "among (the king's) most important merchants" connected with the Indies trade.[24] Writing many years later, Fernand Braudel, the most distinguished economic historian of 16th century Mediterranean trade, came to a similar conclusion. Braudel used the expression "success on a colossal scale" when referring to Mendes family members collectively.[25]

As Aragonese traders, the Mendes-Benveniste family had doubtless been extensively involved in pan-Mediterranean commerce for generations, probably in precious stones imported from the Eastern Mediterranean, a particularly common occupation among such families. Jews had long been prominent in Mediterranean commerce as they normally spoke Arabic as well as their local tongue. They were also culturally better able to act as intermediaries with their Arab counterparts. It is no coincidence that many of the earliest gem dealers stationed in the Portuguese colony of Goa, established around this time, were Jews or *conversos*.[26]

Because they were Jews, the form in which the family would have held its wealth would have differed from the Christian aristocracy. While the medieval nobles displayed their wealth in castles and lands and utilized any liquid assets, like rental income, to win honor and status on the battlefield, Jews took the opposite approach. History had taught them that they might have to flee at any moment. So even when they could own land, they were reluctant to sink much capital into land ownership. Rather, the goal was cash not castles. The Benveniste family would have therefore left Spain with a substantial amount of liquid capital—probably in precious stones as well as bills of exchange, since the direct export of gold and silver had been prohibited. Those bills could be readily redeemed in Lisbon for gold or silver, even though they might have lost something in the discount or fee charged for redemption. The gems would have been easily marketable, too.

Their relocation to the hottest commercial spot on the European continent, involuntary though it had been, could not have been more timely. Modern capitalism was just being born. And they faced scant competition from the local nobility whose wealth, as we have seen, was largely locked in the granite walls of their not-so-marketable castles and estates. The brothers had therefore been given a jump start. And they were smart enough and sufficiently motivated to make even more out of whatever they had.

Stealing much of the Oriental import trade from Venice, Portugal had just opened up those lucrative ocean-going routes to the riches of Africa and the Indies. This had quickly led to a radical shift in trading patterns. Traditionally, high-priced wares such as pepper—crucial for disguising the unpalatable taste of rancid meat and equally prized for reputed medicinal ability to improve eyesight, cure dropsy and eliminate liver pains, among other ailments[27]—had been carted along the expensive overland route from the East to Alexandria and from there by ship to Venice. But a chance to gain a foothold in the emerging Lisbon markets, where pepper and other Oriental goods were now being offered for less, had sent some of the importers fleeing from Venice to Portugal. The German and Italian bankers were among the earliest to arrive. They immediately grasped the potential. The population of Europe was on the rise, especially in the first half of the century,[28] together with living standards and an ever-growing tendency towards ostentation that increased market potential. The Portuguese welcomed the foreigners, even offering them preferential trading rights to improve the flow of capital necessary to make the most of the cargoes.[29]

Still, the sheer volume of merchandise arriving at the Lisbon docks soon created shortages in the precious metals needed to pay the Asian merchants who were selling the spices and gems. The Asians had little interest in an exchange of commodities brought from the West. They might occasionally agree to take payment in the form of wine, brocade and western armaments, such as sword or cannon, but they scorned other items like cloth. They preferred payment in gold, silver or copper, especially silver.[30]

Bullion was therefore in high demand to fill the empty cargo holds of the merchant ships on their outgoing journeys. Speculation became so crazed in the first decade of the 16th century—before the imports of precious metals from the newly-discovered mines in the New World—that larger silver coins virtually disappeared from circulation in the Netherlands and France. They had all been sent south where they were worth more.[31] German and Hungarian mines that were turning out European copper and silver could barely keep pace. Anyone in a financial position to bring silver to Lisbon—like the German and Italian bankers—or could afford to amass a sizeable amount of silver, like the Benvenistes and the de Lunas, was onto a very good thing. This was especially so if they could make their bullion purchases while the ships were away. They could then sit on that bullion until demand was at its zenith in the frantic weeks just before the long-distance convoys left Lisbon harbor each March to catch the favorable winds and tides.[32] The "spread" between the cost at low season and prices being paid at high season was considerable. So were the profits available in any credit arrangement made between a silver dealer and a merchant determined to secure a purchase opportunity for the voyage, even though he could not afford to pay for his bullion until several months hence.[33]

Documents from this period confirm that the finance and international trade connected with The Discoveries was quickly monopolized by the *conversos*. Unlike the *conversos* in Spain who had been hounded by the Spanish Inquisition almost from the beginning, those in Portugal had almost 40 years between the forced conversions of 1497 and the establishment of the Portuguese Inquisition in 1536. They operated free of the fear of being denounced by jealous competitors or debtors. Soon the *conversos* became major players in this new global marketplace.[34]

The lengthy hiatus turned out to be an astonishing stroke of good fortune, commercially speaking. It coincided with Portugal's brief hegemony over the spice markets.[35] The know-how and contacts gained became the basis for a global trade network that descendants of these first generation of Portuguese *conversos* developed in the subsequent century among each other as they moved onwards to such centers of international trade as Bordeaux, Bayonne, Antwerp, Amsterdam and the Caribbean.[36]

It was small wonder, therefore, that soon after arriving in Lisbon, Francisco's father was known as a successful merchant banker dealing in spices and precious stones, alongside three very able sons.[37] The pearls and precious stones arriving from India were in particular demand among the German merchants in Lisbon.[38]

Yet it mattered little whether the Mendes clan actually purchased segments of a ship's cargo in bulk when it returned to harbor, for resale at a handsome profit. Or they used their own stockpiles of silver for direct purchase of these commodities in Asia and then utilized the profits to buy even more silver, repeating the cycle again and again. Or, they provided short-term credit at a handsome fee to eager merchants long on hope and short on cash (interest rates were often hidden in service fees and up-front discounts as the church still frowned upon making money from loans). Or they simply acted as brokers dealing in the bills of exchanges that were increasingly enabling large sums of money to be transferred on paper from one country to another through trusted intermediaries. The old medieval way had been to move the equivalent bullion by wagon train along ill-kept roads. Even as late as the end of the 16th century the transport of 100,000 crowns from Florence to Paris required seventeen wagons secured by five companies of cavalry and 200 foot soldiers.[39] The skilled use of these bills therefore gave families like the Mendes a decided edge. Mark-ups were generally so steep, and demand was so hot, that they would have made large profits any which way, even if some of the ships went down or succumbed to pirate attack on the way, as many did. Since Lisbon had become such a multinational trading center, there was also a lot of money to be made in currency speculation, as the values of the respective currencies of each of the European countries fluctuated in relation to others. Francisco seems to have been the family member most closely involved with the arbitrage side of the business.[40]

Like other educated Jews and *conversos* of the day, both father and sons were no doubt fluent in several languages, giving them yet a further edge over many of their competitors. True, others were competing for the same transactions. But Maison Mendes, *père et fils*, had that rare combination of talents and instincts that made it all work just a little better. They soon became the Grand Masters of their commercial Universe.

Those family ties were crucial. A cadre of able sons was one of the only ways to build an international merchant banking house in the earliest days of modern capitalism, especially if each member could operate from a different location. One of them may have even gone to live in Asia for a while. A certain hot-headed young nobleman named Diogo Mendes was sent by the king with several ships under his command to help the celebrated general, Alfonso de Albuquerque, secure Goa and Malacca for Portugal shortly after the turn of the 16th century.[41] Was he the same Diogo from our House of Mendes? Though the idea is highly speculative, the same strong-willed and imperious manner that eventually led this particular Diogo Mendes to be banished from the scene by Albuquerque has echoes in later behavior.

The Diogo of our story would blatantly continue covert activities on behalf of the *conversos* in the 1530's and 1540's, even though it was suicidal to do so. His financial speculations in Antwerp further suggest he was a high roller and a risk-taker. The timing is right because immediately afterwards, in 1512, the family dispatched Diogo to northern Europe to open an affiliate office in the emerging capital markets of Antwerp,[42] while cousins set up smaller operations in Lyons, London, Venice and Ancona.[43]

With their youthful energies and newly-acquired patina of Christianity, the Mendes brothers seemed to relish the idea of conducting commerce free of the constraints that had thwarted their Jewish forebears in Spain. Both Francisco and Diogo exhibited a certain exuberance about playing on a level field with all the other merchants. Gonçalo, the third brother, acted as a sort of behind-the-scenes manager, renting warehouse space, sifting intelligence reports that were useful for trade as well as building a rapport with the king and generally supporting the initiatives of his brothers. On one occasion, Gonçalo was able to warn the king of possible trouble from the Moors in Tangier, based presumably upon intelligence gained from the family's merchant shipping.[44] The horrors of the previous decade were not without their compensations. As legal equals, the Mendes brothers now had a zest for every transaction, every gamble, every high-level contact, every success.

In line with the way family enterprises operated in those days, it would have been their father who educated them about the mechanics of a profitable transaction, introducing them while still in their early teens to the contacts, languages, transaction techniques, bookkeeping, markets, sea-routes, storms, dangers from pirates, the nascent idea of maritime insurance and seasonal fluctuations in prices and costs needed to become a successful merchant banker. And when he died—possibly while the boys were still in their twenties, since there is no mention of him in the records—they were poised to take their know-how and burgeoning capital to an even higher level.[45]

Three factors had to be in place before they could move into the major leagues, which would include making loans to the various royal houses of Europe and buying into the coveted monopoly rights to the most valuable imports of the day. First, they had to have trusted agents in other European commercial centers to negotiate terms, monitor interest payments and oversee the selling of the large quantities of merchandise they would acquire. Second, they needed to form a partnership with other bankers to pool the vast capital needed to operate a monopoly position in a particular segment of the marketplace. And third, they needed personal connections to a monarch who could grant such rights and would be in need of a reliable stream of income on a long-term basis.

Consider how the Mendes handled the profits inherent in the pepper trade. From the beginning, the cargoes of pepper coming to Portugal via the sea routes from Asia had been a crown monopoly. The pepper that arrived at the dock initially belonged to the king. The income to be derived from the pepper was crucial because the kings of Portugal, like those in the rest of Europe, mismanaged their finances and were perennially in debt.

Court circles were becoming larger and more luxurious. This raised the cost of everything from housekeeping to diplomacy. The perpetual wars—still being fought on the medieval belief that success on the battlefield made the reputation of a monarch—had become more costly too. The feudal system's reliance upon a serf's obligation to bear arms for his lord was breaking down. Monarchs had to increasingly rely upon mercenaries who demanded regular payment in coin. These soldiers also had to be equipped with the expensive canon and firearms that were just then being introduced on the battlefield.[46]

Meanwhile, the collection of taxes kept falling further and further behind need. There was only so much that a largely agrarian population could carry. Even King Manual of Portugal—whose reign at the very beginning of the spice trade era made him the wealthiest ruler in Europe [47]—had financial problems in his latter years, mainly from the drain of his continual wars with the Moors along the western coast of Africa.[48] As a result of the predicament he became anxious to monopolize the revenues from the spices coming into Lisbon as well as the re-export trade to the rest of Europe. That meant making deals with the bankers and commodity merchants of Antwerp, where the imports could be distributed directly to the heavily populated areas of northern Europe.

It was therefore crucial for the bankers to have representatives both in Lisbon and Antwerp, a mercantile city so well placed that it had developed connections with Lisbon even prior to the spice trade. This is doubtless why Francisco sent Diogo to Antwerp as early as 1512. Together, they gradually accumulated sufficient capital and expertise to attract the interest of the Affaitatis—a prestigious banking family from the northern Italian city of Cremona that similarly operated out of Lisbon and Antwerp. In Lisbon, Francisco dealt with João Francisco Affaitati while Jean-Charles Affaitati, his nephew,[49] became close friends with Diogo in Antwerp, where the younger generation of merchant bankers from all over Europe had begun to congregate. Jean-Charles and Diogo even lived on the same street.[50] Syndicates like these had become necessary by the 16th century because of the increasing scale of each deal.

The value to the king of giving monopoly rights to a large syndicate like the Affaitati-Mendes group was based upon reliability. From the king's perspective, it was well worthwhile taking a little less than if he had waited for delivery—a golden sack in hand, as it were, rather than two in a leaky boat. For the revenues from these rights, payable at pre-set times of the year, would come due independent of price fluctuations for the spices or trouble with the fleet. By giving the king an infusion of cash even before the convoys floated back into Lisbon or Antwerp harbors, the syndicate was able to purchase the entire cargo at heavily discounted prices.

The syndicate therefore created what was, in effect, an embryonic futures market. At one point the Affaitatis and Mendes were together contributing between 800,000 and a million ducats towards a single shipment; their lesser partners each invested amounts ranging from 10,000 to 20,000 ducats.[51] But it was well worthwhile because the rest of the European merchants were forced to buy from them—and them alone. These merchants included the Germans who had originally been among the leading importers, mainly because they had enjoyed direct access to the silver mines that had provided the bullion that the Asians demanded for their spices and gems.[52] Cornering the market this way was clearly a great way to make money, but not such a great way to make friends, as Diogo would later find out.

By 1521, the Affaitati-Mendes monopoly was poised to assume an even more profitable role. The reign of King João III had just begun. Like most European monarchs of his day, King João III was wildly extravagant. Contemporary accounts talk of a royal household beset by disorder and wastefulness with auxiliary palaces swarming with idlers and innumerable servants, far in excess of need.[53] Aggravating the situation had been the cost of a coveted marriage in 1526 between King João's sister and Charles V, the Holy Roman Emperor, the most powerful monarch of the era. A dowry of 800,000 cruzados had been agreed upon,[54] even though was there was not sufficient money in the entire treasury to make up that amount. Even a few years later, in 1534, King João still only had an annual budgeted income of 620,000 cruzados.

King João III never did climb out of debt. In the twenty years between 1523 and 1543 he ran up a deficit of 3 million cruzados. By 1544, the size of the outstanding loans needed to tide him over had risen to 2.2 million cruzados. He was so deeply in arrears that the rate of interest charged by the loan brokers of Antwerp rose to 25 percent.[55] Among those making the larger loans was the Affaitati-Mendes syndicate.[56] At one time they were providing the king with sums ranging from 600,000 and 1,200,000 cruzados annually.[57]

As half of the crown's revenues, at least throughout the 1520s, emanated from the spice trade,[58] King João became especially protective of those who were operating the monopolies. He seemed to have developed particular trust in Francisco. "He

(Francisco) is a person of very great reputation," the king told his brother-in-law, Charles V, in August, 1532.[59] "In all his (Francisco's) transactions, and most especially in those which during all this time he has carried out in the Indies trade and in many other which he has carried out on behalf of my Exchequer, he is considered one of the most important and the best supplied merchant."

King João's dependent status was made even clearer later in the letter. "In any aspect of service to me," he continued, " he (Francisco) has always served me so satisfactorily that I am most beholden to him. Thus, I have reason to rejoice in bestowing kindness and favor upon him, as upon one who always was and is my very devoted servant."[60]

The seventeen years between 1517 and 1534, just around the time of marriage, were particularly prosperous for Francisco. During that time he deposited over 4,000 kilograms (about 9,000 lbs) of silver in the *Casa da Moeda*, the state-operated safe deposit center that also minted coins for local use. It is virtually impossible to put a comparative sum on this amount to bring into a modern context, since costs and incomes were so very different. Suffice to say it was the largest deposit of any merchant doing business in the city during those years.[61]

The 40 years between the forced conversions and the arrival of the Inquisition was a period of religious transition for the Jewish community in Portugal. The implicit understanding in King Manuel's laws of 1497, stating that there would be no investigations into their private religious practices in the home for at least twenty years, had meant that this particular community of *conversos* delayed severing ties with Jewish practice, and then only doing so gradually. Since rabbinic literature implies that Francisco had become their *de facto* rabbi,[62] and bearing in mind that the Inquisition had not yet begun its malevolent work, there is every reason to believe that Doña Gracia and Francisco Mendes would have had two weddings: a private Jewish ceremony followed by a very public Catholic celebration.[63] Even the contracts drawn up would have fused Portuguese marriage customs with the requirements of Jewish law. Up until the mass conversions, Jewish communities on the Iberian Peninsula had been autonomous and self-governing. Even so, their betrothal and marriage arrangements tended to meld Gentile and Jewish traditions concerning the rights and obligations of both parties.[64]

Francisco's will, written several years later, stated that should he die during his wife's lifetime, his assets—other than those which rightfully belonged to his brother and partner, Diogo— were to be divided among his survivors; one half for his widow and one half for his children.[65] This style of equal partition between spouse and children was customary in the Portuguese marriage laws of the period.[66] Under the circumstances, it is unlikely that Francisco also signed a *ketubah*, a Jewish marriage contract. Had he been able to do so, it would typically have guaranteed the return of Doña Gracia's dowry in the event of his death or divorce. His brother, Diogo, specifically stated in *his* will that his wife was entitled to get her dowry back in the event of his death. So Francisco may have fulfilled his Jewish obligations this way, too.

How long they were formally betrothed is difficult to pinpoint. According to Jewish custom, a wedding had to take place within twelve months of the official betrothal, with the occasion being the time for negotiations between the two families concerning a dowry and other gifts.[67] It would have also been in keeping with Jewish custom for Francisco to give Doña Gracia an engagement or betrothal ring at this time.[68] Portuguese marriage customs were so similar to Jewish practice at this time that there is no question that an official betrothal of this sort would have occurred.[69]

The close-knit marriage arrangements favored by the courtier Jews of Spain would also explain why Francisco chose to wait until he was in his forties before getting married, although late marriage to a much younger wife was customary for any up-and-coming European merchant of the day.[70] It is unlikely that he was married before and was now a widower. Nothing yet found in secular or Jewish records support the possibility, or even children by an earlier liaison.

Before her Jewish wedding, Doña Gracia would have undoubtedly been required by her family to go through purification in a ritual bath—the *mikveh* in Hebrew or *banyo di novia* in the Renaissance Spanish of these Iberian Jews. Even if they could no longer go a public *mikveh*—as would have been customary in each of the three Juderias of Lisbon before the compulsory conversions—it still would have been considered crucial to first generation *conversos* for the bride to be ritually cleansed before presenting herself at the altar. A makeshift arrangement would typically have been set up in her home. Her girl friends or women relatives might have even made it into an excuse for a bridal shower, a festive event known among themselves as a *bogo de baño*.[71]

The Jewish marriage ceremony would have taken place quietly in either the de Luna or Mendes home. Very few people would have been invited, although traditional Jewish law would have required a canopy over the heads of the bridal pair and the blessings to be recited in the presence of a *minyan*—at least ten men. The ceremony would have ended with at least one additional ring being put on the bride's hand and a joining of the hands of bride and groom. It would have been a warm, family occasion.[72]

By contrast, the public Catholic marriage of a man as wealthy and prestigious as Francisco Mendes could have filled Doña Gracia with trepidation, lest she make one false move in a society where socially correct behavior meant so much. Taking place at a private chapel in the Mendes home or perhaps even the Lisbon cathedral, it was doubtless a major social event, attended by important business, social and personal friends as well as relatives on both sides. It would have been followed by a sumptuous meal with music and dancing. So much money was being thrown away on these occasions that by the beginning of the 16th century King Manuel tried to moderate such lavish expenditures with strict local ordinances. "Men spend," he observed, "if not squander, much of their estates" this way. Besides, he added, "the assembling of so many people at such weddings" too often resulted in the sort of carousing that ended in death. Invitations to have dinner with the bridal couple were therefore forbidden to all save close relatives.[73] It is doubtful whether anyone complied with his wishes. The love of ostentatious display was so prized during these years that these requirements would have been disregarded. Even the king himself—by then King João III—may well have attended.

Did she love Francisco? There are tiny clues that she cared and that her later zeal to help her fellow *conversos* may have deepened through her contact with Francisco. Only a handful of years later, while living as a widow in Antwerp, Doña Gracia's aching loneliness was described by an aging doctor.[74] A traveler to the Holy Land some twenty years after Francisco's death described the arrangements Doña Gracia made for the re-internment of her late husband's remains on the Mount of Olives—an extraordinary gesture of concern for his immortal soul that can only be partly explained by the depth of religious concerns.[75]

Married life, short though it was, could have therefore been sweet. In all likelihood, the newlyweds would have settled down on the Rua Nova dos Mercadores, one the finest streets in central Lisbon where the representatives of the most important foreign merchant bankers congregated—their homes and business establishments being one and the same.[76] It would have allowed Francisco to be close to associates like the Affaitati, as well as the royal palace and the wharf, all of which were key to his ongoing success. This long and broad street also bordered the old Juderia Grande. Many of the *conversos* still lived there, making it an ideal location for their lives in general. Further, it was the heart of the city, framed by 400 or so townhouses, 30 silk workshops, a dozen booksellers and haberdashers, at least nine apothecaries and countless other workshops and stores. As many of the shopkeepers were *conversos,* the couple would have felt even more at home.[77]

A substantial portion of Francisco's commercial affairs typically would have been conducted from the first floor of the couple's residence. This would have given Doña Gracia a front row seat on operations; her keen intelligence able to pick up the obvious and the more subtle nuances of his complex dealings and relationships. Assuming that her father had indeed worked alongside Francisco in prior years, she probably already had a fair idea of what was going on. Upon widowhood, she became too savvy, too fast to have spent her married years weaving tapestries in dank rooms.

In July of 1530, two years after his wedding, Francisco was at the zenith of his powers. He obtained a special charter from the king allowing him the same privileges as the German merchants in the city.[78] Among other benefits, these charters conferred priority status on the merchant's goods whenever they were unloaded from the ships in the harbor and processed through customs. It also permitted exemptions from import duties.

The charter had also enabled the Germans to move to the head of the line whenever they needed to process their silver ingots into coins at the *Casa da Moeda.* The Germans had originally won these privileges because the copper and silver coming from their mines in northeastern Europe had been crucial to the Indies trade. The privileges were also a *quid pro quo* for special trading benefits Portuguese merchants had obtained in the Low Countries and German states in the 15th century.[79] As Francisco was dealing heavily in silver, being permitted the same charter was obviously a rare and valuable concession to a local merchant, and attested to his importance in the spice trade.[80]

By 1533, the House of Mendes was so prosperous that it needed larger quarters for warehousing the goods it was importing from the Indies, and selling or re-exporting to Antwerp. A detailed lease, still extant, describes how Francisco's brother, Gonçalo, selected a cluster of adjoining storehouses for the purpose on the nearby Rua de Lava Cabeças.[81]

Its terms cast an interesting light on the way leasing deals were cut at the time. According to the wording of the lease, the property had become available as a result of the death of the previous tenant. To promote the vacancy, an agent of the landlord had walked the city streets and squares over a six month period talking it up. In his hand he carried a green branch, probably from an olive tree—a recognized symbol that alerted the public to the fact that a building, or buildings, were available for rent and that they should inquire further, even making a bid. During that time nobody topped Gonçalo, who was willing to pay fifty percent more than had been paid by the prior tenant. As seems to have been the custom, the olive branch was ultimately placed in Gonçalo's hand, thereby officially awarding the lease to him. The terms, however, still had to be confirmed in writing and signed by all parties.

These were not just temporary arrangements. The leases offered perpetual rights, almost as good as ownership, assuming the tenants paid regularly and on time—in this case twice each year—and kept the house or warehouse in good repair. In the

Mendes lease, the terms included rebuilding the storehouses at the tenant's expense if the structures happened to be destroyed by fire, flood, earthquake or other calamity. While the arrangement therefore carried many of the burdens of ownership, these leases also became valuable assets that could be passed on to family members. This may have been a reason why the lease was taken out in the name of Diogo and not Francisco. Such creative bookkeeping could have safeguarded the asset from confiscation by the Inquisition. As an Antwerp resident, Diogo's property was not as vulnerable.

Although business was booming, the personal outlook for the Mendes clan, as a family of *conversos*, had become decidedly shaky. This is readily apparent from Francisco's frantic negotiations with papal representatives.[82] It also showed up in the earthquake of January 1531 that became yet another excuse to arouse the masses to the satanic aspects of the *conversos* in their midst.[83] Moreover, the likelihood that an Inquisition would finally come to Portugal was evolving from a possibility into a certainty. It was now only a matter of time.

Working hard to make it happen was the king's own lobbyist in Rome, reflecting pressure from home emanating from the Portuguese clergy, the nobility and the masses, all of whom continued to view *conversos* as alien interlopers who had become too wealthy too fast. The job of the king's lobbyist was to bribe key cardinals to keep the matter squarely before Pope Clement VII. Only the pope could issue the required bull needed to officially set up the Holy Office, the agency that would manage trial and punishment in the name of the church.[84]

The *conversos* meanwhile were delaying this attempt by bribing the same cardinals to drag their stocking feet on the identical matter. These efforts were led by Francisco[85] working closely with Diogo in Antwerp. Acting as financial intermediary, Diogo was responsible for funneling the bribe money collected from the Lisbon *converso* community to Vatican officials through the *conversos'* own paid lobbyist in Rome.[86] All this turned the battle into a windfall for the corrupt cardinals. They now had every incentive to work both sides for as long as they could reasonably drag matters out. It was duplicitous games such as these, and so many more, that would enrage Martin Luther. From his base in Southern Germany, Luther had already stirred the first rumblings of the Reformation.

King João III was meanwhile slipping deeper and deeper into debt through his constant financial bumbling.[87] This made the prospect of confiscating the riches of the *conversos* even more enticing. The experience from neighboring Spain over the previous five decades had shown how an Inquisition could become an effective stream of income for the crown. Regulations governing the confiscation of assets were therefore high among the issues being discussed in court circles.[88] What finally tipped the balance in favor of a bull was the king's ability to arrange for senior members of the Portuguese clergy, influential in Rome, to draw life pensions from his nation's wealthiest parishes— long-term annuities that the *conversos* were unable to match with assurances of equal allure.[89] The bull was issued on December 17, 1531.[90]

Earlier the same fall, Francisco became sufficiently concerned for his own safety and that of his family to take two important steps. The first was to acquire the royal charter that put him on a par with German merchants. That move, which he seems to have launched less than a year before the bull was issued, indicates that he may well have had secondary motives in mind. For those privileges also provided him and his family with a fair amount of diplomatic immunity. Unless specifically approved by the king's own agent, nobody could place them under arrest or conduct house searches, or even charge them with a crime. They also had the right to bear arms and go around town accompanied by armed guards.[91] Meanwhile, the German merchants—so long the financial backbone of the Indies trade—had begun pulling out. As Protestants they were equally afraid of running afoul of an Inquisition. By late 1530, one of them had already been denounced for eating meat on St. Bartholomew's Day. Their business dealings with the king had also been deteriorating, making their long-term future in Lisbon problematic.[92]

From a financial standpoint, this left the market wide open for Francisco. But it did not eliminate the fear that came from being a wealthy *converso* with a particularly high profile. Aware that he might need more than just protection from the local authorities, Francisco also arranged—most certainly at a substantial price—for personal protection from Pope Clement VII. Being the wealthiest of all the *conversos*, and having innumerable competitors who coveted his wealth and were eager to get rid of him, Francisco must have recognized that he would become one of the Inquisition's hottest and earliest targets if he did not take preventive action.

His personal exemption from the Vatican, signed in Rome on December 11, 1531, just six days before the bull authorizing the Inquisition, was addressed to senior Portuguese clergy.[93] It positively drooled with compassion and concern for "our cherished children, Francisco Mendes and Beatriz (sic) de Luna, his wife."

Incidentally, this is the first time Doña Gracia's name appears on an official document. It refers to her by her maiden name, Beatrice de Luna—a practice that would last a lifetime. She would never be known by her husband's name; neither during the time she lived in Christian Europe nor when she reverted to her Jewish identity in Ottoman lands. Although historians and novelists have repeatedly referred to her as Beatrice Mendes, it was never the way she was identified. Rather, she adopted a practice that was in keeping with other women of means or nobility in the 16th century. It was not even an expression of feminist independence.

Explaining with surprising candor that the couple was fearful of being arrested, thrown in jail or hauled into court as a result of accusations, the papal exemption began by appealing to the clerics' "feelings of brotherhood for these people." Should the clergy refuse to listen to that plea, it threatened them with reprisals. "By our apostolic authority," it warned, any accusations, sentencing, penalties or confiscations leveled against the couple, their children or other family members without the direct consent of the Holy See could leave the clergymen subject to "threat of censure... and fines."[94]

The mention of children was not theoretical. The couple's first and only surviving child, a daughter named Ana, had been born a year earlier;[95] an event that in itself might have precipitated the request for the exemption. Evolving from a wide-eyed bride into an anxious mother and confident young wife, Doña Gracia could well have begged Francisco to seek the protection. Knowing her persistence in later life, she may have even nagged him to do so.

Trouble was indeed in the air. By the following June, 1532, the climate had deteriorated to the point where a law was enacted prohibiting *conversos* from leaving Portugal even for the Azores or other colonies. Ship captains were being ordered not to carry out any gold or valuables belonging to them.[96] After all, there would be no point establishing an Inquisition if its primary targets exported their wealth or personally took their money and ran. The expected stampede had to be halted before it started.

A month later, in July of 1532, Diogo was arrested in Antwerp. He was charged with secretly practicing Judaism—officially against the law even in that city—and unlawfully monopolizing the spice trade.[97] It was, to say the least, a stressful time for the couple, and particularly for Francisco. His beloved brother and valuable partner was under arrest. His fellow *conversos* were trapped all around him in an increasingly hostile nation. Negotiations with the Holy See were collapsing. And he had become a family man at a moment of heightened personal danger.

Realizing that the future of his business empire—not to mention his personal peace of mind—depended upon getting Diogo freed as rapidly as possible, Francisco hurried to the royal palace upon receiving the news, apparently through the Affaitatis.[98] On the way, he was doubtless savoring the delectable fact that the king had been impatiently waiting for some 200,000 ducats that the Affaitati-Mendes syndicate owed the crown, a sum already promised by the king to his brother-in-law Charles V, Holy Roman Emperor, to help Charles in his ongoing battles on behalf of Christian Europe against the Ottoman Turks.[99]

The money was one of the periodic payments that the Affaitati-Mendes syndicate made to the king for monopoly rights to pepper and other spices arriving from the Indies. Any interruption in this stream of revenue could deal a significant blow to the Portuguese crown.[100]

Diogo had been in the midst of selling a shipment, thereby raising the cash needed to make the current payment by the prearranged date. The arrest had thrown a monkey wrench into these well-ordered dealings.[101] Since Charles had sovereignty over Antwerp, it was easy to figure out how Francisco was going to force the Portuguese king to intervene on Diogo's behalf.

And intervene he did. By the end of August, only six weeks after Diogo's arrest, the Portuguese king was writing to Charles[102] to say that he had been informed of Diogo's arrest by Francisco, whom he warmly described as "my very devoted servant." He said that Francisco had also told him that Diogo's holdings had been seized at the time of the arrest, along with the assets of other Lisbon merchants under Diogo's financial management. Not only were innocent Portuguese merchants being affected. Even more serious, from the king's viewpoint, was the possibility that the anticipated payment—characterized in his own words as "an enormous sum of money"—might not occur unless arrangements were quickly made for the charges to be dropped, allowing Diogo to go about his business as usual.[103]

The king must have panicked because a second appeal was sent at the same time as the first. This letter was written by the king's wife, Queen Catherine, who happened to be Charles' sister. The Portuguese royal couple must have concluded that there was merit in adding a personal plea from a member of Charles' own family. Or was her added missive one of Francisco's shrewd ideas? Addressed once again to Charles, "most excellent Prince and most powerful brother" and dated just two days prior to the one sent by the king, Queen Catherine also implored Charles to intervene.[104]

"I shall accept with singular pleasure," she wrote, "any kindness and favor you may extend to him (Diogo) out of complaisance to me." She must have been personally acquainted with Francisco because she made it clear that she was not only asking on behalf of her husband. "I, too," she continued, "consider the said Francisco Mendes to be a very loyal servant of the crown." On that account she insisted she did not want to see his impeccable business reputation tarnished, or see other Lisbon merchants suffer, should he fail to fulfill his financial responsibilities due to any disruption in sales. Since the Queen seemed to know Francisco well, his presence at court must have included social occasions that wives would have attended. Once again, it makes Doña Gracia's later comfort level with royalty all the more understandable.

Pressure from the Portuguese royal couple was combined

with pleas from their agent in Antwerp. There was also an out-cry from the city of Antwerp, which feared the financial fallout, as well as from Diogo's colleagues at the Antwerp exchange. Charles soon had no option but to back down. By September 17—an incredibly fast turnaround for those days—Diogo was provisionally freed on bail and his possessions restored, on pay-ment of an interest-free, one-year loan to Charles of 50,000 duc-ats.[105] The decision helped line Charles' perennially empty pockets and left plenty of room for backtracking. Such a power-ful monarch was not going to cave in completely, nor back down without getting something in return.

As the release was only provisional, a cloud still hung over Diogo's head. Thus, early the following year, King João III con-sidered changing the way he transported his valuable Indies car-goes to Antwerp. He had been making heavy use of ships belonging to Diogo. His advisors were saying this was now a hazardous policy since, as he noted in one letter, "I have not managed to (totally) free him (Diogo) from the cases from which he was charged in Flanders.... (and) because of risk I could run," if Diogo's belongings were again sequestered.[106]

The letter, dated February 1533, and addressed to the Count of Castanheira, the king's Chancellor of the Exchequer, asks the count to encourage Francisco not to transport so many valuable goods on his brother's ships either. It might be preferable, urged the king, to distribute them among other merchants and ship-pers plying the same seas. The king implied that he had an obli-gation to make these recommendations, since safeguarding Francisco's assets was his royal duty. What he really meant was that he had a duty to protect the financial viability of the man most responsible for making periodic payments crucial to the crown. Francisco was thus caught between the need to fulfill the wishes of the king and still give his brother every possible sup-port. His independence was eroding.

In combination, all these setbacks were taking a toll. Within a year Francisco became seriously ill, eventually dying around the close of 1534[107] while still struggling on his deathbed to keep paying off the Vatican. These bribes were a last-ditch attempt to delay the activation of an Inquisition in Portugal. The picture of a desperate and weakened Francisco spending his last hours trying to keep such a horror from destroying his people is palpable. It shows up in a letter from the Papal Nuncio in Portugal to the Vatican written just a few weeks after Francicsco died. Francisco, said the Nuncio, had been fretting about having to use an unreliable intermediary to pay the appropriate parties on time, yet he was becoming so ill that he could not do it all himself. Nevertheless, "Francisco eventually had to give in to his inevitable death" wrote the Nuncio.[108]

But Francisco's sudden passing soon became as unsettling to the Vatican as Diogo's arrest had been for King João III. "As the richest and most authoritative man among them," declared the Nuncio in the same letter, "his (Francisco's) death has greatly disturbed business." Payments, it seems, were no longer coming through as smoothly as in the past.

The ruthless blackmail that had faced Francisco during his final months of life was evident in the latter part of the same letter. "I have already spent one day debating with some of their leaders…to convince them to continue a service of 10,000 ducats, since that was the intention," continued a distraught but determined Nuncio. "They offered me five thousand, but I will keep pushing for the desired amount and not much less." The cleric seemed certain that the *conversos* would eventually give in, and maybe go as high as 30,000 ducats. He had good reason. As "the Holy See can resolve to start (implementation of) the Inquisition (at any time)," he noted, "they will thus want to serve us."

———••✦••———

The desperation with which Francisco and the other *converso* leaders had tried to hold back the coming of an Inquisition had a lot to do with their first-hand knowledge of the pain and havoc it could unleash. They would have known exactly what was in store from their experiences in Spain, where an Inquisition had been operating for some fifty years. For a start, the assets of the accused were immediately confiscated upon arrest because "everything they have has to be given back to the true God," as a later Vatican document put it.[109]

As well as stripping the prisoner's family of its holdings and livelihood, regardless of innocence or guilt, an Inquisition inflicted horrible bodily pain upon its victims. Apprehended on alleged charges of clandestine Jewish practice, the prisoner would be dragged off to a fetid, damp and rat-infested dungeon, often languishing for months under sickening conditions before being called to a show trial. Clamped into irons, prisoners were rarely allowed to speak to one another. Torture was commonplace to facilitate a "confession," irrespective of the truth.

As churchmen were not allowed to draw the blood of another Christian, even a "New" Christian, all manner of creative alternatives were devised.[110] A prisoner's hands were bound at the back. By means of a rope fastened to those hands, the body would be raised to the ceiling. Having hung there for some time with weights tied to the feet, the prisoner would be let down almost to the ground with abrupt jerks that would disjoint arms and legs. Or, the prisoner would be forced to swallow large quantities of water, after which the body would be squeezed tightly to produce unimaginable pain. Feet would be held to the fire. Cords would be tied to an arm and twisted tighter and tighter until a "confession" was drawn from the victim. The infamous *rack* would stretch limbs to the tearing point. While in the dungeons, legs and feet would be rubbed with raw meat so the rats would gnaw at the person's skin. Under such an ordeal, family members would weaken and implicate other family members, until not a single one was free from the fear that even their own children might speak out against them. Whenever internal family feuds were fed into this satanic brew, it caused everyone within the *converso* community to live in terror, no matter how they conducted their lives, or how much love existed between them.

Children were routinely arrested. So were women, many suffering fearful abuse. They would be shamed by being stripped to the waist before the clerics. Or they would be paraded through the public streets, similarly stripped, before being marched, even pregnant, to the stake, where flames would lick their way upwards from lighted faggots. Burning the flesh was viewed as a way to cleanse and redeem the soul. If the condemned agreed to renounce their "sins" of backsliding into Judaism, they could be pardoned at the eleventh hour. But they were usually so emotionally broken, sick and penniless by then that their lives could never be rebuilt.[111]

Many were never brought to trial. They perished from sickness and neglect while being detained in the dungeons. This led to handy denials by the church that large numbers of *conversos* were ever convicted or burned at the stake.[112]

———••⁙••———

Another matter had to be resolved as Francisco lay dying. It was the terms of his will. The informal arrangements that he always shared with Diogo must have weighed heavily on his mind. It was high time to put something in writing, something he did on his deathbed. "I declare," wrote Francisco in his native Spanish, "that my brother has one half and I, the other (half) of what is with him (assets currently held by Diogo in Antwerp). And although my estate may be greater, he helped me to earn it (and) my intention was thus always."[113] Despite Diogo's recent troubles, the brothers may have decided that a liberal city like Antwerp, where the rule of law was dominated by the needs of merchants rather than the dogma of the church, was a safer place to keep the lion's share of the family assets.

Francisco then concerned himself with contingencies. "I only ask him (Diogo)," continued Francisco, "for mercy's sake, that should he die without a son (heir), that he make my daughter my inheritor," thus giving Ana the portion he was allocating to Diogo.

After that, he turned to the division of his own share. In this regard, Francisco followed Portuguese custom.[114] "I also declare," he continued, "of (my) estate, my wife...has one half and her daughter... two thirds of the other half." The final third was to be set aside to cover the expenses connected with his passing. These would have been substantial, since the family would have been expected to mount a public funeral Mass with pomp and circumstance, even a full-blown procession along the streets, given his high position in Lisbon society and proximity to court circles. By tradition, a portion of this final third would have also been set aside for the customary gifts to charity and church. It would also cover the cost of reciting a Mass for his Catholic soul on each anniversary of his death.[115] Francisco ended by saying that whatever remained after meeting these expenses rightfully belonged to his wife.

In later testimony before the rabbinic courts, when these details were revealed, Doña Gracia insisted that she was not in the room while her husband was writing the will. Francisco had not wanted her to know the contents. Instead, he had handed her the document already tied and sealed. She carefully put it aside for safekeeping, thereby complying with his desire for secrecy until after his death.[116]

What was he worried about? Was he afraid she would resent the amount he was leaving to Diogo and argue with him on this point? She certainly raised the idea that he should not have treated Diogo so generously when the matter came before the rabbis. Was he trying to keep secret the fact that a substantial portion of his estate was safely in Antwerp, under Diogo's name, until he was gone, when it would be too late for anyone to force him to take corrective action? Certainly the fact that the king considered the safety of Francisco's assets important to the crown must have been worrisome. Francisco was well aware that the king was not concerned about the safety of those assets for the family's sake, but for their value, after Francisco's death, to a royal court that was perpetually seeking cash.

The hours just prior to his death must have therefore been tense for more than just emotional and physical reasons. Indeed, one can well imagine the young wife, her small daughter clutching at her long skirts, fearing widowhood not only for its loneliness but for the royal hands that were poised to grab their estate, once someone as powerful as Francisco was gone.

The first risk Doña Gracia had to assume alone was to ensure that Francisco's body would be given the correct ritual treatment for a Jewish male, despite the hazards of doing so at a time of increasing scrutiny from the church. As a first generation convert who had also served as the "rabbi"[117] of the *converso* community, it would have been especially meaningful for Francisco to follow the Jewish rituals of death; attention to the immortal soul carrying a significance that is difficult for the modern

mind to grasp. A contemporary traveler confirmed those feelings by reporting that on his deathbed Francisco begged his
young wife to find ways to bring his remains to Jerusalem.[118]
Later, she honored the request.[119]

Even under extreme scrutiny, the *conversos* routinely found a
way to thwart the authorities on these matters. Men like Francisco would circumvent Catholic last rites by having a relative,
or trusted member of the *converso* community, suffocate them
with a pillow before the priest arrived. Or they would wash off
the consecrated oil that a priest might have applied. Care was
taken to have only close family members around the bedside at
the moment of death, at which time the body would be turned
to the wall, according to time-honored Jewish practice. The
corpse would have then been washed with warm water and
dressed in clean linen, whereupon, in keeping with the customs
of Iberian Jews, a coin or pearl would be placed in the mouth to
facilitate the journey to the next world. The body would have
never been left alone until burial—a Jewish rite still practiced
today.[120] A Jewish funeral would have been an impossibility. Nevertheless, the family could try to make sure burial took place as
fast as possible, as required by Jewish law, and recite Jewish
prayers almost inaudibly, during the Catholic rites, or after everyone had gone home. Finally, if they dared, the family would
return home to a ritual meal of fish, eggs and olives, eaten at a
low table. The customary seven days of Jewish prayers could have
been concealed by holding a daily Mass in the family's private
chapel. A medieval tradition in Portugal would have required
Doña Gracia to dress in undyed homespun and sackcloth for at
least the first year, in contrast to the fine silks and luxurious
brocades then in fashion. And to mourn, even to wail, in full
view of the society in which she moved.[121]

CHAPTER 4

Widowhood

Doña Gracia was now a widow, and widowhood offered exceptional benefits during the 16th century. It was a woman's sole springboard to autonomy.[1] For the first time she could make independent decisions. Fathers ruled women's lives before marriage and husbands ruled them afterwards. Although only 25 years old, any decision about a future husband or lover, any decision concerning the deployment of her immense fortune, any decision concerning the future of Francisco's merchant-banking enterprises, any decision concerning her personal finances was now hers alone, save for any advice she cared to take from family members or business associates.

A widespread awareness of these benefits was reflected in the popular Spanish saying, *antes biuda que casada* ("better a widow than a married woman"). A widow's value to society as the caring adult who could best raise the next generation was so great, and her needs so obvious, that she enjoyed vigorous legal protection of her rights. She also benefitted from a measure of freedom and power unequaled in any other capacity. She was more active and visible in the public realm than a married or single woman. And she had more freedom than during subsequent eras when menfolk were less likely to be away from home for extended periods to trade, to provide personal service to their lord or king and as life expectancy improved.[2]

Even prior to the 16th century, it had not been uncommon for certain women—especially Jewish widows—to regularly serve as moneylenders,[3] as purveyors of merchandise such as embroidered purses, silk, silver or jewels.[4] A few on the Iberian Peninsula even practiced medicine and controlled large sums of money; buying, managing, exchanging and bestowing legacies, dealing in securities, posting bonds and becoming influential members of family or community.[5] Further, they actively protected their rights as widows by filing innumerable lawsuits, even appearing alone and bringing actions before the rabbinic courts.[6]

Still, two obstacles immediately faced Doña Gracia. The first was the problem inherent in remarriage—even a subsequent marriage undertaken for love, since it was a step that would have placed her and her property again under male control.[7] This would have been a serious liability for a woman who now possessed one of the largest fortunes in Europe. What's more, she controlled the financial and personal interests of a daughter who had become an heiress in her own right; a girl who would one day bring a significant dowry to her own bridal bed. Yet without remarriage there could be no more children. Even an openly-acknowledged romantic or sexual dalliance was off limits, given Doña Gracia's prominence in society and the possibility of some form of financial coercion resulting from such a liaison. This would have been agonizing for a 25-year-old woman, still so young and fresh-faced that she would be described as a *demoiselle* in a contemporary document.[8]

The second obstacle involved the not-too-subtle designs of a penniless monarch on the estate. Francisco's executors, who apparently included Doña Gracia, immediately sought royal permission for a four-year delay in compiling the required inventory of assets and liabilities.[9] They probably intended to use the time to get as much money out of Portugal as they could, or move it temporarily into the name of others so it would be out of reach.

But the king was prepared. On January 30 1535, he wrote to the Count of Castanheira saying that he had denied permission to delay the inventory. "I did not let them have the permit," explained the king," because it seemed to me that it could be prejudicial to the orphan girl, daughter of the said Francisco Mendes." He told the count that the executors had insisted that rushing to complete an inventory could undermine the entire operations of the House of Mendes, as they "will not be able to conduct business as in the past." But he suspected otherwise. "(Since) it seems that it must not be for the reason that they give, but for other reasons that will be prejudicial to the orphan (Ana)," he added, "I ask that you write telling me what to do." In the interim, said the king, he was granting the executors a temporary delay of a month until he received a reply from the count.[10]

An important outcome would have been to determine how much of the total assets belonged to Ana, since the formula for partition had been outlined in Francisco's will. It was also well-known that delaying partition traditionally benefitted the widow. She retained the use of the combined capital without interference from family members or court-appointed probate officials. As a consequence, widows frequently sought and obtained a reprieve from the customary demands to divide up the property immediately.[11] There was ample precedent for the request, although the king was not about to concede. In this instance, too much was at stake.

There was further reason for concern among the executors.

Throughout Europe there had long been a tradition, based upon Roman law, that the estate of anyone who was directly indebted to the king could be seized until matters were sorted out.[12] What was worse, King João, like many rulers at that time, considered any widow connected to his court to be chattel, required to do his bidding on command.[13] In that vein, he was determined to grab at least the portion of the estate that rightfully belonged to Ana, however long it took.

Two years later, he was still plotting to acquire a share of this pot of gold. In a letter dated May 12 1537, he told the Count of Castanheira, "I want the daughter of Francisco Mendes, who is well loved, to be brought to the house of the Queen, my most beloved and precious wife, in order for her to grow up and learn all the fine customs." He continued, "I command you to speak with Gonçalo Mendes, his brother, and with other relatives that seem appropriate to you, and tell him on my behalf that I will take pleasure in their sending the daughter of the said Francisco Mendes to the house of the Queen, where she will be very well and at ease." Then the king got to the nub of the issue. "And from here," he added, "with the estate that her father left her, an honorable person will marry her and they will be content."[14] What he meant, of course, was that by bringing Ana into the court he could control her inheritance. He could also control the choice of a husband, who would doubtless be required to agree, in advance, to give a substantial portion of Ana's immense riches to the crown.

Should the carrot not yield the desired results, the king fully intended to use the stick. He indicated that he intended to override any contrary decision that might be made by the orphan's court—a board that supervised the handling of a minor's inheritance.[15] "Tell the same to the orphan's judge who did the inventory of her estate, or to any person who seems appropriate," he commanded the count, "and they should tell her mother, so that she will be glad to do it and be happy." Only at the end of the letter did he concede that he knew his plan might not go as smoothly as he had implied. So he urged the count to "....give them the reasons you consider good ones, so that they enjoy doing it as it will be good for them." He concluded with a note of gratitude, since he knew he was giving the count a difficult task. "And I will take pleasure in this," he assured the count, "and will thank you very much." His overly solicitous manner was probably due to the fact that the count had been designated to supply someone from his own family as the future husband, a fact not revealed in the letter but widely known in court circles.[16]

What were the king's real concerns? Gaining a financial windfall was the most obvious. But the child could have been also viewed as a hostage. Mendes' business contacts and wealth were exceedingly important to the crown. The king may have therefore feared that Doña Gracia might otherwise relocate to Antwerp to work alongside Diogo, away from the Inquisition. And quite soon the entire Mendes trading network could be lost to Portugal. But with the child at the royal palace, the mother would not be inclined to move too far away. And then, once the Inquisition was established, it might be possible to confiscate the mother's inheritance, too. The king might also have seen a Jewish girl child as a potential mistress for himself, even if he first married her off to a nobleman. People of Jewish ancestry were at once reviled and revered for the exotic, cosmopolitan touch they brought to the court.[17]

One can therefore imagine the dazed look on Doña Gracia's face when Gonçalo arrived on her doorstep bearing the fateful news from the king. If she refused she could lose the level of royal protection that had always been there when her husband was alive, placing her in a hazardous position in a gathering Inquisition storm. But to hand over her only daughter to the royal court would force her to give up a child, forfeit half of the family's fortune and lose that child's descendants to Judaism. It would have been anathema to her and all that Francisco and the family held sacred.

Francisco's money was becoming more of a burden than a blessing.

What to do? In this first major crisis of her widowhood, one catches a glimpse of Doña Gracia's emerging iron will and strategic thinking. For a start, she paid off the 5,000-ducat bribe outstanding to the Vatican at the time of her husband's death.[18] At least that would help delay the actual implementation of an Inquisition. The financial clout of Diogo and the power inherent in his spice syndicate was another major asset. The king could ill afford to alienate the entire family. Her next move was therefore to send word to Diogo. She needed to leave Portugal before her enemies could rally their forces to obstruct her departure.

By August 14, less than three months later, Diogo was busy making hasty arrangements for her trip. One of the first things he did was to contact his royal friends in London. He alerted Thomas Cromwell, Henry VIII's chancellor and chief financial advisor, that the widow of his late brother and partner, her family and her servants were on their way and should be offered every courtesy and protection while passing through England on their way to Antwerp.[19]

Diogo had a host of reasons to trust Cromwell and feel secure about dealing with England. A few years earlier he had extended loans to the British Treasury and the British crown would continue to seek out the House of Mendes even after Diogo's death, suggesting there had long been a close financial relationship.[20] Also, Henry VIII had recently broken with the pope in order to marry Anne Boleyn. The British were therefore shifting away from Catholic domination towards an autonomous Church of England. Though Jews had been officially barred from England since 1290—during a fever-pitch of anti-Jewish fervor typical of the Middle Ages—a small community of *converso* merchants had nevertheless been thriving in London and Bristol since the end of the 15th century. Provided they kept their Judaism discreet, they were generally left alone.[21]

Thomas Cromwell had become aware of the value of befriending *converso* merchants during the years he had spent in Antwerp as a young trader. He had arrived, coincidentally, just at the time that Diogo also settled in. He even became friends with Diogo's friends, the Affaitati.[22]

The financial know-how and contacts that Cromwell gained in Antwerp had proven invaluable. His later rise to power in England was based largely on his skill as a money manager. He was also familiar with the financial barons of Antwerp who controlled access to the lucrative markets of continental Europe—vital to the sale of British cloth and other goods. Cromwell also staunchly supported Henry's anti-Catholic policies, including the dissolution of the monasteries in England.[23] Here, indeed, was a friend who had every reason to come through for Diogo.

Though the letter to Cromwell was written ostensibly by the aldermen of the city of Antwerp, it was clearly dictated by Diogo, or compiled from very specific information he gave them. As such, it tells a great deal about what was going on and provides clues to the way the family negotiated its way around public issues affecting the lives of its members. The letter opens by identifying Doña Gracia as the widow of Francisco and the sister-in-law of Diogo, thereby underscoring that she was not just anyone, but someone whose goodwill could mean the continuation of a flow of loans to England. It thus implies how important it was for the British to provide her with safe passage as she passed through on her way to Antwerp, where she was going "to conduct necessary and urgent business" with her brother-in-law Diogo.[24]

Identifying the trip as business-related indicated the alleged temporary nature of her departure from Lisbon. It was a strategy she would employ again a few years later when she sought to leave Antwerp against the wishes of the authorities there, too.

The business ploy may not have been a total fiction. Doña Gracia had a secondary and more personal motive for wanting to reach Antwerp. Later testimony before the rabbinic courts[25] suggests she had become uneasy about the informal arrangements that had existed between the two brothers. Placing so much family money in Diogo's name meant trusting a man she had rarely, if ever, met. Further, by mentioning that Doña Gracia had "urgent and necessary business" to conduct in Antwerp, it confirmed the commonplace nature of widows in business. Otherwise the burghers of Antwerp would have held themselves up to ridicule. Even a letter from a Papal Nuncio in Portugal to the Vatican written around the same time—discussing the continuation of the bribes enjoyed during Francisco's lifetime—expresses the hope that Doña Gracia will now "take a great part of the weight (of her husband's financial obligations) on her (own) shoulders."[26]

In their letter to Cromwell, the burghers explained that the reason Doña Gracia was leaning towards the idea of coming "overland through the English Kingdom to reach her destination" was to due to "the war" which made her "hesitate to put her family and servants in peril on the open seas." The war in question was the on-again, off-again hostilities between Charles V, Holy Roman Emperor and Francis I, King of France, both of whom sought an ever-greater share of European lands under their personal control. Particularly in dispute was Flanders. Francis had invaded in March, 1537, but little progress had been made.[27]

The sea lanes between Lisbon and Antwerp had been affected. Part of Francis' military strategy had been to intercept merchant shipping as it sailed up the coast of France to bring valuable commodities from Portugal to Charles' major port of Antwerp.

Surviving letters of King João III of Portugal are filled with worries about French raids on merchant shipping crucial to his nation's economic welfare.[28] Shortening Doña Gracia's sea voyage, especially in the hotly contested English Channel, by charting a course that would keep her party far from the hostilities, would have been of the utmost importance. Diogo even took the added precaution of sending one of his own ships to Lisbon to fetch the party.[29]

Doña Gracia may therefore have sailed due north from Lisbon to Bristol, rather than take a northeasterly course that hugged the coast of France and turned eastwards into the Channel near Plymouth. The port of Bristol was deep within an inlet along England's western coast and also had a small community of *conversos*, thus making it a particularly safe and hospitable landing spot for Doña Gracia and her party.[30]

From there, they could have traveled by carriage to London and then proceeded along the well-traveled road south to the port of Dover. After that, it was only a scant twenty-two mile sea crossing to Calais, allowing them to traverse the Channel at its briefest and safest crossing point. Calais was in British hands at this time, making the route even more inviting.[31] From Calais, Doña Gracia's party could proceed overland to Antwerp, thereby sidestepping the most hazardous part of their sea journey—the English Channel where Charles' Empire was battling Francis I.

Arrangements for her passage now assured, Doña Gracia's next challenge was to obtain the needed permission to leave Portugal with key family members. Though she doubtless pretended otherwise, the coming of the Inquisition and the designs of the king upon her daughter would have made it foolhardy to even consider returning.

How did she get out? Certainly a woman of her value to the crown, intending to take along a small daughter, her brother-in-law Gonçalo, a sister, two nephews and servants,[32] would not have been able to leave without an exit permit approved at the highest level, either by the pope or the king. Portuguese historians have speculated that it was probably the pope.[33] But she left in such a hurry—learning about the king's intentions in May or June and already on her way by August—that there would hardly have been time for a courier to reach the Vatican and return with a safe conduct before the inclement days of autumn and winter set in, thereby precluding a departure until the following spring.

More likely, she persuaded the king that it was only a temporary voyage, needed to settle some outstanding financial issues. At the same time she could argue that it made sense for her to use the occasion to escort her younger sister, Brianda, who had been promised in marriage to Diogo. Further, it would have been an equally ideal opportunity to safely escort her two youthful nephews, Juan Micas (later known as Don Joseph Nasi) and his older brother Bernardo Micas (later known as Don Samuel Nasi). Both had reached the age of university entrance and were soon to be enrolled in the prestigious University of Louvain, not far from Antwerp. The two youths, who were related to her on both sides of the family, graduated from that institution just a few years later.[34]

Since the king was still dependent upon revenues from the Mendes-Affaitati syndicate and the good will of other spice merchants with whom he was dealing, it would have been counter-productive for him to refuse. He had already witnessed the flight of German merchants. He could ill afford to alienate the rest of his merchant community by confiscating the fortune or arresting one of its leaders simply for requesting the right to travel abroad. So even if he suspected Doña Gracia's true intentions, he would have felt compelled to provide the needed papers. Most likely it was a negotiated settlement, with some money handed over in exchange for the clearance. Much of the family's remaining wealth could be exported later on, through bills of exchange or a complex shifting of debts and credits typical of *converso* business dealings.

For Doña Gracia, this must have been a time tinged with both excitement and sadness—eagerness to enter the enticing business world of Diogo and live among some of the most celebrated intellectuals and artists of the Renaissance, yet clouded with sadness, knowing she would never see Lisbon again, although some family members would follow later.[35]

Though she did not yet know it, Doña Gracia was beginning the first leg of a tragic migration—from Lisbon to Antwerp, from Antwerp to Venice, from Venice to Ferrara and back again to Venice and then on to Constantinople—wanderings that would similarly characterize the rootless lives of hundreds of her fellow *conversos*. By dint of her own peripatetic existence, she would comprehend firsthand how deeply they were suffering.

————···✳···————

They set sail sometime that August,[36] embarking upon a sea journey that in those days would have taken around two weeks, assuming good winds and the class of speedy caravel Diogo would have sent.[37] Conditions for passengers were reasonably good. The captain's cabin and officers' quarters were typically set aside for ladies, unless the ship already had passenger quarters, which many did.

Personal belongings were carried in large sea chests lined with velvet. Heavy woolen capes screened out the harsh Atlantic winds as passengers paced the creaky decks. Singing and dancing were common diversions. Food was plentiful. Barrels brimmed with fresh water, oil or wine and innumerable baskets overflowed with cheeses, onions, flour, dried beans and fish, salted meats, jams and dried fruits, chick peas, rice, sea biscuits, olives and spices from the Oriental trade. Live chickens were kept in cages for fresh meat or to provide eggs, permitting passengers and crew to enjoy a diversified diet.

Cooking was done on deck in a metal firebox fueled with cordwood. Copper cauldrons and cooking pots were mounted on hooks over the flames for boiling. Wooden or iron utensils were the preferred table and serving ware. A private contingent of fighting men and sometimes even an armed fighting vessel accompanied these voyages, taken along for personal security and to fend off a pirate attack. For the same reason the ships typically traveled in flotillas. [38]

Arriving at Bristol, Doña Gracia and her party would have been met by a small *converso* community primarily engaged in the international cloth trade—an occupation that had been part of Iberian Jewish mercantile activity for at least two centuries. Bristol was close to the center of cloth production and also provided a sheltered harbor. It was therefore an obvious place for *conversos* to establish themselves after fleeing Spain. It was a ritually observant community, left untouched by the official rules that no Jews could reside or worship freely in England. Despite a *converso* veneer, it even held services in the house of one of its leaders in none too secret circumstances.

The soul of the Bristol community was another Beatrice—a doctor's wife named Beatrice Fernandes. She was determined to uphold her Judaism regardless of risk or censure. She held classes in Judaism for incoming *conversos* not schooled in their ancestral faith. She dictated Jewish prayers which they probably wrote down phonetically. She observed the festivals and fasts, kept a Saturday Sabbath and strictly adhered to the Jewish dietary laws to the point where she worried about eating at roadside inns while traveling. She personally baked her own matzos for Passover and held a Seder service for the local *conversos* at her home.[39]

The older Beatrice could well have helped to inspire the younger one. Since it was typical for members of the *converso* community to lodge among their own, there is a good chance a meeting took place.

Though Doña Gracia and her party may have intended to move on to London and stay there awhile,[40] their time in the capital city was actually short, possibly because of an outbreak of plague that summer of 1537.[41] Once again, they would have typically lodged among their own. In this instance it would have been the small and relatively new *converso* merchant community of about thirty souls which at the time was clustered near the Tower of London.[42]

(These were the *conversos* who several decades hence used their unique intelligence-gathering capabilities, garnered from family and business contacts still on the Iberian Peninsula, to alert Queen Elizabeth I to the gathering of a Spanish Armada.[43] They were also credited with introducing their favorite dish of Portuguese fried fish into England—the Irish adding the chips later on, thus making Britain's national food a staple of totally foreign origin).[44]

The arrival of Diogo's bride-to-be and the widow of Francisco was surely a major event. For it had been the loans that the Mendes brothers had first made to the English treasury, some thirty years earlier, along with a commensurate need to have their own agents on hand, that had led to the birth of this particularly *converso* community. Other *conversos* had drifted to London, as they had done to Bristol, as refugees from the Spanish Inquisition. Although their presence was known, no investigations into their religious practices had ever been initiated despite at least one plea directly from Ferdinand and Isabella.[45]

The talk of London that summer was the publication of a first Bible translated into the English language—one of Henry VIII's efforts to establish an independent Church of England.[46]

The Catholic Church had never wanted its flock to have this direct knowledge available to them. Having first been distributed that August, this English-language Bible could not have failed to come to the notice of Doña Gracia. It could have been a factor in her later decision in Ferrara to support the publication of a Bible that would have been equally meaningful to her own people. Known as the *Ferrara Bible,* and written in the Spanish vernacular of the Iberian Jews, its aim would be to give all *conversos,* especially those who no longer read Hebrew, a better understanding of the fundamentals of their heritage.[47]

In London, Doña Gracia would have found a secret synagogue in the house of one of their leaders where some twenty London-based *conversos* congregated each Saturday. She would have met a Mendes family relative, Antonio della Rogna, described in a later account as "a tall, middle-aged man with one eye who was the master of Hebrew theology."[48] She would have been introduced to Christopher Fernandes, the Mendes agent who intercepted Portuguese spice ships weighing anchor temporarily at Southampton, or Plymouth. His task was to warn any *converso* refugees on board if it was safe to continue to Antwerp, where the authorities were constantly changing their policies concerning whether or not to admit these illegal emigrants from Portugal.[49] Advance knowledge would determine the length of their stay in England.

It is thus in London that we first brush up against the embryonic escape network being operated by the Mendes brothers to help their *converso* compatriots flee the increasingly hostile atmosphere on the Iberian Peninsula. Reliable numbers are impossible to estimate since it was a clandestine migration. However, the regularity with which the Emperor Charles V and Queen Marie, his regent of the Low Countries, fussed about the influx of these *converso* refugees over a twenty year period that stretched from the early 1530's to around 1550, when Antwerp closed its doors for good, suggests it must have been substantial, running into the thousands.[50]

The ultimate destination of most of the refugees was the Ottoman Empire where many of their relatives had already found refuge under more tolerant Muslim rule. Doña Gracia would later support and expand this escape network with her customary zeal and determination. Since the Muslims were the enemy of the Portuguese, and indeed the whole of Christian Europe, the refugees could not possibly sail directly from Lisbon. They had to carve out a much more circuitous route. Many never made it, as we shall see.

The arrival of Doña Gracia and her sister was even noted in the royal circles of Henry VIII. The intermediary in this instance was Bastian (also known as Sebastian) Rodriguez Pinto, a middle-aged member of London's *converso* community who was later denounced by a Milan Commission as "living according to the Hebrew law."[51] Pinto was such a close friend of the Mendes family that when he moved to Ferrara in Italy a few years later—the only place he could safely live after the denunciation—Diogo would personally guarantee a loan of 3,000 ducats for him against insolvency.[52]

That summer in London, however, Pinto was still considered an upstanding Christian merchant on the periphery of court circles. Knowing that Doña Gracia and her party favored the briefest possible sea crossing, Pinto approached a courtier named John Hussee on their behalf, anticipating that they would cross at the narrowest point—which was from Dover to Calais. Hussee was the shrewd and devoted court representative of a Calais-based power couple named Lord and Lady Lisle. As Lord Lisle was serving as Deputy of this French province then under British rule, it meant living a considerable distance from the seat of royal power. He had therefore hired Hussee to stay close to the king and Cromwell, much like a modern lobbyist. Hussee gained favors or additional stipends for the Lisles whenever he could, a coveted role that also provided Hussee with the elegant but euphemistic title of "gentleman of the King's retinue."[53]

Lord Lisle—actually Arthur Plantagenet Viscount Lisle—was an illegitimate son of Edward IV. He was one of those royal-blooded relatives whose political fortunes rose and fell according to the pleasure of his monarch. It was a precarious way to live, considering how many of Henry's intimates ended up with their severed heads displayed on London Bridge.

In pursuit of political advancement, Lord Lisle had another asset—his wife, Honor. A master manipulator with dynamic energy and a lively wit, she was an accomplished dancer, card-player, horsewoman and a mistress of intrigue; only now being acknowledged for the powerful role she played at Henry's court, albeit from a distance. She was an indefatigable writer of letters. She used her sophisticated pen, thoughtful gifts and personal attention to people of importance passing through Calais to develop and nourish important networks. She sought and obtained favors that provided her with influence far beyond what might have been expected. Ambitious for her children too, she managed to win a coveted post for two of her daughters in the Queen's household.[54]

Like many an aristocrat, Lord Lisle was perennially in debt. Becoming well acquainted with London's money merchants was therefore yet another key role that Hussee played in the lives of the Lisles. This is no doubt how he came to the attention of Pinto. Hussee would have been intimately familiar with the financial benefits that could accrue to his master by offering assistance to Doña Gracia and her party.

But since the matter at hand primarily concerned two important ladies, he initially addressed his plan to the Lady rather than the Lord. "Pleaseth your ladyship," he wrote from London on September 27 1537, in a firm but swift hand, with all the eloquence of Shakespearean English,[55] "that Bastian Rodriguez Pinto, merchant of Portugal, desired me to write unto your ladyship to be good... unto these gentlewomen which he saith are of a principal house of Portugal and doth now repair towards Flanders.... For the one of them shall marry with a rich merchant in Flanders called Diogo Mendes. And...because these gentlewomen are his (Pinto's) friends and he would gladly shew them all the pleasure that lay in him, he hath sundry times desired me to write unto my lord and your ladyship for them."

Hussee then tempted the Lisles with a payoff. "So that if it may please my lord and your ladyship to be good unto them, and make them some cheer (when they land in Calais), it would not be lost, for the said Pinto is minded to give my lord and your ladyship a present of spices, which shall be worth twenty ducats at the least."

Continued Hussee: "If therefore it would please your ladyship at their coming... to welcome them and entertain them as your ladyship shall think meet (fit), the said Pinto would think himself not a little under your ladyship bounden." In other words, Pinto could be counted on whenever a future favor might be needed, perhaps a loan or some commodity in plentiful supply in Antwerp. Moreover, it would not be lost on the quickwitted Lady Lisle that she would thereby meet and connect with one of the richest widows in Europe, as well as a woman who was about to marry one of the wealthiest merchants in Antwerp. Hussee ended by noting that "the said Pinto is a knight," further suggesting the red carpet treatment would be fitting.[56]

How did a secret Jew and a *converso* become a knight? It was no empty boast. A few families of courtier Jews were so honored even prior to the Expulsion. After conversion, even more *conversos* obtained noble status in Portugal and Spain. It was typically bestowed by doing favors for the crown or simply by buying their way into the nobility. If the world was going to force them to live outwardly as Christians, they seemed to be saying, they might as well reap the benefits. Some even created coats of arms. This heraldry can be seen, even today, carved onto the graves of their descendants in Jewish cemeteries in such disparate places as Jodensavanne in Suriname and on the Lido in Venice.[57]

In Calais, Doña Gracia would have had the chance to meet and absorb vital lessons from one of the shrewdest and most independent women of the era. One can only speculate about what they might have discussed amid the warm hospitality of the Lisle compound.

Then, as the warm days of summer faded into autumn chill, the weary travelers embarked on the final lap of their long trip, bouncing for untold hours inside a carriage along rutted roads in a terrible state of disrepair, due primarily to the war effort.[58] The scene visible from the carriage windows is still with us, thanks to the somber landscapes of Pieter Bruegel, the Elder, the Flemish painter who was growing up at the time and already beginning to sketch his celebrated canvases.

What of the Lisles? Three years afterwards, Lord Lisle was arrested as a traitor, accused of plotting to deliver Calais into the hands of the pope. He was imprisoned for twenty months inside the dank and sinister apartments of the Tower of London. Lisle was an old, sick and broken man, only days away from death, when he was finally released. Lady Lisle went mad during his imprisonment.[59]

PART II

ANTWERP: 1537–1545

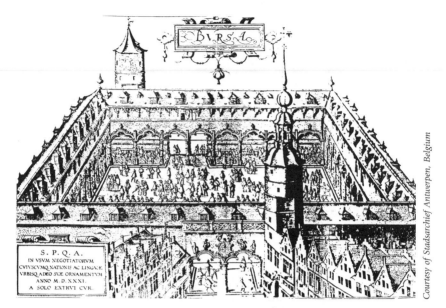

Engraving of the Antwerp Stock Exchange, 1531

Portrait of Charles V, Holy Roman Emperor, by Titian

CHAPTER 5

Among the Money Merchants

As Doña Gracia headed northeast by carriage along the Great Road from Calais, Antwerp must have loomed like a fairy tale city rising out of the incessant mists that permeated the climate of the region. In the distance would have been clusters of pencil-thin houses, two or three stories high, with steep stairs and narrow passages. Built in the Gothic style, they had been designed with overhanging second stories, leaded windows, turrets and crooked facades of wattle-and-daub. They were so uniform in appearance, and so tightly-packed, that they resembled rows of wooden soldiers marching in lockstep up the city's narrow, winding streets. Their tile or slate roofs were pitched in the Dutch vernacular—thatch had already been banned as a fire hazard—and edged with crenelated gables to further prevent flames leaping from house to house. Some did not yet have glazed windows. Thus, when the temperature dropped, as it often did in this dismal, rainy climate—so different from the warmth and sunshine of Lisbon—the creaky shutters would be pulled tightly shut, plunging the living areas into darkness even in broad daylight.[1]

These narrow houses were further squeezed inside a series of crumbling ramparts; the city adding yet another, wider encircling wall each time it ran out of space. These expansions meant that in certain places the old medieval moats were now no more than a muddy ditch. Here and there the skyline was punctuated with higher structures: tall church spires, the highest of all being the 400-foot steeple of the recently-completed Cathedral of Our Lady.

Then there were the grand mansard roofs of the Renaissance guildhalls and the peaked roofs of the new "Spanish towers," the name given to the multi-storey palatial homes, some as high as 80 feet, being built by wealthy foreign merchants, like Diogo Mendes and his friend and neighbor, Jean-Charles Affaitati. Diogo's residence had the added status of also standing next door to the mansion of one of the Welsers, the great German banking rivals of the Fuggers, the foremost bankers of the era.[2] Following the pattern of any financial boom, fortunes were being made by real estate speculators bent upon destroying the remaining large gardens and open spaces to erect these grandiose buildings. Demand was so great that house prices more than tripled between 1500 and 1567, as Antwerp's population exploded from 40,000 to over 100,000.[3]

First settled during the first millennium as a cluster of villages built upon the mud flats of the wide River Scheldt, some 55 miles inland from the North Sea, and criss-crossed by canals, Antwerp was enjoying its Golden Age. In recent years it had become the preeminent financial center of Europe. Since the beginning of the 14th century it had been a financial market of some importance, holding two trade fairs each year that attracted a sizeable number of foreign merchants. These were the medieval fairs, held in key cities all over Europe, that drew merchants together to settle debts, raise capital, cash bills of exchange, swap currencies, buy and sell commodities and generally attend to their business needs before the rise of a quotidian stock exchange or banking as we know it today.[4]

It was not until the middle of the 15th century that Antwerp began her meteoric rise to prominence. The Zwin, a river that served the adjacent port of Bruges, had begun silting up, making it difficult for larger cargo vessels to sail in and out. The merchants quickly turned to neighboring Antwerp, known for importing and re-exporting Baltic grain. Its quay on the river Scheldt had long been a busy place, the British also favoring Antwerp as the best port city in continental Europe for dealing in woolen cloth—that country's most important export product.[5]

After discovering the sea route to the East, Portugal also turned to Antwerp as the ideal port and financial hub for selling and distributing Asian luxuries to the densely-populated cities of northern Europe. Its spices, coming from the Orient, had become as essential to the kitchens of the *nouveau riche* of the Renaissance as a double oven might be in America today. Spices helped preserve food. They protected the nostrils from the stench of putrid meat and the palate from its rotten taste. Cooked foods were virtually buried in spices. At especially refined tables, spices were even passed around on a gold or silver tray. They were drunk as beverages. Some, like ginger, were prized for their medicinal qualities. Because they came from faraway lands they also took on a mythic quality. Paradise was reputed to be a place filled with exotic spices. The best spices, with pepper topping the list, were considered so precious that they were much sought after as gifts.[6]

This is why John Hussee, the representative of Lord and Lady Lisle at the court of Henry VIII, had been so impressed when Sebastian Pinto, the Mendes agent in London, had offered spices as a token of appreciation, and why Pinto chose to give spices rather than cash.

As the entry port for the bulk of the spices now coming into Europe, Antwerp began attracting an ever-rising number of Portuguese, Spanish, English, South German and Italian merchant bankers. This, in turn, drew hither an ever larger share of the continent's trade. The foreign merchants were further encouraged by the city's business orientation: it favored a liberal commercial climate over Catholic fanaticism. The Portuguese were particularly fortunate. Their rights dated back to a treaty signed in the previous century to encourage them to live and trade in the area. Their presence was so highly prized that in 1511 they were given a fine mansion for their consulate.[7] The absolute freedoms, legal protections and guarantees enjoyed by all foreigners trading in Antwerp swiftly became legendary. A stone carving over Antwerp's principal gate highlighted that commitment, proclaiming to all comers that the city was "for merchants of all nations."[8]

All of which meant that the center of product distribution was moving rapidly northwards, away from the republic of Venice which had served as the gateway to and from the European continent for centuries. By the second decade of the 16th century even Hungarian copper, previously exported to the Orient through Venice, was being rerouted through Antwerp.[9] Often as many as 2,500 tall-masted ships or slender galleys crowded the Scheldt, the late-comers having to lay at anchor for two or three weeks before their turn came to unload at the quay. As the century progressed and Antwerp became even more important, up to 1,000 wagons would rattle into town each week laden with provisions and merchandise.[10]

Another reason for the rapid rise of Antwerp had been the general growth of large-scale commodity trading. The ability to raise capital and prevail over the hazards of long-distance shipping were becoming more and more important to the success of any venture. Fleets were not only carrying an ever-increasing volume of goods back and forth from one end of the Mediterranean to the other. They had to be outfitted for similar trade throughout the Orient and the emerging colonies of the New World. The general greed for money, possessions and ostentatious display of wealth—a hallmark of the Renaissance—also meant that a money-based, capital-intensive and credit economy had arisen to replace the older, more localized forms of barter or minor loans. The result was that the modest nature and slower pace of the seasonal fairs were no longer adequate.[11]

There was also a need for rapid and regular infusions of cash on demand to meet the escalating costs of war. The feudal system was breaking down and with it the ease with which a monarch could call upon his nobles to raise an army of vassals, whenever required. This led to hired mercenaries. The hardware of war was also becoming more sophisticated. Expensive artillery, arquebuses, halberds, cannon, gunpowder and muskets constantly needed replenishment. But the revenues from a largely agrarian population were hopelessly inadequate to meet these new financial realities. Besides, collection was slow and often uncertain. A battle could not be postponed until the coffers had been filled. Nor could the monarch count on the loyalty that had prevailed in former epochs when knightly service was viewed as an honor. No money, no troops. No pay, no commitment. And in the 16th century the European powers were at war virtually all of the time—among themselves or against the dreaded Turks.[12]

Raising cash to meet the demands of war had therefore become a royal headache of gargantuan proportions. The only hope was credit. And the only people with sufficient funds to meet those credit needs were the wealthier merchants based increasingly in Antwerp. But what about loan security? While a monarch was alive, his concerns about his own creditworthiness tended to keep him in line. But whenever that ruling monarch died, there was no tradition or law that bound his successor to his debts. So other methods had to be devised. Future revenues from royal lands were mortgaged. So was general taxation income. At times, even the royal jewels, robes of state and other valuables served as collateral. Some royal possessions were sold outright. Even Venice had to pawn her jewels early in the 16th century after constant skirmishes with the Turks had drained her treasury.[13] But the payback was still so uncertain that royal loans were normally floated at interest rates that could rise as high as 25 percent or more. Even so, demand did not cease. The princes were caught between their passion for war and glory— without which they could not strut among their peers or hang onto ancestral lands—and the frightful reality of insolvency. Even as powerful a monarch as Charles V, Holy Roman Emperor, was perennially in debt.[14]

But one person's woe becomes another's golden opportunity. The Fugger family, the great German bankers of the period, built their fortune upon the revenues of Tyrolean silver and copper mines acquired forty years earlier. Charles V's predecessor had desperately needed funds for an Italian campaign and had proffered the royal mines as collateral. Lending to desperate princes could turn into a lucrative enterprise indeed.[15]

The international merchants were becoming increasingly crucial to the military operations of Europe's princes for yet another reason. They could safely and rapidly move money through bills of exchange, drawn on an agent closer to a battlefront that might have been hundreds of miles distant. With pay-hungry troops about to mutiny or pillage, this was critical. All told, it thrust these merchants into positions of power and influence beyond anything they had enjoyed in the past.[16]

The final factor that lifted Antwerp into financial prominence was the sheer volume of foreigners doing business there. In Antwerp it was possible to cash a bill of exchange written from almost anywhere in Europe at any time, float a loan, take an option on merchandise not yet arrived at the port, sell commodities, raise capital or deal in any currency. By 1531, the city of Antwerp had created what economic historians consider the first *bourse*, or stock exchange, bringing an assemblage of business men from different nations into an enclosed area at pre-set hours each day for a common purpose. The name emanated from Bourse Square, a plaza in nearby Bruges where foreign merchants had originally assembled for the purposes of transacting financial business.[17]

The exchange building itself cost the city fathers 300,000 golden crowns.[18] A surviving woodcut dated 1531, soon after completion, shows an enclosed courtyard edged on all four sides by a covered arcade, elaborately carved and decorated and arched in the Gothic style. Cut into the pointed roofs of the arcade were rows of dormer windows filled with leaded glass and finished off with flourishing cornices.[19] These gave unobstructed light to an upper level of shops where the great Flemish painters of Antwerp sold their works.[20] Some of the upper space was no doubt also used by the notaries who recorded every transaction. On ground level, refectory tables and benches were set out under the archways. The central courtyard, open to the skies, was where the merchants and brokers—formally attired in tall hats, dress swords at the hip, frock capes and hose—mingled in small groups in a most gentlemanly fashion. While it may seem strange to create an environment for business in the open air—especially in Antwerp's rainy climate—it had historic and practical roots. Business in those days was typically conducted on the open streets. Moreover, if coin or cloth had to be scrutinized for fraud or fault, it would best be done in daylight rather than a dimly-lit room. Indeed, the tables beneath the archways, standing on diagonally-set tiles, may well have been placed there for rainy day use, or whenever it was necessary to put something in writing.

Antwerp was officially part of the domains ruled by Charles V, Holy Roman Emperor. Despite the imposing title, his realms were no more than a loose confederation of minor German and Italian states plus the Low Countries (present day Belgium and the Netherlands). The aim of the "empire" was to strengthen the hand of a number of the smaller duchies of Europe by uniting them under one supreme leader, elected by the vote of lesser princes. Each vote had been bought seven years earlier at a total cost of one million gold florins (about 300,000 ducats), only adding to Charles V's current financial woes. In addition to the domains under his sovereignty as Holy Roman Emperor, Charles had also acquired dominion over Spain, following the death of his maternal grandmother. The death of other relatives had brought Austria, Hungary and Bohemia under his velvet hat. Not since the days of Charlemagne in the 9th century had one monarch dominated so much of Europe.[21]

An angular man with an elongated face, Charles V had a protruding chin and dark eyes that were full of warmth and compassion. He thought himself ugly, though he was genuinely regal. He was one of the last knightly monarchs who, albeit humorless and some say dour, genuinely tried to carry out his duties with honor and glory. He was also one of the few ruling monarchs in history who had the humility to abdicate three years before his death, rather than hang on until he drew his final breath. He may well have been, as many have said, the foremost gentleman of his age.[22]

As of late, he had been spending most of his energies bumping on horseback through Italy and France, fighting Francis I, his rival monarch in France, over disputed territory. The year Doña Gracia arrived in Antwerp the two kings were finally drawing up an uneasy truce, partly in fear that a divided Europe would fall prey to the dreaded and increasingly powerful Turks. Charles

V considered it part of his divine mission to spare Christian Europe from being overrun by the infidels. He was a staunch Catholic, anxious to preserve the Old Faith. Thus, he also fretted about the growing might of the Protestant Reformation, launched twenty years earlier by Martin Luther, the German theologian.

Back in 1517, Luther had tacked his famous 95 *theses* to the door of a cathedral in nearby Wittenberg, outlining his criticisms of the Catholic Church that had sent shock waves of religious sedition throughout Europe. His outrage had attracted the *converso*s in Antwerp, many of whom initially joined the movement, allying themselves with other enemies of Rome and the Inquisition. Luther's approach also offered a form of Christianity that came nearer to their own Judaism. By 1521, rumors were circulating that the *converso*s were helping to print and circulate Protestant materials.[23] This influenced Charles to act with ambivalence towards the *converso*s in general; a group of people with questionable loyalty who fueled his money machine but didn't quite fit reliably into any known classification.[24]

Still, Charles was several times removed from direct control over Antwerp. As a result of its economic power, the city had won self-governing privileges, acting almost like an autonomous republic. As Charles was dependent upon its capital markets, he respected its autonomy. Besides, there was another layer between him and the city—his sister, Marie, Queen Dowager of Hungary. In 1531, six years before Doña Gracia arrived in Antwerp, Charles had installed Marie as Regent of the Low Countries. He thereby continued a precedent whereby the Low Countries had been repeatedly ruled by strong women; the most recent being Marie's predecessor, Margaret of Austria.[25] Though only 25 years old at the time, Marie was unquestionably equal to the task. She quickly became more than a puppet ruler, opposing Charles V's orders whenever she saw fit. She showed strength, pragmatism and shrewdness, occasionally making Charles appear in his pronouncements like a high-minded fool.[26] A portrait painted around this time shows a striking family resemblance. Marie has the same elongated face and forward thrusting chin. Her clothes and expression suggest a serious woman who had little tolerance for the frippery of the era.[27]

Antwerp was not only a flourishing business center. With its flow of easy money, luxurious living and a certain cosmopolitan flair, it exemplified the cultural flowering of the Renaissance. What better place to attract the era's most talented painters, goldsmiths, silversmiths, tapestry weavers, glass-blowers, sculptors, dramatists, musicians, bookbinders, art printers, diamond-workers, silk weavers, engravers, writers, thinkers, printers, craftsmen and reformers than a tolerant city filled with prosperous merchants who were eager to support the arts, and open-minded enough to embrace radical ideas in science and religion.[28]

It was while staying in Antwerp some twenty years earlier, where he had gone to negotiate certain commercial and diplomatic treaties, that Sir Thomas More, the great English philosopher and statesman, wrote *Utopia*; his master work criticizing the economic and social conditions in Europe at that time, especially perpetual war, oppression of the poor and unjust laws.[29]

More's friend in Antwerp was Desiderius Erasmus, the great Dutch writer and reformer. Erasmus believed, among other things, in the importance of manners as a civilizing agent that paved the way for more compassionate treatment of one's fellow human being.[30] Erasmus also argued against the flagrant abuses and greed within the Catholic Church. By the time Doña Gracia arrived in Antwerp, the city had become one of the most important printing centers for Reformation propaganda, although such an activity was still officially considered an heretical act, punishable by death. Antwerp had begun to dominate the printing trades in general, irrespective of content. This was all the more significant considering that moveable type and mechanical book production had been around for less than a hundred years, fueling Renaissance learning in ways never before imagined.[31]

A few years earlier, Hieronymous Bosch, living along those narrow streets, had just finished transmitting his religious passions onto breathtaking canvases. Albrecht Durer, a particular friend of the Portuguese merchants,[32] had been working on his renowned woodcuts and oil paintings; while Pieter Bruegel, the Elder, was leading the way for Van Dyke and Rubens, Antwerp's most famous painters, to continue the legacy of great Flemish art well into the next century. With a large Portuguese population resident in the city, it was also not surprising that two of its most celebrated intellectuals chose to live there during this period: Rui Fernandes de Almada, the noted diplomat, intellectual and friend of both Durer and Erasmus;[33] and Damaio de Gois, the writer and humanist. They found Antwerp far more appealing than the repressive atmosphere prevailing in Portugal.

Antwerp was also a festive place. Lent was an occasion for rowdy amusement, rather than repentance. A religious procession was an excuse to decorate the streets. Weddings, funerals, christenings and births were all celebrated with gigantic feasts. On most days the markets were crowded. Townsfolk went about their business to the joyous sounds of bells that were rung from the myriad of church towers on every conceivable occasion—to wake them up in the morning, for the daily opening and closing of the city gates and even to announce the official closing of all taverns at eleven o'clock each night.

There were theatricals, dancing schools, fencing schools, basic schooling for both boys *and girls*, skating on the iced-over moats in winter, picnics in the nearby fields in summer, antique forms of hard-ball games and bowling alleys, a *public* library. It was also a shopper's paradise, the Paris or Manhattan of its day;

a delectable emporium offering specialty items and craftsman-
ship, such as its renowned Flemish tapestries. Thomas Cromwell
purchased shirts and furniture in Antwerp.[34] Lady Lisle sent one
of her agents to buy the latest in *stomachers*—an elaborate waist-
coat that was the height of fashion—in Antwerp the very year of
Doña Gracia's arrival.[35]

In every respect it was a banquet for the mind, purse and
body. It was a cultured city that so embodied the true sprit of
the Renaissance that it was dubbed "the Florence of the North."[36]

How did the Portuguese *converso*s, and Diogo in particular,
fit into this flourishing milieu? Antwerp's rapid financial expansion soon attracted the *converso*s, with their international trading networks, especially those like the Mendes brothers who had
become major players in the Indies trade.

What made operations even easier was that Antwerp was then
under Spanish rule. It was part of Charles' Spanish domains.
Many of the Portuguese *converso*s had been born in Spain and
still had family members living there. They had continued to
trade with Spain and its colonies despite its policies of political
and religious enmity. Ongoing commercial connections show
up time and again in Inquisition testimony. Even the Mendes
were still making loans to Spanish officials.[37] The city had a
strong Portuguese flavor, too. Substantial links had been established between Antwerp and Lisbon as early as 1499 when the
Portuguese crown first sent an agent to Antwerp to develop a
distribution hub for its valuable Asian cargoes. By 1508, the king
had established the *Feitoria de Flandres*, a northern branch of his
important *Casa da India*, the Portuguese government agency responsible for assuring the maximum revenues out of the crown's

lucrative Asian trade. It was precisely the same year that the Affaitati—partners of the Mendes brothers—were granted monopoly privileges by the Portuguese crown over the valuable spices coming in from the East.[38]

By 1512,[39] only four years later, two of the younger members of both families, Jean-Charles Affaitati and Diogo Mendes, were being dispatched to Antwerp to run the northern European end of the business. Already 27 years old and in control of one of the larger fortunes, this would have instantly made Diogo a senior member of an energetic crowd of speculation-happy youths, barely in their twenties, who were pouring into Antwerp seeking a speedy road to riches.[40]

As mentioned, Diogo and Jean-Charles were soon contributing 800,000 to one million ducats each to a single shipment from Portugal; their lesser partners investing amounts ranging from 10,000 to 20,000 ducats each.[41] These were spectacular sums, considering the average wage of a mid-level bureaucrat was around 100 ducats *a year* and a modest village home cost about 200 ducats.[42] By pooling their purchasing power, they could not only buy all the spices destined for Antwerp, but almost everything else for sale in Lisbon. By purchasing in advance they acquired the shipments at rock bottom prices. By 1520, the Portuguese crown was so deeply in debt that it desperately needed their advance payments to outfit the following year's fleet, and continue to cover the costs of their monarch's profligate ways.[43] Francisco, carefully stroking his king through personal contact in Lisbon, had been able to further the aims of the syndicate by maintaining such a stranglehold over the crown that other bankers could barely get a fine leather boot through the door.

Diogo was making his own royal loans to hard-pressed monarchs. Early on he made a major loan to the Emperor Maximilian, Charles V's grandfather and predecessor, who died in 1519. He covered a debt of 700,000 Portuguese escudos (roughly 640,000 ducats[44]) owed by King João III's *Feitoria de Flandres*.[45] Diogo also made at least one loan to Charles V just a few years before Doña Gracia arrived in Antwerp,[46] There were probably dozens more.

The *converso* merchants found the city so lucrative that in 1518 they made a payment of 800,000 ducats to the necessary authorities to issue a decree that officially permitted them to stay indefinitely—provided, of course, they lived as good Catholics. By 1526, and again in 1529, they had proved themselves so helpful to the commercial expansion of the city that further decrees were issued encouraging Portuguese (a widely-used code name used throughout Europe during the 16th century for all *conversos*) settlers.

A contemporary Antwerp magistrate commented that the *converso*s were trading in "merchandise of better quality, more precious and needed, than those commonly obtainable." He added: "to these belong spices, sugar, wines, oil, cotton, brazilwood, ivory; all kinds of fruit, including figs, raisins… large quantities of pearls, gems, rings and other items."[47]

At the beginning Antwerp still only knew what it was like to have the cream of the *converso*s —merchant traders who were bringing in substantial capital, skills and unparalleled commercial contacts, along with a close relationship with the Portuguese crown that virtually assured the city's continued preeminence.

It did not stay that way for long. As Portugal proved increasingly hostile towards all *converso*s in its midst, and established its own Inquisition, *converso*s of more modest means and skills began viewing Antwerp as the ideal escape hatch of tolerance, asylum and opportunity. By the time Doña Gracia arrived, the authorities were shifting gears, fearful that the refugees were taking advantage of Antwerp's hospitality as a convenient way station along a roundabout route that was taking them, their possessions and their skills, to the Ottoman Empire. In the process it had unwittingly become an accomplice for the transfer of *converso* money and expertise that strengthened the hand of the dreaded Turks—Christian Europe's most feared enemy.

Starting in 1525, all Portuguese arriving by ship had to first present themselves at the city hall to be interrogated concerning their real reasons for coming to Antwerp. Innkeepers had to provide lists of their guests or face a stiff fine. For a brief period there was a mild reversal of policy, with the refugees being permitted to stay just 30 days to sell, buy or exchange what was needed for an onward journey. But local officials began to panic once the human tide started to swell. By 1532, Charles V officially forbade any further settlement of *converso*s in Antwerp, although this did not stop the flow.[48]

The twenty-four years between the time Diogo first settled in Antwerp and the arrival of Doña Gracia were not only spent getting rich. He lived luxuriously, gave sumptuous parties and supported the arts. Since his friend and partner, Jean-Charles Affaitati, was known to be a patron of Italian and Flemish writers, it was likely that Diogo was inclined in the same direction. If Doña Gracia's later attitudes are any indication, Diogo no doubt favored works by *converso* writers or anything that could expand Jewish scholarship.[49] We know that he was in contact with Daniel Bomberg, the celebrated Renaissance printer of Jewish theological works. Bomberg was not himself of Jewish ancestry, as far as is known, but may have chosen to foster Jewish printing simply because it was good business. Bomberg was born in Antwerp but later moved to Venice, possibly because it was one of the only cities left in Europe where he could freely publish Jewish works at this time.[50]

Like Francisco in the south, Diogo had naturally assumed the mantle of leadership over his fellow *conversos* in the north— a position in keeping with the family's sense of communal responsibility and irrespective of any difficulty it might cause them personally. For there is no doubt that in all that he undertook, Diogo was pursuing a perilous course. At any moment his clandestine and not-so-clandestine activities could prove hazardous, should his fellow merchants, competitors or even Charles V himself decide that there was no longer a need to keep Diogo around. Punishments were severe. Heretics, traitors and thieves were routinely strangled, hanged, burned, boiled alive in oil or water, branded and dismembered.[51]

The peril was acknowledged in the later writings of Joshua Soncino, the great 16th century rabbi living in Constantinople. Reflecting upon the Antwerp period some twenty years later, Soncino's observations have contemporary resonance for diaspora Jews who give generously to Israel, but choose not to live there. Soncino suggested the Mendes brothers were good Jews even if they themselves chose not to return to a place where they could live openly as Jews—a reluctance that normally tended to rankle the Levantine rabbinate. This was because "they were holding onto the hand of those Jews spared from that bitter and impetuous apostasy," explained Soncino, "and were (thus) helping with their bodies and money to make a great nation live." He postulated that the brothers had decided "it was a greater *mitzvah* to benefit others than to save themselves alone." By doing so, opined Soncino, they were also bringing "merit to their (own) souls."[52]

In other words, they could be redeemed for having sinfully enjoyed the fruits of residing and prospering "among the idol worshipers," as the Jews called the Catholics on account of their ubiquitous icons. Such an attitude on the part of at least one rabbi would have had great meaning for covert Jews like Francisco and Diogo. The same guilt-ridden craving for redemption could have helped inspire Doña Gracia to build upon the important rescue work that both brothers had started.

What was the scope of this undercover rescue operation? The overall plan, as Soncino implied, was to prevent the *conversos*— who represented a substantial segment of the Jewish world of the 16th century—from ruin and extermination, thereby helping to ensure the survival of the Jewish people in general. To this end, the Mendes brothers had spearheaded two complimentary strategies. The first was to try to prevent the Inquisition from coming to Portugal, thereby enabling the *converso*s to maintain their property and conduct business without fear of arbitrary confiscation, as well as discreetly practice their ancient rituals until a more tolerant regime came to power.

The other was to build an escape route for any *converso* eager to move on to a more tolerant European city, such as Antwerp, Lyons, Rome, Venice or Ferrara; or if they preferred, join the Ashkenazim in Rhineland cities like Spire.[53] Given the negative attitude towards Jews over many centuries, many felt it would be even more prudent to leave Christian Europe entirely, traveling onwards over the Alps to embark at Venice for Ottoman lands—one of the few ports in Christian Europe where they could do so. Once inside the Ottoman Empire they typically joined relatives in the thriving communities of openly-professing Iberian Jews already established in trading cities like Salonika and Constantinople. To further avoid suspicion or arrest, some even sailed first to Madeira, a Portuguese possession off the Western coast of Africa.[54] They were, after all, not supposed to be leaving the country at all.

The incoming refugees would later tell how they had embarked from Portuguese shores under cover of darkness, usually from a small fishing port, after paying the captain handsomely for the passage. Some of these fees may well have been paid, or advanced, by the Mendes brothers and other wealthy *converso* merchants who participated in the effort. The large spice trade, with its dozens of ships regularly plying the crowded sea lanes between Portugal and Antwerp, made the exodus less conspicuous. The Portuguese authorities seemed to shift course almost as often as the ships themselves. Sometimes they simply looked the other way, sometimes they made arrests and sometimes they just climbed aboard before the ship weighed anchor to "confiscate" any valuables they could find, probably for their own pockets.[55]

Other hounded *conversos* trekked north by foot or river boat, no doubt following the great overland trade routes used by the wagon-trains leaving Lisbon for Bayonne or Bordeaux in southwest France—soon to become yet another center of *converso* resettlement. France never did have an Inquisition at this time. From France they could move by road to the customary embarkation point of Venice, if they so wished.[56]

Though the two brothers were certainly not responsible for the entire exodus, having one of them in the south and the other in the north, at least at the beginning, made them ideal leaders. They had at their command shipping, banking and currency exchange capabilities. And their powerful positions as lenders of international importance also made it less likely that a petty bureaucrat would get in their way. An awareness of their prominence must have surely emboldened the downtrodden who might have otherwise never mustered the courage to leave.

Consider, for a start, how London fitted into the exodus. Almost from the start, Diogo was involved in loan transactions to the British Treasury—loans that soon required sending an agent to reside in London.[57] Henry VIII had inherited a full treasury from his father, but it had quickly been depleted as a result of his own wars against France. As early as 1515, Henry had been forced to borrow from the Antwerp merchants.[58]

Others *conversos* and Mendes' agents soon followed. This made it easy for Diogo to quietly divert one or another of them to assist the refugees who, by the early 1530's, were beginning to flee Portugal in ever-increasing numbers. There was Christopher Fernandes, as mentioned earlier, who warned those on board the incoming spice ships of the potential dangers awaiting them in Antwerp, where official policies towards the incoming hordes similarly shifted as rapidly as the tides; at once viewing them as traders who had made the region prosperous, but fearful of their Turkish sympathies. Fernandes warned the refugees if and when their property might be confiscated on the pretext of it being destined to enrich the dreaded Turk. Would they be arrested and imprisoned and interrogated under torture concerning the true motives for their voyage? Or would they be allowed to settle, even temporarily? Might they be better off tarrying a while in London? It was up to Fernandes to advise.[59]

He was assisted by Antonio della Rogna, the one-eyed man who was reputed to be a master of Hebrew theology.[60] Della Rogna cashed the jewels and other valuables that the refugees had hidden away among chests of clothing and hampers of food taken on board, and even inside the felt hats they typically wore.[61] Money not needed in London or coin that could not legally be exported was swapped for a bill of exchange, payable by the House of Mendes in Antwerp.[62]

Upon arrival in Antwerp, the refugees looked upon Diogo as their "patron and protector," as official accounts would confirm.[63] They would go directly to Diogo's place of business (probably on the ground floor of his house, as was the custom) to cash that bill of exchange. If the refugees did not have any money—perhaps it had been stolen or used to pay a ship's captain—they could apply for a grant or loan from *la bourse de charité*. This was the charity bank set up by local *converso* merchants, under Diogo's leadership, to support the refugee effort.[64]

It was a fund of significant size, reputedly over 100,000 ducats and growing by 45,000 ducats a year.[65] This indicated that it was either being invested at a huge profit, or that the wealthy *converso* merchants of Antwerp were under pressure to regularly contribute. Diogo also used his position as a leading merchant in Antwerp to sign rent guarantees for refugees who lacked the personal or fiscal backing needed to become an acceptable tenant. He arranged for a *converso* physician to welcome them and help them find lodgings.[66] Diogo and the agents of the House of Mendes also acted as the clearinghouse for refugees who reached Ottoman lands and began sending money back to Antwerp to help other family members to join them in safety.[67]

A later account of the reputed espionage activities of Diogo's nephew, Don Joseph Nasi, provides a clue concerning one of the ways in which the escape network's clandestine messages might have been moved from one locale to another. A letter would initially be dispatched to an intermediary and then sent on to yet another intermediary over a circuitous route until it reached its final destination. Only the person handling the final lap would know the true identity of the recipient. And only the recipient would know the true identity of the sender.[68]

Diogo also provided the departing refugees and their children with vital funds—ten ducats for each adult and five for each child—for the onward journey.[69] Moreover, since they had to undertake a hazardous trek over the Alps and through Italy before reaching Venice, their valuables were often sent on separately, concealed among the regular export shipments to Ferrara or Ancona that went out under the commercial seal of the House of Mendes.[70] One such agent used for the transfer of assets was reputed to be Bomberg, the printer of Jewish works. One can well imagine how it might have worked: Diogo would undercharge for a sale, or overpay for a purchase. The excess would be conveyed to its rightful owner. It is likely that Diogo would have wanted to support Bomberg's work anyway, since Bomberg had spent the past twenty years printing biblical commentaries and editions of the Talmud and Mishnah, the codification of rabbinical law.[71]

For *converso*s who were really anxious to cling to the remnants of Jewish practice, there were indications from the testimony of the incoming refugees, as well as local citizens and clergy, that Diogo and his associates hosted religious services in one house or another, and personally blessed them in the Jewish manner.[72] The extent and organized nature of these operations, as noted, fly in the face of the accepted notion that Jews in centuries past never mounted a coordinated or credible effort to fight the consequences of anti-Semitism.

By the 1530's, and possibly even earlier, the House of Mendes in Antwerp, under Diogo's stewardship, but no doubt subordinate to Francisco's direction, also became the clearinghouse for those bribes and other payments being regularly sent by a consortium of Portuguese *converso*s to the Vatican. These were dispatched in the form of bills of exchange, normally in the care of Duarte da Paz, an enigmatic member of the tribe who was operating as the *converso* lobbyist in Rome; a man variously described by both sides as crafty, daring, astute, untrustworthy, eloquent and energetic.[73] Da Paz needed all the aforementioned skills as danger and duplicity were his constant companions. He even took the precaution of wearing a finely tempered suit of armor under his doublet when appearing before the pope. One day early in 1535, immediately after leaving the pope's presence, he was pounced upon by an unknown assailant and stabbed fourteen times. Had it not been for his hidden armor he would have died instantly.

Da Paz immediately protested to King João of Portugal, whom he suspected of arranging the ambush. Replying to an

enquiry sent to the Portuguese court by one of the pope's nephews several weeks after the incident, the king emphatically denied involvement. Had he organized the murder attempt, noted
the king, it would have been arranged differently and da Paz
would not have escaped with his life. The only thing that the
monarch said he regretted was that it all happened, "so near the
presence of the Holy Father."[74] Da Paz recovered, but it damp-
ened his ardor for his mission. There might have been a connection between this audacious act and the death of Francisco, which
had occurred only weeks before. The Portuguese crown was probably trying to undermine the resolve of the *converso*s at a moment when they were especially vulnerable.

Following Francisco's death, the importance of Diogo and
his money-laundering activities in Antwerp became even more
crucial. The clerics soon realized they would have to re-direct
their efforts northwards if the ducats were to continue flowing
with the same predictability. This was clear from a letter dated
March 1, 1536, sent by the Papal Nuncio in Portugal to the
Vatican explaining why the bribes had ceased, or at least were
being delayed.[75]

In this particular letter, the Nuncio commented angrily that
"two or three of them (the representatives of the *converso*s in
Portugal) were to come to meet me in Santarem," a city about
100 kilometers northeast of Lisbon. They were supposed to deliver a promised bribe of 5,000 ducats in the form of a bill of
exchange. But while he was waiting he gained the impression
that there was a problem or disagreement among them. Or
maybe they didn't even have the money, because they ended up
canceling the meeting. With a hint of impatience he then explained that he intended to bypass this hapless group in Portugal and send a demand for the promised bill of exchange "to
Flanders (Antwerp) with my order for *them* to pay Rome." Even
the local *converso* delegation advised him that "in Flanders I will

achieve the resolution of everything." Meanwhile, they promised the Nuncio they would go around Portugal to try to raise the money locally. But this would take some time, they warned, since "they want to record how much each person gives."[76]

Irritated to the core, the Nuncio then went on to say that he was leaning more and more towards Antwerp, adding that if they (Diogo and his associates) did not come through, the conversos must be "the biggest asses in the world." As a consequence, he was more than eager to proceed swiftly with the establishment of a "vigorous" Inquisition in Portugal. Once they understood this was certain, he insisted, prompt payment would surely resume. But just in case, he told the Vatican, he was going to travel personally to Antwerp "as Diogo Mendes is there"— implying that direct contact with Diogo was the only reliable way to keep the spigot open, now that Francisco was dead. In the meantime, the Nuncio wanted the pope to know that he was sending one of his most trusted henchmen to visit Doña Gracia, who was still in Lisbon, to see if she would be willing to take this particular "weight upon her (own) shoulders." It was something, as noted, that she eventually agreed to do.[77] It is interesting how willingly Doña Gracia accepted this responsibility, confirming an early grasp at leadership rather than passing the task on to Diogo, which she easily could have done.

As well as sending money to the dreaded Turks, rumors soon began circulating that Diogo was selling the Turks cannon-balls and other weapons.[78] This was so, noted later accusations preserved among the correspondence of Queen Marie, despite the fact that "the Turk, the enemy of the Catholic faith...has declared open war on the Emperor...and recently entered the Kingdom of Hungary under arms to invade Christianity."[79] It would have been logical for Diogo to be involved in Levantine trade, considering how many of his merchant brethren he was sending to Ottoman lands. Also, Levantine trade was a natural part of Antwerp's international dealings. But just how much of this was because he was trying to help his co-religionists, and how much was normal trade for profit, is hard to say. The extent of the military hardware allegedly involved is also questionable, although all these rumors were no doubt grounded in truth. As a result, claimed the authorities, "a large amount of gold and silver is (thus being) transferred and the Turk…continues to be greatly fortified and strengthened, as much in numbers as in horse and goods."[80]

Certainly a man who was constantly taking high-stakes, high-risk positions in the world of finance and shipping must have been energized by all the intrigue. Diogo shows signs of thoroughly enjoying the thrill of the game, as did Francisco before his untimely death, in contrast to Doña Gracia who also fought back hard, but never with the same sense that she relished combat.

Diogo must have had a gambler's outlook—or an inordinate sense of his own invincibility—because he continued even though his chances of being caught were increasing by the day. The first major salvo against his neatly-planned escape network came with an edict issued by an obviously infuriated Charles V on April 17, 1530. He argued that the *conversos*—whom Charles described as "persons simulating the Christian religion and deceiving Christians under the appearance and garb of Christians"—had for some time been fleeing to the "land of the Turks and other enemies" with all their belongings and "even things not of their own." It had therefore become necessary, he noted, to appoint an official whose job it would be to seize anyone making such a flight or transfer. The edict was designed to cover all parts of Charles V's domain, including his provinces in Italy, France, Belgium and Germany, many of which had to be crossed to reach Venice.[81]

No one was to be spared. Any and all "pretended Christians

preparing to travel to join the Turks," including "merchants found transmitting weapons of offense" henceforth fell under this decree. Information from those seized and suspected could be obtained "by torture if...necessary." The job of organizing the witch hunt was given to Cornelius de Schepperus, a man who would figure prominently in *converso* affairs for years to come, along with Jean Vuysting, who was to serve as his hatchet man. Vuysting would later be described by Samuel Usque, the friend of Doña Gracia and a contemporary observer, as "the cruelest persecutor of Israel since the loss of the Temple....He laid in wait for (the refugees) in the State of Milan and there arrested them by the cartload. Since he did not have the authority to kill them, he despoiled them of even their last garment. He subjected the weak women and wearied old men to a thousand tortures to force them to reveal what possessions they had brought with them, and how many others were to follow, so he could await and arrest them (too)...."[82]

The human tide continued nonetheless. Despite the emotional strength needed to leave the comfort and familiarity of one's homeland and the dangers that lay in wait for any traveler, the specter of burning or rotting in a dungeon in Portugal was deemed more terrifying than the perils of the high seas and mountain passes. Diogo soon became a marked man. The only question was where and when, and under what pretext he could be eliminated. Armed with the new edict, there was a preliminary attempt to arrest Diogo and a handful of his associates in February 1531. It fell apart the same day when the prisoners insisted they were protected by letters of safe conduct granted expressly by Charles himself five years earlier.[83] But not for long. More solid evidence of wrongdoing was now being eagerly sought to build a case against Diogo that could be prosecuted and won.[84]

The opportunity began with one of those incidents that cried out for exploitation. In 1521, a *converso* woman had arrived in Antwerp from Lisbon with her three boys and two girls. She explained that she was running away from her husband, a physician, who was still in Portugal but threatened to come after her. Diogo had been among *converso* leaders of Antwerp who had persuaded her to move to Salonika. Once there, she and her children reverted openly to Judaism, as was customary. The incident passed unnoticed at the time. Then, in May, 1532, some ten years later, one of her sons, now a young man, returned to Italy where he insisted he bitterly resented his desertion from the Catholic faith. In a ragtag and penniless condition, the youth moved on to Antwerp. His intention, he told the authorities, was to board a ship to return to Portugal where he could be reunited with his father. But meanwhile, his father had gone to Salonika, too. Some Antwerp-based friends of the youth's mother tried to persuade the boy to return to Salonika as well, apparently fearing what he might reveal to the authorities in a moment of weakness.[85]

They were right. Tempting the youth with bribes, a former agent of King João III—who bore a grudge over prior dealings with Diogo that had turned sour—encouraged the boy to go to Bruges and repeat the entire story to Charles V's confessor. On July 5, the youth confirmed that Diogo was someone who influenced the *converso*s to revert openly to Judaism by helping them resettle in Ottoman lands. Diogo, revealed the youth, kept the Turks informed of all that was occurring in Christian Europe. Diogo was also a secret Jew, involved in illicit trading that helped his fellow *converso*s transfer their assets into Italy. From there it was easy to make further transfers to Ottoman lands, given the volume of trade between Italian and Levantine ports.

Moreover, Diogo and three of his associates were alleged to be agents of the sultan who were encouraging the *converso*s to take their property out of Christian Europe. Diogo and these

associates were immediately charged by Charles' imperial government with fostering illegal commercial relations that would
enrich and embolden the infidel Turks at the expense of Christian Europe.[86]

As this was the summer when the sultan was amassing an
army of 300,000 foot soldiers and 100,000 horse on the out-
skirts of Vienna,[87]—a summer so fraught with the danger of
Turkish infiltration into the very heartland of Europe that even
the pope talked of fleeing to France[88]—Diogo must have seemed
the embodiment of wickedness and treason.

The accused merchants protested their innocence. They suggested the information was tainted by an undercurrent of ven-
geance. To no avail. A few days later they were arrested. The
charges against the others were soon dropped, but Diogo's goods
were impounded. His ledgers were seized and bailiffs were sent
to his mansion to haul him off to prison.[89] Allegedly found
among his belongings were two books in Hebrew: one book of
psalms and another book of Jewish chants according to the
Ashkenazi rites; all of which, it was implied, underscored his
acts of heresy.[90] In the meantime, three more charges were lodged
against Diogo: that he had falsified exchange rates for his own
profit; that he had lent money at usurious rates; and that he had
operated monopolies that had enriched himself but harmed
others in Antwerp.[91]

Shortly afterwards, on August 23, Diogo asked if his case
could be heard "in prompt and good order, given the heavy
losses" he was incurring due to his imprisonment and the seizure of his goods.[92] At first it looked as though he was going to
be transferred to Brussels to be judged before the Council of
Brabant, the regional governing body that came directly under
the control of Charles V. But this idea was quickly quashed following a protest at Antwerp's city hall by other Portuguese merchants. It also prompted a senior Antwerp official to vigorously

intercede, arguing once again that such action constituted a flagrant violation of the protections that the city had granted its
foreign merchants. Those rights stipulated that no foreign merchants could be jailed unless the charges had first been heard
before a tribunal of municipal officials. Antwerp's leaders were
also aware that the arrest of a leading merchant like Diogo on
charges of questionable commercial dealings could adversely
affect the prosperity of Antwerp and its citizens. It would desta-
bilize the entire community of foreign merchants, shattering the
trust that they had placed in the city fathers to protect and honor
their business dealings. This, in turn, could encourage them to
relocate elsewhere.[93] Moreover, Diogo had financial obligations
outstanding to townspeople. They could face bankruptcy if the
anticipated funds were not delivered on schedule.[94]

Diogo had other powerful friends. Word of the arrest was
immediately dispatched by Jean-Charles Affaitati to Francisco
in Lisbon. With good winds, the journey by sea could have taken
as little as ten days.[95] Another letter must have been rushed to
London, probably addressed to Thomas Cromwell, asking if
Henry VIII would also intervene to help free Diogo. Within
weeks, both the king and queen of Portugal and the king of
England were writing to Charles and Marie pleading for Diogo's
release.[96] The consuls of Spain, Genoa and Florence—places
where the House of Mendes was also doing business[97]—added
their protests. Damaio de Gois, the Portuguese writer and humanist, appealed personally to Marie. So did Ruy Fernandes,
the powerful agent of the Portuguese crown in Antwerp.[98]

Diogo also had his agents approach Queen Marie with a
compromise: would she agree to dismiss all charges for a payment of 10,000 to 12,000 ducats? The queen countered by recommending an interest-free loan for one year of 50,000
ducats—but only as a form of bail until a legal decision on the
case could be issued.[99] The entreaties had evidently enraged

Marie and Charles.

They soon became obsessed with accumulating evidence to prove beyond a doubt, even in the municipal courts, that Diogo was a traitor and a secret Jew. On August 8, less than three weeks after Diogo's arrest, Charles wrote to two of his trusted lieutenants. He wanted them to know that Antonio della Rogna, Diogo's chief of underground activities in London, had been captured, apparently seized while on a mission somewhere in Charles' domains. He was now being held prisoner in "the fortress of Cogel."[100]

Charles was ordering his lieutenants to interrogate della Rogna along with other potential informants arrested at the same time, since "it concerns the safety...of the whole state." The lieutenants were being instructed to find out from the prisoners whatever they could about "the aforesaid Jews (*converso* refugees) and their practices and the manner in which they remove their goods." Evidently della Rogna had confessed "in the presence of the captain and soldiers." Charles wanted the lieutenants to tell him how reliable this information might be. A good deposition, added Charles, "made in legally attested form and signed with your seal" could provide the legal ammunition needed to take the critical steps "for the good of our own state and that of Christendom."[101]

Another propitious opportunity was to fall into Charles' lap. It was the arrival in the area of David Reubeni, the messianic pretender who had shown up in Lisbon during Doña Gracia's teenage years. Ten years later the indefatigable Reubeni was still criss-crossing Europe seeking support for his holy war against the infidel. Coincidentally, he had arranged to meet Charles V in Regensburg, the official seat of government of the Holy Roman Empire, around the same time as Diogo's arrest. Considering Charles' apprehensive mood, it was no surprise that Reubeni was immediately arrested. Charles was eager to find out whether

Reubeni had ever had dealings in the Low Countries. He must have believed that Reubeni was somehow working with Diogo. For Diogo was interrogated during this time about his knowledge of the exotic adventurer and Reubeni's well-known goal of restoring Jewish rule to Jerusalem.[102]

In the end Charles had trouble proving anything at all. On August 13, Diogo was brought to trial.[103] But it was initially before a panel of councillors sent from Brabant to Antwerp by Charles and Marie, not the burghers of Antwerp. In the interim weeks Charles had apparently decided not to bring additional damaging information from the della Rogna interrogations, or use any of Diogo's deposition about Reubeni. Probably the potential economic fallout resulting from Diogo's arrest was beginning to sink in, and Charles had decided it might be wiser to compromise. After all, he had been clearly warned in those royal missives that the credit markets would be thrown into such disarray as to affect him personally.

The tenor of the proceedings quickly shifted in Diogo's favor. Aided by an able lawyer, Diogo claimed that the charge of heresy had to be heard before an ecclesiastical court, not secular judges. Moreover, heresy was a crime specifically exempt under the special protections and privileges granted foreign merchants. By the same token, the other charges belonged under the jurisdiction of the city of Antwerp, since they concerned business dealings. Simply holding these hearings in Antwerp was not good enough. If his arrest and confiscation of goods had therefore been ordered "without proper authority," he and his belongings should be immediately released and damages paid for the inconvenience. Not so, replied the Attorney General. The charges should be heard by the executive judges. No way, countered Diogo.[104]

Concerning the allegations of running a monopoly, Diogo argued that what he had been doing was no different from how his fellow merchants behaved in other areas of trade. Engaging in business with the *converso*s in Italy or elsewhere was again no different from the practices of other Antwerp merchants. Besides, why was exporting *converso* property to Italy a crime? Italy was also a Christian land. Loaning money to *converso*s in Antwerp was similarly no crime, he posited. He was a prudent banker and *converso*s were known to honor their debts.[105]

Ultimately it was decided that both sides should submit their respective jurisdictional claims in writing. Presumably the judges sent by Charles and Marie had become increasingly worried about the possible impact upon the other merchants as they rapidly agreed to drop all allegations of heresy "to which…he will no longer be held to answer."[106]

At the end of August, Marie issued a provisional decree, later confirmed by the Council of Brabant. The evidence was not yet sufficient, it noted, to keep Diogo under arrest, nor to continue to impound his ledgers and assets. Diogo was temporarily released on payment of 50,000 ducats. The only caveat was that certain leading merchants had to guarantee his appearance in person at a subsequent trial (of which no further mention was ever made) and whenever an issue arose concerning the *converso*s and their possessions.[107] He also had to pay court costs. Eventually he received a full pardon.[108] But that would not come to pass for some time.

This did not mean that Charles stopped worrying about the possibility of treason among the *converso* merchants. If he could not get rid of Diogo, then he would have to proceed another way. And proceed he did. The day after the case against Diogo fell apart in the courts, Charles issued an edict denying access to the Low Countries to any *converso* refugee bound for Ottoman lands. Together with his existing commission overseeing *converso* activity, it permitted the interrogation and search of any *converso* refugee arriving in Antwerp to ascertain such a possibility. But once again, the order had scant effect on the human flood tide.[109]

Nor did Diogo stop helping his brethren. Charles and Marie did not give up either. In November of the same year, another *converso* merchant was arrested on the road to Lyons. He was accused, along with some of his colleagues, of similarly aiding the infidel Turks by trafficking with *converso*s.[110] All of which had a chilling effect upon the foreign merchants in Antwerp and particularly the *converso* community. There was talk once again of leaving. This must have worried Charles since he was still dependent upon their credit. It terrified the city fathers. Three years later, in October 1535, the imperial authorities were so worried that they reconfirmed the foreigners' ancient privileges and protections.[111] A memorandum issued by the Council of Brabant gives some insight into the reasons for this constant swinging of the pendulum. On account of the industrious *converso* merchants, it noted, our "inhabitants have become wealthier…properties…have risen in value…merchants and peasants have derived greater profits from their wares and produce and the poor have been more effectively helped and supported."[112]

Two years after that, in February 1537, the year that Doña Gracia arrived, the edict of 1532 refusing entry to those *converso*s found to be headed for Ottoman lands was abolished. It was replaced by another that allowed them to remain indefinitely in Antwerp with their belongings and families.[113] This invitation, together with the prosperity of the region, opened the floodgates even wider. One reason why Charles and Marie kept swinging back and forth can be gleaned from a remark that Marie made to Charles in a letter some ten years later. Complaining about the continued *converso* refugee problem, she remarked that though they posed a threat to Christian Europe on the one hand, "we would do well if we were lucky enough to persuade them to remain here, because of the benefit that would accrue to the country due to their being industrious people."[114]

Diogo's high-profile arrest had nevertheless tarnished his reputation and undermined Francisco in Lisbon. Within a year of the incident, as noted, the Portuguese king decided not to transport so many of his goods on Diogo's ships.[115] Others must have similarly withdrawn to a distance.

———••✂••———

What was the ultimate fate of Diogo's youthful denouncer; Reubeni, the messianic pretender and Antonio della Rogna, the agent being held prisoner in the fortress at Cogel? The youth, who was quaintly termed "game for the gallows" by the Antwerp *conversos*, once they found out what he had done, ran back to Italy where, it was rumored, he became a (successful) thief.[116] Charged with having seduced *conversos* to embrace Judaism, Reubeni was taken to Spain in chains and is believed to have perished in a prison in Badajoz in 1538.[117] As for poor Antonio, he was listed as being back in London around 1540 continuing covert activities as usual.[118] So presumably he was released. Or maybe Diogo bribed the guards, allowing della Rogna to escape in the sort of daring escapade that characterized this flamboyant era.

Statue of Amatus Lusitanus (born João Roderigo), Physician to Doña Gracia, Castelo Branco, Portugal

CHAPTER **6**

A Time for Learning

I t would have therefore been a troubled Diogo—struggling against a chilly climate of suspicion surrounding all his business dealings and a rising tide of distrust against incoming *converso* refugees in general—who would have met the carriages and horsemen bringing Doña Gracia and her party through the Antwerp city gates. His sumptuous mansion in the most fashionable part of town would now begin filling up rapidly as the new arrivals unloaded their trunks and settled in. They would increase in number as time went on and the agony of an Inquisition began to corrode the lives of those who remained in Portugal.

The property was a sprawling urban compound that included two separate wooden houses and nine cottages. It was graced by a gilded fountain that probably stood in the center of an interior courtyard. The estate was situated in what was then known as the street of the cemetery of St. Mary's. It stretched backwards almost to the edge of town and included its own private wooded area. The land had once been part of the Jewish quarter. As such, it carried a special land tax, payable each year on Christmas Day "as a perpetual and hereditary payment in conformity to the arrangements concerning lands belonging to Jews."[1]

This was so even though Jews had been officially barred from Antwerp since 1370 (although selected moneylenders had been permitted to stay on because of their importance to the local economy).[2] According to the details of a later sale, the tax was payable in perpetuity, whether or not Jews resided on the property. After Diogo died and the family left Antwerp, even the incoming buyers of Flemish descent would be required to continue payment.[3]

The ban of 1370 had occurred in the wake of a particularly gruesome, albeit typical medieval pogrom. A certain Jew had been charged with stealing a sacred object. It had ended in the flaying and igniting of a representative handful of the Jewish community in full public display. The rest were banished or chose to convert. In later years these converts would become so numerous and prosperous in the region that some historians believe that their still-bitter descendants helped accelerate Luther's rise to prominence.[4]

Diogo had purchased the property some years earlier from a French merchant named Don Jacob of Marseilles. He may well have been of Jewish extraction, too. He carried the name of Jacob and also came from Marseilles; a city and region that had harbored a significant Jewish population from the time of the late Roman Empire.[5]

Listed as being part of Diogo's household within five months of Doña Gracia's arrival in Antwerp were Diogo himself, Doña Gracia, her daughter, Ana, her sister, Brianda, and Gonçalo Mendes, the third brother.[6] Not mentioned were her two young nephews—Samuel, 15, and Joseph Nasi, 13,[7] then known respectively as Bernardo and Juan Micas. This was probably because the boys had immediately transferred to the University of Louvain where they would have lived—at least during each semester—for the next three or four years. By 1540, the boys' mother would have also joined them in the house.[8]

From what we know about Doña Gracia's strong will and assertive personality, it can be assumed that she and Diogo immediately began working out how they would handle the capital she was bringing in. It represented a substantial chunk of the assets of the House of Mendes—by some accounts, as much as 300,000 ducats.[9] Her later actions suggest she would have been anxious to learn all she could about the business, as well as the inner workings of Diogo's Vatican efforts and the emerging escape network. And it would have been in Diogo's interest to teach her, considering his precarious position and the capital she was bringing to the table.

But she was still only 27 years old. And there are tantalizing hints of more personal concerns taking center stage. Most prominent was the grief she was suffering being far from home and thwarted in her struggle to find emotional happiness.[10] Consider for a start the appeal of a man like Diogo, someone she must have heard about all her life, but never had the chance to know personally. He was brilliant, attractive, cultured and sophisticated. Fifty-two years old at the time of her arrival,[11] he was probably aging in the sort of elegant, alluring way that young women—especially intelligent women—find irresistible. His manners must have been impeccable; his blend of wit, shrewdness and charm cultivated to win over even the most cautious or cantankerous adversary. And she had been alone now for almost three years.

Several historians have postulated that the proposed marriage between Diogo and Brianda may not have been a closed deal when Doña Gracia took her younger sister with her to Antwerp, and that the sisters soon found themselves in competition for the same man. If so, Doña Gracia may have hoped that Diogo would follow the Biblical injunction that favored a man marrying his deceased brother's wife, an act known as a levirate marriage.[12]

However, it was only supposed to apply if the couple did not have children. Even so, Doña Gracia and Francisco had not given birth to a boy; one of the possible contingencies broadening the definition.[13] Under the circumstances, Diogo would have had an awkward choice to make. He ultimately married the younger sister who may well have been prettier, livelier and more fun. For instance, Brianda must have been such an avid shopper that Doña Gracia had to take legal steps, a few years later, to prevent Brianda from spending her entire allowance on herself instead of her child.[14] Moreover, Brianda would never be willing to give up the fun of life in Renaissance Europe to go to the Ottoman Empire, further suggesting that she was enchanted with good living and therefore perhaps more appealing to men.

But a squabble over marriage seems doubtful. In a family of Iberian courtier Jews, marriage partners were decided upon years in advance and mutual attraction had nothing to do with the choice of a spouse. Besides, it runs counter to Hussee's letter, which indicates the decision had been made even before the women left Lisbon.

Still, this does not rule out the possibility of spontaneous combustion on Doña Gracia's part. As a possible fantasy lover, Diogo also makes sense when one realizes that he was one of the few men Doña Gracia could trust. Here was someone who would not ingratiate himself solely for her money. Moreover, if she did fall in love with Diogo during these years in Antwerp, it would help explain the intensity of the bitterness that would subsequently develop between the two sisters—an emotionally-charged rivalry that is hard to understand in financial terms alone.

For curiously, it was not until the spring of 1539[15]—eighteen months after Doña Gracia and her party arrived in Antwerp—that Brianda and Diogo finally married. The marriage contract, drawn up just before the wedding, and probably finalized by Doña Gracia on her sister's behalf since both parents had apparently died, stipulated a dowry of 4,350 ducats.[16]

Why did Brianda and Diogo wait so long? There is no clear explanation. But it would have been long enough to allow a host of emotions to rage inside Doña Gracia (and possibly even Diogo) during the interim period, particularly as they were all living together under the same roof. Even if the marriage had been pre-arranged, it would not have stopped Doña Gracia dreaming and hoping. As she began to learn the technicalities of the business—expertise so skillfully acquired that Diogo would later be willing to assign her, in his will, total responsibility for the future of the House of Mendes,[17]—she may well have reacted like a modern career woman. She could have easily found herself tumbling into love with a senior business associate with whom she was spending long hours, particularly someone who delighted in her skills.

Significantly, at the time of the wedding, we find Doña Gracia accepting the advice of a trusted friend and moving out of the house. The move was made in response to some anguish that the arrangement was causing her. Though there are hints that she was afraid to continue living under the same roof as a marked man, she was also complaining of loneliness.[18] Was it that she could not bear to sleep alone in her room, knowing that the newlyweds were making love just down the hallway? She became so distraught that she was ready to quit Antwerp entirely at this juncture and move to Ferrara[19] where her brother, Aries de Luna, eventually settled and may have already been residing.[20]

At least one historian has speculated that she initially intended to stay in Antwerp only long enough to settle her financial affairs with Diogo.[21] She never did bother to learn French—the official language of the region at that time.[22] A letter, written by Diogo to the duke of Ferrara, in October 1538, putting himself at the duke's disposal, could have been intended to lay the foundations for a move onwards by Doña Gracia, and possibly even the entire Mendes clan. Cash and credit were apparently being traded for legal rights and protections—a time-honored manipulative device that would be continued under Doña Gracia's stewardship. "His Excellency with words and I with deeds will do everything that His Excellency orders," was the delicate way Diogo put it.[23]

Still, she pulled back at the last moment. One reason may have been ill health. She was being treated at the time for digestive disturbances by a medical botanist and innovative *converso* physician named Amatus Lusitanus. [24]

Born in Portugal in 1511, Lusitanus was about the same age as Doña Gracia and may have been related through the Benvenistes.[25] A graduate of the great medical school at the University of Salamanca in Spain, he had also fled the increasingly repressive atmosphere of Portugal, making his way to Antwerp a few years earlier than she did. By this time he had become one of that city's most eminent physicians, treating such prominent citizens as the mayor and the Portuguese consul. In 1536, just before Doña Gracia's arrival, he published his first medical tract called *Index Dioscoridis*. In time, he would be credited with being the first to understand the valves of the veins. His open mind also encouraged him to experiment with the medicinal use of plants being brought back by the Portuguese from India and the East.[26]

Lusitanus, whose real name was João Roderigo do Castelo Branco,[27] was deeply distrusted by the Catholic Church. Not only was he a *converso*, but he was also unusually frank in his descriptions of sexual problems. He was especially outspoken about the difficulties afflicting nuns due to canon law, which dictated abstinence, a requirement he viewed as unnatural. Such passages were later excised by the church from his medical books.[28]

He would remain in Antwerp until 1541 when he was invited to occupy an important medical chair at the University of Ferrara.

By all accounts he was a charming and compassionate physician with a strong personal code of ethics, dedicated to an honorable life and serving humanity.[29] In two different accounts he talks of treating Doña Gracia.[30] He first takes the time to describe her in the warmest terms as "generous and kindly....embellished from birth with all the virtues."[31] On numerous occasions—first in Antwerp and later in Venice—he was called in because she was suffering from severe stomach pains. In the first instance he prescribed a medicinal drink made of "flesh-colored" roses.

He later commented that in Venice another doctor mistakenly gave Doña Gracia a potion made of muscat roses instead, causing her to develop sores and a raw tongue. He found out because she became alarmed. And, in her usual forceful manner, she had called upon her old friend Lusitanus, who discovered the roses had been the wrong variety; which was why, Lusitanus concluded, she was suffering so.[32]

Whatever the sickness, it was obviously reoccurring. Long distance travel along uneven roads was not something anyone would undertake while suffering from a physical ailment, unless forced to do so.

———••❖••———

To fully appreciate the larger reason she was anxious to leave Antwerp in the spring of 1539, yet failed to do so—one has to step back and review other events going on at the time. For a start, Diogo's sincerity as a practicing Catholic was still under strict surveillance.

This would have created insecurities for the entire family and placed Doña Gracia in a particularly untenable position.

Every shred of evidence suggests she harbored strong feelings about her Judaism.[33] She apparently even insisted upon keeping a kosher home despite the dangers involved, assuming that later revelations by Marie, a servant girl in Diogo's household, can be accepted at face value. It also assumes that Diogo was not diligent in his observance until other family members arrived. According to Marie, the family resisted eating any meat brought home from the market, unless it had been butchered by one of their own men, who no doubt knew the techniques of Jewish ritual slaughter.[34]

Doña Gracia also loathed being forced to observe Catholic devotions. An Antwerp priest later complained that she resisted going to church and praying in the true Catholic manner.[35] "When she confessed she always wanted to sit in a chair," maintained the priest, Father Sebastian di Mendis, a Portuguese clergyman residing in Antwerp. He had known her, he later told the authorities, since the days when they both lived in Lisbon. Yet despite his pleadings, she would never go down on her knees, as was the holy Catholic custom. Worst of all, he later told Queen Marie, "the widow" as he called Doña Gracia, would never confess any sins during confession. She would simply say "I love God," over and over. Her attendance at confession, he concluded with an air of disdain, came more from a fear of being accused of not being a genuine Catholic than from a true sense of devotion. Further, he added, "She would eat meat daily without even bothering to find out if it was forbidden on that particular day." This was so, he insisted, even though she had been admonished several times to be more vigilant.[36]

While it would be natural for a priest to speak with contempt about someone he perceived to be mocking his faith—irrespective of the fact that Doña Gracia had been raised as a Catholic by royal edict rather than by choice or heritage—Father Sebastian's observations correspond with other events taking place in the Mendes household at this time. Almost immediately after Doña Gracia's arrival, Diogo applied to Pope Paul III—whose jurisdiction over such matters superceded even Charles V—for permission to allow the entire Mendes family to hold Catholic services and receive communion in their home. The Vatican document, dated February 22, 1538, must have cost the family a pretty ducat or two as it was all-encompassing in allowing them to circumvent a myriad of Catholic rituals.[37]

It allowed members of the family, identified by name, plus six others chosen by Diogo (which may have been an attempt to create a *minyan*), to regularly worship in the privacy of the family mansion. It further permitted them to choose their own confessor. This was especially important since it was becoming a practice among *conversos* to send at least one family member into the priesthood. This way, they could safeguard their secrets at confession and even keep Hebrew texts without arousing the suspicion of the authorities.[38]

The papal document also gave their confessor the right to absolve each of them of any alleged heretical transgressions. It allowed them to have a "portable altar....behind closed doors...with no ringing of bells and keeping...voices down...and in such a way that the celebrants may not be charged with misdeeds." It provided sufficient freedom, in fact, to enable them to hold private Jewish services. At least one witness interrogated at later hearings told of a Jewish wedding ceremony that had taken place in the mansion.[39] Another reported that there was a chapel in the house where Diogo, his wife and three or four others "sing psalms in the Jewish manner."[40] The family was further permitted to eat meat and other prohibited products during Lent, if required on "the advice of a doctor."

Less clear in the document, but more fraught with intrigue, is why Doña Gracia and the other women in the family would have personally sought the right to enter, at least four times each year, a convent and speak to the cloistered nuns. The request was granted, provided they enter with "four other honest women" and was extended to "whichever monasteries of nuns they prefer." This privilege only makes sense when, once again, one realizes that each *converso* family would similarly send a representative number of their girls into a convent for personal safety and the secret preservation of the faith. In a threatening environment a convent was also an ideal hiding place for storing personal papers and even valuables.[41]

If a convent was also critical to the operation of the escape network, it would explain the need for multiple visits at regular intervals. And that was a strong possibility. An international order of nuns had the potential of serving as a web of safe houses or clandestine courier service. Assuming the order had convents throughout Europe—as did the Carmelites, for example —important information destined for a Mendes agent in a distant city could be folded into general correspondence or the internal memoranda that would regularly travel by courier from convent to convent. Since certain convents also served travelers, the refugees could be sure of a warm welcome. A handsome gift of ducats provided by Doña Gracia on a regular basis to help underwrite this cost would have been expected and even sought. Even better, for the purposes of subterfuge, an extra donation here and there would not arouse suspicion. It was considered a Catholic duty to support these holy orders.

The order of nuns most likely chosen by Diogo and Doña Gracia was probably the one dubbed *Les Carmes* by witnesses later giving evidence about *converso* activities in Antwerp.[42] It was located in a neighborhood where many of them lived. *Les Carmes* was probably the local shorthand for Carmelite. In Antwerp this would have been the church of the Carmelites on the Meir. It was also the church favored by the local Spanish bankers.[43] Interestingly, the famed 16th-century mystic and dissident Carmelite leader, Saint Teresa d'Avila, is well-known to have had *converso* origins.

Finally, the papal document permitted the Mendes family to

bury their dead "without funeral pomp." In effect, it would have granted them the privacy of Jewish burial rites.

In all these instances Diogo's name regularly appears alongside that of Doña Gracia as being among those most specifically cited for the privileges. The myriad of references to Doña Gracia by name, plus the timing of the document, suggested it was she who nudged Diogo to get it. Otherwise why didn't Diogo apply sooner? Further, it echoes a similar papal dispensation that her late husband had obtained in Lisbon six years earlier.[44]

At the very least, the document provided room for the family to maneuver if charges of heresy were suddenly thrust upon Diogo again. And they had good reason to think it might happen. An open-door policy towards the incoming *converso* refugees had been issued yet again by Charles V in February 1537. Confirmed by the city of Antwerp in November of that year, it had unleashed a veritable onrush of ships bearing their distressed human cargoes.[45] If trouble ensued in the city as a result, a backlash or search for a scapegoat could not be long in coming.

The new guarantees offered the *converso*s everything except the freedom to openly follow their ancestral faith, or deceive the city by using it as a way station en route to apostasy in Ottoman lands. The hope was that they would stay and help the region prosper. Many of them were therefore no longer in a rush to move onwards. Besides, they were now coming north for more reasons than persecution. As a result of fiscal mismanagement, Portugal was facing a severe economic crisis. Widespread poverty and despair further bloated the human tide of desperate refugees. Antwerp was perceived as the Eldorado of the North, attracting the poorest of the poor, not just those who had assets to protect or even a faith they still cared to follow.[46] And they were fleeing despite an edict from the Portuguese king declaring that all *converso*s were prohibited from emigrating, unless they had his express permission to do so.[47]

The endless stream of downtrodden and penniless *converso*s

were soon giving Doña Gracia first-hand exposure to the misery of her people on a major scale. But she was not yet in charge of the operation. And she had begun casting a covetous eye towards Italy—drawn there, as was her friend Lusitanus, by the liberal policies of Duke Ercole II of Ferrara, a small city-state located some 65 miles southwest of Venice. Ercole II had come to power in 1534, three years before Doña Gracia arrived in Antwerp. One of his first actions had been to confirm the decree that his grandfather, Ercole I, had made immediately after the expulsion of Jews from Spain, welcoming the departing Iberian Jews and *converso*s. They had been classified collectively under the ethnic umbrella term of *hebrei hispani*. Also included were Levantine Jews from Turkey (typically of Spanish origin) who had gone to Ottoman lands, but later chose to return to a place where they could further trade between Europe and the Levant. These Jews and *converso*s were being encouraged to engage in any form of mercantile activity in Ferrara. All of this was in contrast to the indigenous Italian Jews whose endeavors were more tightly restricted.

Duke Ercole II's objective was power and prestige. By making immigration attractive for the *hebrei hispani*, he hoped to build his modest city-state into a financial behemoth like Antwerp. He went so far as to send emissaries to Antwerp in the mid 1530's to actively recruit its leading *converso* merchants. What better prize than Doña Gracia herself and her personal fortune? Her presence could tempt others and potentially provide him with loans.[48]

Gerolamo Maretta, one of the duke's first emissaries, arrived in Antwerp early in 1538, only a few months after Doña Gracia. Ostensibly, Maretta's mission was to acquire horses and other goods for Ferrara. But his main mission was to convince the *converso* merchants of Antwerp that a substantial amount of business could be generated by moving to Ercole's even more tolerant state, located on the river Po. Maretta, a merchant himself, started by establishing relations with his fellow Italian merchants already in Antwerp, specifically Jean-Charles Affaitati, the Mendes partner originally from Cremona. He also contacted Ludovico Guicciardini, a merchant originally from Florence with broad interests and accomplishments who wrote some of the most compelling accounts of Antwerp at this time. From there, Maretta ingratiated himself into the *converso* merchant community. But he soon found that they had a sound reason for not coming to Ferrara. The journey required passing through the duchy of Milan and that was becoming too dangerous.[49]

Following the death of the duke of Milan, three years earlier, the Milanese duchy had come under the direct control of Charles V as a vassal state of the Holy Roman Empire.[50] And Charles V, as noted, had given his agents the right to seize and search any *converso* suspected of traveling through his domains with property or secrets intended for the Turks—a rationale that encouraged local officials, energized by religious zealotry and greed, to seize almost anything from the traveling bands of *conversos*.

When Maretta learned about this hazard, he considered rerouting the *conversos* through France as a less threatening alternative. While considering this option, he also learned of an existing agreement between Charles V and a former French king that allowed "Portuguese merchants" to travel and do business in France, free from harassment. But the *conversos* in Antwerp were not convinced. They wanted the current French king to issue the safe conduct specifically for them. But in attempting to procure such a document, Maretta faced a problem. He did not want to antagonize Charles V by making it look as though he was stealing Antwerp's most valuable *converso* merchants. So Maretta decided to seek the clearance for *conversos* in general, irrespective of whether they were residing in Antwerp at this time, and whether or not they had already lived in the Ottoman Empire.[51]

He failed. The French told him it was redundant to issue such privileges, particularly to *converso* merchants who had already gone to Ottoman lands, because they were already free to come back to France to trade at any time. They had won such privileges through a prior treaty with the Turks. Nevertheless, Maretta must have been given some general assurances because by March 1538, only six months after Doña Gracia's arrival in Antwerp, he was already noting in his dispatches that she was likely to soon relocate to Ferrara, along with a handful of other important *conversos*. He even indicated that he wanted to escort her there personally.[52]

Before she would agree to go, however, she sought her own assurances and favors. She wanted a guarantee permitting any *converso* planning to live in Ferrara to be allowed to return openly to Judaism, without fear of later retribution from the Inquisition. This was something the other *conversos* had sought for some time. She could have limited such a concession to herself and her family, in much the way that the Mendes had obtained personal guarantees in the past. Broadening the guarantee's scope provides a glimpse of her emerging style of leadership: the idea that whenever anyone in a position of power wanted something from her personally, they had to make similar concessions to the *conversos* in general. An Inquisition had not yet been established in Ferrara, nor were there even rumors that there might be one. But it was still a Catholic state. And normal Inquisition practice—if and when it did arrive—would have allowed the Holy Office to immediately arrest all *conversos* who had openly returned to Judaism, charging them with being lapsed Catholics.[53]

On May 30 of the same year, the requested proclamation was issued by Duke Ercole.[54] It allowed any merchant whose native tongue was Spanish or Portuguese, including those now considered Levantine subjects, to reside in Ferrara "as they wish either as Christians or Jews." The decree permitted them to bring all their belongings and merchandise without paying the normal customs duties. With a stroke of the pen, this made Ferrara the only safe haven in Christian Europe where *conversos* could return to their ancestral faith without fear of reprisals. Duke Ercole had thus taken the concept of merchant privileges one step further than Antwerp. Samuel Usque, the writer, would later describe Ferrara at this time with gratitude as, "Italy's safest port where…I might rest from the distressing journeys I have made from Portugal and Spain."[55]

By the spring of 1539, Maretta was again in Antwerp, continuing to build ties to leading *conversos*. One of these connections was with an elderly but distinguished *converso* physician known as Dr. Dionisius.[56] In his younger years in Lisbon, Dionisius had cared for the kings of Portugal and their families. Sometime in the 1530's, probably as a result of being accused of being a secret Jew, he had fled with his three sons to London. His behavior had been considered so shocking he would be burned in effigy in Lisbon in 1542, a fate limited to the most important *conversos* who had escaped to other lands. In 1538, soon after the arrival of Doña Gracia, he had moved on to Antwerp, where he may have actually resided in her house.[57] But he must have been anxious to relocate to Ferrara as it was the finest location for any serious physician of the day.

Maretta moved in fast. During that unhappy spring of 1539, when Diogo and Brianda were arranging their wedding, Maretta took Dionisius to meet Queen Marie at her court in Brussels. He wanted to personally obtain the necessary safe conducts for the doctor and his family to move on to Ferrara without incident. Maretta had similarly gone to Paris to obtain further safe conducts from the French. Meanwhile, he had sent for another set of documents from Duke Ercole for "four Portuguese women" to join them on the journey. It is apparent from this exchange that Doña Gracia had originally planned to move to Ferrara that spring, accompanied by Dionisius and Maretta. But the necessary papers arrived from Ferrara for everyone but Doña Gracia and her party. She was heartbroken at being left behind.[58]

In his dispatch of May 24, Maretta mentioned the problem

to the duke of Ferrara. "I went to (see) Doctor Dionisius and the widow (Doña Gracia)," he wrote. "And since I did not yet have the permit she was very pained to have to wait any longer after the departure of the doctor. It is as if she is left without anyone." Even so, Maretta explained that he planned to leave as soon as possible, perhaps because he feared that otherwise such an outstanding physician could change his mind and Ferrara would lose a distinguished prize. "I have decided to take the doctor," he therefore continued, "because I do not feel right about leaving him (behind). I am (also) confused about whether I should leave the woman alone..."

The letter reveals that something was deeply troubling Doña Gracia that cannot be easily explained, other than to suggest she was having a problem living under the same roof as Diogo and his bride. For, in truth, she was far from "alone." She did have her brother-in-law, sister and daughter with her, plus two young nephews and countless cousins.

The letter further hints that she did not feel equal to men, despite the era's liberal attitudes towards widows of means and her extraordinary wealth and connections. Her later outspoken and imperious manner may have been her way of compensating. "The widow has good reason to be upset," Maretta continued. "She told the doctor, 'you made me get a house alone...leave Diogo Mendes in order to feel more secure here...and now you leave me....'" Maretta reported that she also complained about unfair treatment. 'You give ample papers to the doctor but nothing to me,' she had protested to the troubled emissary. Rather, 'You leave me, a single woman, while you men are well-cared for.' Still, Maretta was not about to change his plans. Despite the outburst he ended the letter by saying, "Absolutely after this holiday I will head off on this voyage, as I have said... and I think everything will go well."[59]

Ironically, Doña Gracia's safe conduct arrived in Antwerp a

month after Maretta and the doctor had left.[60] But she did not use it because after that, there was no more talk of moving on to Ferrara, at least not at this point in her life.

Still, she had helped to expand the business interests of the House of Mendes into Ferrara through her personal connection to Maretta. The timing is irrefutable. Within a few years of this incident Duke Ercole formed a partnership with Sebastian Pinto, the *converso* merchant and friend of the family.[61] The duke was also working with the Affaitatis to import wool from Antwerp. He was receiving sugar shipments from agents of the House of Mendes still in Lisbon. He was receiving loans from the House of Mendes. And many of the *converso* merchants who had come to live in Ferrara were importing wool and other textiles from the Balkans, London, Paris and Holland. All of which put Ferrara on the map as a commercial hub of importance.[62]

But to make this happen Duke Ercole still had to deal with the problem of Jean Vuysting and his henchmen. They had not stopped intercepting *converso* refugees passing through Milan. The duke thus became something of an unintended savior to the tormented refugees. In certain instances he would personally intercede on their behalf, sending emissaries to protest the confiscations. He even managed to get Vuysting arrested on one occasion for improper seizure and misappropriation of goods. He did so by directly contacting Vuysting's superior, the new Spanish governor of Milan, Don Alfonso. Very much the gentleman, Don Alfonso was described by a contemporary as a richly-dressed man known for his charm, generosity, skill at arms, courtesy and kindness, who loved to play "the great lord."[63] Vuysting remained in prison for some time while an emissary from Ferrara—a local Ashkenazi Jew—verified the inventories and goods that had been illegally seized.[64] Bowing to pressure from Ferrara, Don Alfonso later extended safe conducts to all "Portuguese" in transit to Ferrara, even if they did not have special papers from the duke.[65] But not before hundreds had died or were robbed.

———••⚬••———

Doña Gracia's delay in leaving Antwerp turned out to be an unplanned setback that set the stage for her later achievements. Had she gone to Ferrara as originally intended, she would never have had sufficient time to work with Diogo and gain the needed expertise to function as well as she did later on. There is every indication that Diogo was soon making her a close associate. This was not as odd as it might seem. The Antwerp region not only had a tradition of women rulers, it offered an hospitable climate for women of achievement in general. Paintings from the period show women sitting alongside men and conducting business in counting houses, offices and shops. In one of them, the woman's hands rest on an open book (the company ledger?) while she watches intently as a man, probably her husband, weighs coins taken from a pile spread before him. In another, a girl sits at a table weighing gold. Several women portrait painters were taken seriously enough to enjoy great fame. Among them were Katarina de Hemessen, whose delicate work is still honored among the collections of the National Gallery in London, and Anna Bijns who was one of the most popular Flemish poets of the day.[66]

If there was ever a time when Diogo would have welcomed a wise and able kinswoman by his side, it would have been during these few years prior to his death. His advanced age and vulnerability to further harassment seems to have encouraged him to make a conscious effort to teach Doña Gracia all that he could, while introducing her to the supportive role of those men, many of them cousins, who were working alongside him in the House of Mendes.

She would have had to learn techniques like the covert system of personalized wax seals and other marking on goods in transit that *converso* merchants had developed to confirm ownership between themselves. It was their way of eluding confiscation of property, should any of them be apprehended unexpectedly by the Inquisition. This way, their goods could be re-assigned to another family member with the Inquisition being none the wiser.[67] Special bookkeeping techniques also had to be mastered in an environment where capricious harassment could be inflicted upon them at any time. A century later, some of the descendants of these early *conversos* would comment upon a practice whereby "the merchants...keep very few commercial books and make their entries on little pieces of paper in a kind of shorthand which cannot be understood."[68]

More than business would have occupied the pair as they pored over the books under the flickering light of oil lamps. It was now 1540, and the poorest of the poor *conversos* were tumbling from rain-soaked decks and onto the quay. Flotilla after flotilla sailed up the Scheldt with its cargo of misery—the frail and elderly, widows with creased faces, invalids struggling to walk upright, bewildered children in rags—all with barely a ducat or a bundle of meager possessions to their names. What they did own was hidden in the linings of their clothes and their ubiquitous felt hats. All were arrested and interrogated before being allowed in. Their belongings were subject to confiscation if the authorities deemed they were intended to "enrich" the Turks. Too often they were simply robbed. Or, as asserted by Francesco Contarini, the Venetian ambassador in Antwerp, to help fill the coffers of the perpetually bankrupt Emperor. Contarini estimated that at one point the incoming refugees could probably be milked out of as much as 100,000 crowns in all.[69]

Diogo continued to help as best he could. From the testimony of the frightened refugees, we know that those with more than a handful of assets were urged to exchange their valuables or coin in London for bills of exchange made out in the name of Diogo Mendes. These bills would then be brought to Antwerp by a local merchant, presumably not a *converso*, to be returned to them by Diogo after they passed through the dragnet. This ruse was important as any bills of exchange in their possession were fair game for confiscation too. It was a sophisticated operation that suggests a powerful trust in Diogo, since the refugees could never leave a paper trail tracing the money back to its rightful owner.[70]

But the escape network did not operate without losses. An interesting dispatch to Queen Marie from one of the officials in charge of refugee affairs described one such incident that occurred late in 1541. A *converso* woman and two children "laden with gold and silver" arrived in Antwerp one day from Portugal, by way of England, carrying a chest addressed to Diogo. Before the guards could seize and search the chest, the dispatch noted, "it had been broken open with hammers, not the lock but the backside of the chest (and) I could not find out anything from the sailors about who had done this or how." Consequently the official found "nothing worth more than two florins in the chest, except for a...letter of credit for 400 crusados which I enclose..."[71]

During that same month, Queen Marie wrote to Diogo demanding that he hand over 100 ducats to the captain of the guards at a prison where some refugees were temporarily being held. The money, Queen Marie insisted, rightly belonged to a female refugee who may have confessed under torture that her husband had given the ducats to one of Diogo's agents.[72] But it's unlikely that the woman ever saw her ducats again. They probably went straight into the queen's silken pockets or those of her agents.

According to Contarini, it was not only the incoming refugees who were increasingly in trouble. *Conversos* already living in the city and found "in reality (to be) Jews...have been arrested...their synagogues and much other evidence to that effect having been discovered, so they can scarcely excuse themselves. He warned that before too long, "their purses will be cut, especially those of some of the chiefs of them."[73]

For the refugees anxious to get out of Christendom entirely there were added hardships. They still had to trudge with their carts over the Alps to reach Venice in order to board a ship bound for Ottoman lands. And many were losing their lives on the mountain paths "from hardship and travail...and because of their utter helplessness and exposure," according to accounts by Usque, the *converso* chronicler. The terrain and the weather were so rough that "wives were widowed when they were about to give birth...and when they gave birth on those cold and intemperate roads, still a new kind of misfortune was suffered."

They regularly faced Vuysting's traps set up along the roads through Milan.[74] Wholesale arrests and confiscations were now taking place. Ostensibly, it was alleged by the authorities that their pathetic wagon trains might once again be a well-organized effort by Diogo and his associates to enrich the Turks with skilled manpower and goods. In December, a commission was even set up in Milan to explore the issue and formally detain anyone suspected of heresy whose destination was likely to be Ottoman lands.[75]

When the news reached Antwerp, Diogo hurriedly called a meeting in his house to develop a defensive strategy. Antonio della Rogna, his senior agent in London, was summoned to attend, along with three other leading *converso* merchants in Antwerp. The group decided to instruct the Mendes agent in Milan to use every effort to persuade the commissioners to release the suspect refugees and return their property to them. Meanwhile, the agent was to provide for their needs in prison. It was customary in those days to expect family or friends to supply a prisoner's necessities. Otherwise the captive was certain to perish from exposure, neglect and malnourishment. To defray the cost of all this work, the conspirators agreed to contribute to an ad-hoc fund that would operate like the *bourse de charité*. A draft in the amount of 2,000 ducats was dispatched by special courier to Milan.

All these details were leaked to members of the commission by Gaspar Lopez, a cousin of Diogo who was employed by him to serve the House of Mendes in London and Antwerp. Lopez had attended the meeting. Shortly afterwards he had been sent to Milan where he had been arrested on suspicion of being a secret Jew.[76] In truth, the commissioners may have arrested him because they suspected he was one of the conspirators. No doubt under pain of torture,[77] he soon turned informer.

Lopez further revealed that the funds—or at least part of them—were not being raised for humanitarian purposes. Rather, they were intended to cover the cost of paying a man named Gonzalo Gomez (whose name suggests he was also a *converso*), then living in Milan, to assassinate Vuysting. Those implicated by name in the assassination plot were Diogo, Doña Gracia, Brianda, as well as the notorious della Rogna.[78]

The conspirators were all identified by Lopez as secret Jews, a designation that left them wide open to future charges of heresy. It also underscored the probability of a treasonous allegiance with the infidel Turks. That concern was not to be taken lightly. The overwhelming fear of Turkish power among the leaders of Europe at this point cannot be underestimated. Diplomatic correspondence from the era is replete with rumors about the Turks amassing thousands of fighting men and galleys in their ongoing quest to conquer all of Christian Europe.

It is noteworthy that the women were implicated too, suggesting they may well have been full participants. For Doña Gracia, it would have been an ideal opportunity to learn all she could about covert operations, and how to react in the strongest possible way to confrontation and crisis. Was she afraid of repercussions? If so, then she learned to overcome those fears as she was later praised for her willingness "to risk her life to save her brethren."[79]

Though rumors of the plot were reported to Charles V and Queen Marie, proceedings were never initiated against Diogo and his team.[80] Perhaps the crowned heads did not want to be embarrassed a second time, remembering what had happened when they had tried to convict Diogo on conspiracy charges a few years earlier. But a terrible cloud lingered, nonetheless. The family was perfectly aware that given the right circumstances a tidal wave of repercussions could burst forth at any moment with this incident becoming tinder for the fire.

The other difficulty raised by the incident was the fate of the small London community and its activities in aiding the refugees. At this particular moment, Henry VIII had become anxious to foster closer relations with Charles V. What better way for Henry to do so than to go after the *converso*s in his lands too. After being left alone for many years, the tiny *converso* outpost in England suddenly found itself under siege. Officials started intruding into their lives and making arrests.[81]

But not for long. Ironically, within a year or so, Queen Marie had to write to the British authorities in England on behalf of *converso*s being taken prisoner in London. Mendes money and influence may have generated the request, because one letter mentioned that the king and queen of Portugal were also petitioning on behalf of some of these *converso*s.[82] And they would have interceded only if the roundup had inadvertently disrupted their cherished spice trade again.

In Antwerp, Diogo was busy paying bribes for the release of those who managed to get to the Low Countries. This is evident from the wording of a personal letter that Queen Marie sent him during this period in which she addressed Diogo as her "dear and good friend". It mentioned a payment of 100 ducats to release certain *converso*s being detained at Zeeland, the place of entry to the Low Countries for many of them.[83]

Still, it was a particularly bad winter. By December 1540, the same month as the convening of the Milan Commission, a new round of interrogations was being authorized in Antwerp.[84] Its aim was to determine which of the incoming *converso* refugees was a sincere Christian—and thus possibly an industrious worker or merchant for the city—and which were secret Jews whose sole aim was to exploit Antwerp as an oasis of personal replenishment on their way to enemy territory. Even the practices of the Mendes household, and other longer-term *converso* residents, came under review. Ship captains and other Old Christians were asked to supply information as observers, so that the refugees could be implicated by outsiders as well as by their own admission. Torture was liberally applied.

The testimony of these wretched folk, continuing on and off for about four years, shows a desperate attempt to placate their interrogators.[85] Most kept insisting that they were only looking for better opportunities to make a decent living. They tried to sound convincing about the sincerity of their religious beliefs by reciting as much information as they could muster about the validity and rituals of the Catholic faith, which was not very much.[86]

Consider the story told by 49-year-old Pierre de Salva Terra. He insisted he had only come to Antwerp with his wife, Lucretia, and their two small children, to make a better living. He carried no bills of exchange. He had no knowledge of any *bourse de charité*. Rather, he had brought along some Indian cotton which he hoped to sell. If he could not engage in profitable trade in Antwerp soon he fully intended to move on to Cologne. Turkey, it seemed, was not even a possibility. In fact, he said, he had already contacted a wagon driver and hired a cart to go to Cologne.[87]

From all these accounts it becomes clear that it was considered safer to split the family's assets into a number of different forms: coin, bills of exchange and goods for sale such as spices, grain or cloth (which could also demonstrate merchant intent). Witnesses would tell how each family member would also carry along a mattress to sleep on during the 15 to 21-day voyage. The wealthy could rent cabins at fees ranging from 25 to 50 ducats. The others were charged from two to five ducats a head for deck space. All brought their own food for the voyage: apples, bread and biscuits were the most typical fare. At least one passenger asked the captain for some beer. Ship captains confirmed the accounts given by the refugees. They insisted that they, too, had been under the impression that the families were genuinely seeking better economic opportunities. The refugees were not leaving on account of the Inquisition.[88]

However, since most of the shipping trade between Lisbon and Antwerp was controlled by the *conversos*—primarily in a shared system that spread the risk should one of the ships go down—it is unlikely that the captains would have said anything that could have jeopardized their lucrative positions on vessels owned and operated by *converso* merchants.[89]

But others—priests, dock workers, servants and agents of the Portuguese crown—told a more damaging tale. Two city porters reported that certain refugees coming into the port would wait until "after the ringing of the Antwerp bell"—that is, after the night curfew—to slip off the ships and scurry into town, to avoid being arrested, stripped of their belongings and interrogated. Some prisoners confessed to having been circumcised as well as baptized (presumably those who were not old enough to have been legally circumcised in pre-expulsion Spain). A valet in the household of an agent of the Portuguese king gave another reason why the Inquisition had to be responsible for their flight. He explained how it had created a climate where it was impossible for *converso* merchants and moneylenders still in Portugal to collect outstanding business debts. Whenever they insisted upon going to court to force collection, explained the valet, the Old Christian borrowers would threaten to denounce them to the Inquisition as heretics.[90]

There was testimony from informers concerning certain *converso*s who had started out living in Antwerp as seemingly upstanding Catholics, and then surfaced later in Ferrara or Venice as observant Jews. One was seen functioning as a cantor in a Venetian synagogue. Another, who had been a servant in Diogo's household, was reputed to have become a rabbi. Several *converso*s whose acts of heresy had been so blatant that they had been burnt in effigy in Portugal, were reported to be quietly residing in prosperity in Antwerp.

The interrogators heard reports of synagogue services being held in various Antwerp houses, particularly in or around the neighborhood of the Carmelite convent. They were provided with additional testimony suggesting that open land behind the convent was being used to bury *converso*s "on virgin ground...following the manner of the Jews." The *converso*s were even accused of questionable business practices. One particular scam allegedly involved obtaining money by predicting whether a pregnant woman would give birth to a boy or a girl. Finally, despite what they themselves said to the contrary, a summary of the proceedings concluded that those who had fled Portugal had good reason to fear the Inquisition. For they were all, in truth, secret Jews.[91]

The harassment was soon becoming so relentless that even Diogo was ready to quit the city around this time.[92] He and Doña Gracia went so far as to begin settling their affairs in an effort to leave within a year.[93] Their goal was to relocate to one of the great trading cities of Germany, or some other locale—such as Ferrara or the Ottoman Empire—where they could cast aside their veneer of Christianity and live openly as Jews. Doña Gracia was so anxious to get out that she asked Diogo to put the promise in writing. She also asked him to state that if he didn't leave within a year he would turn over the portion of the estate that rightly belonged to her and her daughter.[94] She must have had a hunch that despite any protestations to the contrary, he was now too old, too comfortable and too settled to physically make the move.

For Diogo had also become a father; his young wife, Brianda, having given birth to twins; a boy and a girl.[95] Only the girl survived as there is no further mention of a son. She was baptized in the Cathedral of Our Lady in June of 1540. Jean-Charles Affaitati—a man who had remained one of Diogo's most devoted friends and claimed that he visited Diogo every day—acted as godfather even though he was not in Antwerp for the ceremony. The infant was given the Christian first name of Beatrice, just like her aunt.[96] In private, she took the Jewish first name of Gracia, once again just like her aunt. The family was thereby following the Sephardic tradition of naming a new baby after a *living* relative.[97] Historians have since dubbed the child "Gracia La Chica" (Gracia the Younger) although there is no evidence that this name was ever used by the family. However, for the purposes of our story, and to avoid confusion, the girl will henceforth be known as La Chica.

Diogo used the arrival of his baby daughter to arrange for the release of Blanca Fernandes, his 75-year-old wet nurse who had been rounded up with other incoming refugees. Originally born in Soria in Spain, Blanca had fled to Portugal at the time of the expulsion so she could remain a Jew. Five years later she had been forcibly converted in Portugal along with all the other Jews.

With the coming of the Inquisition to Portugal she had fled, once again, this time to Madeira. From there, she had come to Antwerp with other family members, ending up among the refugees who were being arrested and interrogated.[98] Diogo insisted he needed Blanca to look after his new baby.[99] But in reality he must have made the arrangements on compassionate grounds. Seventy-five would have been too old. And, like so many *conversos* of this era, Blanca had been a wanderer, required by threat, fear or decree to flee from three different countries in a single lifetime. She deserved a little comfort.

Following the birth, Doña Gracia became even more concerned about the way that the assets of the House of Mendes might eventually be divided. She asked Diogo to give her yet another document indicating that even though he had been using her capital for his ongoing commercial enterprises, she and her daughter would always be entitled to half of the entire assets of the House of Mendes. He complied, seemingly with great willingness.[100]

Her eagerness to put all these agreements in writing doubtless stemmed from her business training. A later commercial contract in Portuguese concerning a cloth exporting deal between her nephew, Don Samuel, and a group of Levantine Jewish importers, that was made under her stewardship, is filled with enough contingent penalties to suggest the hand of a modern American lawyer.[101]

Doña Gracia was fast becoming a canny business woman. It was all to the good. She was about to need all the training she could muster.

CHAPTER 7

Crisis

Though he had fought hard to the end, Diogo was close to death.[1] It was now the summer of 1543 and plans to move elsewhere had never materialized. He would die in the city of Antwerp where he had savored his greatest triumphs. Certainly it was not a happy time for the family. The Office of the Council of Brabant—the regional seat of government under Charles V—had just issued a list of the names of everyone executed in Lisbon by the Inquisition over the past few years.[2] There were about 150 names on the roster. It would have undoubtedly included friends and relatives left behind. Like his older brother nine years earlier, Diogo seems to have succumbed at the very moment when his personal world was falling apart.

In keeping with the religious practices of the times, he demonstrated great concern for the eternal life of his soul. He took care to ensure that his last moments were in harmony with Jewish rather than Catholic tradition—once again, assuming that the witness who later described the scene was telling the truth.

When the priest at his bedside tried to administer last rites and talk to him about the death and the passion of Jesus Christ, Diogo reportedly hid his face and shook his head. In the end the priest had to caution the family that because he had refused all attempts, Diogo died as a Jew.[3] Such behavior would have had damaging implications for the preservation of family assets. But perhaps during the last moments Diogo had been beset by less worldly priorities. It was not uncommon to see a flurry of Jewish concerns take precedent at the final hour, even among the most assimilated *conversos* and even if it exposed family members to possible detection and difficulty.[4] Despite the obvious bias of a Catholic informant, it carried a ring of truth.

On June 28, while on his deathbed, Diogo dictated his last will and testament.[5] It was read on July 2, indicating that he must have died that very day, or a day or so earlier.[6] A reading of the will shows, among other things, an eagerness to follow the time-honored custom of foreign merchants in Antwerp and make a special bequest specifically to the needy of the city.[7] In Diogo's case this meant leaving 3,200 ducats for the poor.[8] Out of the income from this capital, two hundred ducats were to be distributed annually for all time, divided into thirds as follows: one third for the needs of indigent prisoners, one third to clothe the destitute and the final third to provide doweries for orphans. If the amount could not be generated from available capital in Antwerp, he wrote, arrangements were to be made through his agents in Portugal to make up the difference.[9] It was probably something Diogo would have wanted to do anyway, although if he had stopped worrying completely about appearances he would have doubtless insisted that the alms be set aside exclusively for needy *conversos*. All three causes were considered as significant in Jewish law as they were among the church fathers.

His family bequests were far less benign. In fact, they would prove explosive. He left Doña Gracia squarely in charge, appointing her as his principal executrix. He also made her the guardian of his infant daughter, La Chica, and administrator of the child's estate until the girl reached adulthood or married. This swept aside any natural control that should have gone to the child's own mother, Brianda.

He further made Doña Gracia administrator of all the firm's capital and obligations "dispersed in many places," so that "what has been done hitherto may be continued."[10] This sounds like a veiled reference to the escape network rather than his business ventures. Indeed, the ever-vigilant Father Sebastian would report not long afterwards that Doña Gracia "receives everyone at her home, and it is said publicly in Antwerp that she has a bank that takes care of those who come from Portugal."[11] Other witnesses also implied that Doña Gracia's house had become a place where *conversos* would gather before starting onwards.[12] It was she who now supplied the cash as well as intelligence reports concerning safe houses and perils on the way. It was she who was now risking her life to continue the covert activities that had already been deemed treasonous by the crown.

To assist in her endeavors, Diogo appointed two of his close aides: Guillaume Fernandes,[13] a senior member of the family firm who must have been related in some way or Diogo would have never given him such responsibility, and Juan Micas (known hereafter in our story as Don Joseph Nasi, the name he would use when he later returned to Judaism).[14]

Don Joseph was one of the two young nephews—related to her on both sides of the family— that Doña Gracia had brought with her to Antwerp. He was destined to play an important role in her life as her confidante and most trusted advisor. His father, who had died of the plague in 1525 while Don Joseph was still a child, had been a physician to the king of Portugal and a medical and philosophy professor at the University of Lisbon.[15] The father's early death may have been a reason why Doña Gracia brought the two boys with her. Don Joseph had already begun working for the House of Mendes in France.[16] He had been sent to Lyons, another major financial center specializing in trade with the Iberian Peninsula. Lyons was where the French crown raised the funds for *its* wars against Charles V and others.[17] Three years earlier, in 1540, presumably while in that city, Don Joseph had negotiated a number of large loans to the French crown. The combined amount was so large—at one point reaching 150,000 ducats[18]—that they became fraught with repayment problems. The French would cite pretext after pretext for not paying them back; excuses that would plague Don Joseph for most of his career.[19]

Contemporaries speak of Don Joseph as being handsome with a great deal of personal charm, although later in life he would develop a reputation for haughtiness, scheming and self-centeredness that would leave him with as many enemies as admirers.[20] Sometime during the family's Antwerp years he served as a cavalry captain in the Emperor's army. He was a college friend and jousting partner of Maximilian, the nephew of Queen Marie and the Emperor Charles who would later become Emperor in his own right.[21] These court connections would prove invaluable for business as well as the ongoing viability of the escape network. In September 1542, a year before Diogo's death, Don Joseph had graduated from the University of Louvain.

His older brother Bernardo Micas (known hereafter as Don Samuel Nasi, the name which *he* eventually used when *he* returned to Judaism) had graduated two years earlier, in April, 1540.[22] It was Don Samuel who told a professor at the University of Louvain how the two brothers had reputedly acquired the Christian family name of Micas.[23] It was, he said, on account of their father. The king of Portugal had named the father Micas, or Shiny, saying it was because he outshone all the other physicians. But there could have been a more subtle reason. The *conversos* were known to play all sorts of games with their baptized names. And Micas—or Miquez as it was also spelled—also happened to be the name given to the portion of the Torah that is read in synagogues at Hanukkah, recounting the story of Joseph and Pharaoh.[24]

Though Don Samuel would be permitted the title of Doctor upon graduation, and had been studying Latin and Hebrew (a permitted course of study especially among enlightened theologians), he never achieved the prominence of his dashing younger brother. Whatever Don Samuel did for the firm and the family was so far in the background as to have eluded the written record.

In the unlikely event that something were to happen to Doña Gracia, Agostinho Henriques, a cousin later known by his Jewish name of Abraham Benveniste, was to replace her at the head of the bank.[25] And, noted Diogo, do "all that which my said sister-in-law with the others may do." Finally, Diogo added firmly, "this (will) cannot be challenged by any court in any other place for any reason because I am convinced that they will be most competent and they will act as I would act and have acted."[26]

What about his young wife Brianda? In keeping with the practice of the era she should have been the executrix. She should have inherited the capital and control of Diogo's portion of the House of Mendes. At the very least she should have been given control of her own daughter's upbringing and the portion of the estate allocated to her daughter. But Diogo obviously did not trust her. He gave her no voice whatsoever. She would struggle against this perceived injustice, and the ridiculous financial position in which it placed her, for the rest of her days.

Diogo's will, like the one of his brother, Francisco, was initially drafted in his native Spanish,[27] although parts of the document were later reproduced in Italian.[28] At one time there may have even been a copy in Old French, which would have been the one originally filed in Antwerp.

———••✜••———

At 33 years old Doña Gracia was now at the helm of one of the greatest fortunes in Europe. Down through the ages those who inherit vast amounts of money or large enterprises at a relatively young age have talked of such moments as being terrifying, the stuff of which nightmares are made. In modern times one has only to consider the sentiments expressed by John D. Rockefeller Jr. or Edsel Ford.

But it was also one filled with promise—that is, if Doña Gracia could fend off the attack dogs that were snarling at her door. If she had appeared vulnerable eight years earlier when her husband died, she became so much more so when she took command of the entire financial empire incorporated into the House of Mendes. Women may have been respected in business, but it was still a man's world. And the burghers of Antwerp may not have felt the same loyalty towards a woman who was also a newcomer to their tight circle. Meantime, the ruling houses of Europe saw in her fortune nothing but ready cash—for them.

But the speed with which they moved in on her was horrifying. On July 5, only three days after the public reading of the will, and probably less than a week after Diogo died, Doña Gracia was hit by the first salvo. Based upon allegations that Diogo had continued to practice Judaism in secret all along, and had been determined to overthrow Christianity through his dealings with the Turks—a charge that was tantamount to treason—all the chests containing Diogo's ledgers and other crucial documents were seized, sealed and sequestered. On July 10, Charles V wrote a hurried note to Queen Marie, his trusted Regent for the Low

Countries, reminding her that, for greater security, all of Diogo's papers should be sealed in strong boxes. To be certain that no tampering took place, there were to be round-the-clock security measures. A representative of the crown was to stay in Diogo's mansion and even sleep next to the boxes, as well as start work on an inventory of the contents within a week.[29]

The aim was to identify Diogo's assets before the family could hide anything. For an additional law decreed that anyone who was convicted of secretly practicing Judaism loses his estate to the crown.[30] Charles was so intent on counting every ducat of the potential windfall that he even added a postscript to his July note. "It is Our wish," he instructed in the same letter, "that the one of you who will be sleeping in the house should sleep in the room containing the strong boxes."

Doña Gracia and the family immediately protested. They argued that if the authorities truly believed Diogo was a traitor, they should have charged Diogo during his lifetime while he could defend himself. Besides, they added, his sincerity as a Catholic had been amply demonstrated by his bequests to the poor and his exemplary death according to the rites of the Catholic Church.[31]

It cost Doña Gracia a "gift" of 40,000 ducats to generate an official exoneration of Diogo's alleged behavior and an interest-free loan of a further 200,000 ducats for two years to Queen Marie to prevent the queen from claiming that surviving family members were secret Jews too.[32] All these negotiations must have taken place with speed, since the exoneration is dated 1543, and there would have been only a handful of months left to the year. The wording of Charles' exoneration insisted, of course, that it was being granted for other reasons. It noted that several "good people" had since intervened on the family's behalf. It heaped praise upon the "services that he (Diogo) had provided to the Emperor." It acknowledged the prosperity that Diogo's

commercial activities had showered upon the residents of
Antwerp. It also mentioned the wise advice Diogo had regularly
provided to the region's Council of Finance. For all these reasons, it stated, the Emperor had decided to free up Diogo's assets after all.[33]

The pardon further spared the entire family from future
charges of heresy, even if they were later found to have relapsed
into Judaism—a promise, incidentally, that was never kept. In
addition, it absolved them, and anyone in their employ, now or
in the future, of charges of having helped those *converso* refugees
who wanted to move on to Salonika. Also forgiven was Diogo's
transgression of serving as the distribution agent for money being sent back by *conversos* already re-established in Ottoman lands
to help their relatives move there too. Finally, the document
acknowledged that these appeals and requests were being made
in part at the recommendation of Queen Marie, and in consideration of funds offered to the crown.[34]

A careful reading of the intent of this document, together
with the observations of Father Sebastian about the level of activity at the Mendes mansion in the period just after Diogo's
death, suggests that Doña Gracia had no intention of curtailing
the family's efforts on behalf of the refugees. Later accounts imply
she did the just the opposite.[35] One could speculate upon her
motives. For one, there was never a hint that she enjoyed making money and still more money for her own account, as her
husband and brother-in-law had done, although she was not
totally altruistic. She would later insist upon the legal right to keep
what she did make in commerce from her own endeavors.[36] But
she had been financially besieged once before in her life. Might
she have been trying to ensure that the assets under her stewardship were used immediately for a purpose of her own choosing,
while she still had the chance? Sooner or later, those rulers would
surely have their way. And the entire Mendes fortune might be

confiscated and used instead to prop up spendthrift monarchs who were heaping abuse and suffering on them all.

She was also the sort of woman who would have wanted to put her personal stamp on the operation as fast as possible. This becomes clear from *converso* accounts of her deeds at this time. No further mention is ever made of Diogo's role, confirming that Doña Gracia must have plunged into the management of the escape network with a zeal and nurturing style that soon gave the mission a very different quality. According to the writer, Samuel Usque, the contemporary chronicler who knew her well, "she generously provided money and other needs and comforts to the refugees who arrived destitute, sea-sick and stuporous in Flanders..." and "hastened to alleviate the miseries caused by the hardship and hazards of their long journey." He praised her personal style in the loftiest manner. "Her inspiration," he observed, "greatly encouraged (the *conversos*) in Portugal who were too poor and weak to leave the fire (Inquisition)." Moreover, he added, she became "a prop for the weary, a clear fountain for the thirsty, a shady tree, full of fruit which has fed the hungry and sheltered the forsaken." Many are reaching safety "on this eagle's outstretched wings."[37]

These words implied a warmth and caring that would have been an emotional life-preserver for refugees who had been torn from their homes, looked upon with contempt by their neighbors and despised by the authorities. "Has anyone ever seen a woman risk her life to save her brethren, as if she inherited Miriam's innate compassion," Usque added, "or govern her people with Deborah's remarkable prudence; or aid the persecuted with Esther's boundless virtue and surpassing piety; or free the besieged from anguish, like the chaste and generous widow Judith, a woman of true-hearted courage?"[38] In an adjoining passage Usque described her as "delicate."[39] So she may well have been a small woman, even by the standards of her time.

————••✄••————

Though Charles V's pardon was generous, Doña Gracia clearly did not trust the document or the current climate that was stepping up its harassment of all *conversos*. In November of the same year she had obtained a safe conduct from the pope that allowed her, along with her recently widowed sister, Brianda, their children and staff to relocate to Rome or any of the neighboring Papal States.[40] They were expressly not to be harmed or charged with heresy, suggesting that their heretical ways were well known throughout Europe. The safe conduct was doubtless needed to get safely passed Vuysting and his henchman, should they travel through the duchy of Milan. Though one might ask why they did not go by sea, it was understood in those days that any sea voyage was fraught with even worse dangers from storms and pirates.

Rome and the Papal States had been the only refuge in Western Europe available to Jews, without interruption, since Roman times. Some say it was because the popes regularly relied upon local Jews for medical and financial expertise and tended to know many of them personally. But even this would not last much longer. Twenty-nine years later, reeling from the impact of the Reformation that was sapping the centuries-old hegemony of the Catholic Church, Jews would be expelled from the Papal States too.

Yet Doña Gracia did not rush away from Antwerp—at least not immediately. There was still much work to be done with the refugees. The short-term loan of 200,000 ducats to Queen Marie was also a matter of serious concern. It represented—at minimum—12 percent of the known assets of the House of Mendes.[41] That they finally left in the middle of 1545, immediately after receiving full restitution from Queen Marie, implies a connection. In the meantime, the safe conduct became a sort of insurance policy, permitting a rapid retreat if needed, but not necessarily something to use right away. At the very least, it indicated an advanced level of strategic thinking on the part of Doña Gracia and her inner circle of advisors.

•••┄┄┅╳╬╳┅┄┄•••

Charles V and Queen Marie were not satisfied with what they had extracted from the deal. As always, they needed ready cash for Charles' continued battles. It was common knowledge that they hoped to squeeze more out of the House of Mendes, and there was no lack of important men about Antwerp eager to serve the crown in such matters.[42] Enter Father Sebastian once again. Knowing that Doña Gracia was suspected of secretly practicing Judaism, he went to her home in May of the following year, 1544, with a plan that he believed would help defend her against breaking the rules. The key, he decided, was to marry off her 14-year-old daughter, Ana, to a prestigious Old Christian.[43]

The suitor he had in mind was Don Francisco D'Aragon, a celebrated Iberian nobleman who had come to Antwerp as an emissary of the crown to investigate the problems surrounding the influx of *conversos*.[44] D'Aragon was an illegitimate descendant of the royal house of Aragon. Eighteen years earlier he had accompanied the Empress Isabella, beloved wife of Charles V and sister of King João III of Portugal, when she first met Charles in Spain. It was a union with such a happy ending that it had left D'Aragon close to both rulers.[45] Doña Gracia and Ana would be well protected forever more.

Two days after talking the matter over with a friend, Father Sebastian paid a call on Doña Gracia. He carefully explained the advantages of such a marriage, saying it would remove any traces of Judaism. But rather than be pleased and even flattered at the notion, she told him she wanted to have him chased from the house with a stick for even raising the idea.[46] She also wanted to know where the idea had originated. Had D'Aragon asked Father Sebastian to speak to her on his behalf? Had the king of Portugal's agent in Antwerp put him up to the task? No, he told her. He had acted totally on his own, as her confessor.

She then made it clear that she had no desire to marry off her daughter.

When Father Sebastian related this story to Queen Marie sometime later, the queen asked him if he had explained that refusing such an important friend of the crown could make both the Emperor and herself extremely angry. No, said Father Sebastian. He hadn't thought of reminding Doña Gracia of such a possibility. And that was not the only mistake he made, he admitted. D'Aragon later rebuked him for having raised the possibility without first approaching him personally.[47]

Nevertheless, the idea delighted D'Aragon. For we know that about two weeks *before* Father Sebastian visited Doña Gracia, Charles V had written to his sister, Queen Marie, with the very same suitor in mind.[48] It had apparently been on the mind of the monarchs too. The Venetian ambassador later reported in a dispatch that a much-hated Florentine named Gaspare Ducchio, another close friend of Queen Marie, had also proposed the idea.[49] Ducchio was deep in debt to the House of Mendes.[50] And he may have viewed the opportunity as a way to extricate himself from some of these debts by acting as the intermediary for a grateful D'Aragon. In fact, Charles had already approached D'Aragon who "let me know that he is hoping to succeed in marrying her."[51]

D'Aragon was so enthusiastic ("as the said D'Aragon might come into great wealth by this means" noted Queen Marie later on),[52] and so certain of success, that he promised Charles an immediate loan of 200,000 ducats should he win the go-ahead from the mother. He told Charles that he could easily raise the funds from the money merchants of Antwerp, once they knew that Ana's portion of the Mendes fortune would soon be under his control.[53]

Charles drooled at the prospect. He wrote to his sister, Queen Marie, from an encampment in Spire. "As you can imagine," he noted with glee, "the loan of the said monies would come at a marvelously propitious time, given the great need I have of them." He sounded so anxious for it to happen, and happen fast, that the purpose of this particular letter was to solicit her help. He gave Queen Marie permission to sign his name to a procurement (presumably of military hardware) from Spain and Naples so he could have his equipment "with dispatch." Then he added with confidence: "I am sure you will be able to settle the matter."[54]

What none of them expected, at least at the outset, was that they would be facing a determined, fearless and outspoken adversary in the mother of the proposed bride—a woman who would not even be brought into line by Charles V, the most powerful monarch in Europe. They must have chosen to ignore what had occurred when a similar scheme had been hatched in Lisbon seven years earlier.

The queen tried her best. On May 12, some two weeks after Charles' request to Marie for her help in the matter, she replied to Charles saying she had already spoken to D'Aragon and offered him "every guidance and assistance." But he had told her flatly that she would not accomplish very much unless she was willing to go to Antwerp (the court normally resided in Brussels), "to discuss the matter with the mother...in person." Marie made it clear to Charles that she was not about to do so, since it would be humiliating and even pointless. She reminded Charles that she had already tried to speak to Doña Gracia about the match on numerous occasions, all without success, Wrote Marie: "Every time I have tried to speak to the mother she excuses herself on the pretext of illness, and she might do it again."[55] It offers us a delectable image: the all-powerful Dowager Queen of Hungary, Regent of the Low Countries and sister of the Holy Roman Emperor, rebuffed by a *converso* businesswoman.[56] But, as everyone who was anyone in Antwerp seemed to know about the "affront" as one official put it,[57] it did not bode well for Doña Gracia. She had made a fool out of the queen.

Marie was indeed enraged. Not only had she been rejected personally, she had tried sending in others to no avail, either. A senior agent of the Portuguese king in Antwerp had been approached to try to persuade Doña Gracia,[58] as had Father Sebastian, suggesting the cleric had been a pawn all along, just as Doña Gracia suspected.

Doña Gracia was probably stalling for time. She could have left Antwerp already had it not been for the forced loan of 200,000 ducats that would not come due for a year. But could she hold out that long? In the same May letter, Marie told Charles that D'Aragon had suggested threatening Doña Gracia if she continued to stonewall their efforts. He had asked "Your Majesty...to take such steps as would not only make her (Doña Gracia) happy to agree to the plan but would make her solicit him (D'Aragon) in order to hang on to the remains of her wealth." But Marie warned Charles that, "Other merchants might take it as a poor precedent, and remove to a place beyond your lands where they are not in the habit of forcing marriages." If that happened, predicted Marie, it might "give rise to a murmuring on the part of your subjects," who would feel the economic downturn."[59]

This did not stop the determined D'Aragon from spreading mischief on his own, dropping hints within the *converso* community that he had the influence to curtail the harassment they were facing daily from the authorities. But he was not of a mind to do so unless Doña Gracia consented to the marriage.[60]

Marie further counseled Charles that keeping up the pressure could result in the "departure of the girl." This was probably a delicate way of saying the departure of the House of Mendes, along with its trade and business, which could adversely affect the city. As a result, declared Marie, "I have put off going to Antwerp until I have been advised by Your Majesty...how I should conduct myself."[61]

Charles immediately backed off, insisting, "I have never meant nor desired that you should assist in this affair but with due courtesy and without using any sort of unreasonable coercion...."[62]

Were the excuses Doña Gracia kept giving the queen totally false? Or was there some basis in fact, even though it conveniently allowed her to stall for time in the hope that the monarchs might tire of asking? We know from her physician, Amatus Lusitanus, that Doña Gracia suffered from recurring bouts of intestinal or stomach pains. Later testimony at one of those relentless interrogations concerning refugee activity makes mention of her having gone to "take the baths" around this time in the medicinal waters at Liège.[63] And when she finally decided to leave Antwerp for good, her customary practice of going to a spa must have been sufficiently well known to Queen Marie to serve as a credible way of acquiring an exit permit.

Meanwhile, the tussle over the marriage was not yet over. By the beginning of July, Queen Marie finally managed to persuade Doña Gracia to come to see her in person. One can picture Doña Gracia, exquisitely attired in one of her many fashionable gowns and satin pumps, striding into an audience with the queen. A letter dated July 9, 1544, sent by Queen Marie to D'Aragon, the rejected suitor, right after the encounter, makes it clear that the meeting was contentious.[64] Both were strong-willed women. Neither was cowed by the other.

Doña Gracia first told Queen Marie how Father Sebastian had suggested the idea of her daughter marrying D'Aragon. But she was so opposed to the match that she "would rather see her daughter drown"—surely an audacious and insulting remark to make to a crowned head of Europe. But Doña Gracia was now in full throttle. She told the queen she was furious that D'Aragon had been going around telling everyone in town that it was on account of Doña Gracia's obstinacy that the *conversos* continued to be persecuted.[65]

Queen Marie assured her that the measures being taken against the *conversos* had nothing to do with D'Aragon and the marriage. The policy was intended to chase away fugitives who wanted to live as Jews, which was contrary to the law of the land. Indeed, any help that D'Aragon had been giving the officials was solely for the benefit of Christendom. Doña Gracia then told the queen that the *conversos* were counting on her and that she had to support them.[66]

Both must have been aware that a punitive new decree, issued two weeks earlier, stated that any refugee from Portugal arriving in the future would be automatically confined to the municipal jail and tried on charges of heresy—the presumption being that the only reason for leaving Portugal would have been because they were indeed secret Jews and feared reprisals from the Inquisition. Forty refugees had been arrested just nine days before. Doña Gracia and other members of the Mendes family had been sheltering large numbers in their houses to keep them out of jail,[67] aware that even a brief time in prison would have placed their tired bodies under such abominable conditions that it would have further undermined their health and their future. But there was only so much that private individuals could do.

The queen refused to yield to any of Doña Gracia's pleadings. Rather, she made it clear that she would continue to support the policies of the Emperor for the good of the land.[68]

Doña Gracia would not yield either. There would be no marriage. As in Portugal, she was certainly not going to marry off her daughter to an Old Christian. Later on, a Levantine rabbi would observe how anxious Doña Gracia had been all along that "the seed of the great and holy" (meaning the Jews in general or, more likely, her own family's distinguished ancestry) not be mingled with that of the Gentiles.[69] Nor was Doña Gracia disposed to hand over Francisco's hard-earned money to a man already past his prime who was doing all he could to make life miserable for the refugees. She had saved Ana once. She would do it again.

But D'Aragon would exact his revenge. A rebuff by a family of *conversos* would have been the worst kind of humiliation. Within days after he received his rejection letter, D'Aragon spent an evening discussing the evil doings of the *conversos* with Cornelius de Schepperus, the senior official in charge of the refugee problem.[70]

D'Aragon laid it on thick. He told Schepperus that the *conversos* arriving daily in Antwerp were fleeing from Portugal because they were afraid of being burnt by the Inquisition. He was clearly trying to refute the idea that any of them were coming in as sincere Christian merchants, which would be the only way they could obtain clearance.

To underscore his point, he told Schepperus that the king of Portugal must have had good reason to persecute them, which in itself implied they were all evil-doers. D'Aragon seems to have been acutely aware of the difficulties of coaxing any captain of a merchant ship, and even the sailors, to denounce the refugees and explain what was really going on. So he disclosed to Schepperus that he had tracked down two informers who might "persuade" the mariners to change their stories. D'Aragon said he was convinced that all the refugees really wanted was to live as Jews in the land of the accursed Turks and take all the goods they could with them. As proof he added that he had interrogated three Portuguese students at Louvain who swore they had seen three different *conversos* in Antwerp who had been burnt in effigy in Portugal—marking them as the most dangerous heretics. D'Aragon then unleashed a tirade about how certain *conversos* were engaged in shabby business deals mentioning, of course, how one was employed as a steward in the Mendes household.[71]

Such a diatribe could not fail to have an impact upon Cornelius de Schepperus. He dispatched a lengthy letter to Queen Marie the very next day, recapitulating in detail the entire encounter. In closing, he made a cryptic remark indicating that Queen Marie knew perfectly well that D'Aragon was an unsavory character, although this had not prevented her from using him to advance her financial agenda. "Concerning Lord Francisco (D'Aragon)," noted Schepperus, "I have heard from the Duke of Arschot what Your Majesty's opinion of him is. To which I can only say that from having spoken to him yesterday for the first time, I noticed nothing about him except that he struck me as acting in good faith. If it is otherwise, he is deceiving me."[72]

It could have been a coincidence, but immediately after the acrimonious meeting between the queen and Doña Gracia the interrogation of incoming *conversos* was stepped up. Thirty-nine prisoners and 65 witnesses were called to testify between the third week of July and the middle of August of 1544.[73]   But if Queen Marie was not going to give up, neither was Doña Gracia. She had already appointed her nephew and close advisor, Don

Joseph, as her intermediary between the refugees and the crown. His charm, intelligence and captivating ways could perhaps prevail where she had failed, particularly as the queen had high regard for him.[74]

In the months that followed, Don Joseph repeatedly intervened on behalf of the refugees, pleading with the queen to permit house arrest instead of prison, pending their hearings. A ship's pilot talked of seeing Don Joseph negotiating for the release of four men and one woman at the nearby town of Vere.[75] Among those he managed to release was Diogo Fernandes Neto, the man who had succeeded Duarte da Paz as the lobbyist for the *conversos* at the Vatican. Neto had come to Antwerp from Rome.[76] He had been found guilty of practicing Judaism behind the backs of the cardinals, which had led to his banishment by the pope.[77] Neto had arranged to meet his wife and children who were coming in with the fleet from Lisbon. But after being reunited, they had all been detained along with dozens of others.

Don Joseph was largely successful. By June 7 of the following year, 1545, together with other senior members of the House of Mendes, he had negotiated bail for all the *conversos* still in prison. The total cost: 1,280 ducats,[78] ostensibly to cover the expenses associated with their imprisonment and interrogations. Three days later the temporary release under bail was made permanent. All received permission to "trade freely and settle permanently" in the Low Countries.[79]

Doña Gracia was beginning to place more and more trust in Don Joseph. Eventually their lives and deeds would become so intertwined that it would be difficult to figure out where one began and other left off—save to say, as has been reported by numerous historians, that she was the mastermind behind all their endeavors.

Later, there was even speculation that a sexual relationship developed between the two. In the early 1990's, Catherine Clément, a French author, created a romantic novel out of the bare bones of the life story of Doña Gracia. She cast Don Joseph as the lover, though she admitted at the time it was pure fiction. However, she was later sent a drawing from Turkey, taken from a 19th century Jewish book published in Istanbul, depicting Doña Gracia and Don Joseph as lovers. Although Clément still dismisses the notion as more legend than fact, it remains a tantalizing possibility, even though Don Joseph later married Doña Gracia's daughter.[80]

But that would not have been a deterrent. These were ribald times. All sorts of sexual practices were acceptable and spoken about as openly and graphically as today. There were gleeful communal ceremonies of putting bride and groom to bed. Accounts of lesbian nuns. Topics selected for books and paintings that were purposely erotic. And through it all the needs and desires of a woman were no less championed than those of a man.[81] So, although a liaison has never been proven, it remains a possibility.

Consider, too, the views of the indomitable Father Sebastian. His testimony before Queen Marie also happened to mention that Guillaume Fernandes, a senior member of the House of Mendes, was living with Doña Gracia in her Antwerp house. "They say he is the husband of the widow of Francisco Mendes," reported Father Sebastian, "even though they do not live as husband and wife."[82] While there was a perfectly honorable reason why Fernandes might have lodged there—Fernandes was the man named by Diogo in his will as one of her most trusted advisers—the wording of Father Sebastian's statement implies that Doña Gracia might well have had men in her life.

All this intrigue did not dim the interest of the wider world in the banking enterprises of the House of Mendes. For them it was business as usual. If there was money to be lent, there was money being sought. The British crown was one such borrower. At the time of Doña Gracia's meeting with Queen Marie, a British envoy in Antwerp wrote back to London to say that he planned to approach "the heirs of Francisco and Diogo Mendes."[83] He was seeking 25,000 crowns from them as part of a much larger loan he was cobbling together from a variety of bankers wary of Henry VIII's constant penury. Raising smaller amounts from a number of lenders was the only way the envoy could fulfill his obligations. Interestingly, Gaspare Ducchio, the Florentine banker who had promoted the marriage idea to Queen Marie, was acting as a loan broker for the British crown at the time. Not only did he have debts outstanding to the House of Mendes, he could have been overextended in other ways too, making it even more likely that a personal financial predicament could have been the driving force behind his efforts to force a marriage between young Ana and D'Aragon.[84]

Portrait of Marie of Hungary, Regent of the Low Countries

CHAPTER 8

Flight

The summer of the following year, 1545, was unusually dry. Rain had not fallen since the middle of June and the drought would last into September. Even the larger rivers were running low and there were pockets of pestilence.[1] Who knew when and if the local people would turn on the *conversos* in a violent and bloody manner. It had happened so many times throughout Europe during periods of drought and plague. And in Antwerp the climate of tolerance had been deteriorating for some time.

Inside the Mendes mansion preparations had been going on since early summer. The sisters, together with their daughters, servants and staff were leaving Antwerp for Venice. If the family and assets of the House of Mendes were to be preserved to help continue the fight, they would have to operate from a safer location. Later correspondence makes it clear that their ultimate goal was the Ottoman Empire.[2] Doña Gracia knew only too well when to leave a party. If her husband and brother-in-law had tarried too long it may have been because they were bewitched by court life. The pragmatic Doña Gracia seems to have harbored no such conflicts.

Just as well. Not only was there a rising climate of hatred towards the *conversos* of Antwerp. Even the openly-professing Jews of Italy—among the most assimilated and educated Jews of the period—were being herded into ghettos and the *conversos* already in Italy were once again facing an Inquisition. It had been introduced into the Italian peninsula in 1542, the year before Diogo's death, ostensibly to fight Protestant heresy.[3]

The choice of Venice rather than Ferrara or Rome made sense. Venice had served for centuries as the crossroads for trade between Europe and the Middle East. It was the main port of departure for *conversos* leaving Christian Europe. It was also one of the few cities in Europe where trade with the Ottoman Empire was actively being fostered. Four years earlier, in 1541, Levantine Jewish merchants residing in Venice had even won special trading privileges, creating an opportunity for new commercial links by the House of Mendes as well as the transfer of capital.[4]

Even before this new opening, funds could most easily be converted and transferred to the Ottoman Empire from Venice, since the volume of trade passing through that city-state was so large. Venice also had a long history of supporting the needs of merchants with the impartial rule of law (as Shakespeare reminds us in *The Merchant of Venice*,[5] written later in the same century). These attitudes pre-dated Antwerp's support of commerce by many years and there was not the same ideological pressure from its overlords. Most of the Venetians, including its leadership, were not fervent Catholics. Indeed, they had been most reluctant to have an Inquisition imposed upon them by the pope. Even the Venetian ambassador in Antwerp noted in a dispatch, written that very autumn, that "there are few places they (the Mendes) can trust for safety other than Venice."[6] With its cosmopolitan environment, someone like Doña Gracia would feel welcome as long as she needed to stay.

Even more important, Venice had been losing its centuries-old hegemony over the Mediterranean to the Turks. It was therefore in an appeasement mode as far as Turkish power was concerned. It could not afford to lose its merchant ships to Turkish raids. This created a safety net for Doña Gracia and her party should there ever be trouble with the Venetian authorities.[7] The Turks would do all they could to assure her safety and ease her onward journey. The House of Mendes—with its riches, superb credit, international intelligence network and formidable presence—had the potential to become as valuable an asset to Ottoman ambitions as it had been to the Christian kingdoms.

In March of the previous year a safe conduct had been authorized by the Venetian authorities for both sisters. It permitted them to bring relatives and staff up to 30 in total. It also confirmed that their possessions would be "safe, free and secure" and that they would be given the same treatment "as the other inhabitants of our city."[8] A later confirmation of this safe conduct would include a provision allowing six members of their household to carry arms—a reminder that the Mendes widows, like members of most wealthy families in those days, regularly hired private guards for their own protection.[9]

Their eagerness to leave was understandable. The year was already half over.[10] If long distance travel was to be undertaken at any time in northern Europe, it was best done during the warmer months. The time was almost over-ripe. The last of the *converso* prisoners had been released. The bulk of this wretched flow of refugees was now moving onwards. Assistance might soon be needed as much in Italy as it had been in Antwerp. Doña Gracia had finally collected on the loan she had reluctantly given to Queen Marie right after Diogo's death.[11] And collection had created an added peril, since it set the stage for Marie and Charles to dream up yet another way to rob the estate, a possibility that deeply troubled Doña Gracia.[12] One does not rebuff the ruling monarchs without fretting over reprisals. Besides, Ana was growing up. The pressures for a marriage partner would be endless. Even Don Joseph and the others in her inner circle had suggested it was best to leave as soon as possible, the group deciding to depart together.[13] Lower level agents could stay behind and handle outstanding debts that could not be collected immediately.

Doña Gracia and her advisors were perfectly aware that Marie and Charles were not going to let a family with so much ready cash and credit wriggle out of their grasp without a fight. The Antwerp mansion was therefore being left behind with its furniture intact. Commercial ledgers were carefully stacked in appropriate places to further emphasize an intent to return.[14] Even their lower-level agents were being ordered to leave as soon as possible, one by one, so as not to generate gossip.[15] This would enable as much as possible of the Mendes fortune to be taken out of the reach of Charles V before the authorities could find out what had happened.

But how to slip away? In Lisbon Doña Gracia had concocted an excuse based upon her need to discuss estate and commercial issues with Diogo in Antwerp. This time it had to be something different. It is at this juncture that Doña Gracia's penchant for "taking the baths" assumed added usefulness. The year before she had obtained Marie's permission to go to Aix-la-Chappelle (today called Aachen), one of the finest local spas known since antiquity.[16] Why not again? If there were drawbacks to being a woman in business there surely were benefits. Though men in those days also visited these baths to improve their health, it was all the more natural for a woman to make regular and leisurely trips to a spa. And surely she would want to take her trusted advisors and family with her, given that most trips in those days lasted for months rather than days or weeks.

Queen Marie agreed to provide the necessary exit permits, particularly as Doña Gracia promised to return, as she had always done in the past.[17] It is possible that the women went ahead and the men joined them later, using Aix-la-Chapelle as a staging spot before moving on. Such a strategy would have lessened suspicion even more.

For all of these carefully orchestrated maneuvers and more, the Venetian ambassador in Antwerp would later applaud Doña Gracia and her party for "showing great skill." It was not easy to leave a city "with an estate of this sort," he commented, especially as it could encourage other *converso* merchants to withdraw themselves and their capital,[18] something the ambassador hinted to his superiors in Venice was already happening. The monarchs' ongoing persecution of the incoming refugees was obviously having an effect on all *converso* residents. Nobody felt safe.

But how best to take out the "estate?" The Mendes fortune was held in a variety of forms: as outstanding loans at varying rates of interest; in bills of exchange and marketable commodities such as cloth; in property, most notably the family mansion and compound in Antwerp; and in jewels, precious stones, plate and coin.[19]

Paper obligations could be readily transferred from one location to another, especially as the House of Mendes had a strong network of agents all over Europe and, no doubt, in the Ottoman Empire too (considering how often Diogo had been charged with such dealings). It was not as easy to transport heavy treasure chests and merchandise over unpaved roads and mountain passes. Thus, Doña Gracia next turned her attention to a portion of their valuables held in a handful of chests, including 23 bales of cloth.[20] She needed to find somewhere to park them for temporary safekeeping, presumably so they could be sent on at a later date. The traveling party also had to guard against the possibility of being waylaid on the road by robbers, or lesser officials who might confiscate their belongings, despite the wording of any safe conduct.

Thus Doña Gracia arranged to have at least three chests of valuables carted by a trading partner named Ledders to the Bavarian mountain town of Fussen.[21] Fussen lay several hundred miles southeast of Antwerp, about a third of the way to Venice. Sending them ahead also shielded the valuables from any hint of Mendes ownership, discovery of which would have immediately tipped border authorities to the real reason for the family trip to the spa. They were to be dispatched by the Ledders' agent in Antwerp, accompanied by a bill of lading declaring a value far below their actual worth. This vastly reduced customs charges and lessened the likelihood of seizure and search. Stuffed into chests were 40 (amended to 46 by one later account) boxes of pearls with an estimated worth of 50,000 ducats and a dozen or so ducat-doubloons (worth about two ducats each). In addition, there were the bales of cloth with a total value of 80,000 ducats; in all a small fortune and another indication of how vast the total Mendes holdings must have been.[22] Once in Fussen, the chests were to be handed over to a trusted local merchant for temporary safe keeping.[23] Other local merchants agreed to send still more chests directly to the Adriatic port of Ancona (another exit point for Ottoman trade), further indicating that their intended future lay in Ottoman lands.[24]

The group set out with a convoy that would have contained numerous carriages, wagons piled high with luggage and mounted guards.[25] The first leg was the 80-mile trip to Aix-la-Chappelle. Traveling in a convoy would have been yet another reason why they could not possibly proceed without exit permits. They were simply too conspicuous.

Around this time and possibly to justify Doña Gracia's move southwards after she left Aix-la-Chapelle, rather than back to

Antwerp, a romantic story arose that young Ana and Don Joseph had fallen in love. Also, that he had seized the chance to elope— "impudently stealing away a maid of noble parentage" as the abduction was quaintly described by a 17th century historian, taking his lady love (where else?) to Venice.[26] A concerned mother would naturally have to catch up with the runaway couple to "save" her daughter from disgrace.[27] Though this tale was surely a rumor deliberately spread by the family to shield its true motives, such a marriage would have also been an ideal way to stop others with designs upon Ana's fortune.

Even the Venetian ambassador spoke of Ana and La Chica being married off at this time "to free themselves from the fear of having to marry others upon request."[28] However, he had his facts somewhat confused. He implied that the weddings, or at least the marriage arrangements, had already taken place. A marriage between Ana and Don Joseph did transpire in the end, although not until the family was safely in Constantinople. Why they waited so long may have been yet another sign of Doña Gracia's implacable adherence to the precepts of her faith. It may have been important for her to have her daughter married in a traditional Jewish wedding, conducted by a rabbi, and with a bridegroom who had been ritually circumcised, which would have been suicidal in Christian Europe.

There was also the legal issue of the validity of a Christian marriage, and any marriage contract that went with it, if and when the couple later reverted openly to Judaism. It was a dilemma regularly faced by the great rabbis of the day, especially in Muslim lands where a large number of incoming *conversos* were returning to their ancestral faith and where Jews lived under their own legal code.[29] Even engaging in a clandestine Jewish ceremony would not have been prudent while family members remained in Christian Europe. At this perilous point they needed to meticulously maintain the appearance of being good Catholics. They could thereby preserve their freedoms, privileges and fortune intact until it was all safely transferred — persons as well as property—to the Ottoman Empire. By then Ana would be twenty-three years old. And it would have been socially unspeakable for a girl from a wealthy and influential family to still be single—unless such plans had indeed been sealed many years in advance.

They were on their way by August. This is clear from a letter that Henry VIII's personal envoy in Antwerp sent back to London in September. The Mendes, he said, had recently left the city, presumably for good.[30] Their departure must have been sufficiently important to the British Treasury or it would not have even been mentioned. But the British envoy also got his facts mixed up. The daughter involved in the marriage controversy that had so angered Queen Marie, according to him, was Diogo's child. The estimate of the size of her dowry was 400,000 ducats—which also sounds excessive.

According to the British envoy, the sisters had become "enraged with the crooked dealings of Gaspare Ducchio against them" and the queen's insistence that a marriage take place. Thus, they "lately gave vale (farewell) to this town and are gone to... Lyons where...they have promised to emprunt (lend) the French king 800,000 crowns for five years without interest." The envoy ended by remarking upon how much traveling cash they had with them. "(They) carried from hence at least seven or eight thousand ducats in ready money,"[31] he added.

———••❦••———

The overland route taken by their convoy through Europe can be stitched together, in part, from the frantic notes that Queen Marie would soon be sending to merchants in various cities along the way, imploring them not to cash any notes or bills of exchange that would benefit the Mendes widows.[32] From Aix-la-Chapelle they traveled due south to Besançon, one of the newer financial centers used by major European banking houses to trade notes and exchange debts and credits.[33] From there, they continued southwards, but turned slightly to the west to skirt the Alps and make their way to Lyons, the other great financial center of Europe where the House of Mendes had been active.

It could not have been a happy band of travelers. They had now become wanderers themselves with no permanent home, bumping endlessly along dusty, uneven or soggy roads just like the refugees they had been helping. And they were being chased by vengeful monarchs who were willing to use torture to exact revenge.[34] They were not sure what would face them in the future. Other unsettling news would have reached them at this point. Gonçalo, the third Mendes brother, had died in Antwerp, sometime late in October.[35] Yet another prop had been pulled from under them.

Physical privations and dangerous circumstances make for troubled relationships. So it is hardly surprising that it was on the road that discord seems to have first erupted outwardly between the two sisters, although it had no doubt been brewing for some time. Brianda was not happy about losing control of her part of the estate, which meant losing control over her future. Venice and Ferrara were glittering centers of Renaissance life. She wanted to remain and enjoy the fruits of these great cities—as subsequent events would show. But Doña Gracia had long been determined to leave Christian Europe and take as much of the Mendes money with her as she could,[36] behaving as though the fortune was a sacred trust, reserved for the benefit of her family and her people and not to be squandered by vengeful monarchs or greedy suitors. If any of these funds came under Brianda's irresponsible control, she later told the rabbis, they "would certainly...be lost."[37] In addition, as the official guardian of La Chica and her inheritance, Doña Gracia had an added duty to see that the girl did not assimilate and marry a local nobleman.[38]

The primary reason for the Mendes party to stop over in Lyons and Besançon would have been to exchange and collect outstanding debts;[39] part of a consolidation of banking activity before transferring assets to Turkish lands. The outstanding French loan originally arranged by Don Joseph in 1540, most of which had never been repaid (the French king was a notorious deadbeat[40]), continued to occupy the attentions of both Doña Gracia and Don Joseph.[41]

An interesting offer would also engage the party during their stay in Lyons. While in transit, secret correspondence had been flying back and forth between the Tuscan emissary in Antwerp and Cosimo de Medici, Duke of Florence who later became the Grand Duke of Tuscany. Like the duke of Ferrara, Cosimo was anxious to lure the capital and know-how of the "Portuguese merchants" to his duchy, whose center was the great banking city of Florence. He had instructed his emissary to seize the moment. Everyone knew, the emissary noted in his letter, that there was no better way of drawing these merchants to his lands than to have the "the leaders" of the House of Mendes in their midst. "If it were possible to attract them to Florentine territory," he wrote, "this could in turn attract many others of their nation, particularly those of means".[42] As soon as the Mendes party arrived in Lyons, the emissary therefore made an offer through a local representative: come and live in that duchy instead. Doña Gracia must have turned them down flat as no more was ever heard of Cosimo's invitation.

The stopover in Lyons would have also been the occasion when Brianda doubtless watched with growing impatience while her sister negotiated repayment of monies that actually belonged to Brianda's portion of the estate. These funds were—in Brianda's eyes—being wrongfully snatched from her grasp and placed under Doña Gracia's control. It had taken a while for Brianda to realize how powerless she had really become, now that Diogo was gone. But after weeks on the road, such powerlessness must have appeared horrifying and humiliating. It meant begging for her every need. It meant watching helplessly while Doña Gracia lavished ducats on a cause to which Brianda may not have been as deeply committed. It meant being implicated in clandestine work that might lead to her arrest at any moment, even if she did not actively participate. It meant that if she preferred to remain in Venice, or even go to Ferrara, and not move on to the Ottoman Empire—which later actions suggested she clearly despised—she would be left penniless and lose her daughter too, if her sister refused to compromise.[43] Worse, she might be forced to continue on to the Turkish realms. And Doña Gracia, as we have already seen, was not the sort to yield to anyone.

Christopher Manuel, a man who was to become one of Doña Gracia's most trusted agents, had been working frantically to collect some very large loans.[44] And these may well have been the catalyst. The thought of so much money piling up under Doña Gracia's control may have been more than Brianda could stand. One can almost see the sisters screaming at one another; Doña Gracia sticking staunchly to her position, believing she had been handed a sacred charge that she was not about to compromise; Brianda reacting like a helpless and hostile adolescent longing to be given the privileges of a mature adult. As Doña Gracia was not an adversary who would easily concede, especially when she felt her rights and authority were being challenged, Brianda must have figured she did not stand a chance.

Or did she? A desperate person takes desperate measures. Matters would reach a climax soon after the sisters arrived in Venice. For now, any resolution or compromise would have to wait until their journey was complete. Winter was drawing in fast and the last leg of their journey would necessitate traveling over the twisting roads close to the Alps.

Their convoy was therefore soon pushing eastwards—straight into the maw of yet another hazard, the trouble-filled Duchy of Milan. Any other route would have added months and hundreds of miles to their trip. Once in Milanese territory, they became a tempting target, despite the many safe conducts they carried. Vuysting's men were lying in wait. Vuysting himself had probably been notified by Charles and Marie to confiscate Mendes property anywhere it showed up Charles' domains.[45] When the convoy arrived in Pavia, some 200 miles west of Venice, Doña Gracia was forced to give up a chest of unspecified belongings including two bales of cloth. It took a year before she could put sufficient pressure on the governor of Milan to release the goods. But even though an agreement was reached, the goods could not have been returned right away because Doña Gracia was still petitioning a magistrate in Pavia for their release four years later.[46] Once again, believing she had been wronged, she was tenacious. Her name, and her name alone, appears on these repeated requests, as it had begun to do on all official requests or documents concerning her family and its banking enterprise.

By the time they reached Venice it was already December.[47]

———••✥••———

Sometime the previous August, probably a month or so after Doña Gracia and her party left for Aix-la-Chapelle,[48] Charles and Marie realized they had been duped. The principals of the House of Mendes were never coming back; their money, prestige, credit and business lost forever to the Holy Roman Empire and the people of Antwerp. Charles was seething.[49] He immediately issued the decree that Vuysting may have utilized, stating that Mendes holdings were to be seized anywhere they were to be found in his domains.[50] The sense of outrage clearly extended to Marie, based upon the fury she was about to unleash in a letter-writing vendetta.

The crown's initial step was to immediately file criminal charges against Doña Gracia and her traveling party, implying that taking an unauthorized flight, without clearance from Antwerp, confirmed that they were heretics and traitors bound for the Ottoman Empire.[51] As they were not present to defend these charges, they were officially declared secret Jews. This gave Charles the legal justification to confiscate all their assets left behind. Under this pretext, the Antwerp mansion was raided. All personal possessions, ledgers and other documents found inside were impounded.[52] The indefatigable Gaspare Ducchio joined in the witch hunt, running around town searching for any debts left unpaid. Such a discovery would have advanced the idea of criminal intent. It would have confirmed that they were actually unrepentant debtors running away from their obligations. Duccio became so caught up in this quest that he failed that month to fulfill his duties to the British in a timely fashion.[53]

Painting them as criminals would have been useful for other reasons, too. The Tuscan emissary had noted in his report how significant the departure of the Mendes was for the entire *converso* community, and especially for the wealthier merchants only lately arriving from Portugal. "The general opinion," he observed, "is that others of their nation are about to follow the Mendes, since they are the leaders and the chief people..." The Tuscan emissary had therefore already begun negotiating with these merchants, recommending that they settle in Pisa as it was close to the Mediterranean coast and well situated for traveling by sea to Spain and Portugal. He assured the leading *conversos* that Pisa was "a fine and abundant place to live... that houses were cheap, that they were many gardens... and that His Excellency (Duke Cosimo) had instituted a fine university (at Pisa)."[54] All of which must have reached the ears of Charles and Marie and made them even more incensed.

Why Doña Gracia and her party left behind so much valuable information is a mystery. By early September their ledgers had been examined, enabling Marie to begin writing a barrage of letters aimed at tracking down all outstanding debts due the House of Mendes. Marie made it clear that repayment of those debts was to be diverted to the crown. If credited to a Mendes account, she warned the recipients, payments would end up among Doña Gracia's holdings and go to enrich the Turks. One of the first of these letters, written on September 3, informed the duke of Florence that substantial sums had recently been posted to the credit of the House of Mendes by three Florentine merchants. She asked the duke to order the merchants in question to hold onto those funds, as the Mendes "are suspected of certain crimes."[55]

On September 13, she similarly wrote to the Margrave of Antwerp saying that she had heard that a courier had just arrived with numerous letters from Lyons for various Antwerp merchants. She ordered the Margrave to gather all the merchants who had incoming letters in the pouch. They were to open the letters in front of him and tell the Margrave if they made mention of any outstanding debts due to the Mendes.[56]

On October 2, yet another letter—this one from the Emperor to a senior commander in the border town of Besançon —noted that the Mendes ledgers had included a reference to a Spanish merchant who had recently received 5,200 ducats payable to the Mendes. The Emperor ordered the commander to apprehend the Spanish merchant and bring him to his office to personally pay the money in question.[57] On October 8, another official order went out in the name of the crown demanding that chests belonging to the Mendes that had been handed to a shipping agent in Antwerp to send directly to Ancona be returned to Antwerp, where presumably they would be confiscated.[58]

In yet another letter, dated October 18, Queen Marie commanded her commissioners to gather all the Antwerp merchants who had accepted bills of exchange payable to the Mendes in Lyons. They were to hand the money to the Emperor, rather than to the Mendes, or face prosecution. She sounded worried that the money might simply disappear in the close fraternity of merchants who were never anxious to cooperate with state officials.[59]

Not a ducat, it appeared, would escape her grasp as long as someone—anyone—might have some Mendes money that she could impound. On November 10 she was similarly chasing a certain Portuguese man who had left town after receiving some money from the Mendes. Marie was asking for him to be apprehended and brought before the Margrave of Antwerp, presumably to give back whatever sums he had acquired.[60] On the same day Marie sent another letter to the viceroy of Naples, explaining the whole story, but twisting the facts to her advantage. The Mendes widows had suddenly fled Antwerp, she explained in a way that implied wrongdoing, together with their senior agents, Don Joseph and Guillaume Fernandes. As all were suspected of (unspecified) crimes, she continued, the Emperor had impounded their belongings and sent commissioners to examine their ledgers. During the examination they discovered that the viceroy and his brother, the Cardinal of Burgos, were to receive 20,000 ducats in June of the following year from the proceeds of an estate; 15,000 ducats of which was payable to the Mendes. She wanted the viceroy to notify his brother to hold onto the entire amount until a final decision had been made concerning Mendes property.[61]

In late November Marie issued the order that gave her the

legal right to sell off all Mendes belongings that had been confiscated.[62] She also authorized a proclamation requiring anyone
holding Mendes property to divulge what they had or face punishment. She further forbade any merchant, or their agents in
Lyons, Rome, Venice, Spain or elsewhere, who owed money to
the Mendes, from honoring a Mendes bill of exchange.

The merchants protested, however, and on November 27 she
temporarily backed down, insisting only that they would face
severe punishment if it ever came to light that "they had colluded
with the Mendes to defraud the Emperor or safeguard the fugitives' money."[63] Bailiffs were then given the right to sell off the
family's furniture and other household items to the highest
bidder.[64]

All of this would have been reported to Doña Gracia by her
own agents who had remained in Antwerp, or by the other merchants. And it would not have been in character for her, as the
head of the House of Mendes, to stand idly by while the family
was being financially raped. She did not. She chose instead to
place her trump card in play. She sent her nephew, Don Joseph,
a personal friend of the royal family and a former military officer in the Emperor's army, to sort things out.

By the spring of 1546, Don Joseph was back in Antwerp on a
mission to save whatever he could. Shortly before Easter, he
obtained an audience with Queen Marie. He opened the conversation by insisting that the authorities had no legal right to
do what they had done. The sisters were not subjects of the
Emperor, he reminded the queen. They had come from Portugal of their own free will to do business in Antwerp. They had
not run away from Antwerp after stealing goods from anyone.

They had paid their debts before departing and had even left detailed instructions with their agents to take care of all matters that could not be concluded immediately.[65]

If that were so, retorted the queen, why had they not answered the summons to appear in court when charges were first raised against them? "They could have been present if they had wanted to," she told him. "They had been summoned with sufficient notice." In their absence, she explained, justice had taken its course and a sentence of banishment and confiscation of goods had been passed. Besides, she reminded him, evidence that they were heretics who were dealing with the enemy had been suspected for years. However, to show that the crown "did not wish to deal with them without due process of justice" Marie conceded that she would be willing to revoke the sentence of banishment, allowing them to "come in person" to answer to the charges before the Council of Brabant.[66]

Don Joseph explained that this was impossible. The sisters were now in Venice where—he did not fail to remind her—"they were held to be good Christians." This being so, he ventured, he would gladly appear before the justices in their place. He invited the queen to make all the investigations she wished about him in Antwerp, Portugal or France, the three countries where he had lived, because he was so sure that she would find nothing damaging.

Besides, he added, leaving Antwerp without formal permission—something he insisted the sisters had thought they were free to do—was not so heinous a crime as to require the confiscation of all their personal belongings and business assets, much less the portion that rightfully belonged to their respective daughters. Since most of the assets did belong to the girls and were only temporarily being held under guardianship, there was even less reason for confiscation. The girls, he added, were not even old enough to be held delinquent. At their age they had no choice but to follow their mothers. Moreover, he warned the queen, some of the assets she had seized actually belonged to other merchants. And if she and the Emperor continued to act in such an arbitrary manner "other merchants would (also) take heed and leave Antwerp"—a reprise of the old threat that he must have known would trouble her. Even so, he said, he was willing to offer 30,000 ducats to settle the matter and allow the House of Mendes to continue doing business in Antwerp.[67]

The queen left him with two options: submit Doña Gracia and her sister personally to justice before the Council of Brabant or agree to a realistic settlement. Anything less than 100,000 ducats would not even be considered. She later said that she based the figure on the fact that her commissioners had estimated that the goods already impounded could produce at least 200,000 ducats, including those allegedly belonging to the girls.

Don Joseph left the audience irate. For the queen later mentioned that he walked from the room threatening to go in person to the Emperor "in the hope of getting a better deal" and that he was also going to write to the "widows" for further instructions.[68]

It was around this time that the three chests of valuables that had previously been shipped to the mountain town of Fussen and had escaped customs duty came to the attention of both monarchs. They were delighted to discover that they had the right to confiscate them too, for customs fraud, separate and apart from all the other belongings.[69]

Meanwhile, Don Joseph was as good as his word, traveling to Regensburg to meet the Emperor, his old fighting buddy. It must have been a warm encounter between two men who both prided themselves on being gentlemen. The Emperor immediately agreed to make full restitution in exchange for a payment of 30,000 gold ducats by August, although later letters suggest the Emperor still intended to press the legal case for heresy. He could not look as if he were giving in entirely.[70]

When Queen Marie got wind of the deal, she became irate. Charles was in the midst of raising an army to engage in a major battle against the German Protestants.[71] It seemed to her that what Charles had done was neither practical nor tactical. In a letter of July 16, she reminded her brother that he had been counting on Mendes money to furnish artillery, build a new fort near a strategic bridge and fix fortifications at Gelders (now part of the Netherlands). "I should (also) warn Your Majesty," she added, in a tone that implied that Charles was behaving stupidly, "of the danger into which would fall Your finances... I have no means of paying other than by availing myself of the said goods." Just in case this line of reasoning did not convince him of his folly, she also raised a legal technicality. The agreement drawn up between Charles and Don Joseph that she had been sent, she told Charles, had been "neither signed nor certified." She also reminded him that the goods and money seized were worth much more than the 30,000 ducats Don Joseph was supposed to provide. She implored Charles once again to think more clearly. "I do not wish to let the affairs over here fall into ruin...(but) I have been obliged to incur new expenses ...due to the troops that are gathering to invade your lands."[72]

It was a battle, incidentally, that the Emperor himself had provoked because he had decided that the Protestants were growing too powerful. And it was escalating into a confrontation of outsized proportions. The Protestants had amassed a reputed 15,000 horsemen, 8,000 foot soldiers, 120 brass cannon and 300 boats to make bridges, among other provisions of war. For his part, the Emperor had raised 10,000 cavalry, 14,000 foot soldiers and 80 cannon.[73] Queen Marie was becoming frantic about the cost of it all. She even suggested to Charles in one of her many letters that he immediately take possession of the three chests of valuables still at Fussen and use the contents to raise instant cash. It could be hazardous to try to haul them all the way back to Antwerp, she cannily implied, given the deployment of enemy troops.[74]

The correspondence between the monarchs continued at a fast clip. The Emperor wanted to stick to the deal he had made with Don Joseph. The queen did not. By August 15, she wrote to tell Charles that restitution was out of the question anyway, since everything collected from the Mendes had been sold and spent. She sounded sick and tired of her brother's continued wars, which she predicted "will be the ruin of Antwerp." All she could offer, she wrote, was the return of "some furniture and luggage that has not been sold."[75]

An inventory taken one month earlier showed that around 300,000 ducats had been raised from the sale of the Mendes pearls, doubloons, miscellaneous merchandise, money owed from ship captains and so forth. A subsequent page of the inventory shows how it had all been spent, with more going out than coming in: for the payment and provisioning of troops, arquebuses, a new fort, the cost of bringing back the chests from Fussen (which they must have decided to do after all), to repay a merchant owed money from a previous loan that the Mendes had syndicated for the Emperor, as well as other miscellaneous items.[76]

Even so, as Don Joseph was in possession of a written agreement from the Emperor concerning restitution, he was not about to give up. If the monarchs could not return the actual items, then at least they could make the family whole with the equivalent ducats. By September 14, Marie was complaining to Charles that Don Joseph and his agents solicit her "daily," although "I have no means on earth to satisfy them." To provide herself with a reason for the delay without admitting "our poverty," she told Don Joseph she was waiting until the widows appeared in person to answer to the charges.[77]

Don Joseph then tried separating the value of the treasure chests from the overall deal by insisting that customs fraud had neither been intended nor committed. The chests contained only pearls and silver which were non-taxable items. By the end of September he had obtained a written receipt from Queen Marie acknowledging that the ducats he had promised to pay the Emperor, in exchange for restitution, had been delivered.[78]

However, a postscript to this document shows just how wily Don Joseph could be. He admitted that "notwithstanding" the wording of the receipt, the ducats had not actually been delivered. He had simply arranged for them to be deducted from the proceeds of the sale of Mendes belongings, if and when those proceeds were returned to him.

One year later these interminable discussions were still going on. The widows remained in Venice. They had no intention of returning to the Emperor's realms to face the interrogations and torture that would be in store for them.[79] The queen was not going to make good either. She did not have the means nor the inclination to do so. The Emperor remained equally determined to stand honorably by his original agreement with Don Joseph.[80]

It was not until July, 1547, a full two years after Doña Gracia and her party had left for Venice, that the two sides finally reached a reluctant settlement. The House of Mendes would provide their majesties with an interest-free loan of 200,000 pounds[81] for one year, fully secured by other crown income. The chests and their contents would remain confiscated, but the official penalties normally imposed for a crime of this nature would be dropped. All other criminal charges and allegations of heresy would be abandoned too. In dropping all charges, Marie reminded Charles how much trouble had been stirred up among the merchant community when they had tried to convict Diogo of wrongdoing fifteen years earlier.[82]

As arrangements for the sale of the Antwerp mansion were mentioned by the family at a later date,[83] one can assume that any possessions not sold off immediately were therefore given back, although that which was returned would have represented only a minuscule portion of what had been lost overall. As Doña Gracia placed tremendous emphasis upon holding onto the family fortune and using it for the welfare of her people, these losses must have been a bitter blow indeed.

PART III

ITALY: 1546–1552

CHAPTER 9

Merchants in Venice

At mid-point in the 16th century, Venice would have loomed like paradise before the eyes of the weary traveler crossing from the mainland to its offshore perch within a gentle lagoon. This would have been particularly true for a cultured woman like Doña Gracia, arriving as she did at the close of 1545. The Italian Renaissance was in full flower. And this picturesque city, built upon a cluster of islands that rose from the sandbanks and shallows at the northernmost end of the Adriatic Sea, was one of its most exquisite jewels.

Over the previous forty years, wealthy Venetian merchants, under the inspiration and personal guidance of Jacopo Sansovino, the great Renaissance architect, had embarked upon a rare spending spree. They had poured ducats by the thousands into the creation and adornment of sumptuous palaces and villas along the Grand Canal and its companion waterways. Under construction or reconstruction, their freshly-cut Istrian marble facades, not yet stained by time and tide, glistened like ice slabs against the sharp sun and indigo skies that characterized this fabled city. Inside these sumptuous dwellings it was as though every successful merchant and patrician family in Venice was trying to outdo the other. They decorated each and every wall, archway and ceiling with breathtaking frescoes, oil paintings or giant tapestries. Not to be outdone, the church had embarked upon conspicuous spending to similarly embellish its buildings, engaging Tintoretto to adorn many interiors. Nearby, some of the greatest art of the era was emerging from the Venetian workshops of Titian and Bellini. In combination, it became a virtuoso performance.[1]

Such brilliant interiors virtually demanded an endless round of masked balls, banquets, card parties, theatrical evenings, pageants, weddings, processions, recitals and other festivities to complete the tableau. Inspired no doubt by such rich surroundings, Venetian men and women were equally beguiled by personal fashion. Venetian clothes, expertly cut and stitched in the finest lace, linens, brocades and velvets, were the envy of all Europe. Even Venetian galley captains strutted around in silk cloaks, ermine and cloth of gold.[2]

The city's fun-loving women, whether aristocrat or courtesan, were free from the puritanical streak that had kept the women in the Low Countries on a somewhat tighter rein. They dyed or bleached their hair, holding it in place with gold or silver pins. They covered the head, neck and fingers with large and costly jewels and decorated their skirts with silver, gold or pearls; the number of layers and fullness of those skirts serving as an indication of wealth and status. Indeed, a woman was not fully dressed unless she carried a delicate handkerchief, fan and perfumed gloves.[3] Though the church railed against such ostentation, and there was an air of decadence about it all, few listened. These fashions were such a symbol of elevated social standing that Doña Gracia would later demand a special exemption from Sultan Suleiman, seeking the right for herself and her household to continue to wear Venetian dress when they moved to the Ottoman Empire seven years later.[4] Brianda would be similarly loathe to give up the city's magic.[5]

For Venice also offered unique sounds, as though such splendor would have been incomplete without a symphonic accompaniment. Giant church bells regularly tolled from each parish tower, creating an uplifting cacophony that survives even into the modern era. Time was marked by their contrasting tones, the sound of the *Maragona* being one of the more traditional morning wake-up calls.[6] Added to that were the hoots and shouts of the boatmen as they punted their gondolas along the rivers and canals; the slap of water against the wooden walls of the canals as river traffic stirred up a wake; the babble of exotic tongues as Italian, Greek, Slav, Armenian, German, Turkish and Arab traders gathered to work out their deals on and around the Rialto bridge.

Venice had always had a self-reliant, almost defiant attitude towards the outside world. Possibly this was because it had been founded by refugees fleeing the repeated waves of invasions that continually plagued the Italian mainland at the close of the Roman period. Through the ages it had remained a haven for refugees, much as in later centuries the United States would also build upon the energy and enterprise of successive waves of immigrants. To make the most of its slender resources—fish, salt flats, subsistence farming—the residents initially grouped themselves into cooperatives that would become the prelude to the establishment of a republic. An oligarchy would later evolve, made up of leading merchant families who ruled by inter-connected councils and committees that tended to balance competing interests. At the helm was the doge, a sort of president chosen successively from among their own. Unlike most of its neighbors, Venice never flirted with royalty or the divine right of kings. What ruled Venetians was its passion for commerce and the sea. It even called itself the Serenissima, the State of the Sea. Once each year, it still holds a colorful ceremony celebrating its "marriage" to the sea. Citizens crowd into barges to watch as a single golden ring is tossed into the waters to seal the union.

Lacking abundant natural resources, Venice was forced early on to look outwards for economic opportunities. These rested in its unique location at one of the most northerly points along the Mediterranean shores—deep enough to bring goods by ship right into the belly of Europe. It was also midway along the ancient shipping routes of the Mediterranean Sea. Such a two-fold geographic advantage virtually assured commercial success—provided it chose to capitalize on its chance to become the indispensable trade bridge between Byzantium in the East and Christendom to the West. It was soon building its own commercial and fighting fleet. It established colonies and fortified outposts to safeguard its shipping. It developed great galleys whose combination of oars and lanteen sails provided speed and agility in battle. Venetian leaders were so protective of its commerce that for years no conflict, no war, no competing ideology, no skirmish between East and West, no strife between infidel or true believer, could interrupt the flow of trade for more than the briefest spell. It was the Switzerland of its time and a merchant power unto itself. The business of Venice was business. Typically, it even had no qualms about shipping pilgrims and Crusaders to Jerusalem and back—for a price. Everything was negotiable.

As these merchants grew rich, they began to live accordingly. They patronized the arts. They indulged in Oriental luxuries that came through the city. They built decorative palaces for themselves in an East-West blend of Moorish and Gothic styles. They attracted scholars, printers, craftsmen, glass makers, goldsmiths, jewelers and artists whose excellence would soon become yet another identifying factor of Venetian life.[7] This in-gathering of merchants from all over the Mediterranean made it as much a cauldron of ideas as a crossroads for trade. By the 16th century it rivaled Antwerp as Europe's leading publisher of books. It had more bookstores and printing shops than any other city. At least fifty publishing enterprises were in existence by the time Doña Gracia arrived.

But after Byzantium was conquered by the warrior-like Muslim Turks in the 15th century, and Portugal established long-distance trade routes that bypassed the Mediterranean entirely, Venice started to lose its supremacy. Eventually the Serenissima was forced to acknowledge competition from both the Turks and the Portuguese.

It was in the early years of a long decline as a center of power and prestige that Doña Gracia arrived on its ornamental doorstep along with the other leaders of the House of Mendes—savvy in the ways of spice trading that no longer relied upon the Mediterranean, sophisticated in the perils and promise of international shipping, in touch with far-flung agents that could supply reliable intelligence from all over the known world, bursting with riches despite their Antwerp losses. If the family were indeed secret Jews, nobody was going to challenge them—provided they observed the outward rituals of Christianity and the strict social conformity expected of an upper-class household. Under these conditions, a warm welcome would be assured. Besides, Doña Gracia was a trophy and an opportunity. In Portugal and again in Antwerp the Mendes fortune had provided loans for the benefit of the state. The ability to do so was the trump card she carried with her into Venice and was eager to play once again at the first the opportunity. Lending vast sums was the ultimate way for a commoner to exercise power in the 16th century. She would use this tool repeatedly.[8]

———··✦··———

What roles had the Jews played in Venetian life and commerce throughout the centuries? Documents record their presence from around the 13th century onwards but long before that time individual Jewish merchants came and went. Jews had been plentiful on the Italian peninsula since the Roman era. There were about 1,300 openly-professing Jews in Venice when Doña Gracia arrived.[9] As it would have been her first encounter with Jews who were formally permitted to practice their religion openly, it must have been an emotional moment, as strong as the one commonly expressed by the modern Jewish traveler arriving on Israeli soil for the first time.

Like the Mendes party, many of these Jews had first come to Venice as refugees, fleeing southwards from the Jewish persecutions in the Rhineland that had followed the plague-ridden years of the Black Death. Others had fled north from oppressive conditions in the Papal States and later after expulsion from Iberian lands and other Spanish-held territories. Jews were not popular even in Venice. But money lending was essential to the Venetian economy. Since Christians had long been denied this role by the church, Jews had been encouraged to take over the vital task of extending credit at interest, and the pragmatic Venetians tolerated them. Money lending, medicine and dealing in second hand goods were the only occupations they could (officially) pursue, thereby preventing them from posing a competitive threat to everyone else.[10]

Land owning, public office, and military service were closed to them. They were even required to wear the hated yellow badge that the pope had decreed for all Jews in Europe—yellow being the traditional color of shame. Still, the rule was only half-heartedly enforced in this less-than-zealous state. Venice, for example, provided an exemption for its Jewish physicians, as well as any Jew who had to travel beyond the confines of the city, where this sort of identification would have been perilous. Still, so many of the Venetian Jews regularly skirted the requirement that by the end of the 15th century the law had to be changed. Venetian Jews were required to wear a yellow hat instead. During all this time, at moments of religious indignation, they were temporarily expelled from Venice and then invited back when it became clear that their absence hurt the city's economy.[11] During the long periods when they did live in Venice, they were permitted to reside anywhere. This did not keep them from petitioning for a district of their own that would offer safety and support. For years their wish was disregarded. But in 1516, some 30 years before Doña Gracia's arrival, they finally got what they wanted, although not in the spirit or manner they sought. At that time, Venice was demoralized. It had taken a terrible beating in a land war against other European powers, forsaking its supremacy at sea for possible expansion on land. The Turks had rushed into the vacuum at sea and were soon attacking Venetian shipping and outposts. This put the Venetians on the defensive both on land and at sea. At home, a plague had broken out. And all around the city there had been fearsome fires.

Preachers began to insist that Venice's survival lay in regaining God's grace by atoning for its sins. One of the most deplorable of all these sins, maintained the clergy, was permitting Jews to live freely and ostentatiously around town. Creating a ghetto—a walled and gated area where the Jews were separated from everyone else and locked in at night—was deemed an act of penance and a plea for rehabilitation into God's graces.[12] Humiliating Jews had been a classic way of seeking God's favor since the Roman Empire had first embraced Christianity as the only true religion.

The area chosen was a swampy lowland that had once been

the site of a foundry. The neighborhood was known as the *geto* in the Venetian dialect, which means "to cast."[13] Only later was the name adopted as the generic term for similar Jewish compounds in other European cities. There was scant space for the all the people who were crowded in. One contemporary source observed how "eight or ten individuals lived squeezed into one place, and with a great stench."[14] Having forced such circumstances upon them, it was then easy to heap scorn and derision upon their behavior and appearance. A century later, the crowding would become so intense that there would be not just one, but three Venetian ghettos.

Nonetheless, a vibrant communal, religious and social life rapidly arose within these walls. There were spacious and ornate synagogues and schools, greengrocers and kosher butchers. Their rabbis were so respected for their learning that they were sought out by emissaries of Henry VIII when he attempted to claim biblical legitimacy for the annulment of his marriage to Catherine of Aragon.[15] By day, Jews and others would regularly go in and out of the ghettos and continued to participate in the general commercial life of Venice. They would find ways of slipping out at night, too, by putting on the black Christian cap and bribing the guards.[16] The broader city even became renowned as a thriving center for the publication of Jewish books, though Jews could not go into the business for themselves and had to seek out non-Jewish publishers to do the printing.[17]

The incoming *converso* refugees were placed in a different category. Ostensibly, they were Christian. So no attempt was made to force them to live in ghettos. This did not sit well with the Venetian Jews who considered the *conversos* insincere and opportunistic, knowing full well that those who intended to move on to the Ottoman Empire would swiftly revert to Judaism once they got there. Having done so, they might even return to Venice as Levantine Jews who would then be given privileges not accorded the Venetian Jews. Thirty years later, in 1580, Chaim Baruch, the man who acted as a consul for the Levantine Jews in Venice, would liken the *conversos* to a "ship with two rudders." The *conversos*, he maintained, would twist and turn in whatever way was most beneficial at any given moment. If they wanted to claim an inheritance that could not pass from Christian to Jew, or collect a debt with similar restrictions, they would profess their love of Christianity. If they became mortally sick and anxious to protect their Jewish souls by dying according to Jewish ritual, they were suddenly Jews.[18] The competing agonies of the Venetian Jew, struggling under degradations of Shakespearean proportions, versus the stateless *converso*, leading a perilous life on the border between two faiths, were so great that neither had much compassion for the plight of the other.

The Venetians felt as ambivalent towards the incoming *conversos* as Charles and Marie. As their numbers swelled, just as in Antwerp, there was constant talk of closing the door, which happened in law although never in practice. The presence of so many people of uncertain faith and even more uncertain social roles and loyalties—even within the same family—disturbed the Venetians' rigid social, religious and ethnic classifications. They gladly welcomed foreigners, but they could never fit these foreigners into a comfortable category. A few immediately headed for the ghettos, despite the hardship, in their zeal to live openly as Jews. Most maintained a Christian facade, seeking the widest possible chance for survival. They gladly went about the streets wearing the respected Venetian black velvet cap and other honorable clothing.[19]

Once again, many of the earliest arrivals were sophisticated merchants with the sort of capital, know-how and contacts that the Venetians sorely needed if they were going to regain their former glory. The power elite of Venice, good Christians one and all, also rationalized that it was preferable to keep the *conversos* and their wealth in Christendom rather than see it all go to enrich the Ottoman Empire.[20] Persecutions for alleged apostasy were therefore sporadic and lukewarm at best.

Still, by 1547, just two years after Doña Gracia's arrival, Venice would yield to papal pressure and agree to establish an Inquisition. But it was mild compared to those in Spain and Portugal, or even the Papal States. A *converso* who had chosen to move into the ghettos would never be hounded for being a traitor to Christianity.[21] The Venetian Inquisition would seek out only those *conversos* whose way of life or blasphemous remarks gave rise to gossip or public scandal. A discreet *converso* had nothing to fear, unless a disgruntled family member or close associate reported an incident. Ordinary Venetians were not coaxed to root out covert Jewish practice as they were doing on the Iberian Peninsula. State officials were reluctant to countenance any move that might disturb a highly valued mercantile community. Even the handful of *conversos* who were convicted and given a death sentence ended up being quietly drowned at sea, rather than becoming a public spectacle at an *auto-da-fé*. Probably the pragmatic Venetians were also being careful not to precipitate Turkish outrage. Former *conversos* were too close to the sultan's court. In the end, most were acquitted or banished.[22]

Doña Gracia likely delegated an aide to find a suitable residence in advance of her arrival in Venice. The Venetian authorities may have even offered to locate a *palazzo* reflecting her importance to the Serenissima, and the possible gains that Venice could derive from having such a prize in their midst. Despite ample evidence of her Jewish sympathies, there was not a hint that she might have to live in the ghetto. She was ostensibly a practicing Christian. And that was all that the Venetians would have worried about.

All available accounts suggest that for much of the time the sisters lived separately, maintaining their own households as they had done in Antwerp,[23] living along the Grand Canal or in its immediate vicinity.[24] Brianda leased the newly-completed Gritti Palace[25] near the church of San Marcuola. At this time it was Gothic in style with five arched windows, balconies overlooking the Canal and two floors of lavish reception rooms.[26] It still stands today diagonally across the Grand Canal from the equally ornate *Fondaco dei Turchi*, the central warehouse and gathering spot for the Turkish community of Venice (also still standing). From the rear door of the Gritti, the ghettos were only paces away. It might also have been the home of Doña Gracia at the very beginning. Certainly it was the most extraordinary location for all her endeavors. Later on, after returning from Ferrara, Doña Gracia maintained her own residence in the San Paulo neighborhood,[27] a more central location closer to the Rialto. Brianda would be living further north in Santa Caterina, and again near the ghettos, although for a while it seems as though she was still occupying the Gritti.[28]

These *palazzos* would have provided the sort of lavish setting that would have allowed full participation in the social and political whirl of Venetian upper-class life; the kind of contact that nurtured personal and business contacts at the highest level. In the peculiar 16th century way in which official dislike never did translate into personal enmity, the sisters even entertained Charles' ambassador to Venice. He was invited to their banquets and was regularly entertained in the homes of their agents.[29]

They clearly needed a socially acceptable explanation for their sojourn in Venice. So they spread the word that they had fled Portugal and the Low Countries because the monarchs of both kingdoms had tried every trick to separate them from their fortune.[30] In a city that had little fondness for the current monarchs of Europe, such an attitude would have also helped generate trust. Even Doña Gracia's well-known desire to go on to the Ottoman Empire would not have compromised her reputation. Rather, the Venetians likely viewed it as a chance to build important commercial connections for future trade.

Having rid herself of the burdens that were plaguing her in Antwerp, she was on the lookout for business opportunities—for which she would later demand the right to keep the profits[31]—even while transferring much of her wealth to Ottoman lands. But these were no longer the glory days of Francisco and Diogo. Dazzling loans and syndications to kings and emperors appear to have faded in favor of more mundane commercial activities.

Everything hinged upon making the most profitable alliances. Venice was operating at this time under stringent laws that kept the best deals for their own leading citizens—defined as anyone who had held citizenship and paid taxes for twenty-five years or more. Among other restrictions, outsiders and new arrivals could not transport goods on the Venetian galleys and ships—critical for the safety of any shipment.

To circumvent this ruling, Doña Gracia and her agents allied themselves with a leading Venetian nobleman named Marco da Molin and his son, Nicolà, both of whom were seen going "everywhere with them."[32] The House of Mendes was willing to pay for the use of their name and energies as front men. On at least one occasion Nicolà was sent to the customs office to pick up a shipment of sugar and pepper that could have only come in under a noble name.[33] Thus, the House of Mendes was able to send and receive merchandise—no doubt at a handsome profit—in a manner that would have otherwise been off limits to non-citizens. The relationship was close. The families even socialized.[34]

There was a further reason why it was important to ship as many goods as feasible under the umbrella of an Old Christian family. Whenever Christian pirates knew that a particular ship was carrying goods belonging to a Jewish merchant, they would step up their harassment, even in the formerly safe waters of the Adriatic Sea. The Jews on board would be seized for ransom and the goods, of course, never seen again.[35]

Obviously, these surrogate arrangements could not be spelled out in written contracts. Therefore, the most likely safeguard was the promise of future collaborations and payoffs—if the Old Christian partners conscientiously fulfilled their end of the bargain. The strategy of placing business deals and property in an Old Christian name would have been familiar to Doña Gracia. It had been common practice among *converso*s in Spain and Portugal whenever they feared imminent arrest by the Inquisition, or needed to circumvent legislation that placed them at a disadvantage.[36] There were probably any number of Venetians eager to oblige—for the right price. All that was needed was a hint or two dropped with finesse at one of the many social gatherings.

Acting as a venture capitalist was another of Doña Gracia's profitable endeavors. These arrangements were also often transacted with merchants of Old Christian descent.[37] Since the era of Francisco and Diogo, the House of Mendes had made a very specific type of loan that allowed certain merchants to repeatedly invest quantities of Mendes silver in a variety of deals. The profits were shared between merchant and banker according to a pre-set formula, although the funds were normally left intact with the merchants to re-invest over a considerable period of time. Only periodically would some of the credits be transferred back to the Mendes.[38]

Analogous arrangements were made with their own agents. One such deal developed at the time of Doña Gracia's departure for Constantinople in 1552. She left 18,000 ducats with Duarte Gomez and Agostinho Henriques, her two senior business representatives. The two men were each supposed to add 3,000 ducats of their own for a total capital pool of 24,000 ducats. After deducting the expenses, half the profits were to go to Doña Gracia and half were to be divided between the two men. In other words, the agents stood to gain 25 percent of the profits for an investment of only 12.5 percent of the capital—clearly an incentive that would encourage enterprise, yet still leave plenty for the bank.[39]

Other dealings grew out of the bank's ability to handle commercial ventures for clients in far-off places. One contract, drawn up by Don Samuel Nasi, Don Joseph's older brother, shows the painstaking detail with which the merchants spelled out their respective obligations.[40] And it demonstrates how little commercial transactions have changed in almost 500 years.

The contract, dated October 1561, and drawn by Don Samuel after he had moved with the family to Constantinople, is written in old Portuguese. Don Samuel had apparently been asked by three Jewish merchants in Constantinople for help in importing some Venetian cloth, a prized commodity in the Levant. Under the agreement, they were to pay Don Samuel 2,000 ducats for the cloth and Duarte Gomez, a Mendes senior agent in Venice, was placed in charge.

In order to procure the goods, Don Samuel promised the three Jewish merchants that Gomez would have access to their 2,000 ducats within 25 days of the signing of the contract, presumably via a written letter of credit sent by courier to Gomez. The credits would enable Gomez to use actual coin, which the contract indicated was needed for the purchase. To discourage fraud, Gomez was to watch while the bales were being made up and sealed with Gomez' personal seal.

Don Samuel agreed to assume the risk for the bales during

shipment across the Adriatic Sea from Venice to Ragusa (modern-day Dubrovnik). The three Jewish merchants bore the costs for the overland trek from there to Constantinople; a combination of sea and land routing considered the safest at that time. Upon arrival, the bales were to be immediately delivered to the merchants.

Payment was to be made at two different times: an initial deposit of 700 ducats at the outset with the balance due on delivery. If the bales were lost in transit, Don Samuel agreed to return the deposit. Even the rate of exchange—53 Turkish aspers for each ducat—is stipulated precisely. Once signed, each party was provided with a copy of the contract which was dated according to the Jewish and Gregorian calendar.[41]

The House of Mendes was also involved in direct import-export deals. Once, while in Constantinople, Doña Gracia sent a ship filled with wheat for her Venetian agents to sell on commission.[42] She also directed shipments of wool, pepper and grains from Constantinople to Venice where fabrics were loaded for the return journey.[43] She would always be forceful about retrieving any lost, stolen or impounded goods in transit, as shown by the tenacious way in which she continued to press, year after year, for the return of those bales of cloth that had been confiscated in Pavia.[44]

During her sojourn in Venice, Doña Gracia also served as a judicial investigator or expert witness in an insurance dispute (maritime insurance having originated in the late 15th century in Portugal). The case involved two Jews of Portuguese descent like herself and it was first brought before a panel of two Jewish arbitrators, also of Portuguese descent, and one Jewish judge. According to the surviving transcript, Abraham Catalan, an importer, had arranged with Moshe ben Hini, an underwriter, to insure a shipment which included transporting a box of 38 pearls from Alexandria to Venice. But calamity struck. The ship *Quirina*, which was bringing the box across the Mediterranean along with other merchandise, "crashed in Cyprus," according to the record left by the Jewish judges of that time.[45] Part of the freight was salvaged, nonetheless, and sent onwards to Venice aboard another ship. Upon arrival, Catalan's box of pearls was discovered inside a sack of pepper. But when the box was opened in front of five witnesses only 13 pearls lay inside. Catalan sued Moshe seeking compensation for the loss of 25 pearls.

Like many insurers even today, Moshe was not eager to pay up. Still, the judicial panel concluded that Moshe had to pay Catalan 70 ducats within two months. Moshe appealed, demanding a hearing before a higher Jewish court; specifically before a Jewish judge named Rabbi Raphael Yoseph. Doña Gracia participated in this higher court hearing.

The surviving text reveals neither the outcome of the appeal nor the exact reason why Doña Gracia was called in. But the incident does indicate that she was actively involved with the openly-professing Jewish merchants of the ghettos. This was not uncommon. Jews, conversos and Christians gathered each day on the Rialto to trade with one another and evaluate shipping risks. Shakespeare took note of this when he had Shylock tell the nobleman, Bassanio, "I will buy with you, sell with you, talk with you..."[46]

Indeed, a new era was emerging in which Jewish merchants of the Levant, many of whom had originally been traders in Spain, were gaining greater prominence in Venice. They helped build a vibrant export market for Venetian glass products, tin, paper, and even foodstuffs, such as the Italian cheeses beloved by Turkish pashas. In return, they were bringing back into Europe, by way of Venice, luminous silks, hides, Turkish tapestry as well as delicacies such as caviar and salted sturgeon.

During the early decades of the 16th century, in an attempt to hold onto its lucrative Levantine trade, the Venetians had been forced to provide special privileges for these merchants whenever they came into Venice on business. In 1541, just five years before Doña Gracia arrived, the Venetian authorities had even granted these Levantine Jewish merchants a special quarter, known as the *ghetto vecchio*, separate and apart from the ghetto occupied by the local Italian Jews. The Levantine Jewish merchants were also exempt from paying customs duties. The Venetian authorities treated them with the utmost care, since there were now so many Jews in high places at the sultan's court that a single incident could have triggered serious repercussions.[47]

Since Doña Gracia was anxious to expand her own shipping opportunities between Venice and Ottoman lands, and transfer capital from Cross to Crescent, the chance to build a close relationship with these Levantine Jewish merchants would have been high on her agenda.[48] Aware of her fortune, they would have been equally interested in building a relationship with her. So her involvement in the incident of the missing pearls is not at all surprising.

But what about her emotional feelings towards these Jews, many of whom would have doubtless known the de Luna and Mendes-Benveniste families in the halcyon days of Iberian life? Could she have slipped into any of the ghettos to visit them, and even attended a worship service, without compromising her position?

Probably. So much banking business—large and small—was based in the ghettos that it would not have been a problem for her to visit, purportedly for commercial reasons. Once there, she could have easily wound her way through the myriad of interior passages that linked one building to another to arrive at a synagogue.[49]

There are even examples on record. Brianda's chief of staff, Licentato da Costa, sent his son into the ghettos to buy kosher meat, eating it openly in Brianda's house.[50] The hearing about the missing pearls must have taken place inside one of the ghettos, too, since it was a Jewish legal proceeding. Equally tantalizing is the fact that the great Spanish synagogue, the largest and most lavish of all the Venetian ghetto synagogues, was completed in the second half of the 16th century, just a few years after Doña Gracia's departure.[51] It raises the possibility that she may well have donated funds towards its construction, the way she would later finance synagogues for Spanish and Portuguese immigrants in the Ottoman Empire.

———••✚••———

Regular contact with openly professing Jews and their rabbis may have aroused in Doña Gracia a sense of unfinished business concerning the mortal remains of her closest kin still lying in Portugal. By April 1548, about two years after her arrival in Venice, she asked the pope for permission to dig up Francisco's bones, as well as those of her late father and mother, from a Lisbon churchyard where they lay. She claimed she wanted to move them from their Catholic resting place to "a chapel she has built in the said city (Venice) for her devotions."[52]

The outline of Doña Gracia's mission is contained in a letter sent on April 27 from the pope in Rome to his Papal Nuncio in Portugal. The Nuncio was being exhorted to do whatever it took to help Doña Gracia's envoy, who "comes under my protection." Added the pope, "Meet with him willingly and give him every help and favor," so the church can assist "this woman" in her "pious and honest desire."[53]

Doña Gracia's real intent, of course, was to have Francisco's bones re-interred on the Mount of Olives, the most sacred resting spot for Jews.[54] And there is no reason to believe she did not do the same for her parents. But why go to all this trouble? For one, there was a compelling need among these stateless and wandering *converso*s to connect with soil that was meaningful for them, especially in death. In an age that took eternal life very seriously, the agony of having one's bones rest for all time in a foreign land, or along an alien roadside, say, in the desolation of the Alps, was palpable.[55] If the *converso*s could not be buried in their beloved Spain alongside their ancestors, then the alternative had to be the Holy Land.

By doing so they could comply with a biblical injunction that viewed the task as a sacred duty, especially among families of noble lineage. "And Moses took the bones of Joseph with him," the Bible notes in Exodus 13:19, and into the Promised Land, rather than allow them to lie for eternity on pagan soil in Egypt. "For he (Joseph) had placed the children of Israel under solemn oath, saying '…and you shall carry up my bones from here with you.'" Among the mystical and devout, having a grave on the Mount of Olives also meant that the deceased would be among the first to be resurrected upon the coming of the Messiah.

Burial on sanctified soil was yet another way for guilt-ridden *converso*s to redeem and make "righteous" their Jewish souls. For this reason, their wills frequently instructed their heirs to choose how and where they should be buried—a veiled way of confirming their wish to be buried as Jews, where possible. Later, if their bones could be transported to the land of their ancestors or to the Holy Land, so much the better.[56]

Portrait of Diane de Poiters

CHAPTER 10

The Enemy Within

The relationship between the two sisters had been deteriorating for some time. Brianda was becoming increasingly agitated as Doña Gracia assumed autocratic control over the family and prepared to move to the Ottoman Empire. For one, Doña Gracia had gone before a Venetian magistrate in May of 1546, only months after their arrival, specifically to re-confirm her personal and financial guardianship of Brianda's daughter under the terms of Diogo's will. This would have been necessary in a new jurisdiction.[1]

The legal maneuver did not sit well with Brianda. She viewed the proceeding as a way for Doña Gracia to spirit away the entire Mendes fortune and La Chica to Constantinople; a place where Brianda absolutely refused to go. Brianda would later insist that unless she agreed to go along, "my cruel sister," as she characterized Doña Gracia, would have left her penniless—"to die of hunger."[2] An exaggeration maybe. But she clearly did not share Doña Gracia's wish to relocate yet again. Brianda probably looked upon the Turks in the same negative way as most of her Christians friends: as a semi-barbaric society with none of the refinements and culture of Renaissance Europe.[3]

About a year or so after their arrival in Venice, plans must have been sufficiently advanced to panic Brianda. By then, she had apparently incurred debts that could never be satisfied unless she had access to substantial sums. What kind of debts is pure speculation.[4] But they could well have resulted from lavish living, a weakness that was obliquely mentioned in her later agreements with Doña Gracia. If she stayed behind she stood to live in reduced circumstances as well as lose her only daughter. It would have been in character for Doña Gracia to play those guardian rights for all they were worth. All that she did and said suggested that she had no intention of leaving her niece behind.

The sisters' dispute ended up in the Court of Foreigners, a legal entity set up by the Venetians to handle disagreements among overseas merchants doing business in the city. In the summer of 1547, some eighteen months after their arrival, Brianda challenged Doña Gracia's role as guardian and administrator in this court, petitioning for an examination into the financial affairs governing Diogo's legacy.[5] A case was formally opened on September 15, 1547.[6] To bolster her case and substitute herself as guardian and administrator of La Chica's inheritance, Brianda denounced Doña Gracia as a secret Jew about to move to Turkey to return to the faith of her ancestors—something that was surely known around town but never officially acknowledged. By contrast, Brianda portrayed herself as pious to the core, telling the court that she and her daughter wanted to remain in Venice where they could continue to live as good Christians. But to do so, she obviously needed legal control over her child and the funds to make their lives viable.[7]

It was the most formidable weapon Brianda could have brandished. And though historians have since characterized her as evil and untrustworthy as a result of this betrayal,[8] the dynamics that pushed her into it are more complex. For one, Doña Gracia comes through in all of her dealings as tough and controlling. It was the only way she could ever have achieved what she did and keep the fortune intact for the mission that was so important to her. But such an attitude could have driven a weaker person to desperate measures. Brianda may have concluded that without the intervention of the courts, Doña Gracia would never have compromised.

Still, it is hard to condone such a betrayal. For the gravity of the allegation must been seen in light of hardening attitudes within the Catholic world. With the rise of break-away movements emanating from the teachings of Martin Luther and his followers, the Catholic Church had been cracking down hard on dissidents, a move that had already brought the Inquisition to Rome in 1542. Then, in the spring of 1547, just six months before the sisters' case was opened, the reluctant Venetians had established an Inquisition in their city, too.[9] It could have emboldened Brianda as it was unlikely that a formal and public charge like the one being made by Brianda could be ignored. It implied that Doña Gracia was a heretic.[10]

Which was probably just what Brianda wanted. Ever since the Inquisition had been established in Spain in the previous century, *converso* families had used it as a mechanism for fighting inheritance and internal property battles. Brianda would have known that if Doña Gracia were arrested by the Inquisition, all the family assets would have been immediately confiscated or at least frozen. As a good Christian and a close relative, Brianda could then have applied to take them over, rather than forfeiting them to the church.[11]

Nevertheless, the entire matter placed the Venetians in an awkward position. The importance of the person being charged could not be overlooked. To arrive at a conclusion that might benefit Venice, without angering either the Turks or the pope, required a Solomon-like decision. Certainly the Venetians did not want to see the Mendes fortune go to the Turks if they had even the smallest chance of keeping some of it in the city.[12] Yet they could not treat Doña Gracia like any ordinary heretic, for fear of reprisals by the Turks.

On the opposing side, the potential financial and personal losses that Doña Gracia was now facing required a dramatic counter-offensive on her part—one that had to go beyond any evidence offered in her own defense, the bribing of local officials or verbal skills during cross-examination.

It is not hard to guess what Doña Gracia was about to do. She remained a woman of action, responding in the same manner as she had done as a young mother in Portugal and again when facing impossible odds in Antwerp. She did not wait for the Inquisition to take up her case. She did not wait around for the Court of Foreigners to come to a decision. She did not even wait around long enough for the court to issue a subpoena for her to testify.[13]

Towards the end the following year of 1548,[14] she "fled one night…and secretly went with her possessions to Ferrara," as Brianda would later describe the departure.[15] By doing so she placed herself and her fortune beyond the control of the Court of Foreigners and the Venetian Inquisition, and any money they might require her to hand over. She must have been tipped off that they were about to find in Brianda's favor and require her to deposit 150,000 ducats in the Venetian Zeccha for the ultimate benefit of La Chica.[16] However, given the size of her usual retinue and the need to obtain a safe conduct from the duke of Ferrara before she left, it is unlikely that Doña Gracia ran away like the proverbial thief in the night.[17]

Whatever the actual circumstances, Doña Gracia took her household and traveled some 60 miles southwest to the independent duchy of Ferrara. Here she could count on finding temporary refuge in the liberal-minded realm of Ercole II—the state that had welcomed the incoming *conversos* from early in the century and where she had once considered living indefinitely.

Since Doña Gracia's intentions were now to move on to Ottoman lands as soon as feasible, she also played her Turkish card. She took the precaution of notifying the sultan, through her agents, that she was still anxious to come to Turkey.[18] Making sure that the sultan was aware of her predicament would have also helped to dissuade the Inquisition from moving ahead.

The sultan reacted with delight to the prospect of welcoming this personal trophy and celebrated international banker to his empire. He dispatched a representative to personally escort her to Constantinople.[19] Meanwhile, rumors conveniently began to circulate that Doña Gracia had promised her daughter, Ana, to a son of Moses Hamon, the sultan's personal physician and one of the most powerful Jews at the Turkish court—shades of a similar story deliberately spread during an earlier crisis. At least two foreign envoys in Venice—the Papal Nuncio and the French ambassador—knew enough about the proposed "marriage" to mention it in their dispatches.[20] Whether or not it was true—and the odds point towards a deliberate subterfuge[21]—it was an excellent way for Doña Gracia to further protect herself.

The letter from the sultan to the authorities in Venice, upon which these rumors had no doubt been based, also noted that Doña Gracia was related to the Hamon family through her late husband and brother-in-law.[22] It may well have been so. Hamon's father had emigrated from the southern Spanish province of Granada to Constantinople (later known as Istanbul) at the time of the expulsion.[23] Hamon also shared the same Benveniste-Mendes sense of obligation to defend his co-religionists against the persecutions that inevitably cropped up even in Turkey.[24] It harkened back to the way all courtier Jewish families had acted for centuries on the Iberian Peninsula.

Meanwhile, the marriage rumors made it even harder for the

Venetians to do anything but let her go, despite what their Inquisition or the Court of Foreigners might have in mind. Hamon himself seemed well acquainted with the feud and anxious to help negotiate an agreement between the sisters as a prelude to departure.[25] It would have been in Hamon's interest to support the marriage as a way to convince the sultan that he had made a special effort to bring Doña Gracia, her fortune and important European contacts, safely into the Turkish fold. Whatever happened later would become a private matter between the two families. Since Ana married Don Joseph almost immediately after the family reached Constantinople, it is safe to assume it was a diplomatic ruse, albeit one that the Venetians would not dare to challenge.

On December 15, 1548, soon after Doña Gracia arrived in Ferrara, the Court of Foreigners issued its decision. It took an artful approach. Significantly, the Inquisition must have been dissuaded from becoming involved, even though it had been handed a valuable opportunity. On the other hand, the court substituted Brianda for Doña Gracia as guardian of La Chica, based on a number of factors: the judges' adherence to the principle of natural descent, the fact that Doña Gracia had fled and could not testify in her own defense and also because of Brianda's display of Catholic devotion.[26] Though these three factors served as solid legal underpinnings for their decision, the judges would have been naturally inclined to lean that way to keep a major portion of the Mendes fortune in Venice.

Brianda immediately used that judgment to assign herself the legal right to begin a barrage of seizures and threats among the merchant community in Venice, Lyons and Paris, as well as other places in Europe, anxious to make sure the estate did not disappear into Turkey before she got her hands on the money.[27] Interference with the collection of debts was something she had probably started doing in a lesser way even before this moment.

Significantly, Doña Gracia sent an aide scurrying to Lyons seven days before the decision.[28] It suggested that either Brianda was threatening action or had already taken it. The records repeatedly indicate that she was making trouble in a number of the different cities where the House of Mendes conducted business, without specific dates being attached to the incidents.[29]

But Brianda soon ran into difficulties. She found that managing these collections was not easy. One of her first moves was to hire Agostino Fenicio, a man from an Old Christian family in Rome who could work in tandem with the legendary and politically powerful Diane de Poitiers.[30] Mistress of the French king, Henry II, she also carried the title of Duchess of Valentinois and was said to eclipse even Catherine de Medici, the king's legal wife who was a powerful force in her own right. The aim of contacting Diane de Poitiers was to seize "a large sum" of money[31] still on deposit in France, arguing that it was part of La Chica's inheritance and should therefore not be handed over to Doña Gracia. It had apparently escaped Brianda's notice that Fenicio was "a completely evil person in the minds of everyone and an infamous denouncer of Jews," as a later account noted.[32]

Fenicio had his own agenda. He had decided he could win glory and riches for Christendom by denouncing both sisters and their daughters to the French as secret Jews.[33] Such a denunciation would permit the French to confiscate, or at least freeze, all the Mendes' assets on deposit in France; both the loans to the crown and funds still in the hands of private merchants. No doubt Fenicio raised this golden opportunity with Diane de Poitiers. In one fell swoop, he could thereby burnish his own reputation with the French court while earning a tidy sum in representation fees from Brianda. It would also confirm the worst fears of Diogo and Doña Gracia. Both had realized long before that as soon as the family fortune, or any part of it, fell under Brianda's control it would inevitably be lost. Indeed, if observations by the French ambassador in Venice are to be believed, the family's distrust of Brianda ran so deep that "both the knowledge (of the money) and the management were forbidden" to her.[34]

They were right. Brianda's interference had a swift and serious impact upon the financial operations of the House of Mendes.[35] Doña Gracia was soon fighting a rear-guard action from Ferrara, eager to sort out the situation and reverse the confiscations in an attempt to rescue the money. She had to send one of her most trusted business emissaries[36] to France once again in the spring of 1549, to remove as much as possible before it was too late. It was a setback that she would later complain cost her a substantial sum in bribes to straighten out.[37]

There were further complications. As soon as the Venetian judges officially decreed that Doña Gracia had to leave a sizeable sum behind for the benefit of Brianda and La Chica, it must have occurred to Doña Gracia that she would never be permitted to depart for the Ottoman Empire without complying—or changing their minds.[38] Thus she may have had second thoughts about calling upon the sultan at such a moment. For there appears to have been a frantic effort on her part, during the early months of her stay in Ferrara, to stop the sultan's representative, known as a *chaus*, from arriving quite so soon to escort her to the Ottoman Empire. She obviously needed time to sort out those frozen debts and conclude an agreement with Brianda that was more to her liking.

Brianda had her own reasons to be unhappy about the imminent arrival of a *chaus*. She must have been worried that as soon as the *chaus* arrived, Doña Gracia might manage to slip away without leaving anything meaningful behind—or worse, force her to go along. Indeed, the French ambassador to Venice was soon suggesting that suddenly both sisters were trying to delay the arrival of the *chaus*. "These women worried themselves greatly when they heard the news that this *chaus* would be coming here," he told King Henry II of France, on July 12, 1549,[39] "and I have it on good authority that they immediately sent people to halt the *chaus*...." The only reason the *chaus* was coming to Venice at this time, noted the French ambassador, was to ensure that both sisters would be permitted to leave immediately.

Troublesome though it all became, the ongoing departure arrangements and sisters' feud did not stop Doña Gracia's continued advocacy on the part of her people. During the same period she also sent three of her agents to Florence to conclude an agreement, dated January 1549, that finally allowed the "Portuguese" official license to dwell and trade in that important center of culture and commerce; negotiations that may have started when Cosimo tried to lure her to his duchy during her flight from Antwerp. Florence had also been an essential banking center for the House of Mendes since the heyday of the two brothers in the 1530's, thus giving her additional leverage.[40] Whether her agents also took the opportunity, during this particular visit, to clear up the financial disruptions created by Brianda's actions is unknown, but likely, as Florence was one of several cities where collection difficulties had arisen.[41]

——••✠••——

Squeezed between the Venetian, Milanese and Papal spheres of influence, tiny Ferrara had jealously guarded its independence for centuries. Under the rule of the sophisticated Estensi family—or d'Este as they were known by the 16th century—this provincial city-state had blossomed into a cultural, literary, scientific and architectural gem, brimming with intellectual energy. Even today, it remains a cultured city of walled gardens, Gothic arches, pilasters, sculptured facades, cobbled alleys, wild poppies and frescoed interiors that fuse nature and art in a harmony of visual splendor.

Just prior to Doña Gracia's hurried arrival, Ferrara had experienced its own golden age of construction under the masterful eye of Biagio Rossetti. New streets had been laid out and fine homes, palaces, convents and churches had spread beyond the old medieval walls as trade flourished, aided by an influx of *converso* merchants who themselves needed houses and gardens befitting their growing wealth. A case can be made that the glory of the later years of Renaissance art, architecture and culture was fueled in part by the riches that these itinerant *converso* merchants helped create in a number of cities. Certainly, as we shall see, they became a financial prop for the cultural Este family.

In Ferrara, the previous hundred years or so had witnessed the arrival of a university, approved by the pope in 1391, that attracted some of the greatest thinkers and innovators of the Renaissance. Poets and painters followed. Supported by a line of enlightened Este rulers, the miniature state soon became identified with a liberal and humanistic outlook. This was especially true under the current duke, Ercole II, after his marriage to Renée, daughter of King Louis XII of France. She was a follower of Martin Luther and in Ferrara had transformed her court into a meeting place for heretics and liberal thinkers. In an official portrait painted around this time, Ercole II appears as an overbearing, middle-aged man with a prominent nose, large ears, high forehead and curly hair. He sports a neatly-trimmed goatee beard.[42] His hauteur may have come from the fact that he had been the despot of the duchy for fourteen years. But he was also an erudite man with a special fondness for music.

The names of Eleanora, Isabella and Lucrezia, the greatest of the Este women who had made their mark a generation or so earlier, still haunt us today: Eleanora of Aragon, the wife of Ercole I (1471-1505), for her intellect and courage and perhaps a role in bringing some of the Jews expelled from her country of birth to her newly adopted state;[43] her daughter, the highly educated Isabella, renowned for her diplomatic skill as well as an unquenchable appetite for books, paintings, gems, portrait medals, statues, bronze figurines, and cameos; and Lucrezia (née Borgia) who was reputedly involved in incest, Vatican orgies and murder before she married Alphonso d'Este, son of Ercole I, in 1501, and became an active participant in the brilliant court life of Ferrara at the dawn of the 16th century. Clever and adventurous women were hardly a novelty in Ferrara.[44]

Neither were Jews. Given its geographic position on a fertile plain and the resulting seasonal agricultural economy that required cash advances for its farmers, Jews had been welcomed since the Roman period. The Este family was unusually pro-Jewish. It had a tradition of providing a refuge for Jews driven out of Spain, Naples, Milan, Central Europe and Bohemia. Este rulers even discouraged the popular medieval practice of having friars preach anti-Jewish sermons—the sort that inevitably led to mob violence.[45]

There was certainly no Jewish ghetto in Ferrara. Rather, Jewish intellectuals—printers, poets, writers, engineers, medical researchers and bankers—worked alongside everyone else. Jews held faculty positions at its university; a rare privilege in Christian Europe. With ten synagogues in lively operation, there was no more hospitable place for Jews and *conversos* in all of Italy.[46] Thus, despite her personal problems and long-term goals, Doña Gracia was about to plunge headlong into its teeming intellectual life. It would have been hard to resist.

••◦❧◦••

Along the Corso Giovecca, one of Ferrara's most important

streets, there is a midpoint where three imposing buildings stand at triangular points to one another: the great medieval castle known as the *Castello Estense,* a Romanesque cathedral, known simply as the *Cattedrale,* and, just a few paces away, the elaborate *Palazzo Magnanini.* One of Rossetti's architectural masterpieces, the *Palazzo Magnanini* was built around 1508 for Gaetano Magnanini, private secretary to Duke Alfonso I, father of the current duke, Ercole II. The palace (still standing today) had remained in this family of ducal retainers ever since.[47]

Doña Gracia's presence, holding the promise of generous cash infusions into Ercole's coffers at every turn and her worldwide contacts, was exceedingly important to the duke. Although she had temporarily lodged with her old friend, Sebastian Pinto, upon arrival,[48] the duke immediately cleared the way for her to take a two-year lease on this magnificent palace for the relatively modest sum of two hundred ducats a year.[49] He pursued the opportunity despite misgivings from members of the distinguished Magnanini family who made the concession simply "to favor him"[50]—suggesting how important it must have been to the duke to provide Doña Gracia with the finest possible accommodations. The lease, ending at Easter 1551, was signed in January, 1549.[51] The rent was fully paid in advance, and in cash.[52]

The Magnanini House, as it was then called, was more horizontal than vertical, spread over low two stories that rimmed a courtyard and loggia. Both the terra cotta façade and the main entrance archway—where carriages rattled through so their passengers could dismount under a *porte cochère*—were lavishly trimmed with white marble cornices, ornamental stone urns and floral motifs. The interior was equally splendid, the living rooms decorated with gilded and frescoed ceilings and walls. There were marble columns and statues in the formal gardens in the rear, cypress trees, an orchard, a vineyard, a granary, a bakery, a furnace, a storeroom for sausage meats, a cold room for butter and an armory, among other amenities.[53]

The organization of Doña Gracia's Ferrara household at this moment further reflected the grandeur of her living style. Her personal quarters were on the upper floor.[54] Her domestic staff consisted of a chief of staff, probably Christopher Manuel, who was responsible for her servants and personal maids. Wages and dowries for the women servants (which she evidently took on as a personal responsibility) were under the management of Duarte Gomez and Guillaume Fernandes, two of her most important business aides. Gomez also served as her in-house physician, having studied medicine in his youth.[55] The language spoken among the young valets and orphaned girls who waited on the "lady" was Portuguese. This suggests that Doña Gracia had kept up the *converso* custom of giving shelter and employment to the less fortunate of her own people, many of whom she had plucked from the ranks of the penniless refugees while still in Antwerp.[56] They therefore had every reason to be trustworthy, grateful and loyal.[57]

Consider the recruitment and financial arrangements surrounding two such servants. About a year after she arrived in Ferrara, she took in Clara Gonzales, a girl of about ten, and Hector Dias, an adolescent boy. Neither had living relatives to care for them. And based upon their names, both were assuredly *conversos*. In the documents setting up the arrangement, Doña Gracia agreed to provide food, clothing and other necessities in exchange for service to all members of her family, in Ferrara or elsewhere, for a stipulated number of years: Clara for twelve and Hector for eight. The terms of servitude were most probably based upon the age at which they would become legal adults. At that point Clara was to receive a dowry so she would have no difficulty finding a husband. The boy was to be given 22 gold scudi—sufficient for a good start in life.[58] Significantly, the document about Clara noted that she might have been otherwise forced to beg or starve. Both minors were also placed under the legal guardianship of Francisco Berra, Doña Gracia's brother-in-law through her deceased sister, Giomar, and a man who would continue to feature prominently in the affairs of the House of Mendes in Italy.[59]

Don Joseph, temporarily returned from his battles in Antwerp, rented a separate residence.[60]

Once established, Doña Gracia moved swiftly to reverse the decision of the Court of Foreigners and reclaim her leadership position at the helm of the House of Mendes. Perhaps instinctively, she understood that power not exercised is power lost. On January 10, the same day as the signing of the lease, a written request was submitted to the duke by one of her agents requesting, in the most obsequious tone, that she be permitted to continue to run the affairs of the House of Mendes as well as act as guardian to La Chica.[61]

Pertinent passages from Diogo's will were even appended to the document to underscore the basis for her authority. One passage hints at the uphill struggle she continually faced as a business woman in a man's world. She first reminded the duke that Diogo had full confidence in her "even as a female." She then noted that the authority Diogo vested in her was re-affirmed by the Antwerp courts and once again upon her arrival in Venice. Mindful of these precedents, it asked for the right to continue in this role "in spite of any law, custom, act or provision to the contrary." It ended with the hope that "other princes in their own states will concede such authority…with…grace"—possibly a veiled reference to the prior actions taken by the Court of Foreigners in Venice.[62]

Within three weeks she received her answer. On January 28, 1549, Duke Ercole II issued a decree re-validating the terms of Diogo's will.[63] It allowed Doña Gracia once again to issue orders and powers of attorney to her far-flung network of agents throughout Europe. The fact that it post-dated any decision of the Venetians courts became the legal prelude to unraveling those seizures that Brianda had begun several months earlier.

Eleven pages of notes accompanied the duke's decision. After he had carefully examined the wording of Diogo's will, "it became clear that Don (Diogo) had the highest opinion of...Dona Beatrice...and that in her more than in others he had placed his hope and trust," wrote the duke. Following an examination of Doña Gracia's record books, the duke further concluded that she had "so far used as much diligence and trust in the administration of the property, possession and affairs of her (ward) as anyone could desire...it (therefore) seems to us that the petition is right and fair and what she asks must be granted."

The duke then considered her unblemished business reputation. "(Nor can we) be insensitive," he added, "(to the) remarkable qualities of her character, her noble customs, her extraordinary moderation and her other rare virtues...(that) have made her name...distinguished everywhere." As a result, "regardless of the fact that Dona Beatrice (Doña Gracia) is a woman and that the duty of guardianship is prohibited to any woman who is not the mother or grandmother of the child...we...are compelled to make an exception."[64]

All of this placed Brianda in a quandary. When the news reached her in Venice it must have been patently clear that winning in court, as many defendants find out, is never quite as solid as winning in reality. The required deposit of 150,000 ducats had not yet been placed in the Venetian Zeccha. Collections were stalled. Nor did it look like anything would happen in Brianda's favor unless she took matters into her own hands, just as her sister had done. "So as to protect my poor daughter," she would later say, "I was forced to go to Ferrara (too)..."[65]

A private letter written to Brianda by Fenicio, the Old Christian emissary she had hired in Venice, explained the larger reason why. Fenicio made it clear that confirmation of the decision of the Court of Foreigners by the Duke of Ferrara, and even by the Council of Ten as the supreme Venetian authority, was critical to its wider validity. Yet neither ratification was easily obtained. Therefore, he had urged Brianda to "arrange (matters) with His Excellency," presumably in person. Meanwhile, he assured her, he would stay in Venice and monitor progress with the Council of Ten, although even these negotiations, he conceded, were falling apart due to intense lobbying by Doña Gracia's agents. Nevertheless, Fenicio promised Brianda he would write to France to assure those involved that the required confirmation should soon be arriving. With dramatic flair, he then ended his missive with a Shakespearean touch, "God save us from traitors!"[66]

The intention appears to have been for Brianda to establish residency in her own right in Ferrara and then petition the duke for an agreement that dovetailed the one in Venice, smoothing the way with an offer of 40,000 gold ducats.[67] It was hardly the kind of pocket change available to someone who had supposedly been left penniless in Venice, unless she intended to take the payment out of La Chica's inheritance or other assets she had repeatedly insisted were her personal belongings.

Meanwhile, the safe conduct which Brianda obtained from the duke to come and live in Ferrara shows the grandeur of her lifestyle, too. It incorporated a dazzling list of belongings that overflowed with the accoutrements of luxury only available to someone who was still living the life of a wealthy woman: dresses, bed coverings, embroidered cloth and cloth of gold, blankets, rugs of many kinds, paintings, draperies, beds, gold and silver pieces, vases, household and personal ornaments, rings, jewels, precious stones and books.[68]

But it would be months before Brianda could formally make the offer to the duke. She arrived in Ferrara sometime in 1549, six months or so after Doña Gracia.[69] And by then she found a city in turmoil. Plague—one of the most terrifying calamities that could befall a tightly-packed urban area—had broken out. Rumors ran wild that this "highly contagious disease" had come to Ferrara from Germany and Switzerland over the Brenner Pass, brought into town by *converso* refugees who were still traveling through that part of Europe on their way south from Antwerp.[70] Emotions ran so high that the duke was forced to take action.

On September 14 of that year, all new "Portuguese" immigrants who had arrived in Ferrara within the preceding four months were expelled from the city.[71] Initially they were required to live in isolation in the *Boschetto delli Ammorbati*, an area earmarked for people carrying contagious diseases. But the action was not taken without serious misgivings on the part of the duke. Before publishing the proclamation he sent a representative to explain to Doña Gracia how it had been impossible to act differently. He seems to have been terrified that she would explode in anger at seeing her people treated as pariahs yet again if he did not at least try to excuse his actions in advance.[72]

Samuel Usque, the *converso* writer then living in Ferrara, insisted that the expulsions were not only limited to new arrivals. Duke Ercole II "tried to placate (his people) by expelling *all* the Portuguese…in the city," he later wrote. "They left under conditions of great hardship and wretchedness, for the populace considered them contaminated and no one could be found to help them with their departure, even for a price."[73]

He continued, "The time set for their departure expired at night…And they were under penalty of losing their possessions (if they did not leave in time). Here in the darkness…you could see weary old men, with their boxes on their backs, falling in the middle of the street, too weak to bear their heavy burdens. Their frail old wives cried beside them and bemoaned their fate. Other people dragged the burdens they could not carry in anguish."

When they finally reached the port of Ferrara, he observed, they were attacked by guards who had been posted to protect them and their possessions. "With bared swords and spears held at their victims' chests," he wrote, "they forced them to surrender the little money they were carrying for their journey." At least, he noted, the duke later punished these guards for their disobedience and greed. Meanwhile, the ships' captains who were taking them to beaches outside the city, made them pay for their passage "with their weight in gold." Miraculously, he added, not one of them became ill—evidence, argued Usque, that they were not carriers of the disease. However, Usque failed to mention that some of them had indeed died while still in the city.[74]

The residents of Ferrara were so terrified, continued Usque, that they insisted it was not good enough for the *converso*s to park themselves on a nearby beach. They wanted them to leave the area entirely. Some set out for Turkey, many of whom were attacked by corsairs and pirates along the way. Others, he reported, "died unsheltered on Italian roads" since "everyone fled from them because they were rumored to be infected with the plague."

Usque concluded his account by trying to bring some meaning into their persecuted and wandering lives. He reminded his *converso* readers of a prediction made by the prophet Jeremiah centuries before—perhaps directed, he implied, at them. It suggested that because they continued to live life as Catholics, unmindful of the dictates of Jewish law, they were doomed to suffer over and over again. The verse he quoted would have had terrifying parallels to their own reality. "I will pursue them with the sword, famine and pestilence," he wrote, quoting Jeremiah 29:18. "I will make them roam in terror unto all the kingdoms of the earth and let them be a curse, an astonishment, a mockery and a reproach among all the nations wither they shall go tired and harried." In their expulsion from Ferrara, and again in the larger exile from Portugal, that fearful prophecy, lamented Usque, had surely been fulfilled.[75]

If that were not enough, the openly-professing Jews of Italy, unaffected by the ban and with an infuriating sense of self-righteousness, identified yet another biblical passage to justify the *converso* condition. "For although they assimilated among those nations entirely," thundered the sacred words in Deuteronomy 28:14, "they will find no peace among them; the nations will always revile and beshame them, plot against them, and accuse them falsely in matters of faith."[76]

Typically, Doña Gracia was not going to allow such suffering to continue without making at least one attempt to fight back on behalf of her people. During the clamor, five prominent *converso* traders had been placed in quarantine, accused of being among those most responsible for the outbreak. She probably knew some of them personally. In any case, she petitioned the duke for their release. To no avail. Feelings ran too high. She was also probably involved in the initiative—led by a group of *converso* leaders in Ferrara around the same time—to transport three hundred of the exiled *converso*s to Valona (now Vlone) and Ragusa (now Dubrovnik) on the opposite side of the Adriatic Sea.[77] From there they could find their way to Salonika or Constantinople.

All the while the plague was purportedly making inroads into her own household, which had not been affected by the order of banishment.[78] Rumors began circulating that plague had erupted in the very suite of rooms in the Magnanini Palace temporarily occupied by Brianda and her entourage. Furious, Brianda insisted it was not true. Rather, she argued, it was another of those convenient stories that Doña Gracia liked to plant; in this case to undermine her morale by manufacturing the excuse needed to eliminate Licentato da Costa, Brianda's recently appointed chief of staff and strategist. Doña Gracia had insisted on dismissing da Costa and his daughter on suspicion of spreading the contagion.[79] The two were already on the way to Bologna when Brianda managed to bring them back. Another victim was Brianda's personal physician who was forced to leave for Turkey.[80]

What was really going on? Was Doña Gracia using the contagion to bring her sister into line? Probably. During da Costa's absence Doña Gracia begged the duke to intervene in a way that would prevent da Costa from returning, arguing that the *"Licentato"* would interfere with any opportunity for the two sisters to reach an agreement in their ongoing dispute.[81] Clearly, she did not like his influence over her sister. Brianda similarly approached the duke, but for the opposite reason. She pleaded instead to deny Doña Gracia's request, complaining that her sister had already taken everything else from her—her honor, her estate and thus her life. Da Costa's counsel and support was all she had left.[82]

Brianda prevailed. Da Costa was permitted to return as the result of a compromise arrangement worked out by the duke. It permitted da Costa to stay in Ferrara only during periods when his legal expertise was critical to the drafting of an amended agreement between the sisters. But in reality, once the door had been opened, it enabled him to stay longer. We know, for instance, that he initially managed to slip back into the city "secretly" one night, irrespective of formal papers.[83]

In apparent retaliation, Brianda managed to have the writer, Samuel Usque, who was close to Doña Gracia at this time,[84] jailed, after putting pressure on him to make pledges he could not possibly keep. It forced Doña Gracia to untangle matters yet again by seeking and winning his release. She did so by personally visiting him in jail and forcing the authorities to accept the fact that he had been bullied and was too afraid to say no.[85] Brianda moved out soon afterwards, probably in a fit of rage over the entire affair. By the following year of 1550 she had a residence of her own.[86]

Meanwhile Doña Gracia's sister-in-law, Anna Fernandes, the widow of Gonçalo Mendes, the third Mendes brother, was riding out the plague on an island in the river Po.[87] The university had closed down. The duke and his court had sought refuge in the countryside. So had a number of long-time Jewish residents.[88] The foulness of death permeated the entire city.

———••⁘••———

Throughout this terrifying period, Doña Gracia remained very much in control, not only within her own family, but as the leader of the wider *converso* community. For a start, during that plague-ridden summer, Don Joseph was once again headed for Antwerp, this time on community business. His current mission was to forestall the implementation of an imperial decree, dated July 17, 1549, that required all *converso*s who had emigrated to the Low Countries during the prior six years, and were believed to be secret Jews, to leave the Low Countries within a month. The decree had infuriated Antwerp's municipal leaders. They stood to see the very foundations of their economy slide downhill if it were fully implemented. And they had sought and obtained a temporary delay.[89]

Queen Marie and the Emperor Charles, no doubt fearful of their old adversary, arranged for Don Joseph to be detained shortly after his arrival. Part of his mission may well have been no more sinister than clearing up some loose ends in connection with the sale of Diogo's house, negotiations for which had taken place that spring.[90] Don Joseph was arrested on an Antwerp street by the night-watch and taken, under escort, to the island-based castle of Rupelmonde, still standing on the river Scheldt, not far from Antwerp. Both the *converso* merchants and Antwerp's leaders protested vehemently, insisting that either Don Joseph be given a prompt trial or released immediately.[91] What, after all, had been his crime?

Wary of repercussions from the merchant community, Marie and Charles had Don Joseph transferred to an inn near the Antwerp town hall. Once there, representatives of both the *converso* merchants and the Antwerp town leaders showed their contempt for the arrest by forcing their way into the inn and sitting down to eat supper with Don Joseph. Marie and Charles must have realized that they had blundered once again. A few weeks later, on September 11, when the Emperor Charles made one of his ceremonial visits to Antwerp, he used the occasion to release Don Joseph as an "act of benevolence." The decree of banishment for all *conversos* was also rescinded.[92] Even if Don Joseph's presence had merely acted as a lightening rod, or an excuse for a display of outrage, it had served the purpose for which it had been intended. This time around Doña Gracia and her nephew could chalk up a victory.

But, as they knew from experience, these sorts of victories tended to be short-lived. The attempted banishment of all *conversos* from Antwerp, and a similar decree a few months later that was enacted in Venice but also never enforced[93]—as well as the temporary one promulgated in Ferrara during the plague— must have made them both realize that a more permanent solution to the refugee problem was needed.

Thus, within the year or so, the peripatetic Don Joseph was placing a radical idea before the Venetian authorities: give the *conversos* one of the islands that belonged to the Venetian Republic as a territory of their own. While a historian writing about Don Joseph's proposal a century later implied that it was supposed to be for the "Jews" this is unlikely.[94] The Italian Jews had their own leaders and agenda. They would have resented *conversos*

like Doña Gracia and Don Joseph raising any issue on their behalf. More likely the historian meant *conversos*, since he also
mentioned a later attempt by the family to do something similar in Tiberias. Suffice to say the Venetian overture was rejected
with "scorn," as the historian put it, and nothing came of the
venture. But like any shrewd leaders, the pair did not drop the
idea entirely, merely biding their time for another opportunity,
in another setting, where they might stand a better chance.[95]

———••⚬••———

Sometime early in 1550 the epidemic began to subside and
daily life in Ferrara gradually returned to normal. Doña Gracia
was still squarely in charge. A trove of notarial documents from
this period gives us some insight into how she dealt with the
daily matters that came before her. For one, the infamous Gaspare
Ducchio—the Florentine merchant who had tried to persuade
Queen Marie to force Ana to marry a shady Spanish aristocrat—
had still not paid his debts to the House of Mendes. Doña Gracia
was now ready to give this long-pending matter the attention it
needed. That meant turning to someone who was actually in
the Low Countries and could confront Ducchio in person. So,
by notarial decree, she officially appointed a man named Gian
Stefano, originally from Ferrara, but now in Antwerp, to "receive and recuperate any and whatever sums of money, as well
as whatever else, the Magnificent Don Gaspare Ducchio owed
and owes to Dona Beatrice (Doña Gracia)."[96]

Among other banking tasks already under review was a deal
that had been made to improve the financial welfare of Anna
Fernandes, the sister-in-law and widow of Gonçalo—the woman
who had temporarily fled for safety to an island in the river Po.
Signora Anna, as she was known, had appointed Don Alvaro

Mendes, identified as a "relative on the paternal side," to assist in the collection of money owed from the days when her late husband worked with his brothers, Francisco and Diogo. Don Alvaro was to obtain "from the Mendes heirs" the money they owed Signora Anna from transactions carried out in Flanders, Venice and Ferrara. The mandate even granted Don Alvaro the legal right to make collections anywhere in the world, probably to protect Signora Anna should Doña Gracia go to the Ottoman Empire before these debts were fully paid.[97]

By March 1550, Doña Gracia had agreed to loan 5,100 ducats from the House of Mendes to cover these obligations. The goal was to use the cash "to trade, deal and bargain" in such as way as to increase the amount for the benefit of Signora Anna.[98]

A companion document, also dated March 5, precisely articulated the amount of money that had been set aside as credits for Signora Anna after Gonçalo's death. Signora Anna's agents were requesting the right to take possession of the entire inheritance on her behalf.[99] Up until then, Doña Gracia, under her stewardship of the family business, had been in charge of untangling the financial web. But five years had elapsed since Gonçalo's death, which had occurred October of 1545, soon after Doña Gracia and Brianda had fled Antwerp. And a great deal of cash due to Signora Anna had apparently still not been turned over.[100]

Like Brianda, or maybe goaded along by Brianda, Signora Anna's agents may have also resented having to go to Doña Gracia each and every time they needed access to a ducat or two that rightfully belonged to their client. They could have been equally afraid that Doña Gracia had every intention of taking Signora Anna's money with her to the Ottoman Empire. On the other hand, all these demands must have been terribly wearing on Doña Gracia. Taking care of relatives is always a thankless task. And she may have indeed been doing her best against preposterous odds.

In this particular document, Doña Gracia further agreed to release 13,700 ducats on Signora Anna's behalf, in addition to whatever had been dribbling in earlier. In turn, Signora Anna agreed that all of this was sufficient. She pledged not to come back another time. Nor would she ever require another examination of the account books claiming that errors in calculation could have occurred and even more should have been paid to her.[101]

The timing of this accord was significant. It transpired during a period when Doña Gracia was renegotiating with Brianda. There could have been a connection between the two requests. Gonçalo had worked a lifetime for the House of Mendes. Some of the money apportioned to Gonçalo could have included funds that Brianda claimed as belonging to Diogo's portion of the estate. Doña Gracia would not have wanted to pay Signora Anna solely out of Francisco's share. It would have thus been appropriate to settle with Signora Anna before settling once again with Brianda, which she was now under pressure to do as quickly as possible.

On January 15, 1550, Brianda had personally asked the duke to begin his intervention and help her regain control of the part of the estate belonging to her and La Chica—something he had promised to do when she first applied for a safe conduct to come to the city the previous year.[102] The figure mentioned was 300,000 ducats, a sum that is mind-boggling even if it only represented half of the known value of the total worth of the House of Mendes.[103]

Brianda had stressed the urgency of moving forward by approaching the duke on an emotional level as well as treating it as a matter of justice. In a rambling letter[104] that seems to have been written in a state of desperation, she argued that continued lack of control over significant capital of her own enabled her sister to inflict terrible psychological pain upon her. She likened being forced to live with Doña Gracia in the Magnanini Palace—due to an apparent inability to raise sufficient ready cash to rent a place of her own right away—to being in "jail."

Doña Gracia, she insisted, had even refused to allow her "a cheap bottle of ink" and a decent bedcover. And when she did find a way of moving out, by begging from friends and taking out a loan,[105] Doña Gracia would not even let her take along some of the household items she had been using. It was therefore critical, she urged, to reach an agreement fast.[106] What seemed especially upsetting to Brianda was the fact that some personal valuables had been kept from her since the time the family left Antwerp, despite endless promises that they would be returned: three boxes of jewels that Diogo had given to her and a chain holding a Portuguese coin of significant worth.[107]

Probably fearing the delay had already given Doña Gracia too much time to squirrel away money in places unobtainable even to a court, Brianda built in an incentive for the duke to move swiftly.[108] Not only did she offer to pay Duke Ercole 40,000 gold ducats out of the proceeds. She also pledged to give him half this amount within four months, assuming that he awarded her the guardianship of her daughter as well as the supervision of her daughter's inheritance, just as the Court of Foreigners had done in Venice.[109] She had probably made it clear that, unlike her sister, she had no intention of moving on to the Ottoman Empire, but would be residing over the long term in Ferrara with her daughter. This would mean—as would become evident later—that their assets would stay in Ferrara and be available to the duke in the form of repeated loans.[110]

But this was the 16th century. Matters could not move all that swiftly. In the interim, perhaps because Doña Gracia was concerned that a negative outcome could continue to delay collection of other debts, Don Joseph was formally appointed to represent both herself, her daughter, Ana, and La Chica in future legal matters or lawsuits, civil or ecclesiastical. In particular, Don Joseph was assigned the task of finally trying to pry loose that debt from Gaspare Ducchio.[111] If Doña Gracia had to place 100,000 ducats or more in the Venetian Zeccha, she seemed determined that it would not diminish cash at hand. It would also be made up of outstanding debts.

It was June before the sisters finally signed a new agreement. The setting for this noteworthy occasion was the imposing St. Catherine's room on the first floor of the *Castello*.[112] On paper at least, Brianda achieved her objective, based upon the substance of the 17-page agreement still extant in the Ferrara archives.[113] Why Doña Gracia agreed to cooperate is not known, although there are clues.

For one, Brianda had been interfering with the sale of the Antwerp mansion. The difficulties must have begun a year earlier in 1549. Doña Gracia had long taken the position that half the proceeds of the sale belonged to Ana and herself, as heirs to Francisco's estate. It was an argument that assumed that half of all Diogo's assets had always belonged to his brother, Francisco, since they had made their fortune as partners.[114]

The possibility that trouble had been brewing was abundantly clear from the fact that Duarte Gomez, Doña Gracia's agent who actually handled the sale, had been asked to provide an "acquittal and release from the widow of the late Diogo Mendes," assuring the three Flemish buyers that Brianda would not put forward any subsequent claims on the house "both on account of (her) dowry or any (other)claim."[115]

The sales contract even contained a penalty of 3,000 florins, personally payable by Gomez, if something were to go awry.[116] And indeed it did. Brianda refused to sign off on the sale, which ended up delaying the actual closing until December 1550.[117] At some point, Doña Gracia must have been so worried that Gomez would become personally liable for the penalty that she called upon one of great legal minds of the period, Don Marco Bruno dalla Anguille of Ferrara. In a tortuous defense that he must have known would have pleased such an illustrious client, Don Marco concluded that Gomez, and thus the House of Mendes, could not be held fiscally responsible for Brianda's independent actions.[118]

The Antwerp property was eventually sold for 16,000 florins—a sum that was probably equal to the same number of ducats. The buyers also agreed to furnish coin and some solid silver flasks and bowls with a guaranteed weight and appraised value, in addition to the florins which were probably being paid in money of account (credits at various merchants).[119] The idea of payment through the actual exchange of valuables had not gone completely out of style. Moreover, considering the total cost, it was no wonder that it took the combined resources of three merchants to afford the property. For now, however, the closing remained in abeyance due to Brianda's reluctance to sign a release. Doña Gracia may well have been eager to secure an agreement with Brianda as a way to gain control over the liquidation of such a valuable holding.

She may have also been under extreme pressure from the duke to cooperate with Brianda. After all, she was living in his duchy at his pleasure. And the duke remained one of the most steadfast supporters of the stateless *conversos*. So it would have been in Doña Gracia's interest to make herself amenable. The framers of the sisters' accords even stated that they hope that it would enable "the sisters (to) liberate themselves from litigations, discord and controversy in order to conserve the sisterly love between them."[120]

There must have also been ongoing negotiations during the months preceding the Ferrara accords because they begin by acknowledging an interim agreement issued by the Court of Foreigners in Venice some six weeks earlier. On April 24, 1550, the Court of Foreigners had repealed all of Brianda's rights emanating from their original decision of December, 1548—the one that had allowed Brianda to tie up so much of the money belonging to the House of Mendes. Such action had probably been a requirement put forward by Doña Gracia before she would even begin to negotiate. As far as the Court of Foreigners was concerned, there was no reason to withhold it—provided both sisters agreed to the change.

These Ferrara accords then list the issues upon which Brianda was willing to compromise. For a start, she promised to cancel and nullify each and every legal act that had been disrupting Doña Gracia's ability to collect debts and credits in the name of the House of Mendes. Brianda also promised that by December of 1550—six months hence—she would eliminate all remaining sequestrations and impediments to debt collection, which probably included signing the necessary documents for the completion of the sale of the Antwerp mansion. Brianda further promised "not to bother or trouble her (Doña Gracia's) person or belongings, nor those of her senior associates, Don Joseph or Guilluame Fernandes, in any place where they might live."[121]

In return, the guardianship of La Chica and her portion of the assets of the House of Mendes were to be turned over to Brianda, because Doña Gracia had "expressed the desire to go and live...outside of Italy" (the term "outside of Christianity" having been crossed out as possibly too inflammatory, given the tenor of the times).[122]

It was clear that neither sister trusted the other because the conditions under which this transfer was to take place were strewn with precautions. The most far-reaching was that Doña Gracia would remain in control until "six months after Brianda has legitimately demonstrated that she has lifted and nullified all of the arrests and sequestrations she had placed on merchants, bankers and other people of good credit."[123] For her part, Doña Gracia was required to deposit 100,000 ducats in the Zeccha in Venice within three months to cover the inheritance due La Chica when she married or came of age. This immediately reduced the original Venetian requirement of 150,000 ducats by a third.

The agreement also covered the return of Brianda's dowry and other funds from her marriage contract—money that had been placed under Doña Gracia's control at the time of Diogo's death. It was customary for a widow to have such sums returned to assist in her upkeep.[124] They were considered of such economic importance that their immediate return was frequently written into a marriage contract; yet another reason to leave Brianda embittered.

To further ensure that each party kept its word, guarantors were appointed—four bankers in Florence and five in Venice. They were responsible for making sure the deposit was made into the Zeccha and that La Chica later received her money.[125] The fact that the document allowed for supervision of the process suggests that Doña Gracia was genuinely afraid that otherwise Brianda might dip into the funds for her own needs. On the opposite side, Brianda seemed equally terrified that Doña Gracia would sneak away to Turkey before making the deposit. Thus, the very last lines of the document reconfirm the fact that La Chica, "will receive this money even if Signora Beatrice (Doña Gracia) were to be absent and leave Italy."[126]

But before the ink was dry it was evident that these Ferrara accords would be yet another doomed attempt at reconciliation. The Venetians were the first to make trouble. Although frantic diplomatic correspondence must have flown back and forth between Ferrara and Venice during the negotiations, the Venetians were reluctant "to accept agreements made outside their territorial jurisdiction," particularly when it came to large sums of money to be deposited in their Zeccha.[127] Had Doña Gracia reached the Venetians with bribes, or some other sort of pressure, as a subtle way to undermine the pact without alienating the duke? She was accused of such tactics five years later, so it was certainly a possibility.[128] Besides, one has to ask why the Venetians were suddenly interpreting the law so strictly after being perfectly willing to compromise only a few months earlier.

Six weeks later, on July 16, Brianda was up to her own mischief. She proclaimed herself the sole guardian of her daughter, irrespective of the terms she had agreed upon.[129]

There was little chance that "sisterly love" would develop after all.

Possibly as a result of that brazen act, the duke seems to have shifted his allegiance back to Doña Gracia. She was, after all, the one with the power, money and prestige that could do the most for his duchy. Or perhaps he simply collected his money from Brianda for concluding the agreement and went back to what he intended to do anyway. There was a lot of talk of honor in those days, but in word rather than deed. He was certainly benefitting from the basic banking services of the House of Mendes. On one occasion around this time Doña Gracia arranged the transfer of his regular papal taxes to the Vatican "at no additional cost"—provided, of course, the cash was deposited with her in advance.[130]

Anyhow, sometime later that year, or early the following one, 1551, Duke Ercole wrote to Diane de Poitiers,[131] the powerful French aristocrat who had been contacted by Brianda two years earlier through an Italian intermediary to prevent Doña Gracia from seizing Mendes money still in France. That intervention, as noted, had turned sour, tying up thousands of ducats. It had also involved the sisters in an ugly lawsuit that the intermediary, Fenicio, filed against them for non-payment of services rendered. Unable to get satisfaction, Fenicio had subsequently attempted to seize funds that were part of La Chica's personal inheritance, as well as funds that belonged to Doña Gracia and Ana as part of their inheritance from Francisco.[132]

The duke's letter appeared to be designed to help Doña Gracia regain control over their frozen assets in France, have the suit dropped and wriggle out of a damaging situation. The other point likely to have been raised would have been a reopening of negotiations for the unpaid royal loans totaling at least 150,000 ducats that the French court still owed the House of Mendes.[133]

In his letter, the duke cited his obligation to help the "widow and underage girls..."[134] Eventually Doña Gracia agreed in writing on April 10, 1551, to settle with Fenicio for an undisclosed sum of money "and put an end to the dispute." The large unpaid French loan must have figured heavily in her decision to settle, as well as the backing that Fenicio had received from Diane de Poitiers. For Doña Gracia admitted "she had no hope of a positive outcome…(due to) the great favor her adversaries enjoy in the kingdom of France."[135]

Diane de Poitiers did, in fact, accept the duke's pleas to intercede with the French authorities on Doña Gracia's behalf, possibly because of a gift of 30,000 ducats from the House of Mendes received at the same time. A royal decree, signed in Amboise on April 30, 1551, and confirmed by the French parliament in Paris a short while afterwards, acknowledged Doña Gracia's claims to Mendes funds still in France.[136] As a result, more than 100,000 ducats belonging to the House of Mendes —formerly confiscated on the grounds that Doña Gracia had clearly shown her intentions to become a Jew—was returned to the books as a genuine debt of the crown. It all smacks of unscrupulous dealings on the part of Diane de Poitiers, although not without precedent in dealing with Jews. For, after arranging for the confiscation for the benefit of France, Diane de Poitiers then arranged to have the amount reinstated for a "fee" of 30,000 ducats.[137]

However, like so many official decrees at the time, it did not mean that the money in France was immediately forthcoming. Though the decree could help release funds held privately by merchants, it could not do much for the outstanding royal loan. That would take another battle, fought by Don Joseph at a later date.[138]

It would be nice to think that Diane de Poitiers and Doña Gracia had enough in common to treat each other with respect. Both women were involved in business and the power politics of their day. Rather, Diane de Poitiers' actions show that she treated Doña Gracia disdainfully, as just another Jew ripe for exploitation.

CHAPTER 11

Patron of the Arts

There was more to the survival of this "remnant" of the Jewish people than simply saving bodies. In the enlightened and cultured milieu that characterized Ferrara during the late Renaissance, Doña Gracia seized the opportunity to nurture the talents of her own people in a way that could produce works capable of enriching their souls and restoring hope to their forlorn and outcast lives.

Qualities that had lain dormant over prior years as Doña Gracia struggled to establish herself as a leader now reemerged. In a moving dedication to her warmth and compassion, composed during her stay in Ferrara, Samuel Usque described her as "the heart in the body of our people…(who has) always shown that you feel our people's sufferings more poignantly than anyone else." He insisted he was not just saying this "out of blind devotion" because he had become a protégé. He truly believed, he said, that "your name and the memory of your goodness will forever be a part of the marrow of (our) bones."[1]

No fewer than four books published almost immediately

following her departure from Ferrara contain very personal dedications to these qualities of leadership: Ortensio Lando's satire
Dialogo..., published in Venice in 1552; Usque's historical lam-
entation for the Jewish people entitled *Consolation for the Tribulations of Israel*, published in Ferrara in 1553; the *Ferrara Bible*, a
translation from Hebrew into Spanish, also published in Ferrara
in 1553; and Bernardim Ribeiro's pastoral novel *Menina e Moça*,
published in Ferrara in 1554. Two additional authors, Alonso
Nuñez de Reinoso and Girolamo Ruscelli speak gratefully of
her patronage, too.[2]

Further dedications imply that she supported the printing
house of Abraham Usque (probably a cousin or brother of
Samuel Usque) and his partner Yom Tob Athias, based in Ferrara
during the early years of the same decade.[3] She was equally supportive of the prestigious printing house of Gabriel Giolito de
Ferrari in Venice, which flourished around this time but ceased
publishing after 1553. Since this was exactly one year after Doña
Gracia left Italy it suggests a severing of financial support once
she was no longer in Europe.[4]

Even inside her own household, the university-educated
Duarte Gomez was spending spare moments translating into
Spanish some of the more notable verses of Petrarch, the Italian
humanist and bibliophile considered the father of the Renaissance. Before fleeing Portugal at the onset of the Inquisition,
Gomez had been a lecturer in the humanities, philosophy and
medicine.[5]

These are merely the literary works that can be traced back
to her. Much more must have been lost as a result of her frequent relocations, or the need to keep the true name of the patron hidden from public view. Though Doña Gracia was
fascinated by Renaissance advances in science and medicine, as
we shall see, nothing came close to her passion for printing and
publishing.

But why concentrate upon printing and not, say, art? After all, fabulous painters like Dosso Dossi were creating breathtaking canvases in Ferrara under the support of patrons. Superlative architects such as Rossetti had been handed handsome sums to design buildings that in themselves were works of art.

Even before the Renaissance, wealthy and aristocratic women —Christian or Jewish—had been able to wield considerable influence by favoring the creation of books, above all else. They used books to pass along to the next generation aspects of their culture or religious beliefs that they felt were important. They commissioned books as wedding presents for their daughters. They commissioned vernacular translations of religious books to help less-educated women follow Latin church ritual. By doing so, they undermined the stranglehold that the male clergy maintained over their congregations. Indeed, some scholars maintain these books became a key element in the spread of the Reformation.[6]

Jewish women had been similarly involved in copying, printing and publishing devotional and other works as a way of influencing a religious, spiritual and intellectual life that was otherwise closed to them.[7] A wonderful tale is told of a Jewish woman in the early 13th century. One day, her husband offered her a gold piece with which to buy a new dress, whereupon the woman decided she had better uses for the money. She recommended that her husband allow her, "to purchase a book or hire a scribe to copy a book for lending to students…" Another story in the same collection tells of a woman who withheld sex from her miserly husband until he agreed to purchase books.[8]

For Doña Gracia to direct her energies towards publishing was thus a continuation of a long tradition and particularly appropriate in Ferrara. It had been the city-state that had nurtured Isabella d'Este, one of the greatest supporters and collectors of books during earlier decades of the Renaissance. Besides, art and architecture were best fostered by those who were permanently rooted. Books, by contrast, could more easily be transported from place to place.

The works she supported show her deep interest in transmitting a Jewish heritage to a generation that had lost contact with its history, beliefs and culture, and was in need of guidance and inspiration. She chose themes and language that would be easily accessible to the masses of people who no longer knew Hebrew, or had not been taught Latin. The fiction she supported heightened awareness of the pain of the *converso* wanderer, and was a socially acceptable way for her to articulate her own anguish. Maintaining a tight focus also demonstrated the classic pattern of someone who has inherited a fortune, rather than building it: she rarely spent her ducats indiscriminately.

The *Ferrara Bible* was one of the earliest works dedicated to her "because," noted the inscription, "your greatness deserves it and because your own birth and love of your land imposes this well-deserved obligation."[9] It rolled off the Ferrara presses of Yom Tob Athias and Abraham Usque two years after she had left the city, billing itself as a meticulous translation by experts from the Hebrew—"so rare a work never before known to this day." Such praise, however, is more 16th century hyperbole than fact. Before the exile, Iberian Jews had already created translations using Latin rather than Hebrew characters. The special value of this particular volume was that it drew upon a Judeo-Spanish dialect in wide use at that time and thus easy for *converso*s to follow. With slight variations, it became one of the most widely reprinted Bibles among the powerful Jewish community to emerge in Amsterdam a century later, some of whom were descendants of the "Portuguese merchants" of Antwerp in the days of Diogo and Doña Gracia.[10]

The *Ferrara Bible* was printed on two different types of paper and in two paper sizes, suggesting a concern about giving it the widest possible appeal. A certain number of copies were respect-fully dedicated to Duke Ercole II. And it was prudently edited so it could serve as part of the Christian Bible too. The title page carefully pointed out that it had been "seen and examined by the Office of the Inquisition." The front cover sported an elabo-rate design, the center of which was a lively drawing of two tall ships with elevated hulls and lateen sails—similar in style to those used by Christopher Columbus. They were being tossed off course and damaged, albeit not sunken, by an angry sea—a metaphor, no doubt, for *converso* life.

A touching note of appreciation in a commemorative edi-tion, published in Culver City, Calif., in 1992, best sums up the aims and impact of this work. "Our edition," say the modern writers, "was prepared as a tribute to the House of Gracia and Joseph Nasi who, in Italy and (later) in the Ottoman Empire, embodied the (ultimate in) spiritual resistance to persecution and forced conversion, the unshaken will to offer new hope and consolation for the…exiles who kept harboring in their hearts their bitter-sweet love for Spain and the Spanish language."[11] And, they might have added, helped the *conversos* reach back into the biblical depths of their Jewish souls. For during the same years—1552 to 1555—the same press was also turning out prayer books and other Jewish liturgical works in Judeo-Spanish.[12]

For *converso*s who continually asked why they had been singled out for such a troubled and rootless life—there were answers in Samuel Usque's *Consolation for the Tribulations of Is-rael*, a sort of guide for the perplexed, published the same year by the same press in Portuguese. Usque opened by recounting the misfortunes that had dogged the Jews since biblical times. Summarizing the ethnic history of the Jews from the late bibli-cal period through the Middle Ages, he pointed out that each and every time the Jews had swayed towards idolatry (then equated with Christianity as well as paganism) they had been made to suffer for this "sin." But, he assured his readers, the suffering of the current generation had been so severe that it had now purged those sins forever. God's favor was still with them. To buttress his point he reminded his readers that mightier nations like Greece, Rome, Egypt and Persia had all been wiped out. Not Israel. Though bruised and battered she still lived, albeit in exile.

And, he exhorted, signs of an imminent rebirth were all around, starting with the rise to power of the Ottoman Turks whose beckoning "gates of liberty...(allow you) to fully practice your Judaism" once again without fear. Ottoman power was also beginning to trammel Israel's current enemies in Christendom. Other blessings had arrived, he noted, in the form of support from rulers like Duke Ercole and leaders like Doña Gracia. The time was ripe for Israel's fortunes to change. The long-awaited messianic era was about to dawn. But to fully participate required remaining steadfast to the teachings of one's ancestral faith.

To the floundering *converso*s who were being harangued by a church that continually insisted that the might of Christianity showed that it was truly the righteous path, these spirited words must have surely helped instill a renewed pride in their own heritage, and consolation for their tormented souls. A year later at least one copy was being eagerly circulated among the family and friends of a *converso* family in Bristol, England. It had been sent there by fellow *converso*s living in London after being shipped from Italy. Doña Gracia was remembered as being associated with the book, although the eyewitness recounting the episode had not been in Italy and was therefore not very sure of her role.[13]

Doña Gracia's support of Ortensio Lando is also revealing. It can be understood by assuming she was someone with a lively sense of humor who liked practical jokes—a clue to such a predilection being the wild stories she invented whenever she found herself in a tight corner. A sharp wit also would have been in keeping with a strong intellect. Lando, a native Italian from an Old Christian family, was a man whose unorthodox religious beliefs scandalized many. A sworn enemy of dogma, he was willing to admit Italy's faults. He was also a satirist who claimed he lived happily (in a possible homosexual relationship) in a "hospital for madmen."[14]

His outrageous iconoclasm would have appealed to someone like Doña Gracia who was forced to live life forever on the edge. He gave voice to thoughts she would have never dared to utter. One of his works is purportedly a letter from a noble Christian woman to the sultan. She is appealing for help to rescue her husband from the prisons of the duke of Ferrara at the improbable moment when the sultan's fleet is about to smash Christendom—a "letter" that has been viewed an inside joke among the circle of writers surrounding Doña Gracia.[15]

Another work by Lando, *Due Panegirici nuovamente composti....*, was a tribute to women, specifically two of the most distinguished Italian women of the day. Curiously, however, it was dedicated to Don Joseph rather than to Doña Gracia. In dedicating the story of *S. Marchesana della Padulla* to Don Joseph, Lando noted (in the florid prose of the day), "I present you with a portrait of a most unique woman…whose wit amazes me with it's good judgement, whose valor stupefies me and whose goodness brings me such great happiness. Now, you all (possibly meaning Doña Gracia and Don Joseph) who have contemplated the best qualities that the women have in Spain, Flanders and France..(I marvel at how) they become religious without superstition, modest without pretense, liberated without affectation, kind-hearted without flattery and generous without any sort of boastfulness…"[16]

Girolamo Ruscelli, a friend of Lando, was also a native Italian and apparently of Old Christian descent. He had probably been introduced into these circles by Duarte Gomez who was mentioned several times in his writings.[17] Together, Ruscelli and Lando would have helped allay suspicion that the Mendes family only supported its own. In Ruscelli's dedication to Doña Gracia, dated April 27, 1552, Ruscelli talked about "the kindness in her soul." Although elaborate tributes were typical of language used at this time to flatter patrons, the same sentiments are so often repeated that there is a sense that behind the impressive words is truth.

Alonso Nuñez de Reinoso, like Samuel Usque, was a family friend although Reinoso actually lived in Doña Gracia's house in Ferrara.[18] He was a *converso* who may well have known Doña Gracia since her childhood in Portugal. His writings indicate that he was born in Guadalajara, Spain, a few years before the Expulsion. He too became a wanderer—fleeing first to Portugal and then onwards along the typical *converso* migration route to Antwerp and then to Italy. Yet Reinoso was not simply a friend. He spent time as a family tutor, probably for Ana and La Chica,[19] and served as a witness for notarial documents being signed in the house.[20] The closeness, respect and admiration he developed for Doña Gracia is mirrored in his works, even though they are actually dedicated to Don Joseph.[21]

In fact, the number of works dedicated to Don Joseph, as well as Doña Gracia, indicate her nephew's own emerging prominence—something that would become even greater after both Don Joseph and Doña Gracia arrived in Turkey.

Reinoso was a poet as well as a novelist. His most famous work, written around this time, was *La historia de los amores de Clareo y Florisea y de los trabajos de la sin ventura Isea*, a novel in Spanish about the sadness of the wandering life. It reflected many of the same feelings expressed in a more scholarly form by Usque.

For some, however, a novel with a plot would have been easier to digest. That could have been why Doña Gracia felt it was important to become his patron, too. Some historians have even suggested that the fictional patron repeatedly mentioned by the narrator, Isea, whom she calls "el gran señor," actually refers to Doña Gracia; the change of gender creating an added disguise, not unusual in the literature of the day.[22]

Reinoso had something additional to offer those who did not have the patience or reading skills to wade through a complete novel—a separate section, appended to the end, made up of seventeen poems that conveyed the loneliness, confused identity, divided religious loyalties and rootlessness of the wandering existence. Despite their sadness, these verses must surely have brought a smile of recognition to many faces. At one point, he even commented how life on the road also meant the lack of appetizing food.

His verses are constructed in a simple rhyming format that could have easily been learned by heart and chanted for solace among illiterate *converso*s. One of the poems has been attributed to Duarte Gomez's brother, Thomas, rather than Reinoso himself. [23] Thomas implies in the poem that Reinoso has become so beset by melancholy that the man can no longer eat, rising from the table midway through meals. Neither can Reinoso sleep. And to top it off, he is avoiding company—a state of mind that today would indicate serious depression. Gomez further suggests that Reinoso's patron might have become irritated by such behavior. He therefore begs Reinoso to stop endlessly bemoaning his fate and start enjoying life in Italy. But Reinoso says he cannot do it; as would have been true of so many of these troubled souls. It is a hint, perhaps, of Doña Gracia's own pragmatic attitudes and impatience with whiners, especially as the work sounds as though it might have been completed during a period of estrangement, perhaps as a way to help Reinoso return to the good graces of his patrons.[24]

Bernardim Ribeiro's pastoral novel *Menina e Moça*, published in Ferrara in 1554, is similar in style and subject matter to Usque. Its basic structure is a lengthy dialogue between a bride and her mother. Ostensibly, it tells the story of two knights who both fall in love, one of whom is willing to abandon his honor and beliefs (Jewish faith?) for the joys of material riches. It once again sounds like a parable on the confused identity and shifting fortunes of the *conversos*. Historians have identified veiled references in the novel to the crucial role that *converso* women played in perpetuating the faith.

Ribeiro was believed to have been a respected member of the Portuguese court before being suddenly dismissed in disgrace for reasons connected to his *converso* origins, or crypto-Jewish activity. He later reappeared in Ferrara where his novel was embraced by an overtly Jewish press, further underscoring the probability that the novel had a subtext.[25]

At least one historian believes Ribeiro belonged to the same circle of *converso* writers, including Reinoso, who knew each other even before they left Portugal. There are other clues in the fact that one of Ribeiro's poems was published eight years earlier in Antwerp; the same crowd following the same trajectory at the same time.[26]

Keeping company with these older, more established writers, would have been the son of Abraham Usque, one of the owners of the Ferrara Press. Known as Salomon Usque or Salusque Lustiano, the young man was working as an assistant in his father's printing establishment while developing his own talents as a poet and playwright. Later, Salomon Usque would move on to Venice where he would write for the theater. From there he would go to Constantinople where he would revive his father's printing house for a while. In later life he would write verse in Italian and Spanish, as well as commentaries on the political situation in Turkey that would find their way to the office of Lord Burleigh, a senior minister to Elizabeth I of England.[27]

Such a literary crowd, augmented by Yom Tob Athias and Abraham Usque, the printers, and talented people from other professions, were sufficient to create a foundation upon which Doña Gracia could develop a salon in the finest Renaissance tradition. Indeed, during her entire six years in Italy, her magnificent homes were known to attract men of science, law, medicine, printing, prose and poetry, in addition to her customary share of ambassadors and aristocrats.[28]

Another frequent visitor was Antonio Musa Brasavoli, university professor, personal physician to Duke Ercole and a man of science and medicine widely known for his observations and experiments that helped further knowledge in botany, pharmacology and biology.[29] His respect for her ideas and erudition comes through in his writings—works that were later translated into German and circulated throughout Europe.[30]

One mention of his conversations with Doña Gracia show up in a discussion he said he was having with his son, Renato, about a botanical remedy beneficial to the liver and intestines.[31] The ingredients were rhubarb and sugar in the form of little pills taken with a particular type of wine from Crete, or dissolved in chicken broth.[32] The source of information concerning the remedy, noted Brasavoli, was Doña Gracia, whom he characterized as "a most remarkable woman." She had given him some of the pills as a gift. Perhaps she had been suffering from her usual intestinal distress and was sharing her views on the dilemma with Brasavoli.[33]

A second reference concerns an extract from a plant named malabathrum (a derivative of cinnamon), that grows as a weed in India. Although known in ancient times and mentioned by Pliny and Horace, it had been abandoned over the centuries

and was no longer available in Italy. Brasavoli remarked that it
was Doña Gracia who alerted him to this particular remedy and
its history, as well as giving orders to her agents for its importation. It was so rare, he noted, that some of his colleagues doubted
that he was really able to obtain some of it.[34]

Doña Gracia was probably introduced to Brasavoli by her
close personal friend and physician, Amatus Lusitanus, who had
met Brasavoli after moving to Ferrara in 1541. Lusitanus had
joined a distinguished medical faculty at the University of
Ferrara—one of the rare seats of learning fostering subjects such
as anatomy that were not sanctioned by the church. Although
Lusitanus gave up the post in 1547 to move to nearby Ancona,
there are indications that he was constantly on the road and
therefore an intermittent visitor. Among others, his patients at
this time included the pope's nephew and the Portuguese ambassador to the Vatican—another example of the curious personal relationships with Portuguese nobles and senior officials
that thrived despite the atrocities being perpetrated upon the
conversos back in Portugal.[35]

Upon closer examination, it is less difficult to understand.
For one, the friendships would have provided an opportunity
for information gathering. They could also help foster an informal dialogue that could mitigate some of the worst excesses of
the Portuguese Inquisition. It had become so frightful that the
conversos remaining in Portugal had been protesting to the pope
about the unspeakable conditions facing each and every prisoner: abandonment for months upon a pile of rotted straw; limbs
raw from being manacled to a wall or stone floor; languishing
day after day in the isolation of a dank dungeon; constant hunger from lack of food and the rape of women prisoners, even
though they were ostensibly being held by a sanctified institution.[36] Who better to plead their case than a physician who could
gain the ear of a top official suffering from an illness that could

well have caused the official to fear for his own immortal soul? Money alone would not have been sufficient motivation for treating the enemy. Around the same time, Lusitanus refused to continue treating a member of a ducal family in Colonna, despite pressure to do so, for a far lesser crime—the patient refused to follow his directions. In that instance, he had stated flatly that no fee, no matter how large, could induce him to go back.[37]

Doña Gracia's familiarity and fascination with botanical treatments was no doubt strengthened from contact with plants being brought back from the Indies by her shipping agents. These new substances also captivated the attention of Lusitanus who, like Brasavoli, was writing books on medical botany and frequently referred to them. In one of his books Lusitanus even mentioned how, at a slightly later time in the Italian portion of Doña Gracia's life, she would spend 130 ducats to purchase a rare pyramid-shaped stone, the color of honey and the size of an egg, from a Portuguese nobleman who had served as a viceroy in India. Formed in the stomach of certain animals, somewhat like a gall stone, a tiny dose of this substance, taken with wine or water, was known to cure high fevers by causing the patient to sweat, or by inducing vomiting and defecation. Known as a "Belzahartic" stone, it was also used successfully, Lusitanus later noted, to eradicate worms in children and as an antidote to poisonous snake bites. The cunning Indian sellers repeatedly refused to divulge the specific species, although it was rumored to form, like a tumor, on the eye of a deer that had just fought and devoured a snake.[38]

In adopting these remedies, Doña Gracia and Lusitanus demonstrated the same open mind towards alien pharmacological treatments as the Iberian Jews who later migrated to the Caribbean; approaches that stood in stark contrast to the contempt for native remedies displayed by so many of the other European settlers who had nothing but disdain for the practices of infidels.[39]

———••⚎••———

Enlightened Jewish physicians like Lusitanus were far from unique. In fact, they were continuing an honored tradition of the Jew as healer and favored court physician that dated back to the early Christian era. An over-representation of Jews in the medical professions is a phenomenon that survives to this day. The Bible itself became the foundation. Filled with exhortations concerning physical well-being, its many nostrums were initially offered up as religious rituals, presumably to foster compliance. They included such well known requirements as washing hands before prayer and meals, as well as regular full body cleansing through bathing (the *mikveh* requires immersion up to the neck). Jews were supposed to don clean clothes for their weekly Sabbath observance and follow strict rituals for the hygienic slaughter of animals whose flesh they would eat. Certain foodstuffs that can readily cause intestinal problems, such as pork and shellfish, were prohibited. Infectious diseases, like leprosy, were kept in check through quarantine. Today we marvel at the foresight of these admonitions in an age that pre-dated scientific knowledge of the transmission of disease. Even the novel idea of a weekly day of rest, first introduced to the ancient world through the Bible, had healthy emotional and physical implications.

All but the weekly day of rest was tossed aside during the early days of the Christian Church. Instead of healing based upon the accumulation of knowledge, the early Christians rapidly shifted to faith-based healing. They were advised to call upon their saints for cures; and indeed often still do so. Particular saints were assigned particular ailments: John the Baptist for headaches, for example, St. Benedict for inflammations. Even today, there are over seventy specific afflictions for which one or more saints can be invoked for relief. Faith in the healing power of Christ and his disciples replaced faith in the healing power of medicine. Though the Jews called upon their God at such times, they were also required to do all they could to preserve life. By contract, the early Christian faithful were taught that it was more important to care for the soul than to save the mortal body (although church leaders, including the popes, were quick to turn to Jewish doctors whenever they fell ill).

Meanwhile, the Jews stubbornly clung to their health-giving rituals. It saved many of them in times of epidemic and plague. But the fact that they tended to die in far fewer numbers was mistakenly construed as witchcraft, leading to fraudulent charges, such as the deliberate poisoning of wells.

As Jews became increasingly dominant in Mediterranean trade throughout the first millennium, they added to their existing base of knowledge through their endless travels and their direct contact with people from distant places, such as India, Africa and the Far East. These communities provided them with a myriad of information about botanical remedies yet unknown in the West. Jewish medical knowledge on the Iberian Peninsula was further enhanced by way of the Arab world, where learning was far more advanced during the early Middle Ages.

The Arabs had translated and adopted the wisdom of the ancient sages, such as Hippocrates, Galen and their own medical genius, Avicenna, at a time when such knowledge was being scorned by Western Europeans, probably because it also came from men classified as infidels. Most of the educated Jews in these early centuries —at least those in the Mediterranean countries—could read Arabic. By contrast, most of the educated Christian community was still confined to reading Latin texts.

It was the Peninsula Jews who first starting translating the early Arabic texts into Latin. These translations paved the way for many of the medical advances that came with the dawning of the Renaissance. By the mid 16th century, physicians of Jewish descent, especially those from Iberian lands who had lived under the Arabs for centuries, were held in particularly high regard. It was also expected that someone with an outstanding reputation like Lusitanus would be far more than a physician. As a university-educated Jew, he was recognized as a scholar whose numerous medical books displayed an erudition in history, Jewish religious practice, a knowledge of Arabic, as well as philosophy. Surely a treasured addition to anyone's salon.[40]

------••⁚--••------

Duke Ercole himself was a guest at Doña Gracia's palace during this period.[41] So was the French ambassador,[42] although his visits probably had more to do with the large royal loans still outstanding to the House of Mendes.[43]

In any event, conversation would have been lively and ideas would have flowed freely, as they did at the nearby court of the duke, without fear of repercussions. The duke's enlightened attitudes fostered a climate of tolerance. Even concerns about nationality or family lineage were less an issue than in other parts of Christian Europe.[44] This permitted intellectual dialogue to flourish free of constraints. These evenings would have also been elegant. Wealthy *conversos*, as well as their openly-Jewish family members, were known for cosmopolitan clothing that followed the Iberian style: trousers cut in the manner of Seville, peaked bodices and flowing country skirts that purposely exposed a few inches of petticoat.[45]

There is every reason to believe that those who were now living openly as Jews and the ones who still lived as *conversos* mingled at these gatherings. The Jewish quarter of town was close to the *Palazzo Magnanini*. Unlike Venice, there were no restrictive laws that would have inhibited social intercourse. Samuel Usque, for one, became a regular visitor at the home of the Abravanels—the leaders of the openly-professing Jewish community in Ferrara at this time. Usque's book echoed the beliefs and ideas of its most illustrious member—Isaac Abravanel, the diplomat, scholar and mystic who had led the Jews out of Spain in 1492. The Abravanels had first relocated to Naples. From there they had gone to Venice where Isaac died in 1508. Later, around the time of the in-gathering of all Venetian Jews into ghettos, they moved on yet again to the more tolerant duchy of Ferrara. Isaac's only surviving son, Samuel, spent his final years in Ferrara. When Samuel died in 1547, he was in possession of his father's celebrated library of historical, mystical and messianic writings. Samuel's widow, the brilliant Bienvenida, probably made them available to Usque to help him compile the rich and detailed historical and religious background for his *Consolation*... Some say that Ycabo, the main character in Usque's work, was modeled on Isaac, since Ycabo's views were so close to Isaac's messianic ideas.[46]

Bienvenida, incidentally, was the daughter of Isaac's brother, Jacob. This meant that she had also married her first cousin—the same destructive marriage pattern followed by the de Luna-Benveniste clan.

One would have assumed that Doña Gracia became close friends with Bienvenida Abravanel—the one woman whose own circumstances most closely resembled her own. The highly intellectual Bienvenida, as mentioned earlier, had also taken over her husband's banking enterprise upon his death. She had similarly used some of her personal fortune to ransom Jewish refugees being captured by pirates in the Mediterranean.[47] Living only a few hundred yards apart, it's difficult to believe that they would have not have met. However, Bienvenida's contempt for *converso*s, including those who subsequently reverted to their ancestral faith, was well known and even articulated in her will.[48]

Thus it is more likely a certain rivalry developed between them that could have left both women inclined to maintain a cautious distance. In Bienvenida, Doña Gracia would have encountered her equal. And her prior actions showed that she so loved being in charge that she was not about to share power or prestige with anyone, even in community endeavors. Bienvenida may have felt equally intimidated. Certainly there seems to have been a sense of competition between the two.

In September 1550, less than two years after Doña Gracia and her representatives finally arranged for the *converso*s to officially live and trade in Florence, completing the overture that Cosimo de Medici had initiated soon after she fled Antwerp, Bienvenida paid 15,000 scudi to an intermediary to conclude a similar deal for one hundred Jewish households to settle in Naples and its territories.[49] Also in 1550, around the same time as Bienvenida had orchestrated the Naples concession, Henry II, the French king, was persuaded to grant the *converso*s sweeping new opportunities for settlement and trade in France, a move that was believed to have been orchestrated by Doña Gracia. Possibly it was a concession for those delinquent loans since the French were still interested in dealing with the House of Mendes, as would become clear when Doña Gracia arrived in Constantinople.[50]

Although Doña Gracia and Bienvenida may have met on important social occasions, there is therefore little likelihood that a warm bond developed. Besides, any friendship would have been aggravated by Doña Gracia's continued mask of Christianity. Bienvenida's banking business was paying a daily price for her family's open adherence to Judaism.[51] She might well have sniffed at Doña Gracia's stratagem, however pragmatic, viewing it as nothing more than another example of *converso* opportunism.[52]

Yet, as so often happens after a generational trauma, the next generation of both families did not harbor Bienvenida's prejudices. Her son, Jacob Abravanel, entertained La Chica and her husband, Samuel Nasi, soon after they were married in Ferrara in 1557.[53] There are notarial documents indicating business dealings between these younger people from that time forward.[54]

———··⋅⋅☼⋅⋅··———

Scholars have disagreed for years over whether or not Doña Gracia returned openly to Judaism in Ferrara, given the duke's invitation to do so and a safe conduct that included permission to have a synagogue in her home.[55] Our research indicates that she did not. For one, the safe conduct that she received from the pope more than two years *after* she came to Ferrara addressed her in the customary manner for a Christian—"to our cherished daughter in Christ, Beatrice de Luna".[56] Nor would the duke have visited her in her own home if she had been living openly as a Jew.[57] Further, her senior agent, Duarte Gomez, testified before the Inquisition a few years later in Venice that she was a Christian at this time, although "that which she was to herself I do not know."[58]

When she briefly returned to Venice before sailing for the Ottoman Empire, her life continued to reflect the circumstances of a noble Christian lady, rather than a Jew who would have immediately had to move into one of the ghettos. Finally, such an ill-timed "outing" could have had serious consequences for the collection of all debts still pending in the Christian kingdoms of Europe. The authorities, and possibly even certain merchants, would have used it as a pretext for nullifying any obligation—as she had already discovered in Antwerp and later in France. Indeed, after she and Don Joseph reached

Constantinople and made no secret of their return to Judaism, the French used it as an the excuse to dismiss, yet again, any move towards repayment.[59]

Courtyard of the Magnanini Palace in Ferrara, Italy

Photo by author

CHAPTER **12**

An Imminent Departure

N early two years after Doña Gracia made her detour to Ferrara there was still no sign of a genuine truce between the sisters. Or the likelihood that all outstanding debts would ever be collected in an efficient manner, given that Brianda continued to build hurdles along the way. Something had to give. Time was running out.

All around were ominous signs that even in Italy, the last stronghold of limited tolerance in any Christian nation (with the exception of some Germanic states and eastern Europe), the general mood was edging closer towards punitive dealings in regard both to *converso*s and Jews. The Protestants were growing in power and influence. And the Catholic Church, in a move that would later be termed the Counter-Reformation, was responding by becoming ever more repressive in its fight against apostasy in its midst. There was talk of herding Jews into ghettos in town after town. Venice had officially banished *converso*s from its midst in 1550, even though the ban had not yet been enforced. There were sporadic outbreaks of ethnic violence.

Ferrara was safe only so long as Ercole II remained alive and nobody dared predict what might happen after that. There were rumors of imminent public burnings of "blasphemous" Jewish books. Jewish physicians were being barred from caring for Christian patients. The Italian Inquisition was growing stronger and bolder. Economic repression against the Jews of Italy had become so harsh that by the end of the 1550's—only a handful of years hence—most of them would be reduced to poverty.[1] In sum, there were haunting parallels to Germany in the 1930's and Spain just prior to the Expulsion of 1492. As usual, some heeded those signs. Others (including Brianda) did not. What none of them knew was how swiftly the axe was about to fall.

Doña Gracia—child of an Inquisition era who had continually faced reality square-on—demonstrated once again an uncanny sense of timing. Against this backdrop she launched two new initiatives. Operating in tandem they were sophisticated in concept.

The first—a safe conduct obtained from the Vatican—protected her from the rising storm of anti-*converso* and anti-Jewish sentiment and even from her own sister. Early in 1551, she sought and won a comprehensive safe conduct from the pope to come and live in Rome or any of the other Papal States, although the privileges inherent in the safe conduct were to prevail whether or not she was actually residing in a Papal State.[2]

The document allowed her to bring along family, business, merchandise, wealth, servants and business staff. It provided immunity from arrest on any charges and expressly forbade any limitations on commercial activity. Most significantly, it permitted Doña Gracia and her household to leave at any time "together with merchandise, wealth, animals, sums of money, and all other things, even valuables, day or night, on sea or land, whatever the journey, direction or place, however unusual, without any impediment to property or person...." In short, she would never need an exit permit to depart from anywhere she happened to be living.

Moreover, these privileges extended "beyond the borders of this dominion" to cover "any other cities, lands...provinces and places, directly or semi-subject to the temporal sway of this Roman church." The privileges were to be sustained even if suits "criminal, civil or mixed" or "contracts and debts" were pending against her or any member of her household. Penalties for violating this papal directive included a fine of 2,000 "gold ducats" and possible excommunication. It was all done in the hope that nobody "directly or indirectly, tacitly or openly...hinder, trouble, harass, inflict outrage, injury...upon you, your merchants...with respect to debts, credits...," including "ministers of justice and all others...both ecclesiastical and secular."[3]

The document even had the potential to checkmate the Venetians who had already indicated they were unlikely to let her go unless she first agreed to leave behind the substantial court-mandated sum for her sister and her niece.[4] For it was drafted in a manner that would have allowed her to explore the alternative of leaving from Ancona, a bustling port in one of the Papal States that had lately become another key transit point for trade and travel between Europe and the Ottoman Empire. The corrupt Catholic Church was ever ready to serve any hand that fed it.

At the same time, Doña Gracia once again placed her Turkish card in play. She appealed to her agents in Constantinople, and possibly even to Moses Hamon personally, for a *chaus* to come to Venice to escort her and her sister (even though Brianda did not yet know it) to Ottoman lands, as she was now really ready to leave. [5] Having her plans conveyed to the Venetians by a representative of the sultan, rather than having them emanate from her own hand in Ferrara, was a shrewd move. Under Suleiman the Magnificent, Turkish power had reached its apex. Its armed ships had been regularly taking prisoners, stealing goods and creating havoc for Venetian galleys plying their trade throughout the Mediterranean.[6] Thus, making certain that the demand was made by the Turks, plus having a *chaus* physically present, would have made it unthinkable for Venice to prevent her from leaving.

Most of this can be gleaned from letters dated November 14 and 21, 1551, written by Ludovico Beccadelli, the papal representative in Venice, to a colleague at the Vatican.[7] Beccadelli reports, with a hint of surprise, that a *chaus* had arrived unexpectedly on the eighth of the month. Though everyone initially thought he had come to discuss matters of commerce, they soon discovered that he had been sent on behalf of "some very rich Portugese women, one of whom has promised her daughter to a son of the sultan's doctor." Beccadelli framed his words as if the sisters were already in Venice.

And indeed they were. During the previous months, Doña Gracia had sublet her Ferrara palace to the French envoy. She then returned to Venice, having apparently received word that the *chaus* was on his way.[8] In a flurry of banking activity that became yet another prelude to an orderly departure, she had also been busy relinquishing control of a handful of other financial guardianships that had been thrust upon her as head of the House of Mendes.

She had arranged, for example, for the release of an inheritance due to William Pinto, an underage relative of Sebastian Pinto, the long-time family friend and business partner of the Mendes from their Antwerp and London days.[9] To be certain the transfer was fully executed, William had to sign a document in Ferrara confirming that he had received all that was due him from the Mendes family.[10]

She appointed Agostinho Henriques to follow up on the April victory in France, whereby she had regained control over the family money still on deposit with merchants in Lyons. She also appointed a Venetian lawyer to represent her before the Venetian courts should there be a need to thwart, yet again, any attempted interference from Brianda concerning the collection of any of these debts. Nothing was left to chance.[11]

Brianda had immediately followed her sister to Venice. For, as she would say later, she was anxious to make sure Doña Gracia did not leave before *her* rightful inheritance and that of La Chica had been placed on deposit.[12]

This put the Venetians in a precarious position. The *chaus* had been commissioned to take *both* women back to Constantinople.[13] It had no doubt been a last-ditch device by Doña Gracia to take Brianda and La Chica along. But Brianda became enraged when she learned of her sister's continued refusal to back off. An official memorandum from the Venetian Senate to the Turkish court, dated November 13, noted that Brianda had asked to "be heard immediately" upon arrival in Venice. Trying to remain impartial, the Senators decided to ask both women to appear before them. Brianda came personally. Doña Gracia sent an agent.[14]

At the hearing, which took place on or around November 17, Brianda insisted "she did not tell (Doña Gracia) to ask for a permit for her…to leave the city, but rather that she would like to live and die as a Christian (here in Venice) and not a Jew," a crucial point noted in a letter of explanation subsequently sent to the sultan to explain why only one sister was arriving.[15] It was the same argument Brianda had used before to convince the Venetians that she was a sincere Christian in need of support, and that Doña Gracia was the hypocrite. Cleverly, the Senators decided to provide Doña Gracia with a permit to depart immediately. But they also informed the sultan they were not about to "force" Brianda to go against her will.

The idea that Venice was going to let Doña Gracia leave for Constantinople infuriated Ludovico Beccadelli, the local papal representative. He saw it as a slap in the face for Christianity. Here was a woman, he informed the Vatican that same week, who has "caused great injury to our religion by publicly leaving it to become Jewish by going to the sultan in his false religion." What was worse, he declared, the Venetians were about "to let her get by without any punishment." In a righteous tone of voice, Beccadelli declared that he could not restrain himself from speaking up about this outrage "as a Christian and a minister of the church," even though he did not think it would do much good. At least, "it relieved my conscience."[16]

That is all it did. The pragmatic and wily Venetians were not about to listen.

Meantime, they knew they could not trust Doña Gracia to settle informally with her sister before sailing, due to the underhanded manner in which she had sneaked away to Ferrara the last time they tried to pry part of her fortune from her on Brianda's behalf.[17] So to be certain that Doña Gracia "should not leave in secret from the city, taking with her the estate of Brianda and Brianda's daughter,"[18] they posted guards at the doors of her house in the nearby district of St. Paul.[19] In short: Doña Gracia found herself under house arrest.

The *chaus* was then called to the Senate and asked to send a dispatch to the sultan relating what had happened and why. That did not please the *chaus*. As Beccadelli would later point out, "his negotiations (were) not working out as he had expected (and) he had been unable to take these women freely."[20] In fact, the entire episode now became so messy that certain influential Venetians began to fear that an internal family dispute between two sisters could draw Venice into a war it could ill afford to fight. One can almost hear the grumbling along the Rialto in anticipation of a possible interruption in trade. "A few propose," wrote the ever-vigilant Beccadelli, "that we send both (sisters) to Turkey so that we avoid getting into a dispute with the sultan."[21]

By the next day, November 18, guards had been posted in front of Doña Gracia residence so that "the possessions that she holds...are not hidden or smuggled out." The same Senate directive further explained that "no one will be allowed to enter or leave the house other than the *chaus*... as guardian of her personage... whom we will concede permission to go and visit... when he pleases."[22] The concern on the part of the Venetians to avoid offending the *chaus* was palpable. Two days later he was awarded 500 gold ducats from the Venetian mint to cover "clothing for himself and his family" among other expenses.[23] Upon his arrival he had already been given a home on the Guidecca (an important island facing San Marco), a fleet of private boats, nineteen men "to accompany him" as security guards, assistants, a daily allowance, plus "all the usual comforts that are... given to ambassadors."[24]

By November 21 the Senate noted that "no one has been let out or in (Doña Gracia's house) for several days."[25] Inside her elaborately frescoed quarters, however, Doña Gracia must have been burning with rage, pacing up and down and weighing her next move. She would have known better than to activate the terms of the pope's safe conduct. That might have put the *chaus* in an embarrassing position, which she was not about to do. After all, the Turks represented her personal safety valve; the future of her people.

Yet a week of restricted movement was more than enough to change her mind. On November 27 she arrived at a decision, possibly after taking counsel from the *chaus*.[26] She told the Senate she would uphold the Ferrara accords that she had signed with her sister eighteen months earlier. Nonetheless, the Senate pointed out in a memorandum that it would be necessary to draw an updated agreement. In doing so, it revealed a weariness over the entire matter. "If Brianda does not want to accept these aforesaid terms," it concluded in frustration by early December, "she can leave and go litigate outside of our state against her sister, where ever she chooses or pleases."[27] The financial and commercial benefits that Venice had hoped to accrue by inviting the sisters to settle in their lagoon had now deteriorated into an endless squabble and a tinder-box.

By the first week of December the Venetian Senate was compelled to write to its representative in Constantinople, known as a *bailo*, about the behavior of the *chaus*, which had gone from bad to worse. Venice wanted the sultan to know the real reasons why they were having trouble dealing with the man. He had scorned the clothing allowance and other gifts and courtesies. He had begun using "strange words and expressions that were ungracious and offensive to our dignity and the great friendship we have with the (sultan)." And he had threatened to beat the armed guards provided for his protection. In response, Venice had withdrawn some of his privileges, including his daily allowance and personal boats.[28]

What had gone wrong? Was he terrified to return to Constantinople with only one sister and, as a result, only a portion of the great Mendes fortune? After all, the sultan's court was a den of intrigue. It was so corrupt that the Venetians were even required to deliver their regular diplomatic messages inside a bag of gold.[29] If a court official fell from favor, it was not unusual for the man to be poisoned or strangled, so that someone else could instantly grab the coveted post. The *chaus* may have feared that his security guards had been bribed to become his assassins, as regularly happened in Constantinople.

For it had become increasingly likely that part of the fortune would be left behind. By December 23, the draft of a new accord, based on the Ferrara model, had been readied by the negotiators for each side. Once again, Brianda promised to stop annoying Doña Gracia's business associates and tying up transactions "anywhere in the world." In return, Doña Gracia agreed to leave behind 100,000 ducats for La Chica's inheritance. Among other payments, an additional 15,000 ducats were to be given to Brianda to cover miscellaneous expenses, plus 1,500 ducats annually to pay for La Chica's living expenses and education.[30] The citing of education costs underscores the concern about educating well-born young women in Renaissance Europe. However, it was a long way short of the 150,000 ducats that Brianda had originally won from the Court of Foreigners and the 300,000 ducats she had demanded in settlement while still in Ferrara.[31]

Doña Gracia said later that she agreed to sign at this point, despite misgivings, because Venice had promised her "within eight days everything would be concluded and I would be rid of all the nuisances in which I found myself."[32] When nothing happened for more than a month, she grew increasingly angry. On January 11, in a statement presented to the authorities by one of her agents, she maintained that the Venetians had defaulted on their part of the bargain.[33] The Ferrara accords had not been ratified by Venice after all. Nor had anyone taken into account the 50,000 ducats she had lost in France due to Brianda's meddling. Moreover, she complained that Brianda was the one who was now delaying a resolution in order to manipulate Doña Gracia into making further concessions. Eight days later the Venetians issued a decree saying that the sisters were free to plead their respective cases in any court in the city.[34] The officials had done all they could to mediate—without success.

Matters were now at an impasse. The unhappy *chaus* may well have been recalled to Constantinople at this juncture, or removed from his mission in a more violent way, as no more was ever heard of him. Not until March was there talk within the Venetian Senate of receiving another *chaus* to act as negotiator—a Jew who had apparently been commissioned directly by Moses Hamon to help conclude a settlement.[35] Venice was delighted with the idea of shifting the burden of reaching an agreement to the Turks. This way, they could no longer be blamed, irrespective of the outcome.

The new *chaus* did not actually arrive until the beginning of June.[36] He went straight to work and by June 18 an agreement had been drawn up with the assistance of a skilled Venetian notary named Paulo Leoncini.[37] Rapidly confirmed and ratified by the Senate,[3] it covered the key points of a more detailed agreement, still extant, that consumes almost 40 handwritten pages and was dated July 19 and 20, some four weeks later, with additional notes carrying an August date.[39] With the conclusion of the agreement and the deposit of 100,000 ducats in the Zeccha to safeguard La Chica's inheritance, both Doña Gracia and Brianda were told they were now free to go and live where they wished. A warm note of thanks was extended to the new *chaus* for his excellent efforts.[40]

The 40-page Leoncini accords[41] provide a goldmine for financial historians of the period. In addition to their relevance to the lives of the sisters and the activities of the House of Mendes, they name many of the major bankers of the era, together with their affiliations. And they offer a glimpse into the financial dealings of those days, conducted as they were part in credits and part in specie, once again suggesting that nobody was yet totally convinced that true wealth could be represented solely by figures scribbled on a sheet of paper.

The range of the financial network operated by the House of Mendes was awesome in scope. Mentioned by name are Portugal, Spain, the Low Countries, France and Italy. The rest are lumped together under the all-embracing phrase "other parts of the world." There are interlocking agreements with bankers and merchants in all these places that had to be accounted for and supervised. To do so while fleeing from country to country would have required massive chests set aside for paperwork alone. The complexity of such a task must have been overwhelming, requiring a highly skilled staff and a genius for organization.

The thousands of ducats listed in the accords, and the guarantees needed so that debits and credits could be reliably shifted from place to place according to the terms of the settlement, were so complicated that at least one Florentine banker, Don Benedicto Bonacioffi Pitti, was listed as being present during the two days in July when the final touches were being made to the documents. In general, Doña Gracia agreed to deposit the controversial 100,000 ducats in the Zeccha for safe-keeping until La Chica was fifteen years old or married. Doña Gracia also agreed to reimburse Brianda 15,000 ducats for the maintenance of her daughter to date and pay her a further 1,500 ducats annually. Brianda was to personally receive 18,123 ducats as reimbursement for her dowry and other marriage commitments, plus accrued interest.[42]

Yet even at this late date Doña Gracia was not about to physically place those 100,000 ducats in the Zeccha before she set sail; mainly because she did not trust the Venetians to give up the money once they had it in their hands. And Brianda would be no match for such pressure.[43] Instead, a handful of merchants who owed money to the House of Mendes were given eight months to come up with the funds. It was they who were charged with making the deposit by March 19, 1553—eight months hence. Other debts were to be paid out of the proceeds of the sale of the Antwerp mansion—credits still on deposit in Antwerp. Nevertheless, it was a deal that Brianda must have found to her liking. Several paragraphs confirm her satisfaction with an arrangement that had the potential of returning all the money due her, with interest, from her original marriage contract. There was also written confirmation that she had regained full guardianship over her daughter. Interestingly, the portions of the accords concerning Brianda's marriage agreement and motherhood rights were composed in the presence of three local clergymen.[44]

Paulo Leoncini, the notary, was careful to make sure that everyone involved fully understood the content and scope of the accords. At one point it was noted that he even read them to the gathering in ordinary Italian, rather than the legal-style Latin in which they were drafted. Although barely 12 years old, La Chica was brought in to listen, presumably to ensure that she was fully aware of the rights she could exercise on her fifteenth birthday. This was also true of Doña Gracia's daughter, Ana. Also present were Don Joseph, nephew and business partner of Doña Gracia, and Guillaume Fernandes, her trusted financial expert. To maintain an excruciatingly even-handed approach, the negotiators arranged for the meetings to be rotated between Doña Gracia's house in the district of St. Paul and the home of Brianda in the district of St. Catherine; one day here and one day there.

The final segments, not drawn up until early in August, covered all past and future dealings that Doña Gracia and the House of Mendes might have with their agents. One of those appointed was Francisco Berra, the husband of Doña Gracia's deceased sister, Giomar,[45] to "obtain from his other brothers and sisters (possibly meaning *in-law*) the due share of the paternal property." Some of the funds that Doña Gracia had withheld may have therefore belonged to Brianda as part of a personal inheritance from a common grandfather—funds left in temporary safe-keeping with uncles and aunts. This could also help explain Brianda's prolonged outrage.

Also named as agents with full legal powers of representation were Agostinho Henriques, the family member delegated by Diogo in his will to step in if Doña Gracia could not continue at the helm; the aging Guillaume Fernandes and the indefatigable Duarte Gomez. One of their initial tasks was the supervision of the implementation of the accords. Henriques was also left in charge of following up on the myriad of outstanding French loans that still burned a glaring hole in Doña Gracia's portfolio.[46] As all these men were remaining in Italy, it must have made the lengthy meetings during the sultry days of July and August an emotional and bittersweet farewell. Doña Gracia was also saying a potentially permanent goodbye to La Chica, the girl she had nurtured through childhood and who was now blossoming into a beautiful young woman—a beauty apparent from a portrait medal that La Chica had crafted in Ferrara when she was eighteen years old; and which is still extant.[47] There was no guarantee they would ever see each other again.

Sometime before she actually left Venice, Doña Gracia requested and received a special exemption in matters of dress. As she had never suffered the humiliations of living as an openly-professing Jew in Europe, she had never had to live under the restrictive dress code imposed upon Jews in those days. And she was apparently not about to do so in the Ottoman Empire either, even though their restrictions for "non-believers" were mild by comparison; usually limited to a hat of a specific color. If she was finally to live publicly as a Jew, she seemed to be saying, she was not going to be debased by that act—a strength of purpose and concern for dignity that would help make her so beloved by the Levantine Jewish world later on.[48]

The right—extended to her entire household—included permission to wear "stomachers and coifs in the Venetian style." This would have allowed her to remain at the height of Renaissance fashion and instantly indicated that she was a woman of high standing at the sultan's court.[49]

Immediately following the completion of the official paper-work, she applied to Venetian authorities for safe passage to Ragusa—the important 16th century shipping port on the east-ern side of the Adriatic.[50] It would have set her down at the near-est point in the Ottoman Empire from which to make her way overland to Constantinople. It was also a key staging point for anyone involved in shipping at that time, and therefore a place where she could have been immediately delivered into the hands of the sultan's trusted guards.

Since the Adriatic was a hotbed of pirates, it was crucial for her to sail under the protection of both Venice and the Otto-man Turks. She requested a rapid departure, possibly because winter was approaching.[51] She may also have sensed that it was critical to get out before it was too late. That summer, Pope Julius III had ordered all Hebrew books in Rome handed over to the authorities for burning. Inspectors had been rifling through Jew-ish homes, throwing book after book into streets and alleyways and then burning them in a huge bonfire that was symbolically lit on the first day of Rosh Hashanah. By October, even the Ve-netians had ignited a mountain of Jewish books in the *Piazza San Marco*.[52] It was no better in liberal-minded Ferrara where copies of the Talmud were also being publicly burned.[53]

Doña Gracia was offered passage in one of only two Vene-tian galleys available at that moment.[54] This light, three-masted ship equipped with banks of oars, a high forecastle at the bow, and lanteen sails could harness speed with freedom of move-ment in any weather. It could outmaneuver almost any type of attack vessel—useful since Doña Gracia was making a voyage some 300 miles down a treacherous sea lane. The commanders of the Venetian fleet were summoned to provide whichever of the two galleys could be brought into the harbor most quickly for the purpose.[55]

The haste may have also stemmed from efforts to placate the powerful Turks. The Venetians were anxious to let the sultan know that they had done everything possible to avoid delaying her departure. Back in August, they had already written to their *bailo* to let him know that she was about to "depart shortly… so that you can prepare that which seems necessary" for the arrival of such an important personage.[56] Later they added, "We wished to aid her passage with our fleet to Ragusa… so as to serve the most excellent (sultan) graciously."[57] In a subsequent letter they even insisted that should she ever wish to return, she and her agents "will always be treated well and embraced out of respect for (the sultan)."[58]

———••✄••———

The moment of departure would have been highly emotional and stressful for Doña Gracia. She had not been able to fulfill the demands that Diogo had placed on her delicate shoulders concerning his wife and his daughter. She was leaving them behind at a time when Italy was becoming increasingly dangerous. She was also leaving behind her most trusted lieutenants and—for the moment –Don Joseph who would not relocate to Constantinople for another year.[59] Her only daughter, Ana, must have been upset too. There are indications in the terms of a will that La Chica drafted five years later that the two cousins were close. In that will, La Chica stated that she was leaving her controversial fortune to Ana if, at the moment of death, she had no living children and her husband had pre-deceased her.[60]

Doña Gracia was leaving the only part of the world she had ever known. She was surrendering a portion of the family fortune that she had always viewed as a sacred trust. She was leaving dozens of unpaid debts on deposit among merchants and monarchs that might never be collected. She was about to enter territory that was favorable to the Jews, yet fraught with barbaric dangers that equaled or surpassed anything the Catholic Church could serve up.

She was facing upheaval once again in a life filled with upheaval. There surely must have been moments of anguish, self-doubt and even terror as she ordered the members of her household to pack their chests yet again. Even the journey itself was alive with danger.

Yet it was also a time to look ahead rather than dwell on the past. And if she did stand on deck in button boots to peer over the rail and watch as the imposing vessel was rowed out to sea, it would be nice to believe that she was looking ahead towards the prospect of a new life among friendlier powers, and not backwards towards the symbols of Christendom rising above the public buildings that faced the Venetian shoreline; reminders of twisted deeds being perpetrated in the name of a gentle leader named Jesus who would never have condoned such behavior.

PART IV

TURKEY: 1553–1569

Portrait of Sultan Suleiman the Magnificent, circa 1560

CHAPTER **13**

From an Ottoman Perch

I have heard of the afflictions, more bitter than death, that have befallen our brethren... of the tyrannical laws, the compulsory baptisms and the banishments which are of daily occurrence... I learn of anguish of soul and body... brothers and teachers, friends and acquaintances, I, Isaac Zarfati... proclaim to you that Turkey is a land wherein nothing is lacking and where... all shall yet be well with you. The way to the Holy Land lies open to you through Turkey. Is it not better for you to live under Muslims than Christians?

Here every man dwells at peace under his own vine and fig tree. Here you are allowed to wear the most precious garments. In Christendom, on the contrary, you dare not even venture to clothe your children in red or blue...without exposing them to insult or being beaten black and blue or kicked green and red... Therefore are ye condemned to go about meanly clad in sad colored raiments. O Israel, wherefore sleepest thou? Arise!
—From a letter written by the 15th century rabbi, Isaac Zarfati of Edirne, to the Jewish communities of Europe.[1]

Centuries earlier, the Turkmen of the vast Eurasian Steppes—grasslands that stretched from southern Russia to the borders of China—had swooped down upon the ancient kingdoms bordering the natural crescent that makes up the Eastern rim of the Mediterranean Sea. These warrior horsemen were reputed to be able to accurately fire a volley of arrows backwards from their elaborate saddles at a rate of three a second, and hurl a lance at a speed that could pierce sheet iron. In time, they managed to overrun an area that spans modern-day Turkey, Asia Minor, North Africa and the Balkans. They also spent the larger part of the Middle Ages grabbing control of the fertile terrain and ancient trade routes that were formerly under the control of Eastern Christendom, otherwise known as Byzantium.[2]

They were a terrifying lot, these Turkmen: merciless in battle, swift as leopards, ready to snuff out any life that stood in the way of their holy conquests, or thirst for power, attained at all times, they would say, for the greater glory of Islam. On a more personal level they were known to be equally determined to match the accomplishments of Alexander the Great. So captivated was the 15th century Sultan, Mehmed II, by this idea that he even commissioned a biography of himself in Greek.

Armed with their fearsome cries, the ominous boom of their marching bands (an Ottoman innovation), a sense of divine mission and death-defying courage, the Turkmen so terrified any defending army that the enemy seemed to melt away, as though even the foe had come to believe that the Turks had destiny on their side. Turkish historians would bolster that belief by producing evidence that their leaders were directly descended from Noah. Subsequent sultans had no difficulty strangling their own sons or brothers to assure an appropriate transition of leadership. They were so utterly convinced they had been divinely chosen to be Masters of the Universe.

Their final symbolic and strategic victory over Byzantium came in 1453, exactly one hundred years before Doña Gracia arrived. After a lengthy siege and hand-to-sword combat, they took Constantinople, Byzantium's glittering capital city. The blood of the faithful—Christian faithful, that is—flowed through the streets as abundantly as rainwater. Their mutilated corpses bobbed out to sea like driftwood. Picking his way through the carnage, the commander of the Turkmen, Sultan Mehmed II—a fat and fleshy man with a reddish beard and a booming voice— rode on a white horse towards the immense doors of Haghia Sophia, the holiest cathedral in Eastern Christendom, built 900 years earlier by the Emperor Justinian. Upon dismounting, he rededicated the sacred site to Allah and his Prophet Muhammad. It was henceforth known, even to this day, as the great mosque of Aya Sofya.[3] After a thousand years of hegemony, the Eastern Roman Empire had fallen.

Besides being a spiritual base, Constantinople was a priceless commercial gem in a matchless setting. Lying at the epicenter of East-West trade, it offered an extensive deep-water port at the juncture where the easternmost reaches of the Mediterranean squeeze through a narrow waterway known as the Bosphorus, before flowing onwards into the Black Sea, the maritime gateway to central Asia. Overland camel trains and caravans carrying bales of silk, bundles of furs and other luxuries converged upon the city. So did merchants traversing the spice routes to and from the Orient. It was the ultimate crossroads of the known world. It was also a booty-rich treasure-house filled with gold, precious stones, ancient manuscripts and the classical sculpture for which Byzantium had long been famous. It was a prize beyond imagining.

But these Turkmen knew more than how to fight and conquer. They knew how to manage a burgeoning empire. Beginning with Osman Gazi, the ruler who would give his name to the Empire (Ottoman in English; Osmanli in other languages), they produced a series of outstanding sultans who were able to create order out of chaos and allow an assortment of ethnic groups and religions to preserve their distinctive heritage while flourishing for six centuries under a single canopy: Greeks,

Franks, Kurds, Serbs, Arabs and Armenians, among others.

One of their secrets was to harness the diverse skills of these diverse people for everyone's benefit, selecting the best customs, skills, talents and manners from among all the nations, rather than cursing their differences. Ottoman culture soon became a luxuriant amalgam of Arabic script (for their steppe-based, Ural-Altaic tongue), Persian ceremony, Byzantium pageantry and Greek learning. Though none of the minorities was ever permitted to achieve the same status as the Turks themselves, unless they converted to the Muslim faith, they were prized and promoted and even welcomed in marriage into the inner sanctum of the Sublime Porte, the name given to the reigning sultan's court.[4]

All of which opened new opportunities for the scattered Jewish communities that had been in the region since the biblical period. Under centuries of Byzantine rule they had suffered the same humiliations and restrictions imposed upon Jews in every other part of Christendom—the Eastern Orthodox Church having been as contemptuous as Western Christendom.

The Turks looked upon them in a different light. Here was another minority group with much to contribute. As they were not Christian, they could be counted on to be more reliable than any of the Eastern Orthodox Christians the Turks had been conquering. They could even act as a counter-force to that population, since the Christians were constantly trying to convert the Turks.

The Jews were also experienced traders. They could provide the merchant class that the Turks, still a nomadic, warrior and peasant people, were lacking.[5] The Jews were accustomed to speaking several languages and could help as translators or *drago-*

men—a vital skill in a multi-lingual empire. They had banking and writing skills and international trading contacts among their kinsmen in other countries. And they could act as a buffer in any district or city where the presence of too many Christians posed a security risk.

All they asked from their new masters in return was to be permitted to live in their own communities and be governed by their own internal legal code—a measure of autonomy that the multi-cultural, multi-national flavor of the Ottoman Empire was fostering anyway. Besides, as far as the Muslims were concerned, the Jews, like the Christians, considered Abraham as their patriarch and honored some of the same prophets. They deserved to be treated as protected peoples or *dhimmi*. Though the Jews lamented the fact that they were soon forcibly being transferred to cities where their presence and skills were most in demand— a system of mandatory relocation the Turks called *surgun*—they nonetheless flourished.

The letter (quoted above) that Rabbi Isaac Zarfati wrote to his countrymen in other parts of Europe, especially Germany, around the time of the conquest of Constantinople, may therefore not have been an isolated act of good intention. Historians now believe it was written at the behest of the sultan.[6] The aim was to dilute the local Christian population with reliable and grateful Jewish immigrants. Zarfati may have initially raised this idea with the sultan. But there is no doubt that the tidal wave of Jewish immigration that followed could not have been possible without the sultan's prior knowledge and approval. And the sultan would not have agreed unless it offered him some political advantage.

Jews were soon filtering in from the Iberian Peninsula, Germany, Italy, Sicily, Bavaria, Slovakia, Hungary, Poland and other places that were becoming less and less hospitable. The expulsion from Spain in 1492 created the largest and most educated

group of refugees. Some reports say the sultan even sent his admiral, Kemal Reis, with Turkish ships to ferry as many as he
could carry to the other end of the Mediterranean.[7] These immigrants were followed in subsequent decades by the *conversos*
fleeing the Inquisition. Very soon, Spanish culture and the Ladino language of the incoming Iberian Jews eclipsed the indigenous Jews,[8] who spoke Greek, and those from Ashkenaz, who
spoke a German dialect eventually called Yiddish. There were
only 3,000 Jews in Constantinople before 1492. By 1510 there
were 8,000.[9]

By 1553, the time of Doña Gracia's arrival, Jews were firmly
rooted in the public life of the Empire and positions of authority. Their chief rabbi was considered a high state official—higher
even than the Patriarch of the Greek Orthodox Church.[10] Jews
minted coins. They purchased concessions to collect customs
duties down by the wharves. They became tax farmers, paying
the sultan a guaranteed sum in exchange for the right to collect
taxes in a certain region. Sometimes they collected more, which
they could keep as profits, and sometimes they came up short.
Many of these enterprises required partnerships or syndications
to pay the substantial sums required by the government for the
rights or monopolies. The ability of so many of them to afford
such enterprises attested to their rising prosperity.[11]

Jewish physicians, especially those from Spain with an honored tradition of Arab and botanical treatments, were favored
by the sultan and his harem. At least one of them, Moses Hamon,
who had intervened on behalf of Doña Gracia while she was
still living in Italy, was described by a contemporary as a "personage of great authority... esteemed... for his goods (and) knowledge and renowned for his honor."[12] Hamon had risen to a
position where he became more diplomat than physician.

Jewish women were also prominent at court. Some years
earlier, Helga, a Jewish woman from Hungary, had married Sul-

tan Selim I. In time she became the mother of Sultan Suleiman the Magnificent, ruler at the time of Doña Gracia's presence in the Empire.[13] Then there was Esther Kyra, mentioned earlier as one of several Jewish women who served as business manager for the women of the harem. "If you wish to stand in high honor on the sultan's threshold," moaned a Turkish poet during the reign of Mehmed II (1451-1481), "You must be either a Jew, a Persian or a Frank (Western European)."[14]

There was a flowering of Jewish learning, especially after the arrival of celebrated scholars from Germany and Spain. Books that had been started in Spain were completed in Turkey. Aided by this influx of learned men, Jewish schools and academies sprung up seemingly overnight. There was a blossoming of works on Jewish law.[15]

Their teeming and prosperous presence was noted by several travelers. Nicholas Nicolay, a chamberlain to the king of France who was in Constantinople with the French ambassador around the time of Doña Gracia's arrival, was in awe, although he was quick to reflect the prevailing view of his countrymen that the Jews remained a "detestable nation." He conceded nonetheless that, "They have in their hands...the greatest (amount of) merchandise and ready money...in all Levant." Likewise, he added, their homes are more richly furnished than those of any other group in Constantinople. Their artisans, he continued, especially the *conversos,* are "most excellent." They "have set up printing not before seen in those countries," and learned to speak "all the other languages used in the Levant which serveth them greatly" for commerce and diplomacy. However, he lamented that the *conversos* arriving regularly from Spain and Portugal were doing great "damage to Christianity" by teaching the Turks how to manufacture "engines of war...artillery, arquebuses, gun powder, shot and other munitions."[16]

The Jews, he further observed, were allowed to dress in caftan-like "long garments" like everyone else in the Turkish realms, although they were required to wear a distinguishing yellow turban or hat in contrast to the Turks who wore white turbans.[17] That requirement, however, does not seem to have been uniformly observed. Nicolay observed that Hamon, like other physicians, walked around in a tall red hat.[18] Rabbi Joseph ibn Leb, one of the leading rabbis of the day, said that the turbans worn by the Jews in the Macedonian city of Salonika were green.[19] Exemptions could always be bought at a price. But these distinctions were not peculiar to the Jews. There were dress codes for all minorities, mainly centered upon the distinguishing color of headgear and shoes.

Hans Dernschwam, an agent in Constantinople for the Fugger banking house, was similarly awed and appalled at the way the Jews had prospered and proliferated under the Turks. By 1553 he noted that there were some 15,000 Jews on the tax rolls in Constantinople alone, "not counting women and children." This was double the combined number of Greeks, Armenian and other Christian minorities.[20]

The Jews were so numerous that he described them as "thick as ants." Many were living, he said, in "the lowest part of the city near the sea." He was probably referring to neighborhoods known today as Haskoy and Balat, with frontage on the Golden Horn, that had been renowned for their large Jewish presence since the Byzantine era. Nicolay observed that some were also clustered outside the main city in Galata, also known as Pera, which would have been ideal for overseas trade since it was alongside the Bosphorus.[21] Indeed, until a few decades ago, the Galata quarter still rang with the songs and street-game chants of Jewish children speaking Judeo-Spanish.

In the 16th century, Galata was also where Venetian, Genoese and other foreign merchants lived. "Just as soon as a foreign ship comes in from Alexandria, Kaffa (a town in the Crimea),

Venice and other places," continued Dernschwam, "the Jews are the first to clamber over the side." Moreover, he added in astonishment, they were free to travel anywhere they wished in the Empire and beyond—from Egypt to Hungary and from Persia to Poland. The restrictions that had dogged the business lives of openly-professing Jews in Europe for centuries were totally absent here.

Dernschwam noticed that the Jews also made a living in a profusion of local trades and crafts, once again defying the norms of Christian Europe. They had become "goldsmiths, lapidaries, painters, tailors, butchers, druggists, surgeons, cloth-weavers, wound-surgeons, barbers, mirror-makers, dyers...silk workers, gold-washers, refiners of ore, assayers, engravers," and so on, he wrote.[22] And, he reluctantly conceded, they were charitable, at least among their own people, and had well organized communities. Many had remained poor, yet "the Jews do not allow any of their own to go about begging," he wrote. Instead, "they have collectors who go from house to house and collect a common chest for the poor." The funds are also used, he added, for a home for their destitute and sick.[23]

Jewish women were equally active in many of these trades. Another traveler, a Frenchman named Pierre Belon who visited Turkey at this time, told of Jewish women selling towels, kerchiefs, spoons, belts, cushions, bed canopies and bed linens, among other items in the markets. They also worked as brokers for Muslim women who were forbidden, by their religion, to trade in public, selling all manner of goods for them.[24]

The first leg of Doña Gracia's long trip to Constantinople—the 300-mile voyage down the Adriatic Sea from Venice to

Ragusa—which she undertook in the fall of 1552[25] should have taken less than a week. This assumes that the galley that she and her household had been assigned by the Venetian authorities was able to maintain an average speed of seven knots during daylight hours. Much would have depended upon winds and weather and how often it pulled into port along the way, if at all.

It should have been a comfortable trip, since these vessels were substantial and well provisioned. And a relatively safe journey, too, even though they were traveling through pirate-infested waters. The galley carrying Doña Gracia would have been heavily armed. Prior to her departure the Venetians had made it perfectly clear they did not want to provoke an incident with the Turks due to careless transport. Allowing the vessel to be waylaid by pirates would have been foolhardy indeed.[26]

Normally, these galleys were filled to capacity with a mix of cargo and passengers. Canon Pietro Casola, an Italian priest who made a similar voyage down the Adriatic Sea some 50 years earlier, described them as being about 160 feet in length and about 40 feet wide at their broadest point.[27] Barrels of wine, bales of cloth and other carefully-packed merchandise would be strapped to a wooden platform that extended outwards all around like a ledge, reported Casola. Also projecting outwards from the main vessel would be a special place set aside as a latrine. The bottom of the hull would be stabilized with sand and gravel; the sand also used to help secure casks of wine for the passengers.

The entire galley could accommodate around 300 individuals. On Casola's galley there were 170 pilgrims and about 140 sailors, plus a handful of merchants. Nobody would believe, noted Casola, that such a vessel could carry so much merchandise *and* passengers. Nor were passengers necessarily subjected to cramped or bleak conditions. The cabins and enclosed passenger quarters were roomy. Meals could be eaten at tables in a main hall where mattresses were spread around for sleeping at night. Crossbows, bows, swords and other arms were hung from the ceiling to be used as defensive weapons in case of emergencies. At least thirty pieces of artillery with powder and cannon balls were typically carried aboard for the same purpose.

The wealthiest passengers—precursors of First Class today—would sleep in a separate bank of cabins reserved for them alone. Another specific area would be set aside for the storage of foodstuffs—sausages made of fish or meat, some cheeses and other preserved edibles. Another designated section was reserved for a kitchen so well equipped it possessed large and small cauldrons, roasting spits, frying pans and soup pots: sufficient utensils to create a gourmet feast. Live animals would be transported in cages and killed for fresh meat.

Another Mediterranean traveler, a Jew by the name of Eliahu of Pesaro—who sailed the same route on a Venetian galley some ten years after Doña Gracia's crossing—paints a comparable picture of shipboard life.[28] Eliahu, a merchant and scholar of about 50 years of age who was sailing from Venice to Cyprus, was equally impressed with the services provided, remarking that private cabins were readily available for rent for an additional payment of three ducats, on top of the cost of passage. Moreover, "in each boat," he wrote, "you will find two doctors, one a physician and the other a surgeon, an apothecary, a barber, a notary, a priest, a tailor, a carpenter, a blacksmith, a cobbler, a butcher, a shepherd to take care of the animals (live sheep, oxen, calves, poultry)... You will be able to purchase all kinds of merchandise...wine, oil, eggs, herring, salted meats, fruit, vegetables, pocket-shaped pastry and all sorts of dessert." And this was in addition to catered meals.

There were three classes of service at mealtime, he wrote. Yet no matter what level was chosen, the food was "always in abundance... as for a king." The notable Christians on board could dine with the captain for a monthly payment of ten ducats. A lesser meal was served to those who could pay only five ducats. For a relative pittance, a third class had to wait until all the others had been served before they were fed. No matter what class, all diners had a great time. "In front of them blow and scream (the musicians, playing on) trumpets, flutes, drums, harps, violins and all kinds of organs." However, he warned that the storms could be terrifying, "the waves pouring over us so that we feared for our lives." He was especially fearful of pirates who particularly preyed upon Jewish passengers as they were likely to generate the most in ransom money.[29]

Ragusa, the point of disembarkation for Doña Gracia and her party, was situated on a sheltered inlet, midway down the Dalmatian coast directly facing the lower reaches of the boot of Italy.

Since she did not arrive in Constantinople until 1553, she may well have spent the winter in Ragusa before pushing onwards. She had agents and business in Ragusa. It possessed one of the largest merchant fleets in the Mediterranean at that time and provided the safest and most secure gateway for trade between Italy and Ottoman territory. For a while it had been under Venetian sovereignty, although it was most often governed by its own nobles as an independent republic. By 1526, it had been officially absorbed into the Ottoman Empire and was now one of its foremost trading outposts; the Turks' own Venice on the Adriatic. There had been no fighting. Rather, the Ragusans, who were as commercially-minded as the Venetians, offered tribute, negotiating a payment of 12,500 ducats to Sultan Suleiman the Magnificent to leave them in peace. This allowed the city to remain physically and governmentally untouched, with only a nuance of Turkish oversight.[30] As a trading center of international renown, it naturally had a *converso* community, as well as a handful of openly-professing Jews who were never treated particularly well, perhaps because its leaders had remained steadfast Christians. For a while it even had a Jewish ghetto.[31]

Casola, the priest on a pilgrimage, reported that as soon as his galley entered the port of Ragusa it was afforded a typically rousing welcome. Trumpets blew and banners flew and dozens of people flocked to the quay to see what the great galley had brought them. Traders in charge of the merchandise rushed to take their bales off the ship and into the Ragusan markets.

The city itself, he said, was "beautiful in every respect." And safe. Built along the seashore, it was protected by 24-foot thick walls broken by intermittent watch towers behind which rose a range of mountains. There were streets of well-kept stone houses and shops of all kinds. Buildings and public places were set in gardens shaded with pomegranate and orange trees. The white-washed or marble-clad churches and convents of Byzantium were still in abundance. The frescoed halls of the governor's palace reminded Casola of the doges' palace in Venice. Indeed, in many respects, it *was* a miniature Venice.[32]

Considering Doña Gracia's prominence in shipping and the volume of business that the House of Mendes could generate, it is no wonder that she received an especially warm welcome. Mention of her in Ragusa begins in November of 1552,[33] when her agents, Abner Alfari and Izak Ergas, who were already there, opened negotiations with the authorities. Having her male representatives actually meet officials or other merchants whenever long-distance travel or formal hearings were required, was a pattern she had followed since Italy. Dozens of notarial documents found in Ferrara attest to this strategy. In Ragusa, for the first time, her agents carry Jewish names. Still, her bias towards aiding and employing *conversos*—even as she began life in an established Jewish community—continued. We know for sure about Ergas. He later had his possessions in Ancona confiscated by the church as a relapsed *converso*. The origins of Alfari are less certain.[34]

It would have been crucial for her to cement a solid commercial relationship with the city, as Ragusa provided the shortest and safest sea voyage from Italy for goods destined for the Balkans and the Levant. Thus, her immediate concern was to gain credit privileges for at least six months on customs duties she was facing on merchandise she wanted to bring through this important and strategic port. And she wanted the terms of any agreement to stay in force for at least five years. She must have been hoping to move a large volume of goods this way, or those duties would not have been significant enough to require the need for credit rather than cash. She also asked for permission to rent a warehouse to accommodate her property while it was in transit, as well as immunity from confiscation of this property on any pretext.[35]

Even though Doña Gracia was now technically in Ottoman lands, she still feared further attempts by Brianda to confiscate what actually belonged to her. The problem was certainly on her mind as the possibility was specifically addressed in two separate safe conducts. These were the ones she would seek from the Vatican just one year later, in 1554, permitting her to transport trade goods into the Papal States from the Orient. The expression used was "immunity from financial claims, including those related to the estate of her sister." She had obtained a similar order for passage of goods through the port of Ancona.[36] And she did exactly the same in Ragusa in November of the identical year, explaining that "in the future it could happen that, being far from these places, someone could attempt to create troubles to my business passing through this honorable city of yours." She was therefore seeking a guarantee that, "no magistrate on behalf of any authority of any kind could, under any circumstances, take (my property)." Otherwise, she warned, "I would be forced to ...pass through other places where I would be safe from these obstacles."[37]

Her application to the Ragusan authorities had a certain wistfulness to it, penetrating the shield of legal language enveloping so many of her official pleadings. She talked about how she was "accountable for everything to everybody," and how she was always willing and able to pay "whatever I should to everybody I owe anything."[38]

As usual, she was playing it safe and thinking ahead. She also showed remarkable resilience by continuing her business activities without missing a beat, though she had left her most trusted senior aides in Italy.

She gained further exemptions from the Ragusans for any additional customs duties likely to be payable on merchandise that she intended to re-export anywhere in Ottoman territory. In return, she agreed to pay the city a fine of 500 ducats in gold coin if she failed to use Ragusa as a transit point over the next five years. As a further inducement, her agents promised city officials they would try to persuade their colleagues to use Ragusa as well, to the obvious advantage of the city's economy. Judging by Doña Gracia's later expressions of appreciation for all the help that the Ragusan authorities gave her, and her willingness to lend money to their ambassadors in Constantinople, expedite bills of exchange and intercede, when needed, with the central Ottoman authorities on their behalf, she got what she wanted and cemented a useful business alliance.[39]

On a later occasion, in June, 1555, the Ragusan authorities even arranged to speed up a shipment of fabric from Venice that she was anxious to obtain—items (possibly personal ones) that might have otherwise been delayed for months. Indeed, the Ragusan authorities must have found it so beneficial that in 1557 they were willing to renew the original privileges for a further five years.[40] Her activities in Ragusa thereby evoke the image of a consummate business woman in the modern sense. Even a journey taken for an entirely different purpose included some commercial activity along the way.

While in Ragusa, she may have also had preliminary discussions concerning a tax farming concession she eventually operated in that city-state under the administration of Alfari and Ergas.[41] She obtained assurances from the Ragusan authorities that these agents would not be molested in any way. The two men were even granted the right to live outside the ghetto which had confined other Jews in Ragusa since 1545, although they were required to pay the high rents and other taxes expected of the Jews. If she indeed always made sure her agents were well cared for this way, it would have been a smart business move as well as a compassionate one. No wonder when the dispute with her sister flared anew in the Jewish courts a few years hence, she would be so anxious to argue that she had the right to keep some of the profits from the family capital she had tried to preserve with sound business ventures.[42]

The rest of the journey must have been taken overland, since there is no mention anywhere of further sea voyages, and she rode into Constantinople in a carriage.[43] That overland trek— covering an additional 600 miles—would have logically been made along the legendary Via Egnatia. This was the ancient east-west trade route, originally carved out by the Romans, that had been used for centuries by pilgrims, Crusaders and merchants carrying wagon-loads of wares. It still had *mutationes*—command posts to patrol and protect travelers from bandits and *hans* or *caravansaries* for their lodging needs. But it must have been uncomfortable, tedious and tiring nonetheless.

Starting to the south of Ragusa at the coastal city of Durres, the Via Egnatia followed a path due east by way of Lake Ochrida in the Balkans and onwards to the great Macedonian port of Salonika. From there it hugged the coast to Constantinople. Why she did not go the entire way by sea may be explained by the greater perils of sea-going travel in an age of privateers and the relentless eruption of hostilities between Venice and the Turks. Besides, on land she could be accompanied and protected by *janissaries*, the personal troops of the sultan who were routinely assigned to protect Jewish and Christian dignitaries.[44] Don Joseph was shielded by *janissaries* for his journey a few months later. Doubtless the same protection would have been provided for her journey, too.[45]

She had to pass through Salonika, the city with the most Jewish inhabitants in the Ottoman Empire. Though we do not know whether she stopped there for any length of time, it would have been likely. Hundreds of refugees from the leading families of Spain and Portugal made their home in this city and she would have encountered old friends. But for someone like Doña Gracia, it would have been inconceivable to live permanently in a provincial capital. She was accustomed to life close to the locus of power. And that precluded any other option but Constantinople.

Her arrival in Constantinople, sometime in 1553, was positively regal.[46] Since she would have been intimately familiar with the mass appeal of colorful street processions regularly mounted by the Catholic Church, and the endless round of carnivals so popular during the period, it may well have been deliberately staged. Andrés Laguna, a contemporary from Segovia who was a prisoner of war in Turkey at the time, mentioned how uplifting it was for the Jews to see her this way.[47] If it occurred to him, it had no doubt occurred to her, too. And indeed, her proud demeanor would become a morale booster for her people.[48] But, added Laguna cynically, the fact that she and her household had been exempt from wearing the headdress assigned to the Jews and had also gained special permission to wear Venetian clothing meant that they would not be molested as Jews.

It was certainly an event full of pomp and circumstance. "One
day," wrote Laguna, "a Portuguese lady called Dona Beatrice
Mendes,[49] who was very rich, entered Constantinople with 40
horses and four triumphal chariots full of ladies and Spanish
servants... she live(s) like a Spanish duke and has the means to
do so." He also commented with admiration that she was personally known to the sultan. "She had been in close contact with
the sultan (Suleiman the Magnificent)," he wrote, "ever since
she was in Venice."[50]

Even Dernschwam was impressed, calling her capable, accomplished and tough and confirming that she was someone
who actually headed a large international banking business.[51]
He grudgingly recognized that "the Jews are very proud of her
(and) call her *La Señora*"[52]—the first mention of the simple title
she would carry throughout the Jewish world for the rest of her
life. But he also brought the prejudices of his upbringing to the
event. He was quick to describe her, somewhat contemptuously,
as "an old Portuguese woman." He wrote off Brianda simply as
the sister who "was supposed to come here, but has somehow
been detained."[53] Still, the fact that both foreign travelers made
any mention of Doña Gracia implies that her arrival created quite
a stir.

Driving for the first time through Constantinople in her carriage, Doña Gracia would have passed clusters of tall cypress
trees that were a hallmark of the city at that time. At every turn,
glistening domes and slender minarets spiked skywards from a
profusion of mosques like newly-sharpened pencils standing

upright in a mug. The sight would have offered a startling contrast to the ever-present church spires of Christendom. So too would the melody of the city—the wailing call to prayer of the *muezzin* at regular intervals throughout the day replacing the pealing of church bells that calibrated life in the cities of Christian Europe. And so too would the attire of the men in the streets—flowing white robes and turbaned heads replacing the embroidered doublet and black cap typical of a Renaissance gentleman.

The wooden Turkish houses were ramshackle by Western standards. They had latticed windows and projecting upper storeys with box-like balconies that hung precariously over hilly alleyways. Here and there the serpentine alleys were so narrow and twisting that the overhanging balconies almost kissed one another. Walls, gardens, courtyards, graveyards, steep stone steps, Byzantine ruins and street stalls overflowing with merchandise veered off in all directions. There was no order to anything, only adding to the sense of being trapped in an Oriental conundrum—chaos within a maze.[54]

Doña Gracia immediately headed for Galata where a country home and gardens lay waiting for her.[55] The rent, according to Dernschwam, was a ducat a day, which would have been a princely sum. It was here, he noted, that she lived in "luxury and extravagance (with) many servants, maids also, among them two from the Netherlands."[56] Later the family would move into an estate set amid the vineyards of Ortaköy to the east, probably built at the behest of Don Joseph, a property known as the Palace of Belvedere.[57] Its name, which means 'beautiful view,' implied a glorious panorama of the waterfront.

Her surroundings at Galata would have been equally attractive. Unlike the tangle of Constantinople, the European colony of Galata, on the northeastern side of the Golden Horn, the peninsula upon which Constantinople stands, resembled a small

Italian city laid out with straight streets, well-built stone houses and piazzas that soaked up the sunshine. Atop the highest hill stood an ancient stone tower (still standing) that was built during the late Roman period and originally used as watch-tower for fires. Later it served as a look-out for merchant ships on their way into port. Galata was renowned for its carnivals, banquets, sensuous and bejeweled women and taverns that boasted beer cooled by snow brought in from nearby mountains. [58] Envoys from every Western nation clustered here. Most of them preserved the manners and customs of Western Europe, as Doña Gracia probably did.

But there were differences. One of her first symbolic acts, like so many *conversos* who had preceded her, was to formally begin using her Jewish name. In the blink of an eye, noted Laguna, Doña Beatrice became Doña Gracia.[59] He was wrong in suggesting that she changed only her first name. Contemporary documents are very clear in confirming that she was henceforth known, even back in Christian Europe, as Doña Gracia Nasi.[60]

Why Nasi? It was not really a family name at all. It might have therefore been chosen to denote spiritual rebirth, which she must have felt strongly at this moment. In both Latin and Portuguese the word *nasi* connotes birth. And *conversos* often adopted made-up names that carried a personal significance.

Yet the word *nasi* had a secondary Jewish meaning that did have personal significance. In biblical times *nasi* had been a title given to an important person, such as a tribal chief or head of an important family. It inferred authority yet fell slightly short of the idea of the absolute power awarded to a king. The *nasi* had been the name given to the secular or political leader presiding over the *Sanhedrin*, the governing body of the Jews at the close of the biblical era. It gave him the right to establish courts, raise funds, spearhead legislation and keep in touch with the Jews of the diaspora - acting somewhat like a modern president.

Yet unlike a contemporary president, the title and authority could pass down through a family, the notion being that anyone who held such an exalted position was entitled to be treated as if descending from the royal house of David.[61]

The 16th century Jewish poet, Sa'adiah Longo, referred to Doña Gracia enigmatically as a "remnant of the house of the Sanhedrin doe" in a subsequent elegy to her. A blood tie to the House of David was not beyond the realm of possibility. A recent scholarly work, "*A Jewish Princedom in Feudal France, 768-900,*" by Professor Arthur Zuckerman, a modern American historian, builds a compelling case centered around the fact that actual descendants of the House of David were invited to come from the Middle East around the time of Charlemagne to rule over a semi-autonomous area of Jewish settlement in the Provençal region of southern France. Some descendants may well have drifted south during the Middle Ages. The Jews of the Provençal region and those of northeast Spain viewed themselves as being from the same locale. For a while they were even under the jurisdiction of the same monarch.

Further, in pre-expulsion Spain, where Jewish communities typically enjoyed the right to govern themselves in matters of everyday life, the title of *nasi* had been bestowed upon those Jews who held special leadership status. They were considered the spokesmen for their people in dealings with the crown. In turn, the crown gave them political power over the local Jewish people. The *nasi* of the day was usually a man of great wealth and learning, but not necessarily a rabbi;[62] such as Joseph el Nasi (Joseph the chief). There is even evidence of a direct connection through a cryptic reference in the Hebrew literature linking Brianda to a father named Abraham de Nasi, as well as a reference to the Hebrew name of Don Joseph's father as Samuel de Joze Naci."[63]

Therefore, when Doña Gracia reverted openly to Judaism,

she may well have been reviving a revered name and title that had been in her family for generations, though there is no evidence to suggest that a woman ever held the designation before. Or she may have felt entitled to it anyway, as a putative descendent of the royal House of David. Moreover, as it had long been the custom among Iberian Jews of her social class to marry kin, she may have inherited the right to the title from both sides.[64] The Benvenistes had clearly been a *nasi* family in Spain.[65] And in Hispanic society there could be no greater status symbol than lineage acquired through birth. Being told as a child that she came from a family with *nasi* connections must have had a profound effect upon her attitudes and actions.

But what is odd is why only Doña Gracia and her nephews, Don Joseph and Don Samuel, formally adopted the Nasi family name at this point. Her daughter, Ana, became Reyna Benveniste,[66] using the Jewish version of her maiden name until the very end, when she finally used her family name of Nasi.[67] In all official documents found in Christian Europe after her formal adoption of Judaism, La Chica is also referred to as Benveniste, the Jewish version of *her* maiden name too, though both girls had married men who had changed their names to Nasi.[68] An exception was La Chica's portrait medal, struck at the time of her marriage. Inexplicably, the Hebrew characters around the rim refer to her as Gracia *Nasi*.

———••✠••———

By November 1553, some six months after Doña Gracia's arrival, Don Joseph was on his way to join the family in Constantinople. Now a mature man of thirty, he had hardly been idle since the departure of his aunt and cousin. Rather, he had been preparing for yet another bizarre episode in the family saga.

We already know that Doña Gracia had been uneasy about having to deposit 100,000 ducats in the Venetian Zeccha, and would have done almost anything to avoid fulfilling this obligation. She had probably therefore given Don Joseph, along with Duarte Gomez and Agostinho Henriques, the task of making sure it never got there. The result: a brazen abduction and sham marriage.

During lengthy negotiations just before her departure, everyone had understood and agreed that certain debts had to be collected before the ducats could actually be made available. Even Aries de Luna, Doña Gracia's brother in Ferrara, was busy that year appointing legal representatives to collect unpaid obligations in Lyons and Pesaro. It was obviously troublesome because Aries had found it necessary to appoint people with the power to initiate lawsuits and have "debtors arrested, detained and imprisoned...and denounce (any) suspected of planning an escape."[69]

A deadline of March 1553 had been agreed upon for the collections to reach the agreed-upon level of 100,000 ducats.[70] Was it therefore so surprising that on or around January 5 of that year,[71] two months prior to the deadline, and under cover of the dense fog that regularly rolls into the Venetian lagoons on wintry nights, a boat glided along the portion of a canal that led to Brianda's house. On the boat was Don Joseph and his brother, Don Samuel, as well as a handful of accomplices and oarsmen. They lifted the 13-year-old La Chica aboard and proceeded at full speed out of the lagoons. If Brianda's later testimony before the Venetian Inquisition is to be believed, they had originally tried to kidnap both mother and child. But somehow the mother slipped from their grasp. "My cruel sister," Brianda would insist a year later, "got her Juan Miches (Don Joseph) to try to kidnap me and had my poor daughter kidnaped in ... violation of the freedom that this city's greatness and authority had provided me in terms of liberty and security."[72]

La Chica must have been willing and even eager. Perhaps the conspirators convinced her that it was the only way to save her inheritance. Or maybe she secretly harbored a desire to run off with her debonair cousin and was willing to play along.

From there, Don Joseph, Don Samuel and La Chica fled south to the Papal States. On January 22, two weeks after the abduction, they were captured at Faenza by papal officials who had been alerted by the Venetians, and led away to Ravenna. Since Don Joseph and his brother had good connections with the Vatican, they escaped being locked up and quickly arranged a "wedding" ceremony. Don Joseph and La Chica were then "married" in front of the Ravenna cathedral in the presence of a large crowd; their marriage consummated that very night—at least according to gossip that was artfully planted and later incorporated into ambassadorial missives. Interestingly, there is no suggestion during any of this period that La Chica was the unhappy or reluctant victim, which opens up all manner of interpretation about her relationship with her mother.[73]

The next day a courier from the Venetian government came galloping into Ravenna demanding that the papal authorities hand over Don Joseph and the young girl immediately, no matter what had transpired. The mother, they reported, was beside herself with grief and anxiety. In fact, secret deliberations had taken place at the highest levels. A senior group of Venetian officials had decreed the arrest of all the abductors; the decree itself having been proclaimed on public posts at the San Marco and Rialto piers, as well as other boat stops throughout the city. Anyone found harboring the kidnapers or their accomplices was to be hanged and forfeit all their personal possessions. Anyone who could lead the authorities to the abductors would be given a reward of 1,000 ducats.[74]

But the Venetians were not going to grab their men that easily. While papal officials agreed to turn over the girl, and armed boats were sent to fetch her from an inn where the couple were staying,[75] Don Joseph managed to persuade them to allow him to go to Rome to plead for the validity of the marriage. Without its validity he could not gain any rights to the glittering dowry. And keeping the dowry from being deposited in the Zeccha had been the point of the caper in the first place. The papal officials permitted that concession.

By March, it became clear that the papal authorities were not about to give in to the demands of the Venetians and return Don Joseph for justice. There was never much love between the two states. The Venetians therefore decided to offer an even larger reward—3,000 ducats to anyone "to bring him (Don Joseph) back alive." Two thousand ducats would be awarded anyone who brought him back dead. At the same time, Don Joseph was banished forever from their city. If he dared enter nonetheless, he was to be hanged "between the two columns of San Marco until his death." He was then to be beheaded and quartered, his dismembered parts put on display around the city. Don Samuel similarly faced hanging and perpetual banishment, with 2,000 ducats offered to anyone who could bring him back alive; 1,500 ducats if dead. The other conspirators received lesser sentences, including Agostinho Henriques who had also participated in the abduction.[76]

Why had the Venetians reacted with such severity? Was it the result of a frenzied and brutal act of revenge led by a single patrician who had been counting on winning the fabulous dowry?[77] "Everyone in Venice," wrote the ambassador in Venice to the court of Charles V, "save those who coveted the girl and her dowry, finds the sentences harsh."[78] Indeed, it could well have been an awareness of the nuptial intentions of a highly determined aristocrat that spurred Don Joseph and his conspirators into taking such bold action in the first place.

Despite the "marriage," the Venetian government refused to give up the dowry. Don Joseph even offered King Henry II of France another loan if the French would intervene on his behalf with the recalcitrant Venetians. The French demurred.[79] However, they were willing to provide Don Joseph with special papers to take to the Turks to see if the Turks could persuade the Venetians to provide restitution.[80]

This was ostensibly the reason why Don Joseph left for Constantinople in November of 1553. Three men accompanied him, one of whom was his brother, Samuel.[81] The moment was recorded by Don Alphonso de Lencastre, the Portuguese emissary to the Vatican. He wrote from Rome to tell King João III of Portugal (who was still on the throne) that Doña Gracia had sent a ship filled with soldiers from Ragusa to Ancona where Don Joseph was waiting for transport (he obviously could not leave from Venice). Along with the ship were letters of safe conduct and instructions for the *janissaries* who were to accompany him for the land portion of the journey. As personal guards of the sultan, the *janissaries* were colorfully attired. Don Alphonso described one who "was wearing trousers of black velvet, Italian style, and gold buttons with a crimson satin doublet and a crimson shirt of fine linen."[82]

Even more interesting was a clue buried in the text of the letter that explains the way the House of Mendes may have traded information for favors. The letter contained a portion in code concerning classified information about Portuguese holdings in and around Goa, a Portuguese colony on the West Coast of India. Lencastre noted that Doña Gracia had recently sent him a special warning concerning a threat to the security of a Portuguese-held island near Ormuz (where the strategic straits of Hormuz enter the Persian Gulf—a key junction that controlled the trade routes from the Orient to the Mediterranean). Turkish fleets had attacked the area one year earlier.[83] In addition, said

Lencastre, Don Joseph had promised to provide the Portuguese with any other news he could pick up in Turkey about India (the Portuguese were facing problems with incursions into several of their colonies there), upon his return to Ancona two months hence.

The trading of sensitive information once again seems to have been a way for the House of Mendes to maintain close contact—and pry favors from—a nation where hundreds of *conversos* were living under the daily threat of the Inquisition; a continuation of the way the family had served the Portuguese crown in Lisbon decades earlier.[84] Helpful, too, were the small personal favors that they were always ready and willing to provide kings and princes. On one occasion, after having been alerted to a royal craving for Parmesan cheese by Lencastre, Don Samuel arranged to send the Portuguese king two Parmesan cheeses on a Mendes ship bound from Italy to Lisbon, specifically for his personal consumption.[85] On another, Don Joseph was asked by Duke Ercole to help retrieve five horses and a mare that the duke had purchased specially from the Ottoman Turks—known for their fine breeding—but which had been stolen in transit on their way from Constantinople to Italy.[86]

Don Joseph reached Constantinople early in 1554, according to Dernschwam, the Fugger agent in Constantinople. From the start, he lived in princely fashion, just like his aunt. In a rare physical description of Don Joseph at this juncture, Dernschwam observed that he was a large man with a neatly trimmed black beard.[87]

Don Joseph also traveled to Constantinople in regal fashion, reported Dernschwam, entering the city with over twenty of his own liveried *converso* servants and followed by a convoy of some 500 *converso* refugees.[88] He favored silk clothes lined with sable—ideal for the chill of winter in Constantinople. Whenever he rode around the city he was protected by two mounted *janissaries* with staves, according to Turkish custom. He had brought with him all sorts of firearms for jousting and target practice—armor, helmets, lances, battle-axes and muskets. He delighted in this sport, said Dernschwam, holding festive sporting events in the garden of the family's home in Galata.[89]

It did not sound like the baggage of a man who was about to go back to Italy two months hence. Besides, going back would have been suicidal. Don Joseph now had a steep price on his head. The French in Constantinople even commented that his prior desire to pursue his rights in the abduction incident by involving the sultan had cooled, even though this avenue of restitution was still open to him through the letters of concern he had brought with him from the French ambassador in Rome.[90] In sum, he never did follow up. Just as Doña Gracia had capitulated when she knew she had been bested by Diane de Poitiers, she may well have counseled Don Joseph that it was an ill-conceived plan from the outset, and they should get on with their lives while seeking other ways to solve the problem.

Laguna similarly included some lines about Don Joseph's arrival in his travelogue. He agreed that Don Joseph cut an impressive figure. Here was someone, wrote Laguna, with important connections in Spain, Italy and the Low Countries—"a gentleman... very well read, a man at arms and a friend of France." Don Joseph, he noted, had been knighted sometime early in life by Charles V.[91] Although there is no other corroboration of this fact, Charles V could well have made him a minor knight. It was certainly something that was happening to *conversos* elsewhere, as previously noted, especially those who had served the crown in Spain and Portugal.[92]

But Laguna and Dernschwam were both aghast when the knightly Don Joseph, so close to some of the most important aristocrats at the royal courts of Europe, immediately arranged to have himself and his male servants circumcised, so that he could live in the future as a Jew. It was judged an outrage so scandalous that several Western historians were still including it in their writings a century later.[93] It was yet another signal that he had no intention of returning.

Dernschwam was certain Don Joseph would regret circumcision, especially if he ever wished to go back and live in Christian lands where it would have been a sure sign of apostasy.[94] Laguna insisted that he visited Don Joseph almost every day during those initial weeks, begging him not to do it. To no avail. Dernschwam concluded that the act was all connected with the chance to marry Ana, now known by her Jewish name of Reyna.

Yet even though Don Joseph promised Laguna he would remain a Christian, and stay out of the way of his (now openly-Jewish) aunt and future mother-in-law, he ended up making the Faustian pact. In April, claimed Laguna, Don Joseph sold his soul and body to the devil so he might become eligible for 300,000 ducats in dowry money. He even changed his name from Juan Micas to Joseph Nasi. "When I asked him why he had done this," wrote Laguna, "he said that it was so that he should not remain subject to the Inquisition." It was a weak excuse. After warning Don Joseph that such an act made him even more subject to allegations of apostasy, Laguna cautioned him that he would soon regret this devilish deed.[95]

Within two months, insisted Laguna, his prediction proved accurate. He claimed that he watched as Don Joseph wept over his sin, but was consoled by the thought of having so much money. There is some truth to these allegations. Neither Don Joseph nor his brother, Samuel, inherited any family money of their own. Don Samuel publicly admitted with humility, four years later, that all *his* wealth derived from marrying an heiress.[96] What would have been true for one brother would doubtless have been so for the other.

But the sum of 300,000 ducats was a gross exaggeration.

Documents connected with the division of the family's wealth, compiled during Doña Gracia's negotiations with Brianda in Italy, repeatedly cited 300,000 ducats as an approximation of half the total assets of the House of Mendes. Later French accounts placed the dowry closer to 90,000 ducats, in addition to a quantity of pearls and precious stones. The valuables may have been added to make sure both girls—La Chica and Reyna—were provided with a dowry of equal value. It would certainly make the later figure cited by the French much closer to reality.[97]

What about the prior plan, circulating in Italy, that Reyna had been promised to the son of Moses Hamon? A report by Duke Ercole's ambassador to the court of the sultan made it clear that a union to a *converso* girl who had been brought up as a Catholic, even though it had occurred involuntarily, would have never been sanctioned by the pious Dr. Hamon. As many in Christian Europe probably suspected all along, it had only been a ploy.[98]

What about Don Joseph's "marriage" to La Chica? No problem, either. The rabbis of Constantinople would not have fretted over a hasty Christian ceremony, followed by a questionable consummation. For one, they considered all *converso* marriages performed in Christian countries null and void, unless a companion ceremony had been performed according to Jewish ritual and in the presence of at least ten men (*a minyan*). In addition, the Sephardic rabbinate had never accepted the formal ban on plural marriage issued by a 10th century Ashkenazi rabbi.[99] They certainly were not going to mount objections that would fly in the face of the intentions of a wealthy woman who could do them so much good. The Turks would not care, since the Jews had the right to live under their own domestic code.

The wedding of Reyna and Don Joseph took place in June, with Doña Gracia hosting lavish parties before and after the event.[100] One can well imagine her joy. Two of the young people she loved most were being wed in a traditional Jewish ceremony. It was something that she herself had been denied. And it must have brought deep emotions to the surface. Even the French ambassador to the sultan's court came over to Galata late in August to help celebrate with the family.[101]

How did Reyna feel about marrying her sophisticated cousin? She was thrilled, according to Stephan Gerlach, a preacher to the German colony in Galata, although he remarked that her friends were opposed to the match.[102] Gerlach implied that this was because she was so much richer than he was. It was also possible that Don Joseph had a darker side that Jewish historians have tended to dismiss. Dernschwam repeatedly used the word "rogue" when referring to him. And despite Don Joseph's later diplomatic achievements on behalf of the Ottoman Empire, and Doña Gracia's obvious confidence in him, he went down in Turkish history as a conniving opportunist with no scruples whatsoever.

It was Don Joseph, insisted the Turks, who made Suleiman's successor, Selim II (who ruled from 1566 to 1574) into a drunkard. Selim's drinking was so heavy that he later became known as Selim the Sot. Don Joseph, so the story goes, plied Selim with drugs and alcohol while arranging repeated orgies that combined heterosexual and homosexual activity (the sultans would sexually exploit youths so they would not have too many heirs and thus create a conflict for succession rights). Don Joseph would have been expected to participate. The Turks also maintained that Don Joseph exerted a perverted influence over Selim by pandering to the worst of his excesses.

Moreover, it was rumored, Don Joseph had an illegitimate daughter, Rachel, whom he "gave" to Selim for his harem. Following her conversion to Islam, this beautiful girl was later known as Nur Banu. Not only did she become one of Selim's wives, she also became the mother of the future sultan, Murad

III. (The story seems outrageous except that it may have had a close parallel, at least in Don Joseph's mind, with the biblical tale of Esther). Conniving with her father, so the story continued, Nur Banu then stole money from the royal treasury for their personal business projects.[103]

Don Joseph was also accused of being responsible for humiliating the Turks in October, 1571, by persuading them to confront the combined forces of Christian Europe at the great naval battle of Lepanto, where they suffered awesome losses. But these derogatory tales must be taken with a large grain of salt. He was, after all, a Jew. And even the Turks felt ambivalent towards the Jews. However, even Jewish historians admit he would have had to have been ruthless to further any of his goals at the sultan's court of the day.[104] Interestingly, Doña Gracia would have needed to be equally tough to accomplish what she did, too. Yet there was never the same disdain or unsavory rumors connected to her actions.

At the family's home, however, one gets a different portrait of this enigmatic man. Together with Doña Gracia, Don Joseph was feeding up to eighty impoverished Jews a day. The pair were also donating thousands of ducats to support the Jewish home for the poor and sick in Constantinople.[105] In addition, Don Joseph was speedily becoming a trusted royal advisor on foreign affairs at the Sublime Porte, thanks to a taste for intrigue and his past dealings with many of Europe's most powerful monarchs. Because the Turks had no official representation at the courts of the Christian monarchs of Europe, these relationships made him especially valuable.[106]

———••✶••———

If the crowned heads of Christian Europe thirsted after the

Mendes money, so did the sultan. Upon her arrival in Constantinople, Doña Gracia was immediately asked to provide a loan of 10,000 ducats.[107] Lencastre, the Portuguese ambassador, put it as high as 40,000 ducats. This may have been the rationale for his insistence in the early days that she was "remorseful" for having made the decision to move to Turkey and return to Judaism.[108] There is also the enigmatic letter in the Venetian archives, dated November 1553, that suggests she was taking steps to make certain she would be welcomed back, should she ever need or wish to return to Venice.[109] But it could have simply been her lifelong habit of always having an exit strategy.

Certainly her actions indicate she had entered the Ottoman Empire for the duration of her life. For one, Doña Gracia's negotiations in Ragusa implied forward preparations for the long term. And her flourishing business opportunities—she applied for an extension of her customs privileges with the Ragusan authorities twice[110] over the next decade—would have outweighed any mandatory loans she was forced to make to the sultan. Indeed, the House of Mendes was soon shipping large quantities of wool, pepper and grain to Venice and other parts of Italy.[111]

For the first time we also hear of Doña Gracia buying rental property—something she probably feared to do during her peripatetic life in Europe.[112] Whether it was done purely for profit, or as a way to provide housing for the continual flow of incoming refugees is uncertain. But it would certainly have helped the resettlement effort—assuming, of course, that the rents were subsidized. She also involved the House of Mendes in shipbuilding.[113] Whether this was simply as a banker, as part of her normal venture capital endeavors and for her own shipping needs, or for the wine importing concession that Don Joseph was shortly to develop, is not known.[114]

In those early years Doña Gracia also applied for a tax farming concession in Constantinople. The privilege was actually purchased in her own name, along with her "agent and partner" *Salamon* and *Yasef*.[115] Don Joseph would have been *Yasef*. *Salamon* was possibly Salomon Usque, the young member of the publishing family from Ferrara who had also moved onto Ottoman lands.[116] Significantly, she was the only woman whose name has so far been found in the tax records of the time, other than the women of the harem and wives of the sultan who gained these special privileges by virtue of their position.[117]

It was a renewable, three-year concession. It allowed the House of Mendes to collect the taxes on all wine and other alcoholic beverages being brought into Constantinople—a trade that was off-limits to the Muslims because of the Islamic ban on consuming alcohol. The partners made their first payment to the Sublime Porte in November, 1556, representing half the full amount due, regardless of what they actually collected. The large initial payment enabled them to also obtain a monopoly on all barrel lumber being brought into the city, which they would have needed as containers, including shipments going directly to the dockyards.[118]

Later on, in a move that demonstrated how they combined leadership of the Jewish community with shrewd business dealings, they would permit the Jewish cloth merchants of Salonika to pay some of their taxes in wool textiles, rather than in cash. This way the cloth could be obtained at a lower cost. And the merchants were not depleted of precious cash.[119]

To organize these collections required someone, or several people, at the helm with outstanding organizational and management skills, a network of trusted agents and functionaries and a keen eye for fraud, as is still true today.

How did she do it? For one, any attempt to disrupt business was treated firmly, with a response at the highest level of authority administered as fast as possible. On one occasion, for example, she impressed upon the sultan, through a messenger, the need to write to the Bey (governor) of Semendria, a commercially important Serbian town on the Danube, demanding an investigation into the unexplained death of six of her business agents who had been traveling by boat from Belgrade to Vidin, another town on the Danube. The captain and crew had denied any knowledge of the matter.

The sultan began his letter to the Bey by asking whether the perpetrators had since been identified and punished. If not, and they turned out to be soldiers, he sought assurances that they would be sent to prison. If they were common criminals, he wanted them punished according to the precepts of Muslim law, which probably included maiming and execution, "so there will be no repetition of such act," noted the sultan.[120]

On the same day, her messenger also complained to the sultan that a boat belonging to four men in Doña Gracia's service had been pillaged by thieves in the port of Santorino in the Cyclades, a cluster of exquisite Greek islands under Ottoman control. The thieves had made off with all the trade goods the four men had in their possession, selling them to residents of the nearby island of Naxos. The person who had sold the stolen goods had already been caught and required to make good. And a portion of the goods (presumably those not yet sold) had been returned to her agent, Samuel.[121] The value of the remainder had been offered as vouchers. But those vouchers, she complained, had never been honored. The sultan was now demanding that the thief pay up, as promised, so that the situation did not give rise to any "further grievances."[122]

One other item of unfinished business needed Doña Gracia's attention during those initial years in Constantinople: the reburial of her late husband's bones on sacred soil in Jerusalem. Although we have no specific mention that this ceremony included the bones of her parents, it is unlikely that she would fail to give them the same consideration, especially as she had brought the remains of all three family members to her home in Venice, presumably in anticipation of carrying them on-wards.[123]

The reburial took place on the Mount of Olives in Jerusalem, reported Dernschwam, with the required rituals performed by Jews (he probably meant rabbis) with the interment "accompanied by a large contribution," presumably to the poor, as was the tradition. Dernschwam added that this was something that Francisco had begged his wife to do on his deathbed.[124]

This she did for him in 1554, in keeping with her characteristic sense of duty.

CHAPTER **14**

Tragedy in Ancona

he news from Italy was not good. In May 1555, Gian
Pietro Carafa—who readily admitted he had never done
a kindness to anyone and could not imagine why he
had been selected by the cardinals[1]—ascended to the Holy See.
At the advanced age of seventy-nine he became Pope Paul IV.

Despite his seeming surprise, the reason was clear. These were
troubled times. The Catholic Church was rapidly losing adherents to the Protestants. Muslim armies had reached the gates of
Vienna. And *conversos* all over Italy had been reverting openly to
Judaism under the very noses of outraged clerics. In Carafa, the
church could count upon an extremist known for his zeal in
controlling defections; who had repeatedly praised work of the
Spanish Inquisition; who had been a close advisor to the Spanish monarchs, Ferdinand and Isabella; who had turned the relatively mild Italian Inquisition into an instrument of terror and
submission. One could hardly have elected a more fitting individual to lead the church at a precarious moment in its longstanding hegemony over the souls of Europe.[2]

Those who put him on the throne of St. Peter were not to be disappointed, especially in his dealings with the Jews and *conversos* in the Adriatic port of Ancona, an important gateway to the lucrative pan-European and Levantine trade in cloth, hides, oil and wines. Annexed to Rome some twenty years earlier, it had come under the direct jurisdiction of the Vatican. Prior popes, seeing what had happened in Ferrara and Antwerp, had initially fostered *converso* settlement as a way to bring wealth to the Papal States too. In fact, Ancona soon became so important to the finances of the region that by November 1540, Pope Paul III publicly demanded that the local Catholics treat the *conversos* kindly and acknowledge their Jewish origins. He wanted to encourage them to stay and build Ancona as a competitor to Venice. Pope Julius III reconfirmed this decree in 1553, stating that the *conversos* were entitled to the same freedom of worship as the indigenous Jewish residents of the region, whose families had lived there for centuries.[3] That meant they could revert openly to Judaism without fear of reprisals. Everything pointed to Ancona as a protected and prosperous place to live.

The indigenous Jews were soon mingling freely with the *conversos* and even former *conversos* now living as Jews, as well as Levantine Jews who would temporarily visit for trading purposes. It was hard to tell them apart. They dressed alike, lived in the same neighborhoods, worked together on local and international business and were active in the property market. They made good money by acquiring and managing homes for rent because of the large transient population. Unlike other city-states in Italy, Ancona had no functioning Inquisition and no burnings of Jewish holy books. Should any *converso* be accused of deviation in matters of faith, that person was allowed a year's freedom to depart before any action could be taken. Ancona's city council and papal officials, many of whom had grown wealthy as a result of the rising prosperity, were perfectly happy to ignore behavior that would have raised eyebrows elsewhere.[4] Ancona was considered secure enough, one should recall, to have been the port chosen by Don Joseph as the optimum place to wait for a ship to take him to the Ottoman Empire, after Venice put a price on his head for the abduction of La Chica.

But some people still worried about possible reprisals, as so often happens when Jews grow wealthy and flaunt their new-found riches. A few of the more devout among them insisted that too much wealth led to a neglect of the Torah and its teachings and there would surely be a price to pay. "The Jews' behavior," noted Benjamin Nehemia ben El-Natan, a rabbi from the neighboring community of Civitanova, "ha(s) become overbearing...they live securely in their beautiful dwellings, courts and palaces, every one going to his vineyard or field and carrying his gold and silver with him. But they forget the Lord and do not set aside any time for study..."[5]

The freewheeling atmosphere was certainly blasphemous to Pope Paul IV. He loathed Jews and viewed all *conversos* as apostates. Less than two months after being confirmed in office he launched his first attack—a papal bull entitled *Cum Nimis Absurdum*. "It is both absurd and inappropriate," he wrote on July 14, 1555, "that Jews, whose guilt (for their ancestors' alleged betrayal of Jesus) has condemned them to perpetual serfdom, should prove so ungrateful..." He continued: "For (our) mercy they pay (us) back with insults... their insolence has gone so far in our capital city of Rome and in several other cities (and) villages... that they not only venture to live mixed with the Christians... in the vicinity of churches, without any distinction in their attire, but also dare to rent houses in the choicer streets and squares... They...own property, employ wet-nurses, maids and other Christian servants and commit many other acts to the shame and contempt of the Christian name."[6]

Henceforth, he announced, the age-old segregation policies

of the church would be reinforced with renewed vigor. Employment of Christian servants by Jews was to be strictly forbidden. Jews now had to wear their badges at all times. No Christian could address a Jew as "sir." Only one synagogue would be permitted in any city; the others had to be converted into churches. Jewish moneylenders were placed under restrictions so punitive that it would soon become impossible to make a living. Jewish physicians could no longer minister to Christian patients. Jews could no longer own property, nor engage in local commerce, save dealing in secondhand goods.

Within weeks, the Jews of Rome were being rounded up and shunted into a ghetto. Others cities followed, including Ancona, although trading privileges were left intact, at least for the moment.[7] But a special catastrophe awaited the unfettered *conversos* of Ancona. Ignoring the rights and privileges granted and reconfirmed by his predecessors, the new pope had his agents swoop down upon them with horrifying swiftness. An ad-hoc arm of the Inquisition began rounding up those who had blatantly reverted to Judaism, despite any promises of protection that had made been in the past.[8] At least one contemporary observer insisted that beliefs had nothing to do with the decree. Rather, it was a cynical device that permitted the pope, and his scheming nephew, Carlo Carafa, to get their hands on the bountiful riches that had been acquired over a relatively short time by the incoming *converso* merchants of Ancona.[9]

For Doña Gracia it became a personal tragedy. Jacob Morro, one of her local agents, was arrested without warning at the beginning of August, and slammed into prison for alleged apostasy.[10] Her representative in Ragusa, Izak Ergas, had his possessions in Ancona confiscated and may also have been temporarily detained, having been in Ancona at that moment.[11] Her old friend and physician, Amatus Lusitanus, either fled moments ahead of the arresting officers or was briefly imprisoned, too.[12] The good doctor was forced to abandon everything he owned—"gold, silver, my professional clothes, my precious robe and not a few pieces of furniture," as he later put it.[13] This was in addition to his beloved medical books and the manuscript of an almost-completed medical text he had been writing—the fifth book in a series of case studies called *Centuriae* (as each consisted of one hundred remedies). Also left behind in the rush to escape were the drafts of his commentaries upon a medical tract by Avicenna, the 10th century Arab physician who had been centuries ahead of his time in understanding the human body and disease.[14]

Doña Gracia must have known other prisoners, too. Connections with the *conversos* and Jewish merchants of Ancona had been constant since her days in Antwerp and Ferrara. On at least one occasion she supervised a financial transaction for a Jewish widow from Ancona named Stella. The woman had turned to Doña Gracia to manage some 400 gold ducats. The intent was to use the capital to help generate interest income for Stella's family through loans and syndications. The arrangement, made during Doña Gracia's stay in Ferrara, provides at least one illustration of the agreements being made between openly-practicing Jews and *conversos*—just the type of interchange that the pope found so unsettling.[15] This particular Stella may have even been among those arrested in Ancona, as her dealings with Doña Gracia stipulate that she had been married to a *converso.* And a woman known simply as "Stella" was included among the relapsed *conversos* whose possessions were confiscated.[16]

Some 90 men and women were arrested in the first roundup, including those like Ergas who now lived elsewhere, but happened to be staying over in Ancona on business. It soon became a deadly combination of religious zeal mixed with an irresistible opportunity for personal enrichment. First, the Vatican asked for 30,000 scudi to re-validate the *conversos'* original privileges. The remainder of the *converso* community countered with an offer of 15,000 scudi.[17] It began to look suspiciously like the underhand maneuver so often used during these times: withdraw a privilege or confiscate an asset and then demand a payment to have it reinstated.

The bargaining was no use anyway. Before the leaders could negotiate further, the Vatican ordered the prisoners tortured to gain confessions of apostasy and relapse into Judaism.[18] It was ridiculous, argued the pope, for them to insist they had always been Jews, like the indigenous Jewish population. Everyone knew that for the past sixty years no Jew had been allowed to live in Portugal, unless he or she had been baptized. It was clearly time for those *conversos* still at large to flee elsewhere, many going to Pesaro, another Adriatic port city some 37 miles to the north.

Pesaro was a city-state, like Ferrara, renowned for its art, architecture and culture. Raphael had grown up there. Titian would paint a portrait of its current ruler, Guidobaldo II, a delicate man of letters and learning and considerable military skill. But Pesaro had never developed the volume of international shipping trade that had made Ancona wealthy. And this was exactly what the refugees had to offer. Guidobaldo seized the moment.

Meanwhile, between August and November, Inquisition officials took detailed inventories of the belongings that the prisoners and the fleeing *conversos* left behind in Ancona. These were summarily confiscated on a presumption of guilt, in typical Inquisition manner, for the benefit of the church. Forty-eight of the inventories survive, offering an intriguing portrait of the household and trade items in their possession. It shows, for example, that the merchants typically used their homes for storing goods as well as personal possessions; also, that they tended to dress in black.[19]

Jacob Morro had merchandise that included bales of furs, dried beans and Cordovan (leather) goods for a total of 544 trade pieces in all. For his own domestic use, he had a chest filled with 22 earthenware plates, undefined clothing and cloaks, 11 pieces of wool and cashmere garments, some fine linen and cotton, tables, some 25 drinking glasses, iron utensils for his fireplace, two beds and two rugs.[20]

Amatus Lusitanus had a more refined household. He and his wife occupied two rooms. Typical of the times, they kept most of their belongings in moveable chests, some made of iron. His wife had a coat of black velvet and a number of dresses: two made of damask, one trimmed with velvet and another two in purple as well as a plethora of accessories such as separate sleeves, shirts, furs and caps. There were also two cloaks, one trimmed with leather, a wolf skin fur, black cloth from Flanders, purple Venetian fabric, linen handkerchiefs and dozens of books, at least 22 of which were medical tracts.[21]

A predictable physician's concern for cleanliness and hygiene is apparent. Their household items included a "new rug," a feather bed with mattress, sheet and bedspreads, several additional bedspreads including two in white and one in wool, a second bed, mattress and bedspread, extra sheets, face cloths and "other rags." Among their kitchen items was a pot "with a plate inside," silver and bone spoons, an ordinary bucket as well as a "bucket with holes" that could have served any number of purposes, possibly even medicinal use as a means to create steam by throwing water over hot coals placed inside. Furnishings included two brass candelabra, several brass sculptures (undefined except that one sported a gun), linen table napkins and tablecloths.[22]

The listing of the belongings of Joseph Oef Amato, who may have been the doctor's brother, was punctilious enough to note that one of his velvet-trimmed coats had coffee stains on it, and a chest with a "German" lock could not be opened.[23]

Izak Ergas' possessions, as expected, consisted primarily of trade goods belonging to himself and others—sheepskins, cloth from Bombay for making turbans, bundles of buttons, small embroidered napkins. This was not surprising since he had already moved to Ragusa. However, he probably kept a room or two in Ancona for storage and temporary housing. After his inventory was taken, the notary made mention of the fact that the door to Ergas' room was locked.[24]

Stella's belongings were kept in an upper floor room in a variety of chests and strong boxes made of iron, two of which were painted. One had been lying open. There were also five wooden chairs and a bedstead.[25]

Debts due the prisoners were ferreted out, collected, catalogued and confiscated. To ensure nothing they owned was overlooked, the pope's agents examined the municipal registers where all commercial transactions were recorded.[26] So many assets were available for the taking that the opportunity for outright stealing must have been overwhelming. By October, the pope's man in charge, Giovanni Vincenzo Falagonio, had fled to Genoa where he was subsequently arrested for accepting a bribe of 16,000 ducats from the *conversos*[27]—probably to delay further arrests and facilitate some of the periodic escapes occurring among the prisoners. He may also have been caught making off with some of the confiscated property for himself.[28]

These confiscations and arrests threw normal commercial dealings into turmoil. Substantial and reliable merchants were suddenly impoverished. Trade was interrupted as all merchandise entering the port was checked by the newly-appointed Inquisition officials to determine whether any of it belonged to the *conversos*. Anyone owed money by one of the *converso* merchants who had been arrested found it impossible to collect, which further stalled trade. Inquisition officials meantime insisted there was nothing to fear. All goods or credits that rightfully belonging to an Old Christian or a member of the original Jewish community would be restored. But these disruptions, plus the grisly spectacle of prisoners being marched through the streets chained for torture, brought commerce to a standstill.[29]

Jewish legal courts were soon being petitioned to hear disputes in which the parties to many of the intricate deals within the Jewish world could no longer fulfill their pledges. Who was at fault and who was liable to make restitution?[30] At least one of the rabbis, Samuel de Medina of Salonika, expressed profound grief and indignation over the injustices.[31] Still, a ruling was important since it had the clout to force the losing party into submission, or face excommunication and thus a loss of business.[32]

Even Doña Gracia herself felt the chill of the financial chaos that ensued. Her agent, Isak Ergas, had been involved at the time in a three-way transaction with Jacob Morro and Naham Cohen, another Mendes agent. A year before the troubles began, the deal had been confirmed in writing in the customary manner in Ancona, and again in the spring of 1555. The capital being used belonged to Doña Gracia as banker and venture capitalist, making her the ultimate creditor. She was also entitled to a portion of the profits. But because of the disruptions and confiscations, Ergas fell into debt. His outstanding obligations to Doña Gracia, involving a debt of almost 1,000 ducats, lingered for seven years. Eventually, in 1562, the redoubtable Duarte Gomez, who was still acting as Doña Gracia's personal representative in Italy, intervened and arranged to release Ergas from most of the debt. The absolution, recorded by a notary in Ferrara, required Ergas to pay just 270 ducats as a compromise. The parties further agreed that no action could be taken in the future against Ergas, or any of his heirs.[33]

All these complications became matters of serious concern for Ancona's commercially-minded city council, since its Christian population was being hurt economically, too. During the autumn of the roundups, it sent a representative to the Vatican to plead for a chance to save Ancona's traffic and trade. But the pope told the representative that he "did not want them (the *conversos*) in Ancona at all."[34] The only concession made by the pope was to reaffirm and reestablish the commercial rights of the indigenous Jews, and those from the Ottoman Empire who had temporarily come to live and trade in Ancona. The pope's mood was implacable. In October, he issued a brief reserving the right of the Inquisition to arrest and sentence all *conversos* still at large in Ancona and confiscating their property too. But they must have all bolted by this time because a senior Inquisition official was sent to Pesaro to ask Guidobaldo to hand them over. The duke refused.[35]

From the baroque apartments in his ducal palace in Ferrara, Duke Ercole was closely following the events. And he did not sit idly by. In December he wrote to the leaders of all the *conversos* being "persecuted by Paul IV," offering them the option of relocating to his duchy, too. He sweetened the deal with exemptions from any of the customs and taxes they were accustomed to paying in Ancona. "We promise to embrace them and treat them well," he insisted, "and give them honor and justice at all times."[36]

Ferrara had grown wealthy and influential from *converso* money and it was an opportunity not to be missed.[37] From past experience it was also an offer the *conversos* knew they could trust. In fact, the *conversos* actually in Ferrara had no doubt lobbied the duke to extend the offer. Many of them, like the Mendes, were bankers whose financial future was caught up in the events at Ancona. But the trouble was that Ferrara was up the Po river. Although it was a navigable river, it was even less practical than Pesaro for the size and volume of merchant shipping that regularly pulled into Ancona.

With the arrival of ship after merchant ship into the ports of Salonika and Constantinople, the grim news slowly made its way into the Ottoman Empire and into the home of Doña Gracia too. She reacted decisively. After all, the pope had arrested her personal agents and confiscated property that rightly belonged to the House of Mendes.

Sometime that winter she visited Sultan Suleiman. In reality, she may have sent her plea through Don Joseph as her senior male representative. However, it is interesting that a contemporary observer, Joseph ha-Kohen, insisted that Doña Gracia personally sought an audience.[38]

The aim was to beg the Grand Turk, as he was often called, to intervene on behalf of her agents, her property and the relapsed *conversos*[39] languishing in prison, some in terrible pain from torture and all facing the probability that they would soon be led to the stake.

What kind of man was she facing? For one, Suleiman was a brilliant military strategist, feared by virtually every monarch of his day. This was no mean feat at a time when the world's rulers included such giants on the stage of world history as Charles V, Ivan the Terrible and Henry VIII. Yet Suleiman towered over even these legendary personalities. By this time he had reigned unchallenged for 35 years. He had annexed Hungary, seized Belgrade, taken over the strategic island of Rhodes, laid siege to Vienna, marched into Iran, Syria and Tripoli. His admiral (some say infamous pirate) Barbarossa, operating from a base along the Barbary (North African) coast, had become the terror of the Mediterranean.

There was a lot more to the 61-year-old Suleiman than military genius. To his own people he was revered as *Kanuni*, the Lawgiver; the man who codified the responsibilities and rights of his subjects and cemented a structure that would allow the

Ottoman Empire to survive for another four hundred years.

He was also a builder. Suleiman lavished his capital and Empire with sumptuous mosques, baths, bridges, clinics, colleges, covered markets and aqueducts. He wrote poetry in an ornate Persian style that was a form of high art in itself. He was fond of study, well read in history, the Koran, precepts of good governance, science, astrology and skilled as a goldsmith. He was known to be pious and fair. Yet he could be ruthless when challenged, able to summarily execute a close friend or order his most promising son, Mustafa—after the young man was reputed to be plotting a coup d'état—strangled with a silken garotte while he watched from behind a screen.[40] A garotte had to be used because it was forbidden to draw royal blood.

Yet this complicated man was frugal and temperate in his personal habits. He refused to enjoy the pleasures of his many concubines after developing a passion for Roxelana, a Russian slave of great beauty and sunny disposition. She had originally been purchased for his harem, but he eventually married her and was strongly influenced by her. Her sons became eligible to succeed as sultans in their own right. She became a woman of immense political power and prestige.[41] Some of Doña Gracia's dealings with Suleiman concerning Ancona may well have been negotiated through Roxelana—woman to woman.

Because exotic stories have circulated for centuries about the Turkish royal practice of maintaining a harem, it is often believed that women in Turkish society lacked political power. Not so, at least at the top. The mothers of the various sultans became extremely influential whenever their sons were more addicted to worldly pleasures than worldly power. Some of these mothers were wily enough to intoxicate their sons with endless delights. Indeed, royal women were so influential at this particular moment that when Roxelana brought the harem inside the very walls of the sultan's palace, she initiated a 100-year period of female influence that was so powerful it was dubbed The Sultanate of the Women.[42]

It is therefore likely that Doña Gracia gained influence at this particular court by forming close relationships with the women at the top: Roxelana, wife of Suleiman; her daughter-in-law, Nur Banu, the equally ambitious wife of Suleiman's heir apparent, Selim, and a woman Doña Gracia may have known all along. Certainly a special relationship existed between Nur Banu and Don Joseph.[43] This was probably one reason why Don Joseph eventually supported the succession fight of Selim against one of Selim's half-brothers. Another factor favoring a close alliance was the reputed Jewish origins of Nur Banu.[44] Still another possible avenue of influence was the friendship that quickly grew between Don Joseph and one of Suleiman's most trusted viziers. The vizier had married one of Suleiman's daughters, and this particular daughter could have provided yet another path of infiltration for Doña Gracia.[45]

An official portrait painted around this time shows Suleiman as a thickset man with regal bearing, warm yet shrewd eyes, a long, slender nose, tight lips, a grey moustache and a lengthy, albeit neatly-trimmed grey beard. On his head he is wearing the obligatory tall white turban with horsetails, a royal emblem. His pine green caftan, probably made of silk and mohair, is covered with an ermine-trimmed cape. A scimitar with a decorated handle is tucked into a jeweled belt.[46]

When not leading his disciplined troops on a military campaign, Suleiman lived at the legendary Topkapi Palace. Built upon a breathtaking promontory along Constantinople's waterfront, it had been completed a century earlier by his great grandfather, Mehmed the Conqueror, who had sent to Italy for the great Renaissance architect, painter and portrait medalist, Matteo de Pasti, to help design the project. Wars and differences in faith did not prevent him, or any of the Turkish sultans, from importing the best craftsmen from Europe. In 1502, Mehmed's son, Bayezid I, had invited Michelangelo to design and build a bridge over the Golden Horn. This particular project, however, did not materialized due to a plethora of complications.

Topkapi, which overlooked the water on three sides, was a vast estate comprising a series of geometric courtyards, enclosed gardens and exquisite pavilions. More than a palace, it was the seat of government for a sprawling empire, as well as a statement of Ottoman grandeur and power. Each day, ten cavernous kitchens fed from 3,000 to 8,000 courtiers, servants, state officials, *janissaries* and diplomats. Each building enclosed a labyrinth of rooms, corridors, porticos and covered walkways.

Lace and floral-patterned tiles, typically blue-on-white or green-on-white, adorned many of the walls and vaulted ceilings. Finely-woven Oriental rugs in a rainbow of hues were spread over stone or marble floors, on top of which the most senior dignitaries and—in separate quarters—the women of the palace would recline on softly cushioned platforms covered with embroidered silk coverlets. The result was an ambience that was lighter, more airy and colorful than the gloomy castles and baroque palaces of Europe.

To present a plea at the court of Sultan Suleiman the Magnificent, Commander of the Faithful, Shadow of God, Lord of the Lords of the World, was a formal act encased in pomp and ceremony. A diplomat or official emissary of the importance of Don Joseph would typically arrive on horseback and enter through the Imperial Gate. Once inside the first courtyard, the emissary would be required to dismount before going through the double-turreted Middle Gate. A vizier would then meet him and lead him past rows of bowing courtiers and *janissaries* standing at attention. Finally reaching the sacred innermost sanctuary where the throne room was situated, he would be greeted by a terrifying silence—"the silence of death itself" as eyewitnesses described it.[47]

The "gifts" for the sultan, which he would have been expected to bring along, would now be inspected. All around would stand an immense crowd of courtiers wearing turbans wrapped in countless folds of the whitest silk. High-plumed *janissaries,* still as statues, would be poised to react at the least transgression. Even so, chamberlains would grasp both of the emissary's arms as he entered the throne room—a chamber so heavily decorated with gold, silver and precious stones that it dazzled like a jewel-box. They would not let go until the audience was over, a practice dating back two hundred years to the time when a Croatian had sought an audience with Murad I and tried to kill him.

Upon entering, the emissary would be led forward and pushed down to kiss the sultan's feet before the proceedings commenced. Afterward, he would be led backwards to stand against a wall facing the sultan, thereby avoiding turning his rear to such an exalted ruler. Protocol required him to remain on his feet throughout the audience.

Sultan Suleiman conducted these audiences from a jewel-studded throne, or seated on a cushioned platform in time-honored Turkish fashion. After the emissary stated his purpose the sultan would listen, but he would be unlikely to give an answer right away. A lot would depend upon the views of his senior advisors. As Don Joseph was rapidly gaining influence over those advisors, the nature of his concerns would have doubtless been discussed in advance. Later, he himself would become one of the court's most trusted counselors.[48]

The intervention led by Doña Gracia was a success. On March 9, 1556, the sultan sent a strongly-worded letter to Pope Paul

IV. At the request of Don Joseph this valuable letter was personally delivered by the secretary to the French ambassador in
Constantinople.[49] The French had been acting as intermediaries between Christians and the Ottoman Turks since early in the
16th century as they had been willing to deal with the Turks when
other Christians nations would not.[50]

The arguments put forth in this letter for the release of the
prisoners provide a hint of the strategy that must have been used
to entice the sultan to become involved.[51] Suleiman began by
complaining that Ottoman subjects had been among those
seized—an obvious violation of Ottoman sovereignty and dignity. What irked him even more, he noted, was that his treasury
was facing a loss of 400,000 ducats in taxes and customs duties
that could no longer be paid, due to the confiscation of goods
and property that rightfully belonged to the prisoners. Part of
the loss, he explained, were the periodic payments pledged by
his tax farmers—possibly a veiled reference to a lump-sum payment that Don Joseph and Doña Gracia might have temporarily
withheld as a form of leverage.

In order to repair the damage, the sultan requested the release of "our subjects...with all the property which they had
and owned." In this way, "they will be able to satisfy their debts
and the...customs officials will no longer have an excuse for
their failure to pay, by virtue of the arrest of the said prisoners."
By doing so, he added, "you will give us occasion to treat in a
friendly fashion your subjects and other Christians who traffic
in these parts"[52]—a subtle threat that implied possible reprisals.
The message was reinforced by a personal letter from the French
ambassador in Constantinople to the pope's powerful nephew,
Carlo Carafa.

It did little good. In his reply to the sultan in June, the pope
said that only the prisoners who had previously resided in the
Ottoman Empire and were therefore considered Levantine sub-

jects were being released and their possessions and credits restored. He flatly refused to grant clemency towards those relapsed *conversos* who had never moved to Ottoman lands. He specifically mentioned Jacob Morro, saying that he could not even make an exception for an agent of the House of Mendes, especially as the man refused to repent.[53] However, bearing in mind the goodwill he felt towards Doña Gracia personally ("regarding the good business that was done with her...which benefitted good Christians"), he did agree to return the goods that Morro was holding on her behalf, said to be worth 45,000 ducats, provided she sent an envoy from Constantinople to take possession in her name.[54]

Part of his diffidence may have been due to the fact that the onrush of events had overtaken diplomacy. Between August and October of the previous year, soon after the mass arrests, some 38 of the prisoners had managed to escape. It typically happened when guards were bribed to look the other way. Around 27 others agreed, no doubt under torture, to repent their relapse into Judaism and had been consigned to work as galley slaves—a common sentence in an era when few were willing to undertake this suicidal work voluntarily. But they had also escaped, this time while on their way to the galleys at Naples, probably because other members of the *converso* community found a way to bribe the guards who were taking them there. This left 25 unrepentant souls manacled in the dungeons, including an elderly woman. Unwilling to face torture, one of them committed suicide by jumping out of a window. By June, all the rest had been burnt at the stake, including the old woman.

Some scholars believe that Jacob Morro was the man who committed suicide since his name never showed up on the lists of those executed. Nor was there any evidence that he escaped.[55] They further believe that this was the reason that the pope had to tell the sultan he could not make an exception, since the suicide had already taken place. In addition, since the executions took place during March and June of 1556—the months that correspond to the sultan's letter and the pope's reply—they were probably carried out with haste to spare the pope from any more troublesome appeals from Suleiman.[56] But the identity of the person who committed suicide is far from sure. Lusitanus talks of a surgeon named David Romero who also jumped from a prison window—a man who was severely depressed because his 8-year-old son had died following an operation that the father himself had administered.[57]

Despite Doña Gracia's inability to save her agent, it would have not been in character for her to have relied solely upon a single written plea from the sultan. Other avenues were being pursued simultaneously. Sometime in December 1555, agents of the House of Mendes, together with their long-time Florentine bankers, had been helping to remit a large sum of money to the Vatican that had been collected by the *conversos* in an attempt to save their brethren through yet more bribes.[58] The process echoed the kind of dealings that routinely took place in the days when Francisco and Diogo were trying to delay the arrival of the Inquisition in Portugal. Though the ducats arrived too late to save the martyrs, or failed to make a difference to the pope's objective, they probably had something to do with the "good business" that the pope would later mention in his letter to the sultan. It certainly would have influenced his decision to restore Doña Gracia's property to her—a woman whose ability to supply the Vatican with ongoing cash was still too important to deny her outright.

During that winter of 1555, the pope's agents in Ancona also found themselves facing the first of two representatives of the sultan sent directly to the city at the urging of Doña Gracia.[59] This mission was directed at local Inquisition officials, in the hope that they might use their discretionary powers to restore confiscated property. In addition, the two envoys were given the special task of looking out for goods and credits that were due "that rich Jewish woman…who was a resident of Constantinople."[60] They further tried to tempt the local population to be more forceful in its protests to the pope, by making it clear that the disruptions were likely to encourage the Levantine merchants to favor alternative ports.

The pope refused all of these pleadings, and stubbornly carried out the executions—an affront to Sultan Suleiman, and by association Doña Gracia and Don Joseph. Suleiman was not the sort of man to be rebuffed without venting his anger on those who had got him into the predicament in the first place. His prestige had been undermined. A fear of those repercussions could help explain the zeal with which Doña Gracia subsequently pursued a boycott in the city of Ancona.[61] But to suggest that Doña Gracia herself initiated the boycott, as certain historians have done, is an exaggeration, as we shall see.

———••❧••———

Though it was not easy to replace the layout and location that had made Ancona such an important center of trade with the Eastern Mediterranean, a boycott would have been an obvious way to draw city officials more deeply into the crisis. A boycott would also demonstrate the importance of the *conversos* and former *conversos* to the commercial life of the city and the activities surrounding the port, especially in connection with its vital textile trade. However, Jewish sources indicate that the idea of a boycott was initially urged upon the Levantine Jewish communities by the *converso* refugees who had managed to flee to Pesaro; and that it was brought to Turkey by Rabbi Judah Faraj, one of their leaders.[62]

Re-routing all trade through Pesaro was the best way for the *conversos* to maintain their ongoing business arrangements with relatively little interruption. It would also help ingratiate them with Duke Guidobaldo, their host. Not only had the duke given them refuge at the expense of his own reputation with the pope, he had probably done so in return for promises implying a quick boost to the stature and economy of his minor city-state. The refugees may have even bragged that they could easily persuade the Levantine merchants to move their ships through Pesaro instead. Revenge "for the spilled blood of our brethren"[63] was another motive. The fleeing refugees wanted to see the people of Ancona, and indirectly the pope, suffer the consequences of the outrage. And they were afraid that if they could not generate the promised trade, the duke would be quick to anger and deny them the right to stay.[64]

To make such a transfer effective required the cooperation of all the Levantine shipping agents—from Salonika to Bursa—not just a handful. Pesaro was an inferior port and would not have been attractive purely from a financial viewpoint, especially as the indigenous Jews and their Levantine brethren in Ancona could readily take over the functions of the departing *conversos*. A meaningful boycott required the full support of all the Jewish merchants in Ottoman lands. And that meant appealing to Jews of diverse backgrounds: Sephardic Jews who had come directly to Turkey from Spain after the Expulsion, former *conversos* who had trickled in later on, indigenous Italian Jews who were fleeing Italy, Ashkenazi Jews fleeing persecutions in Eastern Europe and the local Romaniote Jews who had been there for centuries. Not all had close connections with the *conversos* or cared about problems in Ancona.

Yet another potential hurdle stood in the way of united action (modern Jews might argue that cooperative action among Jews in general has always been difficult to achieve). It was the concerns of the long-standing Jewish population of Ancona. They were horrified when the wharfs began to empty, the flow of ships started to thin out and it became clear that it was happening on account of the actions of those refugees who had fled Pesaro. City officials were equally panicked. They rushed off a plea to the pope, saying "if Your Goodness does not help us, this most faithful city of yours, which used to be full of commerce and exchanges like any other noble city of Italy, will (become) destitute and abandoned." They further warned the pope that the refugees had "such power that they (are) able to convince some Jews and rabbis" to heed their requests.[65]

Meanwhile, the indigenous Jews of Ancona, led by Rabbi Moses Basula, their aged and distinguished leader,[66] wrote their own letters to the communities of the Levant. They warned the rabbis and other communal leaders that such action would ruin them financially and trigger reprisals from a pope whose "anger will nearly boil and his rage will come out like fire." He will think that "your brothers living in Turkey are laughing at me and mocking me."[67] Besides, they argued, the port of Pesaro was not capable of handling the goods. Pesaro was also suffering from an outbreak of the plague, which would further ruin trade.[68]

To underscore their point, the Jews of Ancona reminded the Turkish communities of a recent anti-Semitic incident that had occurred in Pesaro. By implication, the Jews of Ancona were arguing that it was ridiculous to help anyone who would have been foolish enough to go to Pesaro. The incident in question concerned a group of young troublemakers, led by the duke's brother, who had marched into a synagogue one night and dragged its Torah scrolls from the Ark, tearing them and wrapping them around a pig before placing them back inside the Ark. The Jews of Ancona also implied that it would be beyond the power of the refugees to compel the merchants of the Levant to change their long-standing and profitable shipping arrangements.[69]

The refugees in Pesaro countered that Pope Paul IV's anti-Jewish decrees were already so harsh that it was absurd to suggest that a boycott of Ancona could make life any worse for the Jews still there.

Tracing the truth was not easy, and certainly not when critical events were happening so far away and communication was limited and slow. The incident of the pig, for instance, shows up in Usque's *Consolation* as having happened a full three years earlier, with no mention of the duke's brother being involved. According to Usque, there were two incidents, not one. And they were the work of a group of ruffians without official sanction. In the first incident one of the scrolls had been "dashed…against the ground and left there." Other scrolls had been carried outside and thrown into the yard. Four nights later the vandals marched into a different synagogue, breaking an iron gate to get in. They removed the scrolls from that Ark too, whose "sacred bands and mantles they (then) rolled and wrapped in a loathsome swine…" After this, they "put this filthy animal into the Ark" leaving the scriptures lying on the floor.[70]

The rabbis were caught in between, not knowing which faction to believe. They also had to consider the implications for loss of life. If there were no boycott, the refugees now in Pesaro might face a serious predicament, since Duke Guidobaldo's hospitality towards them had already ruptured his close relations with the pope. In practical terms, it may have cost the duke his existing appointment as captain-general of the papal armies.[71] Moreover, as he had also undertaken an expensive renovation of the existing harbor to accommodate the expected increase in traffic, his anger would know no limits. On the other hand, if there were a boycott, the indigenous Jews of Ancona might face expulsion, massacre or penury, brought on by the wrath of a furious pope.[72]

With both viewpoints to consider, and varying degrees of

compassion towards those "Portuguese" merchants who chose to remain and grow rich in Christian lands, the Jewish communities of the Levant and their leadership soon became fragmented. At the outset there had been enthusiasm. Rabbi Judah Faraj must have been a charismatic man who had been able to present the pro-boycott position in compelling terms. This had been augmented by the fact that his first port of call had been Salonika—home to the largest numbers of Jews who had come directly from Spain or Portugal, as well as former *conversos*. Both would have felt a kinship to those who had been persecuted in Ancona and therefore been sympathetic.

The communities of Salonika quickly agreed that they should divert trade to Pesaro as fast as possible. The only condition was that the communities of Constantinople, Adrianopole (modern Edirne) and Bursa—the other great trading centers—must join in. They felt it was only just that everyone had to put up with the same losses and disadvantages. Moving on to Constantinople, Rabbi Judah initially met with similar enthusiasm. One of the city's most powerful rabbis, Joshua Soncino, reported that his eyes were overflowing with tears when he first heard the story, after which the city's congregations unanimously agreed to a boycott, too. But they were equally insistent that all other Levantine communities join in. Until this could be achieved, they also decided to make their boycott temporary, giving it a time limit of eight months—from the late summer of 1555 to Passover of 1556—by which time they hoped to give the boycott permanent status. If not, it would simply expire.[73]

But that was as far as it went. There was not the same level of enthusiasm elsewhere. Most of the other Jews had never experienced an Inquisition. If anything, they felt a closer link with the indigenous Jews of Ancona. The Jews of Adrianopole were divided. The Jews of Bursa rejected the idea outright, saying they could not afford the losses that their merchants might sustain because of Pesaro's inferior docking facilities.[74] Meanwhile, certain Jewish shippers pretended to be headed for Pesaro but changed course at the last moment, for which any number of excuses could be given.[75] Some even encouraged others to do so, by entrusting consignments to them.[76]

Soon, the looming chaos had more to do with heritage and personal economic concerns than it did with presenting a united Jewish front against aggression. This was so even though such a front may well have demonstrated the kind of muscle that the early settlers in modern Israel, some five hundred years later, were determined to show to the world; a level of determination that could make Christian leaders, and even Muslim rulers, think twice before persecuting the Jews with such abandon.

It was at this point that Doña Gracia became involved, responding initially to the pleas from her people in Pesaro who knew she was in their corner.[77] She had personally honored the idea of a boycott from the beginning. Ships laden with her merchandise were no longer docking in Ancona, and she had already moved her own operations to Pesaro.[78] Further, she had very personal reasons for favoring the pro-boycott faction. She had spent her life fighting attacks on *converso* life. She had lost one of her agents to a terrible death. Her friend and physician had suffered irretrievable losses. Her ongoing business had been undermined by the upheavals. And punishing Ancona could give both herself and Don Joseph a chance to regain credibility with Suleiman.[79]

Doña Gracia was therefore soon leading a vigorous effort to patch together a boycott that would hold. On her instructions, Rabbi Joseph ibn Lev, one of the leading rabbis of the city, approached each of the other rabbis of Constantinople, one by one, "so as not to gather to discuss the matter among themselves."[80] The aim was to convince them to sign a statement requiring all Jews to respect the boycott. Rabbi Abraham

Yerushalmi, the rabbi of the Romaniote Jews even gave his support on his deathbed.[81] For it was, as some have since observed, a matter of *pikuah nefesh*—the obligation to save lives; one of the crucial tenets of Judaism. Once again, noncompliance was not simply a matter of opinion. It could carry significant drawbacks for any merchant who transgressed.

Ibn Lev was doing fine until he approached Rabbi Joshua Soncino, arguably the most influential of them all. Soncino refused to sign. He said that he had since heard from the Jews of Ancona. And he had had time to look at both sides of the argument.[82] It is worth noting that Soncino came from a distinguished family of Italian Jewish printers of German origin.[83] His natural sympathies would have been with the indigenous Jews of Ancona, whether he was willing to admit it or not.

His *responsa* 39 and 40, written at this emotional and stressful time, provide a window into his thinking on the topic. He was particularly critical of the fact that the refugees chose to resettle in Pesaro, presumably to continue getting rich, instead of going directly to the Ottoman Empire. Had they gone instead to Ottoman lands, he argued, there would have been no need to ask other Jews to make sacrifices on their behalf. "They didn't have to establish for themselves a dwelling place in the land of the Gentiles," he remarked.[84] Like so many of the openly-professing Jews of Italy and the Ottoman Empire, he had scant patience with the misfortunes of the *conversos*. They had no right to save themselves at the expense of their Jewish brethren. They were seen, as usual, as a money-grubbing, amoral people. Besides, noted Soncino, he was not at all sure which faction was telling the truth. And this would make it difficult to impose sanctions on anyone. He was also worried that something as financially significant as a boycott would end up causing perpetual friction among the Jews themselves.

If he suspected that Doña Gracia might be angry, he was right.

Even a distinguished rabbi like Soncino was not beyond being called to task by a woman who had defied kings, popes and princes. And she was becoming more imperious as she grew older. The tone and details contained in his *responsum* (legal opinion) No. 40 is the clearest lament that we have concerning how withering it must have felt to publicly defy the will of *La Señora*.

Soncino tells us that he and two other rabbinic leaders of his congregation were initially summoned to a meeting with Don Joseph. However, arriving at the appointed hour, they immediately learned that Don Joseph was leaving the same day for Adrianopole, probably to follow the sultan's court. So it would have been clear in advance they were not about to deal with a man sufficiently relaxed and clear-headed to appreciate the other side of the question.

The encounter was stormy. Under pressure, Soncino finally agreed to sign, but with one caveat. If the version of the story put out by the Jews of Ancona turned out to be true, he would be free to let all the other rabbis know that his signature did not imply agreement with the boycott, and the ban would presumably lapse. Don Joseph lost patience with this sort of fence-strad-dling.[85] He told Soncino it was better to "sit still and do nothing... and (not) write anything to anyplace."

Doña Gracia did not agree with her impatient nephew. A few days later she sent for the president of Soncino's synagogue and gave him the task of personally making sure that Soncino signed the document. The leaders of the congregation held a meeting very soon thereafter. They decided that Soncino, along with five distinguished members, should go to see Doña Gracia in person and apologize—a daunting task since she was as feared as she was respected. In a *responsum* written a year or so earlier, Soncino had observed that the elders of the community had been terrified when he had been late in submitting certain written arguments to her. "The Jewish nobles," he wrote, "the judges of the community...trembled greatly that I was late (in heeding) the voice of her...and they bade me haste."[86]

Soncino began by reminding Doña Gracia that Don Joseph seemed perfectly satisfied that he "sit and do nothing." He implored her not to put added pressure on him, because he was truly worried about the impact upon the Jews of Ancona. That may be so, she shot back. But she would not be mollified until he had signed. Nothing he could tell her about his rabbinic problem of signing something in the name of the Almighty when he was uncertain of the facts did any good. The meeting went nowhere. "She did not cool down," he later wrote, "and we rose from her presence and left."[87]

Both Doña Gracia and Soncino now dug in their heels. Doña Gracia saw the boycott as a politically important response to tyranny and trouble. Soncino was equally determined to stand up for what he believed was the correct solution based on Jewish law, and for the Jews of Ancona who had sent further letters suggesting Rabbi Faraj had been telling lies.[88] Soncino even offered to send an emissary at his own expense to the leaders of the Jews of Venice and Padua, to ask them to investigate the matter impartially and see who was really telling the truth. He would later say that Doña Gracia refused this offer, insisting that he was fully able to make a determination from the facts at hand. "The heart knows if it is examining crookedness or perverseness" was the way Soncino described her words.[89]

Meanwhile Doña Gracia decided to bypass the intractable Soncino entirely. Her agents arranged for the Sephardic congregations of Constantinople—by far the largest and most influential in the city—to proclaim the boycott anyhow, along with a willingness to enforce the decree under threat of excommunication. They were joined by a smaller Ashkenazi congregation that ratified the boycott over the protests of at least one member who had commercial dealings in Ancona. Initially, that congregation had declined. But when Don Joseph flexed his financial muscles and threatened to withdraw the family's financial support, they fell into line, too. They could not find anyone else to cover the costs if the funding was withdrawn. "For there wasn't anyone," reported Soncino, "who could provide a large provision like this." The Romaniote congregation followed along as well. It was easy for them. None of their members traded with Ancona, so a boycott would not affect them one way or another.[90]

Soncino could hardly remain idle. He issued a carefully worded statement showing that on two counts such a decree had no legal standing in Jewish law. For one, consent had been secured under pressure. In addition, it violated the Talmudic principle that one person cannot protect himself at someone else's expense. During his deliberations, Soncino raised the curious idea that the lives of the victims of the Ancona *auto-da-fé* should be considered less important to the Jewish world than the desecration of the synagogues in Pesaro. He maintained that going to Pesaro after what had happened was indefensible, since disrespect for the sacred scrolls was even "more serious" a crime than the loss of human life, for "there is no greater insult in all of Israel."[91]

His only concession was to raise a compromise, put forward by a few of the Jewish leaders, that it might be a good idea to compensate Duke Guidobaldo for his hospitality (and presumably placate his anger) with a "gift" of 20,000 ducats. The leaders recommended raising the sum by levying a special tax on the Jewish community as a whole. They also suggested explaining to the duke that because there was no king of Israel it was impossible to force compliance.[92]

Doña Gracia meantime implored the rabbis of all the major Levantine communities to support their brethren in Pesaro, whom she feared would surely face annihilation at the hands of an angry duke if the promised riches failed to materialize. The well-being of the *conversos* in Pesaro, she reminded the rabbis, should be considered more important than any temporary financial loss. The highest religious authorities of the era, Joseph Caro and Moses di Trani, both of whom were living at the time in Safed, the celebrated center of Jewish learning in the Holy Land, spoke out in favor of her argument. Di Trani said he had faith in the fact that the Pesaro refugees would compensate the Jewish merchants in the Levant for any losses that resulted from the transfer. And, he noted, Doña Gracia herself had already compensated some of them.[93]

Even the combined voices of these two outstanding rabbis was not enough. Without united action and total obedience, the boycott was destined to fail. The divided Jewish community did not even raise the 20,000 ducats to appease the angry duke.[94] Nevertheless, however limited in scope, the temporary boycott did ruin dozens of Old Christian merchants.[95]

Though it was something of a pyrrhic victory and Ancona slowly returned to normal, Doña Gracia's strategy was vindicated in the end. Her evaluation concerning the possible consequences of a failed boycott was correct. By 1558, some two years later, Duke Guidobaldo decided that his future lay in rebuilding ties to the pope, not rebuilding a port that lay empty. Under relentless pressure from the Vatican, he issued an edict banning the *conversos* from his lands.[96] But he did not turn them over to the papal authorities. In this respect he lived up to reputation as an independent-minded leader.[97]

What was harder to evaluate was the likely impact upon the Jews of Ancona had the boycott prevailed. Would the Christian world have developed greater respect for the Jews? Or would the pope's fury have unleashed yet another bloody pogrom?

And what about Lusitanus? After arriving in Pesaro, the physician had been determined to retrieve his beloved manuscripts, if nothing else. If only he could pry these works out of the hands of the Inquisition, he later said, he could accept the loss of all his other possessions. Talking the matter over with a friend, he decided to write and ask. And he discovered that a merchant from Salonika had persuaded one of the Italian officials to hold onto them. Ultimately his *Centuria V* manuscript was returned to him and he finished this work in Pesaro. He even revised it "at great leisure" when he moved on to Ragusa a few years later before ending up in Salonika. His commentaries were never returned.[98]

The complicated financial arrangements needed to restore assets and credits belonging to the local *converso* merchants—some of which Doña Gracia claimed as her own as a way to help the refugees get back what they were owed—were handled by the same Florentine bankers that had been associates of the House of Mendes for years, and had acted as brokers for the bribes offered by the *conversos* in December of 1555.[99]

It must have been especially disheartening for Doña Gracia to discover that the Jewish world she cared about so deeply placed factional feelings ahead of cooperative action. Cooperative action had been the core philosophy of life and leadership handed down by her husband and brother-in-law and probably even her parents. Further, Jewish historians have pointed out that it was the first occasion since biblical times that Jews had responded to persecution with something more demanding than prayers, tears, bribes or flight. If Doña Gracia's leadership role in this attempt at retribution had been her only contribution, it would have been significant in itself.

But even a failure as public and humiliating as this one could not dim Doña Gracia's sense of purpose, or allow her to believe she had no place acting as a leader in a man's world. She was stubborn enough to move forward, nonetheless.

CHAPTER **15**

A Time of Trial

Inside the *Palazzo Gritti*, in the San Marcuola district of Venice,[1] La Chica was growing up. If the portrait medal struck of her a few years later is any indication, she was becoming a beautiful young woman.

The medal shows her in profile: fashionably dressed, her features regular and well-proportioned, her mood serious—almost frighteningly so—for someone so young. She is wearing a luxuriant gown. Typical of late Renaissance style, it has a tight bodice that rises upwards to finish in a low, square-cut neckline. Attached at the sides are ballooning sleeves. Its rich fabric appears to be velvet or brocade. Tucked into the deep neckline is a symbol of modesty—a gauze chemise, obscuring her lifted breasts, that sweeps up to culminate in a stand-up collar. Over the chemise hangs a large pendant pearl. Her shoulder-length hair is adorned with two rows of cascading and twisted pearls. They are sewn into a delicate French hood that frames the front of the face, but allows her long tresses to flow freely from the rear.[2]

As the exquisite gown indicates, Brianda was raising her daughter in upper-class style, underwritten by the allowance that she had pried out of her reluctant sister.[3] Officially, Brianda's home was a Christian one, yet there were hints of Jewish practice and the kind of ambiguity typical of a *converso* lifestyle. If Brianda's motive for remaining in Venice had indeed been to live as a sincere Christian, it was not apparent from the way the household had been operating.

Her resident business manager, Licentato da Costa, would later admit that he was, in fact, living as a clandestine Jew; eating only fish, eggs and fruit when he dined with Brianda, and obtaining his meat from the nearby ghetto butchers. Both he and his son, who also served the household, had been circumcised. But, like everyone else in residence, they were known by their Christian names and would occasionally recite Christian prayers.[4]

Meanwhile, Brianda refused to go to church, taking confession instead from a Spanish priest (who was probably one of the many *conversos* who had gone into the church for just such a purpose). During Lent, she managed to get two doctors to admit she was sick and needed meat—hardly the act of a committed Christian. If she kept any religious images in her home, as would have been expected, they were certainly not prominently displayed in the public rooms.[5]

But the leading families of Venice probably did not care. They were only concerned with the spectacular dowry. For both mother and daughter, being courted by the cream of Venetian society must have been a heady experience. During this time, as Charles V's ambassador observed,[6] Brianda was seriously considering a match that would have wed her daughter to an aristocrat.

The fortune itself, in pure gold coins, had meanwhile been placed in two locked boxes inside the Zeccha, each with three different keys. Trustees and intermediaries for Brianda and Doña

Gracia, as well as representatives of the Venetian authorities, had been on hand to count the coins as the payments gradually came in—restitution of debts left over from the halcyon days when Diogo was making loans to monarchs, bishops and merchants alike. These deposits had been proceeding according to the schedule outlined in the Leoncini accords of July 1552. Even as late as March 1555, officials were confirming the fact that the inheritance could be withdrawn freely by the girl and her mother as soon as La Chica turned fifteen.[7]

Still, it would have been an unhappy and anxious time for both mother and daughter. Italy in general, as has been noted, was stepping up its persecution of *conversos* and openly-practicing Jews. Although Brianda and La Chica, along with members of their household, had been living under a 12-year-old safe conduct that protected them from allegations of apostasy by the Inquisition,[8] events unfolding in Ancona suggested that such protection could be rendered worthless at any time.

The pivotal moment came during the months leading up to June 1555—the date when La Chica turned fifteen. As she was not yet married, La Chica and her mother had every right to withdraw the much-fought-over dowry from the Zeccha. But they must have known that Doña Gracia would not easily let 100,000 ducats pass into Brianda's unreliable hands, even at the eleventh hour. Nor would Doña Gracia permit Diogo's only daughter to marry a Venetian nobleman who would give her Christian children. Instead, Doña Gracia would try once again to lure them back under her wing.[9]

From her perch in the East, Doña Gracia was indeed pursuing two new strategies simultaneously. One involved appealing to the Jewish courts in the Levant to confirm, once and for all, that the family fortune rightfully belonged to her and her own daughter, Reyna (Ana).[10] It was the most audacious claim she had yet made regarding the House of Mendes. At the very least, it would reaffirm her stewardship of the money within the autonomous Jewish world, should Brianda start trouble again. The court decision could also be used to retrieve the dowry and other funds from Brianda, should she and her daughter ever revert openly to Judaism and come under Jewish law. The timing of the appeal to the Jewish courts leaves little doubt that it was tied somehow to the coming of age of La Chica.[11]

Second, Doña Gracia turned to Agostinho Henriques, the senior member of the House of Mendes still in Venice who had been designated to replace Doña Gracia should something happen to her. Henriques' task was to bribe the appropriate Venetian officials to prevent the dowry money from being released on time.[12] In addition, Henriques wrote directly to the authorities at the Zeccha arguing against Brianda's fitness to receive the money.[13] All of this pressure must have been effective because a note in the Venetian records, dated June 20 1555, suddenly reversed all previous declarations. It insisted instead that La Chica *could not* withdraw the money. Nor could her mother, "without the authorization of all the attorneys for the benefit of this young girl."[14]

No reason was given for the change of policy, but parallel events suggest an explanation. It seems that both Henriques and Duarte Gomez, the other senior agent of the House of Mendes in Venice, had tipped off the Office of Heresy, the administrative arm of the Inquisition, that da Costa was living secretly as a Jew inside Brianda's house.[15] This fact was probably among allegations made in Henriques' letter to the authorities at the Zeccha, arguing against Brianda's fitness to receive the money. Obviously, if the Inquisition felt there was evidence to suggest that the household was knowingly harboring an apostate, there would be every reason not to release such a valuable fortune— or at least to delay its release until the matter had been fully investigated. It is possible, but unlikely, that the two men decided upon this course of action without consulting Doña Gracia.

Rather, she had probably encouraged them onwards. This was a close family matter and also a strategy that could have been authorized from a distance.

Moreover, it smacks of Doña Gracia's work since it was not the first time that she had tried to remove da Costa. Knowing how dependent Brianda was upon his learned counsel, Doña Gracia had already attempted, one will recall, to get rid of him during the time of the plague in Ferrara, albeit without success.[16] Da Costa later maintained that the only reason Henriques and Gomez had stayed behind in Venice for so long was that Doña Gracia was still determined to bring Brianda and La Chica to Turkey.[17]

Then suddenly, during that same spring of 1555, the tables were turned. Da Costa denounced Henriques and Gomez to the Inquisition as clandestine Jews. Da Costa even admitted to the Inquisitors that because the two agents were going after him, he went after them.[18] All three Inquisition trials—those of Henriques, Gomez and da Costa—took place in Venice virtually back-to-back during the same terrifying summer of 1555 when atrocities against *conversos* were being launched with abandon in nearby Ancona.

The deliberations of the Jewish judges on the sisters' dispute, in Hebrew and Aramaic, fill dozens of pages. Five of the most learned and respected rabbis of the day expounded on the case. The combined effect of these voices was to lend the outcome exceptional weight. A sixth, Rabbi ha Cohen, died before he could complete his discourse and was replaced by Joshua Soncino.[19] The rabbis' review took place just prior to the Ancona incident and therefore before Soncino's dispute with Doña Gracia.

As noted, Soncino was a man of Italian descent and the religious leader of one of Constantinople's major synagogues. In this instance he had been charged by Doña Gracia with bringing together the "leading and lofty sages"of the day.[20] The aim was to deliberate upon the question as it played out in Jewish law. His self-admitted eagerness to please Doña Gracia on this earlier occasion suggests that it must have taken enormous courage and conviction to oppose her later on.[21]

Before getting down to the matter at hand, he positively wallowed in obsequious praise for her character and deeds. To our ears it seems excessive, even allowing for the hyperbole normally granted leaders in this period of history. "(Weighing heavily) upon me (to make a decision)," wrote Soncino, "was the hand of the lady, who wore the…headdress of kingship…(who) crowns the crown of glory and the armies of Israel…who with her strength and her wealth held the hand of the poor and wretched to save and pacify them in this world and the world to come…;" and, what is more, defied the Gentile world that demanded their death.[22]

Also among the group of learned rabbis was Moses di Trani (sometimes called Mitrani). Born in Salonika in 1500, di Trani's immediate ancestors had come from Spain. Di Trani did not stay in Salonika for long, spending most of his life among the great mystics and rabbis of Safed in the Holy Land where he became one of the leading authorities on Jewish law.[23]

A third was Samuel de Medina. Born in Salonika some five years later than di Trani, Medina also came from a family that had fled Spain at the time of the Expulsion. Medina grew up poor. He had watched helplessly as his sister, two sons-in-law, an older brother and a son died of sickness while he lived on, losing even more than most in an era when death was a constant visitor. He was exceptionally hard-working. By the time he was twenty-five, he was already considered a noted rabbi and *responsa* authority. In 1552, just a few years before he commented on the sisters' dispute, he had been appointed the head of a *yeshiva* (religious academy) founded by Doña Gracia—a position that brought him even wider recognition. Perpetually strapped for cash, he was forced to travel frequently to help augment his income, since he had to support the many family members who had lost their breadwinners. He was known for brevity of language and logical reasoning. A compassionate and kindly man, he was especially sensitive to the complex issues raised by the incoming *conversos*.[24]

The fourth, Joseph Caro, was born in 1502 on the Iberian Peninsula, probably in Portugal. Like di Trani, he had spent most of his adult life in the learned circles of Safed while earning a living as a pearl merchant. He had a talent for leadership, but was equally renowned for his legal decisions and his treatises on Jewish mysticism.[25]

Rounding out the group was Joseph ibn Lev. Born in Monastir, north of Salonika, about the same time as the others, and probably also of Spanish heritage, Lev started out as a rabbi in Salonika. He then moved to Constantinople shortly before Doña Gracia's arrival there. He eventually headed yet another *yeshiva* that she founded in Constantinople and was considered so wise and learned that he was regularly consulted by rabbis throughout the Jewish world.[26]

Though distinguished, it was hardly an objective group in the modern sense. Yet, while they lavished praise upon Doña Gracia's leadership and commitment in the public sphere, they made every attempt to remain impartial in their findings on this family matter. In general, they supported the idea that Doña Gracia was entitled to half the Mendes assets, and probably more. In coming to this conclusion they focused upon the vast sums she had spent to keep the fortune from falling into the hands of "the Gentiles" and to rectify the disruptions caused by Brianda's interference.

An exception was Joseph Caro.[27] He decided that the entire estate belonged to Reyna (Ana), Doña Gracia daughter, as the rightful and singular heir. Caro's argument hinged upon the fact that Jewish law did not recognize the rights of a widow to her husband's estate. Instead, the assets were routinely awarded to the male heirs. If there were none, the assets belonged to the deceased's daughter or daughters. Moreover, argued Caro, Francisco's estate included all the assets of the House of Mendes.

The other rabbis disagreed. They insisted that according to Talmudic principals, the law of the land in which the testator died took precedent over Jewish law. Since Francisco lived and died in Portugal *as a converso*, not as a Jew, this meant adhering to the precepts of Portuguese inheritance practices, rather than Jewish law. Francisco and Doña Gracia did not even have a *ketubah*, a Jewish marriage contract, only a civil one. And, under Portuguese law, a testator could not will his property to others if he had surviving sons and daughters.[28] Only a small portion could be set aside for outsiders. That being said, the rabbis nevertheless took into account the fact that Francisco had clearly stated in his will that he wanted his brother, Diogo, to have *half* of the assets as "he helped acquire (them)."[29]

So they hemmed and hawed in typical rabbinic style. Indeed, they were so equivocal that even historians cannot agree upon exactly what was decided. In general, however, they found in favor of Doña Gracia, awarding her and her daughter the entire assets of the House of Mendes, including the right to seize some of La Chica's dowry to cover the expenses forced upon them by Brianda's actions. Other scholars have argued to the contrary.[30] But it really did not matter. The net result was that nothing changed. Doña Gracia continued to control the assets. And Brianda and La Chica were left with what had been granted to them in Venice when the sisters parted.

It is clear from their arguments that Brianda had been consulted, as would have only been equitable; and that she mounted
a strong defense. Soncino writes that Brianda declared that if
Doña Gracia really believed that Diogo and his family were never
entitled to inherit any of the assets of the House of Mendes, it is
curious that she had not mentioned this fact earlier on.[31] On the
other hand, Soncino and di Trani argued that Doña Gracia had
an added right to the remaining assets because she had to spend
so much time, money and energy to protect them from the Gentile world, and the mischief of her sister.

In a stab at the dowry, Doña Gracia insisted that she was
entitled to take these costs out of the inheritance that La Chica
was due to receive, should Brianda have insufficient personal
funds to cover them. It was as though Doña Gracia had already
decided that even if the rabbis concluded that some of the fortune did indeed belong to Brianda and La Chica, she had a right
to it anyway.[32] Her reluctance to reveal that she had known all
along that she and her daughter were entitled to the entire fortune, she said, was because most of the money was in Diogo's
hands at the moment of her husband's death. Diogo, she said,
might falsely claim that some of it was lost due to business re-
versals, bad debts and missing merchandise (although this does
not explain why she did not speak up after Diogo's death).[33]
Medina was dismissive of her defense on this point, saying that
Doña Gracia and Diogo engaged in commerce together in
Antwerp. And during this time they exchanged documents that
appeared to confirm an acceptance by Doña Gracia that half of
the assets of the House of Mendes rightfully belonged to Diogo.[34]

Di Trani posited that Francisco could have made the shared
arrangement in his will to purposely ensure that some of the
estate would be managed by Diogo in a seasoned manner. It
would also better protect Doña Gracia and her daughter (presumably by placing at least a portion of the fortune beyond the

reach of the Portuguese crown or the Inquisition). Coming from a rabbi, this assumption is interesting in that it shows how the thinking of those times was affected by a need to constantly consider the threat of confiscation as a rationale for all sorts of financial maneuvers. By the same token, Medina argued that the funds that were in Diogo's hands at the time of Francisco's death should not necessarily be considered part of the assets that rightfully belonged to Doña Gracia and her daughter.

Medina also addressed the question of whether Doña Gracia had a right to keep all the profits generated through her own hard work and enterprise; or whether they should be shared among the heirs, since the gains resulted from the use of the original assets of the House of Mendes. He maintained that she must share the profits proportionately.[35] Some additional comments made by Medina imply that Doña Gracia tried to persuade the rabbis that Diogo had no interest whatsoever in his Jewish heritage and therefore did not merit the bequest under Jewish law—an astonishing allegation based upon what is known about Diogo's life.

It is a hint of the desperation she must have felt in her quest to win a favorable ruling from the Jewish courts. And it again shows a darker side of her character. But the allegation could not have stemmed from greed. She had given away too much of the Mendes fortune for that. Still, ends now justified means, regardless of the harm she might do to Diogo's memory. Had the vicissitudes of Doña Gracia's wandering life and the enormous efforts she had exerted to conserve the family fortune taken their toll? As it turned out, she need not have stooped so low. How Diogo conducted himself had no bearing in Jewish law in this kind of a situation, noted Medina.[36]

Beyond Doña Gracia's obvious feud with her sister, the timing of the appeal to the Jewish courts suggests another possibility. Following Reyna's marriage to Don Joseph, Doña Gracia may have also been using the rulings to seek clarification concerning the amount of money that she would now have to transfer to her son-in-law as financial custodian of the inheritance of his young wife. Doña Gracia was not a woman to relinquish control easily—certainly not the control of large sums of money, and even to a man who was her partner. In order to continue working closely with Don Joseph, such a ruling could have helped to put their own financial house in order.

———···⁙···———

The testimony of the three hapless Inquisition defendants—Duarte Gomez and Agostinho Henriques and Tristan da Costa—and the witnesses giving evidence at their trials, gives us a colorful glimpse into the lives of three typical *converso* merchants, and how they eluded the undercurrent of danger and Catholic commitment that stalked them daily.

Licentato Tristan da Costa was fifty-eight when he was first brought before the Venetian panel of Inquisitors in June 1555,[37] led during this period by a Franciscan friar. Other panel members typically included the pope's senior representative in Venice, as well as three nobles of untarnished Catholic piety, appointed by the doge. They were known as the Three Sages on Heresy, and they acted as intermediaries between Venice and Rome. Their unofficial role was to try to restrain the excesses of the church. Nobody wanted the kind of public display of torture and burning so prevalent elsewhere; it would be terrible for business. Indeed, one will recall, Venice had been reluctant to have an Inquisition at all. The actual power of sentencing lay with the ecclesiastical judges. Even so, the possibility of an *auto-da-fé* would have been out of the question. Better, as mentioned earlier, to consider a discreet drowning or banishment.

The questioning normally took place over a period of days. Yet each of the days set aside for a particular prisoner could be weeks apart. The panel tried 1,560 cases during the 16th century, only fourteen of which resulted in sentences of death by drowning and four in executions that prudently took place hundreds of miles away in Rome. Not all the accused were apprehended for practicing Judaism in secret. Rather, a majority of cases heard in Venice were aimed at Catholics who had become followers of Luther or Anabaptists.[38]

The trials took place at the doges' palace, an ornate Gothic-style structure festooned with carved arches and exquisite statuary that stood at an imposing juncture facing the entrance to the Grand Canal and adjacent to the *Piazza San Marco*. The palace was the administrative seat of Venice as well as the residence of the doge. Audience rooms, senate meeting chambers, state ballrooms, stairwells and hallways were all adorned from floor to ceiling with friezes, paneling, frescos, *trompe l'oeil* and paintings. There were canvases by such artists as Jacopo Tintoretto and sculpture by masters like Giovanni Bellini.

Until later in the 16th century, prisoners awaiting trial were also kept in the palace, either in tiny stone cells carved in a dank basement that could flood whenever the waters of the lagoon surged, or in airless and cramped spaces under the roof. There prisoners shivered endlessly in the winter or gasped for relief from the heat in the summer. They spent their days in poor light behind barred windows and doors, with meager food, and tormented by rats and insects that overran their quarters and bodies. The interrogation and torture room were one and the same, presumably for psychological purposes.[39]

When he appeared for his hearing, da Costa sported a long, grey beard and was dressed "as a foreigner," according to the official account, which probably meant he was not fashionably attired like most Venetians of the same social standing.[40] Though he had been arrested in April, he did not appear before the Inquisitors until June. One can well imagine the suffering he had undergone. Brianda would later plead for the chance to take him home while matters were being decided, pledging a fine of 10,000 ducats if she failed to present him for sentencing. She requested the favor "so that my affairs do not go to ruin."[41] But the dreadful conditions must have been on her mind, even though at the onset of the trial the judges had allowed him to be transferred, on a surety of 1,000 ducats, to safekeeping in a religious institution that they themselves selected, probably at Brianda's pleading.[42]

Da Costa told his accusers that he came originally from Viano do Castelo, a prominent port in northern Portugal. He had been born into a family that had been forcibly baptized at the time of the mass baptisms of 1497. His father's Hebrew name was Isaac Habibi, Even though he had been "torn from my mother's chest and baptized" as a baby, he doubted if his mother had ever formerly gone through baptism. At home there was no overt Christian practice.[43]

He was amazingly candid—almost contemptuous—when repeatedly asked for proof that he had lived as a Christian while growing up. It was as though he was certain that Brianda's safe conduct of 1544 covering her entire household, gave him license to taunt his accusers. At one point during the interrogations he even sighed impatiently at the repetitiveness of some of the questions.[44]

He had gone to Mass in Portugal, he said, but only "out of fear that they would put me in jail if I didn't go." As a youth, he told them, he studied law, Latin and sciences at the great University of Salamanca in Spain. While there, he and his fellow *converso* students would tell others that they were going to Mass, "but we did not actually go." After obtaining his degree, he had returned to his home town and married a *conversa* named

Francesca Pereira. They were married in church but only "out of fear of the Inquisition." Later, he made sure his three sons and two daughters were baptized, but once again, only out of fear of the Inquisition and not, he implied, as the act of a true believer.[45]

Around 1543, he and his family left Portugal for Antwerp, ostensibly to find work. From there they moved to Ferrara where they lived openly as Jews. They had been forced to leave most of their property behind (so many *conversos* had been fleeing Portugal on account of the Inquisition that the authorities had been stepping up the enforcement of injunctions preventing them from taking assets with them, since these departures were becoming a serious drain on the economy). But even these rulings could be circumvented, he admitted.

Da Costa went on to explain how this was done. Most of his holdings were in rental buildings. And he had thwarted the law by putting them in his brothers' names (typically the proceeds would then be transferred through bills of exchange that the seller could cash in Antwerp from friendly bankers like the Mendes).[46]

It was in Ferrara, he recalled, that Brianda first approached him for professional help, saying that she was suing her sister. He later moved with her to Venice, on the understanding that he would be fully protected by the safe conduct she had received for herself and her household—a document he believed would protect them all from charges of heresy.

When they asked him, yet again, if he were a Jew or a Christian, da Costa was non-committal. "I don't do Christian acts," he said. "But, on the other hand, he insisted, he had never performed any Jewish ceremonies or said any Jewish prayers since he had been in Venice. Did he use a Christian or Jewish name? The name Tristan da Costa served him in both worlds, he said. "I never declared that it was a Christian or a Jewish name," he mocked, "and I have never been asked." However, he did concede that in Ferrara he had been known as Abraham Habibi, but the name of Licentato Costa was "more appropriate for the business I handled for the lady, since I was not using a name that was explicitly Jewish."[47]

The fact that he regularly wore Christian clothing and the black hat of the Christians (Jews still had to wear red or yellow hats) was done, he said, because he felt certain he was protected by Brianda's safe conduct. Had he ever been to church in Venice? "No," he conceded. Then he added with a certain air of insouciance, "I could have been inside at one point, just passing through." Had he shown respect by kneeling and taking off his hat? "No, sir," he added, implying he had only gone inside because it looked like a useful shortcut through town. Even when he was in Portugal, he said, he had never taken communion, though he had felt obligated to go to Mass. But once there, he had eluded the actual act by getting lost in the crowd. It was during these hearings that da Costa revealed that Brianda herself might not be a sincere Catholic either.[48]

Da Costa's own fluctuating religious identity was confirmed by a Spaniard named Don Gottardo Archaro. He maintained that rather than being Christian or Jewish, da Costa actually "has no faith at all." However, Gottardo added that da Costa was probably closer to the Jews, as shown by the fact that his wife was now living in Salonika and "all of the business partners… are Jewish."[49]

———••❖••———

Amazingly, Gomez managed to delay *his* trial until August, arguing that he was too busy to offer himself for cross-examination in July when originally called—surely a brazen act of hubris or perhaps his personal stand against tyranny. Instead, he offered to provide a bond of 2,000 ducats under the surety of a Florentine nobleman who did considerable business with the House of Mendes. This would assure the court that he would be present at the later date and even appear repeatedly until at least the end of October.[50]

At the time of the hearing, Henriques and Gomez were living in a large house above an engraver's shop in the Castello district of Venice; an area that produced the storage chests used for the extensive shipping trade that passed through the lagoon. Witnesses said that their rooms were a beehive of *converso* activity and that many Jews and women visited the house. Among the pair's immediate neighbors were painters and cabinetmakers.[51]

A Portuguese friar named Simon, who served as a witness, said he had originally met the pair while on a trip to Jerusalem—underscoring once again the extensive travel that seems to have common among *converso* merchants in general. Simon said he had been particularly grateful to the men because Gomez had helped him recoup some money he had unfortunately handed to a less-than-honest merchant. But he "sensed they (were) Jews" because, despite being baptized, they "do not frequent the natural-born Portuguese." And he had seen Henriques with "Jews who wear caps and turbans" (Jewish merchants from the Ottoman Empire). Moreover, he was certain that Gomez had a brother named Guglielmo who now lived and worked as a Jew in the employ of Doña Gracia in Constantinople. And, he said—implying it was something everyone knew—*she* was now living as a Jew. He had a hunch that if the home of Henriques and Gomez were searched, the Inquisitors would find many prohibited books.[52]

Gottardo, the Spanish merchant who also testified against da Costa, was not as certain. He said he had seen the pair accompany the Spanish ambassador[53] to Mass at St. Mark's Cathedral on several occasions. Gottardo had eaten with them at their home, in his own home and also shared a meal at the home of the ambassador. At no time had they ever refused to eat any particular foods. But even though their outward appearance and behavior suggested they were good Catholics, he admitted to harboring doubts. On one occasion, Gottardo recalled, when he was discussing the differences between the ceremonies of the Christians, Muslims and Jews with the two men, he had argued that the Christian ones were the most beautiful. Instead of agreeing with him, Henriques and Gomez had remained silent.[54]

Called to testify on his own behalf, Gomez was far more agreeable and respectful towards his Inquisitors than da Costa, giving them answers they undoubtedly wanted to hear. He said that he was 45 years old and the father of four sons and four daughters. The three oldest children were living with him in Venice. The others were with their mother in Ferrara. He had been born in Lisbon as a Christian. His parents were already Christians by that time, he said, as they had also been baptized during the mass conversions of 1497. He readily admitted having three brothers who formerly lived as Christians but were now living in Constantinople as Jews. Although he was a merchant, he told them that he had originally studied the humanities, philosophy, medicine and theology. In fact, he had been a lecturer in Lisbon with a royal stipend before leaving Portugal.[55]

He was firm about being an active Catholic, insisting he was diligent about taking communion and going to confession, although the Inquisitors found it strange that he seemed to take confession in a number of different churches, rather than attaching himself to a particular parish. He was asked for confirmation of his piety, and later produced a cleric and a merchant, both of whom vowed that he went to confession. One of them told the Inquisitors that Gomez even had images of the saints in his house, and would conduct business on a Saturday. When Gomez entertained Jews in his home, argued this witness, they talked of nothing but trade. They never spoke Hebrew. A hand-ful of other witnesses produced by Gomez, including a secre-tary to the duke of Florence, also confirmed that Gomez lived the life of a sincere Catholic. He was well-versed in Christian topics, they insisted, and regularly conducted business on Sat-urdays.[56]

One can only speculate how many ducats such a detailed confirmation of Catholic piety must have cost Gomez.

Gomez told the judges that his colleague, Henriques, was equally conscientious. When asked whether either of them had contact with Jews, he reported that they did, but only "in order to do our affairs and for nothing else." In any discussion con-cerning the two religions he always said "that the Jewish reli-gion is in vain and the Christian religion is good and holy."[57]

Gomez admitted having some Talmudic books in his pos-session, although at least one of them, he argued, was a book that a cardinal had been anxious to obtain. However, a later compilation of the titles of these supposed books on the Tal-mud actually included parts of the Old Testament in Spanish, some writings of Martin Luther, a work on opera and another on cosmology.[58]

As had happened at the trial of da Costa, the court received conflicting opinions concerning whether Gomez was circum-cised or not. They knew that it was unquestionably the mark of a Jewish man, yet they seemed ignorant of the anatomical signs. Even a practicing physician called to examine Gomez in his home (where some prohibited Jewish texts were indeed found) ap-peared uncertain. The physician said he thought Gomez had been circumcised. But another witness insisted he was not.[59]

Henriques did not show up for his hearing until September of that year, at which time he apologized for not coming for-ward sooner, saying he had been in Ferrara and had not been well. Now, he insisted, he was eager to answer the charges against him.[60] Unlike da Costa, neither Gomez nor Henriques appear to have been held in jail. We do not have the personal testimony of Henriques.

••••☙••••

What was the fate of the three alleged apostates? Da Costa was immediately and permanently banished from Venice.[61] Gomez, however, was formally and publicly acquitted. "Nothing…brought in front of us has been proved with regards to the accusations against Don Oduardo (Duarte) as being a heretic and judaizing," noted the judges.[62] Henriques must have also been acquitted because he stayed on in Venice and did not formally take up residence in Ferrara for several years after his trial.[63]

However, the most dramatic finale to the trials did not come from these verdicts, but from the involvement of Brianda. While da Costa was under detention, she petitioned the court to testify on his behalf, addressing her remarks to the ruling Council of Ten, rather than directly to the Inquisitors.[64] She began by pouring out her heart over the troubles she had faced on account of her "cruel sister" who was still trying to get her to go to Constantinople where she and her daughter could live as Jews.[65]

She explained that this was the real reason Henriques and Gomez had made accusations to the Office of Heresy against her chief of staff, da Costa. "They did this in order to put me in a position of desperation," she told them, "to make me underhandedly say that I wanted to go to Constantinople." Henriques and Gomez arranged for their denunciations to be even more compelling, she said, by bribing a senior church official to actually make the accusations. Moreover, "they had the most reverend monsignor…slander me by saying that (da Costa) was a

Christian living as a Jew (in my house)." Even if that were so, she explained, she was asking them to honor the safe conduct she had obtained years earlier. "I beg that the justice of this safe conduct," she said, "is reinstated for my agent and a hand is put over him in protection."[66]

Sir Melchior Michael, the church official who had allegedly been bribed, then testified. He provided information that created an awkward situation for Brianda. According to Sir Michael, La Chica was so anxious to live as a sincere Christian that she had asked to be removed from Brianda's house and placed in a convent. The implication was that the presence of people like da Costa, living as secret Jews in a none-too-pious household, had become anathema to the young girl. She needed the help of the authorities to get out. But the story has a suspicious ring to it, as though Henriques and Gomez dreamed it up (and managed to sell it to Sir Michael) in a final attempt to break down Brianda's defenses by taking her daughter from her.[67] The idea would have appealed to Sir Michael. It would have meant that he had personally helped to save a Christian soul as well as safeguard the girl's fortune for the benefit of one of Venice's own sons. If he could be paid for telling the tale, so much the better.

Probably seeking to be even-handed, the Council of Ten immediately called upon Brianda and La Chica to testify personally about these new allegations. It was a pivotal moment. "She (Brianda) is called to make the Council understand that she and her family live Christianly," noted the official record.[68]

All of this took place in August, the same month as the mass arrests of relapsed *conversos* in nearby Ancona. The Venetian officials would later confirm that they had been keenly aware that the new pope would no longer tolerate such behavior. If prior assurances and safe conducts could be wiped off the books in Ancona, they could certainly be annulled in Venice. Pope Paul IV's arbitrary actions in another part of Italy were starting to provide legitimacy for similar practices elsewhere.[69]

Brianda now faced the daunting task of defending the actions of her household and holding onto her daughter—all without the help her most trusted advisor. But she was not without her own resources. The Council first summoned Brianda to respond to the question of whether she was indeed living according to Jewish law, as had been intimated by da Costa's testimony. She was given the unusual benefit of being told in advance what would happen if they did find her guilty. She would be banished.[70] As before, the Venetians may have feared creating an incident with the Turks if they went too far in punishing a member of such an important family. It was one thing for the pope to arrest one of Doña Gracia's agents. It was quite another for Venice to deal brutally with her sister.

They also told Brianda that despite the outcome, La Chica would have the right to withdraw the dowry money at any time. Furthermore, "the directors of the Zeccha are ordered to precisely count in full every part of the money that the said (La Chica) wants to withdraw."[71] So that this could happen without impediment, the temporary freeze placed on the funds in June was being lifted.[72] It was beginning to sound like a carefully crafted compromise settlement hammered out behind close doors in advance of a public appearance or pronouncement.

Brianda was first asked to appear on her own, separately from her daughter. She began by reading a statement. "Most illustrious sirs," she said. "I left... the land... where I lived well in order to escape the Inquisition. For this cause, I looked for a way to come to this city, thinking of the liberty the city offered. With a safe conduct in order to live peacefully, I came and obeyed the leadership as if I were St. Francis." But, she said, "I have many persecutors that have always tormented me."[73]

She was then asked what she meant by saying that she had always obeyed the leadership. She replied that she was a *New*

Christian, which meant that she was living as a Christian only because she had to do so. In her heart, she said, she had always lived as a Jew. And this was how she wanted to live in the future. Such a public confession must have stunned the Council members, especially as Brianda had spent over a decade begging them for protection from her scheming sister, so that she might have the chance to live the remainder of her life as a sincere Christian. She was immediately asked to go into an anteroom while her daughter was questioned by the Council.[74]

La Chica started by saying that she hoped that the Council members would help her in whatever she desired to do. All that *she* wanted, she declared, was "to live under the law of my mother." They asked her what she meant by this.

She replied, "Jewish law,"[75] a simple phrase that must have also echoed like the swish of a rapier through that most Christian of chambers.

The Council members then told both mother and daughter to wait in another room while they discussed the implications of what they had just heard. As she left the room, Brianda cried out, "Our money, sirs?"[76] They assured her that the money would now be made available for the taking. They then asked Brianda to confirm her daughter's age. She told them that the girl had already turned fifteen and was going on sixteen.[77]

Later, when the Council members called Brianda back into the hearing room, she was told that she had been banished from Venice. She and her household, including La Chica, were to leave by the end of the month. She complained that there was not sufficient time for her to organize her affairs.[78]

Then she dropped another bombshell. She asked instead if they would "let me stay here in the ghetto with the other Jews." They flatly refused.[79] After all, the possibility of La Chica marrying one of their noble sons was now out of the question, as a Christian could not legally marry a *Jew*. So there was no point wasting any more time on the family. And this may well have been Brianda's strategy all along. She had won the right to leave—and depart with the precious dowry intact.

She was now ready to plead once again on behalf of her chief of staff. She asked for information about the prisoner, da Costa. He had already been held for nearly four months, she complained, even though he had been living in her household under a safe conduct. At this point the Council agreed to release da Costa, on condition that he immediately leave Venice with her.[80]

A report of the outcome sent by Venetian officials to papal authorities several days later shows how much they had wanted to please the new pope on matters of faith, and how angry they were about being deceived by Brianda and her daughter. "They (and their behavior) will not be tolerated in any of our dominions in any way," noted the report. It confirmed the annulment of the safe conduct issued in 1544 for Brianda and her household. Also, that following a public declaration by both mother and daughter that they wanted to live (and indeed had probably been living) as Jews, the entire family had been banished, along with servants, staff and property. Da Costa was cited separately as having been banished, too. All of this was being reported to Rome, "so that his sanctity can remain well-informed and satisfied with our transaction made in the glory of our lord God."[81]

But official condemnation and a detailed report to the pope did not necessarily mean the closing of all Brianda's options. On account of certain loans and other business matters she had been conducting with France (and perhaps dangling the option of lending, at interest, some of the dowry money as soon as she could get her hands on it), she managed to persuade the French ambassador to intervene and see if he could arrange for her to stay in Venice as a Jew, or at least lobby for an extension until the following April.[82] The French, one will recall, had long been on close terms with member of the House of Mendes, even though they had their disagreements. Brianda seemed ready to do almost anything at this point to avoid leaving her beloved Venice.

The Venetians acceded to French entreaties by allowing her an additional month.[83] A few days later the Council of Ten wrote to the French court explaining why this was the limit of what they were prepared to do.[84] Following Brianda and La Chica's confessions of Judaism, they said, they had been left with no choice, especially in light of the current sentiments of Pope Paul IV. "We ordered that which the...pontiff had ordered for the *(conversos)* in his state (Ancona) so as not to support this type of activity." The Council refused to budge, calling Brianda highly deceitful.[85]

During these final few weeks, Brianda did manage to conclude some business. She collected a long overdue payment of 3,000 ducats from the proceeds of some property still owned in Antwerp.[86] She also applied to Duke Ercole for a safe conduct allowing her and her daughter to return to Ferrara, one of the only places left in Italy that still welcomed *conversos* who had brazenly become openly-professing Jews. The duke complied in language that suggested he was delighted. He later explained that he extended the courtesy in part because of the "countless (and) innumerable benefits...that (Doña Gracia)...allowed to occur when she was in Ferrara." He wanted to be equally gracious towards her sister and niece.[87]

He was also perfectly aware that La Chica was now a rich woman in her own right. Thus his chances of securing any number of sizeable loans was virtually assured. In fact, such assurances were no doubt part of the negotiations. Within a few weeks of their arrival, the women had granted two loans of 2,000 ducats each to the duke's brother, Ippolito Cardinal Este.[88] The duke further guaranteed that their property would be protected from any claims made by anyone, even from "abroad;" no doubt a reference to possible further attempts by Doña Gracia. The safe conduct was also sufficiently extensive to permit them to leave Ferrara with all their property at any time they wished to do so.[89]

Thus, late in 1555, as wintry winds began to gust around the lagoon, they packed their belongings and moved back to Ferrara.[90] Unofficially Brianda would now be known by her Jewish name of Reyna Nasi.[91] Her daughter would henceforth be listed in notarial documents under *her* Jewish name of Gracia Benveniste.[92] Based upon later Ferrara documents implying that La Chica was now an extremely rich young woman, the dowry went with them, exactly as the weary Venetians had promised.[93]

Biblioteca Estense and Universitaria, Modena/courtesy of Beth Hatefutsoth Museum, Tel Aviv, Israel

HERCVLES ESTENSIS, Ferraria pulchra, secundis
Hæc quarti, e Ducibus forma sutique, tuus.

Portrait of Duke Ercole II of Ferrara

Courtesy of the Jewish Museum, New York (gift of the Samuel and Daniel M. Friedenberg Collection).

Portrait medal of Doña Gracia's niece in her
18th year, struck in Ferrara, Italy (1558)

CHAPTER **16**

Unfinished Business

The wily duke of Ferrara was not only after La Chica's fortune when he welcomed both mother and daughter back into his duchy.[1] Even greater riches, he must have known, would surely await him in the form of a substantial loan, or an outright gift, as soon as he sought a token of gratitude from La Chica's aunt. He wasted no time. By November, only weeks after their arrival, the duke was already negotiating with Duarte Gomez to solicit funds that would "give proof of the goodwill you (Doña Gracia) always meant to show me."[2]

Doña Gracia had something to gain, too. With the duke in her debt, she might secure a second chance for control over the future of her niece. According to the guardianship customs of the era and the laws of Ferrara, ducal consent was needed before a marriage could take place. With the duke in her debt, she would once again be in a position to have a say in a potential match for La Chica.[3] Also, if anything should happen to Brianda, Doña Gracia might become La Chica's guardian again.

As it turned out, both eventualities would soon come to pass.

Less than a year after returning to Ferrara, Brianda died. Her death occurred during the early weeks of July 1556, presumably from natural causes.[4] It was as though all those years of struggle to gain the dignity of financial independence had been for naught. She had been given only three years on her own, none of which were peaceful. The struggle had continued. Now, at last, as the rabbis would have said, her tormented soul could rest in peace. At least she had gained the right to a Jewish burial.

As required by law, and specifically requested by the duke, an inventory was immediately taken of Brianda's belongings. They included a spellbinding cornucopia of possessions.[5] There was a hoard of 27,000 gold coins in 27 pouches, plus another 300 ducats inside a purse of its own; an unspecified number of silver goblets and silver spoons, a silver salter, a decorative silver piece of sport armor with chimes, at least one silver serving vessel, a bronze and silver stepping stool and additional silver spoons inside a separate wooden box.

Clothes and fashion textiles were in abundance. A chest encased in iron fittings was found packed with fabric, including a dress of stiff black cloth and another one in red. A second trunk was also filled with fabric and a third with clothes. Two more chests were crammed with "goods from Flanders," which doubtless meant even more textiles and lace. Additional boxes were brimming with furs and lace. Her opulent cache stood in stark contrast to the simple clothes worn by the wife of Amatus Lusitanus. Indeed, Brianda's more-than-ample wardrobe of Renaissance finery would stand as mute testimony to her profligate ways.

So would her unpaid debts. Even before her death she had gained a reputation as someone who could be infuriatingly tardy in paying her bills. Consider the complaints of three *conversos* who alleged they had been seduced several years earlier by lavish offers from Brianda to help her in her dispute with her sister.

They had housed her and her daughter in Ferrara during much of the first time she lived there, they said, and advanced 4,000 ducats to Brianda to cover her immediate cash needs. But they had never been paid for their time or their outlay. Upon her return, they were so desperate that they approached the duke himself for help in forcing Brianda to pay up.[6]

Thus it was hardly surprising that she left a slew of other unpaid obligations. There were sums of money due an employee named Don Lazaro Navario, described in his petition as "a Portuguese Jew…residing in Ferrara."[7] This would have placed him in the same category as dozens of other *conversos* who had reverted openly to Judaism after reaching Ferrara. According to his testimony, Don Navario entered Brianda's service in 1546 (the year Brianda first arrived in Venice), providing legal and other strategic counsel. At first, his labors were focused upon her dispute with her sister. Yet he later complained that "he (had never) received a salary for his toil, service and legal advice, although many times…he was promised that he would be paid and that he would be given back the many sums of his very own money that (he) had spent in those times for Brianda…" The cash, he explained, had gone for "things that she needed because of the quarrel between her and her sister and because of other reasons…" but always "with the clear understanding and intention of getting such money back…."

Don Navario argued that some of the funds had been laid out "for food, drink and accommodation (for the other) men in the service of Brianda" who had come to Ferrara to help support her case and who had been lodged in Don Navario's house. He had also paid money out of his own pocket to free certain people who had been put in prison "on account of Brianda"—a tantalizing hint of how overheated the disagreement must have become. The total bill: 1,000 gold ducats.[8]

The five children of da Costa—Isaac, Jacob, Vita, Formosa

and Benjamin—had the same complaint. They sought 1,050 gold ducats in settlement of "salary debts and (other) debts" left unpaid when their father died around the same time as Brianda.[9] In both instances the petitioners were furious because La Chica seemed as reluctant as her mother to make good.

But this was not unexpected. Almost immediately following Brianda's death, La Chica became entangled in a myriad of claims and counter-claims concerning debts still outstanding. The cash sought by Don Navario and the da Costa children might not have been readily available. Nevertheless, their claims must have been valid because La Chica was required to pay them in the end.[10]

••••◦✕◦••••

The news of Brianda's death would have reached Doña Gracia within weeks of learning that her agent in Ancona, Jacob Morro, could not be pardoned and was likewise destined to die in the summer of 1556. Both deaths would have caused emotional suffering in their own way. And both would have required political and financial maneuvering on her part. To the Morro death, and the outrage meted out against all the other condemned *converso* merchants, she had responded by throwing her full support behind a boycott. To the death of her sister, and the prospect of a young heiress of only sixteen living alone in Italy with few reliable relatives to help and support her, she responded as might have been anticipated.

She dashed off a letter to her old friend, Duke Ercole, recommending that she be re-appointment guardian.[11] By the time her letter arrived, the process of appointing a guardian had already begun. On August 13, only weeks after Brianda's death, La Chica and her advisors had written directly to the ducal palace on the same issue. La Chica's notary, Domenico Zaffarini, requested permission to "appoint someone who will aid and assure that she (La Chica) will rightfully (receive)…the entire quantity of money and property that are owed to her." La Chica reminded the duke that she was not able to make these arrangements herself because of restrictive "statutes of Ferrara regarding contracts for minors and women."[12]

On the same August day, Zaffarini drew up a companion document alerting the duke to the importance of the guardianship request, so that La Chica could speedily obtain all that was due "without any damages, debts and serious entanglements."[13] La Chica wanted the collections to be made public, he noted, along with the fact that she intended to take full control of her assets as soon as she reached the legal age of twenty-five. There was further talk in yet another document, drawn by Zaffarini at the same time, explaining that "she does not know if the inheritance…(will) bear a profit or a debt and she is implicated in debts and problems and therefore wishes to act cautiously and judiciously."[14] This could have been a further reference to Brianda's unpaid bills and faulty financial management.

Brianda did not even leave a will, noted Zaffarini.[15] Though one can assume that all her property would have gone to La Chica anyway, it does give the impression of a woman sufficiently self-absorbed, or lacking in foresight, that she did not even worry about providing bequests for her loyal servants. Many of them, like da Costa, had served her for years. Nor did she bequeath alms for the poor, as would have been customary for either a Jew or a Christian.

Moreover, only a week after the official inventory of Brianda's possessions had been completed, 15,000 ducats from La Chica's existing holdings (possibly part of her dowry money) had to be deposited in the duke's personal chest in the castle—a deal that must have been made well in advance and for reasons that were not explained.[16] Another item of special concern to La Chica and her counselors was the potential income from Diogo's remaining properties in Antwerp—a matter that had been handled up to the present by Brianda, in partnership with an agent in Venice, and for which no alternatives seem to have been made to ensure that La Chica would continue to benefit from the arrangement. The drafting of all these documents took place in the San Guglielmo neighborhood of Ferrara, in a residence that Brianda had rented for the entire household, including quarters for Licentato Costa and his family.[17]

Meanwhile, the matter of a guardian was moving forward. By October, Duke Ercole was able to write a warm reply in his own hand to "Snra. Gratia de Luna" in Constantinople. He wished her "all the best" and promised that "he would decide according to her request," noting that it "appears to me convenient from all points of view that you can well imagine..."[18]

His intent soon became abundantly clear. La Chica would be encouraged to formally request that her aunt, Doña Gracia, be named guardian, along with her uncle, Aries de Luna (Doña Gracia's brother), who was still living in Ferrara. Agostinho Henriques, a cousin and one of her aunt's most trusted agents, was to act in Doña Gracia's absence, "with full authority and power to do whatever he sees fit."[19] Later documents would speak of Aries de Luna as a beneficiary, too.[20]

Up until this time there had been very little mention of Aries and nothing is known about his prior life. He must have been considered trustworthy because he was collecting debts on behalf of the House of Mendes as early as 1553.[21] His handling of a complicated loan arrangement with merchants in Venice and Lyons at that time appears to have been exemplary.[22] Further, Doña Gracia initially seemed comfortable enough to engage him as a local guardian for her niece. Unfortunately, as La Chica would soon find out, he turned out to be someone who could not resist getting his hands on more of her riches than had been intended. But that was in the future.

The redoubtable Duarte Gomez was given power of attorney by La Chica to estimate how much money was due from two Florentine merchants in Venice who had loans outstanding to the estate. The merchants had been given loans by Brianda to invest in commerce. It was now important to know when the capital would be repaid and how much interest it would generate. Gomez had apparently not encountered any difficulty staying on in Venice and would operate from that city for at least another eight years.[23]

Early the following year, in January 1557, Aries and Henriques offered the duke a loan of 43,000 ducats on explicit orders of Doña Gracia. The previous December the duke had written a very personal letter to her and another to Don Joseph (whose influence on Doña Gracia the duke acknowledged as the reason for sending the second letter) imploring them to rescue him at a moment of dire financial need.[24] The stated purpose was to support him in his war effort.[25] The war in question was a combined enterprise by the pope and the king of France to align themselves against the growing muscle of Spain under Charles V. The previous summer, Pope Paul IV had tried to expel the Spanish from their long time hegemony over southern Italy. The Spanish had retaliated by invading the Papal States. Duke Ercole, fearing a possible encroachment by the Spanish into his own duchy, had joined the anti-Spanish alliance the previous November. He was now required to pay 300,000 ducats towards the cost of troops.[26]

In framing his words the duke was the quintessence of charm, probably because he had no intention, as we will see, of paying the money back despite the usual guarantees. "Dear lady," he wrote, "many times you showed goodwill to me and promised to lend me a good amount of money. Now that there is a war against me I need that money. I will use my personal income to assure you that the money will be returned...you can trust me...you won't receive any damage from this loan and I will be grateful and...remember your help."[27]

By now Doña Gracia must have known his habits all too well. But she also must have thought it prudent to forward the money anyway, no doubt because of the deteriorating climate against *conversos* in other parts of Italy and because her niece was still under his control. In doing so, she acknowledged the "innumerable benefits" she had received from the duke, both during her stay in Ferrara as well as afterwards. She noted that "his excellency, with his utmost care and diligence, helped to save the estate" of her niece, presumably by providing a refuge for Brianda and La Chica and acceding to her wishes. She sounded especially grateful because she even mentioned how vulnerable La Chica's dowry had been since it "consisted mainly of cash."[28]

As usual, the actual cash amount of the loan was not forthcoming all at once. There was to be an initial payment of 25,000 ducats, with the remaining 18,000 due at the end of the year, part of which was to come from the dowry. The duke had asked for a further loan of 50,000 ducats (25,000 free of interest and a further 25,000 at six percent per annum) for business deals that he had always looked to the *conversos* to help him finance. Still, Doña Gracia would not have been expected to consent to such massive loans without attaching certain strings. Using both the carrot and the stick, she promised the duke that La Chica and her fortune would remain in Ferrara, as he had requested, for at least six years—if, for the same number of years, he would promise to allow "the Portuguese nation (the *conversos*) to stay on and live without any impediment on the part of the pope or others and without being expelled."[29]

But Doña Gracia was far from forthright in her offer. She

surely did not expect La Chica to stay on in Italy, given the increasingly hostile climate for Jews and *conversos* and her own past attempts to bring her niece to Constantinople. But she dangled that possibility before the eager duke anyway. Persuading the duke to give the *conversos* a six-year pledge was vital in the wake of the savage Ancona incident, and the fear of even more reprisals by the pope.

True, Ercole ran an autonomous state. But it still fell under a certain amount of papal pressure as part of the Christian world. One will recall that under coercion, the duke had allowed copies of the Talmud to be publicly burned in Ferrara back in 1553. And there was always the fear that one day Ferrara might be absorbed into the Papal States like some of the neighboring duchies—something that indeed came to pass at the close of the 16ᵗʰ century.

Further, Doña Gracia wanted assurances that his decree would permit the newly-appointed guardians to maintain control over the selection of a husband for La Chica. The duke had to promise in writing that "he (would) not intervene directly or indirectly in the eventual marriage."[30]

Her broader plan now became evident. Around the same time—in January, 1557—Don Joseph sent a letter to the duke from "the vineyards of Pera,"[31] the other name for Galata, the neighborhood outside Constantinople where the family was living. It sought assurances that the duke would agree to the petition that either Henriques or Gomez were about to put before him in person "rather than (entertain) any others." The letter made it clear that it would be in the duke's interest to reach an agreement "with the agents of my lady…(rather) than with others." Underscoring his point Don Joseph then evoked the wisdom of the ages by adding, "there is no prince so great that he does not need something at a certain point, nor a man so poor that he cannot be useful at a certain point."[32] In short: if the duke played along he could expect even more money or an extension of existing debt.

The issue on the table was the choice of a husband for La Chica. Suitors—honorable and not-so-honorable—must have been pressuring the duke for the opportunity to become the lucky spouse. These suitors may well have been among the unspecified concerns raised by Zaffarini in his declarations concerning the future and control of La Chica's inheritance. No wonder Henriques and Gomez needed to visit the duke personally on the matter. They had to make it perfectly clear to the duke that their decision would be final. No other suitor would even be considered.

The husband the family had selected was none other than Don Samuel, the older brother of Don Joseph.[33] It was a choice that may well have been made years earlier by Doña Gracia, and could have been yet another reason why Doña Gracia had fought so hard to keep La Chica under her guardianship. The marriage would perpetuate the family's long tradition of marrying among themselves. And it would allow Doña Gracia to maintain a tight rein over the future of the child that Diogo had placed under her protection. Neither of the young people was likely to raise objections. It would have been an expected participation in a time-honored family custom. Don Samuel, one will recall, had gone to Constantinople with his brother in 1554. He now had an important reason to return.

The family must have believed that it was essential for La Chica to be married off as soon as possible and not only for financial reasons. La Chica had gone through a difficult time immediately following the death of her mother. Alone in the house except for her servants, she quickly became "very lonely."[34] Initially, she had tried to fill the void by inviting a close cousin to stay with her for a few days to "console me and give me the solace I need." The cousin happened to be the wife of Aries de

Luna, her uncle. But the notaries handling her affairs may have already suspected that Aries and his wife were up to no good. They sent the cousin away even though, according to La Chica, she "was harming no one." They would not let the woman stay even though La Chica pleaded with them to do so.[35]

On October 11, 1556, less than three months after her mother's death, La Chica had become so distraught that she wrote a personal letter to the duke, asking him to intervene directly. "Therefore, most Illustrious and Excellent lord," she wrote, "with as much reverence and humility as I owe…I beg (you to let me) keep this cousin of mine by my side because her company is very gratifying and of great comfort." La Chica ended by adding, "If your most Illustrious Excellency does this, you will grant me a huge favor, aside from the fact that what I request is both honorable and natural."[36]

The Duke apparently did not agree, for soon afterward La Chica solved the problem by moving into the home of Aries de Luna and his wife on the Contrada di San Romano. The notaries' suspicions proved well founded. During her period of residence, La Chica "was maliciously deceived by her uncle's cunning," as she later put it. Moreover, "because of her natural reverential awe (for him)," she was persuaded to sign a document that was highly detrimental to her estate.[37] But it took a while for her to find this out.

Don Samuel arrived in Ferrara the following spring and likewise moved into the home of Aries de Luna. The duke authorized the marriage rites "according to the Law of Moses and of Israel."[38] Nobody seemed bothered by the fact that La Chica had been "married" to Don Joseph four years earlier. Everyone probably viewed it as a sham—in the same way that no obstacles had been raised when Don Joseph subsequently married Ana. The wedding took place that summer, at the end of the official mourning period for Brianda.[39] It would have been a time of mixed emotions for the bride. Neither her father nor her mother was alive. Her cousin Ana, who had been at her side since she was born, was now a continent away. So too was her aunt, Doña Gracia and her other cousin, Don Joseph. Though friends and relatives in Ferrara would have worked hard to create a lively round of festivities and celebrations, they must have all felt the terrible void.

La Chica was now seventeen years old. The couple had a Jewish ceremony with a traditional *ketubah*, or Jewish marriage contract. It was drawn up in Hebrew script and recorded the fact that La Chica was entrusting her dowry to her bridegroom, Don Samuel, who was given permission to use the money for trade, under strict supervision of Aries de Luna, her uncle and guardian. Later, Don Samuel would also be permitted to collect outstanding debts.[40] Two major loans to the duke were made during the time of the wedding: one for 27,000 ducats and a second for 25,000 ducats.[41] Though they may well have been the 50,000 ducats promised the previous January, it was clear that even the duke was not above extracting his pound of flesh.

Duke Ercole may have also negotiated the loans as a way to ensure that La Chica would honor her six-year residency commitment.[42] Until the loans were repaid, the couple—together with their riches and the ensuing trade that could thereby be generated by the duke as a result of the cash—would be unlikely to depart for Constantinople. But even these loans were not sufficient surety for a worried duke. Shortly after the wedding, the bridegroom was required to sign an additional guarantee assuring the duke that if he and his new wife left Ferrara early they would owe the duke a penalty of 25,000 ducats—unless he agreed to release them from this obligation.[43]

Historians believe that the famous portrait medal of La Chica that is still extant was struck in celebration of the wedding that summer. Her age around the rim, "in the year of her life eighteen," was recorded in Latin. This probably meant that she had passed her seventeenth birthday and was in the eighteenth year of life, since these medals tended to be struck to celebrate an important milestone.[44]

Though all subsequent legal documents continued to refer to her as "Gracia Benveniste," she used the Nasi family name on the rim of the medal, as noted, which was engraved in both Hebrew and Latin characters. The medal was reputed by experts who had studied it to have been designed by Pastorino de Pastorini, a craftsman from Sienna who was arguably the most renowned portrait artist of the day.[45] During this period he was serving as a master craftsman at the Ferrara Mint and was producing medals for other Jewish clients.[46] Pastorini worked mostly in bronze, the metal used for La Chica's medal. He was particularly celebrated for his development of new techniques and the use of materials that gave a more realistic look to hair and skin.

Having a portrait medal struck was a stylish gesture; the height of fashion. These medals had revived an art and custom that had been dormant since classical times. In an era of conspicuous consumption, they satisfied a narcissistic urge among the upper classes to immortalize their profiles, as well as create a very personal gift of lasting value for friends. All the great princes and luminaries of the age were commissioning and collecting portrait medals: Erasmus, Sultan Mehmed II, Catherine de Medici, Charles V and the renowned German banker, Jacob Fugger.[47]

Only a handful of La Chica's medals are still extant, mostly in private hands. It is likely that La Chica had the medal fashioned in part to give something very personal and special to her new husband; in the way that delicately-painted portrait miniatures were given as tokens of lifelong affection in the 19th century. It also illustrates the way she was dealing with the cross-cultural inconsistencies in her Catholic-Jewish life. On the one hand she proclaimed her new Jewish identity on the medal using Hebrew script. On the other, she violated the biblical injunction against "graven images." Probably that is why the medals struck at this time for Jewish clients were created mostly for rich *conversos* or former *conversos*.[48] Once again, they were straddling both worlds. Certainly La Chica would not have dared initiate such a commission had her formidable aunt still been in Europe, or if her father had still been alive. The medal, then, shows a young girl moving towards her own independent interpretation of a complex heritage. It also helps explain why we do not have portraits of other family members, in an era when portraits painted by the great masters were *de rigueur* in fashionable circles.

———••⠅••———

As soon as they were married, the couple drew up documents to remove Aries de Luna from their affairs, although at what point they both grew to dislike and distrust him is uncertain. They started the process on August 12, 1557, within weeks of the wedding, replacing him with Henriques Nunes, a young cousin in his late twenties.[49] Nunes, nicknamed Righetto, was the son of Nuno Henriques who, like Francisco Mendes, had struggled in Lisbon to prevent the Inquisition from coming to Portugal.[50] Righetto would later win infamy of sorts when he came before the Venetian authorities in 1572 suspected of passing state secrets to Don Joseph. He would also face the Venetian Inquisition charged with being an apostate.[51]

Righetto was a colorful character. The son of a rich merchant, he was a playboy of minimal beliefs but maximum daring. By the time he was arrested in Venice, he had squandered a fortune of his own with "splendid abandon and little remorse," as one historian put it.[52]

Filled with passion for adventure and gaming, Righetto was determined to live the incorrigible life of a titled Iberian Christian gentleman, a *fidalgo*, despite his Jewish origins. It was exactly the sort of lifestyle that had earned so many successful *conversos* the enmity of both Jews and Christians. His spirited defense before the Inquisition was the inspired rhetoric of someone who had been blessed with the finest education and a brilliant mind. His dashing escapes from the doge's prison, on two separate occasions, were worthy of a Hollywood movie; as was the man himself.[53]

Obviously, he was not the most prudent choice as a replacement for the couple's disgraced uncle Aries. Rather, they needed a team of guardians with the integrity and skill to recover and conserve an estate that included both the dowry and assets that had been signed over to Brianda—providing, of course, this money could be collected.

Eight days later, the couple confirmed in writing that Don Samuel had replaced Aries as an administrator of La Chica's estate. Aries also agreed to part with the precious "goods and money" that had been stored at his home for safe-keeping as part of La Chica's overall inheritance. In the future, the items were to be stowed in the city's high court building or given to her husband, Don Samuel.[54] They included a combination of valuables and registered debts, some dating back to the time when Brianda was lending for profit: over 3,000 golden ducats in a variety of pouches and boxes, notarized loans to various merchants and churchmen, the rental of a house in Antwerp (possibly other than the family mansion), bundles of letters, copies of safe conducts, rental agreements, an account book "written in the hand" of Doña Gracia, other account books and assorted financial guarantees.[55]

The couple's disagreements with their uncle must have been

exceedingly bitter because they sued Aries.[56] And it was later made perfectly clear, again in writing, that "Don Samuel and (La Chica) wish to see an end to what has by now become a controversy that has lasted too long." Also, that they wished from now on-wards to "be at their own liberty to dispense and handle matters on their own through this agreement."[57]

At the same time, a local official who appears to have been appointed at the suggestion of Aries to help in the collections, was fired.[58] He was replaced by Don Jacob Abravanel, grandson of the famous Don Isaac Abravanel, the financier and statesman who had negotiated with Ferdinand and Isabella at the time of the Expulsion.

It is understandable that a close friendship might develop between the younger generation of Benvenistes and Abravanels, two of the most distinguished Iberian Jewish families of the period. The newlyweds visited Don Jacob in his Ferrara home as well as working with him.[59] But even this new combination of guardians would fall apart. By June of the following year, Jacob Abravanel would get into such a monumental row with Righetto that the authorities would be forced to issue a restraining order keeping them both apart.[60]

The next important step for the young couple was to find an independent home. Early in September, just weeks after their wedding, they rented a house in the Contrada di Santa Maria del Vado. It was a fine piece of property with a courtyard, an orchard, garden and stable. The rent was 300 ducats for three years—or 100 ducats a year with 130 ducats payable in advance. But it was either in chronic need of repair or it had never been completed, which may well have been its attraction. For, as part of the rental agreement, the landlord promised to immediately start construction of an upper floor. A stairway was to be built connecting the two floors and new ceilings were to be finished in the elaborate fashion of the era. There was to be a parlor, or dining hall, on the new upper floor, as well as various other rooms, all adorned with whitewashed walls and doors and windows made of solid wood. New glass windows were to be added to both floors, with the entire job reaching a standard that would be considered "inhabitable according to the judgement of a 'good man'" (a concept that is still with us in the form of building codes and the legal doctrine of the 'prudent man'). Finally, in a clause that would bring a smile of recognition to the face of any modern tenant fearing endless delays and landlord excuses, there was strong language to the effect that if the construction was not finished by the end of October, as promised, the landlord would have to give the rental advance back to Don Samuel. The couple arranged to move in three weeks after the agreement was signed.[61]

An additional guardian, a *converso* named Hieronimo Lopes, was meanwhile appointed to arrange for the collection of specific debts still lingering in Venice, including money sought from a particular Florentine merchant and a Levantine Jew.[62] In addition, Agostinho Henriques, who was acting as a proxy guardian in Doña Gracia's absence, was granted his own safe conduct, independent of any member of the Mendes family, to come and live in Ferrara in his own right.[63]

Of interest during this period is how the Ferrara notaries dealt with the religious sensibilities of their Jewish clients who had to sign a municipal document that required a Christian oath. For instance, when Don Jacob Abravanel became La Chica's guardian, he was permitted to swear his oath of consent "on the Jewish Bible" and according to "the Law of Moses."[64] Similarly, the children of da Costa, now living openly as Jews, were allowed to take their vows by actually touching the Hebrew Bible and swearing "on the Holy law that was given to Moses on the mountain of Sinai." To emphasize the import of their intent, their actions were administered and witnessed by a local rabbi.[65]

The flurry of guardianships to facilitate debt collection had a purpose. The window of opportunity was closing fast throughout Italy. During the following year of 1558, Duke Guidobaldo, one will recall, finally yielded to the pope's wishes and expelled all *conversos* from Pesaro. Trade was in chaos. Jewish life throughout the peninsula was under siege. It was therefore no surprise when, in February 1558, a *chaus* arrived in Ferrara with a letter from Selim, the son of Sultan Suleiman—the heir apparent to the Turkish throne who had become a close friend of Don Joseph. The mission of this *chaus* was to make sure that the duke allowed La Chica and Don Samuel to leave for Constantinople despite any prior promises. The *chaus* stayed many months, and rumors circulated that he was lingering because the duke could not find a trustworthy interpreter to translate Selim's letter. But it may have been a ruse. The *chaus* probably had orders not to leave until the duke released the young couple.[66]

By May, Don Samuel and La Chica had obtained permission to depart with all their goods. Left unresolved, however, was the matter of the penalty of 25,000 ducats for leaving early. Soon after the wedding Righetto, as a newly-appointed guardian, had pledged his personal funds as surety for the penalty—payable, one will recall, if they left sooner. So Righetto was soon climbing the hill to the duke's personal chambers in the castle to ask if the obligation could be wiped off the books. The duke agreed.[67] He doubtless did not want to push his luck, especially as a *chaus* was on the scene.

Also outstanding was the loan of 50,000 ducats given to the duke around the time of the wedding. And what about the additional 43,000 ducats given him prior to the marriage? Had any of these debts ever been repaid in part or in full? Unlikely. For one, the duke was another perpetually insolvent ruler who needed continuous infusions of cash to keep his duchy afloat; a man so obsessed over his financial troubles that never stopped complaining that he was broke.[68] For another, his ambassador to the Vatican would complain a year later that the Ancona upheavals had resulted in difficulties collecting money owed to him by other creditors.[69] The ripple effect was probably the reason why collections in general were not proceeding smoothly enough to allow the couple to leave as quickly as they, and their anxious aunt, might have wished. Certainly the 43,000 ducats could not have been repaid because Don Joseph had to enlist the help of the sultan to plead for repayment several years later.[70]

Uncle Aries had meanwhile interfered with the collection of debts due La Chica in a similar fashion to Brianda some years earlier. A further representative had to be appointed to move matters along, particularly in Venice, and find ways to circumvent his interference.[71] Had Aries sustained personal losses from the Ancona cataclysm that resulted in obligations he was now frantically trying to cover? Since he had been viewed as an upstanding merchant in earlier years, this may well have been so.

Amid the financial turmoil, an important meeting with the notaries was called in May 1558, in the couple's newly-renovated house on the Contrada di Santa Maria del Vado. The assembled group named yet another legal representative to try to extract the money due from Venice. The couple also drafted their wills. The notaries and judges present considered it such a significant occasion that they begged the venerable Agostinho Henriques to attend. But he complained that he was too busy to be present to ratify these moves. Instead he sent word that he thought La Chica was now perfectly capable of managing her affairs "without me." Despite having said this, the group waited until six o'clock in the evening, hoping he might change his mind.[72]

But there was more to Henriques' absence than a scheduling conflict. He was also later found to be skimming funds that rightfully belonged to the House of Mendes. With Doña Gracia far from the scene, and economic opportunities in turmoil for the *converso* merchants of Italy, the liquid assets of the House of Mendes must have seemed tempting bounty indeed. Significantly, the safe conduct granted to Henriques the previous October to come and live in Ferrara had included a passage allowing this privilege "in spite of his debts," and safeguarding him from liabilities in any other domain.[73] So he must have been in financial trouble for quite some time.

Some months earlier Uncle Aries had also run away, heading for Florence,[74] no doubt to dodge any number of law suits likely to be lodged against him too, as a result of his own questionable dealings. Significantly, just prior to his departure, Aries appointed a local lawyer described as a "respected and famous legal expert" to represent him in "any suits, whether civil, criminal or mixed…that (he) might have with individuals, groups or communities, either in front of an ecclesiastic or lay tribunal."[75] Due to his prior behavior, such action had likely been required by the authorities, and possibly even the duke himself, before Aries was granted permission to leave.

Contempt for Uncle Aries must have also been foremost on La Chica's mind when she worked on her will that spring day in May.[76] She devoted more words to him than any other. "Don Aries de Luna and all his descendants…," she stated, "in perpetuity should not..acquire anything ever of the estate..and if (any of her)…heirs dares to give and hand over anything…under any pretext…such people…shall be deprived …of (their) part." Her wrath may well have been the catalyst for drafting her will at this particular moment.

Still, her will covered other issues too. In typical 16th century style, the preamble was wholly concerned with spiritual thoughts, as well as covering the religious concerns paramount to anyone who had lived life as a *converso*. She "commended her soul to the Omnipotent God, her Creator," whom she hoped would "deign to ascribe her to the place of salvation." In the same mode she gave instructions "for her body to be buried in the place usually ascribed to Jewish burials in the city, town or place where she would chance to die." Also in keeping with 16th century attitudes, she instructed her heirs to "give…alms for her soul and for the remission of her sins to the people and places that will seem more appropriate."

She disposed of the rest of her ample assets according to the norms of the day. She designated as her heirs all the sons she might have with Don Samuel, and any future husband she might take, in equal shares, with the proviso that these sons bear the responsibility of marrying off and providing dowries for any daughters that might be born. If she had no living sons at the moment of her death then her daughter or daughters were to become her heirs. If she bore no children, then her husband, Don Samuel was to become her heir. If he pre-deceased her, then she appointed her cousin, Reyna Benveniste,[77] (Ana) as her heir. If Reyna had already died then the inheritance was to go to Reyna's sons. If there were no sons, then the money was to be shared between Reyna's daughters. If they were no longer living, her next closest relatives would become eligible—barring, of course, her uncle Aries and all his issue.

If none of these heirs were living then the money was to go to "the poor among the Jews of Safed and the entire Holy Land."[78] Her familiarity at such a young age with the Jews of Safed and others in the Holy Land is not as curious as it may seem. Safed was not only the greatest center of Jewish mysticism and learning during this time, it was an administrative capital under the Ottoman Turks. Religious emissaries had been coming to Italy for decades seeking contributions for these settlements among the wealthy Italian Jews. Willing one's property to the poor of the Holy Land was also a way of winning penance for a soul that may have sinned; thus ensuring elevation to heaven after death.[79] And, as was well known, the *conversos* had a deep sense of sin for their outward lives as Catholics, making it more than likely the suggestion of a bequest to the poor of the Holy Land was raised by La Chica's rabbi in Ferrara.

Still, she could just as easily have left the money to the poor Jews of Ferrara, Venice or Constantinople. Thus, the statement gives credence to a theory that has circulated among historians for years that the family, and Doña Gracia in particular, were much taken with Jewish mysticism, as were so many Jews of that era.[80] It also suggests that despite outward conformity with Catholic life, Doña Gracia must have felt strongly about raising both Ana and La Chica with a strong Jewish consciousness.

Don Samuel's will,[81] drafted at the same time, centers on his position in relation to the inheritance of his rich young wife. For one, it confirmed that he had brought no inheritance of his own to the marriage, which would therefore have been true of Don Joseph's marriage to Reyna. Thus, since all Don Samuel's wealth came from his wife, it was to be returned to her upon his death. "The testator declared…," notes the will, "by acknowledging the property (he has acquired from his wife) both on account of relieving his conscience and of acting in the best possible way…(thereby makes) provision to restore the dowry to his wife after his death."

Regarding the scant possessions he personally owned, or might own in the future, Don Samuel bequeathed them along the same lines as La Chica: sons first, daughters next, including any children born to a subsequent wife. Failing that, he wanted to leave whatever he owned at the moment of his death to his younger brother, Don Joseph. Or, if Don Joseph was already deceased, to his brother's heirs.

Notaries were also summoned to the couple's home to draw up the necessary papers revoking all agreements that Aries de Luna had encouraged the two of them to sign. Over the intervening months, the dispute had come before the duke and his counselors. Initially, they had said they could do nothing, since the documents appeared to have been drawn and signed in a perfectly legal manner.[82] But eventually they found in favor of the young couple, determining that they had indeed been deceived. The decision paved the way for the newlyweds to make a full renunciation of any commitments made at that time. The couple must have been so anxious to ensure that these renunciations were watertight that separate documents were drawn for Don Samuel and La Chica.[83]

———••⋅⏝⋅••———

Six months later they were still in Ferrara, tying up loose ends. In the customary interweaving of financial obligations that were a hallmark of *converso* merchant dealings, Don Samuel had finally admitted that maybe the Florentine merchant in Venice did not owe the estate anything after all as the merchant had used the money to pay another merchant who had been waiting patiently to be paid by the Mendes.[84] Possibly fearing that matters would never be satisfactorily sorted out, Doña Gracia dispatched Don Salomon Dordeiro, a Levantine Jew,[85] to remain in Ferrara to represent the House of Mendes after the couple had left; a problem of debt collection that continued into the early 1560's.[86] Dordeiro's other mission was to ensure that the duke would not throw up any last-minute hurdles impeding the couple's departure.[87] Particularly at issue was an unpaid personal loan that La Chica had made to the duke for 10,600 ducats, "not a single penny" of which had been paid back. Acting on La Chica's behalf, Dordeiro was now claiming that the young woman had been forced to take out loans of her own to cover immediate cash needs. As collateral for this loan, the duke had deposited jewelry with a Mendes agent in Venice. But under the circumstances, La Chica had apparently been reluctant to take possession of the jewelry and liquidate it to cover the delinquent sum.[88]

The pair were clearly anxious to leave because a year earlier, Don Samuel had sought and won a limited safe conduct from the Venetians, good for only one occasion and strictly for transit. It allowed him and his household to pass through Venice on their way to Constantinople. It had been reluctantly granted with restrictions because, one will recall, Don Samuel had been perpetually banished from Venice following the abduction affair in 1553. The consent was probably given because his brother, Don Joseph, was growing so powerful with the Turks that they did not dare refuse. It had also been requested in person by the *chaus* who had gone to Ferrara to fetch the newly-weds.[89]

During these final months of their stay in Ferrara, which took place in the first half of 1559, Don Samuel arranged to sell his bay horse, *Il Baio Capitano* (the Captain), to another local gentleman for 500 ducats. Such a name implies a sentimental attachment to a spirited beast, as well as an owner with a wry sense of humor; a rare intimate glimpse of Don Samuel. As usual, no actual cash was payable immediately. The first installment of fifty percent was not due until September, around the time of their actual departure and possibly when the horse actually changed hands. The rest was to be paid to Dordeiro, as the Mendes agent, the following Easter; the dating of financial obligations being typically ascribed to a Saints' Day, rather than the numerical calendar.[90]

Finally, during the fall of 1559, the newlyweds, together with their belongings and all the assets they had been able to muster, left for Constantinople by way of Venice. It was not a moment too soon. This was also the year when Duke Ercole died, leaving the *conversos* who remained in his duchy in the hands of his son, Alfonso II; a far less powerful and charismatic leader and one who never quite managed to keep the dictates of the Vatican at arms length.

———••⊹••———

It had always been difficult for Doña Gracia to collect debts. Those later years in Italy demonstrate the point better than any other and also begin to shed light on one of the many ways in which the family fortune withered to a fraction of its former size. Despite her other accomplishments, Doña Gracia never commanded the stature of her late husband or brother-in-law in this regard. It certainly did not help that she was a woman, although as time went on she came to rely more and more on the power of her nephew, Don Joseph, and his close connections to the sultan. Nor did it aid her cause to be forced to rely upon agents in distant places who themselves were facing persecution and financial setbacks.

One particular case in point was the business deal she had struck with Henriques and Gomez in Italy just prior to her departure in 1552. She had invested, one will recall, 18,000 ducats as seed capital for a trading partnership. The two agents had added 3,000 ducats each of their own money, bringing the available capital to 24,000 ducats. They had all agreed that half the profits would go to Doña Gracia as she had put up most of the capital. For the following four years Henriques had submitted regular accounts outlining what had been going on. But after the Ancona incident Doña Gracia was worried. As a local *converso*, any assets held in Henriques' name might be confiscated at any time. As a precautionary measure she therefore wrote to Henriques asking him to obtain a letter from her Florentine banking agents confirming in writing that the money belonging to this particular deal actually belonged to her. No other persons had any right to any part of the capital.[91]

Henriques ignored her request. He also stopped sending her financial reports. For a further eighteen months Doña Gracia kept on asking. There was still no response. Finally, she dispatched Dordeiro to investigate and persuade Henriques to hand over his reports. Henriques refused once more, arguing that it was not dignified for him to deal with a messenger.

Anticipating trouble as a result of his own truculence, Henriques quickly obtained a personal safe conduct, as previously mentioned, protecting him from foreign debts. When Doña Gracia discovered what he had done she was outraged. She sent him an angry letter saying that she had done him "many favors, which were well known to many people," as a later report explained, "and (for her troubles) he had rewarded her with attempts to rob her of her money."[92]

Henriques responded by insisting he had been forced into numerous outlays connected with La Chica's estate. Doña Gracia did not buy this excuse. "All the expenses you say you had for my niece's business, which you claim I owe you, are baseless," she thundered back. "You never informed me that you had (these) expenses…(And) I never asked you to spend my money on that business…as you will find in the letters I have written to you."[93]

She might have been persuaded to refund all that he claimed he had spent on La Chica, she conceded, if he had not tried to trick her by suggesting that Dordeiro could not be trusted. But having behaved in such a deceitful fashion, Henriques should now watch out for her wrath. "I will use all my power and ability to pull the prey from your teeth," she warned him, "to the extent that you might have to save your own money from my grip." One can almost hear her shouting as she added, "Don't try to pretend that you don't hear or see and ignore responding to my messages, " she barked, "because If I don't receive your response by the time it is supposed to arrive, I will force you to respond whether you like it or not." This angry exchange, recorded in a surviving *responsum* of Joshua Soncino, gives us some of the best insights into her reaction to dishonest practice. Interestingly, she once again stressed, as she had done so often before, that she considered it a point of honor to repay her own (legitimate) debts.

The letter was sent to Henriques sometime during March or April, 1558. It may have arrived just at the moment when Henriques refused to turn up at that all-important May meeting at La Chica's home—the day when the couple's wills and other documents were being drafted and signed.[94]

Even though Henriques later said he would only deal with Gomez, as his partner, he ultimately refused to do even that when directly approached by Gomez to produce the reports. As Doña Gracia implied, it had been a ruse all along. Instead, he filed a counter-suit in Ferrara a year later complaining that false rumors were spreading all over Turkey that he owed 35,000 ducats to the House of Mendes and that he intended to rob Doña Gracia of her money by obtaining a legal release from Duke Ercole. The extra money, on top of the original 18,000 ducats, appears to have been old loans that he had managed to collect from France—one of the tasks he had been assigned when Doña Gracia left for Constantinople. He was hoping the Ferrara suit would clear his name.

To do so, it was first necessary for him to void the section of his original safe conduct that had protected him from "foreign" debts. It was his way of showing honorable intent. He then insisted that part of the money in question was still with the French crown. The rest was being held by the Florentine agents of the Mendes. When those agents were contacted by Doña Gracia, they confirmed that they indeed had 12,000 ducats that rightfully belonged to her. But they were willing to place it at her

disposal only on condition that they first received 16,000 ducats that Henriques owed them. Their response contained a detailed list of all the items included in the 16,000-ducat debt.

At this point Doña Gracia became aware that Henriques had
done more damage than she had initially realized. It was time
to make good on her threats. She personally contacted the Sub-
lime Porte, the sultan's court, asking them to send a *chaus* to
Ferrara to bring the matter before the duke. The *chaus* arrived in
Ferrara late in 1560, carrying a letter from Don Joseph. Addressed
to the new duke, Alfonso II, it came as a direct command from
Selim, Suleiman's son. The letter reminded Duke Alfonso that
Henriques still owed 35,000 ducats to the House of Mendes.
And "one hopes that you will not wish to leave to rest a
debtor…making every diligence (to) do what you may to make
(Henriques) aware of his debt and ready to repay it." The letter
also stated that the current duke was responsible for paying back
a loan of 43,000 ducats that had been granted to his father, Duke
Ercole, at the time of the negotiations concerning La Chica's
guardianship and marriage.[95]

But the clever Henriques still had another gambit. To avoid
facing municipal justice he declared himself a Jew, henceforth
to be known as Abraham Benveniste. As a Jew, he demanded
the right to be judged under Jewish law, even in Ferrara, as there
were certain aspects of Jewish law that he had thought would
treat the matter more favorably.

Doña Gracia countered by seeking a rabbinic opinion as to
whether she was now required to litigate with Henriques in the
Jewish courts. The matter came before the righteous Soncino.
He argued that because the entire matter had occurred while
Henriques was operating as a Christian in a Christian world, he
"could not try to litigate in a Jewish court…to avoid paying his
obligations." Doña Gracia was therefore fully within her rights
to further her claims in Ferrara's municipal courts.[96] But noth-

ing was ever apparently collected.

In addition, only 3,650 ducats of any of the duke's debts was actually forthcoming in the end. And since the sum was payable directly to La Chica, it probably represented the repayment of a different debt. Moreover, part of this small amount was immediately set aside to cover the outstanding money due to the heirs of da Costa.[97] In July of the following year, Duke Alfonso finally acknowledged receipt of additional demand letters from Selim. He defended the seeming lack of resolution by assuring Selim that he had been fully attentive to Doña Gracia's needs. If there had been delays, Duke Alfonso explained to Selim, it was not for want of trying. In fact, he had finally been left with no other choice than to punish Henriques by revoking the earlier safe conduct that had allowed Henriques to live and work in Ferrara— "an act that had never before occurred in our state."[98] There was no further mention of the loan of 43,000 ducats furnished directly to Duke Ercole. It was probably not paid back, either.

Sinyora Giveret Synagogue, founded with funds provided by Doña Gracia, Izmir, Turkey

Sinyora Giveret Synagogue, interior

CHAPTER **17**

A Benevolent Lady

F rom the moment she stepped out of her elaborate carriage and into her new residence at Galata, Doña Gracia enjoyed a status among the Jews of the Ottoman Empire that resembled a crowned head of state. It went far beyond her previous standing with the *conversos*. Indeed, there is evidence that she may have attained an official position equal to a *nasi* in pre-expulsion Spain; or, earlier still, in the time of the *Sanhedrin*, the governing body of the Jews at the close of the biblical era. It was an astonishing feat for a woman, and even more so for a former *conversa*.

Contemporary Hebrew sources repeatedly refer to her during this period as "the crowned" or "crowning lady."[1] The Hebrew term *ha-gevirá*, by which Doña Gracia was known during the Ottoman segment of her life, can connote a queen or queen-dowager, as well as simply a rich woman.[2] Rabbi Soncino wrapped her in "the headdress of kingship" and portrayed her as a mediator.[3] Every day, he reported, "she set out to expound everything difficult between one law and another (and) words of disagreement." She would "bring to light justice without stealing anything from the labors of others."[4]

Sa'adiah Longo, the poet, characterized her as "the supreme leader..." who "nursed (the Jews) from her breast."[5] Samuel Usque, the *converso* writer, had already likened her to Deborah, the great woman prophet and judge in ancient Israel.[6] All of which invokes a picture of an endless stream of supplicants waiting in ante-rooms, anxious to gain an audience with her or deliver a written appeal. Her concept of leadership went far beyond the impact of money. She may have been acting out the theory, popular in the medieval Hebrew literature of the Iberian Peninsula, and among certain Jewish mystics of her day, that it was part of the divine plan to bestow wealth and important political connections upon certain specific individuals for the express purpose of helping their people.[7]

Her deeds during these early years in the Jewish world further indicate that she was a leader with innovative and astonishing modern ideas and was anxious to create practices and policies with a long-term impact.

She established or supported homes for the poor, synagogues and centers of learning in the major cities of the Empire. In Balat, one of the oldest Jewish neighborhoods in Constantinople that dated back to the Byzantine period, she founded a *yeshiva*, entrusting its leadership to the great rabbinic scholar, Joseph ibn Lev. Before long, it had expanded to include a synagogue known as the synagogue of La Señora or Crowned Lady (*Shel ha-Geveret ha-Ma'atirah*).[8]

Doña Gracia was determined that any Jew who wanted to worship in the synagogue of La Señora could attend—a revolutionary idea in a city where it had been obligatory for Jews to maintain membership in a congregation where they or their family had always belonged. The controversy became passionate because the tithes of the synagogue of La Señora were unusually low as so many costs were covered by its generous patron. As a consequence, it was soon drawing members from other congregations. Doña Gracia had especially sought Jews from the nearby synagogue of the Spanish Exiles. Its leaders soon panicked over the defections. The matter was finally adjudicated by the renowned rabbi, Samuel de Medina. He decided in favor of the freedom to join any synagogue at any time, noting that there had never been any communal ban against switching, simply a tradition.[9] Besides, he added, such a prohibition was impractical in a large city. Doña Gracia then convinced Constantinople's other Jewish leaders to allow residents the freedom to change their regular place of worship at any time. The modification was adopted.[10]

One can speculate on her motives for seeking the change. Certainly it freed former *conversos* from the discomfort of being tied to a congregation that did not sympathize with their special dilemmas, or where they were heavily outnumbered and perhaps even scorned. She may have believed that the prevailing system caused hardship to many, while bolstering the power of the few. Or she may have sought the opportunity to quickly fill a house of worship that she had endowed, thereby underscoring her personal power and prestige. But the pressure for change must have angered the rabbis since it lessened the control they maintained over their flock. And coming from a woman it must have been even harder to accept.

Her charitable deeds extended westward to the great textile center of Salonika, the only Ottoman city where Jews were in the majority.[11] Though Jews had lived in the city since biblical times, the refugees from the Iberian Peninsula soon became the most numerous. The first to arrive were the ones who had left Spain as Jews in 1492. They were later joined by the *conversos* who poured into the city during the early and middle years of the 16th century.

Salonika's Jews were separated into even more rigid divisions. Immigrants were corralled into specific congregations, based upon the city or region of their origin. Separate congregations emerged for people from Castile, Provence, Aragon, Catalonia, Italy, Majorca, North Africa, Evora, Lisbon and Sicily, among other places. The influx was so rapid between the late 15th and mid 16th century that it paralleled the onrush of Jewish refugees into the United States at the turn of the 20th century. At the outset, two or three families often shared a home. Crowding became so intense that epidemics and fires were constantly breaking out. Congregations swelled to a point where they needed to split in two and then split again, such as the one representing the Jews and former *conversos* from Lisbon—*Lisbonne Yashan* (old) and *Lisbonne Hadash* (new).[12] These congregations, augmenting pre-existing ones of Romaniote and Ashkenazi Jews, served the immigrants' social, regulatory and welfare needs as well as conducting the customary religious services and acting as tax collectors. But they also hindered assimilation and cooperation between the various Jewish factions by perpetuating the customs and dialects of each segment, creating instead a metropolis of feuding Jews. But even this had its bright side. The Turkish authorities took advantage of their wide range of languages for administrative and diplomatic purposes.[13]

Some disputes became particularly heated because there was also a range of opinion among the rabbis as to how Jewish law should treat the *conversos*. Were their original (Catholic) marriage vows still valid? Could those who had never come to the Ottoman Empire (or never returned to Judaism) inherit the Jewish estate of a deceased relative in, say, Salonika? What about the children of mixed marriages where the woman had been partially from Old Christian stock? Was the painful act of adult circumcision mandatory for full participation in a congregation?[14]

The synagogue founded in Salonika by Doña Gracia was for the *conversos* from Portugal whose cause she had championed most ardently from the beginning. It was originally called *Livyuat-Hen*, reminders of Grace (Gracia), after the name and deeds of its founder. Don Joseph handled the initial negotiations and managed the project. The distinguished judge, orator and commentator, Rabbi Moses Almosnino, was appointed as rabbinic leader and gave the opening sermon in December, 1559[15] He told the gathering that the name was most appropriate as *Livyuat* also signified connectedness and unity, and Doña Gracia was a "glorious" woman who had led those present towards a connection with God and unity with the Jewish world. Almosnino's overarching theme was inclusiveness—a topic that was clearly directed at former *conversos* struggling to become part of the larger Jewish community. He emphasized that there was no right or wrong path towards God. Every path was acceptable. Yet he also recognized that "all beginnings are hard."[16]

Its strict but enlightened regulations, some of which were included in the sermon, were either based upon Almosnino's personal beliefs, or those of the synagogue's benefactor. All members were required to attend services on Mondays and Thursdays, when readings from the Bible were included in the ritual, as well on Saturdays (a reflection, perhaps of the rigid rules concerning attendance at Mass that Doña Gracia had lived under as a Catholic). No quarrel between members could last for longer than two to three days without being submitted to an arbitrator (yet another sign of the contentiousness of Salonika's Jews). Those involved in the conflict had to seek forgiveness from those they had hurt, regardless of social status. Its humbler members were to yield to the views of the richer and more powerful members, while those with money had an obligation to relieve the poorer members of the financial burden of paying the communal taxes and expenses associated with membership. This, noted Almosnino, was the fairest way to allocate the resources and responsibilities of the congregation.[17]

Doña Gracia also founded a *bet midrash* (academy) in Salonika for the study of rabbinic literature, signing over for its upkeep the rents from some local houses that she owned.[18] The idea of rentable property supporting a religious institution is still practiced in present-day Turkey. At least one synagogue in the old quarter of Izmir (formerly Smyrna) that might have long since been abandoned because of costly upkeep, relies in part upon the commercial rents from adjoining stall-holders whose shops sit on synagogue land.[19]

The pattern under which the *bet midrash* was organized was unusually democratic for its day. Instead of a permanent base of scholar-rabbis who were regularly attached to the institution, learned men (so far as we know participation was limited to men) who were accepted could attend only for a limited period. These scholar-rabbis then went back into the community to spread their expanded knowledge among their congregants, leaving room for others to benefit from the chance for a sabbatical or further education, as it would be known today. Such a rotation enabled a large number of religious leaders to attend. The only permanent member was its leader, Rabbi Samuel de Medina, the respected Talmudist, who served as academic director. The post brought this modest man recognition as one of the most prominent rabbis of the day and helped relieve him of some of his ongoing financial difficulties.[20] Once again, the academy appears to have reflected Doña Gracia's wish to help educate a broad range of her people as well as her cautious attitude towards perpetuating entrenched hierarchies. It also neatly complemented the educational work she had begun in Ferrara.

She founded another synagogue in Izmir, a maritime city that lies along the Aegean shores of Western Turkey (Anatolia). This one was named *Sinyora Giveret* (Our Great or Crowned Lady). It is the only synagogue bearing her name that has remained in continuous operation until the present. Though it does not appear in documents from those times—and a known community of Jews in Izmir came about somewhat later—the fact that it was created by Doña Gracia is a fundamental part of its oral tradition. The structure itself has been rebuilt over the years, due to decay and fire, but the strong belief remains that it owes its existence to her generosity. If so, one can assume that it was originally created for *conversos* who had chosen to settle in Izmir; a city where they could engage their exceptional skills in international trade.

Another charitable tradition deeply implanted in the life of the Mediterranean Jews during this period, and fostered by Doña Gracia, was the ransoming of Jews taken captive by pirates. Such deeds, known as *pidion schevouyim*, were considered high priority because they involved the actual saving of lives.

The need was particularly acute in Salonika where sailing vessels filled with Jewish merchants would regularly leave the protection of the port, only to be seized upon by maritime bandits who might be Turkish, Arab, Maltese, Greek or even Croatians from the Adriatic. She contributed heavily to this cause, as sometimes the price for ransoming the captives could reach 500 ducats a head.[21] The ransom money was often too much for even a few wealthy families to bear, resulting in the need for constant, community-wide fund raising. In 1552, for example, the Knights of Malta seized a ship leaving Salonika with 70 Jews aboard and demanded 200,000 Turkish aspers for their release. (The amount can be judged by measuring it against the 55 aspers a day that Don Joseph received, later in the decade, as an advisor to the sultan. And a wealthy man was someone who owned property worth 60,000 aspers). On this particular occasion the need was deemed so critical—perhaps some important Jews had been on board—that Rabbi Almosnino begged the Jews of Salonika to unite, if only to carry out this special *mitzvah*. In subsequent years other rabbis continually rallied their members for the same cause.[22]

Even as late as the 19th century, the Jewish community of Izmir maintained a booth down by the docks where a rotation of representatives waited around the clock to ransom and assist any Jewish captive arriving at the port. Some came from Ashkenazi communities, and certain synagogues would offer to follow the Ashkenazi rite of prayer to make them feel at home. There was a society of women to take care of their needs and help them get established. The arriving refugees were given names like *Mizrahi* (from the East) or *Behar* (Arabic for 'from the sea') when they could not provide genuine family names; a custom that helps to explain a source of two common Jewish surnames. To make sure reserves were always adequate and available, the leaders would impose a special tax on personal property. [23]

Doña Gracia's efforts on behalf of *conversos* harassed by the Inquisition did not cease either. A document tucked away in an obscure section of the Vatican's Inquisition archives shows the changing nature of her work in this regard.[24] In the spring of 1560 she was approached by some of her own contacts in Salonika and Pera to intercede with the sultan on behalf of a certain clergyman named Friar Giacomo. He had apparently been charged with heresy. Giacomo had managed to get word to his good friends in Salonika and Pera and they were now alerting Doña Gracia. No doubt he had such friends because he had been one of the many *conversos* encouraged years earlier to take the cloth as a way to surreptitiously serve his own people.

Giacomo was being held by the local office of the Inquisition on the Greek island of Chio in the Aegean Sea. Although it was part of the Ottoman Empire, Catholic clergy in Ottoman lands still came under the purview of the Inquisition since the church was given substantial autonomy over its internal ecclesiastic affairs. Friar Giacomo had been apprehended in Zakinthos, an island due west of Chio in the Ionian Sea, where he had been discovered disguised as a peasant—perhaps to escape church authorities. Church officials feared they would be forced to hand over their wayward friar and take him to Doña Gracia in Pera, should Doña Gracia obtain an order from the sultan that superseded their normal rights (nobody seemed in any doubt that she could obtain this sort of favor).

In the particular missive, Friar Antonio Veneziano, the senior church official in the region, was writing to Cardinal Alessandrino, the Supreme Inquisitor in Rome, concerning plans to move Friar Giacomo to Crete "very cautiously... for reasons we know" to avoid complying with the order.[25]

In addition to these rescue, housing and educational efforts, Doña Gracia, as mentioned earlier, was feeding around eighty people day at her Galata residence and distributing ducats to poor Jews and the Jewish home for the sick.[26]

Doña Gracia was also credited once again during this period with subsidizing Hebrew printing, as she had done in Ferrara.[27] The Usques, for example, had sailed for Turkey after Hebrew books had been publicly burned in Rome in 1553, and a subsequent rabbinical conference in Ferrara imposed such strong self-censorship that the production of Hebrew works was no longer feasible. No more was ever heard of Abraham Usque, who was probably about sixty and may have not been well enough to travel. Salomon Usque, his son who became a literary figure in his own right, later proceeded to Constantinople. Once there, he kept up the family's printing tradition by publishing several works in the old Ferrara type that he brought with him. These books were among those most likely to have been subsidized by Doña Gracia.[28] Samuel Usque, author of Consolation... ultimately settled in Safed in the Holy Land.[29]

Later in the century, the interest of the House of Mendes in supporting Hebrew printing was one of the few public functions kept alive by Reyna (Ana), following the death of her mother and husband. Reyna did this for about seven years. She started in 1593 when she was in her late fifties, publishing religious books that were initially prepared at her Belvedere Palace. Yet none had the cutting edge of the works that her mother had championed during their halcyon days in Ferrara.[30]

Doña Gracia Street, Tiberias, Israel

CHAPTER **18**

The Tiberias Project

It was early spring…Joseph Nasi had already issued a proclamation in the harbours of Europe that the oppressed of Israel were to arise and make themselves ready to return to the land of their fathers under his protection… Men and women and children gathered up their few moveable goods and filtered through the long-mired dangerous roads and forded rivers and crossed mountains….

"For the angel of death was holding his wing over Donna Grazia Nassi. She was not yet old and she had ailed a little…(but) she had set all her heart upon the rebuilding of Tiberias…
    —From the historical novel *The Last Days of Shylock,* by Ludwig Lewisohn[1]

Situated along the western shore of the inland Sea of Galilee, in the northern reaches of the Holy Land, Tiberias has always held a special place in the hearts and souls of the Jewish people. It was first mentioned in the Bible as the region allotted by Joshua to the tribe of Naphtali. For a long time it was no more than a cluster of crude settlements. Not until the days of Roman domination and the provincial governorship of Herod Antipas—the ruthless Herod of the New Testament—was it carefully laid out and constructed in the Greco-Roman manner on a beautiful strip of flat land between the sparkling waters of the Sea of Galilee and the triangular contours of the adjacent mountain slopes. Herod named the new city after his Emperor, Tiberius Claudius Nero, ruler of the vast Roman Empire from 14 B.C.E. to 37 C.E.[2] It immediately became the capital of the Galilee. Yet it was not the city itself that was initially so important to the Jews. It was the ground beneath. It had been a burial site since the time of the ancient Israelites. And it continued to serve the children of Israel in this capacity.

The great sage and first century rabbi, Johanan ben Zakkai, chose burial in Tiberias. Legend has it that Ben Zakkai escaped from Jerusalem during the chaotic days when it was under siege by the Romans in 68 C.E. He did so by hiding in a coffin while his disciples pretended they needed to leave the city in a hurry to bury their deceased master. Ben Zakkai then set up a rabbinic academy in exile that helped preserve the cornerstones of Jewish faith, customs and laws. Not surprisingly, the entire Jewish way of life was most vulnerable following the destruction of Jerusalem and a Roman interdict banishing them forever from their sacred city as a punishment for their repeated uprisings.

Ben Zakkai inspired a glittering roster of early sages and leaders who studied and wrote and were buried in Tiberias. Soon it became a leading center of Jewish learning. The Mishnah (the codification of oral Jewish law) was compiled in Tiberias, as was the Palestinian Talmud, completed in the fourth century C.E. The martyr and mystic, Rabbi Akiva, who studied under the disciples of Rabbi Ben Zakkai, was buried in Tiberias; as were Akiva's disciples.

In 235 C.E., Tiberias became the seat of the *Sanhedrin*, the ruling body of seventy elders under the leadership of the *nasi* (reputed descendants of the great House of David). But this government in exile did not last long. Eventually it lost its hegemony over the scattered and contentious Jewish communities of the diaspora and was disbanded by the Eastern Roman (Byzantine) Church in 425 c.e. But not before Tiberias had taken hold of the Jewish imagination. Its soil was considered so sacred that the bones of Maimonides, the Spanish-born physician-philosopher, were re-interred there following his death in Cairo in the 13th century. Likewise, the bones of nameless Jews from other distant towns and villages would regularly arrive by camel train to be set down near the burial places of the holy greats. Tiberias soon rivaled Jerusalem in popularity and significance, especially as it was reputed to be the city from which the Messiah would emerge. The prophecy was based upon interpretive tales from the Bible (*midrash*) and the Zohar—the writings of the early mystics—and confirmed by Maimonides in his writings.[3] Those buried nearby were thereby destined to be among the first to be resurrected.

It was also a pleasant place to live. Cool breezes wafted off the waters. The views were spectacular. The healing properties and sensuous pleasures of its celebrated hot springs had been enjoyed since antiquity. So had the riches to be derived from the teeming multitudes of fish that coursed through the Sea of Galilee. Sugar cane grew readily in the region. Silk could be cultivated from the silkworms that feasted on its mulberry trees.

Yet all this was cast into oblivion when the Jews fled the city following its capture by the Crusaders at the dawn of the second millennium. The crusaders were followed by the Mamelukes, nomadic Arabs so lawless and unpredictable that Jews were not inclined to return to the city. Only when the Ottoman Turks conquered the Holy Land in 1516 did the potential for re-settlement reemerge. But by then Tiberias had fallen into ruin, laid waste by years of abandonment and a devastating earthquake. Pilgrims and travelers who passed through in the early years of the 16th century reported that little remained in the derelict city but toppled pillars and fractured stones. It had become a desolate moonscape, inhabited only by snakes that slithered unimpeded through the silent ruins.[4] "No man can go there for fear of the Arabs," wrote Moses Basola, a Jewish traveler, in 1522, "except at the time of the caravans."[5] By 1547, a few Jewish fishermen were eking out a living by the shore.[6] But there was not much more.

Even so, the potential remained, especially as it lay along the major caravan and trade route that stretched from Damascus to Cairo.[7] In the nearby highlands during the same period, the growth of the regional capital of Safed had been nothing short of a miracle. A number of the exiles from the Iberian Peninsula—especially those with messianic expectations, kabbalistic leanings and deep religious feelings—had sought re-settlement in the Holy Land and had selected Safed as the location of choice.

Returning to the holy city of Jerusalem had been replete with difficulties. Poverty remained widespread and it was a far more dangerous place. The Jews arriving in Jerusalem also faced a backlash from a Christian establishment keeping watch over its own holy sites. Describing the scene in Jerusalem at the end of the 15th century, Francesco Suriano, head of the local Franciscan order, wrote: "These dogs, the Jews, are stepped upon, are beaten and tortured, as well they should be. They live on this land in conditions of submission that no words can describe." He continued, "And it is instructive that in Jerusalem, where they committed the crime for which they were dispersed in the whole world, God punishes them more than anywhere else in the world…the Muslims (even) treat them like dogs."[8] Still, a number of Jews were determined to reside there anyway.

Far more popular was the hill town of Safed with its narrow, winding streets and close sense of community. It was also walled and well protected from marauding bands of Bedouins. With so many advantages it rapidly developed as the Holy Land's thriving center of tanning, weaving, dyeing, cloth manufacture and tailoring—wealth-producing crafts that the enterprising new settlers brought with them. Raw Merino wool was shipped to them by the wealthier merchants of Constantinople. The immigrants handled the rest, spinning cloth on home-based looms inside their hilltop houses. Many of these textile producers were also learned men (being a mystic and a merchant were not incompatible).[9] There was little pretense, even among the great scholars. "None among them" wrote one traveler around this time, "is ashamed to go to the well and draw water, or go to the marketplace to buy bread, oil and vegetables. All the work in the house is done by themselves."[10]

Safed soon became renowned throughout the Jewish world for its academies and lively religious discourse, led by the most outstanding sages of the day. The atmosphere of learned debate was exhilarating and broad enough to embrace some of the great kabbalists who lived there, such as Solomon Alkabetz, Moses Cordovero and Isaac Luria. Before ushering in the Sabbath at sunset, the faithful would march out into the fields where barley, beans, cotton and figs were growing, and sing praises to the Lord. The spiritual setting inspired the famous Sabbath song of joy, *Lekha Dodi*, written by Alkabetz at this time and still sung regularly at services today. To Alkabetz, the Sabbath was a living reality that deserved to be embraced after a week's absence with the same eager expectation that a grooms meets a bride.

In 1525 there were only 233 Jewish households in Safed. By the mid 1560's there were nearly 1,000.[11] By day they made cloth. By night or before dawn they would rise and discuss the holy books, seeking meaning in the divine through patterns they discerned in the universe. An estimated ten thousand bolts of finished fabric were being produced each year,[12] in addition to countless learned and mystical tracts that are preserved to this day.

Still, compared to other places in the Ottoman Empire, the number of incoming Jews was small and specialized. There was no centrally organized *aliyah*. Rather, the newcomers consisted

of lone individuals or small gatherings of *conversos* and Jews attracted by the highly erudite milieu.[13]

Others were drawn by the messianic fervor of the times. The
conquest of the Holy Land by the Ottomans earlier in the century, following the great cataclysm of expulsion and exile from
Iberia, had been viewed, as noted, as twin signs that the Messiah was definitely on his way. Calculations, special prayers and
religious acts performed by the kabbalists were aimed, in part,
at hastening his impending arrival.

In 1538, adding fuel to the fires of messianic speculation in
Safed, was the reintroduction of the official ordination of rabbis by Jacob Berav, one of the city's most influential sages. The
rite had not been practiced since the demise of the ancient
Sanhedrin. Informal ordination, exercised individually by each
scattered community, had sufficed in the interim, leading to a
situation—so painfully illustrated by the failure of the Ancona
boycott—where nobody could claim absolute authority over the
entire Jewish world. As the massive influx of sages into Safed
seemed to augur the revival of this fundamental pillar of statehood, it was important to bring the idea to fruition.[14]

Berav's appointment was approved by a vote of the leading
scholars of his academy. But it soon proved little more than a
symbolic act, since nobody outside Safed was interested in relinquishing local autonomy. Nevertheless, the sages of Safed
continued to believe it was authentic, and possibly even preor-
dained. It thus transmitted a powerful signal. A supreme judicial authority was viewed as yet another requirement, predicted
in Isaiah,[15] that had to be in place before the Messiah could
appear and the Messianic Era could commence.[16]

For the *conversos*, the possibility of an imminent Messianic
Age offered very personal benefits. Many feared they would otherwise be burdened in perpetuity with the biblical curse of *karet*—
divine punishment for indulging in idol worship and failing to

fulfill the commandments, even though their 'sins' had occurred under extreme duress. Their only hope lay in the redemptive environment of the land of Israel.[17] As Samuel de Medina pointed out: "For our sages have maintained that... he who walks four cubits within the Holy Land, his sins are forgiven."[18]

———••✄••———

The ferment and promise of Safed could not fail to catch the observant eye and fertile mind of Doña Gracia in Constantinople. As an aging *conversa* who had lived long past most of her contemporaries, it may well have touched her very deeply. The first documentary evidence that she was responding in a manner that was totally true to character—reluctant to remain on the sidelines while others took the lead—came in the form of an official order. Dated July 17 1560, it was sent by a representative of the sultan to his regional governor in Damascus.[19] It acknowledged that a petition had been presented to the sultan concerning the subdistrict of Safed known as Tiberias.

The area in question was described by the petitioning party as having subterranean structures and empty houses. Constructed in pre-Islamic times, these buildings were located inside its ancient and now crumbling city walls. Nearby, it noted, was a large lake and hot springs... "where salubrious water spouts (out of the earth)." It also had "a ruined bath... (and) innumerable date palms and places suitable for the production of silk and for planting sugar cane..." It further noted that "one, two or three thousand Muslims, Jews and Christians come there every year and go into the bath." Also, that the local Turkish deputy collected a handful of aspers for every fish caught in the lake and every person who came through on a "pilgrimage." This was presumably a reference to the Jews, since they often visited the neighboring tombs of the holy greats as well as the medicinal hot springs.[20]

The petition then tempted the sultan with a tantalizing proposal. "If such a (large) number of people come together while (the place) is ruined, how much revenue would be obtained if it were (re)built?" It ended by seeking the right to farm the taxes, with a guarantee that after ten years the petitioner would pay ten times the taxes that the area now yielded.[21]

The sultan's representative began by asking the local governor to comment upon the facts laid out in the petition. Assuming they were correct, he told the governor that the authorities intended to turn the subdistrict into a *waqf*—an area whose income would be used for charitable purpose, such as feeding the hungry. In this instance the purpose was probably the soup kitchen in Jerusalem established eight years earlier by Roxelana, the second wife of Sultan Suleiman. These soup kitchens were normally endowed from landed property—in this case from various parts of the Holy Land and administered from the regional headquarters in Damascus.[22]

Modern historians are unanimous in agreeing that the petitioner was Doña Gracia.[23] Though her name was not found on this initial petition (of which parts are missing), it appeared many times over in subsequent *firmen* (official decrees) and correspondence connected with the plan. The actual words used were either "Gracia Nassy" or "a Jewish woman by the name of Gracia who is the tax collector of Tiberias."[24] Even so, it was wrongly assumed for centuries that the project was spearheaded by her nephew, Don Joseph. This was probably because the Jewish historian, Joseph ha-Kohen, in his *Vale of Tears*, written at that time, gave the nephew all the credit, as did the French.[25] But newly-found Ottoman documents are clear in naming Doña Gracia as the actual tax farmer, and thereby the person in authority. Even more significant was that Don Joseph's name did not appear alongside her own, despite the fact that he was becoming more and more prominent in his own right.[26]

It could have been that he preferred concentrating on matters more closely tied to his role at court.[27] By contrast, the personal appeal of the project for someone like Doña Gracia was undeniable: an opportunity once again to assume an important leadership role, the symbolic value of reintroducing a settlement in a place where the *nasi* had presided in antiquity, the attractions of a city offering a natural spa, burial among Israel's most sagacious souls, a chance for redemption and first in line to savor the euphoria of the Messianic Age. She may have viewed it the safe harbor for her people that she had sought for over a decade; from the time Don Joseph first petitioned the Venetians for an island in the lagoon. From a biblical perspective the Tiberias project enabled her to complete the circle: not only leading her people out of captivity (out from under the cruel and capricious whim of the Inquisition), but literally into the Promised Land.

Tiberias was also a settlement over which she could maintain some political control, as tax farming carried a myriad of legal rights. The tax farmer was immediately considered a minister or officer of the state. He or she could set the fines payable by anyone who was delinquent in their taxes. They could automatically assume possession of any vacant land for agricultural or building purposes. Further, anyone convicted of breaking local laws could not be punished without the prior consent of the tax farmer.[28] In sum: it could serve as a semi-autonomous province in which Jews could settle in safety.

Tiberias thus fitted perfectly with her pragmatic approach to community leadership. It had the potential of becoming as prosperous as Safed, and thereby self-supporting. It also enjoyed an honored tradition as a place of learning—traits she had always valued highly.

The concession was readily granted. The sultan was even willing to assume a large burden of the start-up costs. He commanded the governor in Damascus to begin by providing the materials and manpower needed to rebuild the city walls at an estimated cost to his treasury of 5,000 gold pieces. Without first securing the city with a protective wall, any other undertaking would have been useless. Sultan Suleiman even agreed to pay for the cost overrun when construction turned out to require an extra 500 gold pieces. However, in a frugal afterthought, his officials did caution the governor "to…try to complete (it) with a smaller expense."

In turn, Doña Gracia was required to immediately supply the *waqf* with an annual sum of "one thousand gold pieces," six times the amount collected when she had originally applied in 1560.[29] Regular market days were to be revived. In return, all the taxable income she could collect from the designated area, including seven nearby villages, belonged to her. It was also up to her to bring the nearby spring waters to the city at an estimated personal cost of "800 gold pieces."[30]

In Lewisohn's fictional account it was Shakespeare's infamous Shylock—whom Doña Gracia had cunningly spirited out of Venice after his trial so he would not have to live life as a Christian—who was sent to oversee preparations. In the story, Shylock had been serving as a Venetian agent for the House of Mendes. And Doña Gracia had insisted that he set aside a portion of his profits to ransom captive Jews from the pirates. In reality, the overseer was Rabbi Joseph ben Adret (also called ibn Ardut) of Constantinople, according to 16th century Jewish historian, ha-Kohen. Turkish documents also talk about a physician named David acting as a supervising agent.[31] Adret's salary, 60 aspers a day, was payable by the sultan. He was given eight attendants, who were possibly armed guards, along with sealed orders from the sultan requesting that both the governor in

Damascus and the local overlord in Safed do whatever possible to aid Adret in his mission. Orders were immediately given for all available "porters and builders" in the Galilee to go to Tiberias and work on the defensive wall, with penalties for those who failed to sign up. The residents of nearby villages were assigned the job of making the mortar, using sand from the shores of the lake. The hordes of discarded stones were gathered and reused for the walls.[32]

But the indigenous Arab population was horrified when it discovered the underlying reason for the call up. Its reaction began to resemble the disputes that have continued to this day. One of their aging sheiks—a sort of 16th century Yasir Arafat—insisted that he had found a passage in an ancient text that prophesied the end of the local Arabs, and even Islam, once Tiberias was rebuilt. "Our faith will be lost and we will be found wanting," was the way the historian, ha-Kohen, recorded the sheik's warning. Little wonder that they refused to sign up. Adret immediately reported the mutiny to the governor in Damascus. Fearing the sultan's wrath, the governor quickly ordered the execution of two of the leaders of the rebellion, hoping that a fear of further reprisals for this blatant disregard of royal orders might soften the attitude of the rest.

But it was not only the Arabs who were horrified. The French consul in Constantinople was equally alarmed. Writing to his superiors in Paris in September 1563, at the time of construction, he noted that Tiberias was to be a place "where only Jews will be allowed to live"[33]—something that had never been articulated in writing by the Ottoman Turks, but could have been part of an informal agreement. It would help to explain the local Arabs' explosive reaction.

What was especially worrisome to the French was the belief, echoed in the consul's September letter, that when restoration was complete, Don Joseph would set himself up as "king of the

Jews."[34] The idea that Jews would consider regrouping as a nation—even an embryonic one—seemed to horrify the Christian world. Though the observation may have been designed to discredit a man the French disliked and distrusted anyway, it certainly bolsters the opinion of historians who have since maintained that the Tiberias project was part of a larger attempt to revive statehood. Significantly, as the French dispatch also noted, the concession had been structured to last beyond the reign of Sultan Suleiman, to cover the administration of his son, Selim, and Selim's son, Murad: in short, into the foreseeable future.

Despite the outpouring of opposition, Suleiman attached great importance to the project. This was underscored by the size of Adret's salary, which almost reached the amount paid a court physician,[35] plus the alarm shown by the governor in Damascus when he thought he would not be able to complete the wall as commanded. The reason was that the rebuilding of Tiberias would have fallen within the larger aims of the Ottoman Empire at this time, which was to foster stability, security and economic growth in remote, troublesome and unproductive areas. Doña Gracia may well have understood this point and used it to her advantage when presenting the idea. It would have been politically astute, as it would have positioned her and Don Joseph in the position of promoting Ottoman interests, rather than their own.

The perimeter wall, about three-quarters of a mile in length, was completed around December, 1564.[36] Its relatively short span suggests a modest beginning. Still, the restoration of the city could now begin. During excavations, a crypt of an ancient church, with altars and marble statues still intact, was discovered underground. Workers also found three bronze church bells that had been hidden by Crusaders before they left, three centuries earlier. These were refashioned into cannon for protection.[37]

Mulberry trees were planted in and around the city to provide the necessary environment to raise and feed silkworms. Arrangements were made to bring wool from Spain to manufacture textiles in the Venetian fashion, since these would have been the most popular on the European markets.[38] Orange groves and date palms were cultivated commercially. Some of the Jewish settlers also worked as beekeepers.[39]

Don Joseph then sought craftsmen to build the industries, dispatching representatives and ships to the beleaguered Jews of the Papal States, and probably elsewhere, inviting them to settle in Tiberias. One group that responded to this call was the small Jewish community of Cori, some 40 miles southeast of Rome. The Jews of Cori had suffered severely under the restrictions imposed by Pope Paul IV. First, they had been shunted into a walled ghetto. Then the papal bull reducing their right to participate in a wide variety of commercial pursuits, including handicrafts, had so seriously hampered their opportunities to earn a living that they could no longer feed their families. When they could not even cover their most basic obligations, papal officials condemned some of them—presumably as debtors—to the galleys or execution. "We became a heap of bones," they lamented. "We (were) brought very low... our eyes have welled with weeping and the tears on our cheeks have given us no respite..."[40]

Some sought relief by converting to Christianity. Others were tempted by news of the Tiberias project. Ships, they learned, were being sent by Don Joseph to Venice and Ancona to take Italian Jews to the Holy Land—"especially (those) who are craftsmen, so that they may settle and establish the land on a proper basis." Jews from other communities had already set sail. Thus they were "stirred with a single heart" to make the journey under the leadership of their rabbi, Malachi Gallico. But they had no money to travel even to the ports. So they sent two emissaries to beg for contributions from Jewish communities that had not yet been brought quite so low. No record remains of the fate of these Jews from Cori, but some may well have made it. The surname of Cori would subsequently be identified with Jews from Turkey rather than Italy.[41]

In Tiberias, the newcomers were soon taking over abandoned structures, renovating deserted houses, restoring gaping roofs, clearing the rubble and quarreling in typical Jewish fashion. By 1564 the revival was sufficiently far along that yet another traveler recalled that the scent from the date palm, orange and pine trees was so overpowering that it was almost suffocating. Yet another talked effusively of a wilderness turned into a "garden of Eden."[42] Almost all of the residents, noted one of these travelers, were former *conversos* from Spain and Portugal,[43] suggesting only a handful of the Italian Jews ever got there in the end.

An ancient synagogue was reopened next to the section of the wall that bordered the lake.[44] Doña Gracia personally supported, and may have even founded, a *yeshiva* headed by Eleazer ben Yohai, a sage from Safed. He was thought to have been of Spanish origin and a member of the Benveniste family. Once again, this suggests that she maintained her pattern of turning to other family members whenever a suitable opportunity arose. Its doors remained open for about eighty years after her death, supported by diaspora Jews.[45] Eventually almost seventy scholars studied at the *yeshiva*, according to rabbinic documents.[46] Another *yeshiva* operated outside the city walls.[47]

By the mid 1560's, a Yemenite traveler saw "elderly and honorable men" studying Torah, Talmud and mysticism in a synagogue that may have been one and the same, since he talks of it being within the walled area and close to the shores of the lake. The traveler, Yahia-al-Ahir, had chanced upon the men, he wrote, on the afternoon prior to the Sabbath. Before sundown "they hurried to the hot springs" to cleanse themselves. Afterwards, they returned "to the prayer house" and lit candles. Then the cantor sang psalms to the gathering from atop a wooden tower built for the purpose.[48]

Close to the hot springs "beautiful buildings" began to take shape. A German traveler, Christopher Fürer von Haimendorf, confirmed that they were being constructed "by a wealthy Jewish woman with the permission of the Turkish emperor."[49]

One historian has insisted that among those structures was a mansion being readied for Doña Gracia herself, although none of the travelers and pilgrims wandering through at the time corroborate this fact.[50] What was certain was that she was expected, so it is likely that a fine house was indeed being made ready. "She will come from Constantinople next summer with all her family to live in Tiberias," noted the Portugese friar, Pantãleo de Aveiro, who made a journey to the Holy Land around this time. "Together with her will come all the Jews who wish to follow her." That such an important personage would come and live among them had tremendous symbolic impact. Continued de Aveiro, "This news caused great happiness among the Jews in the Land…"[51] They clung to it, he added, as yet another sign that the Messiah was on his way.

However, there was no mention from any source that she actually arrived. Maybe she was already too infirm. Or perhaps she was warned to stay away as the settlement was increasingly being burdened with setbacks. Less than a year after the completion of the wall the sultan's lieutenants were alerting the district ruler in Safed that vandalism was widespread—presumably from reports sent to Constantinople by Doña Gracia or her agent at the site, the physician named David. It was happening because nobody, it appeared, had ever been assigned to tend the gates. In an angry letter to the district ruler, an official at the Sublime Porte reported that, "Scoundrels from outside (have been entering) during the night and (stealing) objects from the houses of certain people," causing violence to the residents.[52] The missive then reminded the local overlord, somewhat sarcastically, that, "the closing of (the two gates) from evening and their opening in the morning...as is practiced in other fortresses, (would) be of benefit to the residents." For that reason the correspondent ordered the district ruler in Safed to ensure that the gatekeeper in Tiberias opened and closed the gates, as was customary elsewhere.[53]

A second and expanded version of the same *firman*, sent directly to the governor in Damascus, suggested that the reason for the carelessness was because a *firman* on the topic had never been received in Safed. Safety was so crucial to the embryonic settlement, the order explained, that the sultan's counselors wanted two *janissaries* appointed from the constabulary in Damascus to open the gates at the time of the morning prayers, and close them during "the evening prayers." The cost of maintaining the guard was to come out of the money collected for the soup kitchens.[54]

Even this failed to remedy the problem of internal security. In May 1566, just five months later, Doña Gracia had to bring a further complaint to the notice of officials in Constantinople. This time the gatekeepers were not doing their job. The sultan's correspondent directed his ire at the commander of the *janissaries* in Damascus, asking that he personally undertake an investigation. If the gatekeepers were indeed "negligent and slack in the fulfillment of their tasks," he said, the commander was obligated to find other "righteous people" from among the *janissaries* and replace the current slackers.[55]

That was not all. The area's Arab residents were continuing to throw up hurdles to orderly development. During the same year, a dispute arose over claims by the local Arabs in connection with a parcel of unused land that extended from a mosque and its adjacent cemetery. As a result, Doña Gracia decided it

THE TIBERIAS PROJECT   447

would be prudent to build a fence to mark the boundary so that the Arabs could not later claim ownership of any buildings she might wish to put up. The judge in Tiberias was commanded by the central authorities in Constantinople to ascertain that the boundaries were correct. He was then to make certain that Doña Gracia was able to develop the land without further hindrance and in a manner that did not arouse the anger of the local Arabs. Thus "You are obligated to be cautious," he was told by the sultan's emissaries.[56]

Some, if not all, of these raids and quarrels may have been a continuation of the tensions that had simmered between the incoming Jews and the local Arab population from the beginning. The ease with which Doña Gracia was able to repeatedly persuade the sultan to support her needs would have only accentuated their original misgivings.

During this period, Doña Gracia further alerted court officials that the local Turkish bureaucrats were permitting outsiders to farm some of the land in the nearby villages that was included in her tax concession—activity that was interfering with her ability to raise the expected taxes. The governor in Damascus was commanded to ban such people from entering the area. The errant bureaucrats were admonished to stay away. Meanwhile, the governor was required to make sure that Doña Gracia and her agents could go about their business unobstructed.[57]

A sense that Doña Gracia was intimately involved in micromanaging her Tiberias concession could easily be interpreted as a sign that she was physically present. But she had previously shown that she was perfectly willing to conduct business overseas—Italy, for example—without actually being on the spot. So it would be unwise to assume from these reports that she had arrived in Tiberias.

Whether present or not, there is only so much that any one

person, or even a group of influential people, can accomplish when the odds are stacked so heavily in favor of the combined agenda of the opposing forces. And the local Arabs were not the only ones who were unhappy with the new settlement. The Franciscans, based in Jerusalem, were even more hotly opposed. More troublesome still, they had the ear of high officials at the Sublime Porte.

Central to the Franciscans' concerns, not unlike the local Arabs, were their existing rights and status. They feared these would be undermined by an influx of Jews, especially if it became the precursor of a larger plan for Jewish nationhood. Under the Ottoman Turks they had already seen their position deteriorate. Their monastery on Zion Hill, legendary site of the Last Supper and King David's tomb, had been confiscated. It had taken special help from the French—as customary intermediaries between the Christian and Muslim worlds—to obtain a monastery from the Armenian Christians in Jerusalem, called St. Salvador, to replace the one they lost. At this time the Franciscans were led by Bonifacio de Ragusa, a charismatic and effective leader. Experienced in court intrigue, he spread rumors that the Jews were planning to create a separate nation under Don Joseph as their king. Even if this were a lie, it created some misgivings within the Sublime Porte. Bonifacio also warned that the new arrivals wanted to convert the church of St. Peter, one of Tiberias' most ancient sanctuaries, into a synagogue. He was so distraught about this that he sought an official promise from governor of Damascus, as well as one of the most senior officials at the Sublime Porte, that it would not happen.[58]

It is significant that during this time an unknown person was spreading rumors in Constantinople maligning Brianda, albeit that she had been dead for almost a decade. She was being accused of behavior ill-fitting a pious Jewess following her return to Judaism in Ferrara. The rumors must have been potent enough to have required the intervention of Rabbi Abraham Rovico, a leading rabbi in Ferrara. He was moved to write indignantly to the "officials and leaders (of the Jews) in Constantinople" assuring them that the rumors were unfounded. "For the sake of the woman," he wrote, "I come before your exalted eminences to raise my voice loudly in anger...to tell you that anyone who speaks ill of her, namely that her religion and customs and ways were hanging from the rods of the Gentiles, and other words of that nature, he slanders her....because I knew her customs and ways...she was a perfect Jewess..."[59]

It may also have been one of the occasions, mentioned earlier, when rumors circulated suggesting that Don Joseph and Doña Gracia had once been lovers.[60] All of which could have been a conscious effort to discredit the family within and outside the Jewish community of Constantinople.

Such lobbying behind the scenes could have also been a reason why the *janissaries* assigned to guard Tiberias did not actively defend its gates. It could explain why the local Turkish authorities seemed so indifferent about making sure that the new colony was secure and without incident. With enemies like these working the corridors of power, and the French equally opposed, it would have been reason enough for Don Joseph to decide that it would be prudent to distance himself from the Tiberias venture. This would have been particularly devastating to Doña Gracia.[61]

Yet another stumbling block was the lack of immigrants. Prospects for increased settlement were continually being sabotaged by the ever-present threat of traveling on a ship that might be boarded at any time by pirates, consigning the immigrants to slavery. One eyewitness told of Jewish immigrants to the Holy Land being "stripped to the skin and paraded naked" before being taken into captivity. On this occasion, "eighty Jews, included two women, a mother and daughter, were (taken)...and with them the venerable wise old man, Rabbi Jacob Marcus of Salonika."[62]

True, the number of taxpayers in the Tiberias region increased significantly between 1555 and 1573, and the income from taxes almost doubled.[63] But it was a brief flicker of activity before the settlement began a rapid tumble into oblivion. It certainly did not flourish as had been expected. After the death of Doña Gracia in 1569, the descent became even more rapid. Caught up with the fame and power that accompanied his court life, Don Joseph showed every sign of having cooled to the settlement once the pressure was off. Ottoman power was passing its peak, suggesting that Turkish control over the area was also weakening, leaving the residents at the whim of lawless nomads.[64] An outbreak of Bedouin violence in 1575, reported in rabbinic sources, was the final blow. Many of the wealthier Jewish residents simply fled, abandoning their property for plunder and leaving their taxes unpaid.[65]

"I came to Tiberias on May 19, "reported the German traveler, Salomon Schweigger, in 1581, just twenty years after its auspicious rebirth, "and there was only a travelers' inn, and next to it just a few houses."[66]

The only saving grace was that Doña Gracia did not live long enough to suffer the pain of watching its eventual collapse.

CHAPTER 19

Ebb Tide

A decade or so of life in Constantinople had proven spectacular for Don Joseph. As Doña Gracia grew increasingly aged and may have also become infirm, it was now Joseph, nicknamed The Great Jew,[1] who moved into the spotlight. Yet, while his aunt had always kept her sights squarely upon the needs of her people, the nephew behaved more like a landed aristocrat, with a keen appetite for the sophistry of the diplomatic game, the lavish lifestyle and direct involvement in affairs of state.

True, being a man gave Don Joseph greater freedom of action. He also had better opportunities to attain a leadership role at the sultan's court than he would have had at any court in Christian Europe. Later, he would even garner a title and a personal fiefdom to match his ambitions—unparalleled, up to this point, in diaspora Jewish history. In contrast to his aunt, he seemed go out of his way to covet a crown. Perhaps the French warning on the true nature of aims for Tiberias was not so far from the truth.[2]

The family had first arrived in Constantinople during a dynastic dispute between the three sons of Sultan Suleiman. Mustafa, the sultan's brilliant and popular son by his first wife, had just been strangled by a mute, after being suspected of plotting to seize the throne from his aging father. The alleged plot had been artfully concocted by Suleiman's second wife, Roxelana, to insure that one of her two sons, Selim or Bajazet, would become Suleiman's successor.

At the outset, Don Joseph made friends with both surviving sons. The younger men were, after all, his contemporaries. He ingratiated himself so well that within few years even the physician, Lusitanus (who by this time had also left Italy and relocated to Salonika) remarked on "how much you count at the court of Suleiman...and to his sons."[3] Then, when the old man was already "rotting, fat, made up and suffering from an ulcerous leg,"[4] as one historian put it, Don Joseph threw his support behind Selim.

The elder of the two, Selim was favored by his father but by no means the sure winner. It proved a shrewd move. Perhaps Don Joseph saw in Selim, the weaker of the two brothers, a better chance to become the indispensable counselor he obviously wanted to be. How much his aunt's exceptional understanding of the exercise and transfer of power influenced this decision is not known. But, as mentioned, she may well have worked the salons of the *saray,* or women's palace, at the highest levels and passed along vital information that led to the decision.

The best way to assure Selim's support and devotion was to befriend him at a crucial juncture in his life. In 1559 (the same year that Samuel and La Chica came to Constantinople), Don Joseph obtained permission to visit Selim at his official residence in Kutahia, in Anatolia, prior to an actual battle that was to be fought between the two brothers over succession rights. Don Joseph brought along vital supplies—arms, horses, and a reputed treasure trove of ducats. This enabled Selim to be better equipped than his younger brother. The battle rapidly turned in Selim's favor. Bajazet fled to Persia, but was later handed over for execution.

Selim was the ideal instrument for Don Joseph's agenda. The decadent, overweight son of an overpowering father, described as "the most imbecile prince ever to rule a state,"[5] by a French ambassador, and "gluttonous and slothful"[6] by a Flemish diplomat, Selim was addicted to his pleasures. One of them was wine. Yet as a Muslim, Selim was supposed to abstain. The door was thereby swept wide open for Don Joseph. As a wine grower —he was rumored to possess his own vineyards—and an outsider to the Muslim faith, Don Joseph was perfectly poised to become the man who could keep his prince well supplied and his own lips sealed. Nobody likes to drink alone. The two soon became fast friends.

Friendship with the future sultan, and an intimate knowledge of the workings of Europe's foremost royal courts, catapulted Don Joseph into a senior position at the Sublime Porte even before Suleiman died. He could offer early access to news, delivered by the far-flung commercial agents of the House of Mendes. After the humiliations he and his family had received as *conversos* in Europe, he could be trusted to turn this information to the advantage of the Turks. As noted, he was given a generous stipend of 55 aspers a day. Soon he was being courted by emissaries and ambassadors who were quick to recognize where real power lay. His name started showing up in diplomatic missives. He was never very far from the court, whether it was sitting in Constantinople or one of its regional seats. The royal corridors of power were such a treacherous environment that it would have been suicidal to remain absent for long.

Then one night in September 1566, while on a military campaign near Belgrade, Suleiman died suddenly as he rested among his troops. Totally worn out, he lay in a tent pitched in the mud. Messengers galloped off to alert Selim, the heir-apparent. The aim was to bring Selim to camp and proclaim him the new sultan before the news spread and further dynastic in-fighting developed. Don Joseph rode with Selim. En route, the new sultan knighted his beloved comrade, making Don Joseph the governor of a cluster of Greek islands formerly owned by Venice. The governorship carried an imposing title: Duke of Naxos, Count of Andros and Paros, Lord of Milos and the islands. Don Joseph never actually lived in his duchy, at least not for any length of time. Instead he appointed a *converso* named Francisco Coronello, to govern the islands. Coronello was a direct descendant of Abraham Seneor, the elderly and distinguished leader of the Jewish community in Spain at the time of the Expulsion. Seneor had converted to Christianity under extreme pressure from Ferdinand and Isabella, taking the name of Fernando Perez Coronel. Though other family members later reverted to Judaism, Coronello lived as a Christian. This made the arrangement ideal, since the people of the islands were mostly Christian.

Don Joseph was also given other valuable commercial privileges, and a monopoly on the importation of wines and tax farms. He had become a prince of the land in every sense of the word. In correspondence, he would even refer to his estate at Ortaköy as the "Ducal Palace of Belvedere."[7] According to local lore, he placed an inscription on his palace entrance that said "Duke of Naxos," after persuading Selim that gentrification would give him greater status in Europe.[8] Whether his wise old aunt was equally thrilled is uncertain. No doubt aware of the possible backlash that can occur when a Jew takes on too high a profile, she may have not been as delighted as one might expect, although it would have surely warmed her heart to hear her daughter addressed as "Duchess."

In Christian Europe the dukedom became a scandal. The

ambassador from the Holy Roman Empire remarked that it was against the Turkish tradition to appoint a non-Muslim to this sort of post, implying that Don Joseph's power was something to worry about. Still, there is no doubt the elevation impressed the Christian monarchs. However, before Don Joseph could use his new powers to the fullest, he had to remove the most embarrassing, life-threatening and humiliating stain still clinging to his person: his perpetual banishment from Venice, along with its brutal death sentence. Less than six months after Selim's accession he therefore dispatched two agents with a written entreaty to the city on the lagoon. It contained a gentle reminder that he was now in a position to help in any matters that needed the attention of the sultan—provided, of course, the city's fathers voted to lift the death sentence and banishment.

Suddenly, all opposition melted. He won a full pardon from the intimidated Venetians who were particularly terrified at this point of an all-out war with the Turks. There was a practical side to his request, too. In order to be effective, from a diplomatic and a commercial standpoint, he needed on occasion to go in person to Venice. He also had benevolent motives. Diplomatic correspondence between the Papal Nuncio in Venice and the Vatican, six months after the pardon, speaks of "200 Jews arriving from Rome (who are) going to visit (Don Joseph)."[9]

This could well have been one of his many attempts to assist the persecuted Jews of Italy. The pardon would have enabled him to negotiate passage through Venice, once he was again permitted to deal directly with the Serenissima. Whether these Jews were bound for the new settlements in Tiberias or on their way to Turkish cities is not known.

There was another benefit. Even before Selim took over, Don Joseph had been working every conceivable avenue of influence to persuade the French to repay the accumulated loans of around 150,000 ducats still outstanding to the House of Mendes.[10] Doña

Gracia had doubtless been consulted at every turn and probably suggested strategies, since her faithful agent, Duarte Gomez,
was dispatched from Venice on one occasion to pursue the matter in person with the French.

At first, Don Joseph had tried to negotiate amicably by providing a succession of French ambassadors in Constantinople
with substantial, interest-free personal loans whenever their own
government left them temporarily bereft. But relations deteriorated nonetheless. The French argued, as before, that any debt
to a Jew could legally be removed from their books, since transactions with openly-professing Jews were illegal in France. The
House of Mendes had previously worked around this dilemma
by funneling its investments through Florentine agents. But the
fiction had been exposed.[11]

Don Joseph then turned to Sultan Suleiman for help. He
explained that he was about to have difficulty meeting the cash
advances due in connection with his tax farming concessions,
as he had been counting on the ducats overdue from the French
loan. The amount was so large that the Turkish government took
this very seriously, sending a *chaus* to France to personally request payment. That did no good either. Nor did personal letters from Sultan Suleiman or a meeting that Selim arranged
between himself and the French ambassador in Constantinople.

The French then tried to suggest that the large outstanding
debt had been fiction all along, demanding documentary evidence that such a debt actually existed. The only reason Don
Joseph was pressing so hard, their envoy in Constantinople told
the French court with contempt, was because he was desperate
for the money to build his kingdom on the shores of the Sea of
Galilee. But even the French ambassador in Constantinople
thought that his nation was asking for trouble by behaving in
such an intractable manner. He recommended that they could
save both face and cash, and even hostilities in the Mediterra-

nean, by offering compensation in kind—bales of cloth, brazil-wood and other items strongly in demand in Ottoman lands. That was when Gomez was dispatched to Paris. Again, to no avail.[12]

It was not until Selim took over in 1566 that matters reached a climax. With Don Joseph at the pinnacle of his power and out of patience, it was time to mobilize the real muscle of the Ottoman Empire. Still insisting he could not afford to pay what was owed the sultan until the French debt was discharged, Don Joseph elbowed Selim into action. First, he managed to persuade the court to harass the new French ambassador in Constantinople until he agreed to acknowledge the debt, payable in two installments six months apart, after which the ambassador was to receive a sizeable payoff in jewels. Selim and Don Joseph were able to force this ambassador's hand because the man had personally accepted funds from Don Joseph that were beyond what he needed for his official operations. He had been living too lavishly and was overextended. No doubt aware that the French king would never release cash to pay off the Mendes loan, the ambassador agreed instead that goods on ships flying the French flag could be seized at Ottoman ports and the contents liquidated until the amount in question had been recouped.

This gave the Turks the justification to begin confiscating the cargo of French ships pulling into their ports, starting with those arriving in Alexandria. Protests flew back and forth. Papal Nuncio dispatches between Venice and the Vatican were especially strong in their anger, suggesting the French were cooling towards their previously cordial relations with the Turks.[13] Others close to Selim became decidedly uneasy. The prospect of embroiling the Empire in a lengthy and serious dispute on account of a personal debt did not seem worthwhile. Within a year the seizure of goods ceased. Trade dealings returned to normal. Less than 70,000 ducats of the indebtedness was paid off. Later, the French even claimed reparations for their lost cargoes and demanded the execution of Don Joseph. The Turks returned the ships, but refused all other requests.

Europe was appalled that a Jew could have wielded such power for his own ends. A few decades later, the Jesuit historian, Flamius Strada, would confirm how it all came about. "Being altogether enslaved by his pleasures," wrote Strada in the 1630's, referring to Selim, "(Don Joseph) knew all the points in the compass of luxury, feeding him every day according to the variations of humor to the height of his appetite with exquisite and new delights....He excelled in the art of flattery, or the artifice of pleasures by so much he preceded all others in the prince's favor."[14]

Even so, Don Joseph's machinations opened the way for some important diplomatic and economic initiatives. He built up the economy of his duchy, gathering some 6,000 ducats in annual taxes for the Ottoman treasury, fifty percent more than had been available in the past. He nurtured trade relations with Poland, especially concerning the export of wine and wax. Some Jewish historians have tried to read into his Polish initiatives a desire to assist a country that was amenable towards the Jews, once again suggesting he tended to act from dual motives. He fostered dynastic marriages designed to further Ottoman ambitions. The Spanish became so afraid of his influence that they tried to have him assassinated. With good cause. The year that the confiscations began, Don Joseph encouraged the Protestants of the Low Countries to rise in rebellion against their Spanish Catholic overlords, assuring them that the Ottoman Turks would make such trouble in other parts of Europe that they could easily win.[15] Some have said it was an act of personal revenge for the humiliation and confiscations that he and his family had suffered under Charles V and Queen Marie. Maybe so, but in this instance the weakening of the Holy Roman Empire, now identified with the leadership of King Phillip II of Spain (son and heir of Charles V) was a goal of Turkish foreign policy too.[16]

This Protestant uprising was especially important to Jewish history because it led to Dutch independence and the beginnings of Amsterdam as the great mercantile center of Europe. Under the influence of Amsterdam's *converso* residents (some of whom were descendants of the families that had originally worked with Diogo in Antwerp), the Jews of the city even won the right to return openly to the faith of their ancestors during the early years of the 17th century. These Jewish mercantile families developed much of the early Caribbean trade in sugar and cocoa, put pressure on Peter Stuyvesant to accept the first shipload of twenty-three Jews who arrived in the port of New York in 1654 and spearheaded the return of openly-professing Jews to England under Oliver Cromwell. Though Don Joseph can hardly be credited with foreseeing any of these events, it does demonstrate the ripple effect of a single course of action.[17]

———••✄••———

We know little about the final years of Doña Gracia's life, other than the documents linking her to the Tiberias project—the last one of which was dated May, 1566, some three years before her death. The only eyewitness account of her environment was recorded by the venerable Salonician rabbi, Moses Almosnino. In 1565 he traveled to Constantinople on an important mission on behalf of the Jewish community of Salonika. The Jews in his city had been suffering under a burden of taxation that violated a special charter granted to them some thirty years earlier by Sultan Suleiman. In one of the great fires that regularly swept that textile center, the original document had been lost and old abuses were creeping back. Almosnino needed someone to take up the matter at the highest levels of government. He chose not to approach Doña Gracia with this particular request, perhaps because she was already ailing or because Don Joseph was now so powerful at court.[18] Moreover, Don Joseph had been particularly active in the Salonician community, offering his services as a mediator to settle disputes on numerous occasions.[19]

Moses Almosnino was a frequent visitor to the family compound at Belvedere during this incident and on other occasions. And the family was doubtless all living at together, given the customs of those times. It would have been unthinkable to leave an elderly widow on her own, especially if married children were living nearby.

Besides, a few years earlier, Rabbi Almosnino reported seeing most of them at Belvedere. Don Samuel was "sitting at (Don Joseph's) right hand"[20] and participating in all that he did. Attending a *Succoth* service in a private synagogue inside the mansion, Almosnino recalled that it was the week when it was customary to recite the biblical passage about Joseph and his dreams. Afterwards, Almosnino said, he got caught up in a conversation with Don Joseph about dreams. The conversation eventually led to a small essay on the topic that Almosnino included within a larger religious tract about living righteously.[21]

Though Almosnino framed some of his descriptions of the mansion as a vision—a typical 16th century literary conceit—it is likely that he was describing the scene exactly the way it was. Exotic carpets, he wrote, covered the floors and hung from the walls. There were two seats of honor in the synagogue: one for Don Joseph and the other for Don Samuel. In an adjoining room, as was customary during religious services, sat their respective wives, Reyna and La Chica, with other female members of the household, including perhaps their infant daughters. Both seem to have had just one daughter each, neither of whom apparently lived long. Gerlach, the German preacher, later refers to Don Joseph's marriage as childless.[22]

Other visitors spoke with equal admiration of this fine residence and its exquisite furniture that blended Western and Turkish styles. It offered a lively, welcoming and cultured environment. Plays based on biblical stories were presented during Jewish festivals. The mouth-watering aroma of Portuguese cuisine no doubt floated in from the kitchens as the chefs prepared the dishes that Don Joseph regularly sent over to his gluttonous friend, Selim, sealed with his personal seal for safety. The family was famous for its hospitality. Receptions spilled over into the gardens, which visitors dubbed "the vineyard" because Don Joseph had abandoned flowers in favor of the grapevines that were his passion. Belvedere also became an important stop on the tour of at least one, and probably many more, musical groups traveling through the Levant. Good music would have been an expected part of social gatherings given by a cultured, upper class household. By day, there was a constant stream of factors, ambassadors, couriers, musicians, rabbis, emissaries, vendors and mendicants shuffling through the hallways.[23]

Lusitanus described Don Joseph during this period as a learned man.[24] Belvedere, reflecting that interest, housed a fine library. Don Joseph regularly purchased manuscripts and books or had them copied at his personal expense, according to scholars who thanked him profusely in the dedications to their books.[25] From 1565 onwards, it was also the site of a small Hebrew printing press that must have been designed more for its contribution to Jewish literature than in its potential income, for it made scant profits.[26] Eight years after Doña Gracia died, Don Joseph became the author—with the help of a ghost writer—of his own small work on piety, called *Ben Porat Yosef*, published in Constantinople in 1577.[27]

It is a strange little volume for a man who spent his life enmeshed in the debauchery, greed, treachery and other intrigues of court life. The book indicates that he may well have been struggling with inner conflicts. The title alludes to the biblical passage where Jacob blesses his sons, including Joseph. The passage implies that Joseph is a "vine" that bears abundant fruit (does good). The book declares at the outset that it is a dispute with a Christian sage concerning the verities of the Torah, all the Torah's inherent commandments *(mitzvot)*, their intentions and how they should be performed. The Torah is normally defined as the first five books of the Bible, but can encompass the larger body of Jewish teachings. It pits all these teachings against the practices that come from a secular life. And it deals with such philosophical questions as why the righteous suffer and evil prospers, free will, reward and punishment.

In reality, it looks suspiciously like the ramblings of an aging man being confronted with ungrateful *conversos* who are uncertain of the value of their reclaimed ancestral faith. He is impatient with them, like Moses dismayed at the sight of his people returning to worship a golden calf after all the miracles that God has performed for them.

The *conversos* in the book have returned to Judaism. But they cannot commit themselves with the same blind certainty as those who had been Jews all their lives. Rather, they are much taken with Renaissance attitudes towards philosophy and science as a way to interpret life and live in the world around them. The disputation continues with Don Joseph promoting the veracity of the commandments and the non-Jewish sage insisting on knowing the world through the study of nature and observation. Was Don Joseph trying to convince himself that Jewish orthodox faith was pure and perfect? Or was he facing disappointment upon being confronted with all the human shortcomings and superstitions of daily Judaism, compared to the idyllic Jewish life that he may have longed to taste while living in lands where it was forbidden? It sounds as though he was trying to convince himself as much as the doubting *conversos*. The book expresses the intention of reaching readers in places like France and Spain, where Jewish life was still forbidden.

⸱⸱•⸱ᵜ⸱•⸱⸱

Where was Doña Gracia while all this was happening? She was certainly still alive when Almosnino visited Belvedere, although he made no mention of her. Reports of her death do not appear until early in the spring of 1569.[28] What exactly was going on? Knowing she was nearing the end, had she embarked, with servants and guards, for Tiberias? Did her party try to make its way to the Holy Land by ship and did the vessel sink, as so many did, in a raging storm? Did they attempt the land route, joining one of the regular camel trains that wound south along the trade routes through Asia Minor, only to be set upon by brigands? Did she suffer prolonged pain or did God take her quickly?

If she stayed in Constantinople, did she die in the fearful winter of 1568-9 when the weather was so bitterly cold that the Bosphorus froze over and city folk could walk upon the waters?[29] Was her body consumed in flames that could have accidentally erupted inside the waterfront mansion, cold beyond comfort, licking at her voluminous skirts as she or her servants stoked fires and stoves to warm her aging bones? Saving bodies from the pyre had been her life-long mission. It would have been a terrible irony for her to die that way. Did she die from an infectious or degenerate disease? Why is the record so empty regarding the death and burial of someone as beloved and important as *La Señora*? Does it imply that something happened that was so dreadful or shameful that people dared not tell? Why is there no mention of a grave site? Was it simply the result of lost records or was there more?

———••⋅✖⋅••———

To gain insights into these competing possibilities, we must briefly leave the tangible world of the serious historian, and its reliance upon the written record, and move instead into the ethereal realm of Jewish mysticism and kabbalistic beliefs. Basic to those precepts is the concept that God's energy reaches the world through ten *sefirot*, or channels. Jewish mystics believe in the constant transfer of divine energy from the heavenly sphere to earth and back again. Also central to these beliefs is the idea that the greatest souls of Israel ascend straight to heaven. There can be no earthly grave.

Nobody was permitted to know where Moses was buried (Deut.34:6). Elijah, the prophet, ascended directly to heaven in a chariot of fire (2 Kings 2:11). Miriam and Aaron have no known earthly graves. Jesus' body disappeared. Parallel to these beliefs is that the greatest souls are sent down to earth to accomplish a specific task and then lifted directly up again. A mystic might argue that Doña Gracia was one of these great souls, sent down at a critical moment to ensure the survival of a large portion of the Jewish people. When her task was accomplished, there had to be a way to lift her up again. That meant some kind of disaster that could take her body along with her soul: a shipwreck, a fire.

There is a further belief that indicates she could never have reached Tiberias, however fervently she might have longed to get there. It comes from the biblical idea that anyone trying to hurry the return of the Messiah is denied access to the Promised

Land. If indeed she had been engaged in kabbalistic rites, this could have been something the mystics around her were trying to accomplish with their secret rituals. Even the Tiberias project could be viewed in this light. She most definitely had contact with the great kabbalists of Safed. The mystical visions of one of them, Rabbi Caro, the humble and gentle man who supported her Ancona boycott and also gave an opinion in the sisters' dispute, has come down to us through such writings.[30] In later centuries, stories would be told of how the Baal Shem Tov, the mystic and founder of the Hassidic movement in Eastern Europe, tried to sail from Constantinople to the Holy Land, only to be swept off course. If Doña Gracia was engaged in the same type of activity could she, too, have been denied entry?[31]

———••✛••———

She did not leave this world without praise. In death there was tribute. It reflected what had been said about her in the *responsa* literature a few years earlier. The first words of praise were given early in 1569 by Almosnino when he mentioned— somewhat casually, as though everyone already knew—that he had recently delivered a memorial sermon following her death. He referred to the incident while delivering another eulogy in Salonika in honor of their mutual friend and sometime adversary, Joshua Soncino, who died around the same time.[32] There were no details. Rather, the sermon dwelt in typical rabbinic manner upon religious concerns—how the study of the Torah leads to a good name which, in turn, leads to the tranquility of the soul.

Though Almosnino did not say so directly, he hinted that Doña Gracia had these qualities. It bolsters the belief of historians who maintain that she was a devoutly religious woman.

Almosnino tells us that he delivered a second eulogy to Doña Gracia in Adrianopole, thirty days after her death.[33] This would have coincided with the end of the month-long period of deep mourning. Neither, however, was preserved. Possibly this was because rabbis did not publish eulogies on women, an idea that was inferred by a cryptic comment Almosnino made a year later. "Sermons on women," he wrote,"...are hidden (or secret) with me."[34] In a Turkish environment, prejudice would have been especially strong within the orthodox rabbinate, as its own Jewish attitudes would have been reinforced by Middle Eastern influences. The rabbis would have been deeply uncomfortable with even a minor amount of feminine empowerment, acknowledging it only when absolutely unavoidable, as in their dealings with Doña Gracia while she was alive.

The most comprehensive tribute came in an elegy to "Doña Gracia of the House of Nassy" written by the poet Sa'adiah Longo, and included in a collection of his elegies published in 1594.[35] Longo was the most important poet of Salonika during the 16th century. He had arrived there as a small child after leaving Spain with his family at the time of the Expulsion. As a young man, he served as a lay reader in the private synagogue of Moses Hamon, the Jewish physician at the court of Suleiman—the same Hamon who had been in contact with Doña Gracia while she was in Italy. Returning to Salonika around 1530, Longo made a living giving lessons and serving in various capacities at synagogues. His poetic subjects were varied. He wrote on plagues, romance, rabbis, famous men, virtuous women, youth. Though much admired, Longo suffered continually from the classic poet's lament—unrelenting poverty. He lived for more than 70 years, finally being reduced to severe penury.[36]

His lengthy, hyperbolic and complicated elegy on Doña Gracia was composed in two parts: the first was styled like a typical lament for Tisha B'Av, the annual commemoration of the great misfortunes that have befallen Israel. In particular he cites the destruction of the first and second Temples in Jerusalem and the expulsion of Jews from Spain; all of which have connections to a late July-early August date (the ninth of *Av* in the Jewish calendar). The second part follows the traditional literary pattern for an eulogy to a Jewish "woman of valor."

That he chose to tie Doña Gracia's passing with something as calamitous as Tisha B'Av says a great deal about the sadness and sense of loss that must have swept over the Jewish world. Without our *"ha-gevirá,* our crowned lady, he kept repeating, "oppression has returned." We are people "with a broken spirit." He then lists the many other occasions when Israel was reduced to tears. Facing what appears to be life at the time of the Inquisition, he says, "we were fuel for the fire, like filthy meat that putrefies, like a man (who) despairs of his life and digs a pit before him...we were a disgrace unto our neighbors, mockery and derision to our surroundings, our souls wept in secret."

He then talks of the coming of Doña Gracia to relieve the suffering. He describes her, as has been mentioned, as a "remnant from the house of the head of the *Sanhedrin"*—implying that she may have indeed been a descendant of the royal House of David. If so, it would help explain why the *conversos,* and indeed the Jews in general, were so ready to accept her as their leader.

Yet it was equally her deeds, he implied, that made her such a towering figure among her own people. She "straightened the path in the wilderness...the passage to an awesome God," meaning, no doubt, her help in guiding hundreds, and perhaps even thousands of *conversos*[37] throughout their long and dangerous journey to the safety of Ottoman lands, as well as reintroducing them to their faith.

His second section revolves around the concept of a woman of valor. He begins by reminding his readers, somewhat chauvinistically, that Jewish women are not like Ammonite women or Egyptian women or Hittite women. They are "full of life and wise." He then offers his most glowing tribute to Doña Gracia. "The Lady did not behave like an ordinary woman," he writes, "but like every man who girds; she girded her belt with the strength of her loins."

He goes on, "From the fruit of her hands she sowed a vineyard; from the fruit of her hands and righteousness she planted a vineyard of the Lord of Hosts, every house of Israel; and she grew a name like the name of the holy greats."

He then provides us with a lengthy account of how the Jews had waxed wealthy and successful on the Iberian Peninsula, only to be struck down, beaten, humiliated and burned. They could not even flee Portugal, he reminded his readers, because the ports had been closed to them. So they cried out for help and God took pity on them. He sent two brothers and two sisters "from the House of Nessiah," one of whom "stood in an open place at the crossroads...to invite in moaning guests returning to the work of their Creator, exhausted and weary, until their knees buckled." And it was she (Doña Gracia) who "birthed them and nursed them from the breast milk of her consoling nipples." Here was a woman, he noted "who fell from heaven." Whether he meant this in the mystical sense, or in the manner in which one normally speaks of a savior who arrives in the nick of time, is unknown.

In any event, he continued, "I will praise her," even "breaking a pot" to demonstrate his overpowering grief. For "the eminent attributes within you were interwoven." Unlike women who are selfish in their pursuits, he says, Doña Gracia was someone whose "doors were (always) open to the guest...(and) the stranger did not slumber outdoors...for this I will shout with a melting heart and broken spirit." It is here that he alludes to her dogged will, which at times must have been overbearing. Speaking of the agents, ministers and other notables in her circle, he admitted that "all heed(ed) her discipline…trembling seized them." Yet, he concluded, it was her wisdom, rather than her wealth, that became in the end the key to her place in heaven. "So while we weep, she now sits for sure in the palace of the king."[38]

There was more praise in an elegy written by Longo ten years later, at the time of Don Joseph's death. In that work he confirmed that it was Doña Gracia who propelled her nephew forward in his work. He called her "the morning star"—the guiding light of her people, with Don Joseph as a companion star reflecting her brilliance. He also returned once again to his complimentary male imagery, saying that Doña Gracia "ceased to be a woman by the virility of her actions." Even so, he added, she still managed to become the mother of all those who wished to return to the faith of their ancestors—combining, as it were, the best of male and female characteristics.[39]

In closing arguments to their *responsa* briefs connected with the sisters' inheritance dispute, two of the rabbis involved left similar observations for posterity. "Many women have done mighty deeds," wrote Moses di Trani, "but Gracia has surpassed them all."[40] Added Soncino: "Her righteousness will stand forever."[41] The writer, Samuel Usque, reached for the mystical explanation by calling her "God's mercy…(appearing) in human garb."[42]

After that—silence, except for the occasional remembrance in Judeo-Spanish literature. But these stories were written in a relatively unknown ethnic language and in an arcane form of Hebrew characters known as Rashi script. As such, they cast barely a shadow over world consciousness.[43]

———···✕···———

Why was she so quickly forgotten? There are several theories that could account for the rapid onset of collective amnesia. First, she was a woman at a time when nobody wrote or published much about women, as Almosnino implied; even the powerful women at the sultan's court. Second, she was a business woman. Had she been a writer or artist, or even a brilliant theologian like St. Teresa d'Avila or a woman of royal blood, her creative accomplishments or officials papers would have survived. And that would have helped enormously. Lack of easily-accessible papers is the bane of historians. Moreover, business personalities did not become the subject of scholarly review until around the 19th century. It was late into the 20th century before they were considered key players on the stage of history. Third, as noted, she was a *conversa*. And there was a great deal of ambivalence about *conversos* in the structured Jewish world. It took several generations before the negative sentiment expended itself.[44]

Her forceful and confrontational style was another strike against her. Jews perceived themselves so heavily outflanked during this period that appeasement was considered a more realistic strategy. Not everyone may have been comfortable with the memory. Finally, there were no direct descendants—the result, no doubt, of the constant inbreeding that must have been going on for generations before the family even left Spanish lands. The cruelest cut of all shows up in the illustration that accompanies her brief entry in the *Encyclopedia Judaica*. It turns out not to be her portrait at all. It is a likeness of La Chica.

Not even legends survived to tell her tale. However, two living tributes remain that may have more meaning than a host of legends or shelves full of books.

For the first we must travel to Israel; to a lonely corner of Tiberias where a steep hill meanders high above the Sea of Galilee. Its name is Doña Gracia Street. It winds past a cobbled courtyard shaded by palms and eucalyptus trees and decorated with crimson hibiscus bushes. It straightens out as it rises sharply towards the crumbling stone walls of an abandoned castle where wild grasses and a lawn play surrogate for a moat. A huge stone wheel that could have been used two thousand years ago as a grinding stone lies against one side of the ancient walls. Restaurants, art shops and a youth hostel line the western side of the street. Halfway down is a shaded courtyard offering benches for the weary traveler, as she offered a refuge for her people. At the lowest end, a simple bronze plaque, affixed to a modern wall, bears her name in Hebrew letters.

Nobody walking the street or spilling off the crowded tourist buses seems to know who she was. She is never mentioned by any of the tour guides. In a nearby booth, a tired old man, with skin like wrinkled parchment, sits hunched over a low stool selling lottery tickets. He shrugs with contempt when her name is mentioned. Why should he even care?

At first, the entire scene strikes the observer as an insult; hardly a fitting tribute to a life devoted to toiling on behalf of her fellow Jews. And yet. The ah-ha moment arrives. It is the perfect metaphor for a woman who spent her days facing scorn and traveling, literally and figuratively, along an endless road. If life is indeed a pilgrimage, then Doña Gracia made the ultimate journey. A statue, locked in the same spot for all time, would not have been as suitable. Nor would an elegant building for much the same reason. Like the founders of the modern state of Israel, she has been commemorated instead with a street named after her. There could hardly be a more apt tribute.

The message inherent in the second memorial is equally appropriate. For this one you have to travel to Turkey. Once there, you must visit Izmir and walk along the winding alleyways of its bustling *souk*, or street market. As you turn the corner into the shoemaker's lane, you will see a shabby sign tacked onto a rusty metal doorway. *"Sinyora Giveret Synagogue,"* it announces, in black letters upon a mustard-colored background. It is one of the many synagogues originally made possible with funds provided by Doña Gracia, though the structure itself, as noted, has been consumed by flames and rebuilt several times. The service going on inside wraps time-honored Sephardic prayers in ancient chants; much as it would have done in her day. The men are shrouded in flowing *tallit* edged with heavy black fringes, tossed back over the shoulder in the oriental manner. They sway rhythmically back and forth.

Around the ark hang a cluster of antique silver filigree lamps. The rest of the sanctuary is lit by crystal chandeliers that descend precariously from a wooden ceiling. The windows are covered with cross bars and are recessed deep inside diagonal niches. Cream-colored interior walls are highlighted with pale blue moldings. Rows of simple chairs and plain wooden benches stand on threadbare Turkish rugs that are scattered throughout. The yellow stucco on the outside is peeling, revealing wooden boards beneath. The building itself is hidden inside a walled courtyard, so that only the doorway is visible from the street.

On certain days, if you are lucky, you can hear the rabbi speak in broken English about the origins of the congregation. He talks of the humility of Doña Gracia, although there is not a shred of evidence that she was shy or humble. He says this humility was why she did not want her full name used for the title of the synagogue; only the words *Ha Giveret*, even though the notion is unlikely. He calls her Doña Gracia Mendes, not realizing that she was never known by her husband's family name. Nor, indeed, was it ever mentioned that anything funded by Doña Gracia would have been earmarked for incoming *conversos* who had lived life as Catholics, rather than people who were already part of the established Jewish community.

All is muddled or forgotten.

And yet. On a seat near the rear sits a teenage girl. The pen-sive look on her face suggests she is deep in thought. She is dressed casually in Nike sneakers, skin-tight jeans and a white T-shirt. Her highlighted hair is squeezed back into a tight pony-tail. She could well be a descendent of those original *conversos*. Certainly she shows every sign of being the Jewish woman of tomorrow; strong, proud and independent-minded. Watching her, the thought comes to mind that she represents the Jewish people that Doña Gracia worked so hard—and ultimately suc-ceeded—in saving.

Epilogue

By the time of Doña Gracia's death the well-worn escape route from the Iberian Peninsula through Antwerp and Italy and onwards to the Ottoman Empire had ceased to exist. Antwerp had finally closed its doors for good and the Ottoman Empire had started its slow economic decline into centuries of decay. Still hounded by a relentless Inquisition, the *conversos* from both Spain and Portugal now turned their sights westwards towards the riches and emancipation seemingly available to them in the nascent colonies of the New World (although Old World attitudes would eventually catch up with them there, too). Others sought out relatives in the protected settlements of Bayonne, Bordeaux and Amsterdam. *Conversos* on both sides of the Atlantic then combined their talents, family networks and energies to emerge as major players in Caribbean and Latin American trade during subsequent centuries.[1] Today there is a major revival of interest among families of European descent in Central and South America and even the southwestern United States to seek out and reclaim their Jewish heritage.

The Mendes-Nasi family itself was not as fortunate. The career of the enigmatic Don Joseph took an immediate and abrupt turn for the worse after Doña Gracia died.[2] The spring following her death was when the confiscations of French cargo in Alexandria were halted on the advice of rivals at the sultan's court. Perhaps they sensed a weakness emerging in their Jewish colleague and were quick to move in. Compounding Don Joseph's grief was the death, only a few months later, of his brother, Don Samuel, in the early months of 1569.[3]

Although Don Samuel never attained the eminence of Don Joseph, he had nevertheless provided unswerving loyalty and assistance, becoming crucial enough to have been given a stipend by the sultan in his own name.[4] According to Longo and Almosnino, having such trustworthy support meant a great deal to Don Joseph.[5] During visits to Belvedere, Almosnino grew particularly fond of Don Samuel. He may well have had a more gentle personality.

La Chica, on the other hand, disappears entirely from the record. We do not know what happened to her, or even if she predeceased her husband. On the other hand, the whereabouts of the venerable physician, Amatus Lusitanus, was well documented. After coming to live openly as a Jew in Salonika in 1558, he tended the sick of the community for ten years. He wrote yet another of his *Centuria* on the patients he tended in that port city before dying during an outbreak of plague one year prior to Doña Gracia.[6] His work is still regularly quoted in medical literature and there have been several books on his life and medical practices.

Don Joseph, by contrast, still had one last dramatic gesture left in his arsenal. Some of his enemies had long insisted that his real ambitions had always been to become "king" of Cyprus, and perhaps use Cyprus as an even more viable region for Jewish immigration. Groups of Jews were, in fact, encouraged to settle there for a while. But first the Turks had to take Cyprus from the Venetians—something they had wanted to do for some time. It was close to their own shores and located in a strategic spot in the center of the Eastern Mediterranean. Morever, it had long been a nest of pirates and a staging point for sabotage, threatening Turkish safety in that part of the Mediterranean. To stave off Turkish attacks, the Venetians had been paying the sultan an annual tribute of 3,000 ducats. When it was raised by Selim to 4,000 ducats, the Venetians balked, giving the Turks the excuse they needed.[7]

In 1570-71, the Turks invaded Cyprus. They argued, on shaky grounds, that they had every right to take over the island as it had once belonged to the Mamelukes of Egypt who had been conquered by the Turks. Legend insists that the Turks were urged onwards by Don Joseph. He still had the ear of Sultan Selim and was eager to humiliate Venice one more time, as it had humiliated him. Legend also maintains that Don Joseph was aided in his quest by Nur Banu, the reputedly Jewish-born wife of Selim, and apparently one of the auxiliary routes by which Don Joseph continued to secure his power base at court.[8]

But this latest exercise of Turkish power threw Christian Europe into a fury. The various European monarchs temporarily set aside their internal disputes and jealousies to make a consolidated foray against the infidel. In October 1571, their combined navies engaged the Turkish fleet off the Gulf of Lepanto, not far from where the Adriatic flows into the Mediterranean. The famous three-hour battle between the forces of the Crescent and the Cross was reputed to be greatest in the Mediterranean since Roman times. Facing a Turkish force of 222 large galleys, 68 smaller ones, 750 *janissaries* and 80,000 fighting men was a united Christian front of 202 large galleys, 6 smaller ones, 30 other ships and 74,000 fighting men. The churning sea turned scarlet from the spilled blood. It became a disaster for the Turks. Among those wounded on the Christian side was the Spanish man of letters, Miguel de Cervantes, who lost the use of his left arm. Both sides laid the blame for fostering the disastrous engagement squarely upon Don Joseph's shoulders. He never recovered his reputation.[9]

His power base slipped even further as Selim began failing, dying in December 1574. Murad III, Selim's son and successor, did not have the same affection for the dashing Jewish courtier. From a diplomatic standpoint, Don Joseph's final years were spent in obscurity. But there were minor tasks still to be undertaken. He took in other aged individuals who were down on their luck. Among them were the scholar, Isaac Akrish, who had lost all his possessions in a fire, and an impoverished French nobleman who had embraced Judaism and fled to the Ottoman capital.[10] He hosted a Tuscan diplomat during a visit to further commercial relations between Tuscany and the Turks. Nur Banu came to his aid by helping him renew his wine monopoly, which he apparently held onto until his death.[11] He died during the first week of August, 1579, from complications from kidney stones—an ailment that had plagued him for some time.[12]

Though historians have pondered for centuries whether he was a saint or a sinner, he was probably neither. He comes through more clearly as an astute pragmatist, eager to support the causes that would foster the needs of the Jews and *conversos* along with his personal yearning for self-importance and respect. At the same time he was responding to the sleazy demands of international and internal intrigue. It was a duplicitous game, but he needed to play it in order to achieve his goals and those of his equally pragmatic mentor and aunt.

Nevertheless, in contrast to Doña Gracia, Don Joseph grew in legend. He was demonized throughout Europe as one of the most despised figures to walk the stage of Mediterranean history during the 16th century. His ability to instill fear in the hearts and minds of Christian Europe was preserved in a number of plays. The most famous was Christopher Marlowe's *"Jew of Malta,"* written thirteen years after Don Joseph's death. Another contemporary (but now lost) play by the British playwright, Thomas Dekker, *"Josef, the Jew of Venice"* was produced at the end of the 16th century. It has led some to argue that there was a connection between Shakespeare's Shylock and Don Joseph. This is unlikely. The two Jews could not have been more dissimilar, but the character of Bassanio in *"The Merchant of Venice"* does bear a close resemblance to a second or third generation *converso*. Several historians have long maintained that Shakespeare would have been well acquainted with the members of the *converso* community in London at that time. Further, Bassano was the name of a family of *converso* musicians from Italy, originally invited into England in 1531 to play at the court of Henry VIII. They stayed on, eventually assimilating into the general population.[13]

As the monarchs of Europe had done in times gone by, Sultan Murad moved in quickly to compile an inventory of all Don Joseph's possessions, casting a covetous eye upon the estate. But this inventory was different from all the others. A year later, the French were reporting that the combined value of the furnishings and cash did not even add up to the dowry of 90,000 ducats that was supposed to be returned to his widow, Reyna.[14]

What had happened to the fortune? Had Sultan Murad and his henchmen, as later reported,[15] quietly stripped the household of everything of value? Had the Turks allowed the Venetians to raid the estate for claims they alleged stemmed from confiscations of Venetian property that Don Joseph had approved in his duchy of Naxos?[16] What about the French who were still hoping to gain compensation for the confiscations of cargo in Alexandria? Was it simply that Don Joseph's extravagant lifestyle, plus the financial demands constantly being heaped upon him, gnawed away at whatever assets he still owned and income he could generate? Even five years before his death he was so hard up, reported the French ambassador, that he was *au saffran* (on the verge of ruin).[17] The expression comes from the yellow badges, or hats, that were traditionally worn by Jews, prostitutes and debtors.

The shimmering fortune that Francisco and Diogo had amassed earlier in the century was now gone. Despite hard work, it had slipped out of the family's control over time, as inherited wealth so often does. But on this occasion it was not the result of mismanagement or irresponsibility. On the contrary, both Doña Gracia and Don Joseph spent an inordinate amount of time and energy trying to preserve what they had. It was more a question of outside pressures that diminished their vast holdings, ducat by agonizing ducat, despite the best of intentions, or sometimes with the best of intentions.

It was spent to appease sadistic popes and desperate monarchs. It dwindled when valuables were abandoned in Antwerp. It slaked an unquenchable thirst for bribes. It suffered from the difficulties inherent in trying to conduct business while on the run; from commercial ventures gone bad; from the corrosive effect of spiraling inflation as gold and silver flowed in from the New World; from loans that were never repaid. It was depleted by the deeds of untrustworthy agents; by economic turmoil that dogged the *converso* merchant community in Europe; by tax farming obligations that could not always be met through collections; by a lifetime of outstretched hands to people in need; an escape network that needed constant funding, donations to support cultural and religious life; the feeding of the multitudes on their doorstep.

It all added up.

Not that Reyna was left entirely empty handed. Some assets were doubtless preserved as part of her an inheritance she probably received from her mother and La Chica. What was left was enough to keep her in comfort for the rest of her days. She was known to have occupied two houses during her widowhood: Belvedere and another home or printing workshop in a nearby village called Kuru-Techesme.[18]

Still, it could not have been a happy time. As the last living member of a noble family that had savored life in some of the most scintillating salons of the era, she had little left but her glorious memories. Surviving childless for some twenty years after the death of her husband, and thirty years after her mother died, she must have felt terribly alone.

Nevertheless, she continued to honor the family's commitment to the Jewish community. She opened her husband's magnificent library to scholars, one of whom was Almosnino.[19] She developed and supported two separate printing presses for Hebrew works; an activity that had always been important to her family, although nothing of significance was produced.[20]

In the early months of her widowhood, Reyna also petitioned the sultan, as her mother would have done, to help a Venetian cousin in trouble.[21] The cousin, Lisabona Berra, appears to have been the child of Francisco Berra, the man who married Doña Gracia's other sister, Giomar. At the time, Lisabona had two grown daughters. One of them, Alumbra de Luna, known simply as "Luna," was exceptionally beautiful. Alumbra had entered into a scandalous marriage with a man named Giovanni (João) Ribeiro—scandalous because it was a prohibited union between a *converso* living publicly as a Christian and an openly-practicing Jewess.[22] Among other prohibited acts, Alumbra would sneak out of the ghetto at night to sleep with Giovanni in his palace at St. Maria Formosa. Interestingly, a witness at Alumbra's Jewish marriage ceremony, which had taken place on the Venetian island of Murano, was Isaac Habibi, son of Licentato da Costa.[23] Alumbra was widowed a few years later and Lisabona was having great difficulty recovering her daughter's dowry. Reyna sought the sultan's intervention to help the family regain possession of the dowry money and also help all three women leave Venice and move to Constantinople.[24]

This incident is worthy of note because it is connected to the Inquisition trial of a sneaky old *converso* named Gaspare Ribeiro. The 87-year-old Ribeiro, a Lisbon-born spice merchant, money-lender and tax farmer, was Alumbra's father-in-law. Late in life he had become miserly and contentious. The trial was triggered by Ribeiro's reluctance to part with Alumbra's dowry money—a tussle that brought the Ribeiro family to the attention of the Inquisition. As Gaspare had allowed his son to marry an openly-professing Jewess it was charged that Gaspare himself must be a secret Jew. But the real reason for the indictment may have had more to do with Gaspare's miserly and cheating ways. Once before Gaspare had been charged with usury and he had made a lot of enemies. Gaspare had also left a lengthy trail of not-so-covert Jewish practice that went beyond the marriage. Typical of the half-hearted ways of the Venetian Inquisition, there was no condemnation, nor even imprisonment. The decision was inconclusive and the old man died of natural causes some months later. The officials of the Inquisition even permitted him reburial, some years later, in a Jewish cemetery.[25]

Despite her best efforts, Reyna may not have succeeded in bringing her cousin, Lisabona, and Lisabona's two daughters to Constantinople. Or if they managed to get there, it was not due to her intervention. Though Reyna did obtain the letter she sought from the sultan—based perhaps on some lingering good will, the amount of the money that the three women could bring into Turkey, or even a bribe—her imperial missive could not have arrived in Venice. If it had been delivered, it should have shown up in the Venetian archives. Instead, in an incident so beloved of novelists, it surfaced as late as the 1950's as part of the private collection of an antique dealer in Istanbul.[26]

However, the fact that it materialized after so many centuries suggests that this may not be the end of the story. Just the end of the story as we know it now.

NOTES

CHAPTER 1

1. See R. Smith's *Vanguard of Empire: Ships of Exploration in the Age of Columbus*, p. 12.

2. For a fuller discussion of the background to the era's explosive mercantile growth see Diffie and Winius, *Foundations of the Portuguese Empire 1415-1580*, as well as Chapter 3 of this book.

3. An analysis of these materialistic attitudes are explained throughout L. Gardine's book, *Worldly Goods: A New History of the Renaissance*.

4. David Raphael's *The Expulsion 1492 Chronicles*, p. 145.

5. Raphael's *The Expulsion...*, p. 146.

6. Raphael's *The Expulsion...*, p. 149.

7. Raphael's *The Expulsion...*, p. 150.

8. Jane Gerber's *The Jews of Spain*, p. 2; also see Richard Zimler's article "Identified as the Enemy: Being a Portuguese New Christian at the Time of 'The Last Kabbalist of Lisbon,'" in *European Judaism*, Vol. 33, Spring 2000, p. 32.

9. David Gitlitz's *Secrecy and Deceit: The Religion of the Crypto-Jews*, pp. 73-75.

10. Gitlitz's *Secrecy and Deceit...*, p. 74.

11. Raphael's *The Expulsion...*, p. 150.

12. Gitlitz's *Secrecy and Deceit...*, p. 75.

13. For a more detailed look at the Jewish experience during the Middle Ages in Europe, particularly on the Iberian Peninsula, see Heinrich Graetz's *History of the Jews* Vol. IV; S.W. Baron's *A Social and Religious History of the Jews*, Vol. XIII; and the early chapters of Gerber's *The Jews of Spain*.

14. Erna Paris' *The End of Days*, p. 35.

15. Yom Tov Assis' *The Jews of Spain: From Settlement to Expulsion*, numerous references.

16. Raphael's *The Expulsion...,*, p. vii.

17. Raphael's *The Expulsion...*, pp. iii-xix; also see the later chapters in Yitzhak Baer's *A History of the Jews in Christian Spain*, Vol. II, and the final sections of Paris' *The End of Days*.

18. Gitlitz's *Secrecy and Deceit...*, p. 74; estimates concerning the actual number of Jews in the Spanish kingdoms at this time varies widely and we had to make a choice among historians, choosing what we felt was an especially reliable source although even this may not be correct.

19. Raphael's *The Expulsion...*, p. 73.

20. Clauses agreeing to the return of certain buildings—provided the owners came back within a year—have been found in the municipal archives of Girona by Silvia Planas I Marcé, Director of the Nahmanides Institute for Jewish Studies in Girona.

21. Observations made by Professor Yom Tov Assis in his course, *Spanish Jews During*

the Reconquista, given at Yale University, Spring Semester, 1997.

22. Raphael's *The Expulsion...,* p. 71.

23. Raphael's *The Expulsion...,* p. 77.

24. Insights gained from interview in July, 1997, with Professor Helder Marcedo, Professor of Portuguese at Kings College, London.

25. It is virtually impossible to translate the relative value of a cruzado at this point in history with today's currencies. The value and use of cash had an entirely different meaning in a century where so much was still traded through an exchange of services and goods.

26. A verbatim translation of the edict is provided at the conclusion of Gerber's *The Jews of Spain,* pp. 285-289.

27. Alexandre Herculano's *History of the Origin and Establishment of the Inquisition in Portugal,* p. 246; translated by John C. Branner. Modern historians have suggested that some of the 600 may well have been motivated less by a dread of conversion and more by a fear of staying in a country where they would now be under the jurisdiction of Inquisition authorities impatient to confiscate their wealth.

28. Herculano's *History of the Origin...,* pp. 234-235.

29. Raphael's *The Expulsion...,* p. 74.

30. Raphael's *The Expulsion...,* p. 77.

31. Herculano's *History of the Origin...,* p. 247.

32. Samuel Usque's *Consolation for the Tribulations of Israel,* (translated by Martin A. Cohen) p. 202.

33. Livermore's *A New History of Portugal,* pp. 131-134.

34. Baron's *A Social and Religious History...,* Vol. XI, p. 257.

35. Herculano's *History of the Origin...,* p. 253-256.

36. Usque's *Consolation...,* p. 203.

37. Herman Prins Salomon's *Deux Etudes Portugaises: Two Portuguese Studies,* p. 34.

38. When interviewing some of the descendants, the author was angrily told, many times, that this could never have happened to *their* ancestors. It became grounds for a heated exchange.

39. Usque's *Consolation...,* p. 203.

40. Elie Kedourie's *Spain and the Jews: The Sephardic Experience 1492 and After,* p. 146.

41. Andrée Brooks' article "Jewish Voyagers to the New World Emerging from History's Mists," in The New York Times, July 29, 1997.

42. See the catalogue, *Lisboa Quinhentista, a imagem e a vida da cidade,* p. 10, published for a special 1983 exhibition celebrating the 500th anniversary. I would also like to thank Richard Zimler, specialist on early 16th century Lisbon, for these observations and many that follow. Three small paperback books were also issued in connection with the anniversary that describe the city from old records: *Lisboa: a cidade e o Espectáculo na Época dos Descobrimentos; Lisboa em 1551 Sumário; Grandeza e Abastança de Lisboa em 1552;* all published by Livros Horizonte.

43. *Lisboa...,* p. 13.

44. No contemporary records have yet been found to confirm this date, although it has been repeatedly used by historians, based upon other factors in her life that sug-

gest it was the most probable year. See, for example, Cecil Roth's *Doña Gracia of the House of Nasi*, pp. 12-13. Nevertheless, without any contemporary corroboration, I use this date with trepidation.

45. The consensus of most historians who have studied the family. It was further underscored in an interview with Professor Doutor Antonio Borges Coelho, a specialist in the period at the University of Lisbon on October 28, 1997. I was also assisted in this research by Professor Herman Prins Salomon of the State University of New York at Albany, whose recent genealogical studies in cooperation with Aron di Leone Leoni of Milan were incorporated into a lengthy academic journal article entitled "Mendes, Benveniste, de Luna, Micas, Nasci: The State of the Art (1532-1558)," in the *Jewish Quarterly Review*, Vol. LXXXVIII, January-April, 1998, pgs.135-213.

46. *Encyclopedia Judaica*, Vol. 12, p. 835 and C. Roth's *Dona Gracia...*, p. 12; the baptized name of Beatrice de Luna is the one repeatedly used in all subsequent Vatican and municipal documents when referring to Doña Gracia Nasi during the Catholic period of her life (see subsequent chapters).

47. Irisalva Moita's *Lisboa Quinhentista*, Part 2, p. 12.

48. Insights into customs of the period were provided by Eunice Relvas and Ana Horem de Melo, specialists in 16th century history with the Gabinete de Estudos Olisiponenses (Library for the Study of the History of Lisbon) in Lisbon. Interview conducted on October 28, 1997.

49. Based upon new genealogical findings in the archives of Brussels, Modena and Ferrara; also confirmed by Salomon and Leoni in their 1998 article in *JQR*, pg.195 doc.13. These documents substantially alter Roth's analysis of the family relationships in his 1948 biography of Doña Gracia, which immediately took on an aura of certitude. For confirmation of the name of Alvaro de Luna as the father see ASF, notary Taurino, matricola 582, pacco 8; doc. dated May 1553. The document provides the name of the father of Doña Gracia's brother, Aries de Luna; thus, it must have been the name of her own father.

50. Vitorino Magalhâes Godinho's *Os Descobrimentos e a Economia Mundia*, Vol.2, pp. 226-259; also see Virginia Rau's *Estudos Sobre História Económica e Social do Antigo Regime*, pp. 69-81.

51. Their role is repeatedly mentioned in Yom Tov Assis's *The Golden Age of Aragonese Jewry*.

52. Godinho's *Os Descobrimentos...*, p. 243.

53. Gitlitz's *Secrecy and Deceit...*, p. 202.

54. Salomon and Leoni's 1998 article in *JQR*, p. 175.

55. Salomon and Leoni's 1998 article in *JQR*, pp. 177-179.

56. Assis's *The Golden Age of Aragonese Jewry*, map 2.

57. Benjamin Netanyahu's *The Origins of the Inquisition in Fifteenth Century Spain*, pp. 217-218.

58. Netanyahu's *The Origins of the Inquisition...*, pp. 217-218.

59. Salomon and Leoni's 1998 article in *JQR*, pp. 177-179.

60. DMSW, University College, London, box CC, folder 8 of Wolf's papers; testimony of Fernando Rodrigues; also see Salomon and Leoni's 1998 article in *JQR*, p. 172, n.119.

61. Weir's *Eleanor of Aquitaine*, pp. 9-13.

62. Assumed by historians from the name she took upon openly reclaiming her Judaism. See Salomon and Leoni's 1998 article in *JQR*, pp. 175-176.

63. A fuller account of the unique position of widows is given at the start of chapter 4 of this book.

64. The opinion of Adrien de Longpérier, a curator at the Louvre Museum in Paris; reported in *Revue Numismatique* in 1858 and quoted by Alice Fernand-Halphen in her article "Une Grande Dame Juive de la Renaissance," in *La Revue de Paris*, September, 1929.

65. James Gairdner's *Letters and Papers, Foreign and Domestic, of the reign of Henry VIII*, Vol. XII, Part II, p. 197, doc. 520; full text reprinted in P. Grunebaum-Ballin's *Joseph Naci, duc de Naxos*, p. 31. n.2.

66. Voluminous correspondence between Marie of Hungary and her brother, Charles V, Holy Roman Emperor, concerning Doña Gracia and the Mendes fortunes. Transcribed by Jacob Reznik in his doctoral thesis, *Le Duc Joseph de Naxos*, Paris, 1936; also found in DMSW, box CC (labeled Antwerp - Marranos) of Wolf's papers; both quote documents from AGR, Brussels.

67. A. H. de Oliviera Marques' *Daily Life in Portugal in the Late Middle Ages*, p. 216.

68. The role of the Virgin Mary in the literature of the times is discussed in Jane E. Connolly's chapter "Marian Intervention and Hagiographic Models in the Tale of the Chaste Wife," in the anthology *Quien Hubiese Tal Ventura*, (Ed. Andrew M. Beresford), pp. 35-43.

69. Pantaleâo de Aveiro's *Itineraro da Terra Sancta e suas Particularidades*, p. 473, among many other sources.

70. Cecil Roth's *The Jews in the Renaissance*, p. 51.

71. Gerber's *The Jews of Spain*, p. 183.

72. Cecil Roth's *The Duke of Naxos of the House of Nasi*, p. 201.

73. Baer's *A History of the Jews in Christian Spain*, Vol. 2, pp. 271-272.

74. Paris' *The End of Days*, pp. 111-112.

75. Paris' *The End of Days*, pp. 108-112.

CHAPTER 2

1. Salomon and Leoni's 1998 article in *JQR*; for confirmation that Brianda was indeed younger than Doña Gracia see also Charrière's *Négociations de La France dans le Levant*, Vol. II, p. 101 (footnote). Aries de Luna also shows up as the brother in Ferrara in ASF, notary Saracco, matricola 493, pacco 29, doc. dated January, 1557; Giomar is mentioned in ASF, notary Taurino, matricola 535, pacco 8.

2. Fernand-Halphen's *Une Grande Dame Juive de la Renaissance*, p. 153.

3. The right to dress as she chose was specifically mentioned in various decrees of safe-conduct provided to her by the authorities as she moved from place to place. See also Galante's *Hommes et Choses Juifs Portugais*, p. 18, concerning her insistence on this point when contemplating a return to Judaism.

4. Renata Segre's chapter, "Sephardic Refugees in Ferrara: Two Notable Families," in the book *Crisis and Creativity in the Sephardic World:1391-1648*, p. 182. The testimony of the wet nurse, Blanca Fernandez, can be found transcribed at DMSW, box CC, folders 2 and 8 of Wolf's papers.

5. ASV, Senato, Deliberazioni Secreta, filza 24, 1551, doc. dated December 23, 1551.

6. Constance Hubbard Rose's *Alonso Nuñez de Reinoso: the Lament of a Sixteenth-Century Exile*, p. 49; also see the discussion in Chapter 11 of this book.

7. See the expression "our Spanish tongue" used in the dedication of the Ferrara Bible, reprinted in Moshe Lazar's (Ed.) *The Ladino Bible of Ferrara: A Critical Edition*, p. 76.

8. Fully discussed and cited later in these pages.

9. Libby Garshowitz's chapter "Gracia Mendes: Power, Influence and Intrigue," in *Power of the Weak: Studies in Medieval Women*, (ed. Jennifer Carpenter and Sally Beth MacLean), p. 105.

10. ASF, notary Conti, matricola 584, pacco 8s, doc. dated November 17, 1562; also see ASF, notary Caprilli, matricola 504, busta 2, undated inventory accompanying doc. dated August 20, 1557, which includes a mention of her personally completing an account book.

11. Segre' chapter "Sephardic Refugees in Ferrara," p. 183.

12. J. D. M. Ford's *Letters of John III*, p. 344, letter 314.

13. Relvas and Melo interviews; also see Willett and Cunnington's *The History of Underclothes*, pp. 46-47 and Ribeiro and Cumming's *The Visual History of Costume*.

14. ANTT, Chancelaria de D. Joâo III, LV. 19, FLS. 69-69V, MF. 1798; doc. dated 1533.

15. Zimler's article "Identified as the enemy...," in *European Judaism*, Vol. 33, spring 2000, p. 33.

16. Relvas and Melo interviews and the various booklets and catalogues (see prior notes) published around the time of the *Quinhentista* celebrations.

17. Additional information on Lisbon, circa 1510-1526 also provided by the Gabinete de Estudos Olisiponenses.

18. Gitlitz's *Secrecy and Deceit...*," pp. 222-223.

19. Samuel de Medina's responsum 327.

20. Charles-Martial de Witte's *La Correspondance Des Premiers Nonces Permanents au Portugal 1532-1553*, Vol. II, p. 588, letter 251, dated April 27, 1548.

21. Brooks' article "When Household Habits Betrayed the Jews," in The New York Times, February 20, 1997, along with information provided by authors' Gitlitz and Zimler.

22. Discussed in works of contemporary authors such as Usque and Reinoso, among others.

23. An explanation of this phenomenon is more fully articulated in Chapter 18.

24. Herculano's *History of the Origin...*, p. 257.

25. Salomon and Leoni's 1998 article in *JQR*, pp. 169-170.

26. *Lisboa Quinhentista...*, Part 2, p. 12.

27. Graetz' *History of the Jews*, Vol. IV, p. 486.

28. Yosef Hayim Yerushalmi's *The Lisbon Massacre of 1506 and the Royal Image in the Shebet Yehudah*, pp. 6-8 and Herculano's *History of the Origin...*, pp. 262-266.

29. Yerushalmi's *The Lisbon Massacre of 1506...*, pp. 9-16 and Herculano's *History of the Origin...*, pp. 262-266.

30. Yerushalmi's *The Lisbon Massacre of 1506...*, pp. 9-18 and Herculano's *History of the Origin...*, pp. 262-266; also captured in fiction in Zimler's *The Last Kabbalist of Lisbon*.

31. Examples of the fear that permeated all Iberian Jews from massacres such as this one, and the constant threats posted by the Inquisition, are reflected in secondary "getaways"—the trapdoor under the *bimah* (the raised platform where the clergy stand) in the Touro Synagogue in Newport, R.I., the secret door behind a bookcase in the Gomez House in Marlboro, N.Y, and the tunnels under houses recently found in Ibiza by Gloria Mound, an Israeli historian who specializes in *conversos*.

32. Herculano's *History of the Origin..*, p. 271.

33. For a summary of messianic concepts see the *Encyclopedia Judaica*, Vol.11, pp. 1407-1427.

34. Salomon's essay in *The Journal of the American Portuguese Cultural Society*, Vol. VI-VII, 1972-1973, pp. 59-74.

35. Herculano's *History of the Origin...*, pp. 275-278 and the introduction to Ford's *Letters of John III*.

36. A photo of this portrait adorns the inside cover of Ford's *Letters of John III*.

37. Herculano's *History of the Origin...*, p. 275.

38. A convincing argument on this topic is outlined by M. D. Cassuto in his article "Who is David Reubini?" in the Hebrew journal *Tarbiz* 32, Jerusalem, 1963, pp. 339-358.

39. DMSW, box CC, folders 7 and 12 of Wolf's papers; testimony of Diogo Mendes concerning David Reubeni, doc. dated 1532.

40. A fuller account of the Reubeni story can be found in Adler's *Jewish Travellers: A Treasury of Travelogues from Nine Centuries*, pp. 272-313 and the *Encyclopedia Judaica*, Vol. XIV, pp. 114-116. For a 16th century account by the Jewish historian, Joseph ha-Kohen, see Jacob Marcus' *The Jew in the Medieval World*, pp. 251-255.

41. Salomon's essay in *The Journal of the American Portuguese Cultural Society*, p. 70, n.11.

42. Adler, Salomon and the *Encyclopaedia Judaica*, as listed above.

43. Transcribed and translated in Adler's *Jewish Travellers...*

44. Adler's *Jewish Travellers...* et al.

45. Herculano's *History of the Origin...*, p. 291.

46. De Witte's *La Correspondance des Premiers Nonces...*, Vol. II, letters: 23, 26, 28, 37,47.

47. Herculano's *History of the Origin...*, p. 400.

48. Paris' *The End of Days*, pp. 181-188.

49. The practice of favoring 18 years as the ideal age for marriage emanates from the teachings of the Mishnah, an ancient Jewish code of law written down in the second century of the Christian Era (CE). It implies, but does not arbitrarily insist, that eigh-

teen years is the optimum year for a Jewish girl to marry. I wish to thank Professor Abraham David of Hebrew University in Jerusalem for pointing this out to me. However, although this date has been widely accepted by historians and it is probably correct, this author could find no contemporary corroboration.

CHAPTER 3

1. Almeida's *Capitais e Capitalistas no Comércio da Especiaria*, p. 45; also see *Encyclopedia Judaica*, Vol.11, p. 1345.

2. An example is the safe conduct issued in Rome on Oct. 22, 1546 by Pope Paul III, as transcribed in Simonsohn's *The Apostolic See and the Jews*, Vol. 6, p. 2554, doc. 2641.

3. *Encyclopedia Judaica*, Vol. 2, pp. 558-560; Isaac da Costa's *Noble Families among The Sephardic Jews*, p. 146; numerous references in Baer's *A History of the Jews in Christian Spain*, Vols. I and II; Paris' *The End of Days*, p. 248; another excellent source of genealogical and biographical information on prominent Jews on the Iberian Peninsula from the 10th to the 15th centuries is the *Diccionario de Autores Judios*, compiled by Angel Saenz-Badillos and Judit Targarona Borras, Ediciones El Amendro, Cordoba, 1988.

4. See, for example, the warm tone used by King João III to describe Mendes in a letter of August 28, 1532, transcribed in Salomon and Leoni's 1998 article in *JQR*, p. 182, doc. 3 (translated into English in the same article on pp. 137-138).

5. Salomon and Leoni's 1998 article in *JQR*, p. 169; also see DMSW, box CC, folders 2 and 8 of Wolf's papers, testimony of Blanca Fernandez; *Encyclopedia Judaica*, Vol. 11, p. 1345.

6. This refutes Roth's conclusion; see Salomon and Leoni's 1998 article in *JQR*, p. 65. Having explored the Ferrara archives, this author agrees with Salomon.

7. Salomon and Leoni's 1998 article in *JQR*, p. 182, doc. 3.

8. Samuel de Medina's responsum 327; also noted in Garshowitz's chapter "Gracia Mendes...," in *Power of the Weak*, p. 114.

9. DMSW, box CC, folder 7 of Wolf's papers, letter dated September 17, 1532; also reprinted in Salomon and Leoni's 1998 article in *JQR*, p. 184, doc.5.

10. Simonsohn's *The Apostolic See and the Jews*, Vol. 4, p. 2084, doc. 1851 dated February 22, 1538; ANTT, Chancelaria de D. João III, LV. 19, FLS. 69-69V, MF. 1798, doc. dated 1533.

11. The fact that she had married her uncle seems to have been common knowledge among the *converso* refugees entering Antwerp. See testimony of refugees, DMSW, box CC, folder 7, of Wolf's papers, blue sub folder; also confirmed by Salomon and Leoni in their 1998 article in *JQR*, p. 172 and 210 (family tree). The idea of an uncle marrying a niece was common enough that it was regularly used as proof that these people still lived as Jews; also see Baron's *A Social and Religious History of the Jews*, Vol. XIII, p. 129. A defense, in their eyes, was the biblical story of Sarah, who is variously described as either the niece or half-sister of her husband Abraham (Genesis11- 23). These families further believed that anything that was not expressly prohibited in the Bible was permitted.

12. Victor Perera's *The Cross and the Pear Tree*, pp. 78 and 138, mentions a similar pattern among the Pereira family. So does the second page of the Introduction to *Bevis Marks Records, Part II: Abstracts of the Ketubot of the (London) Congregation from Earliest Times until 1837*. The same practice is mentioned in "Jews in Elizabethan England," in *The Jewish Historical Society of England, Transactions*, Vol. XI, 1924-1927, p. 7.

13. We have deliberately used the traditional Iberian spelling (Ana). The fact that Doña Gracia originally named her daughter Ana shows up in several documents. Among them see ASV, notary Leoncini, pacco 7818, p. 176r, doc. dated July, 1552; Simonsohn's *The Apostolic See and the Jews*, Vol. 4, p. 2084, doc. 1851, and confirmed by Salomon and Leoni's 1998 article in JQR, pg.149, n. 53. Only when the family reached Constantinople did she change her daughter's name from Ana to Reyna (Reina). See ASF, notary Conti, matricola 584, pacco 8s; doc. dated May 27, 1558, p. 4.

14. Explained in Salomon and Leoni's 1998 article in *JQR*, p. 210 (family tree) and later in this book.

15. Louise Mirrer's *Upon My Husband's Death*, pp. 22 and 322; also see Judith Baskin's *Jewish Women in Historical Perspective*, p. 97.

16. *The Babylonian Talmud* (ed. and trans. by Isidore Epstein) Seder Nashim, Yebamoth 62b-63a, p. 419 including n. 6 on same page; also see *The Mishnah* (ed. and trans. by Herbert Danby), Mishnah Nedarim, 9:10, p. 277.

17. Baskin's *Jewish Women...*, p. 97.

18. Joseph Caro's responsum 81.

19. For a fuller discussion of the sources and implementation of Jewish betrothal traditions see W. Ze-ev Falk's *Jewish Matrimonial Law in the Middle Ages*, Chapter III (The Matrimonial Match), pp. 86-112.

20. Marques' *Daily Life in Portugal in the Late Middle Ages*, p. 173.

21. Almeida's *Capitais e Capitalistas no Comércio da Especiaria*, p. 45.

22. Gitlitz's *Secrecy and Deceit...*, p. 246.

23. Salomon and Leoni's 1998 article in *JQR*, p. 182, doc. 3.

24. Salomon and Leoni's 1998 article in *JQR*, pp. 179-180, doc. 1.

25. Braudel's *The Mediterranean and the Mediterranean World in the Age of Phillip II*, (abridged edition) p. 578.

26. Observations of retired Professor George Winius, co-author with Bailey W. Diffie of *Foundations of the Portuguese Empire, 1415-1580*, in a telephone interview, January, 1999. Also see Yom Tov Assis' *Jewish Economy in the Medieval Crown of Aragon, 1213-1327*, pp. 82-83. Medieval commercial documents retrieved from the Cairo Geniza further confirm early involvement in this activity.

27. Diffie and Winius' *Foundations of the Portuguese Empire*, p. 318.

28. Braudel's *The Mediterranean...*, p. 297.

29. Diffie and Winius' *Foundations of the Portuguese Empire*, pp. 410-415; also see J. Denucé's "Privilèges commerciaux accordés par les rois de Portugal aux Flamands et aux Allemands" in *Archivo Historico Portuguez*, Vol. VII, No. 10 E 11, 82-83, October-November, 1909, Lisboa, 1909, pp. 311-319.

30. *Cambridge Economic History of Europe*, Vol. IV, p. 511, showing that this remained so even two centuries later; also see Diffie and Winius' *Foundations of the Portuguese*

Empire, pp. 318-319.

31. Herman Van Der Wee's *The Growth of the Antwerp Market and the European Economy, 14th-16th Centuries,* pp. 125-126.

32. *Cambridge...,* p. 193.

33. Insights gained from extensive interviews late in 1997 with James Boyajian, accountant and economic historian, who has written several works on Iberian bankers during the 16th and 17th centuries.

34. Tracy's *The Rise of Merchant Empires,* pp. 267-268.

35. Tracy's *The Rise of Merchant Empires,* p. 29

36. The amazing reach and impact of these *converso* networks became the basis for a conference called *The Jews and the Expansion of Europe to the West,* organized by the John Carter Brown Library at Brown University in June, 1997. The deliberations were later incorporated into a book by the same name (Ed. Paolo Bernardini and Norman Fiering).

37. From historical data provided for the exhibition, "Portuguese Jews between the Discoveries and the Diaspora," Fundação Calouste Gulbenkian, Lisbon, June-September, 1997.

38. Herman Kellenbenz's *Os mercadores alemães de Lisboa por volta de 1530,* p. 9.

39. Braudel's *The Mediterranean and the Mediterranean World,* p. 343.

40. Opinion of Marques de Almeida, Professor of History and Director of the Sephardic Studies Program, Lisbon University, based on his own readings; provided in an interview on October 8, 1997.

41. Diffie and Winius' *Foundations of the Portuguese Empire,* pp. 253-255.

42. Almeida's *Capitas e Capitalistas...,* p. 45.

43. See later chapters for the specific roles that would be played by relatives and agents in these cities.

44. Ford's *Letters of John III,* p. 177, letter 134.

45. More from Boyajian interviews.

46. Richard Ehrenberg's *Capital and Finance in the Age of the Renaissance,* pp. 25-30.

47. Livermore's *A New History of Portugal,* p. 142.

48. Diffie and Winius' *Foundations of the Portuguese Empire,* p. 414.

49. Virginia Rau's *Um grande mercador-banqueiro italiano em Portugal: Lucas Giraldi,* p. 5.

50. Grunebaum-Ballin's *Joseph Naci, duc de Naxos,* p. 28.

51. Diffie and Winius' *Foundations of the Portuguese Empire,* pp. 413-414.

52. Diffie and Winius' *Foundations of the Portuguese Empire,* pp. 413-414.

53. Herculano's *History of the Origin...,* p. 281.

54. Herculano's *History of the Origin...,* pp. 279-280.

55. Livermore's *A New History of Portugal,* pp. 146-147.

56. Salomon and Leoni's 1998 article in *JQR,* p. 182, doc. 3.

57. Almeida's *Capitais e Capitalistas no Comércio da Especiaria,* p. 46.

58. Tracy's *The Rise of Merchant Empires,* p. 29.

59. Salomon and Leoni's 1998 article in *JQR,* p. 182, doc. 3.

60. Salomon and Leoni's 1998 article in *JQR*, p. 182, doc. 3.

61. Godhino's *Os Descobrimentos e a Economia Mundia*, Vol. 2, p. 242; the calculation was made by multiplying 17,845 marks by 23 (the factor used in Rau's *Estudos...*, p. 79) to reach the corresponding number of kilograms, and then multiplying the kilograms by 2.2 to reach the equivalent pounds.

62. Samuel de Medina's responsum 327.

63. Garshowitz's chapter "Gracia Mendes...," p. 96.

64. Falk's *Jewish Matrimonial Law in the Middle Ages*, p. 88.

65. Moses di Trani's responsum 80.

66. Moses di Trani's responsum 80.

67. Falk's *Jewish Matrimonial Law in the Middle Ages*, pp. 42 and 86.

68. Falk's *Jewish Matrimonial Law in the Middle Ages*, p. 53.

69. Marques' *Daily Life in Portugal in the Late Middle Ages*, pg.165.

70. Observation of Professor Ivana Elbl of Trent University in Peterboro, Ontario. She has explored the lives and habits of Portuguese merchants during the 15th and 16th centuries; interviewed by telephone on February 3, 1999.

71. Gitlitz's *Secrecy and Deceit...*, pp. 254 and 266, n. 43.

72. Falk's *Jewish Matrimonial Law in the Middle Ages*, pp. 51-53 (n.3), 65.

73. Marques' *Daily Life in Portugal in the Late Middle Ages*, pp. 166-173.

74. Leoni's chapter, "La Diplomazia Estense e L'immigrazione dei Cristiani Nuovi a Ferrara al Tempo di Ercole II," in *Rivista Storica*, May-August, 1994, p. 323, doc.1.

75. Babinger's 1923 edition of Hans Dernschwam's *Tagebuch einer Reise nach Konstantinopel und Kleinasien (1553-55)*, p. 115.

76. Irisalva Moita's chapter in *Lisboa Quinhentista*, p. 15.

77. Zimler's article "Identified as the enemy: being a Portuguese New Christian at the time of 'The Last Kabbalist of Lisbon,'" p. 33.

78. Salomon and Leoni's 1998 article in *JQR*, pp. 179-180, doc. 1.

79. Denucé's "Privilèges commerciaux accordés par les rois de Portugal aux Flamands et aux Allemands," in *Archivo Historico Portuguez*, Vol. VII, No.10 E 11, 82-83, October/November 1909, pp. 310-319.

80. A.A. Marques de Almeida's article "Judeus e Cristâos-Novos Portugueses," in the Portuguese journal *Oceanos*, January, 1997, p. 31. He incorrectly stated that this charter was given in 1533 when, in fact, it was given in 1530 according to a date actually written into the text of the charter.

81. ANTT, Chancelaria de D. Joâo III, LV. 19, FLS. 69-69V, MF. 1798; doc. dated 1533.

82. De Witte's *La Correspondance des Premiers Nonces permanents au Portugal, 1532-1553*, Vol. II, letters 7, 23, 26, 28.

83. Herculano's *History of the Origin...*, p. 299; also see Baron's *A Social and Religious History...*, Vol. XIII, p. 53.

84. For a fuller explanation of the struggle see Herculano's *History of the Origin...*, Chapter III.

85. Francisco's role is evident from *La Correspondance des Premiers Nonces permanents au Portugal 1532-1553*, letters 7, 23, 26,28.

86. Herculano's *History of the Origin...*, p. 474.

87. Diffie and Winius' *Foundations of the Portuguese Empire*, pp. 414-415; also see Livermore's *A New History of Portugal*, pp. 146-147.

88. Gitlitz's *Secrecy and Deceit...*, p. 51.

89. Herculano's *History of the Origin...*, pp. 625-627.

90. Herculano's *History of the Origin...*, p. 348.

91. Denucé's *Previlèges commerciaux accordés...*, pp. 310-319.

92. Kellenbenz's *Os mercadores alemâes...*, p. 11.

93. Salomon and Leoni's 1998 article in *JQR*, pp. 180-181, doc. 2.

94. Salomon and Leoni's 1998 article in *JQR*, pp. 180-181, doc. 2.

95. DMSW, box CC, folder 9 of Wolf's papers, testimony of Father Sebastian di Mendis, a confessor of Doña Gracia in Antwerp, who gives her age as 14 years on or about 1544. A second mention is made in a letter of King João III to the Count of Castanheira dated January 30, 1535, immediately following the death of Francisco. See Ford's *Letter of John III*, p. 65. But no age is given.

96. Livermore's *A New History of Portugal*, p. 147; Herculano's *History of the Origin...*, pp. 312-313.

97. DMSW, box CC, folder 1 and 7, of Wolf's papers; doc. dated September 17, 1532.

98. Goris' *Étude sur Les Colonies Marchandes Méridionales*, p. 200. Goris insists that the Affaitati were the ones to tell the news to the king, but the king's letter of August 28 to Charles V contradicts this assumption, suggesting it was Francisco himself.

99. Grunebaum-Ballin's *Joseph Naci, du de Naxos*, p. 29.

100. Salomon and Leoni's 1998 article in *JQR*, p. 135.

101. Salomon and Leoni's 1998 article in *JQR*, p. 182, doc. 3.

102. Salomon and Leoni's 1998 article in *JQR*, p. 182, doc. 3.

103. Salomon and Leoni's 1998 article in *JQR*, p. 182, doc. 3.

104. Salomon and Leoni's 1998 article in *JQR*, pp. 183-184, doc. 4.

105. Goris' *Étude sur Les Colonies...*, p. 567; Vroman's *L'Affaire Diego Mendez*, pp. 26-27. There is some discrepancy on the dated documents pertaining to Diogo's release. The hearing that permitted the release is dated August 24 and the Portuguese letters are dated August 28. Yet historians agree the pressure from Portugal was paramount. Possibly this is due to a clerical mistake in the dating of one document or the other, or a transcription error.

106. Ford's *Letters of John III*, p. 96, letter 57.

107. This assumption is based upon a letter of the king dated January 30, 1535 (Ford's letter 165) referring to Francisco's death as having recently taken place; also see de Witte's *La Correspondance des Premier Nonces...*, Vol. II, p. 88, letter 23 dated February 12, 1535, from Marco Vigerio della Rovere, Papal Nunico in Portugal, to Ambrogio Ricalcato, his superior at the Vatican.

108. De Witte's *La Correspondance des Premiers Nonces...*, Vol. II, p. 88, letter 23.

109. ACDF, S.O., St.St. UV-12: *S.O. Alexandro VII. Doctrinalia, criminalia, civilia*, XVII century—fascicles 41-43.

110. Henry Kamen's *The Spanish Inquisition: An Historical Revision*, p. 190.

111. Fuller accounts of Inquisition torture can be found in many histories of the period. See, for example, Roth's *A History of the Marranos*, pp. 99-143; Paris' *The End of Days*, pp. 190-208; Herculano's *History of the Origin...*, pp. 532-566.

112. The Vatican's "examination of conscience" in connection with the Inquisition began in the spring of 1998 in a spirit of pre-millennium repentance. See a Web posting of the *"American Atheist"* dated April 18, 1998 and The New York Times, Section A, page 3, October 31, 1998; among other reports.

113. Moses di Trani's responsum 80.

114. Joseph ibn Lev's responsum 23.

115. Marques' *Daily Life in Portugal in the Middle Ages*, p. 276.

116. Joshua Soncino's responsum 12.

117. Samuel de Medina's responsum 27.

118. Dernschwam's *Tagebuch einer Reise...*, p. 115.

119. De Witte's *La Correspondance des Premiers Nonces...*, Vol. II, pp. 558-589, letter 251 dated April 27, 1548.

120. From research by Richard Zimler, a writer on this period, provided in an interview in Lisbon, November, 1997; also see Gitlitz's *Secrecy and Deceit...*, Chapter XI (Death and Funeral Customs)

121. Marques' *Daily Life in Portugal in the Middle Ages*, pp. 277-279.

CHAPTER 4

1. Mirrer's *Upon My Husband's Death*, p. 322.

2. Renée Levine Melammed's chapter, "Sephardi Women in the Medieval and Early Modern Periods," in Judith Baskin's (Ed.) *Jewish Women in Historical Perspective*, pp. 115-134; also see Erler and Kowaleski's (Ed.) *Women and Power in the Middle Ages*, p. 2 and Margaret Wade Labarge's *A Small Sound of the Trumpet*, Chapter 4.

3. Mirrer's *Upon My Husband's Death*, p. 123.

4. Howard Adelman's review of Shlomo Simonsohn's *The Jews in the Duchy of Milan* in *JQR*, Vol. LXXVII, Nos. 2-3, October 1986-January 1987, p. 202; also see Maria Giuseppini Muzzarelli's comments concerning practices among Jewish women in her chapter "Beatrice de Luna, Vedova Mendes, Alias Donna Gracia Nasi," in the anthology *Rinascimento al Femminile*, pp. 102-6.

5. Melammed chapter, "Sephardi Women...," pp. 120-124; Heath Dillard's *Daughters of the Reconquest*, p. 13; Ginio's *Jews, Christians and Muslims in the Mediterranean World after 1492*, pp. 246, 262-263.

6. Baskin's *Jewish Women in Historical Perspective*, p. 109.

7. Mirrer's *Upon My Husband's Death*, pp. 10, 294.

8. Gairdner's *Letters and Papers, Foreign and Domestic...*, Vol. XII, Part II, p. 197, doc. 520; full text in P. Grunebaum-Ballin's *Joseph Naci, duc de Naxos*, p. 31, n.2.

9. Ford's *Letters of John III*, p. 206, letter 165.

10. Ford's *Letters of John III*, p. 206, letter 165.

11. Dillard's *Daughters of the Reconquest*, p. 101.

12. Michael M. Sheehan's article "English wills and the records of the ecclesiastical and civil jurisdictions," in the *Journal of Medieval History, (1988)* Vol. 14, pp. 3-12.

13. Labarge's *A Small Sound of the Trumpet,* Chapter 4; also see Mirrer's *Upon My Husband's Death,* p. 37.

14. Ford's *Letters of John III,* p. 344, letter 314.

15. The right of the king to insist upon the marriage of a member of his court to anyone of his choosing was underscored in an interview on October 27, 1997 with Professor Maria Helena Carvalho dos Santos, a professor at the New University of Lisbon who has written extensively on the Jews of Portugal.

16. DMSW, box CC, folder 5 of Wolf's papers, testimony of Diogo de Redondo, a Portuguese merchant of Old Christian lineage in Antwerp.

17. Analysis of the predicament provided by Professor Carvalho.

18. Herculano's *History of the Origin...,* p. 400. This book uses the term "escudos" while others have stuck with ducats. There was scant difference in the value and one must assume it was one and the same.

19. Gairdner's *Letters and Papers...,* Vol.XII, Part II, p. 197, doc. 520; full text in P. Grunebaum-Ballin's *Joseph Naci, duc de Naxos,* p. 31, n. 2.

20. Lucien Wolf's *Essays in Jewish History,* p. 75; also see J. Gairdner and R. Brodie's *Letters and Papers, Foreign and Domestic, of the Reign of Henry VIII,* Vol. XIX, Part I, pp. 513, 514, 550; letter 822 dated July 2, 1544 and letter 887 dated July 10, 1544.

21. David Katz's *The Jews in the History of England,* p. 1-7.

22. DMSW, box CC, folder 7 of Wolf's papers.

23. Jasper Ridley's *Henry VIII,* pp. 196-197.

24. Gairdner's *Letters and Papers...,* Vol.XII, Part II, p. 197, doc. 520; full text in P. Grunebaum-Ballin's *Joseph Naci, duc de Naxos,* p. 31, n. 2.

25. Moses di Trani's responsum 80 and Joshua Soncino's responsum 12.

26. DMSW, box CC, folder 7 of Wolf's papers.

27. Jervis Wegg's *Antwerp 1477-1559,* pp. 212-213.

28. Ford's *Letters of John III,* repeated mentions.

29. Gairdner's *Letters and Papers...,* Vol.XII, Part II, p. 197, doc. 520; full text in P. Grunebaum-Ballin's *Joseph Naci, duc de Naxos,* p. 31, n. 2.

30. Katz's *The Jews...,* pp. 10-13; also see Wolf's *Essays in Jewish History,* p. 86. This routing was never considered by historians, such as Roth, who simply assumed her ship pulled in at Southampton or London. Others have based their ideas upon later interrogations at Antwerp, which suggested a prolonged stay that is refuted by the dating of the Lisle letter. Moreover, this testimony was simply hearsay and neither the facts, nor geography, back it up.

31. Gairdner's *Letters and Papers...,* Vol. XII, Part II, p. 271, doc.757; letter of John Hussee to Lady Lisle dated September 27, 1537. Transcribed in Muriel St. Clare Byrne's *The Lisle Letters,* pp. 412-413.

32. Tallied from a compilation of sources: Simonsohn's *The Apostolic See and the Jews,* Vol.4, p. 2084, doc. 1851, dated February 22, 1538, listing those members of the family living in Diogo's house within a few months of her arrival in Antwerp. Brianda's name is included in the Cromwell letter; also see Salomon and Leoni's 1998 article in

JQR, p. 152, n. 43, concerning her two nephews and Chapter 6 of this book for further details.

33. Noted in an interview with Professor Doutor Antonio Borges Coelho in Lisbon in October, 1997.

34. Salomon and Leoni's 1998 article in *JQR*, p. 152, n. 43.

35. A brother, Aries de Luna, is mentioned as being active in business in Ferrara by the mid 1550's - see ASF, notary Saracco, matricola 493, pacco 29, doc. dated January, 1557. Francisco Vaz Beirâo (later called Berra), who married Giomar, shows up in Venice in 1552 - see ASV, notary Leoncini, 7818 (1548-1556), p. 194-195 covering accords of July-August, 1552. Countless other members of the Mendes Benveniste family enter the record in Antwerp and Italy (see later chapters).

36. An assumption based upon the dating and content of the Antwerp and Lisle letters.

37. Donald Lach's *Asia in the Making of Europe,* p. 124.

38. Roger Smith's *Vanguard of the Empire,* pp. 143-146 and Shatzmiller's article "Traveling in the Mediterranean in 1563: the Testimony of Eliahu of Pesaro" in *The Mediterranean and the Jews: Banking, Finance and International Trade (XVI- XVIII Centuries),* Ed. Ariel Toaff and Simon Schwarzfuchs.

39. Details from testimony by Thomas Fernandes, a nephew of Hector and Beatrice Nuñes, before the Lisbon Inquisition. He had returned to Portugal where he was arrested in 1556. Processo (case) 9449 in the Arquivo de Torre do Tombo, reprinted in English in Roth's article in *The Jewish Historical Society of England: Miscellanies, Part II,* 1935, pp. 32-56. Though Fernandes' recollections concern a period about eight years later, there is every reason to suspect the practices were the same in 1537.

40. The probability of a lengthy stay was noted by both Roth and Wolf, based upon hearsay testimony given at a later investigation of incoming refugees in Antwerp. The dating of these London letters (Antwerp and Lisle) suggests otherwise.

41. Ridley's *Henry VIII,* p. 300.

42. Lucien Wolf's article "Jews in Elizabethan England," in *The Jewish Historical Society of England, Transactions,* Vol. XI, p. 11.

43. Katz's *The Jews in the History of England,* pp. 58-69.

44. Roth's *The Middle Period of Anglo-Jewish History Reconsidered,* p. 5. This author is indebted to Claudia Roden, the London-based Jewish food historian for the finding.

45. Wolf's chapter, "Jews in Tudor England," in his *Essays in Jewish History,* pp. 74-76.

46. Ridley's *Henry VIII,* p. 303.

47. See Chapter 11 of this book for details.

48. Wolf's chapter, "Jews in Tudor England," in his *Essays in Jewish History,* p. 79.

49. Wolf's chapter, "Jews in Tudor England," in his *Essays in Jewish History,* p. 77.

50. See Chapters 5,6 of this book for further details.

51. Wolf's chapter, "Jews in Tudor England," in his *Essays in Jewish History,* p. 79.

52. Salomon and Leono's 1998 article in *JQR,* p. 204, n. 148; also worth noting is that the celebrated British playwright, Harold Pinter, claims that his ancestors were *conversos* named Pinto.

53. Byrne's *The Lisle Letters,* p. 8

54. For further details about the lives of Lord and Lady Lisle, from which this summary was taken, see Byrne's *The Lisle Letters*; Hanawalt's chapter "Lady Honor Lisle's Networks of Influence" in Erler's *Women and Power in the Middle Ages* and Ridley's *Henry VIII*, pp. 296, 318-319, 330- 331, 340, 363.

55. Public Records Office, London, Doc. S.P.3/12, 106 (for original); brief reference to same in Gairdner's *Letters and Papers, Foreign and Domestic of the Reign of Henry VIII*, p. 271 doc.757. Shakespeare was born 27 years later, in 1564.

56. Byrne's *The Lisle Letters*, pp. 412-413.

57. Andrée Aelion Brooks' article "A Jungle Journey" in *Reform Judaism Magazine*, spring, 1999.

58. Wegg's *Antwerp 1477-1559*, p. 140.

59. Ridley's *Henry VIII*, pp. 340, 363.

CHAPTER 5

1. For more on the appearance of Antwerp see Fonds Mercator's *Crowning the City: Vernacular Architecture in Antwerp from the Middle Ages to the Present Day;* also see *Antwerp's Golden Age: the Metropolis of the West in the 16th and 17th Centuries (exhibition catalogue, City of Antwerp, 1973).*

2. Grunebaum-Ballin's *Joseph Naci, duc de Naxos*, p. 28.

3. Guido Marnef's *Antwerp in the Age of Reformation: Underground Protestantism in a Commercial Metropolis*, pp. 5-6.

4. Ehrenberg's *Capital and Finance in the Age of the Renaissance*, pp. 54-56, 236-237.

5. Ehrenberg's *Capital and Finance...*, pp. 233-236.

6. Wolfgang Schivelbusch's *Tastes of Paradise: A History of Spices, Stimulants and Intoxicants*, Chapter I, provides a fuller treatment of importance of spices at this time.

7. E. R. Samuel's "Portuguese Jews in Jacobean London," in *The Jewish Historical Society of England, Transactions*, Vol. XVIII, p. 173.

8. Diffie and Winius' *Foundations of the Portuguese Empire 1415-1580*, p. 412.

9. For a fuller account of the rise of Antwerp as a commercial center see Ehrenberg's *Capital & Finance...*, pp. 233-280.

10. Wegg's *Antwerp 1477–1559*, p. 323.

11. Ehrenberg's *Capital and Finance...*, pp. 21-63.

12. Ehrenberg's *Capital and Finance...*, pp. 26-30.

13. Ehrenberg's *Capital and Finance...*, pp. 34-46.

14. See copies of the numerous letters that flew between Charles V and Marie, Regent of the Low Countries, concerning the need for her money - DMSW, box CC of Wolf's papers, reprinted verbatim from AGR, Brussels; also found in the footnotes throughout the early chapters of Reznik's *Le Duc Joseph de Naxos*.

15. Ehrenberg's *Capital and Finance...*, pp. 64-87.

16. Ehrenberg's *Capital and Finance...*, pp. 21-63.

17. Ehrenberg's *Capital and Finance...*, pp. 237-238.

18. Wegg's *Antwerp 1477–1559*, p. 98.

19. Goris' *Étude sur les Colonies Marchandes Méridionale*, p. 108 (illustration).

20. Wegg's *Antwerp 1477–1559*, p. 98; as a result of the proximity of the artists' shops to the trading floor it is logical to assume that the wealthier merchants vied to have the best artists paint their portraits; as a result, it is conceivable that a portrait of Diogo Mendes exists, perhaps in a private collection. Doña Gracia's religious leanings might have prevented her from sitting for a portrait.

21. Tyler's *The Emperor Charles the Fifth*, pp. 20, 322-325.

22. Tyler's *The Emperor Charles the Fifth*, pp. 277-285 and illustrations.

23. Wolf's article "Jews in Elizabethan England," p. 8.

24. For a fuller treatment of Charles' life and times see Tyler's *The Emperor Charles the Fifth*. For Charles' changing attitudes towards the *converso*s see Baron's *A Social and Religious History of the Jews* Vol. XIII, pp. 119-121.

25. Labarge's *A Small Sound of the Trumpet*, p. 80; also see Wegg's *Antwerp 1477-1599*, pp. 190, 210-211.

26. The characters of both Charles and Marie will be more fully explored when their actions directly affect Doña Gracia. See for example, copies of their numerous letters preserved at DMSW among Wolf's papers.

27. Tyler's *The Emperor Charles the Fifth*, p. 312 (illustration).

28. Marnef's *Antwerp in the Age of Reformation...*, p. 3 and noted throughout Wegg's *Antwerp 1477–1559*.

29. For more on *Utopia* see Peter Ackroyd's *The Life of Thomas More*.

30. Norbert Elias' *The History of Manners*, pp. 56-57.

31. Marnef's *Antwerp in the Age of Reformation...*, p. 39; also see Wegg's *Antwerp 1477-1559*, pp. 165, 201.

32. J. M. Lopes' *Les Portugais à Anvers au XVI Siècle*, p. 17.

33. Barata's *Rui Fernandes de Almada*, pp. XI, XII.

34. DMSW, box CC, folder 7 of Wolf's papers, quoting a letter dated August 29, 1529, from Stephen Vaughan, a British envoy in Antwerp to Thomas Cromwell in London.

35. City of Antwerp's *Antwerp's Golden Age...*, p. 21; also see Marnef's *Antwerp in the Age of Reformation...*, p. 33; Wegg's *Antwerp 1477-1559*. pp. 84, 92, 131, 149, 179, 287; DMSW, Wolf's papers, box CC, folder 7.

36. Lopes' *Les Portugais...*, p. 17.

37. ASV, notary Leonicini, busta 7818, doc. dated July-August, 1552, p.191 (back) covering the agreement between the sisters before Doña Gracia departs for Constantinople.

38. Van de Wee's *The Growth of the Antwerp market and the European Economy (14-16th centuries)*, Vol. II, pp. 128-129.

39. Wolf's chapter "Jews of Tudor England," p. 75.

40. Goris' *Étude sur les Colonies...*, p. 27.

41. Diffie and Winius' *Foundations...*, p. 414.

42. Fernand Braudel's *The Mediterranean and the Mediterranean World in the Age of Phillip II*, pp. 321-323.

43. Diffie and Winius' *Foundations...*, p. 414.

44. The exchange rates given are only rough estimates, since there were fluctuations then as there are today. My thanks to James Boyajian of Madera, Calif., an economic historian of the period, for providing those rates.

45. Salomon and Leon's 1998 article in *JQR*, p. 142.

46. Ehrenberg's *Capital and Finance...*, p. 264.

47. Baron's *A Social and Religious History...*, Vol. XIII, p.121.

48. Herbert Bloom's *The Economic Activities of the Jews of Amsterdam in the Seventeenth and Eighteenth Centuries*, p. 2; also see Baron's *A Social and Religious History...*, Vol. XIII, p. 119 and DMSW, box CC, folder 6 of Wolf's papers.

49. Grunebaum-Ballin's *Joseph Naci, duc de Naxos*, p. 28

50. Goris' *Étude sur les Colonies...*, p. 566; also see David Werner Amram's *The Makers of Hebrew Books in Italy*, Chapter VII.

51. Wegg's *Antwerp 1477-1559*, p. 145-148.

52. Joshua Soncino's responsum 12.

53. DMSW, box CC, folder 9 of Wolf's papers; transcription of testimony of Diego Manuel. The intermingling of some of these Sephardic refugees with the already-established Ashkenazim of the Rhineland merits further exploration.

54. Roth's article "Why Anglo-Jewish History?" in *The Jewish Historical Society of England, Transactions*, Vol. XXII, p. 23.

55. DMSW, box CC of Wolf's papers; refugee testimony to this effect can be found in many of the folders.

56. Braudel's *The Mediterranean...*, p. 158-159; also see Wolf's chapter, "Jews in Elizabethan England," p. 3.

57. Wolf's chapter "Jews in Tudor England," p. 77.

58. Wegg's *Antwerp 1477-1559*, p. 183; also see Katz's *The Jews in the History of England*, p. 3; the first Mendes agent in London was Jorge Añes, a native of Valladolid in Spain, who arrived with his wife and children around 1521.

59. Wolf's chapter "Jews in Tudor England," p. 77.

60. Wolf's chapter "Jews in Tudor England," pp. 77-79.

61. DMSW, box CC, folder 9 of Wolf's papers, testimony by Agnes Gomez, a refugee and Antoine Cardoso, an employee of the Portuguese crown's agency in Antwerp.

62. Wolf"s article "Jews in Elizabethan England," p. 4.

63. DMSW, box CC, folder 8 of Wolf's papers, transcribing doc. dated August 23, 1532.

64. DMSW, box CC, folder 1of Wolf's papers, testimony of Jean Lopez; the existence of this loan bank is repeatedly mentioned by the refugees and can be found in other folders.

65. DMSW, box CC, folder 1 of Wolf's papers, testimony of Gaspar Lopez.

66. DMSW, box CC, folder 5 of Wolf's papers, testimony of Govaert van Londerseel, vicar at the Cathedral of Our Lady, and a man named Nicolas Fernandis.

67.DMSW, box CC, folder 8 of Wolf's papers, transcribing a document of Charles V dated 1543. Issued after Diogo's death, it absolved him and anyone connected with his operation, from accusations that they distributed such funds to help *converso*s move on to Salonika, a city which had become a catch-all term for Ottoman lands.

68. Baron's *A Social and Religious History of the Jews,*Vol. XVIII, pp. 475-477, n. 47.

69.DMSW, box CC, folder 11 of Wolf's papers, testimony of Gaspar Lopez.

70. Goris' *Étude sur les Colonies...,* p. 566; also see DMSW, box CC, folder 1 of Wolf's papers, testimony of Francisco Gomez.

71. Amram's *The Makers of Hebrew Books in Italy,* Chapter VII.

72. DMSW, box CC, folder 1 of Wolf's papers, testimony of Gaspar Lopez; this witness also mentions the charity bank.

73. Herculano's *History of the Origin...,* p. 319.

74. Herculano's *History of the Origin...,* pp. 396-397.

75. De Witte's *La Correspondence des Premiers Nonces...,* pp. 170-173, letter 47 from Marco Vigerio della Rovere in Braga, Portgual to Ambrogio Ricalcato at the Vatican.

76. De Witte's *La Correspondence des Premiers Nonces...,* pp. 170-173.

77. This payment was mentioned in Chapter 4 of this book and in Herculano's *History of the Origin...,* p. 400. However, Heculano mistakenly implies that Doña Gracia was already in Antwerp.

78. DMSW, box CC, folder 5 of Wolf's papers, testimony of Professor André Balenus. Also reprinted in Latin in Salomon and Leoni's 1998 article in *JQR,* p. 189, doc. 7. Also see Jean Vroman's *L'Affaire Diego Mendez,* p. 14.

79. DMSW, box CC, folder 7 of Wolf's papers, doc. dated September 17, 1532.

80. DMSW, box CC, folder 7 of Wolf's papers, doc. dated August 23, 1532.

81. DMSW, box CC, folder 1 of Wolf's papers, doc. dated April 17, 1530.

82. Usque's *Consolation...,* p. 208.

83. Grunebaum-Ballin's *Joseph Naci, duc de Naxos,* p. 29.

84. DMSW, box CC, folder 7 of Wolf's papers, doc. dated September 17, 1532

85. Goris' *Étude sur les Colonies...,* pp. 562, 566; also see Vroman's *L'Affaire Diego Mendez,* pp. 14-17; the youth's name was Luiz Garcia.

86. Goris' *Étude sur les Colonies...,* pp. 562, 566; also see Vroman's *L'Affaire Diego Mendez,* pp. 14-17.

87. Francisco López de Gómara's *Annals of the Emperor Charles V,* p. 91.

88. Tyler's *The Emperor Charles the Fifth,* p. 139

89. DMSW, box CC, folder 8 of Wolf's papers, docs. dated August 23 and September 10, 1532.

90. DMSW, box CC, folders 4-5 of Wolf's papers, testimony of André Balenus.

91. DMSW, box CC, folder 1 and 7 of Wolf's papers, doc. dated September 17, 1532.

92. DMSW, box CC, folder 8 of Wolf's papers; doc. signed by a functionary named Boudewyns and dated August 23, 1532.

93. Vroman's *L'Affaire Diego Mendez,* pp. 16-20.

94. Grunebaum-Ballin's *Joseph Naci, duc de Naxos,* p. 29.

95. Wegg's *Antwerp 1477-1559,* p. 175.

96. DMSW, box CC, folder 1 and 7 of Wolf's papers, doc. dated September 17, 1532.

97. The Mendes and their connections to these commercial houses are covered in subsequent chapters.

98. Vroman's *L'Affaire Diego Mendez*, p. 26.

99. DMSW, box CC, folders 1 and 7 of Wolf's papers, doc. dated September 17, 1532.

100. DMSW, box CC, folders 4 and 6 of Wolf's papers, letter of Charles V dated August 8, 1532.

101. DMSW, box CC, folders 4 and 6 of Wolf's papers, letter of Charles V dated August 8, 1532.

102. Salomon and Leoni's 1998 article in *JQR*, p. 144.

103. DMSW, box CC, folder 8 of Wolf's papers, doc. dated August 23, 1532.

104. DMSW, box CC of Wolf's papers, docs. dated August 23, 1532 (folder 8) and September 17, 1532 (folder 1,7); the lawyer's name was Jehan van den Dycke.

105. Goris' *Étude sur les colonies...*, p. 566.

106. DMSW, box CC, folder 8 of Wolf's papers; doc. dated August 23, 1532.

107. DMSW, box CC of Wolf's papers, docs. dated September 10, 1532 (folder 8) and September 17, 1532 (folders 1,7); also see Vroman's *L'Affaire Diego Mendez*, p. 28 and Goris' *Étude sur les colonies...*, p. 567

108. Reznik's *Le Duc Joseph de Naxos*, pp. 70-72, n. 6; letter from Marie to Charles dated July, 1547.

109. Roth's *Dona Gracia...*, p. 36.

110. Goris' *Étude sur les colonies...*, p. 568; the merchant's name was Antonio Fernandez.

111. Goris' *Étude sur les colonies...*, p. 570.

112. Baron's *A Social and Religious History...*, Vol. XIII, p. 122.

113. Goris' *Étude sure les colonies...*, p. 571.

114. Reznik's *Le Duc Joseph de Naxos*, p.71, n.6.

115. Ford's *Letters of John III*, p. 96, letter 57, dated February 13, 1533.

116. Vroman's *L'Affaire Diego Mendez*, p. 17.

117. *Encyclopedia Judaica*, Vol.14, p. 115.

118. Wolf's article "Jews in Tudor England," p. 79.

CHAPTER 6

1. ASF, notary Giacomo Conti, matricola 584, pacco 4, docs. dated August 30, 1549 and December 11, 1550.

2. Bloom's *The Economic Activities of the Jews of Amsterdam...*, p. 1.

3. ASF, notary Conti, matricola 584, pacco 4, doc. dated December 11, 1550, p. 5.

4. Ephraim Schmidt's *Geschiedenis van de Joden in Antwerpen*, pp. 21-24; also see Usque's *Consolation...*, p. 185.

5. The history of Provence as a Jewish region is explained in Arthur Zuckerman's *A Jewish Princedom in Feudal France, 768-900*.

6. Simonsohn's *The Apostolic See and the Jews*, Vol. 4, p. 2084, doc.1851 dated February 22, 1538. For confirmation that Doña Gracia lived in the same house, see Leoni's

article "La diplomazia estense e l'immigrazione dei cristiani nuovi a Ferrara al tempe di Ercole II," in *Nuova Rivista Storica*, March-August, 1994, p. 323, doc. dated May 24, 1539.

7. Salomon and Leoni's 1998 article in *JQR*, p. 152, n. 43.

8. Salomon and Leoni's 1998 article in *JQR*, p. 152, quoting university registers; also see DMSW, box CC, folder 7, testimony of Diego de Redondo. For the arrival of the mother see the testimony of André Balenus (same folder).

9. Leoni's article "La diplomazia estense...," p. 301.

10. Leoni's article "La diplomazia estense...," p. 323, doc. 1 dated May 24, 1539.

11. DSMW, box CC, folder 12, testimony of Diogo Mendes in 1532 in connection with the arrival of David Reubeni, during which Diogo gives his age.

12. Grunebaum-Ballin's *Joseph Naci, due de Naxos*, p. 32; Salomon and Leoni's 1998 article in *JQR*, pp. 151-2, n. 42; Leoni's article "La diplomazia estense...," p. 308.

13. See reference to this idea in Friedenwald's *The Jews in Medicine*, Vol. I, p. 382. Some Jewish families believed that a soul could not be saved unless a son, or at the very least a male child of a widow who becomes the wife of the deceased husband's brother, is able to pray for that soul.

14. ASF, notary Batista Saracco, matricola 493, pacco 29, doc. dated June 4, 1550, f. 9r.

15. Salomon and Leoni, 1998 article in *JQR*, p. 151, n. 41.

16. Salomon and Leoni, 1998 article in *JQR*, p. 151, n. 41.

17. ASF, Saracco, matricola 493, pacco 29, doc. dated June 4, 1550.

18. Leoni's "La diplomazia estense...," p. 323, doc. 1 dated May 24, 1539.

19. Leoni's "La diplomazia estense...," p. 323, doc. 1 dated May 24, 1539.

20. ASF, notary Taurino, matricola 535, pacco 8, document dated May 8, 1553 and notary Saracco, matricola 493, pacco 29, doc. dated January, 1557 (where he is identified as Doña Gracia's brother by virtue of his being called her niece's uncle, as well as bearing the family name of de Luna). Based upon Inquisition concerns, it is logical to conclude that Aries had probably already been there for a while.

21. Grunebaum-Ballin's *Joseph Naci...*, p. 33; also see Reznik's *Le Duc Joseph de Naxos* p. 31.

22. ASF, notary Conti, matricola 584, pacco 4, doc. dated August 30, 1549.

23. ASM, Cancelleria Ducale, Patricolari, busta 885 (sub folder titled "Mendez'); also see Salomon and Leoni's 1998 article in *JQR*, p. 204, n. 148.

24. Lusitanus' *Dioscorides I*, part 120.

25. See the Hebrew book *Makor Baruch* by Baruch Epstein, a Lubavitch rabbi from Vilna, who lived and worked in the first half of the 20th century.

26. A comprehensive account of Lusitanus' life can be found in Friedenwald's *The Jews in Medicine*, Vol. I, p. 332-390; also see Friedenwald's *Amatus Lusitanus.*

27. Jane Gerber's *The Jews of Spain*, p. 160. In the typical way in which the *conversos* played games with their names and Christian identities, he had changed over to a Latin name meaning "The beloved from Portugal."

28. Dov Front's unpublished monograph, *"The Expurgation of the Books of Amatus Lusitanus."* Dov Front is chairman of nuclear medicine at the Rambam Medical Cen-

ter in Haifa, Israel.

29. Friedenwald's chapter "Amatus Lusitanus," pp. 638-641.

30. Lusitanus' *Dioscorides I*, part 120 and *Dioscorides* II, part 39.

31. Lusitanus' *Dioscorides I*, part 120.

32. Lusitanus' *Dioscorides I*, part 120.

33. This is the general consensus of historians based upon her actions and subsequent facts in her life. It is also implied in the testimony (biased though it may have been) of Father Sebastian di Mendis, her confessor in Antwerp. DMSW, box CC, folder 9 of Wolf's papers (the year incorrectly given as 1548 instead of 1544, a mistake that probably occurred in transcription).

34. DMSW, box CC, folder 9 of Wolf's papers, interrogations of incoming *conversos*. Although the testimony of any servant or neighbor under such circumstances must always be treated with skepticism, the details provided by Marie strike an authentic note as she even gave the name of the man (Robyn Pinto) who handled the ritual slaughter.

35. DMSW, box CC, folder 9, testimony of Father Sebastian di Mendis.

36. DMSW, box CC, folder 9, testimony of Father Sebastian di Mendis.

37. Simonsohn's *The Apostolic See and the Jews*, Vol. 4, p. 2084, doc. 1851 dated February 22, 1538.

38. The Sephardic journal *Los Muestros*, (Brussels), issue of December, 1998, pp. 19-20. The practice dates back to pre-expulsion Spain.

39. DMSW, box CC, folder 2 of Wolf's papers, testimony of Augustinho Henriques.

40. DMSW, box CC, folder 1 of Wolf's papers, testimony of Gaspar Lopez.

41. Rose's *Alonso Nuñez de Reinoso : the Lament of a Sixteenth-Century Exile*, pp. 90-91. As Doña Gracia did not yet have the luxury of a permanent place of settlement, free from the threat of harassment or persecution, this writer is of the belief that some of her most intimate papers may yet be found in a convent either in Antwerp, Venice or Ferrara. A convent was also the only public institution run by women at that time, and thus could have been especially meaningful for Doña Gracia.

42. DMSW, box CC of Wolf's papers; see particularly the testimony of Jaspar Centurion (folder 7), Manuel Bernaldis and Antonio Paulo (folder 9); also see the summary of findings issued by the Council of Brabant (folder 5), undated.

43. Information provided to the author on August 2, 1999, by Herman Coppens, head of the State Archives of Antwerp.

44. Salomon and Leoni's 1998 article in JQR, p. 180, doc. 2 dated December 11, 1531.

45. DMSW, box CC, folder 8 of Wolf's papers, doc. dated November 19, 1537.

46. Goris' *Étude sur les colonies...*, pp. 571-572.

47. DMSW, box CC, folder 8 of Wolf's papers.

48. Leoni's article "La diplomazia estense...," pp. 294-297.

49. Leoni's article "La diplomazia estense...," pp. 296-306.

50. Tyler's *The Emperor Charles The Fifth*, p. 64. The duke who died was Francesco Sforza.

51. Leoni's article "La diplomazia estense...," pp. 294-308.

52. Leoni's article "La diplomazia estense...," pp. 294-308.

53. Leoni's article "La diplomazia estense...," pp. 294-308.

54. Leoni's article "La diplomazia estense...," p. 302, doc. 3.

55. Usque's *Consolation...*, p. 213

56. Leoni's article "La diplomazia estense...," pp. 306-307

57. Roth's article "The Middle Period...," p. 4; also see Wolf's *Essays in Jewish History,* p. 78 and Leoni's article "La diplomazia estense...," p. 323, doc. 1.

58. Leoni's article "La diplomazia estense...," p. 323, doc.1.

59. Leoni's article "La diplomazia estense...," p. 323, doc.1.

60. Leoni's article "La diplomazia estense...," p. 308.

61. Pinto is also mentioned by Amatus Lusitanus in his medical tract, *Dioscorides I,* Part 120, as already living in Ferrara while Diogo was still alive.

62. Leoni's article "La diplomazia estense...," pp. 318-321.

63. Gómara's *Annals of the Emperor Charles V,* p. 126.

64. Leoni's article "La diplomazia estense...," pp. 313-314, which gives the name of the Jew as Salomon della Ripa; also see Salomon and Leoni's 1998 article in *JQR,* pp. 173 and DMSW, box CC, folder 1, of Wolf's papers.

65. Leoni's article "La diplomazia estense...," p. 313.

66. Wegg's *Antwerp 1477–1559,* pp. 226, 243, 244, 341.

67. Information gleaned from James Boyajian, an economic historian of the period, in an interview in Carmel, Calif., on August 17, 1999.

68. Bloom's *The Economic Activities of the Jews of Amsterdam,* p. 91.

69. Rawdon Brown's *Calendar of State Papers and Manuscripts relating to English Affairs existing in the Archives and collections of Venice, etc...,* Vol. 5, p. 88, letter 229.

70. Goris' *Étude sur les colonies...,* p. 572; see also DMSW, box CC, folders 2,5,7 of Wolf's papers; see particularly the testimony of Fernando Rodrigues in folder 8 and reprinted in Salomon and Leoni's 1998 article in *JQR,* p. 190, doc. 8.

71. DMSW, box CC, folder 8, doc. signed by Jerome Zandelin and dated October 8, 1541.

72. DMSW, box CC, folder 8 of Wolf's papers, doc. dated October 17, 1541.

73. Brown's *Calendar of State Papers...,* Vol. 5, p. 88, letter 229.

74. Usque's *Consolation...,* p. 208.

75. Wolf's *Essays in Jewish History,* pp. 79-83.

76. DMSW, box CC, folder 1 of Wolf's papers; testimony of Gaspar Lopez; also see Roth's *Doña Gracia...,* p. 37.

77. A program of interrogation, also in December of 1540, authorized in Antwerp by Queen Marie, casually advises torture as a customary means of getting at the truth, suggesting it was commonplace. See also DMSW, box CC, folder 7 of Wolf's papers, doc. dated December 6, 1540.

78. Salomon and Leoni's 1998 article in *JQR,* pp. 174-175, n. 124; also see DMSW, box CC, folder 1 of Wolf's papers, testimony of Gaspar Lopez.

79. Usque's *Consolation...,* p. 230.

80. Wolf's *Essays in Jewish History,* p. 82.

81. Katz's *The Jews in the History of England*, pp. 5-8.

82. Gayangos' *Calendar of Letters, Despatches and State Papers relating to Negotiations between England and Spain*, Vol.VI, Part II (1542-1543), p. 270, letter 114.

83. DMSW, box CC, folder 8 of Wolf's papers, letter dated October 17, 1541.

84. DMSW, box CC, folder 7 of Wolf's papers, questionnaire dated December 4, 1540.

85. In transcript and modern French at the DMS Watson library, University College, Gower Street, London; and in their original form at *Archives Générales du Royaume* in Brussels.

86. Goris' *Étude sur les colonies...*, p. 572.

87. DMSW, box CC, folder 1 of Wolf's papers. While the mention of Cologne may have been given to avoid admitting that the family intended to move onto the Ottoman Empire, it could well have been true. A number of these refugees did end up in Germany. Traveling onwards was, after all, replete with danger.

88. DMSW, box CC, folders 5,8 and 9 of Wolf's papers.

89. Information provided by James Boyajian, economic historian of the period, in an interview in Carmel, Calif., on August 17, 1999.

90. DMSW, box CC, folders 5,8 and 9 of Wolf's papers; testimony of Francisco Baradan.

91. DMSW, box CC, folders 5,8 and 9 of Wolf's papers.

92. Vroman's *L'Affaire Diego Mendez*, p. 33.

93. Moses di Trani's responsum 80.

94. Moses di Trani's responsum 80.

95. Norman Rosenblatt's 1957 doctorial thesis, *Joseph Nasi, Court Favorite of Selim II*, p. 8, n. 37.

96. Grunebaum-Ballin's *Joseph Naci, duc de Naxos*, pp. 32-33, based upon a later deposition given by Affaitati.

97. Salomon and Leoni's 1998 article in *JQR*, p. 201-202, doc. 17. By this time the young girl had returned to Judaism and signed the letter with her full Jewish name (Gracia Benveniste). We found the same combination of first and last names for the girl on numerous documents in the Ferrara achives, even after her marriage to Don Samuel Nasi.

98. DMSW, box CC, folders 2 and 8, testimony of Blanca Fernandes.

99. Grunebaum-Ballin's *Joseph Naci, duc de Naxos*, p. 33.

100. Moses di Trani's responsum 80; also see Samuel de Medina's responsum 329.

101. ASF, matricola 584, pacco 9s, doc. dated 1562.

CHAPTER 7

1. The approximate date of death has been determined by placing two dates side by side: the date of the original writing of Diogo's will (June 28, 1543) as mentioned in ASF, notary Saracco, matricola 493, pacco 29, coupled with a document from ASV, notary Lioncini, 7818, 1548-1556; p. 176 (front) that talks of the will being "published" on July 2.

2. DMSW, box CC, folder 4 of Wolf's papers.

3. DMSW, box CC, folder 9 of Wolf's papers, testimony of Father Sebastian di Mendis.

4. Gitlitz's *Secrecy and Deceit*, p. 278.

5. The will was dictated to Antwerp notary William van Strict. We have used the Saracco date (see note 1 of this chapter) for the drawing up of the will, although Salomon and Leoni in their 1998 article in *JQR* argue that the will was drawn on July 27. We favored Saracco as we have personally reviewed this document. We further know that Diogo wrote it on his deathbed because Moses di Trani's responsum 80 makes particular note of this fact.

6. ASV, notary Lioncini, 7818, 1548-1556, doc. dated July 19, 1552, p. 177.

7. Goris' *Étude sur les colonies...*, p. 549.

8. The will actually speaks of 1,600 Flemish pounds. In keeping with the primary use of ducats, or their equivalent, throughout the book, we have used the exchange rates provided by James Boyajian, economic historian of Madera, Calif.

9. Lopes' *Les Portugais à Anvers...*, p. 40, n.

10. ASF, notary Saracco, matricola 493, pacco 29, June 4, 1550; this document contains the most complete copy of the will that we have available to us.

11. DMSW, box CC, folder 9 of Wolf's papers, testimony of Father Sebastian.

12. DMSW, box CC, folder 7 of Wolf's papers, testimony of Marie de Haza.

13.The name William is normally Guillaume in Old French and Guglielmo in Italian or Spanish. We have used the most appropriate form depending upon circumstances.

14. This portion of Diogo's will was written into Moses di Trani's responsum 80, as previously mentioned. Two further translations are available; see DMSW, box CC, folder 7, box CC of Wolf's papers for a segment taken from M. A. Levy's *Don Joseph Nasi, Herzog von Naxos*, Breslau, 1859, p. 38 It was also partially reproduced, as noted earlier, in Ferrara by notary Saracco, matricola 493, pacco 29, doc. dated June 4, 1550.

15. Salomon and Leoni's 1998 article in *JQR*, pp. 170 and 189, doc. 7; also see DMSW, box CC, folder 2 of Wolf's papers, testimony of André Balenus.

16. Reznik's *Le Duc Joseph de Naxos*, p. 53, n. 2, letter of Queen Marie to Charles V dated April 6, 1546 (mistakenly marked 1545 but copied with correct date into DMSW, box CC, folder 9 of Wolf's papers).

17. Ehrenberg's *Capital and Finance in the Age of the Renaissance*, p. 281, chapter on Lyons.

18. Grunebaum-Ballin's *Joseph Naci, duc de Naxos*, p. 107, n. 3.

19. Riccardo Calimani's *The Ghetto of Venice*, p. 95; also see Roth's *The Duke of Naxos*, p. 27.

20. See Chapters 13 and 19 for further details.

21. Grunebaum-Ballin's *Joseph Naci, duc de Naxos*, p. 38; also see Reznik's *Le Duc Joseph de Naxos*, p. 43.

22. Grunebaum-Ballin's *Joseph Naci, duc de Naxos*, p. 38.

23. DMSW, box CC, folder 2 of Wolf's papers; testimony of André Balenus.

24. Michael Molho's *Usos Y Costumbres de Los Sefaradies de Salonika*, p. 235.

25. Leoni and Salomon's 1998 article in *JQR*, p. 152, n. 45; also see Zorattini's *Processi del S. Uffizio di Venezia Contro Ebrei E Giudaizzanti (1548-1560)*, Vol. I, p. 225, testi-

mony of March 26, 1555.

26. ASF, notary Saracco, matricola 493, pacco 29, June 4, 1550.

27. The parts of the will that are copied verbatim into responsum 80 of di Trani are inserted in Spanish, while the rest of di Trani's deliberations are in Hebrew. This suggests that the entire will was originally written by Diogo in his native Spanish.

28. ASF, notary Saracco, matricola 493, pacco 29, doc. dated June 4, 1550.

29. DMSW, box CC, folder 8 of Wolf's papers, doc. dated July 10, 1543.

30. Moses di Trani's responsum 80.

31. DMSW, box CC, folder 8 of Wolf's papers, transcribing an undated edict (only the year 1543 is given) from Charles V.

32. ASV, Ital VII, 992 (9606), pp. 240 a-b, dispatch from Venetian ambassador, Bernardo Navagero, in Brussels dated September 5, 1545. Confirmed in Grunebaum-Ballin's *Joseph Naci, duc de Naxos,*, p. 35. This updates an assumption made by Roth in his *Doña Gracia...*, p. 43. The documents mention 200,000 florins. But since florins and ducats are used interchangeably we have continued our policy of referring to all these references as ducats.

33. DMSW, box CC, folder 8 of Wolf's papers, letters patent of the Emperor Charles V, 1543.

34. DMSW, box CC, folder 8 of Wolf's papers, letters patent of the Emperor Charles V, 1543.

35. Usque's *Consolation...*, p. 37 and 230; the praises of the rabbis in their various responsa, plus the poetic tributes of Sa'adiah Longo in his elergy on Doña Gracia in *Shivrei Lukhot*, ref. Opp 8N 1074 (3), ff.42-47, Bodleian Library, Oxford, England.

36. Samuel de Medina's responsum 327.

37. Usque's *Consolation...*, p. 230.

38. Usque's *Consolation...*, p. 230.

39. Usque's *Consolation...*, p. 230.

40. Salomon and Leoni's 1998 article in *JQR*, p. 192, doc. 9 dated November 20, 1543.

41. Based upon the estimate of 600,000 ducats that Ambassador Navagero gives in his dispatch of September 5, 1545, although it's doubtful whether he would have known the full value, given their understandable need for secrecy.

42. ASV, Ital VII, 992 (9606) pp. 240 a-b, dispatch from Venetian ambassador, Bernardo Navagero, at Brussels dated September 5, 1545.

43. A first-hand account of Father Sebastian's attempts to persuade Doña Gracia to marry her daughter to D'Aragon are incorporated into an account of his interrogation in the presence of Queen Marie; DMSW, box CC, folder 9 of Wolf's papers, doc. dated May-December 1544 or 1545 (incorrectly typed as 1548).

44. *Archivio Historico Portuguez*, Vol. VIII, p. 26, letter LX, from João Rebélo, agent of the Portuguese crown in Antwerp to the king in Lisbon, dated July 16, 1544.

45. Roth's *Doña Gracia...*, p. 43; also see Reznik's *Le Duc Joseph de Naxos*, p. 48.

46. Interrogation of Father Sebastian (see details above).

47. Interrogation of Father Sebastian (see details above).

48. Reznik's *Le Duc Joseph de Naxos*, p. 48, letter dated April 28, 1544.

49. Dispatch of the Venetian ambassador dated September 5, 1545 (see details above).

50. ASF, notary Conti, matricola 584, pacco 4, doc. dated December 11, 1550.

51. Reznik's *Le Duc Joseph de Naxos*, p. 48, transcribing a letter dated April 28, 1544.

52. Reznik's *Le Duc Joseph de Naxos*, p. 49, n. 5, transcribing a letter dated May 12, 1544.

53. Many of these letters have been copied from the archives in Brussels as footnotes into Reznik's *Le Duc Joseph de Naxos*; see particularly pp. 48-50. Some can also be found in box CC among Wolf's papers.

54. Reznik's *Le Duc Joseph de Naxos*, p. 48, letter dated April 28, 1544.

55. Reznik's *Le Duc Joseph de Naxos*, p. 49, n. 5.

56. Roth's *Doña Gracia...*, p. 44.

57. *Archivio Historico Portuguez*, Vol. VIII, p. 26, letter LX.

58. *Archivio Historico Portuguez*, Vol. VIII, p. 26, letter LX; the agent was João Rebélo.

59. Reznik's *Le Duc Joseph de Naxos*, p. 49, n. 5, transcribing a letter from Marie to Charles dated May 12, 1544.

60. DMSW, box CC, folders 1 and 12 of Wolf's papers, transcribing a letter dated July 9, 1544, from Queen Marie to D'Aragon.

61. Reznik's *Le Duc Joseph de Naxos*, p. 49, n. 5 (see above).

62. Reznik's *Le Duc Joseph de Naxos*, p. 50, n.11, letter from Charles to Marie from Spire dated May 25, 1544.

63. DMSW, box CC, folder 5 of Wolf's papers, testimony of Diego de Redondo.

64. DMSW, box CC, folders 1 and 12 of Wolf's papers, transcribing a letter dated July 9, 1544.

65. DMSW, box CC, folders 1 and 12 of Wolf's papers, transcribing a letter dated July 9, 1544.

66. DMSW, box CC, folders 1 and 12 of Wolf's papers, transcribing a letter dated July 9, 1544.

67. Salomon and Leoni's 1998 article in *JQR*, pp. 153-154.

68. DMSW, box CC, folders 1 and 12 of Wolf's papers, transcribing a letter dated July 9, 1544.

69. Samuel de Medina's responsum 331.

70. DMSW, box CC, folder 8 of Wolf's papers; letter dated July 22, 1544, from Schepperus to Queen Marie.

71. DMSW, box CC, folder 8 of Wolf's papers; letter dated July 22, 1544.

72. DMSW, box CC, folder 8 of Wolf's papers, letter dated July 22, 1544.

73. Salomon and Leoni's 1998 article in *JQR*, p. 154.

74. Strada's *History of the Low Country Wars*, p. 138-139.

75. DMSW, box CC, folder 7 of Wolf's papers, testimony of Emmanuel Carrerro.

76. *Archivio Historico Portuguez*, Vol. VIII p. 26, letter LX.

77. Herculano's *History of the Origin...*, p. 519.

78. The documents speak of 200 Carolinian florins and 600 Flemish pounds; in keeping with our policy of using ducats throughout we have again exchanged them for ducats using the formulas supplied by James Boyajian.

79. Salomon and Leoni's 1998 article in *JQR*, p. 154; also see DMSW, box CC, folder 8 of Wolf's papers, doc. dated June, 1545.

80. Fax from Catherine Clément to the author dated June 14, 1997. Further information was not forthcoming from Clément to make a search for this drawing feasible.

81. John Hale's *The Civilization of Europe in the Renaissance*, p. 428-438.

82. DMSW, box CC, folder 9 of Wolf's papers, testimony of Father Sebastian.

83. J. Gairdner and R. Brodie's *Letters and Papers, Foreign and Domestic, of the Reign of Henry VIII*, Vol. XIX, Part I, pp. 513,514, 550, letters 822, 887 from Stephen Vaughan, British envoy in Antwerp.

84. Gairdner and Brodie's *Letters and Papers...*, Vol. XIX, Part I, pp. 513,514, 550, letter 822, 887.

CHAPTER 8

1. Wegg's *Antwerp 1477-1559*, p. 259.

2. Reznik's *Le Duc Joseph de Naxos*, p. 68, n. 5, letter of Marie to Charles dated April 3, 1546 and p. 60, n. 14, letter from Marie dated July 16, 1546; DMSW, box CC, folder 9 of Wolf's papers, doc. dated October 8, 1545. This one concerns chests that Doña Gracia sent to the port of Ancona, underscoring the long-range intent of the move.

3. Calimani's *The Ghetto of Venice*, p. 58.

4. Benjamin Arbel's article "Venice and the Jewish Merchants of Istanbul in the Sixteenth Century," in *The Mediterranean and the Jews: Banking, Finance and International Trade (16-18th Centuries)* Ed. Toaff and Schwarzfuchs, p. 45.

5. Antonio's speech at the end of Act III, Scene III.

6. ASV, Ital VII, 992 (9606), pp. 240 a-b, dispatch from the Venetian ambassador Bernardo Navagero in the Low Countries dated September 5, 1545.

7. The evaluation of the situation in Venice was provided by Professor Amos Luzzato, an expert of Jewish -Venetian history and Reinhold Mueller, an expert on Venetian economic history, in interviews in Venice on May 28-29, 1998.

8. Zorattini's *Processi del S. Uffizio di Venezia Contro Ebrei e Giudaizzanti (1548-1560)*, Vol. I, p. 341; also see ASV, Ital VII, 992 (9606) pp. 246b, dispatch from Navagero dated September 21, 1545. Another safe conduct was recorded on December 30, 1545, just about the time they arrived in Venice. See ASV, Consiglio dei Dieci, Lettere dei Capi, filza 48, p.600, doc. dated December 30, 1545.

9. Segre's chapter "Sephardi Refugees in Ferrara...," p. 182.

10. Moses di Trani's responsum 80 mentions the departure as being two years after Diogo's death. This would place it the middle of 1545. Since Ambassador Navagero writes about the departure in several dispatches in the fall of 1545, one can assume they left in the summer soon after the loan of 200,000 ducats came due. Also, by September, Queen Marie was already writing to various cities on their route to try to intercept any transfers of funds. Also see Gairdner and Brodie's *Letters and Papers, Foreign and Domestic, of the Reign of Henry VIII*, Vol. XX, Part II, p. 148, letter 334, dated September, 1545.

11. Reznik's *Le Duc Joseph de Naxos*, p. 60, n. 14, letter from Marie to Charles dated

July 16, 1546.

12. Moses di Trani's responsum 80; also see ASV, Ital VII, 992 (9606) pp. 246b, dispatch from Navagero dated September 21, 1545.

13. Moses di Trani's responsum 80; also see DMSW, box CC, folder 9 of Wolf's papers transcribing a letter from Marie to the Viceroy of Naples dated November 10, 1545.

14. ASV, Ital VII, 992 (9606) pp. 240a-b, dispatch from Navagero dated September 5, 1545; also see DMSW, box CC, folder 9 of Wolf's papers; letter of November 27, 1545.

15. DMSW, box CC, folder 9 of Wolf's papers transcribing a letter from Marie to the Viceroy of Naples dated November 27, 1545; also see ASV, Ital VII, 992 (9606) pp. 240a-b, dispatch from Navagero dated September 5, 1545.

16. Grunebaum-Ballin's *Joseph Naci, duc de Naxos*, p. 36.

17. ASV, Ital VII, 992 (9606), pp. 240a-b, dispatch from Navagero dated September 5, 1545.

18. ASV, Ital VII, 992 (9606), pp. 240a-b, dispatch from Navagero dated September 5, 1545.

19. DMSW, box CC, folder 9 of Wolf's papers, transcribing a letter from Marie to the duke of Florence dated September 3, 1545 (incorrectly listed as 1548).

20. DMSW, box CC, folder 9 of Wolf's papers, transcribing an inventory of Mendes belongings dated July, 1546.

21. Reznik's *Le Duc Joseph de Naxos*, p. 53, n. 2, letter dated April 6, 1546 (mistakenly marked 1545) but copied with correct date into DMSW, box CC, folder 9 of Wolf's papers.

22.Contents listed in a letter from Queen Marie to Charles V dated July 16, 1546, transcribed in Reznik's *Le Duc Joseph de Naxos*, p. 60, n. 14. The bales of cloth were mentioned in a separate inventory dated July, 1546 from the Viennese archives found in DMSW, box CC, folder 9 of Wolf's papers.

23. Reznik's *Le Duc Joseph de Naxos*, p. 57, n.8; letter dated June 22, 1546; the merchant was Jeronimus Soller of Ausburg.

24. DMSW, box CC, folder 9 of Wolf's papers, transcribing a note from the Margrave of Antwerp dated October 8, 1545.

25. This assumption is based upon an eyewitness account of how Doña Gracia and her party entered Constantinople. It assumes the mode of travel would have been similar and also typical of long-distance travel among the upper classes of the time.

26. Strada's *History of Low Country Wars*, p. 138.

27. The various versions of this "love" story are discussed in Reznik's *Le Duc Joseph de Naxos*, pp. 75-77; also see ASV, Ital VII, 992 (9606), pp. 246b, dispatch from Navagero dated September 21, 1545.

28. ASV, Ital VII, 992 (9606) pp. 240a-b, dispatch from Navagero dated September 5, 1545.

29. Samuel de Medina's responsum 327 discusses the validity of a Catholic marriage.

30. Gairdner and Brodie's *Letters and Papers...*, Vol. XX, Part II, p. 148, letter 334 from Stephen Vaughan to Sir William Paget dated September, 1545.

31. Gairdner and Brodie's *Letters and Papers...*, Vol. XX, Part II, p. 148, letter 334.

32. DMSW, box CC, folder 9 of Wolf's papers; transcription of letters dated September 13, October 2, 8 and 18, November 6 and 27, 1545.

33. Hale's *The Civilization of Europe in the Renaissance*, p. 177

34. Reznik's *Le Duc Joseph de Naxos*, p. 68, n. 5, letter from Marie to Charles dated April 3, 1546.

35. Salomon and Leoni's 1998 article in *JQR*, p. 154, n. 50.

36. Moses di Trani's responsum 80; ASF, notary Batista Saracco, matricola 493, pacco 29, June 4, 1550.

37. Samuel de Medina's responsum 331.

38. Samuel de Medina's responsum 331.

39. ASV, Ital VII, 992 (9606) pp. 246b, dispatch from Navagero dated September 21, 1545.

40. Gómara's *Annals of The Emperor Charles V*, p. 132.

41. Roth's *The Duke of Naxos*, (mentioned throughout); also see Calimani's *The Ghetto of Venice*, p. 95.

42. ASFM, Mediceo del Principato, 1170a, Insert III, ff. 171r-172v, letter from Giorgio Dati in Antwerp to Pier Francesco Riccio in Florence dated October 1545.

43. ASF, notary Batista Saracco, matricola 493, pacco 29, doc. dated June 4, 1550 and ASV, notary Lioncini, 7818, July 18, 1552, pp. 178-195; see also Zorattini's *Processi del S. Uffizio...*, Vol. I, p. 342-343, testimony of Brianda de Luna.

44. ASV, notary Leoncini, busta 7818 (1548-1556), p. 177.

45. Moses di Trani's responsum 80.

46. Simonsohn's *The Jews in the Duchy of Milan*, Vol. II, docs. 2528, 2529, 2530, 2770.

47. Leal's *Os Actos e Relações Politicas e Diplomaticas de Portugal*, Vol. VI, p. 14, dispatch from Balthasar de Faria, Portuguese ambassador in Rome to King Joâo III of Portugal dated February 16, 1546.

48. The date has been determined by placing correspondence concerning confiscation of their assets, beginning in September, alongside the probable date of the loan coming due, which would have been in July or early August.

49. Moses di Trani's responsum 80.

50. Moses di Trani's responsum 80.

51. Reznik's *Le Duc Joseph de Naxos*, p. 53, n. 2, letter from Marie to Charles dated April 6, 1546.

52. DMSW, box CC, folder 6 of Wolf's papers, transcribing a proclamation by Marie dated November 27, 1545.

53. Gairdner and Brodie's *Letters and Papers...*, Vol. XX, Part II, p. 148, letter 334, dated September, 1545.

54. ASFM, Mediceo del Principato, 1170a, Insert III, ff. 171r-172v, document dated October 1545 from Giorgio Dati in Antwerp to Pier Francesco Riccio in Florence.

55. DMSW, box CC, folder 9 of Wolf's papers, transcribing a letter from Queen Marie to the duke of Florence dated September 3, 1545.

56. DMSW, box CC, folder 9 of Wolf's papers, transcribing a letter dated September 13.

57. DMSW, box CC, folder 9 of Wolf's papers, letter from Charles to Major de Léon Cobos dated October 2, 1545; the Spanish merchant was Jean Jacomo Spinola.

58. DMSW, box CC, folder 9 of Wolf's papers, official order dated October 8, 1545; the shipping agent was Hieronymo Diodati.

59. DMSW, box CC, folder 9 of Wolf's papers, announcement from Marie to her commissioners dated October 18, 1545.

60. DMSW, box CC, folder 9 of Wolf's papers, letter from Marie to Sandelin dated November 10, 1545; the man was Lope de Probenza.

61. DMSW, box CC, folder 9 of Wolf's papers, letter from Marie to the Marquis of Villa Franca, Viceroy of Naples, dated November 10, 1545.

62. DMSW, box CC, folder 6 of Wolf's papers, announcement dated November 27 concerning Mendes' belongings.

63. DMSW, box CC, folder 9 of Wolf's papers, declaration dated November 27, 1545, concerning Mendes' belongings.

64. DMSW, box CC, folder 6 of Wolf's papers, announcement dated November 27, 1545.

65. Details of this meeting can be found in a footnote to Reznik's *Le Duc Joseph de Naxos*, p. 53, n. 2, transcribing a letter from Marie to Charles dated April 6, 1546 (incorrectly written 1545). Another copy can be found in DMSW, box CC, folder 9 of Wolf's papers.

66. Reznik's *Le Duc Joseph de Naxos*, p. 53, n. 2, letter from Marie to Charles dated April 6, 1546.

67. The document of April 6, 1546 (see above) actually says (Flemish) "pounds"; we have made the exchange.

68. Reznik's *Le Duc Joseph de Naxos*, p. 53, n. 2, letter from Marie to Charles dated April 6, 1546.

69. Reznik's *Le Duc Joseph de Naxos*, p. 60, n.11, letter from Marie to Charles dated July 16, 1546.

70. DMSW, box CC, folder 6 of Wolf's papers, declaration of Marie dated September 29, 1546, with notes appended by Don Joseph.

71. Wegg's *Antwerp 1477-1559*, p. 259; also see Gómara's *Annals of the Emperor Charles V*, pp. 123-124.

72. Reznik's *Le Duc Joseph de Naxos*, p. 60, n. 14; letter from Marie to Charles dated July 16, 1546.

73. Gómara's *Annals of the Emperor Charles V*, pp. 123-124.

74. Reznik's *Le Duc Joseph de Naxos*, p. 60, n.14, letter from Marie to Charles dated July 16, 1546.

75. Reznik's *Le Duc Joseph de Naxos* p. 63, n. 16, letter from Marie to Charles dated August 15, 1546.

76. DMSW, box CC, folder 9 of Wolf's papers, transcribing an inventory of Mendes belongings dated July, 1546.

77. Resnik's *Le Duc Joseph de Naxos*, p. 64, n. 1, letter from Marie to Charles dated

September 14, 1546.

78. DMSW, box CC, folders 6 and 9 of Wolf's papers, transcribing a declaration by Juan Micas (Don Joseph) dated September 29, 1546.

79. Reznik's *Le Duc Joseph de Naxos*, p. 68, n. 5, letter from Marie to Charles dated April 3, 1546.

80. DMSW, box CC, folders 1 and 9, letter from Charles to Marie dated June 20, 1547.

81. In this instance it is unclear how to translate these "pounds" into ducats, since the national origin of these particular pounds is not given.

82. Resnik's *Le Duc Joseph de Naxos*, p. 70-72, n. 6, letter from Marie to Charles dated July, 1547.

83. ASV, notary Leoncini, busta 7818 (1548-1556) 189r, agreement between the sisters dated July, 1552, mentioning the sale of the Antwerp house with Antonius van Malle, Antwerp notary, recording the sale. Numerous documents from Ferrara further confirm that the family sold the house.

CHAPTER 9

1. For a more complete account of Venice, its appearance and history, see Patricia Fortini Longworth's *The Rise and Fall of Venice*, chapter XI, plus general commentary in Philip Brown's *Art and Life in Renaissance Venice*, and George Bull's *Venice: the most Triumphant City*.

2. Longworth's *The Rise and Fall of Venice*, chapter XI plus general observations in Brown's *Art and Life in Renaissance Venice*, and Bull's *Venice: the most Triumphant City*.

3. Cesare Vecellio's *Habiti antichi er moderni di tutto il mondo*, general comments.

4. André Laguna's *Viaje de Turquia*, in the anthology, *Autografias y Memorias*, Ed. Serrano y Sanz, p. 131.

5. Zorattini's *Processi del S. Uffizio...*, Vol. I, p. 346, testimony of Brianda de Luna.

6. Calimani's *The Ghetto of Venice*, p. 33.

7. Longworth's *The Rise and Fall of Venice*, early chapters.

8. Segre's chapter "Sephardic Refugees in Ferrara...," p. 178.

9. Calimani's *The Ghetto of Venice*, p. 2.

10. Pullan's article "A Ship with Two Rudders: Righetto Marrano and the Inquisition in Venice," p. 39.

11. Calimani's *The Ghetto of Venice*, chapters 1-2.

12. Calimani's *The Ghetto of Venice*, pp. 31-34.

13. Calimani's *The Ghetto of Venice*, p. 129.

14. Calimani's *The Ghetto of Venice*, p. 135.

15. Katz's *The Jews in the History of England*, p. 26.

16. Zorattini's *Processi del S. Uffizio...*, Vol. 5, trial of Gaspare Ribeiro, 1579.

17. Calimani's *The Ghetto of Venice*, p. 80-82.

18. Pullan's article "Righetto Marrano and the Inquisition in Venice," pp. 37-38.

19. Muzzarelli's chapter "Beatrice de Luna, Vedova Mendes...," in Niccoli's *Rinascimento al Femminile*, pp. 97-100.

20. Albert de Vidas' bulletin *Erensia Sefardi*, Vol. 6, No. 1, winter, 1998, p. 2.

21. Pullan's *The Jews of Europe and the Inquisition in Venice*, p. 176; also see Pullan's article "A Ship with Two Rudders: Righetto Marrano and the Inquisition in Venice," p. 57.

22. Calimani's *The Ghetto of Venice*, chapter 5; also see Zorattini's article "Anrriquez Nunez alias Abraham alias Righetto," p. 295.

23. Zorattini's *Processi del S. Uffizio...*, Vol. I, p. 255, June 27, 1555, testimony of Tristan da Costa. A separate residence for each sister is also mentioned in the Leoncini accords, see ASV, notary Leoncini, busta 7818 (1548-1556), 189r., section of sisters' accords dated July 18, 1552.

24. Gunebaum-Ballin's *Joseph Naci, duc de Naxos*, p. 47, n.1; also see Salomon and Leoni's 1998 article in *JQR*, p. 155 and Kellenbenz's article "I Mendes, I Rodrigues...," p. 147.

25. Zorattini's *Processi del S. Uffizio...*, Vol. I, p. 254, testimony of Tristan da Costa.

26. Giuseppe Cristinelli's *Cannaregio: Un Sestiere di Venezia*, p. 108.

27. ASV, notary Leoncini, busta 7818 (1548-1556) 189r. ASV, section of sisters' accords dated July 18, 1552.

28. Conflict between the version supplied by da Costa's testimony in Zorattini's *Processi del S. Uffizio...*, Vol. I, pp. 254-255, and the one mentioned in the Leoncini accords of July-August, 1552.

29. Grunebaum-Ballin's *Joseph Naci, duc de Naxos*, p. 47, n.; the ambassador was Juan de Mendoza.

30. Leal's *Corpo Diplomatico Portuguez: Os Actos e Relações Politicas e Diplomaticas*, Vol VI, p. 14, letter of Balthazar de Faria to the king in Portugal dated February 16, 1546.

31. Samuel de Medina's responsum 327.

32. Pullan's *The Jews of Europe and the Inquisition in Venice*, p. 178.

33. Zorattini's *Processi del S. Uffizio...*, Vol. I, p. 256, testimony of Licentato Costa. Also see Pullan's *The Jews of Europe and the Inquisition of Venice, 1550–1670*, p. 178, n. 48.

34. Zorattini's *Processi del S. Uffizio...*, Vol. I, p. 232, testimony of Oduardo (Duarte) Gomez.

35. Arbel's article "Venice and the Jewish Merchants of Istanbul...," p. 51.

36. Zorattini's *Processi del S. Uffizio...*, Vol. I, pp. 259-261, testimony of Licentato Costa on July 15, 1555, for one particular example.

37. ASV, notary Leoncini, 7818, p. 176 (back) ASV, section of sisters' accords dated Tuesday, July 18, 1552. The names mentioned that connote Old Christian ancestry include Carolus de Antenoriis; Averardo and Petro de Salviatis; Antonio, Ludovico and Vincenzo Bonvisi, Bartholomeo de Panciatis and Joannes Baptista de Carnesecchis; all of Florence, London or Lyons.

38. ASV, notary Leoncini, 7818, p. 176 (back) ASV - accords between the sisters dated Tuesday, July 18, 1552.

39. Baron's *A Social and Religious History of the Jews*, Vol. XVIII, p. 82; also see Joshua

Soncino's responsum 20; the unfortunate outcome of this particular deal is covered in Chapter 16.

40. ASF, notary Conti, matricola 584, pacco 9s: commercial contract dated October, 1561, personally signed by Samuel Nasi. The merchants in question were Abraham Abentaben, Haim Cohen and Yom Tob Mocco. The author is grateful to James Boyajian for this difficult translation.

41. ASF, notary Conti, matricola 584, pacco 9s, contract dated October, 1561.

42. Zorattini's *Processi del S. Uffizio...*, Vol. I, p. 232, testimony of Odoardo (Duarte) Gomez.

43. Kellenbenz's article "I Mendes, I Rodrigues...," p. 148.

44. Simonsohn's *The Jews in the Duchy of Milan*, Vol. II, docs. 2528, 2529, 2530, 2770.

45. See Abraham David's article "New Jewish Sources on the History of the Members of the Nasi-Mendes Family in Italy and Constantinople," in the Italian (Jewish history) journal *Henoch*, Vol. XX, October 1998, pp. 179-188.

46. Shakespeare's *The Merchant of Venice*, Act I, Scene III.

47. Arbel's article "Venice and the Jewish Merchants of Istanbul...," pp. 40-45.

48. Kellenbenz's article "I Mendes, I Rodrigues...," p. 147.

49. The opinion of Michaela Zanon, director of the Venetian Ghetto Museum, in an interview with the author on May 28, 1998.

50. Zorattini's *Processi del S. Uffizio...*, Vol. I, p. 255, testimony of Tristan da Costa.

51. Calimani's *The Ghetto of Venice*, p. 34.

52. De Witte's *La Correspondance des Premiers Nonces..., 1532-1553*, pp. 588-589, letter 251; also see Simonsohn's *The Apostolic See...*, p. 2622, doc. 2573.

53. De Witte's *La Correspondance des Premiers Nonces...*, pp. 588-589, letter 251.

54. Babinger's 1923 edition of Dernschwam's *Tagebuch einer Reise...*, p. 110.

55. Rose's *Alonso Nuñez de Reinoso: the Lament of a Sixteenth-Century Exile*, p. 77 (excerpt of a poem).

56. Segre's chapter, "Sephardic Refugees in Ferrara...," p. 167; also see Gitlitz' "Secrecy and Deceit...," p. 103-115. The Papal Nuncio was Giovanni Ricci and Doña Gracia's envoy was Christopher Manuel.

CHAPTER 10

1. Segre's chapter "Sephardic Refugees in Ferrara...," p. 166.

2. Zorattini's *Processi del S. Uffizio...*, Vol. I, p. 341, testimony of Brianda de Luna.

3. Grunebaum-Ballin's *Joseph Naci, duc de Naxos*, p. 47.

4. ASF, notary Saracco, matricola 493, pacco 9, document dated 1550 (date illegible); Brianda defense of her need to recover her portion of Diogo's estate.

5. All contemporary sources found by this author agree that Brianda made the allegations concerning the Judaizing of her sister. This has been interpreted by historians as evidence that she was the one who first approached the court. However, one of the documents ("Information on the Mendes to the Bailo in Constantinopoli" ASV, Deliberazioni Secreta- Senato Filze 24, November 21, 1551) specifically says that Doña

Gracia was the first "to seek recourse from our judges." The historian Grunebaum-Ballin makes the same assumption. So it cannot be assumed that just because Brianda made the damaging allegation that she was necessarily the one who first approached the court for a resolution.

6. ASF, notary Saracco, matricola 493, pacco 29, document dated June 4, 1550, 1v.

7. Moses di Trani's responsum 80; Samuel de Medina's responsum 331; Joshua Soncino's responsum 12. Interestingly, there is no disagreement between the Jewish and Christian accounts of what happened between the two sisters in Venice, making it less likely that anyone was exaggerating.

8. This accusation was made many times by Cecil Roth, among others.

9. Calimani's *The Ghetto of Venice*, p. 58.

10. Charrière's *Négociations de La France dans le Levant*, Vol. II, pp. 101-102, n. 1, letters of July-August, 1549.

11. Rose's *Alonso Nuñez de Reinoso...*, pp. 76-77. Further insights were gained from an interview with Professor Rose in Cambridge, Mass., on October 17, 1998. She studied *converso* family behavior in connection with the Inquisition for her doctoral thesis on Alonso Nuñez de Reinoso.

12. Grunebaum-Ballin's *Joseph Naci, duc de Naxos*, p. 47; also see Samuel de Medina's responsum 331.

13. ASF, notary Saracco, matricola 493, pacco 29, document dated June 4, 1550, 1v.

14. Charrière's *Négociations de La France...*, Vol. II, pp. 101-102, n. 1, letters of July-August, 1549.

15. Zorattini's *Processi del S. Uffizio...*, Vol. I, p. 341, testimony of Brianda de Luna.

16. Zorattini's *Processi del S. Uffizio...*, Vol. I, p. 342, testimony of Brianda de Luna; also see Salomon and Leoni's 1998 article in *JQR*, p. 156.

17. Salomon and Leoni's 1998 article in *JQR*, p. 156, n. 57.

18. Charrière's *Négociations de La France...*, Vol. II, pp. 101-102, n. 1, letters of July-August, 1549.

19. Charrière's *Négociations de La France...*, Vol II, pp. 101-102, n. 1, letters of July-August, 1549

20. Charrière's *Négociations de La France...*, Vol II, pp. 101-102, letters of July-August, 1549; also see Franco Gaeta's *Nunziature di Venezia*, Vol.5, pp. 316-318, letter 198 dated November 21, 1551. The Papal Nuncio was Ludovico Beccadelli and the French ambassador was M. de Morvilliers.

21. Moses Hamon was known as an orthodox Jew, which made it highly unlikely that he would have promised his son to a girl who had spent her entire life as a Catholic. Renata Segre is one historian who shows the depth of feeling in this regard in her chapter "Sephardic Refugees in Ferrara..."

22. Heyd's chapter "Moses Hamon, chief Jewish physician to Sultan Suleyman the Magnificient," in the journal *Oriens*, Vol.16, p. 159.

23. Heyd's chapter "Moses Hamon, chief Jewish physician...," p. 155.

24. Heyd's chapter "Moses Hamon, chief Jewish physician...," p. 161.

25. ASV, Senato, Deliberazioni Secreta, 1552-1552, Registro. 68, p. 2 (front) document dated March 12, 1552 and p. 4 (back), doc. dated March 16, 1552, both of

which concern the flow of information between Venice and the Turks.

26. ASF, notary Saracco, matricola 493, pacco 29, doc. dated June 4, 1550, 1v; also see Segre's chapter "Sephardic Refugees in Ferrara...," p. 169.

27. ASF, notary Saracco, matricola 493, pacco 29, doc. dated June 4, 1550, 1v.

28. Salomon and Leoni's 1998 article in *JQR*, p. 156, n. 57. The aide was Christopher Manuel.

29. ASF, notary Saracco, matricola 493, pacco 29, doc. dated June 4, 1550, 1v, 2r, 4r. 6r.

30. ASF, notary Conti, matricola 584, pacco 5, doc. dated April 20, 1551.

31. Moses di Trini, responsum 80.

32. Moses di Trini, responsum 80.

33. Moses di Trini, responsum 80.

34. Charrière's *Négociations de La France...*, pp. 101-102, n. 1, letters of July-August, 1549.

35. ASF, notary Saracco, matricola 493, pacco 29, doc. dated June 4, 1550, 1v and 2r.

36. Charrière's *Négociations de La France...*, pp. 101-102, n. 1, letters of July-August, 1549; the emissary was probably Christopher Manuel.

37. Samuel de Medina, responsum 332.

38. ASV, Senato, Deliberazioni Secreta, Registro 67; 172v, memorandum of November 17, 1551.

39. Charrière's *Négociations de La France...*, Vol. II, pp. 101-102, n. 1, letters of July-August, 1549; the French ambassador at this time was M. de Morvilliers.

40. Segre's chapter "Sephardic Refugees in Ferrara...," p. 175.

41. ASF, notary Saracco, matricola 493, pacco 29, agreement dated June 4, 1550, 7v.

42. Description taken from a mid-century engarving of the duke in the Biblioteca Estense and Universitaria, Modena, Italy.

43. This is speculation, but it makes sense since the invitation was made by her husband and involved so many of the Jews that she must have personally known from her youth in Aragon.

44. See entries for Ferrara and the Este family in the *Encyclopedia Britannica* and Gundersheimer's *Ferrara: the Style of a Renaissance Despotism*.

45. *Encyclopedia Judaica*, Vol. 6, p. 1231.

46. For general background on the Jews of Ferrara see *Encyclopedia Judaica*, Vol. 6, pp. 1231-1234; multiple mentions in Roth's *The Jews in the Renaissance*, and Gundersheimer's *Ferrara: the Style of a Renaissance Despotism*. For information on the synagogues see Moses Shulvass' *The Jews in the World of the Renaissance*, p. 192, n. 2.

47. Carla di Francesco and Marco Borella's *Ferrara: the Estense City*, pp. 100, 159

48. ASF, notary Bonsignori, matricola 569, busta 3, doc. dated December 10, 1548; also see Segre's chapter "Sephardic Refugees in Ferrara...," p. 169, n. 33.

49. The documents use the term scudi. Because they also use scudi interchangeably with ducats, we have continued to use the more universal 16th century monetary term.

50. ASF, notary Taurino, pacco 8, doc. dated January 11, 1549, accompanying the

rental document.

51. Salomon and Leoni's 1998 article in *JQR*, p. 195, doc. 13; also see ASF, notary Taurino, matricola 535, pacco 8, doc. dated January 11, 1549; the lease was signed by Christopher Manuel on Doña Gracia's behalf.

52. ASF, notary Taurino, matricola 565, pacco 8, document dated January 11, 1549; also see Segre's chapter "Sephardic Refugees in Ferrara...," p. 166.

53. Segre's chapter "Sephardic Refugees in Ferrara...," p. 181. Caution: we could not locate the document in the Ferrara archives associated with this list under the citation given by Segre and presume an error either in the notary name or date.

54. ASF, notary Conti, matricola 584, pacco 5, document dated April 20, 1551.

55. Zorattini's *Processi del S. Uffizio...*, Vol. I, p. 230, testimony of Duarte Gomez; also see DMSW, box CC, folder 9 of Wolf's papers for testimony during the interrogations of 1544, by a man named Jores Pieterssen van Gootens, suggesting Gomez and Fernandes were brothers.

56. Laguna's eyewitness accounts in *Viaje de Turquia*, within Serrano's anthology *Autografias y Memorias*, p. 131, describe them as "Spanish" which would imply *converso*.

57. Segre's chapter "Sephardic Refugees in Ferrara...," p. 182.

58. ASF, notary Conti, matricola 584, pacco 4, doc. dated December 1, 1549.

59. Salomon and Leoni's article 1998 in *JQR*, pp. 174-175, n. 124 and the genealogical table on pp. 210-211 of the same article. For confirmation that Giomar was indeed deceased see ASF, notary Taurino, matricola 535, pacco 8.

60. Salomon and Leoni's article 1998 in *JQR*, p. 156, n. 58.

61. ASV, notary Saracco, matricola 493, pacco 29, 1549, docs. A and B dated January 10, 1549

62. ASV, notary Saracco, matricola 493, pacco 29, 1549, docs. A and B dated January 10, 1549

63. Segre's chapter "Sephardic Refugees in Ferrara...," p. 170, n. 35,36.

64. ASV, notary Saracco, matricola 493, pacco 29, undated notes accompanying doc. dated January 10, 1549.

65. Zorattini's *Processi del S. Uffizio...*, Vol. I, p. 342, testimony of Brianda de Luna.

66. ASM, Cancelleria Ducale, Patricolari, busta 496 (sub folder Fenicio), letter from Fenicio to Brianda dated June 20, 1550.

67. Salomon and Leoni's 1998 article in *JQR*, p. 158, n. 63.

68. ASM, Cancelleria Ducale, Patricolari, busta 885 (sub folder titled "Mendez"), undated draft of a ducal safe conduct with language indicating that it was prepared at this particular moment as it refers to a recent decision of the Venetian court and its validity in Ferrara.

69. Salomon and Leoni's 1998 article in *JQR*, p. 157, n. 61.

70. Usque's *Consolation...*, pp. 213-214.

71. Salomon and Leoni's 1998 article in *JQR*, p. 158.

72. ASM, Cancelleria Ducale, Carteggio degli ufficiali camerali, busta 2, doc. dated September 14, 1549 from the "Ufficiale Camerale" to the duke.

73. Usque's *Consolation...*," pp. 213-214.

74. Segre's chapter "Sephardic Refugees in Ferrara...," p. 171.

75. Usque's *Consolation...*," p. 214.

76. Rose's *Alonso Nuñez de Reinoso...*, p. 90.

77. Segre's chapter "Sephardic Refugees in Ferrara...," pp. 170-171.

78. Salomon and Leoni's 1998 article in *JQR*, p. 158, n. 62.

79. Segre's chapter "Sephardic Refugees in Ferrara...," p. 171, n. 42. Brianda's obvious attachment to this man was so great in later testimony before the Venetian courts (see Zorattini's *Processi...*, Vol. I, p. 344) that one wonders if he was also a lover.

80. Segre's chapter "Sephardic Refugees in Ferrara...," p. 171, n. 40.

81. ASM, Cancelleria Ducale, Carteggio degli ufficiali camerali, busta 2, doc. dated December 1, 1549, from the "Ufficiale Camerale" to the duke.

82. ASM, Cancelleria Ducale, Patricolari, busta 747 (sub folder titled "de Luna"), unsigned documented dated December 2, 1550.

83. ASM, Cancelleria Ducale, Patricolari, busta 747 (sub folder titled "de Luna"), undated document from Brianda to Duke Ercole.

84. See Chapter 11 for the works they were developing together.

85. ASF, notary Conti, matricola 584, busta 4, doc. dated September 22, 1549; also see Salomon and Leoni's 1998 article in *JQR*, p. 157, n. 61 and Segre's chapter "Sephardic Refugees in Ferrara...," p. 168.

86. ASF, notary Saracco, matricola 493, pacco 29, end of doc. dated 1550 (month/day illegible).

87. Salomon and Leoni's 1998 article in *JQR*, pp. 154-155, n. 50.

88. Segre's chapter "Sephardic Refugees in Ferrara...," p. 171, n. 40.

89. Salomon and Leoni's 1998 article in *JQR*, pp. 156-157.

90. ASV, notary Leoncini, busta 7818 (1548-1556), doc. dated July 20, 1552, p. 189 front/back, notes a sales contract dated April 12, 1549.

91. Salomon and Leoni's 1998 article in *JQR*, pp. 156-7.

92. Salomon and Leoni's 1998 article in *JQR*, pp. 156-7

93. Calimani's *The Ghetto of Venice*, pp. 47-48

94. Strada's *History of the Low Country Wars*, pp. 138-139 and Grunebaum-Ballin's *Joseph Naci, duc de Naxos*, p. 49.

95. Strada's *History of the Low Country Wars*, pp. 138-139. The island incident is also mentioned in Reznik's *Le Duc Joseph de Naxos*, pp. 78, 79, 85; also see Rose's *Alonso Nuñez de Reinoso...*, pp. 55-56.

96. ASF, notary Conti, matricola 584, pacco 4; doc. dated December 11, 1550.

97. ASF, notary Conti, matricola 584, pacco 4; doc. dated October 22, 1549.

98. ASF, notary Conti, matricola 584, pacco 4; two docs. dated March 5, 1550. Currency given in scudi. But as the term *ducat* and *scudi* are used interchangeably, we have continued to use ducats throughout. However, it is confusing. On one of the documents (p. 5), ducats are translated as being worth 2.6 scudi each.

99. ASF, notary Conti, matricola 584, pacco 4, doc. dated March 5, 1550, p. 6.

100. ASF, notary Conti, matricola 584, pacco 4, doc. dated March 5, 1550, p. 3.

101. ASF, notary Conti, matricola 584, pacco 4, doc. dated March 5, 1550, pp. 5-6.

102. ASM, Cancelleria Ducale, Particolari, busta 747 (sub folder titled "de Luna") undated letter from Brianda to the duke apparently written at the time of her arrival.

103. ASF, notary Saracco, matricola 493, pacco 29, doc. dated 1550 (month/day illegible).

104. ASM, Cancelleria Ducale, Particolari, busta 747 (sub folder titled "de Luna"), personal letter from Brianda to the duke dated January 15, 1550.

105. ASM, Cancelleria Ducale, Particolari, busta 747 (sub folder titled "de Luna"), undated doc. concerning financial favors granted by Ferandes, Botteglio and Dias.

106. ASM, Cancelleria Ducale, Particolari, busta 747 (sub folder titled "de Luna"), personal letter from Brianda to the duke dated January 15, 1550.

107. ASM, Cancelleria Ducale, Particolari, busta 747 (sub folder titled "de Luna"), undated statement from Brianda to the duke listing what she personally hopes to get out of an amended agreement.

108. ASF, notary Saracco, matricola 493, pacco 29, end of doc. dated 1550 (month/day illegible).

109. Salomon and Leoni's 1998 article in *JQR*, p. 158, n. 63 and p. 196, doc. 14.

110. ASF, notary Saracco, matricola 493, pacco 29, doc. dated January 18, 1557.

111. ASF, notary Conti, matricola 584, pacco 4, doc. dated March 19, 1550.

112. ASF, notary Saracco, matricola 493, pacco 29, doc. dated June 4, 1550, 1r.

113. The Ferrara archives are housed today in a deteriorating palace of vaulted ceilings and faded frescoes that belonged to Guido Borghi, an attorney reputedly of Jewish descent. This was before the persecutions of World War II turned it into a headquarters for fascist torture and violence.

114. Samuel de Medina's responsum 329.

115. ASF, notary Conti, matricola 584, pacco 4, 19-page doc. dated December 9-11, 1550; the buyer were Franciscus Werner, Petrus van der Wallen and Johannes Dubois.

116. ASF, notary Conti, matricola 584, pacco 4, 19-page doc. dated December 9-11, 1550

117. Marco Bruno dalla Anguille's *Consiliorum sive Responsorum illustris ac praestantissimi iureconsulti*, Vol. I, edited by Thomas Cananus, Zenari, Venice, 1583, Vol. I, pp. 360-362; also see ASV, notary Leoncini, busta 7818 (1548-1556), p. 189 (back).

118. Marco Bruno dalla Anguille's *Consiliorum sive Responsorum illustris ac praestantissimi iureconsulti*, Vol. I, pp. 360-362.

119. ASF, notary Conti, matricola 584, pacco 4, 19-page doc. dated December 9-11, 1550, pp. 5-6.

120. ASF, notary Saracco, matricola 493, pacco 29, doc. dated June 4, 1550, 3r.

121. ASF, notary Saracco, matricola 493, pacco 29, doc. dated June 4, 1550, 6r.

122. ASF, notary Saracco, matricola 493, pacco 29, doc. dated June 4, 1550, 7r-8r.

123. ASF, notary Saracco, matricola 493, pacco 29, doc. dated June 4, 1550, 7v.

124. ASF, notary Saracco, matricola 493, pacco 29, doc. dated June 4, 1550, p. 8v.

125. ASF, notary Saracco, matricola 493, pacco 29, doc. dated June 4, 1550, 7v.

126. ASF, notary Saracco, matricola 493, pacco 29, doc. dated June 4, 1550, 17r.

127. Salomon and Leoni's 1998 article in *JQR*, p. 158 and n. 64.

128. Zorattini's *Processi del S. Uffizio...*, p. 343, Vol. I, testimony of Brianda de Luna.

129. Salomon and Leoni's 1998 article in *JQR*, p. 158 and n. 65.

130. ASM, Cancelleria Ducale, Carteggio di consiglieri, segretari e cancellieri, busta 10b, doc. dated May 26, 1551.

131. Segre's chapter "Sephardic Refugees in Ferrara...," p. 172, n. 45; also see ASM, Cancelleria Ducale, Patricolari, busta 747 (sub folder titled "de Luna").

132. ASF, notary Conti, matricola 584, pacco 5, doc. dated April 20, 1551, p. 3

133. Roth's *The Duke of Naxos*, p. 27-28; also see Grunebaum-Ballin's *Joseph Naci, duc de Naxos*, p. 107, n. 3, quoting the figure mentioned by Sultan Selim as being still outstanding a decade later.

134. ASM, Cancelleria Ducale, Patricolari, busta 747 (sub folder titled "de Luna").

135. ASF, notary Conti, matricola 584, pacco 5, doc. dated April 20, 1551, p. 3.

136. Segre's chapter "Sephardic Refugees in Ferrara...," p. 175, n. 45.

137. Grunebaum-Ballin's *Joseph Naci, duc de Naxos*, pp. 99-103.

138. Roth's *The Duke of Naxos*, pp. 27, 28, 62, 63.

CHAPTER 11

1. Usque's *Consolation for the Tribulations of Israel*, p. 37.

2. Rose's *Alonso Nuñez de Reinoso...*, pp. 43, 50, 56, 163.

3. Roth's article "The Marrano Press at Ferrara, 1552-1555," in *Modern Language Review*, Vol. 38, 1943, pp. 307-317.

4. Rose's *Alonso Nuñez de Reinoso...*, pp. 53, 56.

5. Roth's article "Salusque Lusitano," in *JQR*, Vol. 34 (1943-44) pp. 67-69. Some historians have argued that Gomez and Salomon Usque, the son of the printer-poet, Abraham Usque, were actually one and the same person, but Roth makes a strong case refuting that theory. For Gomez's other achievements see Zorattini's *Processi del S. Uffizio...*, Vol. I, p. 230, testimony of Oduardo (Duarte) Gomez.

6. Susan Groag Bell's chapter "Medieval Women Book Owners," pp. 158, 165, 179 in *Women and Power in the Middle Ages* (Ed. Erler and Kowaleski).

7. Roth's *Jews in the Renaissance*, p. 52; see also Baskin's *Jewish Women in Historical Perspective*, p. 101.

8. Baskin's *Jewish Women in Historical Perspective*, p. 107.

9. Moshe Lazar's *The Ladino Bible of Ferrara (1553): A Critical Edition*, p. 76.

10. Lazar's *The Ladino Bible of Ferrara...*, Preface and Introduction.

11. Lazar's *The Ladino Bible of Ferrara...*, Preface and Introduction.

12. Roth's article "The Marrano Press...," p. 317.

13. Roth's article "The Marrano Press...," p. 314.

14. Rose's *Alonso Nuñez de Reinoso...*, p. 50, n. 63.

15. Rose's *Alonso Nuñez de Reinoso...*, pp. 50, 55-57.

16. Lando's *"Due Panegirici nuovamente composti...,"* Segno del Posso, Venice, 1552, pp. 37-38; special thanks to my research assistant, Emily Zaiden, for locating a copy

in Venice.

17. Rose's *Alonso Nuñez de Reinoso...*, p. 57.

18. ASF, notary Conti, matricola 584, pacco 5s, doc. dated April 20, 1551, p. 1.

19. Rose's *Alonso Nuñez de Reinoso...*, p. 49.

20. ASF, notary Conti, matricola 584, pacco 5s, doc. dated April 20, 1551, p. 1.

21. Rose's *Alonso Nuñez de Reinoso...*, pp. 48-49.

22. Rose's *Alonso Nuñez de Reinoso...*, p. 42, n. 50.

23. The fact that Duarte Gomez indeed had a brother, Thomas, who also worked as an agent for Doña Gracia is confirmed in Zorattini's *Processi del S. Uffizio...*, Vol. I, p. 230, testimony of Oduardo (Duarte) Gomez.

24. Rose's *Alonso Nuñez de Reinoso...*, pp. 14, 89, 139, 163.

25. For a more detailed discussion of Bernardim Ribeiro and his novel, see Helder Macedo's article "A Sixteenth Century Portuguese Novel and the Jewish Press in Ferrara," in *European Judaism*, Vol. 33, No.1, London, spring 2000, pp. 53-58.

26. Rose's *Alonso Nuñez de Reinoso...*, p. 50. Bernardim Ribeiro may have been an uncle of a man named Joâo (Giovanni) Ribeiro who shows up in Venice thirty years later as the bridegroom of a cousin of Doña Gracia (see Epilogue). Significantly, Joâo's father, Gaspare, was known to have had a brother and sister living in Ferrara. Bernardim Ribeiro could therefore have been a family member.

27. Roth's article "The Marrano Press...," pp. 307-317.

28. Segre's chapter "Sephardic Refugees in Ferrara...," p. 183.

29. Segre's chapter "Sephardic Refugees in Ferrara...," p. 183.

30. Background provided by Emily Zaiden, my research assistant in Italy, who researched Brasavoli's life while she was in Ferrara and Venice.

31. Antonio Musa Brasavoli's *Medici Ferrariensis - De medicamentis tam simplicibus, quam compositis catharticis, quae uniciuq; humorisunt propria*, Venice, 1552, p. 12.

32. Possibly the earliest historical reference to Jewish mother using chicken broth for medicinal purposes!

33. Brasavoli's *Medici Ferrariensis - De medicamentis...*, p. 12.

34. Antonio Musa Brasavoli's *Medici Ferrariensis - Examen Omnium Trochiscorum Unguentorum, Ceratorum, Emplorum, Cataplasmatumque....*Venice, 1551. pp. 42-44.

35. Friedenwald's *The Jews and Medicine: Essays*, Vol. I, pp. 332-390; the Portugese ambassador was Alfonso de Lencastre.

36. Herculano's *History of the Origin...*, pp. 540-561.

37. Friedenwald's *The Jews and Medicine: Essays*, Vol. I, p. 339.

38. Lusitanus' *Discorides II*, Enarr. 39, p. 269.

39. Brooks' article on the history of the Jews of Suriname in *Reform Judaism Magazine*, spring, 1999.

40. For a fuller treatment of the history of Jewish involvement in the medical professions see Michael Nevins' *The Jewish Doctor: a Narrative History*.

41. Confirmed by Renata Segre, the Italian historian who has studied this period, in an interview with this author in Venice on October 22, 1997.

42. Roth's *The Jews in the Renaissance*, p. 55.

43. Roth's *The Duke of Naxos*, p. 27.

44. Rose's *Alonso Nuñez de Reinoso...*, p. 59.

45. Muzzarelli's chapter "Beatrice de Luna, Vedova Mendes...," in Niccoli's *"Rinascimento al Femminile,"* p. 99.

46. Usque's *Consolation...*, pp. 16, 275-284.

47. Roth's *The Jews in the Renaissance*, pp. 54-55.

48. Segre's chapter "Sephardic Refugees in Ferrara...," pp. 184-185.

49. Segre's chapter "Sephardic Refugees in Ferrara...," p. 177; also see ASFM, Mediceo del Principato, 1170a, Insert III, ff. 171r-172v, doc. dated October 1545 from Giorgio Dati in Antwerp to Pier Francesco Riccio in Florence.

50. Segre's chapter "Sephardic Refugees in Ferrara...," p. 178. Also see Bernardini's *The Jews and the Expansion...*, p. 271.

51. Segre's chapter "Sephardic Refugees in Ferrara...," p. 175.

52. Conclusions developed following the author's October 1997 interview with the Italian historian, Renata Segre.

53. Segre's chapter "Sephardic Refugees in Ferrara...," p. 182.

54. ASV, notary Conti (incorrectly filed under Codegori, matricola 582, pacco 8); doc. dated August 18, 1557, and notary Conti, matricola 584; pacco 9s, doc. dated September 11, 1562, among others.

55. Muzzarelli's chapter "Beatrice de Luna, Vedova Mendes...," p. 95.

56. Simonsohn's *"The Apostolic See and the Jews,"* Vol. 6, p. 2771, doc. 2981.

57. Confirmed by Renate Segre in an interview with the author in October, 1997.

58. Zorattini's *Processi del S. Uffizio...*, Vol. I, p. 231.

59. Roth's *The Duke of Naxos*, p. 28.

CHAPTER 12

1. Roth's *The Jews of Italy* provides a fuller account of this period.

2. Simonsohn's *The Apostolic See and the Jews*, Vol. 6, p. 2771, doc. 2981 dated March 17, 1551.

3. Simonsohn's *The Apostolic See and the Jews*, Vol. 6, p. 2771, doc. 2981 dated March 17, 1551.

4. ASV, Senato, Deliberazioni Secreta, Filze 24 (1551), letter dated November 20 1551.

5. ASV, Senato, Deliberazioni Secreta, Filze 24 (1551), letter dated November 20 1551.

6. ASV, Senato, Deliberazioni Secreta (1552-1553) Registro 68, p. 5, memo dated March 16, 1552.

7. Gaeta's *Nunziature di Venezia*, Vol. 5, pp. 313-316, letter 197, dated November 14, 1551.

8. Segre's chapter "Sephardic Refugees in Ferrara...," p. 171, n. 34.

9. ASF, notary Conti, matricola 584, pacco 5s, doc. dated November 27, 1551.

10. ASF, notary Conti, matricola 584, pacco 5s, doc. dated January 12, 1552.

11. ASF, notary Conti, matricola 584, pacco 5s, docs. dated September 17 and Sep-

tember 21, 1551; the Venetian lawyer was Don Hieronimo Trecio.

12. Gaeta's *Nunziature di Venezia*, Vol. 5, pp. 316-318, letter 198 dated November 21, 1551.

13. ASV, Senato, Deliberazioni Secreta, Filze 24 (1551), letters dated November 17 and 20, 1551.

14. ASV, Senato, Deliberazioni Secreta, Filze 24 (1551), docs. dated November 13 and 17, 1551.

15. ASV, Senato, Deliberazioni Secreta, Filze 24 (1551), letter dated November 17, 1551.

16. Gaeta's *Nunziature di Venezia*, Vol. 5, pp. 316-318, letter 198 dated November 21, 1551.

17. ASV, Senato, Deliberazioni Secreta, Filze 24 (1551), doc. dated November 21, 1551.

18. ASV, Senato, Deliberazioni Secreta, Filze 24 (1551), doc. dated November 17, 1551.

19. ASV, notary Leoncini, busta 7818, p. 180, doc. dated July 19, 1552.

20. Gaeta's *Nunziature di Venezia*, Vol. 5, p. 325, letter of December 5, 1551.

21. Gaeta's *Nunziature di Venezia*, Vol. 5, pp. 313-316, letter 197 dated November 14, 1551.

22. ASV, Senato, Deliberazioni Secreta, Filze 24, doc. dated November 18, 1551.

23. ASV, Senato, Deliberazioni Secreta, Registro 67, p. 174, doc. dated November 21, 1551.

24. ASV, Senato, Deliberazioni Secreta, Registro 67, p. 179, doc. dated December 2, 1551.

25. ASV, Senato, Deliberazioni Secreta, Filze 24 (1551), memo dated November 21, 1551.

26. ASV, Senato, Deliberazioni Secreta, Registro 67, p. 178, doc. dated November 21, 1551.

27. ASV, Senato, Deliberazioni Secreta, Filze 24 (1551), memo dated December 5, 1551.

28. ASV, Senato, Deliberazioni Secreta, Registro 67, p. 179, dispatch to the Venetian *bailo* dated December 2, 1551.

29. ASV, Senato, Deliberazioni Secreta, Registro 67, p. 179, dispatch to the Venetian *bailo* dated December 2, 1551.

30. ASV, Senato, Deliberazioni Secreta, Registro 67, p. 185, doc. dated December 23, 1551.

31. ASF, notary Saracco, matricola 493, pacco 29, request from Brianda to the duke of Ferrara concerning her inheritance, dated 1550 (month/day illegible).

32. ASV, Senato, Deliberazioni Secreta, Filze 24 (1551) deposition dated January 11, 1551 (1552 by the regular calendar since Venice started its new year in March at this time).

33. ASV, Senato, Deliberazioni Secreta, Filze 24 (1551) deposition dated January 11, 1551 (actually 1552, see above).

34. ASV, Senato, Deliberazioni Secreta, Filze 24 (1551) memo dated January 19, 1551

(actually 1552, see above).

35. ASV, Senato, Deliberazioni Secreta, Registro 68 (1552-1553), p. 2, doc. dated March 12, 1552.

36. ASV, Senato, Deliberazioni Secreta, Registro 68 (1552-1553), p. 32, doc. dated June 4, 1552.

37. ASV, notary Leoncini, busta 7818 (1548-1556), p. 192.

38. ASV, Senato, Deliberazioni Secreta, Registro 68 (1552-1553), p. 37, doc. dated June 18, 1552.

39. ASV, notary Leoncini, busta 7818 (1548-1556), 176r to 199r.

40. ASV, Senato, Deliberazioni Secreta, Registro 68 (1552-1553), pg 37, doc. dated June 18, 1552.

41. ASV, notary Leoncini, busta 7818 (1548-1556), pp. 176-197, sisters' accords of July/August 1552.

42. We have once again used ducats rather than scudi or other currencies, assuming, where apparent, that the alternate currencies actually meant ducats.

43. Samuel de Medina's responsum 331.

44. ASV, notary Leoncini, busta 7818 (1548-1556), p. 197; the clergymen were Father Marco de Armano of the church of St. Felix, Father Hieronimus de Belli, deacon of the church of St. Maria Formosa, and Father Aloysio of St. Martialis Ventus.

45. Salomon and Leoni's 1998 article in *JQR*, pp. 174-175, n. 124 and the genealogical table on pp. 210-211.

46. Joshua Soncino's responsum 20.

47. Background on this medal in chapter 16.

48. Sa'adiah Longo's later elegy to Doña Gracia in his *Shivrei Lukhot*.

49. Laguna's *Viaje de Turquia* in *Autografias y Memorias*, p. 131. The rarity of this privilege was noted by Nicholas Stavroulakis, an historian of the Ottomans of the period who was the founder and former director of the Jewish Museum of Greece; given in a telephone interview with the author in the spring of 1999.

50. ASV, Collegio. Notatorio, Registro 28, doc. dated August 12, 1552.

51. ASV, Collegio. Notatorio, Registro 28, doc. dated August 12, 1552

52. Calimani's *The Ghetto of Venice*, p. 85.

53. *Encyclopedia Judaica*, Vol. 6, p. 1232.

54. ASV, Collegio. Notatorio, Registro 28, doc. dated August 12, 1552.

55. ASV, Collegio. Notatorio, Registro 28, doc. dated August 12, 1552.

56. ASV, Senato, Deliberazioni Secreta, Registro 68 (1552-1553) p. 56, doc. dated August 13, 1552.

57. ASV, Senato, Deliberazioni Secreta, Registro 68 (1552-1553) p. 65, letter dated September 11, 1552.

58. ASV, Senato, Deliberazioni Secreta, Registro 68 (1552-1553) p. 173 (back) letter dated November 27, 1553

59. Charrière's *Négociations de La France dans le Levant*, Vol. II, p. 403; also see Laguna's *Viaje de Turquia*, p. 131.

60. ASF, notary Conti, matricola 584, pacco 8s; doc. dated May 27, 1558.

CHAPTER 13

1. Bernard Lewis' *The Jews of Islam*, pp. 135-136.

2. Jason Goodwin's *Lords of the Horizons*, Chapter 1.

3. Phillip Mansel's *Constantinople: City of the World's Desires*, Chapter 1.

4. Goodwin's *Lords of the Horizons*, Chapter 1; see also Mansel's *Constantinople...*, Chapter 1.

5. Morris Goodblatt's *Jewish Life in Turkey in the Sixteenth Century*, p. 5.

6. Mark Alan Epstein's *The Ottoman Jewish Communities and their Role in the Fifteenth and Sixteenth Centuries*, p. 22; further confirmed in a seminar tour called "The Jews of Turkey" given in Turkey by Professor Yom Tov Assis of Hebrew University in June 2000.

7. Harry Ojalvo's *Ottoman Sultans and their Jewish Subjects*, p. 36.

8. Epstein's *The Ottoman Jewish Communities...*, p. 24.

9. Statistics quoted on seminar tour in Turkey given by Professor Assis.

10. Goodblatt's *Jewish Life in Turkey...*, p. 4.

11. Epstein's *The Ottoman Jewish Communities...*, pp. 108-113.

12. Nicolay's *The Navigations, Peregrinations and Voyages Made into Turkey*, p. 130.

13. Ali Kemal Meram's *Padishah Analari*, p. 168; confirmed during Assis' seminar tour.

14. Mansel's *Constantinople...*, p. 24.

15. Goodblatt's *Jewish Life in Turkey...*, p. 5.

16. Nicolay's *The Navigations, Peregrinations...*, p. 130.

17. Nicolay's *The Navigations, Peregrinations...*, p. 132.

18. Nicolay's *The Navigations, Peregrinations...*, p. 93; also see F. Babinger's 1923 edition of Dernschwam's *Tagebuch einer Reise...*, pp. 106-116.

19. Goodblatt's *Jewish Life in Turkey...*, p. 127.

20. Dernschwam's *Tagebuch einer Reise...*, pp. 106-116.

21. Nicolay's *The Navigations, Peregrinations...*, pp. 49-50.

22. Dernschwam's *Tagebuch einer Reise...*, p. 113.

23. Dernschwam's *Tagebuch einer Reise...*, p. 116.

24. Ruth Lamdan's *A Separate People*, p. 119.

25. See the end of the previous chapter for departure documents.

26. See reasons in previous chapter.

27. Casola's *Canon Pietro Casola's Pilgrimage to Jerusalem in the year 1494*, Chapter VI, translated by M. M. Newett. Corroboration of his observations can be found in Richard Unger's *The Ship in the Medieval Economy, 600-1600*, p. 211.

28. Franz Kobler's *Letters of Jews Through the Ages*, pp. 351-359; also see Joseph Shatzmiller's chapter "The Testimony of Eliahu of Pesaro," pp. 237-241 in Toaf's *The Mediterranean and the Jews*.

29. Shatzmiller's chapter, "The Testimony of Eliahu of Pesaro," pp. 237-241.

30. General history taken from a variety of encyclopedia-based sources.

31. Jorjo Tadic's *Jevreji u Dubroniku*, pp. 439-445.

32. Casola's *Canon Pietro Casola's Pilgrimage...*, Chapter VI.

33. Tadic's *Jevreji u Dubroniku*, pp. 322-325.

34. Segre's article "Nuovi Documenti sur Marrani d'Ancona (1555-1559)," in *Michael* IX, Tel Aviv, 1985, p. 185, inventory 17.

35. Tadic's *Jevreji u Dubroniku*, pp. 322-325.

36. Simonsohn's *The Apostolic See and the Jews*, Vol. 6, p. 2924, doc. 3219 and p. 2934, doc. 3233.

37. Tadic's *Jevreji u Dubroniku*, pp. 430-431 (Cons. Rog LII 154'-155': doc. in Italian dated November 9, 1554).

38. Tadic's *Jevreji u Dubroniku*, pp. 430-431.

39. Tadic's *Jevreji u Dubroniku*, pp. 322-325.

40. Tadic's *Jevreji u Dubroniku*, pp. 322-325.

41. Tadic's *Jevreji u Dubroniku*, pp. 322-325.

42. Samuel de Medina's responsum 327.

43. Laguna's *Viaje de Turquia*, p. 131.

44. Busbecq's *The Turkish Letters of Ogier Ghiselin de Busbecq*, p. 89.

45. Leal's *Corpo Diplomatico Portuguez - Os Actos e Relações Politicas e Diplomaticas de Portugal*, Vol. VII, p. 272.

46. Laguna's *Viaje de Turquia*, p. 131.

47. Laguna's *Viaje de Turquia*, p. 131.

48. Sa'adiah Longo in *Shivrei Lukhot*.

49. This is the only contemporary mention found by the author where the name Mendes is attached to her first name. Significantly, it is the name attached to her by an outsider, rather than being an appellation she used herself, or was used to identify her in any official document.

50. Laguna's *Viaje de Turquia*, p. 131.

51. Dernschwam's *Tagebuch einer Reise...*, p. 115. The fact that he calls her capable modifies a long-standing error. An incorrect translation of the German word *geschwindtz* crept into an English version of Dernschwam's diaries (see Jacob Marcus' *The Jew in the Medieval World*, p. 415), perpetuating the idea that he was describing her as "dangerous."

52. Also confirmed in Fr. Pantaleâo de Aveiro's *Itineraro da Terra Sancta e suas Particularidades*, p. 473. However, the title *"La Señora"* that has come down to us through history probably started out as *"A Señora"*—the Portuguese version of the same expression.

53. Dernschwam's *Tagebuch einer Reise...*, p. 115.

54. Mansel's *Constantinople...*, p. 36.

55. Dernschwam's *Tagebuch einer Reise...*, p. 115.

56. Dernschwam's *Tagebuch einer Reise...*, p. 115.

57. Gad Nassi's *Jewish Journalism and the Printing Houses in the Ottoman Empire and Modern Turkey*, p. 81; see also Roth's *The Duke of Naxos*, p. 11, n. 1. The neighborhood

of Ortaköy lies east of Galata.

58. Mansel's *Constantinople: City of the World's Desires*, pp. 12-14.

59. Laguna's *Viaje de Turquia*, p. 131.

60. ASF, notary Conti, matricola 584, pacco 8s; p. 4, doc. dated May 27, 1558.

61. *Encyclopedia Judaica* ,Vol. 12, p. 835.

62. Baer's *A History of the Jews in Christian Spain*, Vol. I, pp. 54, 92, 398.

63. Salomon and Leoni's 1998 article in *JQR*, pp.163 (n. 84), 170 (n. 110).

64. Further thanks for this deduction to recent research by Salomon and Leoni.

65. Baer's *A History of the Jews in Christian Spain*, Vol. I, pp. 94-95.

66. ASF, notary Conti, matricola 584, pacco 8s; p. 4, doc. dated May 27, 1558.

67. Roth's *The Duke of Naxos*, p. 218.

68. ASF, notary Conti, matricola 584, pacco 8s; p. 4, doc. dated May 27, 1558.

69. ASF, notary Taurino, maricola 535, pacco 8; doc. dated May 8 and July 14, 1553. These must have been debts due to the House of Mendes, rather than personal obligations, since Don Joseph is mentioned as being involved, among other clues.

70. Further details in Chapter 12.

71. Gaeta's *Nunziature di Venezia*, Vol. 6, pp. 196-197, letter 314 dated January, 1553.

72. Zorattini's *Processi del S. Uffizio...*, Vol. I, p. 342, testimony of Brianda de Luna.

73. For a highly detailed and annotated account of this episode see Benjamin Ravid's article "Money, Love and Power Politics in Sixteenth Century Venice," in pp. 159-181 of *Italia Judaica*, May 1981; also see Salomon and Leoni's 1998 article in *JQR*, p. 154.

74. ASV, Consiglio dei Dieci. Criminali, Registro 8, 21r, 22v, 23 r-v, 28r-30v, 32r-v; docs. dated January 17 through March 16, 1553.

75. Gaeta's *Nunziature di Venezia*, Vol. 6, pp. 196-197, letter 314 dated January, 1553

76. ASV, Consiglio dei Dieci. Criminali, Registro 8, 21r, 22v, 23 r-v, 28r-30v, 32r-v; documents dated January 17 to March 16, 1553; also see Gaeta's *Nunziature di Venezia*, Vol.6, pp. 213-214, letter 323 dated March, 1553.

77. Grunebaum-Ballin's *Joseph Naci, duc de Naxos*, p. 54.

78. Grunebaum-Ballin's *Joseph Naci, duc de Naxos*, p. 54, quoting a letter by Dominique de Gaztelu dated March 13, 1553, preserved in the state archives in Vienna; also see Ravid's article "Money, Love and Power Politics in Sixteenth Century Venice" p. 174.

79. Grunebaum-Ballin's *Joseph Naci, duc de Naxos*, pp. 68-69.

80. Charrière's *Négociations de La France dans le Levant*, Vol. II, pp. 403-404, footnote; the offer was made through M. Louis de Lansac, the French ambassador in Rome.

81. Laguna's *Viaje de Turquia*, p. 131.

82. Leal's *Corpo Diplomatico Portuguez...*, Vol. VII, p. 272.

83. Merle Severy's article, "The World of Suleyman the Magnificent," in the November 1987 issue of *National Geographic*, p. 562.

84. Ford's *Letters of John III*, p. 177.

85. Leal's *Corpo Diplomatico Portuguez...*,Vol. VII, p. 495.

86. ASM, Cancelleria Ducale, Patricolari, busta 893 (sub folder titled "Miches"), letter from Duke Ercole to Don Joseph dated October 6, 1555.

87. Dernschwam's *Tagebuch einer Reise...*, p. 116.

88. Dernschwam uses the word Spanish, but they must have been *converso*.

89. Dernschwam's *Tagebuch einer Reise...*, p. 116; also see Roth's *The Duke of Naxos*, p. 7.

90. Jean Chesneau's *Le Voyage de Monsieur D'Aramon, Ambassador pour le roy en Levant,* pp. 48-49 in Vol. 8 of *Recueil de Voyages et de Documents pour servir a L'histoire de la geographie depuis le XIIIe jusqu'a la fin du XVIe siecle,* Paris, 1887.

91. Laguna's *Viaje de Turquia,* p. 131.

92. Sebastian Pinto, one should recall, was also considered a "knight."

93. Grunebaum-Ballin's *Joseph Naci, duc de Naxos,* p. 70, n.1.

94. Dernschwam's *Tagebuch einer Reise...*, p. 116.

95. Laguna's *Viaje de Turquia,* p. 131.

96. ASF, notary Conti, matricola 584, pacco 8s, document dated May 27, 1558; the family later arranged for Don Samuel to marry La Chica. See Chapter 16 for details.

97. Charrière's *Négociations de La France dans le Levant,* Vol. III, p. 808.

98. Grunebaum-Ballin's *Joseph Naci, duc de Naxos,* p. 71; the Ferranese ambassador was Hieroniumus Jeruffino.

99. Baron's *A Social and Religious History of the Jews,* Vol. XVIII, p. 86.

100. Grunebaum-Ballin's *Joseph Naci, duc de Naxos,* p. 70.

101. Dernschwam's *Tagebuch einer Reise...*, p. 116. The ambassador at the time was M. d'Aramon.

102. Gerlach's *Turkisches Tagebuch...*, p. 303.

103. Conclusions of Beki Bahar, the Turkish historian and poet, based upon local histories, particularly the Turkish book *Padishah Analari;* recounted in an interview with the author in Istanbul on April 24, 2000. Also see Goodwin's *Lords of the Horizons,* p. 160.

104. Epstein's *The Ottoman Jewish Communities...*, p. 92.

105. Dernschwam's *Tagebuch einer Reise...*, p. 116.

106. Grunebaum-Ballin's *Joseph Naci, duc de Naxos,* p. 72.

107. Grunebaum-Ballin's *Joseph Naci, duc de Naxos,* pp. 67-68.

108. Leal's *Corpo Diplomatico Portuguez...*, Vol. VII, p. 272.

109. ASV, Senato, Deliberazioni Secreta, Registro 68 (1552-1553), p. 173 (back), letter dated November 27, 1553.

110. Tadic's *Jevreji u Dubroniku,* pp. 322-325.

111. Dernschwam's *Tagebuch einer Reise...*, pp. 115-116.

112. I. S. Emmanuel's *Histoire des Israélites de Salonique,* p. 217.

113. Aveiro's *Itineraro da Terra Sancta e suas Particularidades,* p. 473.

114. Baron's *A Social and Religious History of the Jews,* Vol. XVIII, pp. 88, 98.

115. Epstein's *The Ottoman Jewish Communities...*, p. 89.

116. Roth's article "Salusque Lusitano," p. 78.

117. Epstein's *The Ottoman Jewish Communities...*, p. 92.

118. Epstein's *The Ottoman Jewish Communities...*, p. 90.

119. Epstein's *The Ottoman Jewish Communities...*, pp. 88-92.

120. Galante's *Documents Officiels Turcs Concernant les Juifs de Turquie*, pp. 185-186. There is a conflict in the dating of the documents. They carry a date of January 1565, but they also say that Doña Gracia had only recently arrived from Flanders. This suggests the incidents might have taken place considerably earlier and the confusion may have been a fault of transcription or translation.

121. Galante believes the Samuel in question was Samuel Usque, the writer. But if the date of 1565 is indeed correct, it could have been Samuel Nasi, the brother of Don Joseph, as he had moved to Constantinople in 1559 (Chapter 16).

122. Galante's *Documents Officiels...*, pp. 185-186.

123. See Chapter 9 for details.

124. Dernschwam's *Tagebuch einer Reise...*, p. 115.

CHAPTER 14

1. Baron's *A Social and Religious History...*, Vol. XIV, p. 33.

2. Baron's *A Social and Religious History...*, Vol. XIV, pp. 32-35.

3. Segre's article "Nuovi Documenti sur Marrani d'Ancona (1555-1559)," in *Michael* IX, Tel Aviv, 1985, pp. 130-135.

4. Baron's *A Social and Religious History...*, Vol. XIV, pp. 32-35; also see Segre's article "Nuovi Documenti...," pp. 130-135.

5. Baron's *A Social and Religious History...*, Vol. XIV, p. 43.

6. Baron's *A Social and Religious History...*, Vol. XIV, p. 34.

7. Baron's *A Social and Religious History...*, Vol. XIV, pp. 32-35; also see Segre's article "Nuovi Documenti...," pp. 130-135.

8. Freehof's *The Responsa Literature and a Treasury of Respona*, p. 151.

9. Pullan's article "A Ship with Two Rudders: Righetto Marrano and the Inquisition," p. 51.

10. I. Sonne's article "Une source nouvelle pour l'histoire des martyrs d'Ancone," pp. 360-369 in *Revue des Études Juives*, No. 89, Paris, 1930.

11. Segre's article "Nuovi Documenti...," p. 185, inventory 17.

12. Sonne's article "Une source nouvelle...," p. 371 conflicts with Amatus' own account, where he says he sacrificed all his possessions to avoid getting caught.

13. Dedication of Lusitanus' *Centuriae V*, dated 1559 (since reprinted).

14. Dedication of Lusitanus' *Centuriae V*. Lusitanus' brief comments about the situation in Ancona in *Centuria V* help us further understand the reason why the previous popes had been so accommodating to the *conversos*. Lusitanus mentioned, for example, how one of his friends who had also been arrested had been to India and China, suggesting such worldly experience was not unusual among *converso* merchants. Moreover, during their travels, merchants had acquired detailed knowledge about certain medicinal herbs and cures, further confirming that these travelers became a source for the advanced medical knowledge that made Jewish and *converso* physicians so popular. Medical historians might find it worthwhile to explore the

role of the Sephardic diaspora, and particularly the spread of the *converso* merchants throughout Europe in the early 16th century, in introducing certain botanical cures previously confined to the Orient or Muslim world.

15. ASF, notary Conti, matricola 584, pacco 5s, doc. dated May 26, 1551. The agent in charge of the deal was Fernando Mendes, a Florentine judge; see also Segre's chapter "Sephardic Refugees in Ferrara...," p. 175.

16. Segre's article "Nuovi Documenti...," p. 172, inventory 8.

17. Segre's article "Nuovi Documenti...," p. 137.

18. Segre's article "Nuovi Documenti...," p. 138-139

19. The list can be found in Segre's "Nuovi Documenti...," pp. 170-226.

20. Segre's article "Nuovi Documenti...," pp. 181-183, inventory 14.

21. Segre's article "Nuovi Documenti...," pp. 211-215, inventory 37.

22. Segre's article "Nuovi Documenti...," pp. 211-215, inventory 37.

23. Segre's article "Nuovi Documenti...," pp. 169-171, inventory 6.

24. Segre's article "Nuovi Documenti...," pp. 185-186, inventory 17.

25. Segre's article "Nuovi Documenti...," pp. 172-173, inventory 8.

26. Marc Saperstein's article "Martyrs, Merchants and Rabbis...," p. 217, in *Jewish Social Studies,* Summer/Fall 1981.

27. Baron's *A Social and Religious History...,* Vol. XIV, p. 38.

28. Segre's article "Nuovi Documenti...," pp. 140-143.

29. Segre's article "Nuovi Documenti...," pp. 144-145.

30. Solomon Freehof's *The Responsa Literature and a Treasury of Respona,* pp. 154-155.

31. Goodblatt's *Jewish Life in Turkey...,* p. 114.

32. For an example of one of these complicated cases, for which no satisfactory conclusion could be reached, see Freehof's *The Responsa Literature...,* p. 153-154.

33. ASV, notary Conti, matricola 584, pacco 8s, doc. dated November 17, 1562.

34. Segre's "Nuovi Documenti...," p. 138-139; the Ancona representative was Giovanni Trionfi.

35. Segre's article "Nuovi Documenti...," p. 142-143.

36. Leoni's *La diplomazia estense e l'immigrazione...,* p. 326, doc. 6.

37. Leoni's *La diplomazia estense e l'immigrazione...,* p. 315-317.

38. Pilar León Tello's Spanish translation of Joseph ha-Kohen's Hebrew work *El Valle Del Llanto (Emek ha Bakha),* p. 154.

39. Sonne's article "Une source nouvelle...," p. 367, quoting the words of Joseph ha-Kohen.

40. Severy's article "The World of Suleyman the Magnificent," pp. 352-374.

41. Severy's article "The World of Suleyman the Magnificent," pp. 352-374.

42. Goodwin's *Lord of the Horizons,* p. 160.

43. Goodwin's *Lord of the Horizons,* p. 160.

44. Author's interview with Nikos Stavroulakis, founder of the Jewish Museum of Greece and an Ottoman scholar, on December 31, 2000; see also *The Encyclopaedia of Islam,* 1995 edition, p. 124.

45. Baron's *A Social and Religious History...*, Vol. XVIII, p. 474, n. 43; the vizier was Rustem Pasha.

46. Ojalvo's *Ottoman Sultans and their Jewish Subjects*, p. 64.

47. Severy's article "The World of Suleyman the Magnificent," p. 571

48. Busbecq's *The Turkish Letters of Ogier Ghiselin de Busbecq*, pp. 59-66; also see Severy's article "The World of Suleyman the Magnificent," pp. 352-374 and Mansel's *Constantinople*, pp. 61-65.

49. Grunebaum-Ballin's *Joseph Naci, duc de Naxos*, p. 77. The secretary at this time was Baron Pierre Cachard.

50. Reznik's *Le Duc Joseph de Naxos*, p. 120.

51. Baron's *A Social and Religious History...*, Vol. XIV, p. 39.

52. Baron's *A Social and Religious History...*, Vol. XIV, p. 39.

53. Grunebaum's article "Notes et Mélanges," p. 14 in *Revue des Études Juives*, No. 24, Paris, 1894.

54. Segre's article "Nuovi documenti...," pp. 144-145; also see Reznik's *Le Duc Joseph de Naxos*, pp. 242-243, doc. 6.

55. Roth's *Doña Gracia of the House of Nasi*, p. 205, n.5.

56. Sonne's article "Une source nouvelle...," p. 364-368.

57. Lusitanus' *Centuriae V*, p. 56.

58. Segre's chapter "Sephardic Refugees in Ferrara...," p. 175.

59. Segre's article "Nuovi documenti...," pp. 144-145.

60. Segre's article "Nuovi documenti...," pp. 144-145.

61. Sonne's article "Une source nouvelle...," p. 369.

62. Joshua Soncino's responsa 39, 40, Moses di Trani's responsum 237, Joseph ibn Lev's responsum 54 and Samuel de Medina's responsum 59 all discuss Ancona; also see Saperstein's article "Martyrs, Merchants and Rabbis...," p. 221.

63. Joshua Soncino's responsum 39.

64. Saperstein's article "Martyrs, Merchants and Rabbis...," p. 218-219; also see Sonne's article "Une source nouvelle...," p. 369 and Joshua Soncino's responsum 39.

65. Reznik's *Le Duc Joseph de Naxos*, p. 125, n. 34.

66. David Kaufman's article "Deux Lettres Nouvelles," p. 232 of *Revue des Études Juives*, No. 31, Paris, 1895.

67. Joshua Soncino's responsum 39.

68. Kaufman's article "Deux Lettres Nouvelles," p. 232.

69. Saperstein's article "Martyrs, Merchants and Rabbis...," pp. 218-219.

70. Usque's *Consolation...*, p. 215.

71. Joshua Soncino's responsum 40.

72. Saperstein's article "Martyrs, Merchants and Rabbis...," p. 218.

73. Saperstein's article "Martyrs, Merchants and Rabbis...," p. 225; also see Joshua Soncino's responsum 40.

74. Freehof's *The Responsa Literature..*, p. 155, quoting a responsum of Moses di Trani.

75. Saperstein's article "Martyrs, Merchants and Rabbis...," pp. 221-222.

76. Roth's *Doña Gracia...*, p. 160.

77. Saperstein's article "Martyrs, Merchants and Rabbis...," p. 222; also see Joshua Soncino's responsum 40.

78. Grunebaum-Ballin's *Joseph Naci, duc de Naxos*, p. 77.

79. Sonne's article "Une Source Nouvelle...," p. 369.

80. Joshua Soncino's responsum 40.

81. Joshua Soncino's responsum 40. Two other rabbis mentioned were Rabbi Solomon ibn Beya and Rabbi Samuel Saba.

82. Joshua Soncino's responsum 40.

83. *Encyclopedia Judaica*, Vol. 15, p. 142.

84. Joshua Soncino's responsum 39.

85. Joshua Soncino's responsum 39, 40; also see Saperstein's article "Martyrs, Merchants and Rabbis...," p. 223.

86. Joshua Soncino's responsum 12.

87. Joshua Soncino's responsum 40.

88. Joshua Soncino's responsum 40.

89. Joshua Soncino's responsa 39, 40.

90. Joshua Soncino's responsum 40.

91. Baron's *A Social and Religious History...*, Vol. XIV, p. 42.

92. Joshua Soncino's responsum 40.

93. Roth's *Doña Gracia...*, pp. 170-171.

94. Baron's *A Social and Religious History...*, Vol. XIV, p. 320, n. 39.

95. Goodblatt's *Jewish Life in Turkey in the Sixteenth Century*, p. 115.

96. Baron's *A Social and Religious History...*, Vol. XIV, p. 42.

97. Roth's *Doña Gracia...*, p. 172.

98. Lusitanus' dedication to Don Josef Nasi in *Centuria V*; also see Friedenwald's *The Jews and Medicine*, pp. 340-342.

99. Segre's chapter "Sephardic Refugees in Ferrara...," p. 175.

CHAPTER 15

1. Zorattini's *Processi del S. Uffizio...*," Vol. I, p. 254, testimony of Tristan da Costa.

2. The medal of La Chica has been widely used, copied and reprinted; the likeness is sometimes mistakenly attributed to Doña Gracia herself. By the time it was struck La Chica was married, or about to marry and living as a Jew. So the assumption is that she would have been known as Gracia Nasi, since she had wed Don Joseph's brother, Samuel Nasi. Yet documents of this period all indicate she continued to be known by her (Jewish) maiden name of Gracia Benveniste. An original is in the Jewish Museum in New York City.

3. Zorattini's *Processi del S. Uffizio...*, Vol. I, p. 255.

4. Zorattini's *Processi del S. Uffizio...*, Vol. I, pp. 251-260.

5. Zorattini's *Processi del S. Uffizio...*, Vol. I, pp. 261-262.

6. Grunebaum-Ballin's *Joseph Naci, duc de Naxos*, p. 54. The ambassador at this time was Dominique de Gaztelu.

7. ASV, Consiglio dei Dieci, Parti Secrete, Filza 9, 1555-1558, docs. dated November 29, 1553 and March 10, 1555.

8. Zorattini's *Processi del S. Uffizio...*, Vol. I, p. 341, reiterating the safe conducts of March, 1544.

9. Zorattini's *Processi del S. Uffizio...*, Vol. I, pp. 342-344.

10. Freehof's *The Responsa Literature...*, Part II, p. 153.

11. In his responsum 80, Moses di Trani talks of some 11 years having passed since Diogo's death in 1543.

12. Zorattini's *Processi del S. Uffizio...*, Vol. I, p. 343.

13. Zorattini's *Processi del S. Uffizio...*, Vol. I, p. 257.

14. ASV, Consiglio dei Dieci, Parti Secrete, Filza 9, 1555-1558, doc. dated June 20, 1555.

15. Zorattini's *Processi del S. Uffizio...*, Vol. I, p. 343.

16. Segre's chapter "Sephardic Refugees in Ferrara...," p. 171, n. 42.

17. Zorattini's *Processi del S. Uffizio...*, Vol. I, p. 257.

18. Zorattini's *Processi del S. Uffizio...*, Vol. I, p. 255.

19. Joshua Soncino's responsum 12.

20. Introduction to Joshua Soncino's responsum 12; the fact that Doña Gracia, rather than Brianda, must have been the first to request a new adjudication, is supported by the introductory remarks of Caro in his responsum 81 on the topic.

21. Introduction to Joshua Soncino's responsum 12.

22. Introduction to Joshua Soncino's responsum 12.

23. David's *To Come to the Land*, pp. 164-165.

24. Goodblatt's *Jewish Life in Turkey...*, pp. 24-31.

25. David's *To Come to the Land*, pp. 156-157.

26. Goodblatt's *Jewish Life in Turkey...*, p. 18.

27. Joseph Caro's responsum 81; also see Garshowitz's article "Gracia Mendes: Power, Influence and Intrigue," pp. 108-110.

28. Garshowitz's chapter "Gracia Mendes...," p. 104.

29. The wording of will was reproduced in Moses di Trani's responsum 80 (*Avqat Rokhel*).

30. These differences show up, for example, in the conflict between the writings of Freehof and Garshowitz while Roth believes they favored Doña Gracia.

31. Joshua Soncino's responsum 12.

32. Moses di Trani's responsum 80.

33. Moses di Trani's responsum 80.

34. Samuel de Medina's responsum 329.

35. Samuel de Medina's responsum 317.

36. Samuel de Medina's responsum 328.

37. Zorattini's *Processi del S. Uffizio...*, Vol. I, p. 252.

38. Calimani's *The Ghetto of Venice*, pp. 58-59.

39. Brianchi, Righi and Terzaghi's booklet *The Doge's Palace in Venice*, and Franzoi's booklet *The Prisons of the Doge's Palace in Venice.*

40. Zorattini's *Processi del S. Uffizio...*, Vol. I, p. 252.

41. Zorattini's *Processi del S. Uffizio...*, Vol. I, p. 344.

42. Zorattini's *Processi del S. Uffizio...*, Vol. I, p. 256.

43. Zorattini's *Processi del S. Uffizio...*, Vol. I, pp. 252-253,258.

44. Zorattini's *Processi del S. Uffizio...*, Vol. I, p. 258.

45. Zorattini's *Processi del S. Uffizio...*, Vol. I, pp. 252-253.

46. Zorattini's *Processi del S. Uffizio...*, Vol. I, p. 260.

47. Zorattini's *Processi del S. Uffizio...*, Vol. I, pp. 254,258.

48. Zorattini's *Processi del S. Uffizio...*, Vol. I, pp. 252,255,258.

49. Zorattini's *Processi del S. Uffizio...*, Vol. I, p. 228.

50. Zorattini's *Processi del S. Uffizio...*, Vol. I, pp. 228-229; The Florentine was Don Luca de Albicis, a man whose name appears frequently in notarial documents connected with the House of Mendes and was particularly evident in the Leoncini accords (see Chapter 12).

51. Zorattini's *Processi del S. Uffizio...*, Vol. I, p. 225.

52. Zorattini's *Processi del S. Uffizio...*, Vol. I, pp. 226-227.

53. The Spanish ambassador at this time was Francisco de Vargas.

54. Zorattini's *Processi del S. Uffizio...*, Vol. I, pp. 227-228.

55. Zorattini's *Processi del S. Uffizio...*, Vol. I, pp. 229-231.

56. Zorattini's *Processi del S. Uffizio...*, Vol. I, pp. 231,238,239,243; the secretary was Don Pietro Gelido, a cleric.

57. Zorattini's *Processi del S. Uffizio...*, Vol. I, p. 232.

58. Zorattini's *Processi del S. Uffizio...*, Vol. I, p. 234.

59. Zorattini's *Processi del S. Uffizio...*, Vol. I, pp. 232- 233.

60. Zorattini's *Processi del S. Uffizio...*, Vol. I, p. 246.

61. Zorattini's *Processi del S. Uffizio...*, Vol. I, p. 263.

62. Zorattini's *Processi del S. Uffizio...*, Vol. I, pp. 244-246.

63. See Chapter 16 concerning Henriques' later dealings in Ferrara.

64. Zorattini's *Processi del S. Uffizio...*, Vol. I, p. 342.

65. Zorattini's *Processi del S. Uffizio...*, Vol. I, p. 342.

66. Zorattini's *Processi del S. Uffizio...*, Vol. I, pp. 343-344.

67. Zorattini's *Processi del S. Uffizio...*, Vol. I, p. 344.

68. Zorattini's *Processi del S. Uffizio...*, Vol. I, p. 345.

69. Zorattini's *Processi del S. Uffizio...*, Vol. I, p. 347.

70. Zorattini's *Processi del S. Uffizio...*, Vol. I, p. 346.

71. Zorattini's *Processi del S. Uffizio...*, Vol. I, p. 346.

72. Zorattini's *Processi del S. Uffizio...*, Vol. I, p. 346.

73. Zorattini's *Processi del S. Uffizio...*, Vol. I, p. 347.

74. Zorattini's *Processi del S. Uffizio...*, Vol. I, p. 347.

75. Zorattini's *Processi del S. Uffizio...*, Vol. I, p. 347.

76. Zorattini's *Processi del S. Uffizio...*, Vol. I, p. 347.

77. Zorattini's *Processi del S. Uffizio...*, Vol. I, p. 347.

78. Zorattini's *Processi del S. Uffizio...*, Vol. I, p. 347.

79. Zorattini's *Processi del S. Uffizio...*, Vol. I, p. 347.

80. Zorattini's *Processi del S. Uffizio...*, Vol. I, pp. 348-9.

81. Zorattini's *Processi del S. Uffizio...*, Vol. I, p. 348.

82. Grunebaum-Ballin's *Joseph Naci duc de Naxos*, pp. 63-64; also see Salomon and Leoni's 1998 article in *JQR*, p. 162; the French ambassador was M. de Gabre.

83. Zorattini's *Processi del S. Uffizio...*, Vol. I, p. 349.

84. Zorattini's *Processi del S. Uffizio...*, Vol. I, p. 349.

85. Zorattini's *Processi del S. Uffizio...*, Vol. I, p. 350.

86. Segre's chapter "Sephardic Refugees in Ferrara...," p. 179, n. 66.

87. ASF, notary Saracco, matricola 493, pacco 29, doc. dated January 18, 1557.

88. Segre's chapter "Sephardic Refugees in Ferrara...," p. 179, n. 66.

89. Salomon and Leoni's 1998 article in *JQR*, p. 196, doc. 15. No firm date given but it was doubtless many months before their estimated date of January, 1556, since Brianda and La Chica had to leave almost immediately.

90. Grunebaum-Ballin's *Joseph Naci, duc de Naxos*, p. 65.

91. Salomon and Leoni's 1998 article in *JQR*, p. 163, n. 84.

92. The name of Gracia Benveniste is repeated many times as the official Jewish appellation for La Chica in the Ferrara documents used for Chapter 16. Brianda, however, is repeatedly referred to as Brianda de Luna, just as before.

93. ASF, notary Conti, matricola 584, pacco 8s, document dated May 27, 1558, outlining the terms of the will of Don Samuel Nasi, in which he discusses his bride's exceptional dowry.

CHAPTER 16

1. Salomon and Leoni's 1998 article in *JQR*, p. 163, confirmed by many of the following docs. from the Ferrara archives.

2. Segre's chapter "Sephardic Refugees in Ferrara...," p. 179, n. 67.

3. Segre's chapter "Sephardic Refugees in Ferrara...," p. 181.

4. ASF, notary Zaffarini, matricola 606, pacco 3, appendix to doc. dated December 22, 1556.

5. ASF, notary Zaffarini, matricola 606, pacco 3, doc. dated December 22, 1556; the inventory, taken on July 10 and recorded on August 12, 1556, is attached.

6. ASM, Cancelleria Ducale, Particolari, busta 747 (sub folder titled "de Luna"), undated petition from Piero Fernandes, Francesco Botteglio and Manel Dias to Duke Ercole.

7. ASF, notary Conti, matricola 584, pacco 8s, doc. dated March 16, 1559.

8. ASF, notary Conti, matricola 584, pacco 8s, attachments to doc. dated March 16, 1559; the actual wording talks about gold scudi, which would have been the same as ducats.

9. ASF, notary Conti, matricola 584, pacco 9s, doc. dated September 11, 1562; once again the words gold scudi are used.

10. ASF, Conti docs. of March 16, 1559 and September 11, 1562 (as above).

11. Segre's chapter "Sephardic Refugees in Ferrara...," p. 179 .

12. ASF, notary Zaffarini, matricola 606, pacco 3, docs. dated August 13, 1556.

13. ASF, notary Zaffarini, matricola 606, pacco 3, docs. dated August 13, 1556.

14. ASF, notary Zaffarini, matricola 606, pacco 3, docs. dated August 13, 1556; also see Salomon and Leoni's 1998 article in *JQR*, p. 198, doc. 16.

15. Salomon and Leoni's 1998 article in JQR, p. 198, doc. 16.

16. Segre's chapter "Sephardic Refugees in Ferrara...," p. 179, n. 68. Again, the documents speak of scudi. Segre insists the deposit was a payback to the duke for receiving Brianda and La Chica into his territories. But they had already been there for over six months. It is possible, but questionable.

17. ASF, notary Conti, matricola 584, pacco 9s, doc. dated September 11, 1562, f.13.

18. ASM, Cancelleria Ducale, Patrticoliari, busta 885 (sub folder titled "Mendez"), doc. dated October 15, 1556 from the duke to "de Luna Donna Grazia."

19. ASF, notary Saracco, matricola 493, pacco 29, doc. dated January 10, 1557.

20. ASF, notary Saracco, matricola 493, pacco 29, docs. dated August 12 and August 20, 1557.

21. ASF, notary Taurino, matricola 535, pacco 8, docs. dated May 8 and July 14, 1553.

22. ASF, notary Andrea Cocchapano found in the file of notary Taurino, matricola 535, pacco 8, doc. dated August 3, 1557.

23. Charrière's *Négociations de La France...*, Vol. II, pp. 772-773, quoting a French diplomatic letter, dated 1564, mentioning that Gomez was still in Venice.

24. ASM, Cancelleria Ducale, Particolari, busta 747 (sub folder titled "de Luna"), docs. dated December 6 and 7, 1556 (6 crossed out and replaced incorrectly by 7).

25. Segre's chapter "Sephardic Refugees in Ferrara...," pp. 179-180. Segre talks of a donation, but our research suggests it was more likely to have been a loan (see later in this chapter for Don Joseph's attempt to collect this sum as a debt). Once again the documents speak of scudi.

26. Luciano Chiappini's *La Corte Estense alla meta' del Cinquecento - I Compendi di Cristoforo di Messiburgo*, p. 25; also see Tyler's *The Emperor Charles the Fifth*, p. 348. Again the historians talk of scudi but continually refer to ducats in an interchangeable fashion.

27. ASM, Cancelleria Ducale, Particolari, busta 747 (sub folder titled "de Luna"), docs. dated December 6 and 7, 1556 (6 crossed out and replaced incorrectly by 7).

28. Segre's chapter "Sephardic Refugees in Ferrara...," pp. 179-180.

29. Segre's chapter "Sephardic Refugees in Ferrara...," p. 180.

30. ASF, notary Saracco, matricola 493, pacco 29, doc. dated January 19, 1557.

31. As we shall see later, it is significant that Don Joseph, who had a passion for wines, took the trouble to identify his residence as being among vineyards.

32. ASM, Cancelleria Ducale, Patricolari, busta 797 (sub folder title "Nasi"), doc. dated January 27, 1557; also see Segre's chapter "Sephardic Refugees in Ferrara...," p. 180.

33. Segre's chapter "Sephardic Refugees in Ferrara...," pp. 179-180.

34. Salomon and Leoni's 1998 article in *JQR*, p. 201, doc. 17.

35. Salomon and Leoni's 1998 article in *JQR*, p. 201, doc. 17.

36. Salomon and Leoni's 1998 article in *JQR*, p. 201, doc. 17.

37. ASF, notary Conti, matricola 584, pacco 8s, doc. dated October 20, 1558.

38. Salomon and Leoni's 1998 article in *JQR*, p. 164.

39. Salomon and Leoni's 1998 article in *JQR*, p. 163.

40. ASF, notary Conti, matricola 584, pacco 8s, doc. dated November 20, 1557 (may be found mistakenly filed under notary Codegori, matricola 582, pacco 8).

41. Segre's chapter "Sephardic Refugees in Ferrara...," p. 180; again we have used ducats where scudi are specified.

42. ASF, notary Sarraco, matricola 493, pacco 29, doc. dated January 19, 1557.

43. ASF, notary Saracco, matricola 493, pacco 29, doc. dated August 12, 1557.

44. Raymond B. Waddington's article "Graven Images: Sixteenth-Century Portrait Medals of Jews," in *The Expulsion of the Jews: 1492 and After,* (Ed. Waddington), p. 94

45. Fernand-Halphen's article "Une Grande Dame Juive de la Renaissance," p. 165; also see Grunebaum-Ballin's *Joseph Naci, duc de Naxos*, p. 74, n.1.

46. Waddington's article "Graven Images...," p. 95.

47. For a more detailed treatment of Renaissance medals see Jardine's *Worldly Goods*, pp. 416-420. For current owners of La Chica's medal see Daniel Friedenberg's *Jewish Medals from the Renaissance to the Fall of Napoleon*, pp. 128-129.

48. Waddington's article "Graven Images...," pp. 97-99.

49. ASF, notary Conti, matricola 584, pacco 8s, doc. dated August 18, 1557 (may be misfiled under notary Codegori, matricola 582, pacco 8).

50. Herculano's *History of the Origin...*, pp. 408, 409, 507.

51. The full story is in Brian Pullan's article "A Ship with Two Rudders: 'Righetto Marrano' and the Inquisition" in *The (British) Historical Journal*, issue 20, Vol. I, 1977, pp. 25-58.

52. Pullan's article: "A Ship with Two Rudders...," p. 26.

53. Pullan's article: "A Ship with Two Rudders...," pp. 25-58.

54. ASF, notary Saracco, matricola 493, pacco 29, doc. dated August 20, 1557 and ASF, notary Caprilli, matricola 504, busta 2, doc. dated September 6, 1557.

55. ASF, notary Caprilli, matricola 504, busta 2, undated inventory accompanying doc. dated August 20, 1557.

56. ASF, notary Conti, matricola 584, pacco 8s, doc. dated October 20, 1558.

57. ASF, notary Conti, matricola 584, pacco 8s, doc. dated August 18, 1557 (may be misfiled under notary Codegori, matricola 582, pacco 8).

58. ASF, notary Conti, matricola 584, pacco 8s, doc. dated August 18, 1557 (may be

misfiled under notary Codegori, matricola 582, pacco 8). The official was Don Hieronimo Canano.

59. Segre's chapter "Sephardic Refugees in Ferrara...," p. 181.

60. ASF, notary Saracco, matricola 493, pacco 9; doc. dated June 8, 1558.

61. ASF, notary Conti, matricola 584, pacco 8s, doc. dated September 3, 1557 (may be misfiled under notary Codegori, matricola 582, pacco 8). The landlord was Don Jacob d'Imola.

62. See notary Conti, matricola 584, pacco 8s, doc. dated September 15, 1557 (may be misfiled under notary Codegori, matricola 582, pacco 8). The Florentine merchant was Don Luca d'Albicis and the Levantine Jew was named Abram Catelano.

63. Leoni's article "Documenti e Notizie...," pp. 131-132, doc. 3.

64. ASF, notary Conti, matricola 584, pacco 8s, doc. dated August 18, 1557 (may also be found under notary Codegori, matricola 582, pacco 8).

65. ASF, notary Conti, matricola 584, pacco 9s, doc. dated September 11, 1562, pp. 6, 16. The rabbi named was Samuel Zarfalino.

66. Leoni's article "Documenti e Notizie...," p. 120. The incident is dated 1556 rather than 1558. But it could not possibly have occurred before the couple were married. Besides, in 1556 Samuel was in Constantinople (Salomon and Leoni's 1998 article in *JQR*, p. 163). The date of 1556 must therefore have been an error.

67. ASF, notary Saracco, matricola 493, pacco 29; doc. dated May 16, 1558.

68. Grunebaum-Ballin's *Joseph Naci, duc de Naxos*, p. 75, n.3.

69. Segre's article "Nuovi Documenti sur Marrani d'Ancona (1555-1559)" p. 152

70. Leoni's article "Documenti e Notizie...," p. 134, doc. 7.

71. ASF, notary Conti, matricola 584, pacco 8s, doc. dated May 25, 1558.

72. ASF, notary Conti, matricola 584, pacco 8s, second doc. dated May 27, 1558.

73. Leoni's article "Documenti e Notizie...," pp. 130-131, doc. 3 dated October 1557; the reason for this becomes apparent later in this chapter.

74. ASF, notary Conti, matricola 584, pacco 8s, third doc. dated May 27, 1558.

75. ASF, notary Andrea Cocchapano, but found in the file of notary Taurino, matricola 535, pacco 8, doc. dated July 7, 1557. The lawyer was Don Hieronimo Cornaro.

76. ASF, notary Conti, matricola 584, pacco 8s, fourth doc. dated May 27, 1558.

77. La Chica clearly uses the Beneveniste family name when referring to her cousin, Reyna, rather than Reyna's married name of Nasi.

78. ASF, notary Conti, matricola 584, pacco 8s, fourth doc. dated May 27, 1558.

79. David's *To Come to the Land*, p. 44.

80. Grunebaum-Ballin's *Joseph Nasi, duc de Naxos*, p. 80.

81. ASF, notary Conti, matricola 584, pacco 8s, fifth doc. dated May 27, 1558.

82. ASF, notary Saracco, matricola 493, pacco 29, doc. dated August 20, 1557.

83. ASF, notary Conti, matricola 584, pacco 8s, docs. dated October 20 and 21, 1558.

84. ASF, notary Conti, matricola 584, pacco 8s, doc. dated March 16, 1559.

85. Leoni's article "Documenti e Notizie...," p. 121; Dordeiro is sometimes listed as de Ardeiro.

86. AFS, notary Conti, matricola 584, pacco 9s, docs. dated February 4 and June 18,

1561.

87. Leoni's article "Documenti e Notizie...," p. 121.

88. ASM, Cancelleria Ducale, Patricolari, busta 885 (sub folder titled "Mendez"), undated doc.

89. Ravid's article "Money, Love and Power...," pp. 177-178; also see Grunebaum-Ballin's *Joseph Nasi, duc de Naxos*, p. 75.

90. ASF, notary Conti, matricola 584, pacco 8s, second doc. dated March 16, 1559.

91. Joshua Soncino's responsum 20; I am especially grateful to Hanania Cohen for a difficult and lengthy translation that summarizes the details of the entire dispute.

92. Joshua Soncino's responsum 20.

93. Joshua Soncino's responsum 20.

94. Joshua Soncino's responsum 20.

95. Leoni's article "Documenti e Notizie...," p. 133-134, docs. 6 and 7, dated October-November, 1560.

96. Joshua Soncino's responsum 20.

97. ASF, notary Conti, matricola 584, pacco 9s, doc. dated September 11, 1562, pp. 11 and 17.

98. Leoni's article "Documenti e Notizie...," pp. 135-136, doc. 8.

CHAPTER 17

1. Examples are in the introduction to Joshua Soncino's responsum 12 and the naming of the synagogue in Izmir (see later in this chapter).

2. I am grateful to Dr. Aviva Ben-Ur, a Sephardic scholar, for this insight.

3. Introduction to Joshua Soncino's responsum 12.

4. Introduction to Joshua Soncino's responsum 12.

5. Sa'adiah Longo's elegy to Doña Gracia in his *Shivrei Lukhot* (sometimes known as *Seder Zemanim*)

6. Usque's *Consolation...*, p. 230.

7. Baron's *A Social and Religious History...*, Vol. XVIII, p. 82.

8. Baron's *A Social and Religious History...*, Vol. XVIII, pp. 82-83.

9. Baron's *A Social and Religious History...*, Vol. XVIII, pp. 82-83.

10. Roth's *Doña Gracia...*, pp. 125-126.

11. Baron's *A Social and Religious History...*, Vol. XVIII, p. 201.

12. Michael Molho's booklet *Les Synagogues de Salonique.*

13. A fuller account of conditions in Salonika can be found throughout I. S. Emmanuel's *Histoire des Israélites de Salonique.*

14. Goodblatt's *Jewish Life in Turkey...*, pp. 112-113; also see Baron's *A Social and Religious History...*, Vol. XVIII, pp. 60-67.

15. Molho's *Les Synagogues de Salonique*, p. 37; also see Goodblatt's *Jewish Life in Turkey...*, p. 117 and Emmanuel's *Historie des Israélites...*, p. 217.

16. Almosnino's *Sefer Me'ametz Ko'ach* (Collection of 28 sermons), pp. 174-179, Sermon 22.

17. Almosnino's *Sefer Me'ametz Ko'ach* (Collection of 28 sermons), pp. 174-179, Sermon 22 (I am grateful to Dr. Hagitte Gal-Ed of New York City for the translation); also see Roth's *Doña Gracia...*, p. 129.

18. Emmanuel's *Historie des Israélites...*, p. 217.

19. Visited and noted by this author in June, 2000.

20. Emmanuel's *Historie des Israélites...*, p. 217; also see Goodblatt's *Jewish Life in Turkey...*, pp. 25-29.

21. Goodblatt's *Jewish Life in Turkey...*, p. 117; also see Emmanuel's *Histoire des Israélites...*, pp. 217, 223-225.

22. Emmanuel's *Historie des Israélites...*, pp. 183, 223-224.

23. Information provided by local scholars and guides during a visit by this author to Izmir in June 2000.

24. ACDF-SO S.O., St.St. Q3-b (Archivio della Congregazione per la Dottrina della Fedde) Rome. Lettre di vescovi dalla Dalmazia e dal Medio Oriente (1557-1629); file labeled *La Signora*, doc. dated July 12, 1560.

25. ACDF, doc. dated July 12, 1560 (as above).

26. Dernschwam's *Tagebuch einer Reise...*, p. 116.

27. Goodblatt's *Jewish Life in Turkey...*, p. 17.

28. Roth's article "The Marrano Press at Ferrara," pp. 315-317.

29. Roth's article *Salusque Lusitano*, p. 78; this author is not totally convinced, suspecting that the Samuel in question may have been Samuel Nasi.

30. Nassi's "Jewish Journalism and Printing Houses...," p. 81.

CHAPTER 18

1. Ludwig Lewisohn's *The Last Days of Shylock*, pp. 134, 157.

2. We have used the newer designation B.C.E. (Before the Christian Era) and C.E. (Christian Era).

3. Baron's *A Social and Religious History...*, Vol. XVIII, p. 110; also see David's *To Come to the Land*, p. 104.

4. For a fuller treatment of the history of Tiberias see Helga Dudman's *Tiberias*.

5. David's *To Come to the Land*, p. 30.

6. Nathan Schor's article: "An Attempt to establish a Jewish State in Tiberias by Doña Gracia Mendes and Don Joseph Nasi and its foiling by the Franciscans," in Vol. 9 of *Et-Mol*, October 1987, Israel (Hebrew), p. 44.

7. From the map entitled "Palestine in the Sixteenth Century" that faces inside title page of Uriel Heyd's *Ottoman Documents on Palestine: 1552-1615*.

8. Schor's article "An Attempt to establish a Jewish State in Tiberias...," p. 48.

9. Neil Asher Silberman's *Heavenly Powers: Unraveling the Secret History of the Kabbalah*, Chapter 5.

10. Solomon Schechter's chapter "Safed in the Sixteenth Century," in his *Studies in Judaism* p. 236.

11. David's *To Come to the Land*, p. 99.

12. Silberman's *Heavenly Powers...*, p. 145.

13. David's *To Come to the Land*, pp. 95-114.

14. Silberman's *Heavenly Powers...*, pp. 148-152.

15. Isiah 1:24-26.

16. Silberman's *Heavenly Powers...*, pp. 149-150.

17. Silberman's *Heavenly Powers...*, p. 147.

18. Goodblatt's *Jewish Life in Turkey...*, p. 175.

19. Heyd's *Ottoman Documents on Palestine...*, pp. 141-143.

20. Heyd's *Ottoman Documents on Palestine...*, p. 141, n.6.

21. Heyd's *Ottoman Documents on Palestine...*, pp. 141-143.

22. Heyd's *Ottoman Documents on Palestine...*, p. 142.

23. Baron's *A Social and Religious History...*, Vol. XVIII, p. 110; also see David's *To Come to the Land*, p. 31.

24. Heyd's article "Turkish Documents on the Rebuilding of Tiberias in the Sixteenth Century," in *Sefunot*, Vol. 10, pp. 204-209, and his *Ottoman Documents on Palestine...*, p. 139.

25. Charrière's *Négociations de La France dans le Levant*, Vol. II, p. 734.

26. Heyd's article "Turkish Documents on the Rebuilding...," pp. 204-209.

27. A fuller account of Don Joseph's diplomatic activities during these years will be taken up later.

28. Schor's article: "An Attempt to establish a Jewish State in Tiberias...," pp. 44-45; also see Heyd's article "Turkish Documents on the Rebuilding...," pp. 193-201.

29. Introduction to the Hebrew journal, *Sefunot X* (1966), p. 14.

30. Heyd's article, "Turkish Documents on the Rebuilding...," p. 204, doc. B.

31. Heyd's article, "Turkish Documents on the Rebuilding...," p. 204, doc. B.

32. David's *To Come to the Land*, p. 30, quoting a lengthy account compiled at the time by Joseph ha-Kohen.

33. Charrière's *Négociations de La France dans le Levant*, Vol. II, p. 734.

34. Charrière's *Négociations de La France dans le Levant*, Vol. II, p. 734.

35. Baron's *A Social and Religious History...*, Vol. XVIII, p. 113.

36. David's *To Come to the Land*, pp. 30-31; also see Roth's *The Duke of Naxos*, p. 115.

37. Marcus' *The Jew in the Medieval World*, p. 322, quoting ha-Kohen's account.

38. Marcus' *The Jew in the Medieval World*, p. 322, further quoting ha-Kohen.

39. Dudman's *Tiberias*, p. 199.

40. Roth's *The Duke of Naxos*, pp. 126-127, quoting a verbatim statement from community of Cori, Italy.

41. Roth's *The Duke of Naxos*, pp. 128-130.

42. Roth's *The Duke of Naxos*, p. 118.

43. Grunebaum-Ballin's *Joseph Naci, duc de Naxos*, p. 79.

44. Roth's *The Duke of Naxos*, p. 115.

45. David's *To Come to the Land*, pp. 32-33, 145.

46. Roth's *The Duke of Naxos*, p. 120.

47. David's *To Come to the Land*, p. 33.

48. Yahia-al-Ahri's *Travels in the Land of Israel (1567)*, Notebook 23; pertinent page provided by Beth Hatefutsoth Museum, Tel-Aviv, from the original in the Jewish National and University Library in Jerusalem

49. Schor's article "An Attempt to establish a Jewish State in Tiberias...," p. 47.

50. The "mansion" is mentioned in Roth's *The Duke of Naxos*, p. 116, and again in his *Doña Gracia...,*"p. 182; however, there is no source note and this fact could not be corroborated.

51. Aveiro's *Itineraro da Terra Sancta e suas Particularidades*, p. 472.

52. Heyd's article "Turkish Documents on the Rebuilding...," p. 206, docs. C and D.

53. Heyd's article "Turkish Documents on the Rebuilding...," p. 206, docs. C and D.

54. Heyd's article "Turkish Documents on the Rebuilding...," p. 206, docs. C and D.

55. Heyd's article "Turkish Documents on the Rebuilding...," p. 207, doc. E.

56. Heyd's article "Turkish Documents on the Rebuilding...," p. 208, doc. F.

57. Heyd's article "Turkish Documents on the Rebuilding...," p. 209, doc. G.

58. Schor's article "An Attempt to establish a Jewish State in Tiberias...," p. 49.

59. A responsum of Rabbi Abraham Rovico, as reprinted in David's article, "New Sources on the History of the Members of the Nasi-Mendes Family...," in the journal *Henoch*, Vol. XX, pp. 184-185.

60. Previously mentioned in Chapter 7 and based upon a written memo from Catherine Clément, the French novelist and author of *La Señora*, to the author dated June 14, 1997.

61. Roth's *The Duke of Naxos*, p. 132.

62. David's *To Come to the Land*, p. 17.

63. Schor's article "An Attempt to establish a Jewish State in Tiberias...," p. 48.

64. Baron's *A Social and Religious History...*, Vol. XVIII, p. 116.

65. Roth's *The Duke of Naxos*, p. 132.

66. Baron's *A Social and Religious History...*, Vol. XVIII, p. 489, n. 76; also see Schor's article "An Attempt to establish a Jewish State in Tiberias...," p. 50.

CHAPTER 19

1. Baron's *A Social and Religious History...*,Vol. XVIII, p. 104; also see Grunebaum-Ballin's *Joseph Naci, duc de Naxos*, p. 151. Since the sultan was known as "The Grand Turk" Don Joseph's nickname may have been a colloquial way for the Jews to refer to the person they considered the most powerful among them.

2. For a more thorough treatment of the career of Don Joseph see Reznik's *Le duc Joseph de Naxos*, Grunebaum-Ballin's *Joseph Naci, duc de Naxos*, Roth's *The Duke of Naxos*, Baron's *A Social and Religious History...*, Vol. XVIII, pp. 84-109 and Goodwin's

Lord of the Horizons. The general highlights on the following pages are taken from these works.

3. Dedication to Don Joseph in Lusitanus' *Centuria V.*

4. Goodwin's *Lord of the Horizons,* p. 89.

5. Baron's *A Social and Religious History...,* Vol. XVIII, p. 479, n. 52.

6. Busbecq's *The Turkish Letters of Ogier Ghiselin de Busbecq,* p. 164.

7. Roth's *The Duke of Naxos,* p. 96.

8. From Turkish histories, as recounted by the historian Beki Bahar during an interview with author in Istanbul in April, 2000.

9. Gaeta's *Nunziature di Venezia,* Vol. 8, letters 106, 110, 152.

10. Grunebaum-Ballin's *Joseph Naci, duc de Naxos,* p. 107, n. 3, mentions the amount in a letter from Selim to the French king; the identical sum of 150,000 is also cited by Facchinetti, Papal Nuncio in Venice, in correspondence to the Vatican on January 19, 1569 (Gaeta's *Nunziature di Venezia,* Vol. 8, letter 337).

11. Grunebaum-Ballin's *Joseph Naci, duc de Naxos,* pp. 103-105.

12. Charrière's *Négociations de La France dans le Levant,* Vol. II, pp. 772-773.

13. Gaeta's *Nunziature di Venezia,* Vol. 8, letters 334, 350.

14. Strada's *History of the Low Country Wars,* pp. 138-139.

15. Strada's *History of the Low Country Wars,* pp. 138-140.

16. See note 2 of this chapter for the combined sources for this general history.

17. A comprehensive treatment of the Amsterdam and the Caribbean trade can be found in Bloom's *The Economic Activities of the Jews of Amsterdam....*

18. Roth's *The Duke of Naxos,* pp. 169-173.

19. Emmanuel's *Histoire des Israélites de Salonique,* p. 217.

20. Roth's *The Duke of Naxos,* p. 166.

21. Almosnino's "Tratado de los sueños" in his *El Regimiento de la Vida.*

22. Roth's *The Duke of Naxos,* pp. 249-250, n. 48, quoting Almosnino.

23. Grunebaum-Ballin's *Joseph Naci, duc de Naxos,"* pp. 152-155.

24. Dedication to Don Joseph by Lusitanus in his *Centuria V.*

25. Roth's *The Duke of Naxos,* pp. 174-175.

26. Rosenblatt's *Joseph Nasi, Court Favorite...,* p. 152.

27. *Ben Porat Yosef* was reprinted by Mashabim, Jerusalem, 1952.

28. Almosnino's *Mamats Ko'akh,* pp. 62b-74b; the mention came in a eulogy delivered on 11 *Nisan* (Jewish calendar) in the Ashkenazi synagogue in Salonika and became part of a collection of his various speeches and sermons entitled *Mamats Ko'akh,* published in Venice in 1588. I am grateful to Dr. Aviva Ben-Ur for this research and translation.

29. For the weather I am indebted to Beki Bahar, the Turkish historian who checked the historical weather records for that winter.

30. Silberman's *Heavenly Powers,* pp. 132-135.

31. I would like to thank Rabbi Leah Novick of Carmel, Calif., for helping me through the concepts of Jewish mysticism as they may have related to the life and death of Doña Gracia.

32. Almosnino's *Mamats Ko'akh*, pp. 62b-74b.

33. Almosnino's *Mamats Ko'akh*, p. 134a, quoting the eulogy that Almosnino gave late in the fall of 1570 for a man named Astruc ibn Sahal.

34. Almosnino's *Mamats Ko'akh*, p. 134.

35. See Longo's *Shivrei Lukhot*, ref. Opp 8N 1074 (3), ff.42-47, Bodleian Library, Oxford, England; this may be the only extant copy now available.

36. Emmanuel's *Histoire des Israélites de Salonique*, pp. 194-197.

37. Statistics are simply not available, given the secrecy surrounding their departure from Portugal, the many years over which these migrations took place and the number of deaths that ensued along the way.

38. Longo's *Shivrei Lukhot*.

39. Grunebaum-Ballin's *Joseph Naci, duc de Naxos*, p. 165.

40. Moses di Trani's responsum 80.

41. Joshua Soncino's responsum 12.

42. Usque's *Consolation...*, p. 230.

43. Examples include *Una Princhipesa en Israel*, written in Rashi script and published by El Pueblo, Salonika, 1929 (now in the private collection of the Besso family of Miami, Fla. and located for this author by Dr. Aviva Ben-Ur). No author is given for this work, which is typical of this genre.

44. Baron's *A Social and Religious History...*, Vol. XVIII, p. 471, n. 35.

EPILOGUE

1. Bernardini's *Jews and the Expansion...*, Chapter 8.

2. Rosenblatt's *Joseph Nasi, Court Favorite...*, p. 106.

3. Roth's *The Duke of Naxos*, p. 66.

4. Emmanuel's *Historie des Israélites...*, p. 183.

5. Roth's *The Duke of Naxos*, p. 236, n. 17 and 18.

6. Emmanuel's *Historie des Israélites...*, pp. 202-204.

7. Baron's *A Social and Religious History...*, Vol. XVIII, p. 480, n. 55.

8. Goodwin's *Lords of the Horizons*, p. 160.

9. In keeping with the earlier synopsis of Don Joseph's career, these generally accepted historical events are listed in note 2 of this chapter.

10. Rosenblatt's *Joseph Nasi, Court Favorite...*, p. 158.

11. Grunebaum-Ballin's *Joseph Naci, duc de Naxos*, p. 165.

12. Charrière's *Négociations de La France dans le Levant*, Vol. III, p. 809.

13. Emilie Roi's article "Double Masks," in the Hebrew drama quarterly, *Bamah*, Israel, 1992.

14. Grunebaum-Ballin's *Joseph Naci, due de Naxos*, p. 166.

15. British newspaper The Jewish World, issue of January 2, 1885, p. 3.

16. Charrière's *Négociations de La France dans le Levant*, Vol. III, p. 809

17. Grunebaum-Ballin's *Joseph Naci, duc de Naxos*, pp. 128, 167

18. Grunebaum-Ballin's *Joseph Naci, duc de Naxos*, p. 167; also see Roth's *The Duke of Naxos*, pp. 216-219.

19. Baron's *A Social and Religious History...*, Vol. XVIII, pp. 477-478, n. 48.

20. Grunebaum-Ballin's *Joseph Naci, duc de Naxos*, p. 167; also see Roth's *The Duke of Naxos*, pp. 216-219

21. Paul Wittek's article "A Letter of Murad III to the Doge of Venice, of 1580," in the *Bulletin of the School of Oriental and African Studies*, Vol. XIV, pp. 381-383, University of London, 1952.

22. Zorattini's *Processi del S. Uffizio...*, Vol. V, pp. 26-29.

23. Isaac appears in the record twice: ASF, notary Conti, matricola 584, pacco 9s, doc. dated September 11, 1562 and in Zorattini's *Processi Del S. Uffizio...*, Vol. I, p. 253.

24. Zorattini's (Ed.) *L'Identità Dissimulata: Giudaizzanti Iberici Nell'Europa Cristiana Dell'età Moderna*, pp. 215, 225.

25. Brian Pullan's lecture "The Inquisition and the Jews of Venice: The Case of Gaspare Ribeiro, 1580-1581," given at the John Rylands University Library, Manchester, England, in January 1979, and reprinted in the *Bulletin of the John Rylands University Library*, Vol. 62, 1979, pp. 207-231; the full trial is transcribed in Zorattini's *Processi Del S. Uffizio...*, Vol. V.

26. Wittek's article in the *Bulletin of the School...*, Vol. XIV, p. 381.

BIBLIOGRAPHY

BOOKS

Ackroyd, Peter, *The Life of Thomas More*, Vintage Books, London, 1999.

Adler, Elkan Nathan, *Jewish Travellers: A Treasury of Travelogues from Nine Centuries*, Herman Press, New York, 1966.

Almeida, A. A. Marquis de, *Capitais e Capitalistas no Comércio da Especiaria*, Edições Cosmos, Lisbon, 1993.

Almosnino, Moses, *Extremos y Grandezas de Constantinopla*, Francisco Martinez, Madrid, 1638.

Almosnino, Moses, *Me'amets Ko'ach* (book of sermons), Venice, 1588.

Amram, David Werner, *The Makers of Hebrew Books in Italy*, Greenstone, Philadelphia, 1909.

Anguille, Marco Bruno, *Consiliorum sive Responsorum illustris ac praestantissimi iureconsulti*, Vol. I, edited by Thomas Cananus, Zenari, Venice, 1583.

Assis, Yom Tov, *The Jews of Spain: From Settlement to Expulsion*, Hebrew University/ World Zionist Organization, Jerusalem, 1988.

Assis, Yom Tov, *The Golden Age of Aragonese Jewry*, The Littman Library, London, 1997.

Aveiro, Fr. Pantaleâo de, *Itineraro da Terra Sancta e Suas Particularidades*, Coimbra, Impresa da Universidade, 1927 (original 1565).

Baer, Yitzhak, *A History of the Jews in Christian Spain*, Vols. I and II, Jewish Publication Society, Philadelphia, 1961.

Barata, Maria do Rosario, *Rui Fernandes de Almada*, Coimbra, 1973.

Barnett, Lionel D., *Bevis Marks Records*, Oxford University Press, 1949.

Baron, Salo Wittmayer, *A Social and Religious History of the Jews*, Vols. XI, XIII, XIV, XVIII, Columbia University Press, New York, 1967-69.

Baskin, Judith R., *Jewish Women in Historical Perspective*, Wayne State University, De-troit, 1991.

Bernardini, Paolo and Fiering, Norman, *The Jews and the Expansion of Europe to the West, 1450-1800*, Berghahn Books, New York, 2001.

Bianchi, Righi, and Terzaghi, *The Doge's Palace in Venice*, Electra, Milan, 1997.

Bloom, Herbert I., *The Economic Activities of the Jews of Amsterdam in the Seventeenth and Eighteenth Centuries*, Bayard Press, Pennsylvania, 1937 (reprinted by Kennikat Press, Port Washington, New York, 1969).

Bosworth, et al, *The Encyclopaedia of Islam, New Edition*, E. J. Brill, Leiden, 1995.

Brasavoli, Antonio Musa, *Medici Ferrariensis - Examen Omnium Trochiscorum Unguentorum, Ceratorum, Emplorum, Cataplasmatumque....*Venice, 1551.

Brasavoli, Antonio Musa, *Medici Ferrariensis - De medicamentis tam simplicibus, quam compositis catharticis, quae uniciuq humorisunt propria,* Vincenti Valgrisi, Venice, 1552.

Braudel, Fernand, *The Mediterranean and the Mediterranean World in the Age of Phillip II,* translated by Siân Reynolds, HarperCollins, 1972 (abridged edition in one volume).

Brown, Patricia Fortini, *Art and Life in Renaissance Venice,* Abrams, New York, 1997.

Brown, Rawdon, *Calendar of State Papers and Manuscripts relating to English Affairs existing in the Archives and Collections of Venice,* Vol. 5 (1534-1554), Longman & Co. and Trubner & Co., London, 1873.

Bull, George, *Venice: The Most Triumphant City,* St. Martin's Press, New York, 1981.

Busbecq, Ogier Ghiselin, *The Turkish Letters of Ogier Ghiselin de Busbecq,* translated by E. S. Forster, Clarendon Press, London, 1927.

Calimani, Riccardo, *The Ghetto of Venice,* Rusconi Libri, Milan, 1988.

Casola, Pietro (or M.M. Newett), *Canon Pietro Casola's Pilgrimage to Jerusalem in the Year 1494,* translated by M. M. Newett, University of Manchester Press, 1907.

Charrière, E., *Négociations de La France dans le Levant,* Vols. II and III, Burt Franklin, New York, 1966.

Chesneau, Jean, *Le Voyage de Monsieur D'Aramon, Ambassador pour le roy en Levant,* in *Recueil de Voyages et de Documents pour servir a L'histoire de la geographie depuis le XIIIe jusqu'a la fin du XVIe siecle,,* Vol 8. Ernest Leroux, Paris, 1887.

Chiappini, Luciano *La Corte Estense alla meta' del Cinquecento—I Compendi di Cristoforo di Messiburgo,* Belriguardo, Ferrara, 1984.

City of Antwerp *Antwerp's Golden Age: the Metropolis of the West in the 16th and 17th Centuries,* Buschmann, Antwerp, 1973, circulated by the Smithsonian Institution, 1973-75.

Clément, Catherine, *La Senora,* Calmann-Levy, Paris, 1992 (fiction).

Cristinelli, Giuseppe, *Cannaregio: Un Sestiere di Venezia.* Venice, 1987.

Da Costa, Isaac, *Noble Families Among the Sephardic Jews,* Oxford University Press, London, 1936.

Danby, Herbert, *The Mishnah* (in translation), Oxford University Press, 1933.

David, Abraham, *To Come to the Land,* University of Alabama Press, 1999.

Dernschwam, Hans, *Tagebuch einer Reise nach Konstantinopel und Kleinasien (1553-1555),* in *Studien Zur Fugger-Geschichte,* Vol. 7, edited by Babinger; Verlag von Duncker & Humblot, Munich-Leipzig, 1923.

Diffie, Bailey W. and Winius, George D. , *Foundations of the Portuguese Empire, 1415-1580,* University of Minnesota Press, 1977.

Dillard, Heath, *Daughters of the Reconquest,* Cambridge University Press, 1975.

Dudman, Helga, *Tiberias,* Carta, Jerusalem, 1988 (English).

Ehrenberg, Richard, *Capital and Finance in the Age of the Renaissance,* translated by H.M. Lucas, August M. Kelley, New York, 1963.

Elias, Norbert, *The History of Manners,* Urizen Books, New York, 1978.

Emmanuel, I. S., *Histoire des Israélites de Salonique*, Librairie Lipschutz, Paris, 1936.

Epstein, Mark Alan, *The Ottoman Jewish Communities and their Role in the Fifteenth and Sixteenth Centuries*, Klaus Schwarz Verlag, Freiburg, 1980.

Epstein, Baruch, *Mekor Baruch (Barukh)*, Vilna, 1928, reprinted in New York, 1994.

Epstein, Isidore, *The Babylonian Talmud* (in translation), Soncino Press, London, 1936.

Erler, Mary and Kowaleski, Maryanne, *Women and Power in the Middle Ages*, University of Georgia Press, 1988.

Falk, W. Ze'ev, *Jewish Matrimonial Law in the Middle Ages*, Oxford University Press, 1966.

Francesco, Carla di and Borella, Marco, *Ferrara: the Estense City*, Italcards, Bologna, Italy (not dated).

Franzoi, Umberto, *The Prisons of the Doge's Palace in Venice*, Electra, Venice, 1997.

Freehof, Solomon, *The Responsa Literature and A Treasury of Respona*, Ktav Publishing House, New Jersey, 1973.

Friedenberg, Daniel M., *Jewish Medals From the Renaissance to the Fall of Napoleon*, Clarkson Potter, New York, 1970.

Friedenwald, Harry *The Jews and Medicine: Essays*, Vol. I, Johns Hopkins Press, Maryland, 1944.,

Friedenwald, Harry, *Amatus Lusitanus*, reprinted as a separate book from the *Bulletin of the Institute of the History of Medicine*, Vol. 5, July 1937.

Ford, J.D.M., *Letters of John III, King of Portugal, 1521-1557*, Harvard University Press, Cambridge, Mass. 1931.

Front, Dov, *The Expurgation of the Books of Amatus Lusitanus*, (unpublished monograph provided to this author).

Gaeta, Franco, *Nunziature di Venezia*, Vols. 5,6,8, Instituto Storico Italiano, Italy, 1967.

Gairdner, James, *Letters and Papers, Foreign and Domestic, of the Reign of Henry VIII*, Vol. XII, Part II, Eyre and Spottiswoode, London, 1891.

Gairdner, James and Brodie, R. H., *Letters and Papers, Foreign and Domestic, of the Reign of Henry VIII*, Vol. XIX, Part I and Vol. XX, Part II, Mackie and Co., London, 1903 and 1907.

Galante, Avram (Abraham), *Documents Officiels Turcs Concernant les Juifs de Turquie*, Haim, Rozio & Co., Istanbul, 1931.

Galante, Abraham, *Hommes et Choses Juifs Portugais en Orient*, Société Anonyme de Papeterie, Constantinople, 1927.

Gayangos, Pascual de, *Calendar of Letters, Despatches and State Papers relating to the Negotiations between England and Spain*, Vol. VI, Part II, Henry VIII, 1542-1543; Eyre and Spottiswoode, London, 1895.

Gerber, Jane, *The Jews of Spain: A History of the Sephardic Experience*, The Free Press, New York, 1994.

Gerlach, Stephan, *Turkisches Tagebuch (Stephan Gerlachs des aeltern Tage-Buch der von zween glorw....)* Johann-David Zunners, Frankfurt, 1674 (copy at Rare Book Library, Colgate Rochester Divinity School and photocopy at Dumbarton Oaks Library, Washington, D.C).

Ginio, Alisa Meyuhas, *Jews, Christians and Muslims in the Mediterranean World after*

1492, Frank Cass, Portland, Ore. 1993.

Gitlitz, David M., *Secrecy and Deceit: the Religion of the Crypto-Jews*, The Jewish Publication Society, Philadelphia, 1996.

Godinho, Vitorino Magalhâes, *Os Descobrimentos e a Economia Mundia*, Vol. 2, , Editoria Arcádia, Lisbon, 1965.

Gómara, Francisco López de, *Annals of The Emperor Charles V*, Oxford University Press, 1912 (a contemporary chronicle edited and introduced by Roger Bigelow Merriman).

Goodblatt, Morris S., *Jewish Life in Turkey in the Sixteenth Century*, Jewish Theological Seminary of America, New York, 1952.

Goodwin, Jason, *Lords of the Horizons: A History of the Ottoman Empire*, Vintage, London, 1999.

Goris, J.A., *Étude sur Les Colonies Marchandes Méridionales*, Burt Franklin, New York, 1925 (reprint 1971).

Graetz, Henrich, *History of the Jews*, Vol. IV, The Jewish Publication Society, Philadelphia, 1967.

Grunebaum-Ballin, P., *Joseph Naci, duc de Naxos*, Mouton, Paris, 1968.

Gundersheimer, Werner L., *Ferrara: the Style of a Renaissance Despotism*, Princeton University Press, 1973.

Ha-Kohen, Joseph, *El Valle Del Llanto (Emek ha Bakha or Vale of Tears)*, Spanish translation by Pilar León Tello, Riopiedras Ediciones, Barcelona, 1989.

Hale, John , *The Civilization of Europe in the Renaissance*, HarperCollins, London, 1993.

Herculano, Alexandre, *History of the Origin and Establishment of the Inquisition in Portugal*, translated by John C. Branner, Stanford University Press, 1926, reprinted by Ktav Publishing House, New Jersey, 1972.

Heyd, Uriel, *Ottoman Documents on Palestine: 1552-1615*, Clarendon Press, Oxford, 1960.

Jardine, Lisa, *Worldly Goods: A New History of the Renaissance*, Doubleday (Nan Talese), New York, 1996.

Kamen, Henry, *The Spanish Inquisition: An Historical Revision*, Weidenfeld & Nicholson, London, 1997.

Katz, David S., *The Jews in the History of England*, Clarendon Press, Oxford, 1994.

Kedourie, Elie, *Spain and the Jews: The Sephardic Experience 1492 and After*, Thames and Hudson, London, 1992.

Kellenbenz, Hermann, *Os mercadores alemães de Lisboa por volta de 1530*, Faculdade de Letras da Universidade de Coimbra, 1961.

Labarge, Margaret Wade, *A Small Sound of the Trumpet*, Beacon Press, Boston, 1986.

Lach, Donald F., *Asia in the Making of Europe*, University of Chicago Press, 1965.

Lando (Landi), Ortensio, *Dialogo di M. Ortensio Lando nel quale si…*, Al Segno del Posso, Venice, 1552.

Laguna, Andrés, *Viage en Turquia* in *Autobiografias y Memorias* edited by M. Serrano y Sanz, Libreria Editorial de Bailly-Bailliere e Hijos, Madrid, 1905 (wrongly attributed to Cristóbal de Villalón).

Lamdan, Ruth, *A Separate People: Jewish Women in Palestine, Syria and Egypt in the*

Sixteenth Century, Brill, Leiden/Boston, 2000.

Lazar, Moshe, *The Ladino Bible of Ferrara, 1553: a Critical Edition,* Labyrinthos, Culver City, Calif., 1992.

Leal, José da Silva Mendes, *Corpo Diplomatico Portuguez—Os Actos e Relações Politicas e Diplomaticas de Portugal,* Vol. VI and Vol. VII, Lisbon, 1884.

Lewis, Bernard, *The Jews of Islam,* Princeton University Press, 1984.

Lewisohn, Ludwig, *The Last Days of Shylock,* Harper & Brothers, New York and London, 1931 (fiction).

Livermore, H.V. , *A New History of Portugal,* Cambridge University Press, 1976.

Lopes, J. M, *Les Portugais à Anvers au XVI Siècle,* Buschmann, Antwerp, 1895.

Longworth, Philip, *The Rise and Fall of Venice,* Constable, London, 1974.

Lusitanus, Amatus, *Discorides I and II* and various *Centuriae;* diverse editions available from academic libraries, including the historical medical library at Yale Medical School, New Haven, Conn.

Mansel, Philip, *Constantinople: City of the World's Desire 1453-1924,* Penguin Books, New York, and London, 1997.

Marcus, Jacob R., *The Jew in the Medieval World: A Source Book, 315- 1791.* The Sinai Press, Cincinnati, 1938.

Meram, Ali Kemal, *Padisah Analari,* Ozyayin, Istanbul, 1980.

Marnef, Guido, *Antwerp in the Age of Reformation: Underground Protestantism in a Commercial Metropolis,* Johns Hopkins University Press, Baltimore, 1996.

Marques, A. H. de Oliveira, *Daily Life in Portugal in the Late Middle Ages,* translated by S.S. Wyatt, University of Wisconsin Press, 1971.

Mercator, Fonds, *Crowning the City: Vernacular Architecture in Antwerp from the Middle Ages to the Present Day,* Haboldt & Co., Paris, 1993.

Mirrer, Louise, *Upon My Husband's Death,* University of Michigan, Press, 1992.

Moita, Irisalva, et al, *Lisboa Quinhentista: A Imagem e a vida da Cidade,* Exposição Temporaria, Direcção Dos Serviços Culturais da Câmara Municipal de Lisboa, 1984.

Molho, Michael, *Usos y Costumbres de los Sefaradies de Salonica,* Instituto Arias Montano, Madrid-Barcelona, 1950 (English translation by Alfred A. Zara to be published).

Molho, Michael, *Les Synagogues de Salonique,* Clermont-Ferrand, France, 1991; French translation by Agnès Wood. Hebrew edition, Aharon Rousso, Tel-Aviv, 1967.

Nassi, Gad (Ed.), *Jewish Journalism and the Printing Hosues in the Ottoman Empire and Modern Turkey,* Isis Press, Istanbul, 2001.

Nevins, Michael, *The Jewish Doctor: a Narrative History,* Jason Aronson, New Jersey, 1996.

Netanyahu, Benjamin, *The Origins of the Inquisition in Fifteenth Century Spain,* Random House, New York, 1995.

Nicolay, Nicolas, *The Navigations, Peregerinations and Voyages Made into Turkey...* translated by T. Washington the Younger, London, 1585 (in some instances the author's names are spelled with an "h"—Nicholas Nicholay).

Ojalvo, Harry, *Ottoman Sultans and their Jewish Subjects,* Quincentennial Foundation, Baksi Senesi, Istanbul, 1999.

Paris, Erna, *The End of Days: A Story of Tolerance, Tyranny and the Expulsion of the Jews from Spain*, Prometheus Books, New York, 1995.

Perera, Victor, *The Cross and the Pear Tree*, University of California Press, 1995.

Pullan, Brian, *The Jews of Europe and the Inquisition in Venice*, Oxford University Press, 1983.

Raphael, David, *The Expulsion 1492 Chronicles*, Carmi House Press, N. Hollywood, Calif., 1992.

Rau, Virginia, *Estudos Sobre História Económica e Social do Antigo Regime*, Editorial Presença, Lisbon, 1984.

Rau, Virginia, *Um Grande Mercador-Banqueiro Italiano em Portgual: Lucas Giraldi*, Estudos Italianos em Portugal, No.24, , Lisbon, 1965.

Reznik, Jacob, *Le Duc Joseph de Naxos*, Librairie Lipschutz, Paris, 1936.

Ribeiro, Aileen and Cumming, Valerie, *The Visual History of Costume*, Batsford, London, 1989.

Rich, E.E. and Wilson, C.H., *The Cambridge Economic History of Europe*, Vol. IV, Cambridge University Press, 1967.

Ridley, Jasper, *Henry VIII*, Constable, London, 1984.

Rose, Constance Hubbard, *Alonso Nuñez de Reinoso: the Lament of a Sixteenth- Century Exile*, Fairleigh Dickinson University Press, New Jersey, 1971.

Rosenblatt, Norman, *Joseph Nasi, Court Favorite of Selim II*, dissertation dated 1957. UMI Dissertation Services, Ann Arbor, Mich.

Roth, Cecil, *A History of the Marranos*, Jewish Publication Society, Philadelphia, 1932.

Roth, Cecil, *The Jews of Italy*, The Jewish Publication Society, Philadelphia, 1946.

Roth, Cecil, *The Duke of Naxos of the House of Nasi*, The Jewish Publication Society, Philadelphia, 1948 (reissued 1977).

Roth, Cecil, *Doña Gracia of the House of Nasi*, The Jewish Publication Society, Philadelphia, 1948 (reissued 1977).

Roth, Cecil, *The Jews in the Renaissance*, The Jewish Publication Society, Philadelphia, 1959.

Salomon, Herman Prins, *Deux Etudes Portugueses: Two Portuguese Studies*, Barbosa & Xavier, Braga, Portugal, 1991.

Schivelbusch, Wolfgang, *Tastes of Paradise: A History of Spices, Stimulants and Intoxicants*, Pantheon Books, New York, 1992.

Schmidt, Ephraim, *Geschiedenis van de Joden in Antwerpen*, Uitgeverij C. de Vries-Brouwers, BVBA, Antwerpen, 1963.

Schmidt, Ephraim, *L'Histoire Des Juifs à Anvers*, Excelsior, Antwerpen, 1963.

Schreiber, Emanuel, *Jews in Medicine*, Engelhard & Company, 1902.

Shulvass, Moses A., *The Jews in the World of the Renaissance*, E. J. Brill, Leiden, 1973.

Silberman, Neil Asher, *Heavenly Powers: Unraveling the Secret History of the Kabbalah*, Grosset/Putnam, New York, 1998.

Simonsohn, Shlomo, *The Apostolic See and the Jews*, Vols. 1-8, Pontifical Institute of Medieval Studies, Toronto, 1990.

Simonsohn, Shlomo, *The Jews in the Duchy of Milan*, Vols. 1-4, The Israel Academy of Sciences and Humanities, Jerusalem, 1982.

Smith, Roger C., *Vanguard of Empire: Ships of Exploration in the Age of Columbus*, Oxford University Press, 1993.

St. Clare Byrne, Muriel, *The Lisle Letters*, University of Chicago Press, 1981.

Stengers, Jean, *Les Juifs dans les Pays-Bas au Moyen Age*, Palais des Académies, Brussels, 1949.

Strada, Faminus, *History of the Low Country Wars*, translated by Sir Robert Stapylton, London, 1667.

Tadic, Jorjo, *Jevreji u Dubroniku*, Sarajevo, 1937.

Tavares, Adérito and Caldeira, Arlindo, *Lisboa Quinhentista*, Part 2, Oficinas Gráficas da Editorial do Ministério da Educação, Lisbon, 1992.

Tracy, James D., *The Rise of Merchant Empires: Long Distance Trade in the Early Modern World, 1350-1750*, Cambridge University Press, 1990.

Tyler, Royall *The Emperor Charles the Fifth*, Allen and Unwin, London, 1956.

Unger, Richard W., *The Ship in the Medieval Economy, 600-1600*, Croom Helm, London, and McGill-Queen's University Press, Montreal, 1980.

Usque, Samuel, *Consolation for the Tribulations of Israel*, translated by Martin A. Cohen, Jewish Publication Society, Philadelphia, 1965 (page numbers in Notes refer to this version throughout).

Van de Wee, Herman *The Growth of the Antwerp market and the European Economy (14-16th centuries)*, Publication of the Minister of Education and Culture, Louvain, 1963.

Vecellio, Cesare, *Habiti antichi er moderni di tutto il mondo*, Pressio Damian Zenaro, Venice, 1589.

Villalón, Cristobal de, *Viaje de Turquia* in *Autografias y Memorias*, edited by Serrano y Sanz, part of *Nueva Biblioteca de Autores Españoles*, Vol. 2, Madrid, 1905 (see Laguna above).

Vroman, Jean, *L'Affaire Diego Mendez*, privately published in Antwerp, 1937, part of the collections at the library of Hebrew Union College in Cincinnati, Ohio.

Wegg, Jervis, *Antwerp 1477–1559*, Metheun & Co., London, 1916.

Weir, Alison, *Eleanor of Aquitaine*, Ballantine, New York, 1999.

Witte, Charles-Martial de, *La Correspondance des Premiers Nonces Permanents au Portugal 1532-1553*, Academia Portuguesa da Historia, Lisbon, 1958.

Willett, C. and Cunnington, Phyllis, *The History of Underclothes*, Michael Joseph, London, 1951.

Zimler, Richard, *The Last Kabbalist in Lisbon*, Overlook Press, New York, 1998.

Zorattini, Pier Cesare Ioly, *Processi del S. Uffizio di Venezia Contro Ebrei E Giudaizzanti*, Vols. I, V, in the series *Storia Dell'Ebraismo in Italia*, II, edited by Leo S. Olschki, Firenze, Italy, 1980-87.

Zorattini, Pier Cesare Ioly (Ed.), *L'Identità Dissimulata: Giudaizzanti Iberici Nell'Europa Cristiana Dell'età Moderna*, in the series *Storia Dell'Ebraismo in Italia*, XX, Firenze, Italy, 2000.

Zuckerman, Arthur J., *A Jewish Princedom in Feudal France, 768-900*, Columbia University Press, 1972.

ARTICLES, SPEECHES AND CHAPTERS IN ANTHOLOGIES AND JOURNALS

Almosnino, Moses, "Tratado de los sueños" in *El Regimiento de la Vida*, Salonika, 1564.

Arbel, Benjamin, "Venice and the Jewish Merchants of Istanbul in the Sixteenth Century" in *The Mediterranean and the Jews: Banking, Finance and International Trade (16-18th Centuries)* edited by Toaff and Schwarzfuchs, Bar-Ilan University Press, Israel, 1989.

Bell, Susan Groag, "Medieval Women Book Owners" in *Women and Power in the Middle Ages*, edited by Mary Erler and Maryanne Kowaleski.

Brooks, Andrée, "A Jungle Journey" in *Reform Judaism Magazine*, Spring, 1999.

Connolly, Jane E., "Marian Intervention and Hagiographic Models in the Tale of the Chaste Wife" in *Quien Hubiese Tal Ventura: Medieval Hispanic Studies in Honour of Alan Deyermond*, edited by A.M. Beresford, Dept. of Hispanic Studies, Queen Mary and Westfield College, London, 1997.

David, Abraham, "New Jewish Sources on the History of Members of the Nasi-Mendes Family in Italy and Constantinople" in *Henoch*, Vol. XX, University of Turin, October 1998.

Denucé, J., "Privilèges Commercaux Accordés par les rois de Portugal aux Flamands et aux Allemands" in *Archivo Historico Portuguez*, Vol. II No. 10 E 11, October/November 1909, Lisbon.

Fernand-Halphen, Alice, "Une Grande Dame Juive de la Renaissance in *La Revue de Paris*, Trente-Sixième Année, Tome Cinquième, September-October 1929.

Garshowitz, Libby, "Gracia Mendes: Power, Influence and Intrigue" in *Power of the Weak: Studies in Medieval Women*, edited by Jennifer Carpenter and Sally Beth MacLean, Ohio State University Press, Champaign, Ill., 1995.

Grunebaum, Paul, "Notes et Mélanges" in *Revue des Études Juives*, No. 28, Librarie Durlacher, Paris, 1894.

Hanawalt, Barbara A., "Lady Honor Lisle's Network of Influence" in *Women and Power in the Middle Ages*, edited by Mary Erler and Maryanne Kowaleski, University of Georgia Press, 1988.

Heyd, Uriel, "Moses Hamon, chief Jewish physician to Sultan Suleyman the Magnificent," in *Oriens*, the Journal of the International Society for Oriental Research, Vol.16, E. J. Brill, Leiden, 1963.

Heyd, Uriel, "Turkish Documents on the Rebuilding of Tiberias in the Sixteenth Century" in *Sefunot*, pgs. 204-209, Vol. 10, Machon Ben-Zvi, Jerusalem, 1966.

Kaufman, David, "Deux Lettres Nouvelles" in *Revue des Études Juives*, No. 31, Durlacher, Paris, 1895.

Kellenbenz, Hermann, "I Mendes, I Rodrigues d'Evora e i Ximenes nei loro rapporti commerciali con Venezia" in *Gli Ebrei e Venezia*, Sec. XIV-XVIII, Edizioni Comunità, Venice, 1983.

Kobler, Franz, "Elijah of Pesaro's Voyage to Cyprus" in *Letters of Jews Through the Ages*, Hebrew Publishing Company, New York, 1952 (in English).

Leoni, Aron de Leone, "La dipomazia estense e l'immigrazione dei cristiani nuovi a Ferrara al tempe di Ercole II" in *Nuova Rivista Storica*, Vol. LXXVIII, No. II, Perugia, Italy, March-August 1994.

Leoni, Aron de Leone, "Documenti Notizie Sulle Famiglie Benveniste e Nassi a Ferrara in *Rassegna Mensile di Israel*, Vol. LVIII, 3rd Series, Italy, 1992.

Longo, Sa'adiah, Elegy to Doña Gracia Nassy in *Shivrei Lukhot*, published in Salonika in 1594. Only known copy at the Bodleian Library, Oxford; Opp8 1074(3)ff. 42-47.

Macedo, Helder, "A Sixteenth Century Portuguese Novel and the Jewish Press in Ferrara" in *European Judaism*, Vol. 33, No.1, London, Spring, 2000.

Muzzarelli, Maria Giuseppina, "Beatrice de Luna, Vedova Mendes, Alias Donna Gracia Nasi: Un'Ebrea Influente" in *Rinascimento al Femminile*, edited by Ottavia Niccoli. Editioni Laterza, Rome, 1991.

Pullan, Brian, "A Ship with Two Rudders: 'Righetto Marrano' and the Inquisition in Venice," in *The Historical Journal*, Cambridge University Press, No. 20, Vol. I, 1977.

Pullan, Brian, "The Inquisition and the Jews of Venice: the Case of Gaspare Ribeiro, 1580-158l," lecture given at the John Rylands University Library, Manchester, England, on January 10, 1979; reprinted in the *Bulletin of the John Rylands University Library*, Vol. 62, 1979.

Ravid, Benjamin, "Money, Love and Power Politics in Sixteenth Century Venice: the Perpetual Banishment and Subsequent Pardon of Joseph Nasi" in *Italia Judaica, Atti del I Convegno Internazionale, Bari 18-22*, March, 1981, reprinted by the Ministero per i Beni Cultuali e Ambientali Pubbicazioni degli Archivi di Stato, Saggi 2, Rome, 1983.

Rizzi, Guido, "Medici ebrei spagnoli nel mondo veneziano del XV secolo" in *Ateneo Veneto*, Vol. 136, N1, Jan-June, 1952.

Roi, Emilie, "Double Masks," in the Hebrew drama quarterly *Bamah*, Israel, 1992.

Roth, Cecil, "The Middle Period of Anglo-Jewish History Reconsidered" in *The Jewish Historical Society of England: Transactions*, Sessions 1955-59, Vol. XIX, University College, London, 1960.

Roth, Cecil, "Processo 9449 - Inquisition in Lisbon; case of Thomas Fernandez" in *The Jewish Historical Society of England: Miscellanies*, Part II, Purnell and Sons, London, 1935.

Roth, Cecil, "The Marrano Press at Ferrara: 1552-1555" in *Modern Language Review*, Vol. 38, 1943.

Roth, Cecil, "Salusque Lusitano" in the *Jewish Quarterly Review*, Vol. 34, 1943-44, Center for Judaic Studies, University of Pennsylvania, Philadelphia.

Salomon, H. P. and Leoni, Aron de Leone "Mendes, Benveniste, de Luna, Micas, Nasci: the State of the Art (1532-1558)" in *The Jewish Quarterly Review*, Vol. 88, No. 3-4, 1998, Center for Judaic Studies, University of Pennsylvania, Philadelphia.

Samuel, E. R., "Portuguese Jews in Jacobean London," article in *The Jewish Historical Society of England, Transactions*, Vol. XVIII, London, 1958.

Samuel, Edgar, "The Jewish Ancestry of Velasquez," in Vol. 35, 1996-8, *Jewish Historical Studies*, London.

Schor, Nathan, "An Attempt to Establish a Jewish State in Tiberias by Doña Gracia Mendes and Don Joseph Nasi and its foiling by the Franciscans" in *Et-Mol (53-54)*, Vol. 9 October, 1987, Israel (Hebrew).

Saperstein, Marc, "Martyrs, Merchants and Rabbis: Jewish Community Conflict as Reflected in the Responsa on the Boycott of Ancona" in *Jewish Social Studies,* Vol. 43, Nos. 3-4, Summer/Fall, 1981.

Segre, Renata, "Sephardic Refugees in Ferrara: Two Notable Families," in *Crisis and Creativity in the Sephardic World:1391–1648*, edited by Benjamin R. Gampel, Columbia University Press, New York, 1997.

Segre, Renata, "Nuovi Documenti sur Marrani d'Ancona (1555-1559)" in *Michael IX (or Mikhael)*, Tel Aviv, 1985.

Severy, Merle, "The World of Suleyman the Magnificent" in *National Geographic*, November, 1987.

Shatzmiller, Joseph, "Travelling in the Mediterranean in 1563: The Testimony of Eliahu of Pesaro" in *The Mediterranean and the Jews: Banking, Finance and Inernational Trade (XVI- XVIII Centuries)* edited by Ariel Toaff and Simon Schwarzfuchs, Bar-Ilan Press, Israel, 1989.

Sheehan, Michael M., "English wills and the records of the ecclesiastical and civil jurisdictions" in the *Journal of Medieval History*, North Holland Publishing Co., Amsterdam, No. 14, 1988.

Schechter, Solomon, "Safed in the Sixteenth Century" in *Studies in Judaism: Essays on Persons, Concepts and Movements of Thought in Jewish Tradition*, Atheneum, New York, 1970.

Sonne I., , "Une source nouvelle pour l'histoire des martyre d'Ancone" in *Revue des Études Juives*, No. 89, Paris, 1930.

Vidas, Albert de, *Erensia Sefardi, A Bulletin of Sephardic Heritage*, Winter 1998, edition, Fairfield, Conn.

Waddington, Raymond B., "Graven Images: Sixteenth-Century Portrait Medals of the Jews" in *The Expulsion of the Jews: 1492 and After*, edited by Raymond B. Waddington and Arthur H. Williamson, Garland Publishing, New York/London, 1994.

Wittek, Paul, "A Letter of Murad III to the Doge of Venice, of 1580" in *Bulletin of the School of Oriental and African Studies, University of London*, Vol. XIV, 1952.

Wolf, Lucien, "Jews in Elizabethan England" in *The Jewish Historical Society of England, Transactions*, Vol.XI 1924-7, Spottiswoode, Ballantyne & Co, London, 1928.

Wolf, Lucien, "Jews in Tudor England" in *Essays in Jewish History*, edited by Cecil Roth, The Jewish Historical of England, 1934.

Yosef Hayim Yerushalmi's , "The Lisbon Massacre of 1506 and the Royal Image in the Shebet Yehudah" in the *Hebrew Union College Annual Supplements*, No. 1, Cincinnati, 1976.

Zimler, Richard, "Identified as the enemy: being a Portuguese New Christian at the Time of the 'The Last Kabbalist of Lisbon'" in *European Judaism*, Vol. 33, No.1, London, Spring 2000.

Zorattini, Pier Cesare Ioly , "Anrriquez Nunez alias Abraham alias Righetto" in *The*

Mediterranean and the Jews: Banking, Finance and International Trade (XVI-XVIII Centuries) edited by Ariel Toaff and Simon Schwarzfuchs, Bar-Ilan Press, Israel, 1989.

Notes on sources of responsa literature used: Much of the responsa literature was generously furnished in photocopy form by Professor Libby Garshowitz of the University of Toronto. The photocopies came from the following sources: The writings of Rabbi Moses di Trani and Joseph Caro from *Avqat Rokhel* in an edition edited by Yeruham Fischel (Leipzig, 1859); Samuel de Medina from *She-elot u-Teshuvot me-ha-Rashdam* (Lemberg, 1862); Joseph ibn Lev from the second volume of *She-elot u-teshuvot*, Vols. 1-2 (reprint Jerusalem, 1958); Joshua Soncino from *Nahalah li-yehoshua* (Constantinople, 1731 also reprinted in Brooklyn, N.Y. in 1970). Collections of *responsa* are normally available at any institution of Jewish learning or university research library. Responsa typically use fictitious names like Reuven or Sarah (though the real names can be easily gleaned from the circumstances of the case).

Notes on exchange rates: for easy reading we have converted most of the currencies mentioned in the documents or secondary literature into ducats, using exchange rates for the appropriate periods provided by James Boyajian, a noted economic historian who lives in Madera, Calif. Sometimes local currency terms, such as scudi or florin, are found in the original documents being used interchangeably with the word ducats – a pan-European currency of that time and the most widely-used standard of the era.

ABBREVIATIONS FOR ARCHIVES, COLLECTIONS OR JOURNALS MENTIONED IN NOTES:

ACDF - Archivio della Congregazione per la Dottrina della Fede (Rome)

AGR - Archives Générales du Royaume (Belgium state archives in Brussels)

ANTT - Arquivo Nacional da Torre do Tombo (Portuguese state archives in Lisbon)

ASF - Archivio di Stato di Ferrara (state archives in Ferrara)

ASFM - Archivio di Stato di Firenza, Mediceo del Principato (Medici Archives) online at: http://www.medici.org/jewish/docs.html

ASM - Archivio di Stato di Modena (state archives in Modena)

ASV - Archivio di Stato di Venezia (state archives in Venice)

ASVAT - Archivio Segreto Vaticano (Vatican archives)

DMSW - Watson Manuscript Library at University College, London

JQR - Jewish Quarterly Review (Philadelphia)

OFCB - Office Fiscal du Conseil de Brabant (papers of the Council of Brabant)

PEA - Papiers d l'État et de l'Audience (state papers of Marie of Hungary)

SO - Sancti Officii (Office of the Inquisition - Rome)

GLOSSARY

alheiras	a Portuguese sausage that substitutes chicken for pork
aliyah	emigration to the Holy Land/Israel undertaken by Jews in the belief it is a holy journey
anusim	Hebrew term for forced converts to Catholicism
apostate	a traitor to the "true" faith; a heretic
arquebus	early type of portable gun (sometimes spelled harquebus) introduced during the 16th century
arriviste	a tycoon of humble origins
Ashkenazi Jew	a Jew of Eastern European origin
asper	unit of Turkish currency
auto-da-fé	public ceremony at which Catholics, or converts to Catholicism, who had repeatedly mocked the faith or done other heretical acts, were burned at the stake
bailo	Venetian envoy to a foreign court
BCE	new term for the period prior to the Christian Era; replaces BC (before Christ)
bet midrash	house of study
bills of exchange	precursors of letters of credit and personal checks
bourse de charité	an ad-hoc pool of money raised by wealthy *converso* merchants in Antwerp to help incoming *converso* refugees fleeing the Inquisition
bull	a papal decree needed before certain actions may be taken by the Catholic church
caravansaries	wayside inns for travelers
caravel	fast-moving and light sailing ship popular in the 16th century
carrack	large, ocean-going sailing ship built to transport heavy cargo; favored by the Spanish and Portuguese in the 16th century
Casa da Moeda	national mint of Portugal where coins were struck and private supplies of silver and gold bullion were stored
CE	new term for the Christian Era; replaces AD (*Anno Domini*, the year of Our Lord)
Centuriae	name given by Amatus Lusitanus, the noted 16th century physician, to his series of books, each of which recounted one hundred cases that he had treated
chaus	Turkish envoy to a foreign court
converso, conversa	a Jew who has been converted to Catholicism either by force or under duress; (*conversa* - feminine form)
Council of Ten	ruling assembly of the Republic of Venice

Counter-Reformation	punitive actions taken by the Catholic Church in the 16th century against break-away factions such as Protestants
crown	British and Flemish unit of currency
cruzado	Portuguese unit of currency
dhimmi	term used by the Ottoman Turks for Christians and Jews, implying a special class of non-Muslims higher than pagans
Discoveries	the voyages of the Spanish and Portuguese that led to the New World discoveries and the sea-going routes to the Orient
Don/Doña	Spanish and Portuguese honorific placed respectfully before the first name of anyone from a prominent or noble family
dragomen	term used by the Ottoman Turks for translators
ducat	pan-European unit of currency normally offered as golden coins of standardized weight; favored during the Renaissance especially for larger international deals
fidalgo	a Spanish gentleman ostensibly of noble birth
firman	official directive/requirement of the Turkish crown
florin	unit of currency used in the Low Countries and England during the 16th century
galley	large, shallow-draft ship propelled primarily by oars used extensively in the Mediterranean Sea until modern times
galliard	popular dance in the 16th century
geto/ghetto	the Venetian word for foundry that eventually became synonymous with substandard residential areas forcibly assigned to Jews
halberd	a staff-like combination of spear and battle-ax popular during the late Middle Ages and Renaissance
Holy Roman Empire	a loose confederation of German states that by the 16th century were far more modest in scope and power that the grandiose name implies
Holy See	Vatican/papal authorities
Inquisition	enforcement agency of the Catholic Church empowered to weed out anyone suspected of undermining the Catholic faith or not living life as a sincere Catholic; special targets were Jews and Muslims who had recently been converted to Catholicism, usually under duress or by force
janissaries	personal troops/guards of the sultan
Judeo-Spanish	the language of Jews from the Iberian Peninsula that was widely used, like Yiddish, until the 20th century
Juderia	a Jewish quarter that was internally self-governed
kabbalist/cabbalist	a student or follower of Jewish mysticism
ketubah	Jewish marriage contract that spells out the financial and legal facets of a marriage
La Señora	based upon the Spanish honorific and informal title ("Mrs" or "Madam"), it was given to Doña Gracia later in life when

	she became so well known that no name was needed after the honorific
Levant/Levantine	countries bordering the eastern crescent of the Mediterranean sea from Greece to Egypt; mostly comprised of Muslims
Licentato	honorific given to someone with a law degree
marranos	Spanish slang word for pigs used as a pejorative for converted Jews
messiah	a savior who would usher in an era of peace and tranquility
mikveh	Jewish ritual bath
minyan	a group of ten men needed before certain Jewish prayers may be recited
mishnah	name given to the codification of Jewish oral law and tradition written down in the second century CE. It covered all aspects of daily living, far beyond what today is considered religious practice; a parallel work compiled at around the same time by an alternate group of rabbis was called the *tosefta*
muezzin	Muslim clerics
mutationes	command posts to patrol and protect travelers from bandits
nasi	Hebrew word for prince or ruler
New Christians	Portuguese term for forcibly converted Jews
nuncio	senior papal representative in a particular country
oud	16th century guitar-like musical instrument
porte cochère	a roof projecting like a canopy or archway over the entrance to a large home or building to protect dismounting visitors from the weather
Portuguese	(or Portuguese merchant) a code name for *conversos* widely used by the authorities throughout Europe during the 16th century when it was in their interest to turn a blind eye to the truth
pound	British and Flemish unit of currency
rabbi anus	Hebrew term for someone who leads secret Jews in prayer
responsum/responsa	Hebrew term for a Jewish legal opinion (plural: *responsa*)
Rosh Hashonah	Jewish New Year festival observed in the fall
saray	women's quarters primarily used for members of the sultan's harem
scudi	unit of currency used in Italy during the 16th century
Sephardic Jew	a Jew whose family originated on the Iberian peninsula (in modern times this definition has been extended to all Jews of non-Ashkenazi origin)
stomacher	type of women's waistcoat fashionable during the 16th century
Succoth	Jewish festival that celebrates the end-of-summer harvest
surgun	term used by the Ottoman Turks for compulsory relocation

	of populations
tallit	Hebrew word for a fringed prayer shawl
Talmud	a collection of writings codifying Jewish religious and civil law that was alleged, during the Counter-Reformation, to include anti-Christian diatribes
Talmud Torah	religious school
vihuela	16th century guitar-like musical instrument
yeshiva	Hebrew term for school for religious studies
Zeccha/Zecca	Venetian mint and safe deposit

INDEX

Page numbers in italics *indicate illustrations.*